The Handicapper's Handbook

Tom Odette

The Handicapper's Handbook

by Tom Ainslie

TRIDENT PRESS • NEW YORK

SBN:671–27015–x
LIBRARY OF CONGRESS CATALOG CARD NUMBER: 69-13515

PUBLISHED SIMULTANEOUSLY IN THE UNITED STATES AND CANADA BY
TRIDENT PRESS, A DIVISION OF SIMON & SCHUSTER, INC., 630 FIFTH
AVENUE, NEW YORK, N.Y. 10020

PRINTED IN THE UNITED STATES OF AMERICA

SECOND PRINTING

ACKNOWLEDGMENT

All handicapping advice published in the United States and Canada is concerned
with the effective interpretation of data published in *The Morning Telegraph,
Daily Racing Form,* and *The American Racing Manual.* Without the detailed
past-performance records, result charts, statistical summaries, and columns of
news and comment that appear in those remarkable publications, the pleasures
of good handicapping would be unattainable. And books like this would be
impossible. The author thanks Triangle Publications, Inc., for its generous
permission to illustrate these pages with certain of its copyrighted past-performance records and result charts. Most especially, the author thanks Triangle for
the unique and indispensable role it has played in the development of Thoroughbred racing as a popular pastime.

Contents

The Handicapper's Handbook

INTRODUCTION:

On the Uses of a Handbook

ONE OF MY FILE DRAWERS overflows with letters that say, "More!" The letters come to me from racing enthusiasts. Some confide that they have found new enjoyment (and have bought new suits and new cars) by using the systematic selection method prescribed in *The Compleat Horseplayer* and *Ainslie's Jockey Book*. Others report with pride that they have vaulted into the inner circle of full-feathered handicappers after absorbing the principles expounded in *Ainslie's Complete Guide to Thoroughbred Racing*. They are happy, but they are not yet satisfied. They all want more.

Few of the letters ask for additional handicapping theory, their writers having been dealt lifetime supplies of theory in my earlier books. The demand is for practical guidance in day-to-day application of the theory. Much as a medical interne upgrades his powers of diagnosis and treatment by watching a more experienced physician at work, my correspondents want to look over my shoulder to see how I do what I do.

They want black-on-white demonstrations of how I handicap actual races. They want full, step-by-step analyses of authentic past-performance records, so that the techniques of locating a winning horse may become fully evident.

I think it is a good idea. There is no doubt that many persons learn more easily by observation than from the study of theory. No doubt, too, someone who has learned theory from a book is sure to benefit from demonstrations of the theory in action.

Accordingly, I now present this handbook, a handicapper's workshop, a compendium of down-to-earth examples which show how someone versed in the principles of Thoroughbred handicapping goes about translating those principles into practice.

Without wishing to drive away any potential customers, I feel duty-bound to state that I have written this handbook on the assumption that its reader (a) prefers to do his own handicapping, as contrasted with playing the choices of newspaper selectors or tipsters, and (b) has at least rudimentary knowledge of the game. If he has already read *Ainslie's Complete Guide to Thoroughbred Racing,* he will find this handbook a most useful supplement—a kind of gymnasium in which to test his own methods against mine. If he has not read my previous works but has a way of analyzing horse races, the examples reviewed in this book will challenge his skill, and the detailed analyses will offer him ample opportunity to spruce up his own knowledge of handicapping theory, should the need exist.

The races discussed in these pages were deliberately chosen to illustrate specific subtleties of handicapping. They were *not* chosen to show what a whizbang I am. They are genuine examples, drawn—as the saying goes—from real life. I actually handicapped the races at my own desk *before* post time. I did the work partly because I had this book in mind, but mainly because handicapping is my hobby. I give it the kind of time and attention that other hobbyists expend on the bridge or chess columns in their newspapers.

The point is that the races discussed in this book are the kinds of examples my readers have been asking for—the kinds of races I ordinarily single out for study, and the kinds of winners I find.

Cynics will enjoy noting that I pick only one loser from the beginning of the book to the end. Let me now spoil their fun by acknowledging that, for every four winners cited in the book, I could have mentioned about six losers that were picked by the very same handicapper (me), using the very same criteria (mine).

The handicapper's losing selections always outnumber his winning ones. This is the inescapable nature of the game, and one of its keenest challenges. As I have written perhaps too often in the past, no handicapper can be sure of cashing any one wager; and no handicapper can be sure of getting even one winner in any given series of five or ten bets; but a good handicapper can be sublimely confident that he will be right approximately 40 percent of the time in the long run. If I confine this book's examples almost entirely to winning choices, it is because I believe that they are more instructive and less confusing than examples in which the horse or its rider loused up the forecast.

The reader for whom this is the first exposure to Ainslie may be surprised and even disappointed to find that the book lacks miracle formulas for dredging up longshot winners. My interest, now as ever, is in styles of play capable of producing substantial annual profits. Longshot systems do not qualify. All claims to the contrary notwithstanding, they offer no miracles to compensate for the dreary successions of losers that offset their occasional 20–1 payoffs.

Let us please agree that the indispensable basis of profitable handicapping is recognition that most races—including a high proportion of the kind that tend to be won by 20–1 shots—are poor betting propositions. Hunting for what he calls "spots," and wagering only on horses that seem to have especially bright prospects, the expert seldom hits a real longshot. Yet he makes much more money than the gambler who pursues miracles.

The horse that wins at a $7 mutuel pays the expert $5 for every $2 he bets. The $2 is in custody of the track's pari-mutuel department for less than ten minutes before it returns to the expert's wallet with its five new companions. If this player manages to cash only one $50 bet in three, at average odds of 5–2 (a rather low winning percentage for a good handicapper whose selections pay such short mutuels), he will realize a profit of $775 on a series of 100 bets. Considering each wager as an investment, his return will be 15.5 cents on the dollar. This enormous rate of profit is obtainable by legal means in no other form of fast-turnover speculation. What's more, barring a string of losses at the beginning of the series of bets, the expert will amass these profits by reinvesting his winnings, which is nicer than digging into one's capital funds all the time, as losers do. Finally, it should be emphasized that a 15.5 percent profit on the wagered dollar is extremely thin soup for a good handicapper. The returns are at least twice that high for many.

Some readers may observe, perhaps with dismay, that I make my selections without resort to the heavily detailed procedures recommended in *The Compleat Horseplayer*. I should explain why. *The Compleat Horseplayer* was an attempt (successful) to show how a beginner, or a habitual loser, could become a winner by practicing a careful method of selecting horses. The detailed procedures were necessary to guarantee such a player a maximum chance of avoiding difficult races, plus the best possible chance of putting his precious money on a worthy horse.

Readers of *The Compleat Horseplayer* will recall that it was even more boastful than this one. I had tested the method personally, with real money, through a full week of racing at Monmouth Park. The profits were considerable (and were duly reported to Internal Revenue). The soundness of the method seemed clear. Thousands of racing fans continue to use it with ample success, further verifying its soundness.

I do not now suggest that they abandon it. If it continues to serve them well, and if they appreciate the sense of security imparted by its carefully codified, highly conservative sequence of operations, there is no reason on earth for them to change. On the other hand, I imagine that most practitioners of the method have by now amended it with rules of their own devising. This handbook may suggest further useful revisions, depending on the tastes and temperament of the individual.

In any event, I do not practice that detailed method in my own handicapping and, at this late date, I feel no compulsion to pretend that I do. Without violating any of the fundamental truths on which the method and all other good handicapping procedures rest, I am able to get to the heart of a horse race by shorter routes. In demonstrating how I do it, I shall be careful to show how each decision relates to the specific factors that were systematized in *The Compleat Horseplayer* and *Ainslie's Jockey Book* and later were microscopically dissected in *Ainslie's Complete Guide to Thoroughbred Racing*.

The process of explanation will consume more time than the actual handicapping required of me. I see no harm in that. To demonstrate a technique without explaining it thoroughly is a waste of everyone's energy. You did not come here merely to see me at work, but to understand why I do certain things and why I avoid certain others. To make sure that you get what you came for, I may occasionally dispense a bit more theory than some of you want or need. It won't kill you.

After handicapping twenty-nine races with you (the largest demonstration of its kind ever published), I shall then take you through eighteen more races—two entire cards of racing—just as if we were together at the track. For that purpose, I have chosen what probably was the greatest racing day in recent decades—the day on which Buckpasser locked horns with Damascus and Dr. Fager. The second program is less glamorous, but equally interesting—an ordinary afternoon at Atlantic City.

Have fun!

PART ONE

Handicapping Allowance Races

THE TYPICAL ALLOWANCE RACE imposes frustration on the handicapper by bringing together horses whose true quality, or class, is less than fully apparent in the past-performance records.

Every horse in the bunch may have competed in nothing but allowance races in each of the eight or ten starts described in the published record. Yet the races themselves may have been of widely varying quality. The term "allowance race" covers a wide spectrum of Thoroughbred class.

The allowance horse with the best-looking record may be outclassed, having been racing for purses much lower than is offered in today's conditions.

Or it may have been beating three-year-olds, whereas it faces older, stronger animals today.

It therefore may be roundly beaten by a horse that has been losing and whose record looks awful. The supposedly inferior horse may have been running in much faster company, for purses larger than today's.

Further complications and frustrations are offered when the allowance field includes an animal that has been losing in handicap races, yet may be the class of today's field.

Or one of the entrants may be an established handicap or stakes winner returning to action after a long rest.

Or, in lesser allowance races, the competition may include horses unsuccessful in allowance fields plus horses that have been doing nicely in top-grade claiming races.

Which horse is the class of the field? And if it is the class of the field, is it in good enough condition to prove its superiority? Is its jockey a winning rider, suited to the assignment? Does it come from a winning barn? Is it likely to benefit from the probable pace of the race? Are the weights reasonable?

If these questions can be answered, the handicapper has a bet.

1. SEVENTH AT GULFSTREAM, MARCH 28, 1967—Track Fast

OUR FIRST CHORE is to read and understand the conditions of the race.

This one is for three-year-old fillies of a special kind. That is, while almost any three-year-old filly in the barns can be entered, the winner of this race is likely to be a pretty nice kind of horse that has already won an allowance or stakes race. Notice, please, that the conditions bar only such three-year-old fillies as have already won *two* races of allowance or stakes grade. In big-time racing, a field of this kind almost always includes several entrants whose records show one allowance victory each, plus an occasional one that has won a single stakes race. Other things being equal, these horses are the logical contenders.

Why? Because the conditions of the race have been designed with them in mind.

To understand this more clearly, pretend for a moment that you are the trainer of a three-year-old filly that has won a maiden-special and an allowance. You want to give her the best possible chance for another victory. The softest touch would be a claiming race, but you would lose the filly to another barn. The hardest proposition would be a stakes race against established stars. A difficult test would be an allowance race for non-winners of three allowance or stakes races: Your filly would have to compete against animals that have won *two* good races, as compared with her one.

So you find her a race like the Seventh at Gulfstream on this particular day. It bars fillies that already have proven themselves superior by winning more than one allowance race. But your filly, having won one, manages to meet the eligibility requirements. By a hair. If she is a pretty good sort, and in sharp condition, your chief worry will be the previous stakes winner that is eligible for the race and that may be ready to win. You also will worry if the field includes a lightly raced, well-bred entrant whose first-rate trainer is giving her a crack at established allowance horses after a recent, unusually swift triumph in a maiden-special-weights event.

We now are ready to go through the past-performance record of the fillies. Our objective is to draw a mental profile of each horse. What has she done to distinguish herself? What has she done lately? Where does she seem to be headed in the racing world? Why is she in today's race? Is she a logical contender? If so, we shall return to her later for a more detailed examination. Otherwise, we shall eliminate her from consideration right now.

7th Gulfstream

6 FURLONGS (Chute). (Alhambra, March 4, 1959, 1.08⅘, 4, 124.) Allowances. Purse $4,500. Fillies. 3-year-olds which have not won two races other than maiden or claiming. Weight 121 lbs. Non-winners of $3,300 since January 17 allowed 2 lbs., $2,925 in 1967, 4 lbs., $2,605 twice since November 19, 6 lbs., a race of any value in 1967, 8 lbs. (Maiden and claiming races not considered.)

(7th GP)—Coupled—Twill Do Maid and Arm-E-Indian.

Secret Promise — Gr. f (1964-Ky), by Warfare—Secret Valley, by Priam II — Mrs. R. L. Reineman — S. M. Edmundson — (R. L. Reineman) — **119**

1967	2	2	0	0	$5,200
1966	3	M	0	0	----

7Feb67–7Hia	fst 7f	.22⅗	.45⅗1.25	f– Allow	4	8	4^6	3^4	1^2	1^4	RUssery		116	4.70	84–13	Secret Promise 116^4 Miss Dilly Dally 118^2 Grand Coulee 116no	Easily 9
24Jan67–4Hia	my 6f	.22⅗	.46⅘1.12⅘	f–MdSpWt	9	12	$8^{8\frac14}$	7^8	2^h	$1^{1\frac12}$	RUssery		118	8.40	80–21	Secret Promise $118^{1\frac12}$ Arm–E–Indian $118^{\frac34}$ A Tip 118^{nk}	Handily 12
7Dec66–5Aqu	fst 6f	.22⅗	.46⅖1.11⅗	Md Sp Wt	2	11	$5^{5\frac12}$	8^{12}	9^{17}	10^{19}	RFerraro		119	21.60	66–24	Fleet Honor 122^6 Tote'm Home 122^1 Mr. Peveron 122^2	Fell back 12
28Oct66–3GS	fst 6f	.21⅘	.45⅖1.12⅘	f–MdSpWt	4	5	$4^{5\frac12}$	4^{13}	6^{11}	$7^{8\frac34}$	DBrumfield	b	116	5.60	71–19	Dancing Mistress 116^h I've 116^2 Hip Hugger 116^3	Tired 12
14Oct66–2GS	fst 6f	.22⅖	.45⅘1.11⅗	f–MdSpWt	1	12	$10^{7\frac14}$	10^{11}	$6^{9\frac12}$	$5^{7\frac34}$	RBroussard		117	11.70	78–13	ChampagneToni $116^{1\frac12}$ Kay'sValentine 116^{nk} Chriscinca 116^1	Dwelt 12

LATEST WORKOUTS   Mar 27 GP 3f fst .36⅗ b   Mar 23 GP 5f fst 1.02 bg   Mar 22 GP 3f fst .36⅖ b   Mar 17 GP 5f fst 1.04⅖ b

She's Very Ultra

B. f (1964-Ky), by Olympia—Sweet Woman, by Roman — 119 — 1967 3 2 0 0 $5,200
Circle M. Farm J. Long (Circle M. Farm) — 1966 0 M 0 0 ——

23Feb67-7Hia gd 6f .22⅕ .45⅘1.12⅖ f- Allow 3 1 13 15 13 1½ DBrumfield 118 *1.80e 82-20 She's Very Ultra 118½ Dana's Flight 1113½ Jaspary 1161 All out 11
9Feb67-4Hia gd 6f .22⅖ .45⅘1.12⅖ f-MdSpWt 11 1 13 14 15 13½ DKassen 118 *1.90 82-16 She's Very Ultra 1183½ Indiscreet 115no Anna Vertex 1182 Easily 12
30Jan67-3Hia fst 6f .22 .45⅗1.12 f-MdSpWt 8 2 11½ 1h 21½ 67½ DKassen 118 10.80 76-15 Perfect Looker 1184 Gracious Roman 1181 Tu-El 1181 Tired 12
LATEST WORKOUTS Mar 25 Hia 5f fst 1.04 b Mar 8 Hia 4f fst .51⅖ b Mar 4 Hia 3f fst .36⅕ h Feb 20 Hia 5f fst 1.00⅘ h

Momma Pierre

Gr. f (1964-Md), by Kinda Smart—Abbestale, by Abbe Pierre — 113 — 1967 3 0 1 0 $1,300
D. J. Sarmento W. A. Croll, Jr. (Mr.-Mrs. C. G. Timanus) — 1966 3 2 : 0 $8,635

23Feb67-8Hia gd 6f .22⅖ .45⅘1.11⅖ f- Allow 6 7 54½ 69 69½ 611 JLRotz 113 2.90 76-20 Just Kidding 112nk Treacherous 1157 Bit Of Dash 115nk Fell back 8
14Feb67-7Hia fst 7f .23⅖ .46⅘1.24⅕ f- Allow 5 3 33 31 12 2no JVelasquez 112 3.00 88-13 Treacherous 115no Momma Pierre 1124 Arrangement 1155 Nosed 7
1Feb67-9Hia fst 6f .22⅕ .45⅖1.11⅖ f- Allow 7 5 42 35 49 46 BBaeza 112 2.50 81-13 Hip Hugger 1151½ Action A Go Go 118½ Miss Vertex 1184 No m'hap 9
6Jly 66-8Mth fst 5½f.22⅕ .45⅖1.04⅘ f-Colleen 8 10 115¾117½ 54½ 26 JVelasquez 114 5.10 87-18 Rhubarb 1146 Momma Pierre 1141½ Betoken 119h Finished well 14
8Jun66-4Mth fst 5½f.22⅖ .46⅕1.05 f- Allow 1 2 11 11½ 12½ 17 DBrumfield 116 7.50 92-11 Momma Pierre 1167 American Dream 1161½ Effayeff 1162½ Easily 7
10Feb66-3Hia fst 3f .22⅖ .34⅕ f-MdSpWt 13 7 4¾ 1nk JLRotz 117 *2.60e 91- 9 Momma Pierre 117nk Rare Coin 117½ Conestoga Babe 117h Driving 14
LATEST WORKOUTS Mar 25 GP 4f fst .49⅕ b Mar 16 GP 4f fst .48⅖ b Mar 11 GP 3f fst .37 b Feb 28 GP 4f fst .51 b

Twill Do Maid

B. f (1964-Ky), by Nashua—Indian Maid, by Rinaldo — 113
Mary D. Keim Mary D. Keim (Mrs. M. Keim) — 1966 4 2 0 0 $8,150

3Sep66-8AP fst 6½f.22⅖ .45 1.16⅘ f-Lassie 5 4 2h 21½ 67 612 JSellers b 119 14.50 80-12 Mira Femme 119¾ Teacher's Art 1192½ Woozem 119¾ Speed, tired 7
24Aug66-8AP fst 6f .22 .45 1.09⅗ f-LassTr'l 3 7 42½ 43 78 88½ WShoemaker b 114 3.10 86-12 Fish House 1142 Deauville 116h Mira Femme 1212 Tired 10
9Aug66-3AP fst 6f .22⅖ .45⅘1.10⅖ f- Allow 3 3 12 11½ 12 11½ WShoemaker b 120 *0.80 91-12 Twill Do Maid1201½ Amerigo Lady1201 Stash It Away120h In hand 7
29Jun66-3AP fst 5½f.22⅖ .46⅖1.04⅗ f-MdSpWt 11 1 13 13 13 13¾ HHinojosa b 115 *1.00 94- 9 TwillDoMaid1153¾ BlossomMorgan 1157 CarrotCake 1153 Easy score 11
Nominated for Kentucky Derby. LATEST WORKOUTS Mar 22 Hia 6f fst 1.13 hg Mar 12 Hia 7f fst 1.25⅖ h Mar 1 Hia 6f fst 1.12⅖ h

Lady Goldie

Dk. b. or br. f (1964-Ky), by Hurry Home—Lady Nita, by Southern Pride — 113 — 1967 5 0 0 1 $365
Walnut Hill Farm J. J. Serna, Jr. (C. Brown, Jr.) — 1966 12 2 1 3 $7,915

23Mar67-4GP fst 6f .22⅖ .45⅘1.11⅗ f- 11000 9 2 42½ 32 33 33 HPilar 116 7.20 83-16 Here's Neptune 113¾ Golden Lamp 1162½ Lady Goldie 116¾ Held on 12
15Feb67-6Hia fst 6f .22⅕ .45⅗1.12⅕ f- 15000 8 4 52 23 34 64½ HPilar 116 3.30 78-16 d-Lady Avalon 112h Ethical 1161 Deepsprings 1182½ Tired 12
6Feb67-7Hia fst 6f .22 .44⅘1.10⅖ f- Allow 4 3 54 57 68 75¾ HPilar 112 103.50 86-14 She'sBeautiful 1151 RegalHostess 1132 Sweet andLow 1181 No sp'd 9
27Jan67-7Hia gd 7f .22⅖ .45⅘1.25⅖ f- Allow 1 4 32½ 44½ 68 717 HPilar 112 52.40 65-23 Dance Dress 1142½ Treacherous 1151 Shirley Heights 1157 Tired 8
2Jan67-4TrP fst 6f .22 .44⅗1.10 Allowance 2 5 1h 21 22 76 HPilar 116 12.00 86-10 Bit of Dash 108nk Salishan 1212½ Game Maid 116½ Used up early 10
14Dec66-9TrP fst 5½f.22 .47⅖1.04⅗ f- H'dicap 12 4 76 33½ 45 47½ HPilar 116 29.60 82-17 Barrie B. 114¾ Hip Hugger 1132¾ Betoken 1214 Bid, tired 14
21Nov66-4TrP fst 6f .22⅖ .45⅘1.11⅗ Allowance 2 6 33 31½ 1½ 11¾ HPilar 114 6.00 85-16 Lady Goldie 1141¾ Scotch Sailor 1153½ Barrie B. 1172½ Driving 12
19Oct66-7Kee gd 7f .23 .45⅕1.25⅗ f- Allow 5 5 1h 1h 2½ 31½ BPhelps 119 12.90 79-19 Quillon 1191½ At Long Last 119h Lady Goldie 119¾ Good effort 10
11Oct66-5Kee fst 7f .23⅖ .46⅘1.25 f- Allow 5 1 1h 2h 35 511 BPhelps 119 4.60 72-18 Carrot Cake 1192½ Quillon 1193 At Long Last 119h Used early 7
LATEST WORKOUTS Mar 15 Hia 5f fst 1.02 h Mar 5 Hia 3f fst .35 h Feb 13 Hia 4f sly .49 b Feb 5 Hia 3f fst .36 h

I've

Ch. f (1964-Va), by Greek Song—Jupey R., by Royal Charger — 113 — 1967 6 1 0 0 $2,600
North Star Ranch T. T. Kelly (Crown Crest Farm) — 1966 10 1 3 2 $4,950

6Mar67-5GP fst 6f .22 .45⅕1.11 f- 12500 3 3 2h 2h 11½ 12¾ JVelasquez b 116 *2.10 89-14 I've 1162¾ Dancing Dale 1221½ Rodarap 1162 Clear under pressure 8
23Feb67-7Hia gd 6f .22⅖ .45⅘1.12⅖ f- Allow 6 4 23 47½ 816 814 JLRotz b 116 5.80 68-20 She's Very Ultra 118½ Dana's Flight 1113½ Jaspary 1161 Tired 11
14Feb67-8Hia fst 6f .21 .45⅗1.11⅕ f- Allow 4 3 1h 3½ 23 47½ JVelasquez b 116 12.90 80-13 GrandCoulee 1181½ RegalHostess 1164½ PerfectLooker1161½ Tired 9
7Feb67-7Hia fst 7f .22⅖ .45⅖1.25 f- Allow 9 1 13 13 34 813 JVelasquez b 116 4.80 71-13 SecretPromise 1164 MissDillyDally 1182 GrandCoulee 116no Used up 9
31Jan67-6Hia fst 6f .22⅕ .45⅗1.11⅘ f- Allow 6 3 1h 11 2h 42 JVelasquez b 116 8.40 83-16 SweetAndLow1181½ GrandCoulee118nk RegalHostess116nk Used up 10
20Jan67-6Hia sl 6f .22 .46 1.12⅗ f- Allow 9 1 1½ 2h 21 56 JVelasquez b 116 11.00 75-19 Hip Hugger 116½ Gala Honors 1181½ Sweet And Low 118h Used up 10
14Dec66-9TrP fst 5½f.22 .47⅖1.04⅗ f- H'dicap 11 5 3nk 55 57 58½ IValenzuela b 114 11.50 81-17 Barrie B. 114¾ Hip Hugger 1132¾ Betoken 1214 Brief foot 14
6Dec66-2TrP fst 6f .22⅕ .45⅗1.11⅖ f-MdSpWt 4 8 31 2h 1h 2no JVasquez b 118 *1.20 85-14 d-One More Kiss 118no I've 1185 Fulcrum's Lass 1183 Bumped late 12
6Dec66—Placed first through disqualification.
8Nov66-3GS fst 6f .21⅘ .45⅗1.11⅘ f-MdSpWt 8 4 1h 2h 3½ 34½ JVelasquez b 117 *2.30 81-20 Hava Nice Day 117nk Hip Hugger 1174 I've 1172 Tired in drive 12
LATEST WORKOUTS Mar 24 GP 3f fst .36⅗ b Mar 17 GP 4f fst .50⅘ b Mar 2 Hia 3f fst .37 b Feb 22 Hia 3f sly .38 b

Barrie B. ×

Ch. f (1964-Ky), by Beau Busher—April Five, by Woodchuck — 115 — 1967 2 0 0 1 $750
Tumblewood Stable H. G. Bockman (W. Floyd) — 1966 6 2 2 1 $8,810

6Mar67-8GP fst 6f .22⅕ .45⅕1.11 f- Allow 4 2 1½ 32½ 511 69¾ KKnapp 119 9.90 79-14 PlumPlum 1174 SweetAndLow 1171 NortheastTrades 113¾ Used up 8
4Jan67-9TrP fst 6f .22 .45⅕1.10⅗ f-H'dicap 2 7 1½ 11½ 11½ 32¼ KKnapp 117 11.00 86-17 T. V.'s Princess 1182½ Forty Merry's 113h Barrie B. 1171 Tired 8
14Dec66-9TrP fst 5½f.22 .47⅖1.04⅗ f- H'dicap 14 1 12 12 11½ 1¾ KKnapp 114 47.40 90-17 Barrie B. 114¾ Hip Hugger 1132¾ Betoken 1214 Hard drive 14
6Dec66-7TrP fst 6f .21⅘ .45⅕1.10⅘ Allowance 5 5 76 88¼ 67 67½ KKnapp 115 3.30 81-14 Game Maid 1151½ Debbie's Tam 1113¾ Deesprings 1151½ Dull try 12
21Nov66-4TrP fst 6f .22⅖ .45⅘1.11⅗ Allowance 7 3 1h 2h 41 35½ JSellers 117 *1.30 80-16 Lady Goldie 1141¾ Scotch Sailor 1153½ Barrie B. 1172½ Weakened 12
27Oct66-4Kee fst 6f .22⅕ .46⅕1.12⅕ f-MdSpWt 3 1 13 15 17 18 KKnapp 117 *1.50 82-21 Barrie B. 1178 Shower of Flowers 117½ Brook Miss 1173½ Easily 11
14Oct66-3Kee fst 6½f.23 .47⅗1.20⅗ f-MdSpWt 5 1 11 21 2½ 21½ DKassen 117 4.30 73-20 Matriarch 1171½ Barrie B. 117h Brook Miss 117nk Gamely 8
1Oct66-8CD my 6f .22⅕ .46⅕1.14 f-MdSpWt 2 2 2h 11 12 2nk MManganello 117 27.00 76-22 Just A Whim 117nk Barrie B. 117h La Contessa 1183 Just missed 12
LATEST WORKOUTS Mar 26 GP 5f fst 1.00⅖ h Mar 3 GP 3f fst .36 b Feb 24 GP 4f gd .50 b Feb 3 GP 4f fst .49⅘ b

Lori Mac

B. f (1964-Fla), by Crafty Admiral—Unified, by Olympia — 113 — 1967 7 1 1 0 $3,525
F. E. Mackle 3d R. W. Lilly (F. E. Mackle, Jr.) — 1966 2 1 1 0 $3,075

22Mar67-8GP fst 6f .22⅕ .45⅕1.11 f- Allow 3 5 41 55 46½ 68 LMoyers 114 6.20 81-19 Lake Chelan 114¾ Plum Plum 117¾ Hip Hugger 1223½ Tired 10
8Mar67-7GP fst 6f .22 .45⅖1.10⅘ f- Allow 5 3 32 11 15 15 JVasquez 116 *1.00 90-11 Lori Mac 1165 Majestic Return 116no Bogota 108no Easy score 8
14Feb67-8Hia fst 6f .21 .45⅗1.11⅕ f- Allow 1 4 2h 2h 44½ 711 JVasquez 116 5.60 77-13 GrandCoulee 1181½ RegalHostess 1164½ PerfectLooker1161½ Tired 9
3Feb67-6Hia fst 6f .22⅕ .45⅕1.11 f- Allow 6 1 1h 1h 1h 2no JVasquez 115 5.90 89-14 Plum Plum 115no Lori Mac 1152½ Greek Song's Get 1217 Nosed 7
20Jan67-6Hia sl 6f .22 .46 1.12⅗ f- Allow 4 4 44½ 54½ 53½ 42 JVasquez 116 14.20 79-19 Hip Hugger 116½ Gala Honors 1181½ Sweet And Low 118h Rallied 10
10Jan67-8TrP fst 6f .21⅘ .44⅗1.10 Allowance 8 5 11 34 1218 1216 LMoyers 109 6.70 76-11 Without A Paddle 1173½ O BeJoyful 117h PiedmontJoy 116½ Stopped 12
5Jan67-4TrP fst 6f .22⅖ .46⅕1.11⅕ Allowance 6 5 32 41½ 56½ 69¾ EFires 112 *2.70 77-14 Royal De Fur 117½ Neecap 1175 Cut And Comb 1142½ Bumped turn 12
4May66-6GS fst 5f .22⅘ .47 .59⅘ f- Allow 1 2 61½ 22 2h 21½ GPatterson 115 5.30 91-16 With a Flair 1171½ Lori Mac 1151½ Bittern 1171 Best of rest 8
18Jan66-3Hia fst 3f .22⅖ .34 f-MdSpWt 4 3 1½ 1nk DBrumfield 117 5.80 92- 8 Lori Mac 117nk Kate's Intent 117nk City Lady 1171 Hard drive 9
LATEST WORKOUTS Mar 27 Hia 3f fst .37 b Mar 21 Hia 3f gd .37 b Mar 17 Hia 4f fst .48 b Mar 7 Hia 3f fst .35⅕ h

Regal Hostess

Dk. b. or br. f (1964-Ill), by Royal Serenade—Mare's Beau, by Your Host — 119 — 1967 4 1 2 1 $6,275
Gray Willows Farm D. Dodson (Gray Willows Farm) — 1966 2 1 0 0 $1,690

2Mar67-9Hia fst 7f .23⅕ .46⅖1.25⅕ f- Allow 6 1 3nk 2h 2½ 1h RBroussard b 116 2.90 83-13 Regal Hostess 116h Bugle Beads 1111 Dana's Flight 1112 Driving 8
14Feb67-8Hia fst 6f .21 .45⅗1.11⅕ f- Allow 2 5 3nk 1h 13 21½ JLRotz b 116 *1.40 86-13 GrandCoulee 1181½ RegalHostess 1164½ PerfectLooker 1161½ Gamely 9
6Feb67-7Hia fst 6f .22 .44⅘1.10⅖ f- Allow 2 5 2h 22 22 21 JLRotz b 113 4.60 91-14 She'sBeautiful 1151 RegalHostess 1132 Sweet andLow 1181 Gamely 9
31Jan67-6Hia fst 6f .22⅕ .45⅗1.11⅘ f- Allow 1 4 2h 31 31 31¾ JVasquez b 116 3.80 83-16 Sweet And Low 1181½ GrandCoulee118nk RegalHostess116nk In close 10
23Dec66-1TrP fst 6f .22⅕ .44⅘1.10⅕ f-MdSpWt 10 2 1h 1½ 12 15½ JVasquez b 119 *3.00 91-11 Regal Hostess 1195½ Hills Best 1193½ Kayshield 1191 Mild drive 12
6May66-2GS fst 5f .22 .46 .58⅘ f-MdSpWt 11 9 129½1215121512 11 WZakoor 116 30.80 84-12 Red Hook 1161½ American Dream 1161 Teaola 116no Trailed field 12
LATEST WORKOUTS Mar 26 GP 5f fst 1.01⅗ b Jan 30 GP 3f fst .37⅗ b

Arm-E-Indian × — B. f (1964-Ky, by Armageddon—Indian Verse, by Noble Hero — Mrs. M. D. Keim — Mrs. M. D. Keim — (Mrs. M. Keim) — **113**

1967	4	1	1	0	$3.200
1966	1	M	0	0	$280

17Mar67-8GP	fst 7f	.22⅗	.45⅘1.25⅗	f- Allow	11	6	6^5	6^7	11^{14}	$9^{5¼}$	EFires	116	2.00	76-22	Fine Call 118^h Majestic Return 116^1 Princess Jupon 111^1	No threat	11
2Mar67-9Hia	fst 7f	.23⅕	.46⅖1.25⅕	f- Allow	4	4	$7^{2¾}$	$7^{7¼}$	$7^{6¼}$	4^3	WHartack	118	*2.20	80-13	Regal Hostess 116^h Bugle Beads 111^1 Dana's Flight 111^2	Late foot	8
16Feb67-4Hia	fst 7f	.23⅖	.46⅕1.24⅗	f-MdSpWt	11	1	$2^½$	1^h	1^2	1^7	WHartack	118	*2.50	86-12	Arm-E-Indian 118^7 Easterborn 118^1 Prejudice 118^1	Mild drive	11
24Jan67-4Hia	my 6f	.22⅗	.46⅘1.12⅘	f-MdSpWt	2	3	6^5	5^6	$4^{2½}$	$2^{1½}$	LAdams	118	10.90	78-21	Secret Promise $118^{1½}$ Arm-E-Indian $118^{¾}$ A Tip 118^{nk}	In close	12
11Aug66-2AP	gd 6f	.22⅗	.46⅗1.11⅘	f-MdSpWt	4	11	$11^{9¼}$	9^9	$5^{8¼}$	4^{11}	HHinojosa	115	12.90	73-22	Galley Queen $115^{3¾}$ Lady Goldie $115^{¾}$ Needle Cushion 115^6	No threat	12

LATEST WORKOUTS Mar 25 Hia 3f fst .36⅘ b — Mar 16 Hia 3f fst .37 b — Mar 12 Hia 4f fst .49 b — Feb 25 Hia 5f fst 1.01 h

Miss Debutante × — B. f (1964-Ky), by Windy City II—Wild Music, by Spy Song — F. H. Lindsay — G. Gay — (F. H. Lindsay) — **113**

1967	1	0	0	0	$150
1966	3	2	0	0	$17,534

6Mar67-8GP	fst 6f	.22⅕	.45⅕1.11	f- Allow	6	5	$3^½$	$5^{7½}$	6^{13}	$5^{7¾}$	LMoyers	113	3.00	81-14	PlumPlum 117^4 SweetAndLow 117^1 NortheastTrades $113^{¾}$	Brief sp.	8
15Oct66-6Kee	sly*7f	.21⅖	.44⅘1.28⅖	f-Alci'des	5	5	$1^{1½}$	1^h	$3^½$	$4^{4½}$	JNichols	119	*1.70	76-22	Teacher's Art $119^{3¾}$ Thong $119^½$ T. V.'s Princess 119^{nk}	Used up	8
26Sep66-8Haw	fst 6f	.22⅕	.45⅖1.10⅘	f-Durazna	2	6	1^1	1^2	1^4	1^7	LMoyers	109	2.40	93-17	Miss Debutante 109^7 Peggy's Liz 118^{nk} Edswinner 111^1	Easily	10
8Sep66-6AP	fst 6f	.22⅗	.45⅘1.10⅘	f-MdSpWt	7	1	2^h	$1^½$	1^3	1^7	JNichols	115	4.00	89-17	Miss Debutante 115^7 Carrot Cake $115^{3½}$ Prejudice 115^4	Ridden out	10

LATEST WORKOUTS Mar 21 TrP 4f fst .49 h — Mar 15 TrP 4f fst .49 hg — Mar 4 TrP 4f fst .50⅗ b — Mar 1 TrP 4f fst .50 hg

Secret Promise: Broke her maiden at Hialeah on January 24, coming from far off the pace in the mud. Returned on February 7 and beat allowance horses after another slow start, this time at seven furlongs. Her absence from racing for the past seven weeks is a bad sign. Three workouts in the past six days suggest that the animal is whole, but workouts are no assurance of the sharpness that should be necessary against the classy kind of recent winner likely to run in a race like today's. Even if the race is untypical, and no really promising filly is entered, I would not bet on this one. Seven weeks is too long a layoff. NO BET.

She's Very Ultra: This Olympia filly has shown traces of Dad's sprinting ability, winning a maiden-special and an allowance with enormous bursts of early speed on off tracks. The five-week layoff, including seventeen days without so much as a workout, disqualifies the filly, however. She probably will have a good deal to say about the early pace of the race, but nothing in her record suggests that she will have much left in the stretch against today's type of field. Especially not after being away so long. NO BET.

Momma Pierre: The unusually capable Jimmy Croll got an allowance race and place money in the Colleen Stakes at Monmouth last year with this one. On February 14, against a field that must have been quite similar to today's, she was on top after three quarters of a mile (today's distance) but lost at the wire. Today's race would seem more favorable to her chances except for that bad effort on February 23, followed by almost five weeks on the sidelines. NO BET.

Twill Do Maid: A Kentucky Derby nominee! Showed no sign of stakes quality in her Chicago efforts last year, however, and has not run since. If the horse had raced like a real Derby candidate during her two-year-old season, she might be a threat today. NO BET.

Lady Goldie: This one hasn't been winning even claiming races lately. NO BET.

I've: Outclassed in every attempt to run with allowance animals. NO BET.

Barrie B.: Only one workout and no races in three weeks are bad news about a young horse entered in a race for sharply conditioned animals of genuine class. Recent tendency to fade in the stretch, combined with long intervals between races and workouts, suggest that this one is in trouble. NO BET.

Lori Mac: That was a smashing victory on March 8, but was sandwiched between two poor efforts for which the sole excuse seems to be a shortage of real class. Notice that the filly won at even money but was badly beaten at higher odds. The higher odds on the days of the beatings indicate that the public recognizes this animal as something less than hot stuff. Functioning on the assumption that a race like today's *should* be won by something with a touch of class, and refusing to bet on the race at all unless a genuinely qualified animal turns up, one might concede Lori Mac a slim chance, but too slim to risk money on. NO BET.

Regal Hostess: Doug Dodson has had this Royal Serenade filly on the pace and in contention at the wire in each of her five most recent races. On February 14 she finished nine lengths ahead of Lori Mac. On March 2 she scored in grand style over seven furlongs. After a hard-fought victory of that kind, a three-week rest is not too much for a filly. As to the sparsity of workouts, note that Dodson—a real horseman—has been getting good results that way. If something contests the early pace with She's Very Ultra, the game Regal Hostess seems classy enough to have an excellent chance in the stretch. CONTENDER.

Arm-E-Indian: In two unsuccessful attempts to win her first allowance race, this one has shown a pronounced lack of speed. NO BET.

Miss Debutante: Front-running winner of a two-year-old stakes at Hawthorne, this filly was short of stamina in her 1967 debut three weeks ago. She could be the class of the field and, if in better shape today, could prove it. CONTENDER.

The only two animals that seem worthy of further consideration are Regal Hostess and the promising Miss Debutante. The latter's work in Chicago last year indicates class. The other's determination, speed, and consistency this year also suggest class, although it must be admitted that she has not yet beaten allowance fillies decisively enough to shape up as stakes material.

Where do we go? To Regal Hostess on several grounds. In the first place she has been running well *this year,* and the other has not. Secondly, even if Miss Debutante is now in condition to run faster and farther than she did on March 6, which seems probable, there is no reason to believe that she has yet recovered her 1966 form. She was so very short in her last race that one can hardly expect her to go all the way today. But one *can* expect that she will be out there winging for a while. This will put her and She's Very Ultra in contention for the lead at some point before the final turn. She's Very Ultra does not figure to survive such a duel but can be counted on to deplete Miss Debutante of valuable energy.

Now for a look at the jockeys. Ray Broussard, on Regal Hostess, is one of the five or six finest stretch riders in the country and should be a particular asset to the filly in today's tough final furlong. Lee Moyers, a topnotch journeyman, has already won with Miss Debutante.

Weights? Regal Hostess has already carried 119 pounds over six furlongs, and toted 116 for seven. Today's weight looks like no problem for her. Miss Debutante should be mighty comfortable with 113.

The Running of the Race

HYPNOTIZED by the status of Twill Do Maid as a Kentucky Derby nominee, the crowd decided to "go to the class" and installed Mrs. Keim's charge as a lukewarm 3–1 favorite. Miss Debutante was second favorite. Secret Promise, off her two 1967 triumphs, was third favorite. And Regal Hostess was a neglected 5–1.

Miss Debutante ran a lovely race, but our handicapping forecast was accurate. The duel with She's Very Ultra took just enough out of the Chicago horse to give Ray Broussard his own way in the stretch drive. Twill Do Maid also ran nicely, and might have given Regal Hostess a bad time at the wire if her rider had been able to keep her out of the switches on the home turn.

The two best fillies in the race were obviously Miss Debutante and Twill Do Maid. But the best one *today* was Regal Hostess, as the handicapping and the result chart showed.

SEVENTH RACE **6 FURLONGS (Chute). (Alhambra, March 4, 1959, 1.08⅘, 4, 124.)**

GP - 30597

March 28, 1967

Allowances. Purse $4,500. Fillies. 3-year-olds which have not won two races other than maiden or claiming. Weight 121 lbs. Non-winners of $3,300 since January 17 allowed 2 lbs., $2,925 in 1967, 4 lbs., $2,605 twice since November 19, 6 lbs., a race of any value in 1967, 8 lbs. (Maiden and claiming races not considered.)

Value to winner $2,700, second $975, third $425, fourth $250, fifth $150. Mutuel pool $131,246.

Index	Horse	Eqt	A	Wt	PP	St	¼	½	Str	Fin	Jockey	Owner	Odds $1
30419Hia¹	—Regal Hostess	b	3	119	9	3	6^{1}	4^{h}	2^{h}	$1\frac{1}{2}$	R Brouss'rd	Gray Willows Farm	5.00
30418GP⁵	—Miss Debutante		3	113	10	2	4^{1}	2^{h}	$3^{1\frac{1}{2}}$	2^{1}	L Moyers	F H Lindsay	4.20
30298Hia⁶	—Momma Pierre		3	113	3	10	7^{h}	7^{1}	5^{2}	$3\frac{1}{2}$	J Giovanni	D J Sarmento	7.60
28626AP⁶	—Twill Do Maid	b	3	113	4	6	5^{2}	$5\frac{1}{2}$	4^{2}	$4\frac{3}{4}$	J Noble	Mrs M D Keim	3.10
30297Hia¹	—She's Very Ul'a		3	119	2	5	$1\frac{1}{2}$	1^{h}	1^{h}	$5^{2\frac{1}{2}}$	D Brumf'ld	Circle M Farm	13.30
30157Hia¹	—Secret Promise		3	119	1	9	10	9^{2}	6^{h}	6^{1}	W Blum	Mrs R L Reineman	4.80
30558GP⁶	—Lori Mac		3	115	8	1	2^{h}	3^{1}	$7^{1\frac{1}{2}}$	$7^{1\frac{1}{2}}$	E Fires	F E Mackle 3d	8.70
30564GP³	—Lady Goldie		3	113	5	7	$8\frac{1}{2}$	10	8^{2}	8^{1}	H Pilar	Walnut Hill Farm	82.20
30418GP⁶	—Barrie B.		3	113	7	8	9^{2}	8^{1}	10	9no	K Knapp	Tumblewood Stable	21.10
30415GP¹	—I've	b	3	113	6	4	$3\frac{1}{2}$	6^{1}	9^{1}	10	B Moreira	Benshoof-Metcalf	14.40

Time .22, .45⅖, 1.11⅘. Track fast.

$2 Mutuel Prices:

9-REGAL HOSTESS	12.00	6.20	3.40
10-MISS DEBUTANTE		6.40	4.80
3-MOMMA PIERRE			6.20

Dk. b. or br. f, by Royal Serenade—Mare's Beau, by Your Host. Trainer D. Dodson. Bred by Gray Willows Farm (Ill.).

IN GATE AT 4.09. OFF AT 4.09½ EASTERN STANDARD TIME. Start good. Won driving.

REGAL HOSTESS reserved off the pace through run down backstretch, continued along outside while advancing on turn and edged MISS DEBUTANTE in a stiff drive. The latter, never far back, moved up boldly on final bend and held on stubbornly in a prolonged drive. MOMMA PIERRE found her best stride too late. TWILL DO MAID saved ground and finished well after encountering close quarters on final bend and in upper stretch. SECRET PROMISE came away sluggishly. LORI MAC was used up early.

Scratched—30518GP⁹ Arm-E-Indian.

One final comment on the importance of basic class in races of this kind: The only stakes winner in the field was Miss Debutante, who would have won if she had been in slightly better trim. The only other stakes horses in the field were Momma Pierre and Twill Do Maid, the third and fourth animals at the finish!

To recapitulate, the best bet in a race like this is a horse of established class and undeniably good present form. The next best is one which, like Regal Hostess, has shown consistency, speed and determination suggestive of class, and is in winning form. In the absence of either type, the race should be passed because an upset is likely.

2. SIXTH AT AQUEDUCT, JUNE 19, 1967—Track Sloppy

NOW THE FUN BEGINS. Here is another allowance race for fillies. Its outcome is predictable, as we shall see, but the prediction is based on considerations different from those that impressed us in the Gulfstream race.

Read the conditions of the race. It is for fillies and mares that have never won three races of any kind—allowance, stakes, or claiming. It is open to the cheapest horses on the grounds and to potential champions—provided they each have won not more than twice. The purse, a plump $9,500, suggests that the winner will be a horse with some class and with condition sharp enough to prove it.

6th Race Aqueduct

6 FURLONGS — AQUEDUCT (Start / Finish)

6 FURLONGS. (Near Man, July 17, 1963, 1.08⅗, 3, 112.)
Allowances. Purse $9,500. Fillies and mares. 3-year-olds and upward which have never won three races. Weights, 3-year-olds 114 lbs., older 123 lbs. Non-winners of two races since March 11, 3 lbs., of a race since then or two races since Jan. 16, 5 lbs.

Gay Gobha

Dk. b. or br. f (1964–Va.), by Besomer—Iarrtas, by Alquest — Mrs. C. MacLeod — C. MacLeod, Jr. — (C. MacLeod, Jr.) — **108** — 1966 6 2 1 1 $9,067

15Aug66–7Sar	fst 6f	.22⅘ .45⅘1.12⅗	f-Adrndck	6	8	98¾	811	89½	75¼	HWoodhouse		115	10.90	80–17	Tainted Lady 115¾ Intriguing 115¾ Silver True 115¾	No mishap	12
3Aug66–7Sar	fst 5½f	.22⅕ .46 1.05	f-Sch'vle	9	7	64¼	63½	65½	44¾	HWoodhouse		116	11.80	87–12	Vanilla 116¾ Northeast Trades 1192 Great Era 1162	Wide	10
12Jly 66–6Aqu	fst 5½f	.22⅘ .46 1.05⅗	f- Allow	3	4	2h	2h	11	1¾	HWoodhouse		119	4.30	85–19	Gay Gobha 119¾ Mopolina 114½ Best Secret 119nk	Hard drive	7
6Jly 66–6Aqu	fst 5½f	.22⅘ .46⅘1.06⅕	f-MdSpWt	7	3	2½	1½	11	12½	HWoodhouse		119	*1.00	82–20	Gay Gobha 1192½ Needles Lady 1194 Imanative 1192	Mild drive	9
29Jun66–5Aqu	fst 5½f	.22⅘ .46⅕1.05⅘	f-MdSpWt	6	6	52¾	53½	21	21½	HWoodhouse		119	3.80	82–17	Vanilla 1191½ Gay Gobha 1196 Henrietta 119no	Wide on turn	12
22Jun66–5Aqu	fst 5½f	.22⅗ .46⅗1.06⅗	f-MdSpWt	3	10	99½	87½	76	32	BFeliciano		119	5.00e	78–20	Green Glade 1191 Sorche 1191 Gay Gobha 1192½	In close, rallied	12

LATEST WORKOUTS Jun 16 Bel 3f fst .35⅖ bg — Jun 13 Bel 7f fst 1.26⅘ h — Jun 9 Bel 6f fst 1.14⅕ h — Jun 6 Bel 7f fst 1.31 h

Camera Tip ×

B. f (1964–Ky), by Tipoquill—Bushthorn, by Boxthorn — T. O. Campbell — W. U. Ridenour — (T. O. Campbell) — **111** — 1967 10 2 2 1 $2,875 — 1966 4 M 1 1 $1,305

27May67–8RD	fst 6f	.22⅘ .45 1.10⅗	Handicap	3	3	83¾	89¼	711	65¾	GPRyan	b	116	7.80	87–17	Rullation 1182 Brave Beau 1221 Counteret 112½	Not a contender	8
20May67–7RD	fst 6f	.22⅘ .46 1.11⅗	Allowance	2	6	32	32½	2½	21½	GPRyan	b	116	6.90	86–17	Sir Bates 1151½ Camera Tip 1131 Bold Copy 117½	Held on gamely	8
29Apr67–8CD	fst 7f	.22⅘ .45⅘1.23⅖	f-Torienne	4	8	66	65½	711	610	MMangan'lo	b	115	74.70	80–12	Furl Sail 1214 Overstreet 1181¼ Gay Sailorette 1151	No threat	8
18Apr67–6Kee	fst 7f	.22⅘ .45 1.23⅗	f- Allow	3	7	68	710	713	614	JLower5	b	105	33.20	76–17	Prim Lady 1163½ Majestic Return 1125 Gay Sailorette 1104	No sp'd	9
12Apr67–7Kee	fst 6f	.21⅘ .45⅕1.10⅗	f- Allow	1	8	711	69½	56½	49	JLower5	b	108	17.20e	81–18	Plum Plum 1162 Alpine Peak 1132 She's Very Ultra 1135	No mishap	8
4Mar67–8FG	fst 1 40	.46⅖1.12 1.40⅘	Handicap	4	6	611	69	715	717	STheall		105	31.50	74–12	Court Her 1163 Jalo Bond 1205 Lucky Roman 1142	Showed little	7
18Feb67–5FD	fst 1 70	.47⅕1.13⅘1.48	Allowance	5	5	310	37½	22	15	JLower5	b	107	2.20	69–18	Camera Tip 1075 Solid Sender 120h Sky Village 112no	Handily	6
11Feb67–2FD	gd 6f	.22 .47⅕1.15⅖	f-MdSpWt	3	10	88	611	33	13½	JLower5	b	113	*0.80	73–28	Camera Tip 1133½ Virgo's Star 1185 Verily 1185	Going away	10
2Feb67–2FD	fst 6f	.22⅕ .46⅖1.11⅘	Md Sp Wt	5	10	85¼	55	43½	25	JLower5	b	108	*1.40	86–11	Rone U. 1185 Camera Tip 1085 Capt. Maltby 118no	Slow start	10
23Jan67–5FD	fst 6f	.21⅖ .45⅘1.11⅘	Allowance	4	6	58½	58	47½	37	JWarner	b	110	7.80	84–14	Prim Lady 1054 Lil' Lija 1183 Camera Tip 1101	Even effort	6
25Nov66–8Lat	sly 1 1/16	.47⅖1.13⅖1.48⅘	f-Clips'ta	5	7	711	67	58	47¼	JWarner		109	7.50e	64–25	Cocktail Music 1131¼ Dun-Cee 1163 Time for School 1103	No threat	8
16Nov66–3Lat	fst 5½f	.23⅕ .48 1.07⅗	f-MdSpWt	6	9	97	610	58½	34	MM'nganello		119	*1.50	80–14	Road Shift 1143½ Sock Hop 119½ Camera Tip 1191½	Belated rally	10
7Nov66–2Lat	my 5½f	.23⅖ .48⅖1.08⅕	f-MdSpWt	2	5	52½	43	33	22	MManganello		119	*1.80	79–23	Super Satin 1192 Camera Tip 1195 Make Me Rich 119nk	Second best	8
27Oct66–2Kee	fst 6f	.22⅗ .47⅖1.13	f-MdSpWt	5	9	85½	66	66	44¾	MManganello		117	44.40	73–21	MartialQueen1172 Vicki'sChoice1171½ Anc'ntProphecy1171¼	Rallied	10

LATEST WORKOUTS Jun 13 Bel tr.t. 5f fst 1.04⅗ b — Jun 10 Bel tr.t. 3f fst .36 h

Prima Ballerina *

Ro. f (1964–Ky), by Royal Vale—Shy Dancer, by Bolero — J. D. Wimpfheimer — W. Sedlacek — (J. D. Wimpfheimer) — **109** — 1967 8 0 2 1 $5,500 — 1966 23 2 1 4 $14,560

2Jun67–6Aqu	fst 6f	.22⅖ .45⅕1.10⅖	f- Allow	3	6	56½	46	36	46½	GMora5	b	104	7.10	84–18	Sumtex 109¾ Jane's Joy 1205½ Blossom Morgan 109nk	Evenly	6
27May67–6Aqu	fm 1 1/16 Ⓣ	1.43⅗	f- Allow	3	4	3½	1½	21	35	GMora5	b	105	5.50	83–12	Forty Merry's 1102 Spire 1113 Prima Ballerina 1051½	Weakened	8
19May67–6Aqu	fst 1	.46⅖1.10⅖1.36⅗	f- Allow	4	4	43	54½	43½	44½	GMora7	b	101	3.70	81–18	Sweet Folly 113h Sumtex 1084 Scottish Heath 113h	Even race	7
13May67–5Aqu	fst 6f	.22 .45⅕1.11⅗	f- Allow	1	8	812	811	64½	22½	GMora7	b	109	5.40	82–16	GreekSong'sGet1212½ PrimaBallerina1092½ Falconry109nk	Rallied	8
5May67–7Aqu	fst 6f	.22⅕ .45⅖1.11⅖	f- Allow	5	6	65	53¼	49	57¾	EBelmonte	b	111	6.40	78–19	Sweet And Low 1135 Dust To Dust 113h Ship Shoal 115¾	No mishap	10
28Apr67–7Aqu	sl 7f	.23⅘ .48 1.26⅕	f- Allow	3	7	64	32	21½	24	EBelmonte	b	112	4.30	71–26	Whiglet 1204 Prima Ballerina 1125 Dust To Dust 113¾	In close	8
21Apr67–6Aqu	fst 6f	.22⅕ .45⅘1.11⅖	f- Allow	2	10	65¾	64	43½	43½	EBelmonte	b	112	31.20	82–22	Great Era 1121½ Vanilla 1101 Sweet and Low 1151	Evenly	12
29Mar67–7Aqu	my 6f	.23⅗ .48⅗1.13⅘	f-H'dicap	3	5	46	65¾	69½	68	EBelmonte	b	112	23.70	66–33	Gr'kSong'sGet112h•SportsEvent113no•She'sB'utiful 120no	Tired	7
6Dec66–6Aqu	fst 7f	.23⅖ .47⅕1.26⅖	f- Allow	4	6	54½	53	1½	1nk	EBelmonte	b	118	6.10	74–26	PrimaBallerina118nk Murmuring1181½ Dunce'sRibbonair1112	Driving	9
24Nov66–6Aqu	fst 6f	.22⅖ .46⅕1.11⅖	f- Allow	2	9	97½	66	79½	57¾	BBaeza	b	118	5.90	78–21	Sumtex 1215 Murmuring 118¾ Bugle Beads 1161½	No speed	10
5Nov66–8Lrl	fst 1 1/16	.47⅖1.13⅕1.45⅖	f-Selima	2	9	85¼	88¼	1012	1019	PIGrimm	b	119	45.30e	71–14	Regal Gleam 122½ Quillo Queen 1192 Thong 1191	Never close	14
25Oct66–7Aqu	fst 6f	.22⅗ .46⅖1.12	f- Allow	2	9	76	77¾	79½	54½	RTurcotte	b	118	3.80	78–18	On the Carpet 1094 Pays to Sing 114½ Wageko 116no	No factor	10

LATEST WORKOUTS Jun 10 Aqu 4f fst .52⅘ b — May 26 Aqu 3f sly .38⅗ b

Up And At 'Em

B. f (1964–Fla), by Hilarious—Auratum, by Blue Swords — Hobeau Farm — H. A. Jerkens — (E. K. Heubeck) — **111** — 1967 2 1 0 0 $5,275 — 1966 8 1 1 1 $4,500

24May67–8Aqu	fst 1	.46⅘1.11⅗1.37⅗	f- Allow	6	1	1½	13	15	13	ECardone	b	110	2.90	80–18	Up And At 'Em 1103 I Be Dandy 113h Chantilly Jewel 1105	Mild dr.	9
10May67–6Aqu	fst 7f	.23⅖ .47 1.26	f- Allow	7	8	77½	88	54	43	ECardone	b	110	11.20	73–21	Heavenly Choir 113no Forty Merry's 1063 I Be Dandy 113h	Rallied	9
6Sep66–1Aqu	fst 6f	.22⅘ .47⅘1.14⅘	f- 11500	3	9	94¼	104¾	42½	2¾	EBelmonte	b	116	*2.10	68–28	Kathleen Gee 111¾ Up And At 'Em 1161 Clemita 1173	Rallied	11
27Aug66–5Sar	fst 6f	.22⅕ .45⅘1.12	f- Allow	4	10	1010	107½	99½	914	ALoguercio5	b	111	12.50	74– 8	Swiss Cheese 121no Treacherous 1162 All too Legal 1213½	No speed	11
3Aug66–7Sar	fst 5½f	.22⅕ .46 1.05	f-Sch'vle	7	6	97	86	77½	66¾	EBelmonte		116	41.70	85–12	Vanilla 116¾ Northeast Trades 1192 Great Era 1162	No factor	10
27Jly 66–6Aqu	fst 5½f	.22⅘ .47 1.06⅕	f- Allow	6	1	44½	41½	32	41	ECardone5	b	114	*1.10	81–18	ShirleyHeights 119½ On theCarpet 119no Pepperwood 119½	Wide str.	7
19Jly 66–6Aqu	fst 5½f	.22⅗ .46⅕1.06⅕	f- Allow	5	5	52	43½	33	3nk	EBelmonte	b	112	*2.00	82–19	Best Secret 112h Gala Honors 119h Up and at 'Em 1122½	Gamely	10
12Jly 66–6Aqu	fst 5½f	.22⅘ .46 1.05⅗	f- Allow	6	6	56	55½	43½	41½	ALoguercio10	b	109	5.10	83–19	Gay Gobha 119¾ Mopolina 114½ Best Secret 119nk	Swerved stretch	7
5Jly 66–4Aqu	fst 5½f	.22⅘ .46⅘1.06	f-Md 12500	6	1	43	43½	2h	12½	ECardone5	b	116	*2.40	83–20	Up And At 'Em1162½ Greek Song's Get1195 Nursemaid1212½	Easily	10
24Jun66–5Suf	fst 5f	.23 .47 .59⅘	f-MdSpWt	7	8	106¼	1116	1010	66¾	WMayorga		118	7.90	85–15	Fragrantly 1184 English Jane 118¾ Dora Mia 118no	No factor	12

LATEST WORKOUTS Jun 14 Bel tr.t. 4f fst .53⅗ b — Jun 10 Bel tr.t. 5f fst 1.02 h — Jun 7 Bel tr.t. 4f fst .50 b — Jun 3 Bel tr.t. 5f fst 1.02 h

Heavenly Choir

Dk. b. or br. f (1964–Ky), by Aureole—Arietta II, by Tudor Minstrel   **114**   1967 4 2 0 0 $8,580
O. Phipps   E. A. Neloy   (O. Phipps)   1966 0 M 0 0 —

19May67–6Aqu	fst 1	.46$\frac{2}{5}$1.10$\frac{3}{5}$1.36$\frac{3}{5}$ f–	Allow 7	3 5^3 4^4 5^5 5$^7\frac{1}{2}$	BBaeza	113	*1.20	78–18 Sweet Folly 113^h Sumtex 108^4 Scottish Heath 113^h	No excuses 7
10May67–6Aqu	fst 7f	.23$\frac{3}{5}$ .47 1.26 f–	Allow 5	7 6$^5\frac{1}{2}$ 6$^5\frac{1}{2}$ 2$^1\frac{1}{2}$ 1no	BBaeza	113	*1.60	76–21 Heavenly Choir 113no Forty Merry's 106^3 I Be Dandy 113^h	Just up 9
29Apr67–1Aqu	fst 7f	.23$\frac{3}{5}$ .47$\frac{2}{5}$1.25$\frac{1}{5}$ f–MdSpWt 11	2 2^1 2$^1\frac{1}{2}$ 1^2 1$^1\frac{1}{2}$	EBelmonte	113	2.60	80–18 Heavenly Choir 113$^1\frac{1}{2}$ Moon Ferry 113^3 Handsome Girl 106^3	Driving 9
22Apr67–2Aqu	fst 6f	.22$\frac{3}{5}$ .46$\frac{1}{5}$1.12$\frac{3}{5}$ f–MdSpWt 11	11 11^{12}11^{11}4^{10}4 7$^6\frac{1}{2}$	WShoemaker	113	*2.40e	74–16 Cynnie 118$^3\frac{1}{2}$ Muse 114^{nk} Gaelic Princess 106^1	Far off pace 11

LATEST WORKOUTS   Jun 17 Bel 4f fst .49$\frac{1}{5}$ b   Jun 9 Bel t.c 5f fm 1.05 b   Jun 5 Bel 4f fst .49 b

Jane's Joy ✳

Ch. f (1963–Va), by Helioscope—Ali Wing, by Alibhai   **113^7**   1967 4 1 2 0 $7,875
Jane Caruso   S. Caruso   (S. Caruso)   1966 12 1 2 2 $5,720

2Jun67–6Aqu	fst 6f	.22$\frac{3}{5}$ .45$\frac{1}{5}$1.10$\frac{3}{5}$ f–	Allow 4	1 1^2 1$^1\frac{1}{2}$ 1^1 2$\frac{3}{4}$	HWoodhouse	120	*1.20	90–18 Sumtex 109$\frac{3}{4}$ Jane's Joy 120$^5\frac{1}{2}$ Blossom Morgan 109^{nk}	Gamely 6
26May67–8Aqu	my 6f	.22$\frac{3}{5}$ .46$\frac{2}{5}$1.12$\frac{3}{5}$ f–	Allow 5	2 1^2 1^2 1^4 1$^1\frac{1}{2}$	ACorderoJr	120	*1.20	81–26 Jane's Joy 120$^1\frac{1}{2}$ Sinking Spring 110^5 Borderline 113$^1\frac{1}{2}$	Mild drive 6
17May67–8Aqu	fst 6f	.22$\frac{3}{5}$ .46 1.12$\frac{3}{5}$ f–	Allow 9	1 1^1 1$^1\frac{1}{2}$ 1^3 2$^2\frac{1}{2}$	HWoodhouse	118	*2.50	81–16 Forty Merry's 109$^2\frac{1}{2}$ Jane's Joy 118^8 Borderline 113^1	Tired 8
3May67–6Aqu	fst 6f	.22$\frac{3}{5}$ .47 1.13$\frac{3}{5}$ f–	Allow 4	1 1$^1\frac{1}{2}$ 1^2 1$^1\frac{1}{2}$ 1$\frac{1}{2}$	DCaraballo^7	113	d12.00	75–21 d–Jane's Joy 113$\frac{1}{2}$ Sweet Folly 113no Forty Merry's 106$\frac{3}{4}$	Bore out 11
3May67—d–Disqualified and placed last.									
29Sep66–6Aqu	fst 6f	.22$\frac{3}{5}$ .46 1.11$\frac{3}{5}$ f–	Allow 9	1 1^3 1^4 1$^1\frac{1}{2}$ 2^{nk}	JRuane	116	19.30	86–18 Wise Lady 114^{nk} Jane's Joy 116$\frac{3}{4}$ Dove Hunt 116no	Made game try 10
14Sep66–6Aqu	gd 6f	.22$\frac{3}{5}$ .46$\frac{3}{5}$1.12$\frac{3}{5}$ f–	Allow 5	1 2$\frac{1}{2}$ 2^2 2^6 5^7	RRoland^7	112	18.50	74–23 Lobelia 119^3 Dove Hunt 116$^2\frac{1}{2}$ Tangle 115$\frac{1}{2}$	Well up, tired 8
17Aug66–8Sar	fst 6f	.22 .45$\frac{4}{5}$1.12$\frac{1}{5}$ f–	Allow 3	2 2^h 2$^1\frac{1}{2}$ 7^7 9^{14}	EBelmonte	118	15.30	73–14 Terrific Traffic 112$\frac{1}{2}$ Tangle 115^h Romanticism 113^h	Stopped 9
10Aug66–8Sar	fst 6f	.22$\frac{3}{5}$ .46 1.12$\frac{3}{5}$ f–	Allow 5	1 1^1 1$\frac{1}{2}$ 2^h 7$^3\frac{3}{4}$	EBelmonte	118	9.70	82–15 Ship Shoal 116$\frac{3}{4}$ Tangle 115^1 Romanticism 113^{nk}	Hard used early 8
5Aug66–1Sar	fst 6f	.22$\frac{3}{5}$ .46$\frac{1}{5}$1.11$\frac{4}{5}$ f–MdSpWt 3	1 1^h 1$^1\frac{1}{2}$ 1$\frac{1}{2}$ 1$\frac{1}{2}$	EBelmonte	118	9.60	90–12 Jane's Joy 118$\frac{1}{2}$ Lobelia 118^6 Hey Dolly 118^h	Won driving 14

LATEST WORKOUTS   May 30 Bel tr.t. 3f fst .37 h   Apr 26 Bel 3f fst .36$\frac{1}{5}$ h   Apr 29 Bel 3f fst .39 b

---

Gay Gobha: Making her first start of the year after ten months of nurture by the breeder-trainer, the patient Colin MacLeod, Jr., this three-year-old showed willing spirit when she beat half the field in the Schuylerville at Saratoga last year. Ran a similar race in the Adirondack as well. Ordinarily, a filly of this kind would return to the races desperately short of stamina, but look at Gay Gobha's workouts. A nice, easy seven-eighths on June 6, followed three days later by a sensible three-quarters, and then, on June 13, the crackdown. Seven furlongs in 1.26$\frac{4}{5}$ is a marvelous workout for a three-year-old filly. It indicates racing readiness. A horse that works so frequently, so swiftly, and at such long distances by comparison with the distance of her scheduled race is a horse prepared for a genuine try, regardless of whether she has had any recent races. Is Gay Gobha a cinch? By no means. We have to wait to see what else is running. But we can be sure that she will be in the chase. CONTENDER.

Camera Tip: Horses unable to win at River Downs do not belong in allowance races at Aqueduct. NO BET.

Prima Ballerina: In her only stakes effort, as a two-year-old, this Royal Vale filly showed nothing. She has been fairly close a few times but has shown no real lick in her eight consecutive losing efforts this year. Might be in the running at some stage, but does not inspire enough confidence to merit selection in a race for a $9,500 purse. NO BET.

Up And At 'Em: The brilliant Allen Jerkens thought so little of this filly as a two-year-old, and for such good reason, that he dropped her into a claimer, which she lost in woefully slow time. In her first start of 1967, on May 10, the filly showed a disposition to come on in the stretch of a seven-furlong race. This apparently prompted the trainer to test her at a mile on May 24. She won after leading all the way. Nothing in her record implies that she has enough early foot to compete against allowance stock at six furlongs. NO BET.

Heavenly Choir: Eddie Neloy's lightly raced filly seems to be comfortable at seven furlongs. She won her allowance race at that distance by a whisker, after dawdling far behind the early pace. Neloy may ask Baeza to try to get off quicker today and to stay as close to the pack as possible, but the horse does not seem capable of changing her style so abruptly. NO BET.

Jane's Joy: The only four-year-old in the race is a confirmed front-runner with a tendency to wilt in the stretch when pressed. As the only front-runner in the field, and carrying a 113-pound feather besides, she might have things all her own way. Especially since the track is sloppy. CONTENDER.

The contenders seem to be Gay Gobha and Jane's Joy. In Gay Gobha's favor are respectable if unspectacular efforts in two stakes races, plus sensational preparatory workouts which indicate an all-out try by MacLeod. The main rap against her is that she will have to catch Jane's Joy, who will encounter little competition during the early going and ought to have a good deal left in the stretch. Although another black mark against Gay Gobha is her long absence from racing, we believe that her workout record cancels that disadvantage.

The negative aspects of Jane's Joy are her status as a confirmed allowance runner with pretensions to nothing better and her invariable weakness in the final yards of the race. However, she has so much more sheer speed than any of her rivals that she shapes up as the logical choice.

How about the jockeys? One look at this factor and the complexion of the race changes. Gay Gobha is to be ridden today by the splendid Hedley Wood-house, who has been the jockey in every one of the filly's earlier races. He was on Jane's Joy in her last start but has abandoned her for Gay Gobha. In his stead, Trainer Sal Caruso has hired Danny Caraballo, a raw apprentice. The theory, of course, is that the kid need do nothing but sit there while Jane's Joy runs in front from wire to wire. The last time Caruso tried this ploy was on May 3. Jane's Joy ran in front all the way against a similar field, carrying 113 pounds, including Caraballo. Unfortunately, the youngster was unable to persuade the horse to run in a straight line. She bore out, interfering with other animals so badly that she was disqualified and placed last. Is there any assurance that she will not bear out again today? No, there is not. Is she worth betting on? Not in my opinion. If Caraballo had been able to keep her on course in the May 3 race, even though losing in the stretch drive, one could expect her to walk away with today's sprint. But since the record shows that she acts badly when the kid rides her, I would not bet a dime on her.

Where does that leave Gay Gobha? All alone as a contender, the rest having been eliminated for good and sufficient cause. Is Gay Gobha worth a bet? I believe so, because that is the way I handicap horse races. True, the pace favors Jane's Joy—bearing out or not. But she had better be running straight ahead in the stretch because the workout record indicates that Gay Gobha is sure to be right on her heels, and gaining fast.

The Running of the Race

JANE'S JOY went off at 7–10, as might have been predicted. Up and At 'Em, because of her recent front-running win (at a mile!) and because Jerkens is among the most deservedly respected trainers in the business, was second choice at 3–1.

Gay Gobha won by a head because Hedley Woodhouse outrode the apprentice Caraballo. Hedley kept his filly on the rail all the way, saving many precious yards of ground. Jane's Joy ran wide on the backstretch, wide on the turn, and wide to the wire, covering just enough extra real estate to permit Woodhouse to

---

SIXTH RACE
Aqu - 31441
June 19, 1967

6 FURLONGS. (Near Man, July 17, 1963, 108⅗, 3, 112.)
Allowances. Purse $9,500. Fillies and mares. 3-year-olds and upward which have never won three races. Weights, 3-year-olds 114 lbs., older 123 lbs. Non-winners of two races since March 11, 3 lbs., of a race since then or two races since Jan. 16, 5 lbs.
Value to winner $6,175, second $1,900, third $950, fourth $475. Mutuel pool $267,325.

Index	Horse	Eqt A Wt PP St	¼	½	Str	Fin	Jockey	Owner	Odds $1
28414Sar7	—Gay Gobha	3 109 1 2	2h	23	24	1h	H Woodh'se	Mrs C MacLeod	6.90
31315Aqu2	—Jane's Joy	4 113 6 1	13	11½	11	22	D Caraballo7	Jane Caruso	.70
31315Aqu4	—Prima B'll'rina b	3 110 3 6	6	6	53	33	J Giovanni	J D Wimpfheimer	11.00
31188Aqu1	—Up And At 'Em b	3 111 4 3	56	52	4½	45	E Cardone	Hobeau Farm	3.30
31150Aqu5	—Heavenly Choir	3 114 5 4	33	34	34	51½	B Baeza	O Phipps	6.90
31089RD6	—Camera Tip b	3 112 2 5	4½	4h	6	6	W Boland	T O Campbell	23.60

Time .23, .47, 1.12⅗ (against wind in backstretch). Track sloppy.

$2 Mutuel Prices:

1-GAY GOBHA	15.80	5.20	4.00
6-JANE'S JOY		2.60	2.40
3-PRIMA BALLERINA			3.40

Dk. b. or br. f, by Besomer—Iarrtas, by Alquest. Trainer C. MacLeod Jr. Bred by C. MacLeod, Jr. (Va.).
IN GATE AT 4.02. OFF AT 4.02 EASTERN DAYLIGHT TIME. Start good. Won driving.

GAY GOBHA, well placed and saving ground from the start, responded to strong handling when kept to the inside for the stretch run and won from JANE'S JOY in the last strides. JANE'S JOY, away fast, raced well off the inner rail the entire trip, held on gamely during the drive but was not good enough. PRIMA BALLERINA lacked early foot but finished strongly in the middle of the track. UP AND AT EM had no excuse. HEAVENLY CHOIR raced wide early and tired during the stretch run. CAMERA TIP disliked the sloppy going.

Overweights—Camera Tip 1 pound, Prima Ballerina 1.

---

get there first. At almost 7–1, Gay Gobha was as sweet an overlay as one ever finds at Aqueduct.

Note well that when a horse is the class of its race and has been prepared for a real crackdown through unusually long, frequent, and rapid workouts, something else needs a pronounced pace advantage to beat it. Gay Gobha, no paragon of obvious class, had nevertheless run better in high quality fields than any of her rivals. I would have gone to Jane's Joy if the past-performance record had not betrayed her rebelliousness toward today's rider, strongly suggesting that inability to save ground would obliterate her pace advantage.

3. EIGHTH AT PIMLICO, MAY 12, 1967—Track Fast

IN SEARCHING for the higher-class animals in an allowance field, there is a tendency to overlook the handicapping wrinkle that produced a good bet on this occasion and that leads to the cashier's window many times a season.

The race is for older fillies and mares that have earned a winner's purse of as much as $3,300 not more than once in their careers. In big-time racing, $8,000 claimers make that much for winning against their own kind.

8th Race Pimlico

▼Start 6 FURLONGS PIMLICO ▲Finish

6 FURLONGS. (I Salute, November 10, 1954, 1.10, 4, 106.)
Allowances. Purse $6,500. Fillies and mares. 4-year-olds and upward which have not won $3,300 twice other than maiden, claiming, starter or optional. Weight 122 lbs. Non-winners of $3,250 twice in 1967 allowed 3 lbs., once 5 lbs., $2,925 twice at any time 7 lbs., once 10 lbs. (Maiden, claiming, starter and optional races not considered in estimating allowances.)

Aunt Tilt ✻
B. f (1963-Ky), by Tulyar—Kerala, by My Babu
Edith W. Bancroft F. Y. Whiteley, Jr. (Mrs. T. Bancroft) **117**
1966 17 2 3 6 $21,962
1965 7 2 1 1 $5,960

19Nov66-8Lrl fm 1 1/16 Ⓣ 1.43⅕ f-Chry'mH 10 10 98¾ 105 810 76½ JBrocklebank 113 42.20 83-10 Swinging Mood 1231¼ Politely 117nk Indian Sunlite 1182 No mishap 10
8Nov66-9Lrl fm*1 Ⓣ .47⅘1.41 f- Allow 9 10 910 74¼ 41 11 JBrocklebank 109 8.80 85-15 Aunt Tilt 1091 Devil's Candy 1163 Angelic Caprice 113½ Driving 12
29Oct66-6Lrl fst 7f .23⅕ .47⅕1.25⅗ f- Allow 9 9 63½ 610 511 512 WShoemaker 112 6.80 79-16 Manya 1131½ Tempt Me Not 1154 Holly-O 122½ Showed little 12
29Sep66-7Aqu sf 1 1/16 Ⓣ 1.46⅗ f- Allow 6 6 66 78 58 56¾ ECardone5 106 15.60 66-27 ShortFall 118¾ MissMoona1114 Swim to Me1181½ No real threat 9
20Sep66-8Aqu fst 7f .22⅗ .45⅘1.23⅘ f- Allow 7 4 46½ 46½ 68½ 411 WShoemaker 112 5.10 76-22 Streamer 1197 Swim to Me 1201 Fatal Step 1163 No threat 7
25Aug66-8AP fst 6f .22⅕ .44⅖1.09⅖ f- Allow 1 6 32 35½ 56½ 54 WShoemaker 116 *2.20 92-13 Misty Swords 1142 Bear Grass 121no Color Me Gone 114¾ Tired 8
11Aug66-8AP sf*170 Ⓣ 1.44⅘ Allowance 5 7 64½ 52¼ 53 44½ JBeebe 109 9.90 80-17 Holiday Wish 1111½ Miss Rincon 114½ Cologne 1092½ Evenly 9
3Aug66-8AP fst 1 .45⅖1.10⅕1.35⅕ f-PckrUpH 4 8 56 89¾ 69½ 310 NShuk 112 33.30 80-12 Swinging Mood 1108 Cologne 1102 Aunt Tilt 112no Hung 12
13Jly 66-8Del fst 170 .45⅖1.10⅖1.40⅗ f-Rosenna 2 4 47 76¾ 54¼ 34½ PIGrimm 111 4.30 92-12 Help On Way 1141½ ShimmeringGold 1113 AuntTilt 111½ Good try 8
13Jly66—The Rosenna run in two divisions, 7th and 8th races.
5Jly 66-6Del fst 6f .22 .45⅖1.11 f- Allow 1 7 44 65½ 44 2¾ FLovato 108 2.90e 89-17 Miss Spin 113¾ Aunt Tilt 1081½ Love Bunowitz 1091 Checked 7
LATEST WORKOUTS Apr 29 CD 5f fst 1.01⅘ h Apr 18 Lrl 4f gd .50 b Apr 13 Lrl 3f gd .38⅖ b Apr 8 Lrl 3f gd .37⅖ b

Wagon Lit ✻
Dk. b. or br. f (1963-Ky), by Amerigo—Dark Sleeper, by Discovery
Christiana Stable H. S. Clark (Pine Brook Farm) **115**
1967 1 0 0 0 ——
1966 9 1 1 1 $5,450

6May67-7GS sly 6f .23⅕ .47⅕1.13 f- Allow 9 2 86 89¼ 62¾ 54 BThornburg 118 34.60 75-23 Tangle 112½ I'm All Ready 115½ Queen Narda 1121½ Late foot 9
28Nov66-7Lrl sly 1 .48⅗1.14⅖1.40⅖ f- Allow 5 3 11 1h 1½ 1nk EMaple5 109 2.10 79-20 Wagon Lit 109nk Tacaro Landing 1121½ Napalm 1165 Just lasted 6
14Nov66-7Lrl fst 1 .48⅖1.14⅕1.40⅖ f- Allow 5 5 32 42½ 41 21½ ENelson 114 3.60 77-26 High Bluff 1181½ Wagon Lit 114½ Tacaro Landing 118no Gamely 7
17Sep66-8Aqu fm 1 1/16 Ⓣ 1.45⅕ f- Allow 3 8 819 815 87 55¾ HWoodhouse 111 87.90 74-20 Barletta 116nk Home Lass 1082½ Angelic Caprice 1163 Late foot 8
6Sep66-8Aqu fm 1 1/16 Ⓣ 1.43⅕ f- Allow 2 8 913 98 87¾ 99 DChamberlin5 107 49.90 81-10 OurDearRuth 111noSilverBright 1131½Shim'eringGold 118½ No speed 10
8Aug66-6Sar fst 6f .22⅗ .46 1.11⅘ f- Allow 3 6 69½ 612 66½ 57¾ DHidalgo5 106 68.00 81-13 Home Lass 1131½ Summer Mark 113nk Fatal Step 1084 Bore out 8
2Jly 66-7Del fst 170 .46 1.11⅖1.42⅗ f- Allow 4 6 67 63¾ 44 35¼ BThornburg 112 17.80 82-16 Sturdy Gerty 115¾ Conqui 1154¼ Wagon Lit 1121 Passed tired ones 7
15Jun66-8Del fst 6f .22⅗ .45⅘1.10⅗ f- Allow 6 2 56¾ 67½ 611 612 ENelson 113 16.90 80-13 Politely 1133 Hilo Hattie 121¾ Midagay 113½ Fell back early 6
26May66-7GS sly 6f .22⅖ .46 1.12⅗ f- Allow 2 4 46½ 59½ 65½ 64¾ PIGrimm 113 7.90 76-24 Shae Maidle 112nk Summer Mark 121¾ Chavalon 113nk Never close 6
18May66-6GS sly 6f .22⅗ .46⅕1.12 f- Allow 4 5 62¼ 77¼ 63½ 52 PIGrimm 114 38.50 82-19 I'm All Ready 1182 Shae Maidle 112no Fizzy 118no No mishap 7
LATEST WORKOUTS May 5 GS 3f fst .38 b May 1 GS 6f fst 1.15⅗ h Apr 26 GS 5f fst 1.04⅗ b Apr 19 Pim 5f gd 1.03⅗ b

Misty's Baby ×
Dk. b. or br. m (1962), by Crafty Admiral—Miss Misty, by Ocean Wave
W. P. Reynolds W. P. Reynolds, Jr. (Beacon Stable) **117**5
1967 7 2 2 0 $9,450
1966 12 1 4 2 $7,785

26Apr67-8Pim sly 6f .23⅗ .46⅗1.12 f- Allow 1 1 1h 2½ 2½ 21½ RKimball 122 2.90 88-16 TemptMeNot 1191½ Misty'sBaby 1224 LongwoodLady 122h Gamely 6
19Apr67-8Pim fst 6f .23⅘ .47⅖1.12⅘ f- Allow 4 2 1h 2h 23 53 RKimball 117 3.00 83-19 PennyPower 115nk PolynesianPlay 1102½ TemptMeNot 115h Wide 7
17Mar67-8Pim my 6f .23⅗ .47⅗1.13⅗ f- Allow 2 1 1h 1h 1½ 11¼ RKimball 119 2.60 82-24 Misty's Baby 1191¼ Pidgin 1141 Penny Power 1172 Drew clear 8
6Mar67-8Pim sly 6f .23⅗ .47 1.13⅖ f- Allow 4 4 1h 1h 1h 12 RKimball 112 4.30 83-26 Misty's Baby 1122 Garden Clubber 1121¼ Dove Hunt 112½ Clear 7
21Feb67-8Bow sl 6f .22⅖ .45⅗1.12⅗ f- Allow 5 5 31½ 32½ 3nk 11¼ RKimball 113 d-8.70 84-30 d-Misty's Baby 1131¼ Zayer Naytik 107¾ Lucy Bean 113nk Bore in 10
21Feb67—d-Disqualified and placed second.
14Feb67-8Bow fst 6f .22⅘ .46⅕1.11⅘ f- Allow 6 9 65½ 57 74¼ 53½ RKimball 117 54.20 84-23 FlashyShot 1141 d-DoveHunt 110nk CherokeeMary 112nk No mishap 11
27Jan67-8Bow sly 6f .22⅘ .46⅕1.12⅗ Allowance 11 2 72½ 1114 1113 1011 JTaylor 113 47.60 73-28 Benedict C. 1151 Nannie's Boy 109¾ Bronze Bout 1161 Tired 12
13Jly 66-8Rkm fst 6f .22⅖ .45⅘1.11⅖ Allowance 5 5 43 57 911 1014 BSorensen 114 41.50 73-18 Acceptance 109¾ Private World 113nk Deep Creek 1192¾ Tired 11
14Jun66-7Suf fst 6f .22⅖ .46 1.11 f- Allow 3 4 1h 2½ 42 69½ JKurtz 112 5.60 81-17 Merispats 115½ Bow's Gal 112no Tune-Swept 120no Speed, tired 7

Zamilu ⊗
B. f (1963-Ky), by Lurullah—Miss Zami, by Nizami II
C. A. Hunt R. L. Young (C. Ortlieb) **117**
1967 4 0 1 0 $1,200
1966 10 4 1 2 $13,295

27Feb67-8Hia fst 6f .22⅕ .45⅘1.10⅘ f- Allow 7 1 31 43 98 86¼ KKorte b 115 4.30 84-14 Athen's Gem 112nk Mandioca 1133½ Foreign Fable 107nk Gave way 12
15Feb67-8Hia fst 7f .23 .45⅖1.23 f-ColumbaH 8 4 41 814 1322 1318 KKorte b 113 127.40f 76-16 Mac's Sparkler 115h Moccasin 1171½ Straight Deal 122½ Tired 14
9Feb67-9Hia sly 6f .22⅖ .46⅕1.11⅗ f- Allow 9 6 45 46 25 23½ KKorte b 115 4.10 82-17 Meadow Stream 1123½ Zamilu 1151½ Boiseana 112h Good effort 12
11Jan67-9TrP fst 6f .21⅘ .44⅗1.10 f-Handicap 7 6 1113 1116 1115 1114 KKorte b 114 18.00 78-14 Little Portress 114¾ Welshwyn 1161¾ Bear Grass 1162½ No speed 11
28Dec66-8TrP fst 6f .22⅖ .45 1.10 f- Allow 4 5 1h 1h 2h 1¾ KKorte b 113 5.50 92-14 Zamilu 113¾ Rare Feather 115h Fizzy 1132¾ Up final strides 12
9Dec66-8TrP gd 6f .22 .45⅗1.11 f- Allow 7 3 32½ 31½ 22 34¼ KKorte b 113 4.90 83-19 Codorniz 1202¼ Neat 'n Sweet 1112 Zamilu 1132¾ Went well 8
23Nov66-9TrP fst 6f .21⅘ .44⅗1.09⅘ f-H'dicap 9 5 21½ 23 34 34¾ KKorte b 113 28.10 88-11 Bacasiwo 1183¾ Bear Grass 1171 Zamilu 113½ Held on gamely 9
13Jun66-8Del fst 6f .22⅘ .45⅘1.11⅖ f- Allow 6 5 66¾ 86¼ 57 55¾ RMikkonen b 118 4.40 82-18 Hot Gossip 1153 Love Bunowitz 115½ Aunt Tilt 105½ No threat 8
20May66-8Pim fst 1 1/16 .47 1.11⅖1.44⅘ f-B-ESus'n 7 ? 23 622 634 E'sd RMikkonen b 121 12.60 —— Holly-O 121½ Chalina 121h Justakiss 1216 Badly beaten, eased 7
LATEST WORKOUTS Apr 14 GP t.c. 7f fm 1.35 b Mar 17 GP 3f fst .36⅘ b

Wayward Star ⊗ — B. f (1962), by Dark Star—Wayward Miss, by Nasrullah. J. G. Kincheloe J. C. Mobberly (H. F. Guggenheim) **117**

1966	17	10	1	1	$13,527
1965	20	2	0	4	$9,363

3Nov66-8Lrl	gd	6f	.23⅕	.47⅘	1.13	f- Allow		12	1	21½	33½	23	32	RAdams	b 112	9.70	85-18	Penny Power 1101 Turf Talk 1071 Wayward Star 1124	Good effort	12
20Oct66-8Mar	sl	6½f	.24⅕	.49	1.23⅕	Allowance		1	2	2h	3nk	3nk	1no	SSmall	b 117	2.50	——	Wayward Star 117no Helioroad 115no Speedy Admiral 1153	Just up	8
8Oct66-9CT	fst	6½f	.23⅗	.47⅖	1.20⅘	Allowance		3	1	21½	2½	13	15	SSmall	b 117	*0.70	85-33	Wayward Star 1175 Rebec 120nk Erin's Joy 108no	Easily best	9
27Aug66-8RD	fm	76f Ⓣ			1.31⅗	f-Rhinel'rH		3	4	11½	3½	75	75	SSmall	b 118	7.80	94- 9	Miss Rochelle 1181 Karola 116nk Miss Hill 1141	Speed, gave way	11
6Aug66-8ShD	fst	6f	.23	.47	1.12⅘	Allowance		3	2	33½	32	21	1no	SSmall	b 117	*0.50	90-17	Wayward Star 117no Crack Back 1221½ Budco 1196	Up closing stride	5
23Jly66-10CT	fst	6½f	.24	.47⅘	1.20⅗	Allowance		2	2	1½	11½	12	11½	AVasil	b 119	*0.50	86-22	Wayward Star 1191½ Jezibel A. 1195 Budco 1147	Handy score	4
2Jly66-10CT	fst	6½f	.23⅗	.47	1.18⅘	Allowance		5	3	21½	2½	11½	14½	SSmall	b 117	1.60	95-15	Wayward Star 1174½ Albergo 113nk Bank Book Sadye 1142½	Handily	6
18Jun66-8CT	fst	6½f	.23⅗	.47⅕	1.20⅘	Allowance		2	2	55	55½	32½	1h	SSmall	b 116	5.30	85-21	Wayward Star 116h Budco 1164½ Bank Book Sadye 114nk	Just up	8
3Jun66-9ShD	fst	6f	.22⅘	.47⅖	1.13⅖	Allowance		6	3	3½	11	12½	14½	SSmall	b 117	*0.70	87-21	Wayward Star 1174½ Jezibel A. 115nk Shining Deer 1145	In hand	6

LATEST WORKOUTS May 6 CT 6f fst 1.16 hg Apr 19 CT 6f fst 1.20 b Apr 13 CT 5f fst 1.05 b Apr 7 Ct 5f sly 1.05 h

Waterloo Bridge * — Dk. b.. or br. f (1963–Md), by Martins Rullah—Goodnight Ladies, by Armageddon. P. Vischer T Simon (P. Vischer) **119**

1967	10	4	2	0	$12,630
1966	17	1	4	1	$7,024

5May67-8Pim	fst	6f	.23⅕	.46⅖	1.12⅖	f- Allow		1	3	46	33½	1½	14	PlGrimm	119	5.70	88-13	Waterloo Bridge 1194 Pidgin 115½ Even Rosier 115h	Mild drive	6
25Apr67-8Pim	fst	6f	.23⅘	.46⅗	1.12⅖	Allowance		2	5	65¾	810	67¾	42¼	PlGrimm	117	49.90	86-14	Namay 108¾ Native Uprising 112h Telepathy 1171½	Late stride	8
8Apr67-4Pim	fst	1⅛	.47	1.11⅖	1.51⅘	Hcp	4000s	2	6	711	611	612	58	PlGrimm	115	3.30	84-14	Fuzzie King 112½ Crown Keys 1141½ Discretion 1045	Dull try	8
30Mar67-4Pim	fst	1 1/16	.49⅕	1.13⅘	1.47	f-	7500	6	2	2h	3½	2½	1h	PlGrimm	115	*2.10	75-19	Waterloo Bridge 115h Acceptance 1081 Two Wings 113h	Driving	7
20Mar67-7Pim	fst	1 1/16	.47⅘	1.12⅕	1.44⅕	Clm	6500	8	3	32	21½	21½	21¼	PlGrimm	114	4.70	88-12	Dodgertown 1141¼ Waterloo Bridge 114½ Corsair II 1221	Gamely	9
14Mar67-5Pim	fst	1 1/16	.47⅗	1.13⅗	1.46⅗	f-	5000	2	6	53¼	2½	1½	12½	PlGrimm	119	4.80	7[illegible] 22	Waterloo Bridge 1192½ Irish Sis 107h Another Spin 1133½	Driving	7
7Mar67-3Pim	my	1 1/16	.50⅕	1.15⅖	1.49⅖	Clm	4000	4	2	21	2h	1h	1½	PlGrimm	114	3.10	63-29	Waterloo Bridge 114½ Dr. Giddings 1152 Fabulous Lee 1172½	Driving	8
20Feb67-2Bow	my	6f	.23	.47	1.13	Clm	4000	5	8	119½	1111	76	23½	PlGrimm	114	10.70	78-22	Hanker 1143½ Waterloo Bridge 114¾ Martin's Ark 1081	Rallied	12
23Jan67-5Bow	fst	1 1/16	.49⅖	1.15⅘	1.49⅕	f-	5000	11	8	817	78¾	614	620	HBlock	113	7.20	47-24	Arctic Queen 1164½ Another Spin 1135 Two Wings 1121	No speed	11
17Jan67-6Bow	fst	6f	.23⅕	.47	1.13⅖	f-	6000	5	9	1111	1213	118½	95	HBlock	114	39.20	75-25	Court Hostess 114nk Go Up 107½ Norma Mathews 109¾	No factor	12

LATEST WORKOUTS May 11 Lrl 3f gd .37 b May 4 Lrl 3f gd .36⅗ b Apr 5 Lrl 4f gd .50 b

Penny Power — Ch. f (1963-Ky), by More Sun—Magic Box, by Escadru. Fiying Lady Stable, Inc. C. C. Heverly (T. Piatt) **119**

1967	4	1	1	1	$5,000
1966	13	4	3	2	$13,770

26Apr67-8Pim	sly	6f	.23⅗	.46⅗	1.12	f- Allow		5	3	33	34½	34½	45½	AAgnello5	117	4.20	84-16	TemptMeNot 1151½ Misty'sBaby 1224 LongwoodLady 122h	Wide	6
19Apr67-8Pim	fst	6f	.23⅘	.47⅖	1.12⅘	f- Allow		3	3	2h	1h	13	1nk	CBaltazar	115	4.20	86-19	PennyPower 115nk PolynesianPlay 1102½ TemptMeNot 115h	Driving	7
5Apr67-8Pim	fst	6f	.23	.46	1.12⅕	f- Allow		4	5	62¾	53	44	22	CBaltazar	115	2.70	87-18	Detente 1072 Penny Power 115h Telepathy 117½	Finished well	7
17Mar67-8Pim	my	6f	.23⅗	.47⅗	1.13⅗	f- Allow		4	3	2h	2h	2½	32¼	CBaltazar	117	6.10	80-24	Misty's Baby 1191¼ Pidgin 1141 Penny Power 1172	Good effort	8
26Nov66-6Lrl	fst	7f	.23	.46⅘	1.25⅖	f- Allow		8	1	2½	32½	57	611	EFires	112	5.80	81-17	Manya 1144 Holly-O. 1225 Definitely Right 107½	Stopped	9
3Nov66-8Lrl	gd	6f	.23⅕	.47⅘	1.13	f- Allow		8	1	11½	13	13	11	CBaltazar	110	*3.20	87-18	Penny Power 1101 Turf Talk 1071 Wayward Star 1124	Safe margin	12
5Oct66-8Haw	fst	6½f	.22	.45⅕	1.16⅕	f-T'bienH		11	1	83½	85¾	53¼	3nk	MHeath	108	15.60	93- 7	Lost Message 112nk Trade Mark 115h Penny Power 108no	Rallied	11
21Sep66-7Haw	fst	6f	.22⅖	.45⅕	1.10⅖	f- Allow		6	9	82¼	76¾	64	41	MHeath	109	27.40	94-10	Money to Burn 117nk Misty Swords 111½ Brave Front 109nk	Rallied	11
3Sep66-7Rkm	gd	6f	.22	.45⅗	1.10⅘	Allowance		3	3	42	64¾	66¾	713	WMayorga	b 111	15.50	77-15	Miss Moona 114nk Sandoval 123½ Naughty Jester 1232¾	Brief speed	7

LATEST WORKOUTS May 10 Pim 4f fst .50⅖ b May 4 Pim 4f fst .51 b May 1 Pim 6f fst 1.18⅖ b Apr 24 Pim 4f fst .50⅗ b

Aunt Tilt: I have long regarded Frank Whiteley as the peer of any horseman alive. But I can't see him getting anything in this race. This filly has not been out since last year, has not been working like an animal ready to win at the first asking, and, in any case, likes longer distances, preferably against mediocre opposition and on grass. Too much has happened to her since her fair tries in the Pucker Up and Rosena last year. While she may have had a touch of class then, she should be credited with none until she displays it again. NO BET.

Wagon Lit: Showed a trace of late run six days ago in her first start of the year. But that was at Garden State, and the filly has not had so much as a workout on the local grounds. Moreover, she is a middle-distance horse, not a sprinter. I have to assume that she is in today's race strictly for conditioning purposes. NO BET.

Misty's Baby: This looks like a mare with an unusual talent for running on off tracks. When the track is fast, she has trouble. It can be predicted that she will be at or near the head end throughout this race. She might even win it, if the rest of the field is as unpromising as what we have seen so far. I don't like her on today's fast track, but we had better not toss her out yet. CONTENDER.

Zamilu: Away since February and unworked since April, this filly presents no threat whatever. Neither should she be credited with intrinsic class superior to that of the other horses in the race. She was completely outfooted in the Black Eyed Susan last year and the Columbia Handicap early this year. She is neither a stakes nor a handicap horse and will not beat allowance fillies today. NO BET.

Wayward Star: Any horse that can win ten times in seventeen starts is a nice meal ticket. But in this case all the victories were at minor bull rings and the horse has not raced in more than six months. NO BET.

Waterloo Bridge: That was a stunning win on May 5. The filly covered the distance with real speed (for allowance horses at Pimlico) and had plenty of energy in reserve at the finish. She should improve today, as horses that win in such style usually do. On the other hand, that string of cheap claiming races makes one wonder whether the last victory was a mirage. Closer examination is necessary. I see at a glance that Trainer Simon is a maneuverer of considerable foresight and talent. On March 7 the filly beat $4,000 males in the mud. He brought her back a week later against $5,000 females—an easier assignment—and got higher odds because the crowd thought he was moving up in class! After six days he tried $6,500 males and got second money. So he waited for ten days and then let her knock over $7,500 girls at an overlay of 2–1. Next he tried an impossible starter handicap, in which she had to carry 115 pounds for a mile and a furlong against males and was soundly trounced. On April 25 she returned to the wars at an apparently unsuitable distance in male allowance company and was eating up the field at the finish before she ran out of room. Then came her latest race, in which she demonstrated that she not only can race against females at six furlongs but can run close to the early pace and capture the lead in mid-stretch. This is an improving filly. CONTENDER.

Penny Power: This is a handy kind of filly, able to handle Misty's Baby on a fast track but not when the ground is sticky. Seems to do best when able to get out front and set a slow pace. CONTENDER.

The contenders are Misty's Baby, Waterloo Bridge, and Penny Power. The past-performance records insist that Misty's Baby is only third best on today's fast track. As the improving horse, coming off her powerful race of last week, Waterloo Bridge would seem to have an edge over Penny Power. That edge becomes more pronounced after an analysis of the probable pace. Assuming that both Penny Power and Misty's Baby are as fit as the record promises, they may lapse into a head-to-head speed duel, favoring the hard-knocking stretch-runner, Waterloo Bridge.

As for the jockeys, all three contenders should be well handled. Phil Grimm has been aboard Waterloo Bridge in each of her last eight starts and is evidently quite able to get the best she has. Penny Power has been switched back to Chuck Baltazar, a real topnotcher who has ridden her to the only victories on her recent list. Misty's Baby is under her favorite jockey, too. Which brings us to weights.

Waterloo Bridge carried 119 last time and is not being asked to carry any more today. Penny Power, who has had to struggle to get into the money when carrying more than 115 pounds, is assigned 119, which may not be a primary cause of defeat but certainly will not improve the prospects of victory. Misty's Baby, however, is the horse in trouble. Originally slated to carry only 117, including an apprentice, she has been switched to Kimball, which means she must tote 122. If the track were wet, she might be able to handle it, but the track is fast and she seems to be the kind of sore-footed Thoroughbred that dislikes a hard running surface.

Waterloo Bridge becomes the solid choice.

The Running of the Race

THE CROWD preferred Misty's Baby, probably because of her consistency. She went off as 2–1 favorite. The smart money was on Waterloo Bridge for a generous 3.30–1. Zamilu took the early lead but perished in the stretch. Whereupon the real racing began. Misty's Baby, close to the lead, as usual, began to tire toward the finish and swerved into Penny Power, preventing that one from getting second money. Once again, a fast track had been too much for the Reynolds horse. Waterloo Bridge, close to the pace all the way, came along on the rail and won by a head. Incidentally, Whiteley's Aunt Tilt might have finished second if she could have found running room in the stretch.

	EIGHTH RACE	6 FURLONGS. (I Salute, November 10, 1954, 1.10, 4, 106.)

Pim - 31080
May 12, 1967

Allowances. Purse $6,500. Fillies and mares. 4-year-olds and upward which have not won $3,300 twice other than maiden, claiming, starter or optional. Weight 122 lbs. Non-winners of $3,250 twice in 1967 allowed 3 lbs., once 5 lbs., $2,925 twice at any time 7 lbs., once 10 lbs. (Maiden, claiming, starter and optional races not considered in estimating allowances.)

Value to winner $4.225, second $1,300, third $650, fourth $325. Mutuel pool $73,896.

Index	Horse	Eqt A Wt	PP	St	¼	½	Str	Fin	Jockey	Owner	Odds $1
31035Pim¹	Waterloo Bridge	4 119	6	5	5²½	2ʰ	2ʰ	1ʰ	P I Grimm	P Vischer	3.30
30897Pim²	Misty's Baby	5 122	3	2	2½	3ʰ	3¹½	2ʰ	R Kimball†	W P Reynolds	2.00
30897Pim⁴	Penny Power	4 119	7	4	4¹½	4²	1ʰ	3¾	C Baltazar	Flying Lady Stable Inc	3.70
29325Lrl⁷	Aunt Tilt	4 117	1	7	6²	5½	4¹	4²	N Shuk	Edith W Bancroft	5.60
31043GS⁵	Wagon Lit	4 115	2	6	7	7	6½	5²	E Nelson	Christiana Stables	9.70
29217Lrl³	Wayward Star	b 5 117	5	3	3ʰ	6²	5ʰ	6⁴	S Small	J G Kincheloe	14.00
30328Hia⁸	Zamilu	b 4 117	4	1	1²	1½	7	7	C Rogers	C A Hunt	13.70

†Five pounds apprentice allowance waived.

Time .23⅖, .47⅗, 1.13. Track fast.

$2 Mutuel Prices:

6—WATERLOO BRIDGE	8.60	4.60	2.60
3—MISTY'S BABY		3.60	2.40
7—PENNY POWER			2.60

Dk. b. or br. f, by Martins Rullah—Goodnight Ladies, by Armageddon. Trainer T. Simon. Bred by P. Vischer (Md.).

IN GATE AT 4.33. OFF AT 4.33 EASTERN DAYLIGHT TIME. Start good. Won driving.

WATERLOO BRIDGE, hustled along to be within striking distance, found an opening along the rail to reach the leaders entering the stretch and outfinished MISTY'S BABY. The latter was a keen contender from the bginning, gaind a slight advatage over WATERLOO BRIDGE under heavy punishment in the last furlong but lost momentum by drifting out sharply ear the finish. PENNY POWER lost a little ground outside the first flight, drove to the front in the early strethc, then could not resist the top pair and was brushed by MISTY'S BABY in the last strides. AUNT TILT, permitted to settle into stride, appeared threatening for the drive but lacked racing room behind the bunched leaders through the entire stretch run. WAGON LIT was outrun. WAYWARD STAR tired. ZAMILU weakened in the drive.

EVENTH AT AQUEDUCT, MAY 18, 1967—Track Fast

THEORY that a good horse can beat a cheap horse at any distance
ers enormous sums of money every year. For example, ordinary
s beat the great Kelso at six furlongs, a distance too short for
sucker bets of the late winter and early spring seasons in Florida,
ornia, New Jersey, and New York are the previous year's leading
when entered in six-furlong allowance races after long winter

progresses, however, the player encounters an occasional oppor-
n on a classy router entered against inferior stock at *seven* fur-
ı is all the distance the class horse needs, especially if it is sharply
is pitted against animals that have their problems going farther
s.

is of this race specify a $10,000 purse for older horses that have
races. This is big money for four-year-olds barely out of the
y. Without a second thought, the experienced handicapper re-
or class—especially hidden class.

---

queduct — 7 FURLONGS AQUEDUCT (Start, Finish)

7 FURLONGS. (Chute). (Rose Net, Sept. 17, 1962, 1.21⅕, 6, 114.)
Allowances. Purse $10,000. 4-year-olds and upward which have never won three races. Weight 124 lbs. Non-winners of two races since March 12 allowed 3 lbs., of a race since then, 5 lbs., of two races since January 16, 7 lbs., of a race since December 10, 9 lbs.

Dk. b. or br. g (1963–Ky), by Stymie—Tweet Fleet, by Count Fleet — 115 — 1967 7 0 1 2 $3,665
Windham Farm E. W. King (Dr. C. E. Hagyard) — 1966 12 2 3 4 $12,420
53⅖ Allowance 7 6 621 610 44¼ 210 EBelmonte 123 12.20 59–24 Blast'gCharge11310SolemnNation123noRuffledFeathers1144 Fair try 7
51⅗ Allowance 4 2 2½ 43½ 34½ 57 EBelmonte 123 15.00 71–20 Dunderhead 1233 Blasting Charge 1102 Trade In 120½ Tired 7
54⅗ Allowance 4 3 511 33 31 32¾ EBelmonte 123 10.00 60–34 Wowzer 1132 Tom Poker 113¾ Solemn Nation 1232 Rallied, hung 7
11 Allowance 1 6 67½ 45½ 46½ 43½ EBelmonte 121 10.80 84–16 Smooth Seas 1211 Velvet Flash 1132½ Irish Dude 113h Sluggish early 6
25 Cl c-14000 5 2 32 33 44½ 37 WShoemaker 117 ♠ 2.50 74–25 Counsellor 1192 Well To Do 1215 ♠Beaustone 1154 Weakened 5

10⅘ Clm 16000 6 6 65½ 54 44 56¾ JTartaglia10 111 9.70 82–16 Two Stelle 121¾ Cuetip 1176 Athen's Gem 116no Began slowly 7
35⅖ Handicap 5 7 98¼104¼ 94½ 85½ RFerraro 117 7.10 —— Thermoject 113no Wiggins Fork 114¾ Wondrascope 1181 No factor 10
52⅗ Allowance 6 2 1h 2h 2h 1¾ EBelmonte 115 *2.10 73–24 Solemn Nation 115¾ Royal Decision 1154 Aerie 123h Came again 8
24⅖ Allowance 5 5 64¾ 76 66 33 LPincayJr 115 *♠1.30 81–23 It's Blitz 117no Emerald Lake 1223 ♠Solemn Nation 1153 Rallied 7

24⅖ Allowance 3 8 69 88¾ 76¾ 32 LPincayJr 122 4.30 83–17 It's Blitz 1101½ Isokeha 115½ Solemn Nation 122¾ Late bid 8
12 Aqu 3f fst .36 h Apr 9 Aqu 6f sl 1.14 h Apr 3 Aqu 6f fst 1.15⅗ h Mar 21 Aqu 5f sl 1.04⅗ b

Ch. c (1963–Ky), by Mamboreta—Way Out, by Alibhai — 115 — 1967 11 0 0 3 $10,450
Blue Streak Stable R. Sechrest (King Ranch) — 1966 18 2 1 1 $9,405
36⅗ DixieH 1 12 1220121512201222 ENelson b 108 78.10 40–38 War Censor 1254 Deck Hand 1142 Needle Him 1112 Trailed 12
51⅗ Allowance 2 7 79¾ 712 78½ 45½ ATCordero b 123 37.70 72–20 Dunderhead 1233 Blasting Charge 1102 Trade In 120½ Late bid 7
44 RiggsH 2 7 714 813 811 913 FAlvarez b 111 74.40 82– 8 Lucky Turn 113no Flag 1203½ Dunderhead 1081½ Never a threat 9
ıp run in two divisions, 7th and 8th races.
36⅕ Allowance 4 9 912 813 815 818 RUssery b 123 14.80 69–16 Brunch 1101½ Dunderhead 1231½ Major Art 1115 Showed nothing 9
38⅘ SanMarino 6 11 11141111 74½ 36¼ APineda b 115 12.00 —— Acknowledge 111nk Galanomad 1186 Walk Out 115½ Closed well 11
48⅘ Allowance 6 9 913 912 86¼ 69 APineda b 118 4.20 82– 7 Lord Byron 120no Road Hog 116no Sette Bello 1164 No speed 9
23⅘ SLuisReyH 3 8 610 86¼ 57½ 49¼ LPincayJr b 111 24.50 93– 4 Fleet Host 1194 Flit-To 1144 Hill Clown 1141¼ No factor 11
Handicap run in two divisions—5th and 8th races.
48⅕ Clm 20000 9 12 1215 93¼ 53 3h APineda b 116 17.60 92– 8 Lord Byron 116no Green Cheese 120h Walk Out 1166 Rallied 12
1Feb67-6SA fst 1⅛.46⅕1.11 1.49⅘ Allowance 3 12 1212 96¾ 57¼ 34½ EBelmonte b 118 6.20 78–18 Galanomad 1134 Atair Noir 114½ Walk Out 1182 Rallied 12
LATEST WORKOUTS Apr 29 Bel tr.t. 4f fst .50 h Apr 19 Bel m.t. 5f my 1.03 b

***Acecho**
Dk. b. or br. h (1961), by Assorted—Chimy, by Chivalric — 115 — 1967 1 0 0 0 ——
Llangollen Farm F. Watkins (Haras Locumba) (Peru) — 1965 3 0 0 1 $529
29Apr67-5CD fst 6f .22 .45⅗1.10⅗ Allowance 8 7 78 812 816 815 JSellers 113 28.00 78–12 Errante II 113h Brilliant Dunce 1131¾ Royal Junction 1162 Far back 8
2May65-Monterrico(Peru) fst*1⅛ 1.51⅘ Special Weights 6 AVasquez 119 *0.60 —— Galanteador 1172¾ Tributo 1191 Payne Guor 1281½ 7
28Feb65-Monterrico(Peru) fst*1⅛ 1.54 Special Weights 32½ AVasquez 119 4.50 —— Gandul 1081¼ New Crack 1281¼ Acecho 119nk 10
21Feb65-Monterrico(Peru) fst*6f 1.14⅕ Special Weights 43 AVasquez 119 *1.50 —— Peruanito 119nk Il Sorpasso 119h Simbal 1192¾ 10
20Dec64-Monterrico(Peru) fst*6½f 1.21⅘ Maiden Special Weights 11 AVasquez 119 *2.40 —— Acecho 1191 Simbal 1191¾ Chan Chan 128nk 12
LATEST WORKOUTS May 13 Aqu 6f fst 1.13⅗ h May 9 Aqu 4f sl .50 b Apr 19 Kee 4f fst :48⅘ bg Apr 8 GP 5f fst 1.00⅖ h

Prisoner's Base *

Dk. b. or br. g (1963-Ky), by Turn-to—Old Game, by Menow — 119 — 1967 4 2 0 0 $5.52
Greentree Stable J. M. Gaver, Jr. (Greentree Stud, Inc.) — 1966 7 M 1 0 $7

2May67-5Aqu fst 7f .23⅗ .46⅘1.23⅘ Clm 27500 5 5 53½ 63¼ 77½ 65½ WTichenor10 b 107 28.00 81-18 Yucatan 1241¼ Simpleton 117nk King's Jest 113h Raced wide
24Feb67-7Hia fst 7f .23⅕ .45⅕1.23⅖ Allowance 1 2 45 44 69¼1014 WBoland b 121 4.80 78-15 Irongate 1211¼ Tom Poker 1138 Wondrascope 1131½ Tired
16Feb67-7Hia fst 7f .22⅗ .45⅖1.23⅗ Allowance 4 5 34 24 12 12 RUssery b 115 *2.30 91-12 Prisoner's Base 1152 Yale Fence 1151 Phantom Island 1211 Handily
6Feb67-3Hia fst 7f .22⅘ .45⅗1.24⅖ Md Sp Wt 7 5 24 22 12 16 BBaeza b 119 3.60 87-14 Prisoner's Base 1196 Two Keys 1141½ Prestidigitator 1191 Driving
2Nov66-1Aqu fst 7f .23⅕ .47 1.25⅖ Md Sp Wt 5 8 51½ 52¾ 53 56½ WTichener10 b 112 9.90 72-19 Sum Farce 1222½ Right Reason 122no Solemn Nation 1171½ No m'h'p
20Oct66-1Aqu sl 7f .23⅘ .48⅖1.27 Md 9000 2 6 62¾ 43½ 1h 21 HGustines b 117 7.80 70-23 Bombax 1171 Prisoner's Base 117½ Bicarb Jr. 1102½ Sharp try
14Oct66-2Aqu fst 6f .23 .46⅘1.11⅗ Md Sp Wt 5 1 33 31½ 44½ 57¾ HGustines b 121 16.50 77-17 Birdsofafeather 1215 Solemn Nation 1211 Sharp 116nk Tired
6Oct66-5Aqu fst 6f .23⅖ .47⅕1.12⅖ Md Sp Wt 10 1 55½ 67¾ 612 518 WTichenor10 111 49.70 63-24 Sermon 12111 Vocalist 121½ Birdsofafeather 1214 Fell back
29Sep66-1Aqu fst 6f .23⅕ .47 1.12⅖ Md Sp Wt 6 6 96½ 99¾ 912 99¾ WTichenor10 b 110 40.30 71-18 Emerald Lake115h Soldier'sStory120½ Birdsofafeather1203½ No sp'd
8Sep66-3Aqu fst 7f .23⅗ .48 1.26⅕ Md Sp Wt 3 3 2½ 3nk 76½ 612 HGustines 120 21.50 63 29 As You Like 1203 Vis-A-Vis 115¾ Counterstroke 1203 Gave way
LATEST WORKOUTS May 14 Bel 7f fst 1.26 h — May 10 Bel 5f fst 1.01 h — May 7 Bel 4f sly .52 b — Apr 30 Bel 4f fst .48 h

Yale Fence

Ch. g (1963-Va), by Swaps—Blue Banner, by War Admiral — 105[10] — 1967 6 0 2 2 $3,72
Rokeby Stable E. Burch (P. Mellon) — 1966 10 1 0 1 $3,75

26Apr67-6Aqu fst 6f .22⅗ .45⅗1.11 Allowance 1 8 65 66½ 56½ 35 JColasacco10 b 107 9.70 83-17 Trade In 1173 Dey Sovereign 1172 Yale Fence 1072½ Wide
11Apr67-6Aqu fst 7f .23⅖ .47⅕1.25 Allowance 2 8 67 67¼ 55 45¼ EBelmonte b 118 6.60 76-27 Blasting Charge 107½ Dandy Steal 1104 Storm Crost 118¾ No mishap
15Mar67-7Aqu sly 7f .23⅘ .48 1.26⅕ Allowance 3 2 21½ 33 35 34¾ BBaeza b 115 1.80 70-24 Lash Back 1154 Guy Zog 124¾ Yale Fence 1151 Evenly in drive
1Mar67-7Hia fm 1 1/16 Ⓣ 1.42⅗ Clm 45000 1 4 78½ 910 89½ 96½ JVelasquez b 116 18.70 85-14 Tom Poker 112no RoundTablePet113nk Wondrascope1141¼ Tired
16Feb67-7Hia fst 7f .22⅗ .45⅖1.23⅗ Allowance 8 1 24 34½ 22 22 JVelasquez b 115 5.60 89-12 Prisoner's Base 1152 Yale Fence 1151 Phantom Island 1211 Gamely
7Feb67-6Hia fst 6f .22⅕ .45⅖1.10⅕ Allowance 2 4 43 44¼ 25 26 BBaeza b 113 8.40 87-13 Irongate 1156 Yale Fence 113no Isokeha 1134 Game try
23Nov66-6Aqu fst 6f .22⅕ .45⅗1.11⅗ Allowance 1 5 33½ 34 45½ 63¾ RTurcotte b 115 26.30 81-17 It's Blitz 1101½ Isokeha 115½ Solemn Nation 122¾ Tired
26Oct66-8Aqu fst 6f .22⅘ .46⅕1.10⅘ Allowance 9 8 74½ 46½ 66¾ 66¾ WBlum b 113 49.40 82-19 Sermon 121h Counsellor 113¾ It's Blitz 1074 Not a factor
17Oct66-6Aqu fst 7f .23 .46⅖1.24⅗ Allowance 6 1 4nk 62½ 77 610 ECardone5 b 110 10.90 73-19 Hurry Khal 115½ Sermon 121h As You Like 1212½ Fell back early
14May66-5Aqu fst 6f .22⅖ .46 1.11⅗ Allowance 4 5 43½ 22 75¾ 87¼ BBaeza b 113 11.90 78-13 First Query 1051 Happy Noble 1121½ Steve's Vow 110nk Tired
19Apr66-8Aqu fst 1 .46⅕1.11⅕1.37 Allowance 2 4 41 41½ 43 43½ BBaeza b 113 *2.30 79-17 Devil's Tattoo 110h Fuerza 114½ Bushfighter 1143 Weakened
LATEST WORKOUTS May 15 Bel 5f fst 1.03⅖ b — May 11 Bel 3f fst .37⅘ b — May 3 Bel 3f fst .36⅕ h — Apr 24 Bel tr.t. 4f fst .49⅖ h

Big Red Rocket *

Ch. c (1963-Ky), by Ribot-Coup, by War Relic — 115 — 1967 10 0 0 0 $1,67
N. B. Hunt F. J. Merrill (J. A. Bell, Jr.) — 1966 22 2 1 2 $21,71

11May67-6Aqu sly 1⅛ .46⅘1.13⅖1.53⅖ Allowance 5 7 723 712 56½ 414 LAdams b 120 5.40 55-24 Blas'gCharge11310SolemnNation123noRuffledFeathers1144 Sluggi'h
22Apr67-9GP fm 1 1/16 Ⓣ 1.11⅕1.43⅕ Handicap 8 9 107½108¾ 65½ 54½ CStone b 113 9.10 84-15 Trish M. 111¾ Climax II 114no Estreno II 1091½ Mild late rally
15Apr67-9GP fm 1½ Ⓣ 1.13⅘2.26 Pan-AmH 7 10 810 77¼ 611 715 BMoreira 111 18.20 84- 5 War Censor 1204 d-Ginger Fizz 1183¼ Voluntario III 113¾ Far back
5Apr67-8GP fm 1½ Ⓣ 1.14⅗2.29⅘ Allowance 4 4 39 55 54½ 33¾ BMoreira 112 7.00 76-13 Base Leg 1173 Circus 117¾ Big Red Rocket 112¾ Passed tired ones
1Apr67-8GP fst 1 1/16 .48⅕1.12⅗1.44 Allowance 3 9 911 89 42 45¼ WShoemaker 112 12.20 83-15 Tara Host 1131¼ Del Bee 113½ Trish M. 1173½ Late rush, hung
11Mar67-7GP fm 1 1/16 Ⓣ 1.11⅖1.42⅖ Allowance 3 7 729 721 716 711 RHernandez 112 20.60 81-11 Murad 115½ Base Leg 1171½ Greek Jab 114½ Trailed thruout
25Feb67-8Hia fm 1½ Ⓣ 2.28⅕ TurfCupH 6 9 710 915 9161017 HGustines 111 13.00 78- 9 War Censor 111h Greek Jab 112no NorthernDeamon113no Far back
11Feb67-8Hia sf 1 3/16 Ⓣ 1.57⅗ Boug'v'laH 9 13 12151211 912 Fell LAdams 112 74.00 —— Tequillo 1101½ War Censor 1101½ Tatao 114½ Hit horse, fell
28Jan67-9Hia sf 1 1/16 Ⓣ 1.45⅘ PalmBchH 4 11 10181115 915 88¾ LAdams 113 31.00 67-25 ThirdMartini111nkNorthernDeamon114hExhibitionist1161 No speed
28Jan67—The Palm Beach Handicap, run in two divisions, 8th and 9th races.
23Jan67-9Hia sly 7f .23⅗ .47 1.25⅕ Allowance 7 6 714 713 712 53½ LAdams 113 5.80 79-19 Saeharf 118½ Beau Legs 113no Wondrascope 1132 Stride late
17Dec66-8Lrl my 1⅜ .47⅗1.13⅖2.20⅖ LaurelCpH 13 10 1115 43¼ 22 42¼ LAdams 113 12.90 101-15 Knighly Manner 1241¼ Green Felt 118h Boll 'n Jac 1131 Hung
LATEST WORKOUTS May 17 Bel 4f fst .51⅖ b — May 10 Bel tr.t. 3f fst .38 b — May 4 Bel tr.t. 6f fst 1.16 h — Apr 19 Hia 4f fst .50 b

Woodcutter

B. g (1963-Ky), by Hill Prince—Bent Twig, by Nasrullah — 115 — 1967 1 0 0 2 $1,00
Pin Oak Stable E. Holton (Pin Oak Stud, Inc.) — 1966 10 2 1 3 $3,52

29Apr67-5Aqu fst 7f .22⅗ .46⅗1.24⅖ Allowance 4 8 711 711 76 513 RMorgan5 116 15.40 71-18 Gaylord'sFeather110h FavorableTurn1178 Counsellor1212½ Slow st.
7Mar67-9FG fst 6f .22⅗ .46⅘1.12 Allowance 5 6 67 64½ 55 43¾ GOverton 115 2.70 87-14 PowerOfDestiny 1171½ CharmingAlibi 1142 DoubleMist 119nk Wide
2Mar67-7FG fst 6f .22 .46⅖1.12⅖ Allowance 5 6 77½ 75½ 63 3h GOverton 114 *1.20e 89-13 Mincing Lane 119h Road Break 114no Woodcutter 114½ Wide stretch
16Feb67-7FG fst 6f .22⅘ .46⅘1.11⅘ Allowance 2 3 45 56½ 59 611 GOverton 115 18.60 81-16 Worthylouk 1182 Third Moon 1133 Juliet's Lover 1132 Fell back
9Feb67-8FG fst 6f .22⅕ .45⅕1.11 Allowance 5 3 35½ 34½ 33½ 35½ DChamberlin 113 7.20 90-11 Worthylouk 1131 Enlightenment 1224½ Woodcutter 1133½ Evenly
3Feb67-8FG fst 1 40 .48⅕1.13⅘1.41⅗ Allowance 3 1 1h 2½ 64 78 MFrederick'n 113 8.10 79-19 I Owe 114½ Wonder Dancer 113nk Viclemen 1143 Used early
19Jan67-8FG fst 6f .22⅖ .46⅖1.11⅘ Allowance 3 5 66½ 54½ 42¼ 43¼ MFrederickson 116 3.20 89-14 Johnie Bound 1212 Gee Ma 109nk Laurentian Way 1101 Raced wide
18Nov66-8Lat fst 1 .47⅗1.13⅗1.40⅖ Allowance 2 6 42½ 31 1½ 11½ RBorgem'ke 112 *2.10 90-18 Woodcutter 1121½ Cajean Princess 104h Sal Allen 1131½ In time
7Nov66-8Lat gd 6½f .23⅘ .47⅖1.19⅖ Allowance 4 5 73¾ 46½ 37 37 RLHancock 113 3.60 81-15 Strawshy 1104 Random Shot 1173 Woodcutter 1136 Even effort
1Nov66-8Lat sly 5½f .22⅘ .47 1.06⅖ Allowance 6 8 67½ 45½ 44 44 RLHancock 117 5.00 86-21 The Wart 1142 Random Shot 1201 Barrel Ahead 1141 No rally
14Oct66-5Kee fst 7f .23⅖ .46⅘1.25⅕ Allowance 7 1 4¾ 3½ 35½ 38¾ RMorgan5 112 11.50 73-20 Bredel R. J. 1175 Dallas County 1193¾ Woodcutter 1122½ Bid, tired
LATEST WORKOUTS May 16 Bel 4f sly .47⅗ h — May 10 Bel 4f fst .47⅖ h — Apr 21 Bel 5f fst 1.03⅕ b — Apr 21 Bel 4f fst .48⅗ bg

*Bitter

Ch. c (1963), by Marc—Beautiful, by Bakersgate — 115 — 1967 5 0 1 1 $13
Mrs. T. C. Christopher Harris Brown (Haras Casupa S.A.) (Uru.) — 1966 13 2 3 2 $2,78

12Mar67-Maronas (Uru.) fst*7½f 1.31⅘ Allowance 3 —— —— —— —— Missing data not available.
12Feb67-Maronas (Uru.) fst*6½f 1.19⅗ Allowance 4 —— —— —— ——
5Feb67-Maronas (Uru.) fst*5½f 1.06 Invitational Handicap 26 —— —— —— ——
21Jan67-Las Piedras (Uru.) fst*7f 1.29⅖ Handicap Unp —— —— —— ——
6Jan67-Maronas (Uru.) fst*6f 1.11⅘ Handicap Unp —— —— —— ——
4Dec66-Maronas (Uru.) fst*1 9/16 2.39⅖ Gran Premio Comparacion Unp —— —— —— ——
LATEST WORKOUTS May 14 Aqu 6f fst 1.14⅖ h — May 10 Aqu 5f fst 1.03⅖ b — May 1 Aqu 5f fst 1.06 b — Apr 26 Aqu 4f fst .51⅗ b

Eagle Lair

Dk. b. or br. g (1963-Ky), by Bald Eagle—Fictitious, by Abernant — 108[7] — 1967 1 0 0 0 $40
Cragwood Stable M. K. Miller (Mrs. J. R. H. Thouron) — 1966 3 2 0 1 $6,855

6May67-5Aqu sly 6f .22⅗ .46⅖1.12⅗ Allowance 1 2 1h 1h 31 49½ RSurrency5 116 5.00 70-27 Irish Dude 111h Bologna Gellis 1141½ Dandy Steal 1148 Used up
24Sep66-3Aqu fst 6f .22⅕ .45⅖1.11⅖ Allowance 3 3 21 21 1½ 13 BBaeza 114 *1.60 86-18 Eagle Lair 1143 SmallTownBoy 1142 Unintentionally 1116 Mild drive
30Jun66-5Aqu fst 6f .22⅕ .45⅖1.11⅗ Allowance 4 2 2h 11 1h 33 WBlum 113 2.20 82-20 Top to Bottom106½ Rego1112½ Eagle Lair113nk Bold bid, weakened
15Jun66-1Aqu fst 6f .22⅖ .45⅗1.11 Md Sp Wt 6 6 21 2½ 1h 1no WBlum 115 *1.20e 88-16 Eagle Lair 115no Smooth Seas 1154½ Age of Reason 11012 Bumped
LATEST WORKOUTS May 3 Bel 6f fst 1.13⅘ h — Apr 30 Bel 6f fst 1.17⅖ b — Apr 25 Bel 5f my 1.03⅖ b — Apr 20 Bel 4f fst .49⅘ b

---

Solemn Nation: No real class here. Everett King claimed the gelding for $14,000 out of a losing race last month and has since made four unsuccessful attempts in ordinary allowance company. NO BET.

Walk Out: Why would Randy Sechrest put this colt into a seven-furlong race when he has been showing no early foot in longer races? Is he sending him out for exercise? Not likely. The horse needs no exercise. He has raced twice in the last two weeks, including a leisurely gallop in the Dixie Handicap only five days ago. Can Sechrest expect to grab today's purse? Could be. Any animal able to finish third in the San Marino Handicap and fourth in the San Luis Rey has class. The 1967 earnings of more than $10,000 for three thirds and two fourths is another sign of class. And the May 4 race, when Angel Cordero helped the colt produce a brisk finishing kick on the dirt, suggests improving form. Seven furlongs would be too little ground for this one against high quality stock, but if he is dropping down in class as much as the conditions of the race imply and if the pace is favorable, there might be a bet here. CONTENDER.

Acecho: Nothing. NO BET.

Prisoner's Base: After two good efforts in February the Greentree gelding withered. Today's switch from a green apprentice to Ussery may help, but the May 2 performance in a mere claiming race was awful. NO BET.

Yale Fence: This one shapes up as a chronic loser that needs to run in claiming races where its touch of quality might pay off. NO BET.

Big Red Rocket: Like Walk Out, this Ribot colt has been doing a lot of work on the grass. Unlike Walk Out, he has been able to win no money during 1967. If class be our main interest today, Big Red Rocket is outdistanced by Walk Out. NO BET.

Woodcutter: Horses that can't win at Fair Grounds can't win at Aqueduct. NO BET.

Bitter: The Uruguayan immigrant needs to become acclimated. NO BET.

Eagle Lair: Mack Miller's Bald Eagle gelding is the only speed in the race. It was woefully short in its 1967 debut a couple of weeks ago and has not worked out since. But the 108-pound impost might help. Last September 24 it ran powerfully enough to encourage the idea that seven furlongs are within its capabilities. CONTENDER.

The contenders are Walk Out and Eagle Lair: the doubtful router and the doubtful sprinter. There really is no reason to believe that Eagle Lair is back in its form of September, 1966. Far more reason to expect it to lead all the way to the stretch and tire. Will Walk Out be able to catch up? He would seem to have an awfully good chance. Disregarding the recent Pimlico race, which was nothing but an exercise gallop, the question is whether the horse will be able to generate full stride within three quarters of a mile. Clue: running on the Santa Anita turf course, around tricky turns, Walk Out got to the three-quarter call of the San Luis Rey as rapidly as Eagle Lair has won at that distance on the swift Aqueduct dirt! If Eagle Lair were in genuine condition, the race would be no contest. As matters stand, however, Walk Out is the sharper animal with the better prospects.

The Running of the Race

THE CROWD was sufficiently suspicious of Eagle Lair's condition to make Prisoner's Base the favorite at a stupefying underlay of 2–1. Eagle Lair was second favorite. Walk Out was overlooked.

Cordero had no trouble hustling Walk Out into third position after half a mile. He collared Eagle Lair in the stretch, beat it thoroughly in a few easy strides, and won going away under a hand ride, as a class horse should in circumstances like these.

In my opinion, Eagle Lair should have been the favorite at about 3–1, and Walk Out should have been no worse than 9–2. Opportunities of this kind turn up three or four times a season.

SEVENTH RACE **7 FURLONGS. (Chute). (Rose Net, Sept. 17, 1962, 1.21$\frac{1}{5}$, 6, 114.)**

Aqu - 31142

May 18, 1967

Allowances. Purse $10,000. 4-year-olds and upward which have never won three races. Weight 124 lbs. Non-winners of two races since March 12 allowed 3 lbs., of a race since then, 5 lbs., of two races since January 16, 7 lbs., of a race since December 10, 9 lbs.

Value to winner $6,500, second $2,000, third $1,000, fourth $500. Mutuel pool $344,320.

Index	Horse	Eqt	A	Wt	PP	St	¼	½	Str	Fin	Jockey	Owner	Odds $1
31089Pim^{12}	Walk Out	b	4	115	2	7	$5^{1\frac{1}{2}}$	$3^{\frac{1}{2}}$	2^{6}	$1^{2\frac{1}{2}}$	ACorderoJr	Blue Streak Stable	25.10
31050Aqu^{4}	Eagle Lair		4	108	8	1	$1^{\frac{1}{2}}$	$1^{1\frac{1}{2}}$	$1^{\frac{1}{2}}$	2^{6}	G Mora^{7}	Cragwood Stable	2.20
31087Aqu^{4}	Big Red R'ket	b	4	115	6	2	8	8	3^{2}	3^{4}	L Adams	N B Hunt	14.40
31014Aqu^{6}	Pris'ner's B'se	b	4	119	4	5	4^{2}	$4^{1\frac{1}{2}}$	4^{1}	4^{1}	R Ussery	Greentree Stable	2.00
31087Aqu^{2}	Solemn Nation		4	115	1	6	$3^{\frac{1}{2}}$	5^{2}	$5^{\frac{1}{2}}$	$5^{2\frac{1}{2}}$	B Baeza	Windham Farm	3.20
30850Aqu^{3}	Yale Fence	b	4	105	5	8	7^{4}	$6^{\frac{1}{2}}$	$6^{1\frac{1}{2}}$	$6^{\frac{3}{4}}$	J Colas'co^{10}	Rokeby Stable	9.60
30876Aqu^{5}	Woodcutter		4	115	7	3	6^{2}	$7^{\frac{1}{2}}$	8	7^{4}	H W'dhouse	Pin Oak Stable	9.90
30705CD^{8}	Acecho		6	115	3	4	2^{3}	2^{3}	7^{1}	8	E Cardone	Llangollen Farm	43.30

Time .22$\frac{3}{5}$, .45$\frac{1}{5}$, 1.10, 1.22$\frac{4}{5}$ (with wind in backstretch). Track fast.

$2 Mutuel Prices:			
2-WALK OUT	52.20	14.00	7.40
8-EAGLE LAIR		4.80	3.80
6-BIG RED ROCKET			6,40

Ch. c, by Mamboreta—Way Out, by Alibhai. Trainer R. Sechrest. Bred by King Ranch (Ky.).

IN GATE AT 4.39. OFF AT 4.39 EASTERN DAYLIGHT TIME. Start good. Won handily.

WALK OUT steadily worked his way forward to the stretch and, responding to mild urging, took command from EAGLE LAIR inside the last eighth and won going away. EAGLE LAIR saved ground while setting the pace and was unable to stay with WALK OUT but was easily second best. BIG RED ROCKET dropped back after beginning fast and was outrun for a half mile, moved to the outside for the drive but could not threaten the leaders. PRISONER'S BASE had no mishap. SOLEMN NATION was finished early. YALE FENCE began slowly. WOODCUTTER showed nothing. ACECHO stopped after a half-mile.

Scratched—Uru. '67-3 Bitter.

---

5. SIXTH AT AQUEDUCT, MAY 2, 1967—Track Fast

A $9,000 PURSE for fillies and mares that have established themselves to the extent of winning as many as two allowances or stakes. At Aqueduct, a chronic allowance runner can win this kind of race, but not if a sharp stakes-winner is entered.

6th Race Aqueduct

1 MILE AQUEDUCT (Start / Finish)

1 MILE (Chute). (Bald Eagle, May 30, 1960, 1.33⅗, 5, 128.)
Allowances. Purse $9,000. Fillies and mares. 3-year-olds and upward which have never won three races other than maiden or claiming. Weights, 3-year-olds 113 lbs., older 123 lbs. Non-winners of a race other than maiden or claiming at a mile or over at any time, allowed 3 lbs.

Renova — Ch. f (1964–Ky), by Reneged—Nova Cain, by Prince Chevalier — A. J. Crevolin — W. H. Dixon — (Mrs. W. Hall) — **113** — 1967 6 3 1 1 $14,512 — 1966 1 M 0 1 $750

3Apr67-7Aqu fst 6f .22⅘ .46 1.11⅕ f-H'dicap 3 6 76¾ 811 812 814 JRuane 110 21.50 73-16 Recall 118no Regal Gleam 1242½ Lake Chelan 113nk Dull effort 8
2Mar67-8GG gd 1 .46⅖1.12⅕1.39⅖ f-Cal.Oaks 2 5 52¾ 4nk 21 1¾ IValenzuela 114 4.40 71-22 Renova 114¾ Miss Midway 113½ Indovina 116½ Long, hard drive 8
8Mar67-8SA fst 7f .22⅖ .45⅕1.23 f- Allow 2 6 53¼ 84¼ 83½ 33 DPierce 114 16.30 85-13 Forgiving 1131½ Amerigo Lady 1171½ Renova 114nk Closed fast 8
4Feb67-6SA fst 6f .22 .45⅕1.11 f- Allow 9 2 32 33½ 32 1½ DPierce 118 5.30 87-15 Renova 118½ Evie Jane 1183 Askew 1181 Under hard drive 11
5Feb67-4SA fst 6f .22⅖ .45⅘1.11 f-MdSpWt 5 6 25 23 13 17 DPierce 115 *1.10 87-16 Renova 1157 Holly Bu 1152¾ Ruahrullah 1151 Speed to spare 12
9Jan67-4SA fst 7f .22⅖ .45⅖1.23⅗ f-MdSpWt 7 3 21½ 3½ 22 26 IValenzuela 115 14.00 79-17 Gay Violin 1156 Renova 1152 Scoop Time 1152½ Held on willingly 12
9Dec66-5SA fst 6f .22⅕ .45⅘1.11⅖ f-MdSpWt 5 12 63 69½ 37 36 IValenzuela 115 *2.50 79-14 She Should Know 1154 Francine M. 1152 Renova 1152 Rallied 12
LATEST WORKOUTS Apr 26 Bel 7f fst 1.32 b — Apr 22 Del 4f fst .50 b — Apr 20 Bel 3f fst .39 b — Apr 8 Bel m.t. 4f my .48⅖ h

Dance Dress × — Ch. f (1964–Ky), by Seaneen—Rave Notice, by Princequillo — Birchfield Farms — N. Combest — (R. C. Wilson, Jr.) — **110** — 1967 6 2 0 0 $6,175 — 1966 12 1 1 1 $4,200

8Apr67-7Aqu my 7f .23⅕ .46⅗1.24⅕ f- Allow 4 5 65¼ 68½ 613 617 ECardone b 110 13.90 68-25 Kate's Intent 113¾ On The Carpet 1136 Arrangement 1134 No m'hap 8
9Mar67-7Aqu my 6f .23⅗ .48⅗1.13⅘ f-H'dicap 2 6 57½ 76¼ 58 56 LPincayJr b 111 9.10 68-33 Gr'kSong'sGet112h•SportsEvent113no•She'sB'utiful 120no No factor 7
7Feb67-6Hia fm*1 1/16 Ⓣ 1.45⅘ f- Allow 7 6 614 713 68¾ 611 JLRotz b 113 4.90 70-16 NancyJr.1122 AmericanDream1122½ GreekSong'sGet112nk No factor 7
8Feb67-8Hia sly 7f .22⅗ .45⅖1.22⅗ f-Mimosa 1 7 713 713 812 79¼ JLRotz b 113 27.60 87-12 Woozem 1195 Quillo Queen 112nk Just Kidding 114no Showed noth'g 9
7Jan67-7Hia gd 7f .22⅘ .45⅘1.25⅖ f- Allow 7 1 712 69¾ 11 12½ JLRotz b 114 11.10 82-23 Dance Dress 1142½ Treacherous 1151 Shirley Heights 1157 Mild dr. 8
0Jan67-7Hia sl 6f .22⅗ .46⅘1.12⅕ f- Allow 8 2 66½ 54 23 11¼ JLRotz b 116 11.30 83-19 Dance Dress 1161¼ Grand Coulee 1184 Rough Decision 1184½ Driving 8
6Dec66-6Aqu fst 7f .23⅖ .47⅕1.26⅖ f- Allow 8 3 75¾ 75¼ 710 79¼ ACordero b 116 16.90 65-26 PrimaBallerina118nkMurmuring1181½Dunce'sRibbonair1112 Far back 9
8Nov66-6Aqu fst 6f .22⅘ .46⅗1.12⅕ f- c-11500 6 2 83¼ 65½ 87½ 45¼ BBaeza b 114 *2.10 77-17 Lady Avalon 1091¼ Sea Nail 1212½ Fairy Good 1171½ No mishap 10
10Oct66-5Aqu fst 6f .22⅖ .46 1.13⅖ f- 12500 8 10 1211 9101010 33 BBaeza 116 6.50 73-17 Native Joy 1163 Nice Princess 116no Dance Dress 116no Rallied 14
LATEST WORKOUTS Apr 29 Aqu 6f gd 1.19 b — Apr 15 Aqu 4f gd .48 h — Mar 8 Hia 5f fst 1.05 b

Arrangement — Dk. b. or br. f (1964–Fla), by Intentionally—Floral Girl, by Noble Hero — Tartan Stable — J. A. Nerud — (Tartan Farm, Inc.) — **110** — 1967 4 1 0 2 $6,050 — 1966 8 2 1 1 $8,195

8Apr67-7Aqu my 7f .23⅕ .46⅗1.24⅕ f- Allow 5 4 44 44 33 36¾ WShoemaker 113 4.50 78-25 Kate's Intent 113¾ On The Carpet 1136 Arrangement 1134 Hung 8
Mar67-7Aqu fst 6f .22⅘ .46 1.11⅗ f- Allow 1 6 59 46 24 1nk WShoemaker 108 *1.90 85-28 Arrangement 108nk Kate's Intent 1085 Ship Shoal 118½ Driving 8
6Mar67-7Aqu sly 6f .23⅕ .47⅗1.13 f- Allow 4 1 2h 2h 31½ 53¾ MYcaza 116 *1.10 74-33 Strong Measures 121¾ Spire 1141½ Sports Event 118h Weakened 6
4Feb67-7Hia fst 7f .23⅖ .46⅘1.24⅕ f- Allow 3 6 67 65¾ 56½ 34 MYcaza 115 5.90 84-13 Treacherous 115no Momma Pierre 1124 Arrangement 1155 Rallied 7
8Oct66-7Aqu fst 1 .45⅖1.10⅖1.37⅖ f-Frizette 5 8 86½ 78 56½ 57 WShoemaker 119 4.30 74-17 Regal Gleam 119h Irish County 1194½ Pepperwood 1192 Swerved 8
7Sep66-6Aqu fst 7f .23 .46⅕1.25⅖ f- Allow 5 8 87½ 74¾ 12 15 WShoemaker 119 *0.90 79-21 Arrangement 1195 Chantilly Jewel 1192½ Shore 107½ Easily 8
2Sep66-5Aqu fst 6f .23⅖ .47⅗1.13⅗ f-MdSpWt 12 6 65 73¾ 4¾ 12½ BBaeza 119 3.50 75-26 Arrangement 1192½ Sports Event 119½ Prima Ballerina 114¾ Handily 12
2Aug66-5Sar gd 5½f.22⅖ .47 1.06⅖ f-MdSpWt 8 7 85 62½ 32 2no DHidalgo5 114 3.60 85-16 Grand Coulee 114no Arrangement 1143 Needles Lady 119h Nosed out 8
7Jly 66-4Aqu fst 5½f.22⅗ .46 1.05⅖ f-MdSpWt 7 5 55 55½ 45½ 44½ DHidalgo5 114 3.30 81-18 Sorche 1192½ Swiss Cheese 1192 Henrietta 114h No late rally 12
LATEST WORKOUTS Apr 27 Bel 4f sly .49⅕ b — Apr 14 Bel tr.t. 5f fst 1.04⅘ b — Apr 8 Bel m.t. 4f my .48⅖ h — Mar 28 Bel tr.t. 4f sl .54 b

On the Carpet — Blk. f (1964–Ky), by Bagdad-Black Discovery, by Discovery — J. W. Schiffer — J. E. Picou — (J. W. Schiffer) — **110** — 1967 1 0 1 0 $2,000 — 1966 15 3 4 2 $24,445

3Apr67-7Aqu my 7f .23⅕ .46⅗1.24⅕ f- Allow 8 1 22 22 21½ 2¾ BBaeza b 113 3.50 84-25 Kate's Intent 113¾ On The Carpet 1136 Arrangement 1134 Gamely 8
9Nov66-7Aqu my 7f .23⅗ .47⅕1.24⅖ f- Allow 4 5 52¼ 53¼ 13 13½ EFires b 114 3.30 84-28 On the Carpet 1143½ Sports Event 116¾ Wageko 1193 In hand 6
6Nov66-7Aqu fst 1 .45⅖1.09⅘1.35⅗ f-Dem'sle 8 6 711 911 710 28 BBaeza b 113 8.80 82-16 Woozem 1198 On the Carpet 113no Amherst 112½ Rallied 9
9Nov66-7Aqu fst 7f .22⅗ .45⅕1.24⅕ f- Allow 1 7 77¼ 78½ 31½ 31¼ RTurcotte b 114 6.70 84-18 With A Flair 1141 d-Bugle Beads 107nk On the Carpet 1143 Rallied 7
9Nov66—Placed second through disqualification.
5Oct66-7Aqu fst 6f .22⅗ .46⅖1.12 f- Allow 10 8 63 45 12 14 ECardone5 b 109 *2.00 83-18 On the Carpet 1094 Pays to Sing 114½ Wageko 116no Easy score 10
8Oct66-6Aqu fst 7f .23⅖ .46⅘1.25⅕ f- Allow 3 8 53½ 52½ 43¼ 43¾ ECardone5 b 111 3.70 76-24 Bless Us 1151½ Sweet and Low 118¾ Kathleen Gee 1141½ No rally 10
1Oct66-6Aqu fst 6f .22⅕ .46⅗1.13⅕ f- Allow 4 7 67 64¼ 42 21½ LAdams b 115 3.70 75-21 Shore 1071½ On the Carpet 115¾ Sweet and Low 118¾ In close 12
7Aug66-5Sar fst 6f .22⅕ .45⅘1.12 f- Allow 11 7 85¼ 96 11111014 LAdams b 118 25.70 74- 8 Swiss Cheese 121no Treacherous 1162 All too Legal 1213½ Wide 11
0Aug66-5Sar fst 6f .22⅖ .46⅕1.12⅗ f- Allow 9 7 812 99¼ 811 86¼ LAdams b 118 4.20 79-10 Spire 1071½ Senesa Compacta 118nk Bittern 109no Fell back early 9
LATEST WORKOUTS May 1 Bel 3f fst .36 b — Apr 25 Bel 1m my 1.42⅗ b — Apr 24 Bel 3f fst .35 h — Apr 16 Bel m.t. 4f sly .49⅘ b

***Equador II** — B. f (1963), by Dionisio--Rain Water, by Nimbus — E. Mittman — W. L. Dorsey — (Mr.-Mrs. W. Whitehead) (Ire.) — **120** — 1967 9 1 2 1 $7,575 — 1966 7 1 0 0 $4,225

3Apr67-7Aqu my 7f .23⅕ .46⅗1.24⅕ f- Allow 3 6 87¼ 811 817 820 ATCordero 120 12.70 60-25 Kate's Intent 113¾ On The Carpet 1136 Arrangement 1134 Far back 8
3Apr67-7Aqu fst 7f .23⅗ .48 1.26⅖ f- Allow 6 4 77 66¾ 55¾ 33 LPincayJr 120 6.60 71-25 Swim To Me 118½ Blended White 1182½ Equador II 1204 Rallied 8
Mar67-6Aqu my 6f .23⅘ .49⅕1.15⅗ f- Allow 3 5 613 714 713 68½ JLRotz 116 7.50 56-46 Double Switch1151 Blended White1164½ Swim To Me1161 No speed 7
5Feb67-8Bow fst 7f .22⅗ .44⅖1.21⅘ f-BFrcheH 4 11 111112191114 1112 CBaltazar 110 50.60 92- 5 Holly-O. 117nk Moccasin 1202½ Lady Diplomat 1112¾ No speed 13
4Feb67-8Bow fst 6f .22⅘ .46⅘1.11⅘ f- Allow 4 5 97¼ 88½ 43½ 41½ CBaltazar 114 *1.80 85-23 Flashy Shot 1141 d-Dove Hunt 110nk Cherokee Mary 112nk Rallied 11
2Feb67-7Bow fst 6f .23⅖ .46⅘1.12⅖ f- Allow 10 1 53½ 55 52¼ 11 CBaltazar 112 *2.50 85-24 Equador II 1121 Phyl's Destiny 1141 Who Cabled 116½ In time 10
0Jan67-8Bow fst 7f .23⅗ .46⅗1.24⅘ f- Allow 5 3 21½ 22½ 22 22 CBaltazar 112 2.60e 87-22 Holly-O 1212 Equador II 1121 Sally Lou 117nk Bore in stretch 7
5Jan67-8Bow fst 6f .22⅘ .46⅖1.11⅘ Allowance 3 4 59½ 58½ 54¾ 56 CBaltazar 111 9.10 82-26 Tetanus 1152½ Old Maestro 1071 Cosimo 117½ Evenly late stages 7
0Jan67-8Bow fst 7f .23⅗ .47⅕1.26⅕ Allowance 4 6 45½ 45½ 22 23½ CBaltazar 113 8.30 78-30 Over Roger 1183½ Equador II 1131½ One Sunday 113¾ Second best 8
LATEST WORKOUTS Apr 29 Bel 5f fst 1.00⅕ h — Apr 14 Bel m.t. 5f fst 1.00⅖ h — Apr 9 Bel m.t. 5f gd 1.03 b — Mar 31 Bel tr.t. 5f hy 1.05 b

Swiss Cheese — Ch. f (1964–Ky), by Dotted Swiss—Affectation, by Citation — C. V. Whitney — I. G. Balding — (C. V. Whitney) — **110**

1967		0	0	0	—
1966	12	3	2	1	$88,57

18Apr67–7Aqu	my 7f	.23⅕ .46⅗1.24⅕	f– Allow	2	7	55	57	59½	513	JLRotz	b 113	6.30	72–25	Kate's Intent 113¾ On The Carpet 1136 Arrangement 1134	No m'hap
16Nov66–7Aqu	fst 1	.45⅖1.09⅘1.35⅗	f–Dem'sle	4	9	914	79¼	410	69½	JLRotz	b 119	6.40	80–16	Woozem 1198 On the Carpet 113no Amherst 112½	No speed
5Nov66–8Lrl	fst 1 1/16	.47⅖1.13⅕1.45⅖	f–Selima	1	11	106¾	66¼	44½	43½	RTurcotte	b 119	5.40e	86–14	Regal Gleam 122½ Quillo Queen 1192 Thong 1191	Wide, rallied 1
29Oct66–4Lrl	fst 1	.47⅕1.13⅖1.39⅘	f– Allow	8	7	54½	47	44½	34½	JLRotz	b 121	1.60	77–16	Court Circuit 1142½ Devotedly 1132 Swiss Cheese 1213½	Bore out
8Oct66–7Aqu	fst 1	.45⅖1.10⅖1.37⅖	f–Frizette	6	5	32½	33	35½	46½	JLRotz	b 119	3.00	74–17	Regal Gleam 119h Irish County 1194½ Pepperwood 1192	Weakened
10Sep66–7Aqu	fst 6f	.22⅘ .46⅖1.12⅘	f–Matron	8	2	97¼	56½	36	1h	JLRotz	b 119	3.10	79–23	Swiss Cheese 119h Great Era 119no Regal Gleam 1198	Driving
27Aug66–5Sar	fst 6f	.22⅕ .45⅘1.12	f– Allow	10	8	98¼	64	42½	1no	JLRotz	121	*1.00	88– 8	Swiss Cheese 121no Treacherous 1162 All too Legal 1213½	Just up 1
15Aug66–7Sar	fst 6f	.22⅖ .45⅘1.12⅗	f–Adrndck	7	10	1212	1012	56½	52¾	JLRotz	115	7.10e	82–17	Tainted Lady 115¾ Intriguing 115¾ Silver True 115¾	Late bid
4Aug66–4Sar	fst 5½f	.22⅗ .47 1.06⅗	f–MdSpWt	4	5	85	45	31	11	JLRotz	119	2.50	85–13	Swiss Cheese 1191 Rosetta Stone 1195 Zeal 1143	Safe margin

LATEST WORKOUTS May 1 Bel tr.t. 3f fst .35 h — Apr 26 Bel 6f fst 1.11⅘ h — Apr 24 Bel tr.t. 3f fst .35⅗ h — Apr 17 Bel tr.t. 3f gd .37 b

Snow Weapon — B. f (1963–Ky), by Arctic Prince—Gaonera, by Brazado — King Ranch — Max Hirsch — (R. Herren) — **123**

1967	1	0	0	0	—
1966	17	3	0	2	$14,73

3Apr67–7Aqu	fst 7f	.23⅗ .48 1.26⅖	f– Allow	8	2	45½	811	814	816	JLRotz	118	17.20	58–25	Swim To Me 118½ Blended White 1182½ Equador II 1204	Fell back
8Dec66–7Aqu	fst 1	.47⅖1.11⅗1.36	f– Allow	4	1	2½	23	512	716	FAlvarez	115	16.80	71–22	Mac's Sparkler 1186 Sailor Princess 116no Nature 1165	Used up
1Dec66–7Aqu	fst 1	.46⅕1.11⅕1.37⅘	f– Allow	6	6	67¼	56½	24	1h	MYcaza	117	12.00	79–23	Snow Weapon 117h First Offence 1123 Sabemar 122½	Driving
22Nov66–7Aqu	fst 7f	.23 .46 1.24⅗	f– Allow	5	5	710	611	69½	66½	EFires	118	10.30	76–23	Omaha Beach 1113 Tangle 121nk Whiglet 1182½	Not a factor
17Nov66–8Aqu	fst 1⅛	.48⅘1.12⅘1.51⅕	f– Allow	6	3	31	32½	33½	36½	WBlum	113	11.40	73–20	Ski Dancer 1182½ Terrific Traffic 1134 Snow Weapon 1132½	No rally
12Nov66–6Aqu	sly 7f	.23⅕ .46⅗1.25⅘	f– Allow	8	4	45½	47	58	43¾	MYcaza	121	18.00	73–29	Darlin Phyllis 115nk Ship Shoal 1171½ Needles Sword 1152	No mish'p
26Oct66–6Aqu	fst 7f	.23⅗ .47⅖1.24⅗	f– Allow	1	5	45½	45	56½	79¾	JLRotz	120	16.10	74–19	SkiDancer1203½ HappyKitten1131½ Through the Mist1151½	Tired
6Oct66–8Aqu	fst 7f	.22⅘ .47 1.26⅕	f– Allow	7	5	53¾	52½	1½	1h	JLRotz	115	10.60	75–24	Snow Weapon 115h Sea Moon 1161½ Tangie 1154	Long hard drive
22Sep66–6Aqu	gd 7f	.22⅗ .46⅕1.26	f– Allow	2	5	85	77	52¾	54¼	EFires	111	14.30	72–23	Song of Rome1141 SeaMoon116no DoveHunt116nk	Mild bid, tired 1

LATEST WORKOUTS Apr 29 Bel tr.t. 1m fst 1.43⅗ b — Apr 27 Bel 3f sly .37 b — Apr 23 Bel 5f fst 1.01⅗ h — Apr 13 Bel m.t. 4f fst .49⅘ b

For Joy * — B. f (1963–Ky), by Johns Joy—Forfeit, by Count Fleet — C. M. Baxter, Jr. — L. Laurin — (C. M. Baxter) — **120**

1967	5	1	0	2	$4,72
1966	14	0	0	2	$1,80

24Apr67–7Aqu	sly 7f	.24⅖ .48⅗1.25⅘	f– Allow	5	1	55	44	46	34	ATCordero	116	20.90	73–24	Belle De Nuit 1184 Fatal Step 118no For Joy 1163½	Good effort
18Apr67–7Aqu	my 7f	.23⅕ .46⅗1.24⅕	f– Allow	7	3	75¼	710	716	718	BFeliciano	b 120	21.20	67–25	Kate's Intent 113¾ On The Carpet 1136 Arrangement 1134	Far back
22Feb67–9Hia	sly 1 1/16	.47 1.12 1.44⅖	f– Allow	2	4	46½	42½	54½	36½	RBroussard	b 121	7.10	74–17	Peony 112½ Ribot Palace 1126 For Joy 121nk	Mild late rally
30Jan67–9Hia	fst 6f	.22⅕ .45⅘1.11⅕	f– Allow	3	12	1217	1210	1011	98¾	RTurcotte	b 112	7.60	79–15	Julie Potatoes 1121½ Royalene 1153½ Little Brown Bar 1121½	No sp'd 1
24Jan67–5Hia	my 6f	.22 .46⅕1.11⅘	f– Allow	9	11	1113	108½	33½	11	RTurcotte	b 112	28.60	85–21	For Joy 1121 Sweety Kid 1142 Tournament Talk 1181½	Driving 1
28Nov66–8Aqu	gd 7f	.23⅕ .46⅘1.26⅖	f– Allow	8	7	1014	1015	912	74½	RTurcotte	b 114	35.10	69–20	Needles Sword 111h Flashy Shot 1072 Whiglet 121h	No threat 1
5Nov66–8Aqu	fm 1 1/16 Ⓣ	1.46⅗	f– Allow	7	6	612	58½	712	611	BFeliciano	b 113	20.70	62–27	River Lady 1136 True Blue 1161 Maggie Fast Step 1163	No speed
24Oct66–7Aqu	fm 1 1/16 Ⓣ	1.45⅖	f– Allow	9	10	1117	1118	913	67¾	BFeliciano	b 113	35.60	71–21	Tagend 1081½ Home Lass 120½ Silver Bright 1063	Never close 1
12Oct66–8Aqu	fm 1⅛ Ⓣ	1.51⅕	f– Allow	7	4	59½	612	815	812	BFeliciano	b 112	3.10	67–21	d–Miss Proctor 1161½ Rope Trick II 116no Sea Moon 1111	Tired

LATEST WORKOUTS Apr 15 Bel tr.t. 5f fst 1.03⅗ h — Apr 10 Bel tr.t. 4f gd .49⅕ h — Mar 24 GP 4f fst .49⅖ b — Mar 16 GP 6f fst 1.16⅗ b

Renova: Won the California Oaks in poor time at Golden Gate Fields, a secondary track. New York debut was unpromising. Likely to be outclassed today and, even if not, shapes up as a loser. NO BET.

Dance Dress: Nick Combest's former claimer may become a stakes winner some day, but has not yet showed any of the earmarks. NO BET.

Arrangement: The poor performance in last year's Frizette should not prejudice us against this filly from a first-rate barn. Neither should her third-place finish in the mud on April 18. Might like today's mile, and might be the class of the field. CONTENDER.

On The Carpet: Consistent last year, with a second-place finish in the Demoiselle Stakes as a certificate of her class, this one ran nicely in her seasonal debut two weeks ago. Whoever wins this race will have to beat her. CONTENDER.

Equador II: Outclassed. NO BET.

Swiss Cheese: After closing powerfully in last year's Adirondack, came on to win the Matron. Did not look very good in the Demoiselle, in which a killing early pace left her far behind and, no doubt, prompted her rider to ease her toward the finish. Yet she crossed the wire only a length and a half behind On the Carpet. Finished much farther behind that one in the mud two weeks ago but has worked sensationally in the meantime. She can be assumed ready to run back to last year's standard, when she won $88,572 in twelve starts. In shape, she is the class of this field. And the presumption must be that she is in shape. CONTENDER.

Snow Weapon: A confirmed allowance horse, penalized with high weight and probably needful of a race or two. NO BET.

For Joy: Outclassed. NO BET.

The contenders are Arrangement (who is scratched), On the Carpet, and Swiss Cheese. The Whitney filly demonstrated superior class last year. Her recent workouts, combined with her easy race in the mud last time out, should make her the favorite today. On the Carpet, the sharp form horse, might make a race of it, but well-conditioned class usually triumphs.

The Running of the Race

ON THE CARPET went off at 1.30–1. Swiss Cheese was second favorite and won like a 1–5 shot.

SIXTH RACE
Aqu - 31015
May 2, 1967

1 MILE (Chute). (Bald Eagle, May 30, 1960, 1.33⅗, 5, 128.)

Allowances. Purse $9,000. Fillies and mares. 3-year-olds and upward which have never won three races other than maiden or claiming. Weights, 3-year-olds 113 lbs., older 123 lbs. Non-winners of a race other than maiden or claiming at a mile or over at any time, allowed 3 lbs.

Value to winner $5,850, second $1,800, third $900, fourth $450. Mutuel pool $309,681.

Index	Horse	Eqt	A	Wt	PP	St	¼	½	¾	Str	Fin	Jockey	Owner	Odds $1
$30788Aqu^{5}$	Swiss Cheese		3	113	5	3	4^{1}	$2^{\frac{1}{2}}$	2^{3}	1^{2}	$1^{5\frac{1}{2}}$	J L Rotz	C V Whitney	1.60
$30788Aqu^{2}$	On The Carpet	b	3	112	3	4	$3^{\frac{1}{2}}$	4^{3}	3^{1}	$3^{1\frac{1}{2}}$	2^{1}	B Baeza	J W Schiffer	1.30
$30716Aqu^{8}$	Snow Weapon		4	123	6	2	1^{1}	$1^{1\frac{1}{2}}$	$1^{1\frac{1}{2}}$	2^{2}	3^{nk}	A DeSpirito	King Ranch	34.10
$30833Aqu^{3}$	For Joy		4	120	7	1	5^{3}	5^{3}	5^{2}	4^{3}	4^{3}	R Turcotte	C M Baxter Jr	11.30
$30788Aqu^{6}$	Dance Dress	b	3	110	2	7	7	7	7	6^{4}	5^{3}	H Woodhouse	Birchfield Farm	37.20
$30788Aqu^{8}$	Equador II		4	120	4	6	6^{1}	$6^{1\frac{1}{2}}$	6^{2}	$5^{\frac{1}{2}}$	6^{12}	A T Cordero	E Mittman	15.70
$30752Aqu^{8}$	Renova		3	116	1	5	2^{h}	$3^{1\frac{1}{2}}$	4^{1}	7	7	R Ussery	A J Crevolin	4.80

Time .23⅘, .47, 1.11⅗, 1.36⅖ (with crosswind in backstretch). Track fast.

$2 Mutuel Prices:			
6–SWISS CHEESE	5.20	2.80	2.80
4–ON THE CARPET		2.40	2.40
7–SNOW WEAPON			4.60

Ch. f, by Dotted Swiss—Affectation, by Citation. Trainer I. G. Balding. Bred by C. V. Whitney (Ky.).
IN GATE AT 4.01. OFF AT 4.01 EASTERN DAYLIGHT TIME. Start good. Won easily.

SWISS CHEESE, well handled, took command from SNOW WEAPON in the upper stretch and won with speed in reserve. ON THE CARPET saved ground but was unable to threaten SWISS CHEESE. SNOW WEAPON set the pace until challenged by the winner and gave way. FOR JOY had no mishap. DANCE DRESS began slowly. EQUADOR II showed nothing. RENOVA stopped after showing early foot and was beaten off.

Scratched—$30788Aqu^{3}$ Arrangement. Overweights—Renova 3 pounds, On The Carpet 2, Swiss Cheese 3.

6. SEVENTH AT AQUEDUCT, APRIL 3, 1967—Track Fast

HERE IS A RACE for a $10,000 purse in which the handicapper's search for a stakes horse proves unavailing. However, something in the race has a clear advantage in the class department, as we shall see. Note the conditions: seven furlongs for three-year-olds and up. Early in the year no three-year-old has a chance against decent older horses at this distance or longer, unless it enjoys a marked edge in class.

7th Race Aqueduct

7 FURLONGS (AQUEDUCT) Start ▼ Finish

7 FURLONGS. (Chute). (Rose Net, Sept. 17, 1962, 1.21⅕, 6, 114.)
Allowances. Purse $10,000. Fillies and mares. 3-year-olds and upward which have never won three races other than maiden or claiming. Weights, 3-year-olds, 113 lbs., older 123 lbs. Non-winners of two races other than maiden or claiming since Oct. 29 allowed 3 lbs., of such a race since Jan. 16, 5 lbs.

Blended White ×

Ch. m (1962), by Top Blend—White Skirt, by Star Pilot
M. Guerrieri A. A. Scotti (M. J. O'Leary) **118**
1967 5 2 2 0 $8,750
1966 20 4 4 0 $20,000

24Mar67-6Aqu	my	6f	.23⅘ .49⅕1.15⅗	f-	Allow	1	3	2^2½	2½	2½	2^1	ECardone	b 116	2.20	64-46	Double Switch115^1 Blended White116^4½ Swim To Me116^1	Gamely	7
22Feb67-5Hia	sly	7f	.23⅕ .46⅕1.24	f-	13000	8	2	1^1½	1^2	1^2	1^3	ECardone	b 112	7.60	89-17	Blended White 112^3 High Bluff 116^1 Color Me Gone 112½	Driving	10
13Feb67-5Hia	gd	6f	.23 .46⅘1.11⅘	f-	12000	5	1	1½	1^1	1^1	2¾	JVelasquez	b 112	*1.10	84-16	Naga 112¾ Blended White 112^1 Bushy Tail 112^4½	Just missed	8
6Feb67-5Hia	fst	6f	.22⅖ .45⅖1.11⅕	f-	9000	3	7	2^1	4^2½	2^1½	1½	JVelasquez	b 112	4.60	88-14	Blended White 112½ Bakery Babe 114^h Color Me Gone 116^4½	Driving	12
6Jan67-5TrP	fst	6f	.22 .44⅘1.09⅘	f-	7500	5	4	2^1½	3^2	3^3	6^5½	JGiovanni	b 116	12.10	87-12	Primfear 114^3 My Marion 116^1½ Vie Eye 113^h	Speed, tired	10
21Dec66-4TrP	fst	6f	.22⅖ .45⅕1:11	Clm	8500	1	4	6^3¼	8^5¾	8^8¼	8^9	JGiovanni	b 113	9.30	78-15	Solid Mike 112½ Good Business 113^2 Gantlet 114^1¼	Gave way	8
21Nov66-6Aqu	fst	6f	.22⅗ .46⅘1.12	f-	12500	4	5	5^3	5^4½	6^5½	6^5½	BBaeza	b 118	*1.80	77-20	Native Twin 116^1 Savannalamar 116^1½ Speedy Lady 111^h	Weakened	7
29Oct66-3Aqu	fst	6f	.22⅖ .46 1.11⅗	f-	Allow	1	2	2^2	2^2½	5^5	6^7	WBlum	b 120	7.20	78-21	BubblesO'Tudor115^1¼ TerrificTraffic120^nk OmahaBeach118½	Stopp'd	6
5Oct66-6Aqu	gd	6f	.22⅗ .46⅘1.12⅕	f-	Allow	3	4	3^nk	2^2	4^2¼	6^9¾	ECardone^5	b 115	*2.30	72-22	Fancy Lace 113¾ Fatal Step 117^h Bubbles O'Tudor 115^4	Tired	11
23Sep66-7Aqu	sl	7f	.23⅕ .46⅖1.26⅖	f-	Allow	11	1	2½	2½	1^2	1¾	ECardone	b 115	*2.10	74-26	Blended White 115¾ River Lady 114^1 Silver Bright 113^h	Driving	11

LATEST WORKOUTS Mar 13 Bel tr.t. 5f fst 1.04⅖ b   Mar 5 TrP 3f fst .39 b   Feb 4 TrP 4f fst .51 h

Zayer Naytik ×

Ch. f (1963-Fla), by Stratmat—Incomparably, by Brookfield or Intent
Starlight Farm L. H. Hunt (M. Feingold) **115^5**
1967 5 1 0 1 $5,230
1966 14 3 3 0 $11,855

21Feb67-8Bow	sl	6f	.22⅖ .45⅗1.12⅗	f-	Allow	8	4	1½	2^1	1^h	2^1¼	RMorgan^5	107	6.80	83-30	d-Misty's Baby 113^1¼ Zayer Naytik 107¾ Lucy Bean 113^nk	Impeded	10
21Feb67—Placed first through disqualification.																		
2Feb67-7Bow	fst	6f	.23⅖ .46⅘1.12⅖	f-	Allow	7	6	3^1½	4^3	4^1¾	4^2½	RKimball	112	8.90	82-24	Equador II 112^1 Phyl's Destiny 114^1 Who Cabled 116½	No rally	10
27Jan67-8Bow	sly	6f	.22⅘ .46⅕1.12⅗	Allowance		5	4	6^2¼	5^5	3^2	5^3	RMorgan^5	106	15.50	81-28	Benedict C. 115^1 Nannie's Boy 109¾ Bronze Bout 116^1	Weakened	12
21Jan67-4Bow	fst	6f	.23⅖ .47⅖1.12⅗	Clm	10500	11	1	3½	1½	2^2	4^2	TKelly^7	103	19.20	82-22	Wide Horizon 106¾ Farmer Boy 116¾ Background 114½	Weakened	12
14Jan67-5Bow	gd	7f	.23⅖ .47⅖1.26⅘	Clm	9500	7	7	7^3½	5^1¾	5½	3^3	TKelly^10	103	10.00	76-27	Farmer Boy 114½ Sum Farce 114^2½ ZayerNaytik103^no	Mild rally	12
2Dec66-8Aqu	fst	6f	.23 .47 1.13	f-	8500	10	1	4^5½	4^5	3^4	2^2½	RMorgan^5	113	17.20	75-23	High Tail 114^2½ Zayer Naytik 113^h Fleet Impelled 112^1¼	Rallied	10
12Nov66-4Aqu	sly	6f	.22⅗ .46⅘1.12⅘	f-	8500	6	1	2^2	2^3	2^1½	1^h	RMorgan^5	111	13.20	79-29	Zayer Naytik 111^h High Tail 114^3 Dulat's Twin 116¾	Driving	8
9Nov66-2Aqu	fst	1	.45⅘1.11 1.37⅗	Clm	8500	9	1	1^1½	1^h	2^1½	7^6	EFires	b 113	25.10	74-18	Poker Table 114½ Am Battle 116^1½ Bombax 116^h	Used up early	9
24Oct66-9Aqu	fst	7f	.22⅖ .45⅘1.25⅗	f-	8500	2	3	2^3	3^4½	4^5½	6^11	JLRotz	b 116	19.90	67-22	Pink Rose 116^3½ Adaptable Miss 116½ High Tail 114^1	Tired	10

LATEST WORKOUTS Mar 11 Bel tr.t. 4f fst .50⅖ h

Strong Measures ×

Dk. b. or br. f (1964-Ky), by Bold Ruler—Who Dini, by Hypnotist II
High Tide Stable L. S. Barrera (E. G. Burke) **113**
1967 5 2 1 1 $12,150
1966 5 1 1 1 $4,670

16Mar67-7Aqu	sly	6f	.23⅕ .47⅗1.13	f-	Allow	1	4	3^nk	1^h	1½	1¾	ATCordero	121	4.80	78-33	Strong Measures 121¾ Spire 114^1½ Sports Event 118^h	Driving	6
1Mar67-8SA	fst	1 1/16	.46⅘1.11⅕1.43	f-	Allow	8	6	5^3	4^2	4^4½	4^11	EBelmonte	116	11.00	77-11	Gay Violin 112^5 Fisn House 118^4 Ellen Gruder 116^1½	Tired	9
22Feb67-4SA	fst	1 1/16	.48⅕1.12⅖1.44⅖	f-	Allow	5	4	4^2	3^1½	2½	1¾	EBelmonte	115	3.50	81-12	Strong Measures 115¾ Kimberly Queen 115^2 Bonaroba 118^1	Driving	9
16Feb67-7SA	fst	6f	.22⅖ .45⅖1.10	f-	Allow	2	6	6^3½	6^4½	6^6½	3^5½	EBelmonte	118	6.50	86-16	Lady Gourmet 118^4 Evie Jane 118^1½ Strong Measures 118^nk	Tired	11
10Jan67-6SA	fst	6f	.22 .45⅖1.11	f-	Allow	5	7	6^5½	5^5	3^3	2^2	BBaeza	117	4.00	85-16	Silver Rullah 117^2 Strong Measures 117^5 Fleet Duchess 117^2	Gamely	12
19Sep66-6Aqu	fst	6f	.22⅖ .45⅘1.11⅘	f-	Allow	8	5	7^5¾	8^10	5^9	4^7	BBaeza	118	*3.00	77-20	GreenGlade115^2½ She'sBeautiful116^1½ GreekSong'sGet118^3	No rally	10
12Sep66-6Aqu	fst	6f	.22⅘ .46⅘1.12⅕	f-	Allow	5	2	2^1	2^h	3^1	4^5	BBaeza	b 116	2.80	77-21	Treacherous 114^5 Senesa Compacta 116no Wageko 114no	Used up	9
5Sep66-5Aqu	fst	6f	.22⅗ .46⅕1.12⅖	f-	Allow	10	5	4^2½	3^2	2^4	3^7	EBelmonte	b 118	5.40	74-25	IrishCounty114^3½ Treacherous116^3½ StrongMeasures118^2½	Fair try	12
20Jly66-5Aqu	fst	5½f	.23⅘ .48⅗1.07⅗	f-MdSpWt		2	4	1^h	1^h	1^h	1^3	BBaeza	119	*0.90	75-23	StrongMeasures119^3ReneKimball119^1OrchestraCircle114^h	Handily	12
15Jun66-5Aqu	fst	5½f	.22⅖ .46⅖1.06⅕	f-MdSpWt		8	5	5^1½	5^4½	3^4	2¾	EBelmonte	119	*2.20	81-16	Treacherous 119¾ Strong Measures 119^2½ Grand Coulee 119^5	Gamely	11

LATEST WORKOUTS Apr 1 Bel tr.t. 4f hy .50 h   Mar 28 Bel tr.t. 4f sl .51 h   Mar 15 Bel tr.t. 3f fst .37⅘ b   Feb 11 SA m.t. 1m fst 1.43 h

Tournament Talk ×

B. f (1963-Ky), by Decathlon—Jenjay, by Brookfield
L. H. Savage M. A. Buxton (L. J. Tutt) **116^7**
1967 5 1 0 1 $3,700
1966 6 2 0 1 $5,345

24Mar67-7Aqu	my	6f	23⅖ .48⅘1.15⅗	f-Corr'tnH		3	2	1½	2^h	2^2	6^8	ATCordero	b 108	2.50e	57-46	Miss Moona 120¾ d-Holly-O. 120^2 Snow Time 108¾	Used up	7
21Feb67-6Hia	fst	6f	.22⅕ .45⅖1.10⅘	f-	Allow	7	2	1^1½	1^1½	1^2	1^1	JVasquez	b 113	*2.00	90-14	Tournament Talk 113^1 Sweety Kid 116^1 Ship Shoal 116¾	Driving	8
8Feb67-7Hia	sly	6f	.21⅘ .45⅕1.11⅖	f-	Allow	4	5	2^4	2^4	3^5	6^6	JRuane	b 115	5.90	81-12	Bear Grass 112^1 Lovely Gypsy 113½ Ultra Quest 121no	Weakened	7
2Feb67-7Hia	fst	5½f Ⓣ	1.05	f-	Allow	12	2	1½	1^2	1^2	5^2	JRuane	b 121	5.30	91-12	Mighty Happy 118½ Sun Play 113^1 Manta H. 112no	Faltered in drive	12
24Jan67-5Hia	my	6f	.22 .46⅕1.11⅘	f-	Allow	2	6	2½	1^2	1½	3^3	JVasquez	b 118	*3.10	82-21	For Joy 112^1 Sweety Kid 114^2 Tournament Talk 118^1½	Weakened	11
19Dec66-7Lrl	sl	6f	.23⅖ .48⅘1.15	f-	Allow	4	1	1^2	1½	1^3	1^3	JVasquez	b 116	*0.60	77-32	Tournament Talk 116^3 Art Form 107^6 Tisamour 114^8	Drew clear	5
5Dec66-7Lrl	fst	6f	.22⅘ .47⅖1.13⅕	f-	Allow	7	1	1^1½	1^1½	2^h	5^5	FLovato	b 118	*0.70	81-17	Queen Narda 107^1½ Art Form 107½ Pidgin 109^1	Gave way suddenly	9
28Nov66-3Lrl	sly	6f	.23 .47 1.12⅗	Md	Allow	6	1	1^4	1^5	1^4	1^7	FLovato	b 115	2.70	89-20	Tournament Talk 115^7 Sharp 114^8 Jice 114^1½	Easily best	7
29Apr66-2GS	my	6f	.22⅖ .47 1.15	f-MdSpWt		7	5	1½	1^1	1^h	4^2	JVasquez	b 115	4.20	67-28	Post Native 115^h May Wonder 115½ Gallant Noralien 115^1½	Weak'd	11
22Apr66-2GS	sly	6f	.23 .48 1.14⅘	f-MdSpWt		4	2	2^1	2^3	3^2	4^6	EMonacelli	b 115	*1.10	66-27	Rose's Needle 115^1 Post Native 115^1 May Wonder 116^4	Tired	8
11Apr66-1GP	fst	6f	.22⅗ .46⅕1.12⅖	f-MdSpWt		3	8	1^h	2½	3^3	3^1	EMonacelli	119	7.30	81-21	Swing Royal 119^1 Arkair 119no Tournament Talk 119^3½	In close	12

LATEST WORKOUTS Mar 31 Aqu 3f sl .37⅕ b   Mar 21 Aqu 5f gd 1.03⅘ b   Mar 15 Aqu 3f fst .36 b   Mar 12 Aqu 4f fst .51⅗ b

Song of Rome — B. f (1963–SC), by Roman Patrol—Inharmony, by Brookfield — S. E. Miron — R. Holton — (Dr. E. L. Wooten) — **118** — 1967 3 0 0 0 —— / 1966 19 3 5 2 $19,290

25Feb67-9Hia fst 6f .22⅘ .45⅘1.10⅘ f- Allow 7 4 88¾ 79½ 812 815 HWoodhouse b 115 52.10 75-20 Nature 1152½ Julie Potatoes 121½ Rose Court 1121¾ No factor. 8
7Feb67-9Hia fst 7f .23⅕ .46 1.23⅖ f- Allow 6 7 74¼ 64 67½ 912 HWoodhouse b 118 59.70 80-13 Maestrina 1121 Sundestine 1152½ Rose Court 112½ No mishap 12
21Jan67-6Hia my 6f .22⅕ .46⅖1.11⅕ f- Allow 2 9 109 86¼ 913 914 RUssery b 118 11.00 74-20 Welshwyn 1154 Galfizzie 1122 Prides Profile 115¾ In close 12
6Dec66-8Aqu fst 7f .23⅗ .47⅗1.26⅗ f- Allow 2 5 33½ 3nk 12 1no EBelmonte b 116 5.20 73-26 Song of Rome 116no Pink Rose 1141 Wiltare 116nk Just lasted 7
29Nov66-8Aqu gd 7f .23⅕ .46⅘1.26⅖ f- Allow 3 8 812 76 77¼ 52¼ JJMartin7 b 111 5.00 72-20 Needles Sword 111h Flashy Shot 1072 Whiglet 121h Rallied 10
19Nov66-4Aqu fst 6f .23 .47⅗1.12⅘ f- Allow 2 11 1012 911 55½ 21¼ ECardone5 b 113 12.40 78-19 Through theMist 1211¼ Song ofRome 113½ ShipShoal 118nk Sh'rp try 12
5Nov66-8Aqu fm 1$\frac{1}{16}$ Ⓣ 1.46⅗ f- Allow 8 7 713 610 59 511 FFont7 b 108 12.80 62-27 River Lady 1136 True Blue 1161 Maggie Fast Step 1163 No speed 8
29Oct66-6Aqu fst 7f .23⅗ .47⅖1.24⅗ f- Allow 2 7 35½ 34½ 44½ 46½ WShoemaker b 117 4.30 76-19 SkiDancer1203½ HappyKitten1131½ Through the Mist1151½ Tired 8
10Oct66-6Aqu fst 7f .23⅗ .47⅕1.24⅗ f- Allow 3 5 52¼ 31½ 41½ 43 WShoemaker b 120 3.30 80-20 Tomeen 111nk Darlin Phyllis 111nk Ski Dancer 1232½ Lacked rally 7
3Oct66-6Aqu fst 6f .22⅕ .45⅘1.11⅖ f- Allow 10 6 65¾ 55½ 22½ 21½ WShoemaker b 120 9.80 84-19 Lobelia 1201½ Song of Rome 1201 Tomeen 1154 Finished gamely 10
LATEST WORKOUTS Mar 31 Bel tr.t. 5f hy 1.04½ h — Mar 26 Bel tr.t. 5f my 1.06 b — Mar 9 Bel tr.t. 4f gd .50⅘ b — Feb 24 Hia 3f fst .37⅗ b

***Equador II** — B. f (1963), by Dionisio—Rain Water, by Nimbus — E. Mittman — W. L. Dorsey — (Mr.-Mrs. W. Whitehead) (Ire.) — **120** — 1967 7 1 2 0 $6,575 / 1966 7 1 0 0 $4,225

24Mar67-6Aqu my 6f .23⅘ .49⅕1.15⅗ f- Allow 3 5 613 714 713 68½ JLRotz 115 7.50 56-46 Double Switch1151 Blended White1164½ Swim To Me1161 No speed 7
25Feb67-8Bow fst 7f .22⅗ .44⅖1.21⅘ f-BFrcheH 4 11 1111 1219 1114 1112 CBaltazar 110 50.60 92- 5 Holly-O. 117nk Moccasin 1202½ Lady Diplomat 1112¾ No speed 13
14Feb67-8Bow fst 6f .22⅘ .46⅘1.11⅘ f- Allow 4 5 97¼ 88½ 43½ 41½ CBaltazar 114 *1.80 85-23 Flashy Shot 1141 d-Dove Hunt 110nk Cherokee Mary 112nk Rallied 11
2Feb67-7Bow fst 6f .23⅖ .46⅘1.12⅖ f- Allow 10 1 53½ 55 52¼ 11 CBaltazar 112 *2.50 85-24 Equador II 1121 Phyl's Destiny 1141 Who Cabled 116½ In time 10
30Jan67-8Bow fst 7f .23⅗ .46⅗1.24⅘ f- Allow 5 3 21½ 22½ 22 22 CBaltazar 112 2.60e 87-22 Holly-O 1212 Equador II 1121 Sally Lou 117nk Bore in stretch 7
25Jan67-8Bow fst 6f .22⅘ .46⅖1.11⅘ Allowance 3 4 59½ 58½ 54¾ 56 CBaltazar 111 9.10 82-26 Tetanus 1152½ Old Maestro 1071 Cosimo 117½ Evenly late stages 7
10Jan67-8Bow fst 7f .23⅗ .47⅕1.26⅕ Allowance 4 6 45½ 45½ 22 23½ CBaltazar 113 8.30 78-30 Over Roger 1183½ Equador II 1131½ One Sunday 113¾ Second best 8
7Dec66-8Aqu fst 6f .22⅗ .46 1.12⅖ f- 13000 1 7 610 612 56 11¼ HWoodhouse 111 28.30 81-24 Equador II 1111½ Bushy Tail 112no Italiana 1182 Driving clear 8
14Nov66-6Aqu fst 6f .22⅖ .45⅘1.11⅗ f- 15000 4 7 712 716 69 66¾ HWoodhouse 114 38.40 78-22 Zeesa Adelle 119½ Native Twin 112nk Savannalamar 115no No speed 7
6Oct66-7Aqu fm 1$\frac{1}{16}$ Ⓣ 1.45⅕ f- Allow 2 4 79¾ 1017 1018 1036 LGilligan 114 35.60 44-20 Winklepicker 1183½ River Lady 1144 Darlin Phyllis 1141½ Tired 10
LATEST WORKOUTS Mar 31 Bel tr.t. 5f hy 1.05 b — Mar 15 Bel tr.t. 6f fst 1.18 b — Mar 11 Bel tr.t. 4f fst .50 h — Feb 21 Bow 6f fst 1.14⅗ h

Swim to Me — B. m (1962), by King of the Tudors—Hukilau, by Native Dancer — Gedney Farm — R. Sechrest — (C. V. Whitney) — **118** — 1967 6 0 0 1 $1,000 / 1966 13 1 1 2 $7,500

24Mar67-6Aqu my 6f .23⅘ .49⅕1.15⅗ f- Allow 4 1 35 35½ 35½ 35½ RUssery b 116 12.30 59-46 Double Switch1151 Blended White1164½ Swim To Me1161 Evenly 7
23Feb67-8SA fm 1¼ Ⓣ 1.11⅖2.00⅗ f-SBar'aH 7 4 22½ 64 97¾ 915 EBelmonte b 112 33.30 79-10 Ormea 114h Maintain 116¾ Miss Rincon 110½ Early speed, tired 9
23Feb67—Santa Barbara Handicap run in two divisions, 5th and 8th races.
4Feb67-8SA fst 1⅛ .47⅖1.12⅕1.50⅕ f-SMrgtaH 5 10 98 1111 1010 96¾ APineda b 111 12.60e 74-14 Miss Moona 118no Maintain 1123½ •Streamer 114no No factor 14
21Jan67-7SA fst 1$\frac{1}{16}$ .46⅘1.11⅕1.42⅖ f-SMariaH 5 11 1011 108¾ 78 57½ APineda b 111 18.00e 83-13 Natashka 1232½ Miss Moona 1181½ Streamer 1152½ Stride late 13
13Jan67-8SA fst 1$\frac{1}{16}$ .46⅘1.11⅖1.43⅗ f- Allow 4 7 56 53½ 55½ 55 PBaeza b 120 34.50 80-15 Swoonalong 118h April Dawn 1174½ Miss Kat Bird 119h No mishap 9
2Jan67-5SA fst 6f .22⅕ .45 1.10⅗ f- Allow 8 7 76½ 65¾ 74 55 BBaeza b 114 2.20e 84-14 Streamer 1164 Trader's Folly 114½ Liz 114½ Showed even effort 9
5Nov66-4Aqu fst 7f .23 .46 1.24 f- Allow 4 5 55¼ 55½ 56 58½ WTichenor10 106 9.10 77-13 Tomeen 118no Ski Dancer 123no Terrific Traffic1217 No mishap 7
31Oct66-8Aqu fm 1⅛ Ⓣ 1.51⅕ f- Allow 2 6 54½ 54¼ 64¾ 73 EGuerin 116 8.60 76-21 Winklepicker 120nk Our Dear Ruth 107½ Sea Moon 116nk No rally 7
14Oct66-6Aqu fst 7f .22⅗ .45⅕1.24 f- Allow 5 7 612 58½ 55½ 47½ EGuerin 118 6.10 78-19 Air Whirl 1152½ Fatal Step 1153½ Omaha Beach 1161½ Broke slowly 7
LATEST WORKOUTS Apr 1 Bel tr.t. 4f hy .51 b — Mar 4 SA tr.t. 5f fst 1.04⅘ h — Feb 21 SA m.t. 4f fst .48⅗ h — Feb 17 SA t.c. 1m fm 1.41⅗ h

Snow Weapon — B. f (1963–Ky), by Arctic Prince—Gaonera, by Brazado — King Ranch — Max Hirsch — (R. Herren) — **118** — 1966 17 3 0 2 $14,730 / 1965 3 M 0 0 $210

8Dec66-7Aqu fst 1 .47⅖1.11⅗1.36 f- Allow 4 1 2½ 23 512 716 FAlvarez 115 16.80 71-22 Mac's Sparkier 1186 Sailor Princess 116no Nature 1165 Used up 7
1Dec66-7Aqu fst 1 .45⅕1.11⅕1.37⅘ f- Allow 6 6 67¼ 56½ 24 1h MYcaza 117 12.00 79-23 Snow Weapon 117h First Offence 1123 Sabemar 122½ Driving 7
22Nov66-7Aqu fst 7f .23 .46 1.24⅗ f- Allow 5 5 710 611 69½ 66½ EFires 118 10.30 76-23 Omaha Beach 1113 Tangle 121nk Whiglet 1182½ Not a factor 8
17Nov66-8Aqu fst 1⅛ .48⅘1.12⅘1.51⅕ f- Allow 6 3 31 32½ 33½ 36½ WBlum 113 11.40 73-20 Ski Dancer 1182½ Terrific Traffic 1134 Snow Weapon 1132½ No rally 9
12Nov66-6Aqu sly 7f .23⅕ .46⅗1.25⅘ f- Allow 8 4 45½ 47 58 43¾ MYcaza 121 18.00 73-29 Darlin Phyllis 115nk Ship Shoal 1171½ Needles Sword 1152 No mish'p 8
29Oct66-6Aqu fst 7f .23⅗ .47⅖1.24⅗ f- Allow 1 5 45½ 45 56½ 79¾ JLRotz 120 16.10 74-19 SkiDancer1203½ HappyKitten1131½ Through the Mist1151½ Tired 8
6Oct66-8Aqu fst 7f .22⅘ .47 1.26⅕ f- Allow 7 5 53¾ 52½ 1½ 1h JLRotz 115 10.60 75-24 Snow Weapon 115h Sea Moon 1161½ Tangle 1154 Long hard drive 9
22Sep66-6Aqu gd 7f .22⅗ .46⅕1.26 f- Allow 2 5 85 77 52¾ 54½ EFires 111 14.30 72-23 Song of Rome1141 SeaMoon116no DoveHunt116nk Mild bid, tired 12
10Sep66-8Aqu fm 1$\frac{1}{16}$ Ⓣ 1.42⅗ f- Allow 5 5 59½ 57½ 68 615 RFerraro 111 27.60 78-17 Miss Proctor 1133½ Lay In 1062½ Buffet Dinner 1113½ No mishap 8
6Sep66-8Aqu fm 1$\frac{1}{16}$ Ⓣ 1.43⅕ f- Allow 10 4 46½ 87½ 98¾ 1011 MVenezia 111 60.80 79-10 OurDearRuth 111noSilverBright 1131½Shim'eringGold 118½ Fell back 10
LATEST WORKOUTS Mar 27 Bel tr.t. 4f my .53 b — Mar 21 Bel tr.t. 3f sl .40 b — Mar 13 Bel tr.t. 4f fst .51⅗ b — Mar 10 Bel tr.t. 3f gd .39 b

---

Blended White: A really sharp mare, well-suited to the distance, but not the kind to bet on in a race of this sort, unless the remainder of the field consists of claiming animals. NO BET.

Zayer Naytik: Idle too long. NO BET.

Strong Measures: A three-year-old, the only one in the race, in fact. Does she have the class? For example, has she ever beaten older horses? The player with access to result charts would shuffle through them and discover that this filly has been running against other three-year-olds. The past-performance record also tells the tale. Note that Strong Measures has invariably been among the highest-weighted fillies in her races. If she had been running against older horses, the weight concessions would be apparent in her record. Does she have the class to beat older fillies at this distance in April? Not as far as the naked eye can see. Note, furthermore, that she is being required to carry 113 pounds which, although not much in a race against other three-year-olds, is maximum weight for her age on the scale specified in today's conditions. She actually is *giving* weight to everything else in the field! She looked sharp in her last outing, however. Maybe the rest of the field is bad enough to give her a chance. CONTENDER.

Tournament Talk: Plenty of speed, but has a tendency to slow down considerably in the stretch. The added furlong makes her a loser. NO BET.

Song of Rome: Has run poorly this year and has not raced in more than a month. NO BET.

Equador II: Needs more racing before qualifying for support in an allowance at Aqueduct. NO BET.

Swim To Me: Sechrest's five-year-old ran a nice, even race in the mud to launch her 1967 New York season. Her strong finish in the Santa Maria Handicap scarcely established her as stakes material, but indicated ability to handle the average allowance animal when in shape. Deserves further scrutiny. CONTENDER.

Snow Weapon: No action yet this year. NO BET.

As between Strong Measures, an undistinguished three-year-old running for the first time against older horses, and Swim to Me, an apparently ready, classy five-year-old with a break in the weights, the handicapper takes the older horse. This is done not simply to "have something going" in the race, but because the older horse—in a race like this one—is a distinctly solid choice.

The Running of the Race

PREDICTABLY, Strong Measures was the favorite, but the shrewdies in the Aqueduct crowd backed Swim to Me down to a strong 3.10–1. The three-year-old was no factor in the running. Swim to Me won on class, outgunning the sharp claimer, Blended White, in the stretch.

SEVENTH RACE	7 FURLONGS. (Chute). (Rose Net, Sept. 17, 1962, 1.21⅕, 6, 114.)
Aqu - 30716	Allowances. Purse $10,000. Fillies and mares. 3-year-olds and upward which have never won three races other than maiden or claiming. Weights, 3-year-olds, 113 lbs., older
April 3, 1967	123 lbs. Non-winners of two races other than maiden or claiming since Oct. 29 allowed 3 lbs., of such a race since Jan. 16, 5 lbs.

Value to winner $6,500, second $2,000, third $1,000, fourth $500. Mutuel pool $367.003.

Index	Horse	Eqt A Wt	PP St	¼	½	Str	Fin	Jockey	Owner	Odds $1
30460Aqu³	Swim To Me	b 5 118	7 8	5½	2h	2⁴	1½	R Ussery	Gedney Farms	3.10
30460Aqu²	BlendedWhite	b 5 118	1 1	1²	1³	1h	2²½	E Cardone	M Guerrieri	4.20
30460Aqu⁶	Equador II	4 120	6 4	7h	6¹	5¹½	3⁴	L Pincay Jr	E Mittman	6.60
30319Hia⁸	Song Of Rome	b 4 118	5 3	6¹	4³	4h	4ⁿᵏ	E Belmonte	S E Miron	17.50
30234Bow¹	Zayer Naytik	4 115	2 5	2³	3½	3¹½	5h	R Morgan⁵	Starlight Farms	29.40
30434Aqu¹	Strong M'sures	3 113	3 7	8	5h	6⁴	6⁶	A T Cordero	High Tide Stable	1.70
30461Aqu⁶	T'rnam't Talk	b 4 116	4 6	3½	7³	7³	7²½	R Russello⁷	L H Savage	7.70
29561Aqu⁷	Snow Weapon	4 118	8 2	4h	8	8	8	J L Rotz	King Ranch	17.20

Time .23⅗, .48, 1.13⅗, 1.26⅖ (against wind in backstretch). Track fast.

$2 Mutuel Prices:

7-SWIM TO ME	8.20	5.20	3.40
1-BLENDED WHITE		5.00	3.20
6-EQUADOR II			4.40

B. m, by King of the Tudors—Hukilau, by Native Dancer. Trainer R. Sechrest. Bred by C. V. Whitney.
IN GATE AT 4.38. OFF AT 4.38½ EASTERN STANDARD TIME. Start good. Won driving.
SWIM TO ME, steadied along early, got through on the inside rallying and wore down BLENDED WHITE while continuing along the rails in the drive. The latter had her speed to open a clear lead early, raced out from the rail into the stretch, held well when challenged and was not good enough. EQUADOR II, slow to settle into stride, finished fast. SONG OF ROME could not menace while finishing outside rivals. ZAYER NAYTIK pressed the pace to the stretch and faltered. STRONG MEASURES was never a factor while between horses much of the way. TOURNAMENT TALK gave way early. SNOW WEAPON fell back early.

---

7. SIXTH AT AQUEDUCT, MAY 30, 1967—Track Fast

HERE IS A really instructive race, illustrating the relationship between class and form, and how to recognize both in circumstances that crop up dozens of times every season.

6th Race Aqueduct

7 FURLONGS AQUEDUCT (Start ▼ / ▲ Finish)

7 FURLONGS. (Chute). (Rose Net, Sept. 17, 1962, 1.21⅕, 6, 114.)
Allowances. Purse $8,000. 3-year-olds and upward which have never won two races other than maiden, claiming, optional or starter. Weights, 3-year-olds 114 lbs., older 124 lbs. Non-winners of a race other than maiden or claiming since March 11 allowed 3 lbs., such a race since Jan. 16, 5 lbs.

Osage

Ch. c (1964–Fla), by Correlation—Court Planting, by Royal Gem II **111**
Kosgrove Stable N. Gonzales (G. Dorland)
1967 6 0 0 1 $800
1966 14 2 1 3 $7,935

22May67–6Aqu	fst	6f	.22⅕ .45⅕ 1.10⅘	Allowance	2	8	910	9½	87½	62¾	LAdams	113	20.70	86–14	VelvetFlash 114no •RightCard 109nk •PriceOfGlory 117nk	Late bid	9
9May67–6Aqu	gd	7f	.22⅘ .46⅗ 1.25⅘	Clm 18000	3	5	69½	78½	65¼	54½	LAdams	116	*2.30	72–25	Big Nash 1121½ Sky Count 1071½ Popsie Doodle 112no	No excuse	8
2May67–4Aqu	fst	6f	.22⅘ .46⅖ 1.10⅘	Clm 20000	7	3	42	42	43½	33¾	LAdams	116	14.30	85–18	Babar 1163½ Will Please 112nk Osage 1162½	Held on gamely	7
14Apr67–4Aqu	fst	7f	.23 .46 1.23⅖	Clm 20000	5	6	69½	68½	613	617	ATCordero	117	5.80	72–18	Pig-Headed 1186 Popsie Doodle 1151½ Lord Robert 1136	Trailed	6
11Feb67–7Hia	fst	7f	.23⅗ .46⅖ 1.23	Allowance	4	8	108¾	1012	714	716	ATCordero	112	53.10	78–20	Ask The Fare1143½ Wedgedale116no Sun Seeker1154	Never close	12
4Feb67–4Hia	fst	6f	.22⅖ .46 1.11⅖	Allowance	10	9	116¾	99¼	119¼	1112	HGustines	112	13.90	75–13	Air Rights 1152 Royal De Fur 1121 Hornbeam 115h	Never close	12
31Dec66–9TrP	fst	170	.46⅕ 1.11⅕ 1.42⅕	C.MiamiH	10	7	105¼	94¼	89	89¾	ACordero	115	46.10	76–16	Fort Drum 115h Biller 1181¾ Pepperwood 1212½	No factor	12
19Dec66–7TrP	fst	6f	.22⅗ .46⅕ 1.11⅖	Allowance	1	8	66	42½	3½	1½	ACordero	117	*1.70	85–14	Osage 117½ Pretty Intent 112nk Royal de Fur 1085	Hard ridden	8
26Nov66–5Aqu	gd	6f	.22⅖ .47 1.11⅘	Allowance	9	9	76½	21½	31	32½	ACordero	122	3.40	81–20	Light the Fuse 122no Misty Cloud 1152½ Osage 1223	Sluggish start	9
14Nov66–7Aqu	fst	7f	.22⅘ .46⅕ 1.24⅖	Allowance	5	5	33½	32½	3nk	32¼	EBelmonte	122	11.20	82–22	Hornbeam 1191½ Shah 122¾ Osage 122½	Bold bid, hung	7
2Nov66–4Aqu	fst	6f	.23 .47 1.12⅖	Md Sp Wt	11	9	78	69	2h	1h	ACordero	122	4.70	81–19	Osage 122h Yarak 1221½ I'm Your Boy 122¾	Reared start, just up	12
26Oct66–3Aqu	fst	6f	.22⅘ .46⅘ 1.11⅗	Md Sp Wt	4	4	56½	56½	56½	54¾	HGustines	122	19.50	80–19	Misty Run 122no Student Driver 122¾ Three Bagger 1223	No rally	13

LATEST WORKOUTS May 28 Bel tr.t. 4f fst .48 h May 17 Bel 4f fst .48⅕ h May 7 Bel 4f sly .49⅗ b Apr 29 Bel 4f fst .47 h

Puntador

B. c (1964–Tex), by Curandero—Turn Out, by Turn-to **114**
King Ranch Max Hirsch (King Ranch)
1967 6 1 1 1 $7,825
1966 5 1 0 0 $2,730

23May67–7Aqu	fst	6f	.22 .45⅗ 1.11⅗	Allowance	4	5	56½	46	1½	1½	JLRotz	113	2.80	85–20	Puntador 113½ Tolk 109no Tartan Dance 119¾	Hard drive	10
8May67–6Aqu	gd	6f	.22⅕ .46 1.11⅘	Allowance	6	1	54½	54½	32	34½	JLRotz	113	5.80	79–21	Babar 1132½ First And Finest 1142 Puntador 1132	Bid, hung	9
1May67–6Aqu	fst	6f	.22⅕ .45⅗ 1.11	Allowance	4	6	75½	54½	57	410	JLRotz	113	3.40	78–20	Dizzy Devil 1131 Pine Hill 1111 I'm Your Boy 1148	No rally	11
22Apr67–7Aqu	fst	1⅛	.46⅖ 1.10⅘ 1.49⅗	WoodMem.	1	7	610	89	812	817	ADeSpirito	126	88.20	71–16	Damascus 1266 Gala Performance 1263 Dawn Glory 1261½	Far back	9
15Apr67–7Aqu	fst	1	.46⅕ 1.10⅖ 1.35⅕	Gotham	1	5	56	55½	612	623	JLRotz	114	47.80	69–14	Dr. Fager 122½ Damascus 1225 Reason To Hail 1147	Weakened	9
13Mar67–6Aqu	fst	6f	.22⅘ .46⅖ 1.11⅖	Allowance	3	6	51¾	41¾	22	2nk	JLRotz	113	3.50	86–18	MisterPitt'sKid122nk Puntador1132½ VictoriaFleetest108no	Gaining	8
24Sep66–5Aqu	fst	6½f	.22⅘ .46⅘ 1.18⅗	Allowance	6	13	118	96½	77½	76¼	JLRotz	119	18.70	81–18	Sun Seeker 115h Rising Market 1222½ Proviso 1221	Slow start	14
6Sep66–6Aqu	fst	6f	.22⅗ .46⅗ 1.12⅖	Allowance	5	4	66	68½	611	612	JLRotz	b 115	14.00	69–28	Disciplinarian 1195 Sun Seeker 115no Right Card 1225	Trailed	6
13Aug66–4Sar	fst	6f	.22⅗ .46⅖ 1.10⅖	Allowance	1	8	77¼	89½	67	616	JLRotz	b 122	11.10	80– 9	Dr. Fager 1178 Bandera Road 1172 Quaker City 1152	Slow start	8
6Aug66–5Sar	fst	5½f	.23⅕ .47 1.06	Allowance	1	2	42½	41½	67	75½	JLRotz	b 122	2.40	81–12	Stamp Act 122nk d-Gay Youth 114½ Backbiter 1101	Roughed on turn	7
8Jly 66–5Aqu	fst	5½f	.22⅗ .46⅘ 1.06⅖	Md Sp Wt	3	2	62¾	41½	31	1½	BBaeza	b 122	5.60	81–21	Puntador 122½ London Jet 1223 One Gem 1224	Up final strides	10

Nominated for Belmont Stakes. LATEST WORKOUTS May 28 Bel 5f fst 1.00 h May 20 Bel 5f fst 1.02⅖ b May 17 Bel 4f fst .47⅘ h

Tanrackin

Dk. b. or br. c (1964–Ky), by Roman Line—Muscidae, by War Admiral **109**
Mrs. T. M. Waller T. M. Waller (Mrs. T. M. Waller)
1967 1 0 0 0 $400
1966 3 2 0 1 $6,855

22May67–6Aqu	fst	6f	.22⅕ .45⅕ 1.10⅘	Allowance	7	5	54½	55½	44½	4nk	RTurcotte	110	5.80e	89–14	VelvetFlash 114no •RightCard 109nk •PriceOfGlory 117nk	Rallied	9
3Dec66–4Aqu	fst	6f	.23⅕ .47⅖ 1.12⅗	Allowance	5	8	53¼	42½	21	1¾	RTurcotte	117	*1.10e	80–20	Tanrackin 117¾ Greek Song's Get 1141¼ Gun Mount 1223	Driving	8
26Aug66–4Sar	fst	6f	.23 .46⅗ 1.11⅘	Allowance	6	6	41	3½	42½	31¾	RTurcotte	119	3.70	87–12	Bandera Road 1141 Backbiter 115¾ Tanrackin 119¾	Wide early	7
15Jly 66–5Aqu	fst	5½f	.22⅖ .46⅖ 1.06	Md Sp Wt	5	8	76¼	67½	33	12	RTurcotte	122	29.30	83–20	Tanrackin 1222 Monitor 1221½ Quiet Town 1221½	Was going away	11

LATEST WORKOUTS May 27 Bel tr.t. 5f my 1.02 h May 19 Bel tr.t. 5f fst 1.04 b May 15 Bel tr.t. 1m fst 1.44 b May 11 Bel tr.t. 5f fst 1.01⅖ b

Fleet Honor

Dk. b. or br. c (1964–Ky), by Count of Honor—That Gibson Girl, by Royal Coinage **111**
Scotch Hills Farm F. E. McMillan (J. Welch)
1967 4 1 0 0 $2,925
1966 5 1 0 2 $3,780

17May67–5GS	fst	6f	.22 .45 1.10	Allowance	2	6	55	612	516	519	DHidalgo	113	16.30	75–18	Mr. Ed P. 1132 Glengary 1137 All At Sea 1222	Showed nothing	6
4Feb67–4Hia	fst	6f	.22⅖ .46 1.11⅖	Allowance	11	2	32	42	3½	54	ATCordero	118	3.70	83–13	Air Rights 1152 Royal De Fur 1121 Hornbeam 115h	Bid, tired	12
28Jan67–6Hia	gd	6f	.22⅗ .46⅗ 1.12⅘	Allowance	7	3	21½	2h	13	15	ATCordero	116	3.30	80–26	Fleet Honor 1165 Mon Zigue 1211 Bold Point 1162	Something left	11
17Jan67–4Hia	gd	6f	.22⅕ .45⅗ 1.10⅗	Allowance	8	4	53½	58¼	714	819	ATCordero	118	10.90	72–13	Balouf 1166 Bold Monarch 1181¼ Wedgedale 1162	Brief factor	10
7Dec66–5Aqu	fst	6f	.22⅗ .46⅖ 1.11⅗	Md Sp Wt	4	3	1h	1½	14	16	ACordero	122	*1.40	85–24	Fleet Honor 1226 Tote'm Home 1221 Mr. Peveron 1222	Won easily	12
30Nov66–4Aqu	gd	6f	.22⅗ .46⅖ 1.11⅘	Md Sp Wt	8	8	106¾	78¼	36	46	RUssery	122	*1.50	78–22	Speedaire1221½MisterPitt'sKid 1222GaelicLancelot 1222½	Bid, hung	14
23Nov66–3Aqu	fst	6f	.22⅘ .46⅕ 1.12	Md Sp Wt	4	2	11½	3nk	11½	3nk	RUssery	122	4.60	83–17	Royal Gallant 122h Royal Medal 122h Fleet Honor 1222½	Gamely	14
16Nov66–4Aqu	fst	6f	.22⅘ .46⅖ 1.11⅖	Md Sp Wt	4	2	12	11½	1½	3nk	RUssery	122	*2.10	86–16	Gun Mount 122no Royal Medal 122nk Fleet Honor 1226	No excuse	10
9Nov66–5Aqu	fst	6f	.22⅖ .46 1.11⅘	Md Sp Wt	14	9	64½	32	58	109½	EBelmonte	122	3.20	75–18	Popsie Doodle 117h Eagle's Spinney 1225 Talboa 122h	Tired	14

Nominated for Belmont Stakes. LATEST WORKOUTS May 27 Bel 6f fst 1.16 b May 23, Bel 3f fst .37⅘ b May 15 Bel 4f fst .48 hg

Devil's Tattoo

B. c (1963–Fla), by Rough'n Tumble—Boodlette, by Boodle **119**
Edith Marienhoff C. Ross (E. Marienhoff)
1967 1 0 0 0 —
1966 10 2 2 1 $8,575

22May67–6Aqu	fst	6f	.22⅕ .45⅕ 1.10⅘	Allowance	6	6	33	34	66½	85	ADeSpirito	119	16.60	84–14	VelvetFlash 114no •RightCard 109nk •PriceOfGlory 117nk	Tired	9
27Apr66–6Aqu	fst	1⅛	.48⅘ 1.13 1.51⅖	Allowance	5	2	21	1h	21½	67¾	PJRuane	110	4.40	71–18	Hail the King 115nk Sea Castle 1133 Enfant Terrible 1203	Used up	6
9Apr66–8Aqu	fst	1	.46⅕ 1.11⅕ 1.37	Allowance	9	3	1½	1h	1h	1h	JRuane	110	17.40	83–17	Devil's Tattoo 110h Fuerza 114½ Bushfighter 1143	Driving	11
2Apr66–8Aqu	fst	1⅛	.46⅘ 1.11⅗ 1.51⅘	Allowance	8	5	58	62¾	44½	513	JRuane	109	10.20	64–19	Neparoo 109½ Highest Honors 1123 Ameri Pilot 1124	No mishap	9
24Mar66–8Aqu	fst	7f	.22⅖ .45 1.23⅖	Allowance	2	3	1½	21	715	825	RUssery	b 122	4.70	64–25	Alexville 1158 Neparoo 1152½ Yale Fence 122h	Speed, tired	9
17Mar66–6Aqu	fst	6f	.22⅕ .45⅘ 1.12⅖	Allowance	7	4	21	22	33½	36	RUssery	b 122	*1.70	75–25	BanderaBeau1133½PlaneCommander1142½Devil'sTattoo1221	Weak'd	7
5Mar66–8GP	fst	7f	.22⅕ .44⅘ 1.22⅘	Hutcheson	11	1	42	44	58	99½	LLoughry5	b 110	45.80	85–15	Bold and Brave 1121¾ Kauai King 1142 All Love 1163	Speed, tired	15
2Mar66–2Hia	fst	6f	.22⅕ .45⅖ 1.11⅕	Allowance	6	2	2h	2h	2½	3nk	LAdams	b 116	*1.70	88–13	Notice Me 116nk d-Sky Duke 116h Devil's Tattoo 116h	Bumped	12
2Mar66—Placed second through disqualification.																	
21Feb66–8Hia	fst	7f	.22⅗ .45⅕ 1.22⅘	FlaBrdrsH	1	8	88¼	77¼	57	56¾	LAdams	b 112	7.40	88–13	Gary G. 1173¼ Native Street 118¾ Handsome Boy 123¾	Slow start	9
12Feb66–5Hia	fst	6f	.22 .45⅖ 1.10⅘	Allowance	6	2	41½	42¼	2h	21	RTurcotte	b 116	4.10	89–17	Sky Guy 1161 Devil's Tattoo 1164 Fairway Ruler 1165	Gamely	12
31Jan66–3Hia	fst	6f	.22⅕ .46⅖ 1.12⅘	Md Sp Wt	11	1	45	32	21½	12½	LAdams	b 119	*0.50	80–21	Devil's Tattoo 1192½ Tullak 1192½ Shanty 1191	Drew clear	12

LATEST WORKOUTS May 29 Bel 3f fst .36 b

Pink Rose — B. f (1963–Fla), by Beau Gar—Bully for Rosy, by Pet Bully — Janley Stable — M. Cohn — (Hobeau Farm, Inc.) — 114 — 1967 6 0 0 0 — / 1966 22 4 4 2 $18,24

31Mar67–7Aqu fst 6f .22⅘ .46 1.11⅗ f- Allow 5 8 816 818 815 711 HGustines 120 18.60 74–23 Arrangement 108nk Kate's Intent 1085 Ship Shoal 118½ No speed
24Mar67–6Aqu my 6f .23⅘ .49⅕1.15⅗ f- Allow 7 7 716 612 611 78¾ RTurcotte 116 11.90 56–46 Double Switch1151 Blended White116½ Swim To Me1161 No speed
25Feb67–8Bow fst 7f .22⅗ .44⅖1.21⅘ f-BFrcheH 7 10 88¼1015 98¾ 77 ORosado 106 97.20 97– 5 Holly-O. 117nk Moccasin 1202½ Lady Diplomat 1112¾ Far back 1
14Feb67–8Bow fst 6f .22⅘ .46⅘1.11⅘ f- Allow 3 11 119¾1112 97¼ 74¼ RMorgan5 109 8.90 84–23 FlashyShot 1141 d-DoveHunt 110nk CherokeeMary 112nk Slug. early 1
30Jan67–8Bow fst 7f .23⅗ .46⅗1.24⅘ f- Allow 7 7 58½ 512 57½ 55¼ RMorgan5 111 3.40 84–22 Holly-O 1212 Equador II 1121 Sally Lou 117nk Raced wide thruout
23Jan67–8Bow fst 6f .23⅕ .46⅘1.12⅗ f- Allow 4 7 67¼ 79 76¾ 53 TLee 118 7.70 81–24 VictoriaRegina II 117nc TerrificTraffic1211½ FlashyShot107h Rallied
6Dec66–8Aqu fst 7f .23⅗ .47⅗1.26⅗ f- Allow 3 6 712 78¾ 34 2no ECardone5 114 *2.20 73–26 Song of Rome 116no Pink Rose 1141 Wiltare 116nk Closed fast
8Nov66–3Aqu fst 7f .22⅘ .45⅖1.24⅗ f- Allow 4 5 513 512 2½ 11½ RUssery 115 2.70 83–18 Pink Rose 1151½ Inspiring 113¾ Sea Moon 116no Wide, drew out
24Oct66–9Aqu fst 7f .22⅖ .45⅘1.25⅗ f- 8500 9 8 99 59 22 13½ RUssery 116 3.20 78–22 Pink Rose 1163½ Adaptable Miss 116½ High Tail 1141 Easily 1
17Oct66–9Aqu fst 7f .23⅕ .46⅘1.26 f- 6250 5 8 99½ 75 32 11½ RUssery 116 3.90 76–19 Pink Rose 1161½ Fleet Impelled 1162 Trijugate 1121½ Driving 1
6Oct66–7Aqu fm 1 1/16 Ⓣ 1.45⅕ f- Allow 4 8 1010 79½ 77¾ 712 ACordero 114 17.80 68–20 Winklepicker 1183½ River Lady 1144 Darlin Phyllis 1141¼ No factor 1
30Sep66–6Aqu sf 1 1/16 Ⓣ 1.45⅘ f- Allow 5 10 913 95¼ 51¾ 44½ ACordero 112 28.70 72–23 Ski Dancer 117½ True Blue 117h For Joy 1124 No mishap 1
LATEST WORKOUTS May 28 Bel tr.t. 4f fst .48⅘ h May 24 Bel tr.t. 5f fst 1.01⅖ h May 20 Bel tr.t. 5f fst 1.02⅘ b May 14 Bel tr.t. 6f fst 1.19 b

Dandy Steal * — B. c (1964–Ky), by Beau Busher—Miss Culprit, by High Bandit — N. Hellman — A. A. Scotti — (L. P.-E. D. Jackson) — 114 — 1967 9 2 4 1 $14,57 / 1966 12 3 3 2 $10,52

22May67–6Aqu fst 6f .22⅕ .45⅕1.10⅘ Allowance 9 9 88¼ 66 56 51¾ RUssery b 114 2.10 87–14 VelvetFlash 114no •RightCard 109nk •PriceOfGlory 117nk Poor start
15May67–6Aqu fst 7f .22⅗ .45⅕1.22⅘ Allowance 2 dense fog 22½ BBaeza b 114 7.20 89–13 Major Art 1092½ Dandy Steal 1145 Dizzy Devil 116h Best others
6May67–5Aqu sly 6f .22⅗ .46⅖1.12⅗ Allowance 2 5 58 56 41½ 31½ WBoland b 114 3.20 78–27 Irish Dude 111h Bologna Gellis 1141½ Dandy Steal 1148 Rallied
24Apr67–6Aqu sly 6f .22⅖ .46⅗1.12⅗ Allowance 2 3 43½ 44½ 1h 12 BBaeza b 113 *1.70 80–24 Dandy Steal 1132 Runny Richard 114¾ Talboa 116½ Ridden out 1
11Apr67–6Aqu fst 7f .23⅖ .47⅕1.25 Allowance 10 3 32½ 3nk 2½ 2½ HGustines b 110 3.80 80–27 Blasting Charge 107½ Dandy Steal 1104 Storm Crost 118¾ Gamely 1
31Mar67–6Aqu fst 6f .22⅗ .46⅕1.11⅗ Clm 20000 2 2 2½ 11 11 12 BBaeza b 116 *1.50 85–23 Dandy Steal 1162 Quaker City 105no Popsie Doodle 1155 Driving 1
25Mar67–8Aqu my 6f .23⅕ .48⅖1.14 Allowance 2 3 1h 1h 21 22½ BBaeza b 112 2.70 70–35 Mister Pitt's Kid 1132½ Dandy Steal 1123 Disembark 121no Gamely
17Feb67–7Hia fst 6f .22 .45 1.10⅕ Cl c-15000 11 2 21½ 21½ 23 24½ WHartack b 116 4.10 88–16 Bold Point 1164½ Dandy Steal 1163 Besieger 116nk Gamely 1
3Feb67–7Hia fst 6f .22⅕ .45⅖1.11⅗ Clm 16000 10 7 41 31 54 66½ MYcaza b 115 16.10 79–14 Persian Blade 1182½ Itsago 1141 Derby Sam 1121 Speed, tired 1
19Oct66–3Kee my 6f .22⅖ .46⅕1.12 Clm 12000 5 3 31½ 2½ 13 17 CHMarquez5 b 114 *0.90 83–19 Dandy Steal 1147 Pride of All 1091½ Village Roan 1192½ Mild drive
13Oct66–5Kee fst 7f .23⅘ .46⅗1.25⅕ Clm 12500 5 4 22½ 22 2½ 23½ KChurch b 119 *0.90 78–19 Poor Luke 1173½ Dandy Steal 1193 Karachi 1165 Second best
30Sep66–7CD sly 7f .23⅗ .47⅖1.26 Cl.. 15000 4 3 2h 21 25 37 RMorgan5 b 114 *1.40 70–26 Breeze Maker 1194 Sky Village 1183 Dandy Steal 114¾ No excuse
LATEST WORKOUTS May 21 Bel tr.t. 3f fst .38⅘ b May 14 Bel tr.t. 3f fst .39⅖ b May 5 Bel tr.t. 3f fst .38 b

Pine Hill * — B. c (1964–Fla), by Intentionally—Pinecrest Miss, by Royal Serenade — Cragwood Stable — M. Miller — (Cavanaugh Associates, Inc.) — 114 — 1967 3 1 1 0 $5.82 / 1966 5 1 1 0 $2,97

16May67–6Aqu gd 6f .22⅗ .46 1.11⅕ Allowance 8 1 13 13 16 16 ECardone 109 2.80 87–22 Pine Hill 1096 First And Finest 1141 Buen Tiro 124¾ Easily
1May67–6Aqu fst 6f .22⅕ .45⅖1.11 Allowance 10 1 1½ 2½ 2h 21 ECardone 111 29.10 87–20 Dizzy Devil 1131 Pine Hill 1111 I'm Your Boy 1148 Good try 1
17Apr67–6Aqu sly 6f .22⅖ .45⅘1.11⅖ Allowance 10 5 45½ 68½ 78¾ 914 BBaeza 113 22.40 72–23 Velvet Flash 1142½ Yarak 115no Dizzy Devil 112nk Wide 1
9Aug66–7Sar fst 5½f.22⅗ .46 1.05⅖ Allowance 3 2 42 45½ 711 717 ECardone5 117 18.90 73–17 Balthazar 1223½ Gay Lord Flynn 1222 Air Rights 116¾ Stopped
1Aug66–5Sar fst 5½f.22⅘ .46⅕1.05 Allowance 3 3 1h 55 68 611 BBaeza 119 8.60 81–11 Yorkville 1192½ Monitor 1222 Balthazar 1222 Brief speed
12May66–6Aqu fst 5f .22⅖ .46⅗ .59⅗ Allowance 4 4 3½ 51¾ 67 69¾ WBlum 122 *0.80 77–20 Reason to Hail 1221½ Curzon 1221 Fort Drum 122nk Ran down, tired
23Apr66–2Kee fst 4½f.22⅖ .45⅗ .51⅗ Md Sp Wt 1 2 13 12 12¾ RGallimore 122 *1.20 101–– Pine Hill 1222¾ Better Bee's Jr. 1227 Pure Spice 1223 Kept driving 1
12Apr66–2Kee sly 4½f.23 .46⅗ .53 Md Sp Wt 6 5 1h 1h 2no RGallimore 122 3.70 94– 4 Mr. B's Lark 122no Pine Hill 1225 Zip Line 122no Sharp 1
LATEST WORKOUTS May 29 Bel tr.t. 3f fst .39⅗ b May 26 Bel 5f sly 1.02⅖ b May 22 Bel tr.t. 4f fst .49 h May 13 Bel 5f fst 1.00⅖ h

Price of Glory — Ch. c (1963–Ky), by Decathlon—Aching Back, by War Admiral — R. C. Peacock — T. H. Heard, Jr. — (F. Roser, Jr.) — 119⁵ — 1967 7 1 2 0 $5,05 / 1966 1 1 0 0 $1,69

22May67–6Aqu fst 6f .22⅕ .45⅕1.10⅘ Allowance 8 4 64¾ 44 31½ 2no GMora7 b 117 22.60 89–14 VelvetFlash 114no •RightCard 109nk •PriceOfGlory 117nk Rallied
22May67—•-Dead heat.
15May67–6Aqu fst 7f .22⅗ .45⅕1.22⅘ Allowance 5 dense fog 47½ GMora7 b 117 10.50 84–13 Major Art 1092½ Dandy Steal 1145 Dizzy Devil 116h No threat
24Apr67–9GP fst 7f .22⅗ .45⅖1.23⅘ Allowance 1 6 1h 2h 22 23 JLeonard b 112 17.90 87–15 Star Hill 1093 Price Of Glory 1122½ Potencial 1221 Game effort
8Apr67–8GP fst 6f .22⅕ .45 1.10⅖ Allowance 6 3 56½ 58 57 66½ CFeagin5 b 108 16.60 85–14 Fleet Admiral 1171¼ Irish Ruler 1221¾ Plodder 122n No mishap
17Mar67–7GP fst 7f .22⅘ .46 1.24⅗ Allowance 10 2 43 21½ 13 13 RSurrency5 b 112 *2.70 86–22 PriceOfGlory 1123 FunnyValentine 1123½ Prevaricate 1171¼ Handily 1
22Dec66–4TrP fst 6f .22 .45⅖1.11 Md Sp Wt 8 2 46½ 511 713 816 RSurrency5 b 108 61.60 83–15 Country Friend 1193 Trish M. 1161¼ Stupendous 1221 Fell back
28Feb67–9Hia fst 7f .22⅗ .44⅗1.22 Allowance 8 11 108¼119½1011 89¾ WHartack b 115 14.80 87–12 U. Bearcat 113nk d-County Monaghan 1161 Slade 113¾ No speed 1
21Feb67–8Hia fm*5½f Ⓣ 1.04⅗ Allowance 5 3 31 1½ 12 11¼ LAdams b 117 *1.70 87–14 Price of Glory 1171¼ O Lady O 1142½ Fireroy 119nk Driving 1
LATEST WORKOUTS May 29 Aqu 3f fst .37⅖ b May 14 Aqu 3f fst .39 b

---

Osage: Used to do fairly well in allowance sprints, but looks as if it might prefer claiming company and a mile or more. NO BET.

Puntador: Max Hirsch's hard-worked colt showed little in the Gotham and Wood, but seems to be coming to hand and must be conceded a good chance in an allowance race. CONTENDER.

Tanrackin: This lightly raced, well-trained animal earns a whopping pace figure off the strong showing he made in his 1967 debut eight days ago. Will almost surely improve today and should benefit from the added eighth of a mile. CONTENDER.

Fleet Honor: Probably needs some racing. In any case, has had numerous chances to show what it can do, and has never come close to matching the performances of Tanrackin or Puntador. NO BET.

Devil's Tattoo: Older colt was badly beaten in the Tanrackin race last week. Might improve a bit today, but not that much. NO BET.

Pink Rose: Probably out for exercise today. This filly has had trouble running with her own sex and has been idle for two months. NO BET.

Dandy Steal: Looks plenty sharp and worth much more than the $15,000 for which Al Scotti claimed him. Should appreciate the seven-furlong distance. CONTENDER.

Pine Hill: Won in a common gallop last out after giving notice of real improvement on May 1. Must be granted a chance to go seven furlongs. CONTENDER.

Price of Glory: Tommy Heard sent this four-year-old after the money three times in slightly more than a month and got its best effort last time, edging Tanrackin by a whisker. The horse figures to show the effects of the exertion of that race. No improvement should be expected. NO BET.

The contenders are Puntador, Tanrackin, Dandy Steal, and Pine Hill, with Tanrackin much the wisest choice. The colt has been managed as if he were a good one and has yet to run a poor race. The power he showed in his first outing of the year was a guarantee of genuine improvement today. As I have been saying for years, and as the Aqueduct crowd agreed on this day, a lightly raced animal with a touch of class can be counted on to produce more than a harder-worked Thoroughbred that has been tested and found wanting. Puntador ran a nice race on May 23, but his pace figures were not in the same league as Tanrackin's and never have been. Dandy Steal ran powerfully enough in the May 22 race against Tanrackin and Price of Glory to be respected today, but his hard recent racing and his claiming background are no recommendation against a colt of the Tanrackin variety. And although Pine Hill has demonstrated improvement after a series of poor efforts in New York, it has yet to display the speed of a Tanrackin.

The Running of the Race

THE CROWD was sufficiently aware of Tanrackin's superiority to make him the favorite, albeit at a juicy 2.40–1. Pine Hill and Dandy Steal were also well backed.

SIXTH RACE **Aqu - 31231** May 30, 1967

7 FURLONGS. (Chute). (Rose Net, Sept. 17, 1962, 1.21⅕, 6, 114.)
Allowances. Purse $8,000. 3-year-olds and upward which have never won two races other than maiden, claiming, optional or starter. Weights, 3-year-olds 114 lbs., older 124 lbs. Non-winners of a race other than maiden or claiming since March 11 allowed 3 lbs., such a race since Jan. 16, 5 lbs.
Value to winner $5,200, second $1,600, third $800, fourth $400. Mutuel pool $720,487.

Index	Horse	Eqt	A	Wt	PP	St	¼	½	Str	Fin	Jockey	Owner	Odds $1
31168Aqu4	Tanrackin		3	111	3	6	5^{h}	4^{h}	$3^{1\frac{1}{2}}$	1^{nk}	R Turcotte	Mrs T M Waller	2.40
31168Aqu5	Dandy Steal	b	3	114	6	1	3^{1}	2^{1}	1^{h}	2^{h}	B Baeza	N Hellman	3.50
31104GS5	Fleet Honor		3	111	4	3	2^{h}	$1^{\frac{1}{2}}$	$2^{1\frac{1}{2}}$	3^{1}	A Cordero Jr	Scotch Hills Farm	27.00
31168Aqu8	Osage		3	111	1	7	7^{4}	7^{4}	4^{3}	4^{8}	J Giovanni	Kosgrave Stable	27.80
31178Aqu1	Puntador		3	114	2	4	6^{3}	$6^{\frac{1}{2}}$	5^{2}	5^{4}	J L Rotz	King Ranch	5.00
30515Aqu7	Pink Rose		4	117	5	8	8	8	8	$6^{1\frac{1}{2}}$	R Ussery	Janley Stable	27.80
31123Aqu1	Pine Hill		3	114	7	5	$4^{\frac{1}{2}}$	3^{1}	6^{1}	7^{1}	E Cardone	Cragwood Stable	2.60
31168Aqu2	Price Of Glory	b	4	119	8	2	1^{h}	$5^{1\frac{1}{2}}$	7^{2}	8	G Mora5	R C Peacock	6.60

Time .22⅗, .45⅕, 1.10⅕, 1.23⅕ (with wind in back stretch). Track fast.

$2 Mutuel Prices:

3–TANRACKIN	6.80	3.80	3.00
6–DANDY STEAL		4.00	3.20
4–FLEET HONOR			7.20

Dk. b. or br. c, by Roman Line—Muscidae, by War Admiral. Trainer T. M. Waller. Bred by Mrs. T. M. Waller (Ky.).

IN GATE AT 4.18. OFF AT 4.19 EASTERN DAYLIGHT TIME. Start good. Won driving.

TANRACKIN steadily worked his way forward and, responding determinedly when set down through the stretch, won from DANDY STEAL in the last seventy yards. DANDY STEAL, well placed early, took command before reaching midstretch and continued gamely but was not good encugh. FLEET HONOR had no mishap in a sharp effort. OSAGE lacked early foot and was unable to better his position during the drive. PUNTADOR, shuffled back early, failed to recover. PINK ROSE began sluggishly. PINE HILL gave way after a half mile. PRICE OF GLORY, rank at the post, began alertly but had a rough trip after losing command to FLEET HONOR.

Scratched—31168Aqu8 Devil's Tattoo. Overweights—Tanrackin 2 pounds, Pink Rose 3.

Turcotte, who had ridden Tanrackin in every start, knew the horse well and proved it. He won from Baeza and Dandy Steal by only a neck but, as the chart shows, had much the better horse. Notice that Pine Hill caved in against superior speed and that Price of Glory was reluctant to run because it suffered from battle fatigue.

PART TWO

Handicapping Maiden Races

WHEREAS THE CLASS FACTOR boobytraps the average racegoer who attempts to unravel an allowance race, his problems with maiden races are quite different. Chief among these problems is one that is not even a factor in real handicapping. I speak of the infield totalisator board and what it discloses about the odds on each horse.

Unable to fathom the scant past-performance information and other perplexities of maiden races, thousands of players have decided in recent years to let the tote board do their handicapping for them. Although it is not a profitable way to play these races, it is very much in vogue and needs to be discussed.

The tote-board player who is faced with a maiden-special-weights event knows that it features the most expensive, most promising non-winners on the grounds. He also knows that insiders have an advantage in judging these fields, being privy to facts about workouts, physical condition, soundness, and other such factors that are not evident in the past-performance records of unraced or extremely lightly raced animals. Furthermore, he has observed that the tote board sometimes gives a reliable tip by revealing a sudden influx of presumably "smart" money on one or another maiden.

But the "smart" money is not always smart. It often is dumb money, stampeded by tips. The chief sources of these tips are, of course, stable personnel and clockers. As soon as a mutuel clerk notices large bets traceable to such insiders, the word spreads among other mutuel clerks and thence to favored persons in the crowd. Within five minutes a colt listed at 7–1 in the track program's morning line may drop to 9–2. At that point the tote-board watchers in the crowd get the message, rush to the windows, and drive the animal down to 2–1.

In New York, New Jersey, Maryland, Florida, Illinois, and California, horses of this description win often enough to command great loyalty among those who bet on them, but not often enough to yield a long-term profit. In the first place, the odds are too low. Secondly, the smart money is wrong more often than it is right and is frequently so divided in its opinion that no tote-board watcher can possibly tell which bet-down horse represents the smartest money. Thirdly, rumors spread so swiftly in racing crowds, and have such a dramatic effect, that a horse may drop from 10–1 to 4–1 without a dollar of smart money—on rumor alone.

The only route to profits on maiden races is through smart handicapping, which is smarter than smart money. Not that I urge you to avoid looking at the tote board—it stands there in front of the stands, staring you in the face, and you might just as well look at it—but *not* for handicapping purposes. I look at it all the time, getting some kind of masochistic pleasure from watching the smart guys bet my choice down from the morning 10–1 to the post-time 3–1. But their betting has no effect whatever on my betting. I bet not because they like a horse, but because I do.

Having disposed of tote-board play—or, at least, having tried to—let me now say that the chief *handicapping* problem of the maiden-special-weights race is usually the first-time starter. Assuming that the race is a sprint for two-year-olds and all entrants have been to the post before, the handicapper need only find the fastest animal or, among those equally fast, the one that has raced most effectively and comes from a good barn. However, suppose there are a few first-time starters in the field and some of them show really good workouts, while none of the horses with previous starts has shown much zip?

Handicap the barns and the breeding! Give preference to the best-bred horse from the best barn. If it's a first-starter running against flawed maidens, it is a good bet. If it has been to the post before and has shown even slight promise, it is preferable to a first-starter of mediocre background. Given two maidens from good barns, favor the one that has run before and shown even a hint of speed. In other words, a previously raced animal has a slight advantage over a first-starter. And, racing being what it is (the rich grow richer and the poor are always with us), the maiden from the good barn has an advantage—even when a first-time starter—over a more seasoned animal which has shown no great speed and comes from a run-of-the-mill stable.

1. FIRST AT MONMOUTH, JULY 17, 1967—Track Slow

A RACE FOR two-year-old fillies whose connections have abandoned hope and are perfectly willing to risk losing the animals at bargain prices.

1st Monmouth

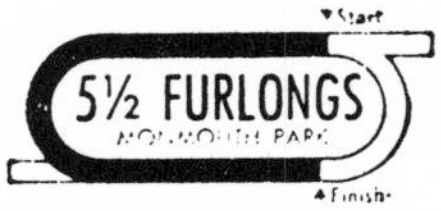

5 1-2 FURLONGS. (I'm For More, June 9, 1961, 1.03⅖, 2, 112.)
Maidens. Claiming. Purse $3.700. Fillies. 2-year-olds. Weight, 117 lbs. Claiming price, $6,500. 1 lb. allowed for each $250 to $5,500.

Apple Mash * $6,500 Dk. b. or br. f (1965–Md), by Crasher—Ray Apple, by Blue Swords **107**10 1967 4 M 1 0 $1,162
Anne W. Niebhur J. W. Boniface (Mrs. A. Niebhur)
28Jun67-1Del fst 5½f.22⅗ .47⅘1.07⅖ f-M 6000 9 6 66½ 51¼ 53 44½ GPierson7 110 3.60 78–13 Discerning 1172½ Nostar 1172 Let It Ring 117no Bid, hung 11
27Apr67-3Pim my 5f .23⅕ .47⅖1.00⅕ f-MdSpWt 5 C 54¼ 68 67½ 68 WJPassmore 118 4.90 85–20 Very Top 1186 Miss Sun Bee 118h Guest Room 118½ Blocked, str'tch 8
7Apr67-3Pim my 5f .23 .47⅗1.01⅕ f-MdSpWt 1 3 21½ 21½ 23 23 CBaltazar 119 6.40e 85–23 Countess Inez 1193 Apple Mash 119no Sue Priam Miss 119½ Gamely 8
31Mar67-3Pim fst 5f .22⅘ .46⅘ .59⅗ f-MdSpWt 5 5 55 47 46½ 512 BPhelps 118 42.60 84–18 Allie'sSerenade1182 CountessInez1183 SuePriamMiss1185 Tired 12
LATEST WORKOUTS Jly 13 Del 5f gd 1.03⅖ b Jly 10 Del 3f gd .37 b Jly 4 Del 3f fst .36⅗ b Jun 25 Del 5f fst 1.04 b

Starcrossed $6,500 Ch. f (1965–Fla), by Alcibiades II—Lynmouth, by Better Self) **117** 1967 0 M 0 0 —
Mrs. A. A. Willcox F. A. Bonsal (Harbor View Farm–Van Tuyl)
LATEST WORKOUTS Jly 13 Mth 3f fst .37⅖ b Jly 8 Mth 5f fst 1.04⅖ b Jly 3 Mth 5f sl 1.03⅗ b Jun 29 Mth 4f fst .52⅗ b

Gay Trouble $5,500 B. f (1965–Fla), by Mr. Trouble—Blue Tammy, by Blue Gay **113** 1967 2 M 0 0 —
Stax Stable J. O'Brey, Sr. (W. M. Pierce)
23Jun67-4Mth sly 5f .22⅖ .47 1.00⅕ Clm 6500 6 9 98½ 811 714 715 MMiceli 107 59.60 74–18 Yankee Dot 1171¼ Grecian Wagon 1172 Aloysius 1171½ Never close 10
13Jun67-2Mth fst 5f .23 .47⅘1.01⅖ f-M 6500 7 12 11131113111131010 BPearl 117 50.90 73–20 Little Chickadee 117no Atop 117½ Craig's Date 117nk No factor 12
LATEST WORKOUTS Jly 15 Mth 5f gd 1.04⅗ b Jly 10 Mth 5f fst 1.02 bg Jly 6 Mth 4f gd .50 b Jun 28 Mth 4f fst .52⅖ b

Belle Landing $6,000 Blk. f (1965–NY), by Landing—Jesrubel, by Mighty Story **115** 1967 3 M 0 0 —
Asbell-Blom A. J. Cochran (M. J. Magde)
13Jun67-2Mth fst 5f .23 .47⅘1.01⅖ f-M 6000 12 2 74¼109 912 98¾ BThornburg 113 28.50 74–20 Little Chickadee 117no Atop 117½ Craig's Date 117nk No factor 12
16May67-3GS fst 5f .22⅘ .47⅕1.00 f-Md 7500 6 8 73¼ 811 717 715 GPatterson 115 7.10 74–18 Pendulous 1153½ Flow Gently 1152½ Chime Song 1153 In close 12
9May67-3GS my 5f .23⅗ .48⅗1.01⅘ Md 7500 12 3 94¼ 74¼ 57 57 GPatterson 112 29.60 73–24 Autumn Joy 115¾ Mark's Flash 115no Senor Irish 112nk No speed 12
LATEST WORKOUTS Jly 8 Mth 5f fst 1.04⅖ b Jly 4 Mth 4f fst .51 b Jun 10 Mth 3f fst .37 b

Princess Jill $6,500 B. f (1965–Ky), by Solar Prince—Fleet's Choice, by Stymie **117** 1967 3 M 0 0 —
Simoff-Telsher D. Dodson (Mrs. A. Zeek)
28Apr67-3GS gd 5f .23⅗ .49 1.01⅗ f-M 8500 5 3 68¼ 68¾ 68¾ 612 JBlock b 113 29.00 69–27 Good Game 1135 Behoove 1132 Ships Singer 1163 Never threat 7
17Mar67-3GP fst 3f .22⅖ .34 f-MdSpWt 9 13 13191316 JBlock 119 33.00f 76– 8 Snoopstep 119¾ Endora 1191 Cape Sable 1193½ Showed nothing 14
2Feb67-3Hia fst 3f .22⅖ .34 f-MdSpWt 12 8 12111212 JGiovanni 116 60.80 80– 8 Miss Hambra 1165 Lachette 116½ Copper Canyon 116nk Trailed 12
LATEST WORKOUTS Jly 10 Mth 3f fst .39 b Jly 5 Mth 5f my 1.06 b Jun 29 Mth 5f fst 1.05 b

Pet Vest $6,500 B. f (1965–Fla), by Petare—Vestwin, by Harvest Reward **117** 1967 1 M 1 0 $740
R. Metcalf R. Metcalf (F. Farro)
27Jun67-3Mth fst 5f .22⅘ .47⅖1.00⅗ f-M 6500 4 7 63¾ 55½ 33½ 2¾ BThornburg 117 5.60 86–19 Dey's Captain 117¾ Pet Vest 1175 Craig's Date 1171½ Bore in 12
LATEST WORKOUTS Jly 12 Mth 5f fst 1.02⅘ b Jly 8 Mth 4f fst .49⅗ b Jly 4 Mth 4f fst .49⅖ b Jun 25 Mth 3f fst .35⅗ h

Rush Rush Rush $6,500 Dk. b. or br. f (1965), by Rasper II—Double Fern, by Double Jay **117** 1967 1 M 0 0 —
Woodside Stud J. B. Bond (Woodside Stud, Inc.)
29Jun67-3Mth fst 5f .22⅘ .48 1.00⅘ Md Sp Wt 6 10 109¼1112118 78 CBaltazar 115 6.00 78–16 Mortek 1182½ Our Golden Lady 1151 Tower Clock 1101 No threat 12
LATEST WORKOUTS Jly 13 Mth 5f fst 1.03 b Jly 10 Mth 3f fst .35⅗ h Jly 5 Mth 3f my .37 b Jun 28 Mth 3f fst .37⅗ b

Ricles $6,500 Ch. f. (1965–Fla), by Alcibiades II—Orevent, by Fervent **117** 1967 0 M 0 0 —
Harbor View Farm I. H. Parke (Harbor View Farm)
LATEST WORKOUTS Jly 15 Bel 5f gd 1.06⅗ b Jly 11 Bel tr.t. 3f fst .37⅗ h Jun 28 Bel 3f fst .37 bg

Lorient $6,500 Gr. f (1965–NJ), by Scotch Bull—In Roses, by Incoming **117** 1967 5 M 0 0 —
W. Siboski C. P. Coco (W. Siboski)
28Jun67-4Mth fst 5f .22⅖ .47 1.00⅘ f-M 9000 10 2 74¾111111141111 MAMar'cio7 b 107 91.60 75–19 Seewinkel 1131½ Charity Baby 1171½ To Win 117½ Dropped far back 12
22Jun67-3Mth fst 5f .22⅖ .47⅘1.01⅕ Md 9000 8 1 64 911 911 913 CBaltazar b 111 12.90e 71–19 Good Advice 1124 Boronia Star 118h Sentinel 1181¼ Far back 9
29May67-2GS fst 5f .22⅘ .47⅖1.00⅖ f-M 7500 8 1 62¾ 79 9161011 MAMarina'o7 b 108 68.90 76–22 Ebbie's Imp 1101 Chime Song 115h Nursey 115h Dropped back 12
5May67-3GS fst 5f .22⅗ .46⅗ .59⅗ f-Md 7500 7 9 77½ 67½ 816 815 MAMarin'o7 b 108 57.20 76–20 Brouillard 1154 Cunning Fox 1151½ Bungalow 1123 No threat 11
25Apr67-3GS fst 5f .22⅘ .47⅘1.00⅗ f-M 7500 3 8 74¼ 68 913 815 MAMar'ccio5 b 108 17.80 71–27 Six Children 1159 Cunning Fox 115nk Instomatic 1152½ No threat 12
LATEST WORKOUTS Jly 13 Mth 4f fst .50 b Jly 5 Mth 6f my 1.17⅖ b Jun 17 Mth 5f fst 1.04 b Jun 12 Mth 3f fst .37 b

Bobbie's Runner $5,500 Ch. f (1965–Md), by Bobbie—Cub Run, by Cosmic Bomb **113** 1967 5 M 0 1 $350
Mrs. L. L. Voigt J. W. Garth (Mrs. L. L. Voigt)
6Jly 67-6Mth fst 5½f.23⅕ .48⅕1.08 f- 10000 11 12 121112171215 1117 RMcDowell5 b 107 77.70 60–26 Little Chickadee 113¾ Dey's Captain 1101½ Pendulous 115no No thr't 12
27Jun67-3Mth fst 5f .22⅘ .47⅖1.00⅗ f-M 6000 3 8 74 67½ 712 57½ MMiceli5 b 108 5.40 79–19 Dey's Captain 117¾ Pet Vest 1175 Craig's Date 1171½ No threat 12
2Jun67-3Del fst 5f .22⅗ .47⅗1.00⅗ f- 5000 2 7 43¼ 32 32 31 TLee b 113 5.20 85–16 Sociable Timi 113h Pied-A-Terre 1131 Bobbie's Runner 1134 Gaini'g 12
17May67-3Pim fst 5f .22⅗ .47⅕1.00⅗ Md 7000 5 12 1216111410 9¾ 67 PIGrimm b 114 32.40 84–15 UnitWit1191½ ShenandoahStar1092 BreezyJeanne1151½ Slow start 12
25Apr67-3Pim fst 5f .22⅖ .46⅕ .58⅘ Md 7000 10 12 1230122512341234 PIGrimm b 114 39.90 66–14 Cockey Miss 1165 Magic Step 1196 Sister Ramona 1142 Far back 12
LATEST WORKOUTS Jly 12 Mth 3f fst .36⅗ b Jly 4 Mth 3f fst .36⅕ b Jun 24 Mth 3f sl .36 h Jun 21 Mth 3fsl .37 b

Bow Tip $5,500 B. f (1965–Pa), by Long Bow—Kilauea, by Volcanic **113** 1967 0 M 0 0 —
J. Nadler A. Gauthier (West Wind Farm)
LATEST WORKOUTS Jly 12 Mth 3f fst .36⅗ b Jun 27 Mth 5f fst 1.02⅗ b Jun 20 Mth 3f my .39 b Jun 15 Mth 5f fst 1.03⅗ b

Here Mary $6,000 Dk. b. or br. f (1965–Md), by Fuzzie King—Mary Zip, by Call Over **115** 1967 2 M 0 0 —
D. Prestileo C. Rodriguez (Mrs. M. Zipkin)
27Jun67-3Mth fst 5f .22⅘ .47⅖1.00⅗ f-M 6000 12 2 117½111612201215 JVelasquez b 113 22.40 72–19 Dey's Captain 117¾ Pet Vest 1175 Craig's Date 1171½ No speed 12
21Apr67-1GP fst 5f .22⅘ .46⅘1.00⅕ Md 10000 11 12 111811191123 1029 CStone b 117 27.20 58–21 Cape Sable 1177 Invalidity 1201½ Mrs. Mehle 1171½ No speed 12
LATEST WORKOUTS Jly 12 Mth 5f fst 1.03⅗ b

Apple Mash: The class difference between Delaware and New Jersey racing has become wider in recent years. Delaware horses rarely win here until dropped drastically in price. This one broke no watches in Delaware, has yet to race or work out here, and can be eliminated. NO BET.

Starcrossed: A first starter which seems to have disappointed the redoubtable Frank Bonsal after he got her from the renowned Harbor View Farm. He will not allow her to be claimed without making a real run at the purse. CONTENDER.

Gay Trouble: A zero so far. NO BET.

Belle Landing: Nothing here. NO BET.

Princess Jill: Away since April. NO BET.

Pet Vest: Ray Metcalf, one of the best in the East, tried with this in her first start and has been working her since. She bore in last time, probably from fatigue (which is not a good sign), but she must be given a chance. CONTENDER.

Rush Rush Rush: Bowes Bond, who was leading trainer at the 1966 meeting here, must not have liked the seventh-place finish against colts. The filly should improve in today's easier company. CONTENDER.

Ricles: Ivan Parke has been winning race after race at Aqueduct with his Harbor View juveniles. If he troubled to send this first-starter over here for a claimer, he wants the purse. That the horse has not worked out here is of little importance. Harbor View and Parke are hot. CONTENDER.

Lorient: Nothing. NO BET.

Bobbie's Runner: Drops in claiming price to a level at which she has failed in the past. The switch to Kenny Knapp from an apprentice may be significant, but not enough to move me. NO BET.

Bow Tip: First-starter of unexciting credentials. NO BET.

Here Mary: Absolutely nothing. NO BET.

The contenders are Starcrossed because of the barn; Pet Vest, for the same reason and because of real speed last out; Rush Rush Rush because of the barn and the prospect of almost certain improvement today; Ricles because of the barn.

If Pet Vest had not ducked in at the finish of her last race, or if Metcalf had put blinkers on the filly today, it would be a hard bet to avoid. But noting the trouble in the last race, plus the added distance today, plus the presence of the Ivan Parke horse, I rule out Pet Vest.

Ivan Parke is a good trainer. Although some of the trainers at Monmouth

Park are equally good, Ivan Parke is with Harbor View, where the rich grow richer. When he sends a horse to Monmouth—especially a first-starter of this kind—it is like a major league ball club farming out a $100,000 rookie to the American Association. The rookie may not bat .400 in Triple A ball, but his class will show.

I therefore pick Ricles over Starcrossed (bred by Harbor View but not *kept* by Harbor View), and Rush Rush Rush.

The Running of the Race

PET VEST was an even-money favorite, as seemed inevitable. Rush Rush Rush was second choice, at 5.10–1. Enough smart money was around to bring Ricles down to less than 12–1.

Ricles won with complete authority. Starcrossed ran a nice race but was not good enough. Pet Vest tired badly.

I regard this race as an excellent demonstration of how the player handicaps the stables in races involving first-time starters.

FIRST RACE	5 1-2 FURLONGS. (I'm For More, June 9, 1961, 1.03⅖, 2, 112.)

Mth - 31718
July 17, 1967

Maidens. Claiming. Purse $3,700. Fillies. 2-year-olds. Weight, 117 lbs. Claiming price, $6,500. 1 lb. allowed for each $250 to $5,500.

Value to winner $2,405, second $740, third $370, fourth $185. Mutuel pool $76,688.

Index	Horse	Eqt A Wt	PP	St	¼	½	Str	Fin	Jockey	C'lg Pr	Owner	Odds $1
	--Ricles	2 117	8	4	4h	3¹	1²	1²	R Broussard	5500	Harbor View Farm	11.70
	--Starcrossed	2 117	2	11	7h	6³	2²	2³	D Brumfield	6500	Mrs A A Willcox	18.80
31642Mth¹¹	Bobbie's Run'r	b 2 113	10	2	12	11h	6³	3⁴½	K Knapp	5500	Mrs L L Voigt	10.30
31492Mth²	Pet Vest	2 117	6	5	3h	4½	5³	4ⁿᵒ	B Thornburg	5500	R Metcalf	1.00
31510Mth⁷	Rush Rush Rush	2 117	7	6	2h	2h	3¹	5¹½	W Gavidia	5500	Woodside Stud	5.10
31492Mth¹²	Here Mary	b 2 115	12	8	11½	9h	8²	6⁴	J Culmone	6000	D Prestileo	42.30
	--Bow Tip	2 114	11	9	9½	8h	9¹	7ⁿᵒ	P Kallai	5500	J Nadler	24.50
30739GS⁶	--Princess Jill	b 2 117	5	12	10¹	12	10¹	8¹½	J Leonard	5500	Simoff-Teltser	26.40
31508Del⁴	--Apple Mash	2 110	1	10	8³	5½	4h	9½	G Pierson¹⁰	6500	Annie Nieburgh	6.90
31502Mth¹¹	Lorient	b 2 117	9	1	5½	7²	11²	10¹	B Pearl	5500	W Siboski	32.10
31383Mth⁹	Belle Landing	2 115	4	3	1²	1²	7h	11½	K Korte	6000	Asbell-Blom	149.10
31466Mth⁷	Gay Trouble	b 2 113	3	7	6h	10½	12	12	J Johnson	5500	Stax Stable	42.70

Time .23, .47⅘, 1.00⅖, 1.07⅕. Track slow.

Official Program Numbers ↘

$2 Mutuel Prices:

8-RICLES	25.40	12.20	8.00
2-STARCROSSED		18.20	13.60
10-BOBBIE'S RUNNER			7.20

Ch. f, by Alcibiades II—Orevent, by Fervent. Trainer I. H. Parke. Bred by Harbor View Farm (Fla.).

IN GATE AT 2.01. OFF. AT 2.01½ EASTERN DAYLIGHT TIME. Start good. Won driving.

RICLES, well placed from the start, was sent around BELLE LANDING to gain in upper stretch and held STARCROSSED safe. The latter, rallied in upper stretch and lacked a further response. BOBBIE'S RUNNER, slow to gain best stride, finished well. PET VEST raced forwardly to the stretch and tired. RUSH RUSH RUSH was never a factor. APPLE MASH saved ground to no avail.

Scratched—Sea Mystery, Sly Wench, 31457Mth¹¹ Bolero Boo Boo, 31492Mth¹⁰ Mosad.

Overweights—Apple Mash 3 pounds, Bow Tip 1.

---

2. FOURTH AT AQUEDUCT, MAY 10, 1967—Track Fast

LET US CONTINUE with the problem of the first-time starters in maiden races for two-year-olds. During May, 1967, Aqueduct presented twenty-three juvenile races in which one or more first-time starters competed. Twenty of the events were won by horses which had raced previously. The only three first-starters to win were trained by Lucien Laurin, Woody Stephens, and Eddie Neloy. Laurin, as observant New Yorkers have learned, wins with two or three first-starters every spring. He specializes in it. Stephens is a recognized master and has the extra advantage of handling the superb stock of Adele Rand. And Neloy is Neloy.

In the race that now interests us, only three of the fillies have ever been to the post before. First-starters are entered by such powerful operatives as Max Hirsch, Mike Freeman (Vanderbilt), Ivor Balding (Whitney), Hirsch Jacobs, Walter Kelley, and Eddie Neloy. Unless the entrants with previous racing have showed promise in those performances, and come from good barns, the handicapper will look among the debutantes for a bet.

4th Race Aqueduct (Start) 5 FURLONGS AQUEDUCT (Finish)

5 FURLONGS. (Bazaar, June 6, 1963, .57, 2, 122.)
Maidens. Special weight. Purse $5,200. Fillies. 2-year-olds. Weight 119 lbs.

(4th Aqu)—Coupled—Yes Sir and Silver Coin.

Many Veils — Dk. b. or br. f (1965–Ky), by Bagdad—Black Discovery, by Discovery — 119 — 1967 1 M 0 0 $250
J. W. Shiffer J. E. Picou (J. W. Schiffer)
12Apr67-3Aqu fst 5f .24 .48⅖1.01 f-MdSpWt 7 8 65½ 65½ 53 42 LPincayJr b 119 *1.20e 78–21 Zoomalong 1191½ Tiegoon 119no Gay Matelda 119½ Closed gamely 10
LATEST WORKOUTS May 7 Bel 4f sly .49⅘ b May 3 Bel 3f fst .36⅘ b Apr 29 Bel 4f fst .48 h Apr 23 Bel 4f fst .47⅕ h

Wiggins — Ch. f (1965–Cal), by Cavan—Lady Sophia II, by Chanteur II — 119 — 1967 0 M 0 0 —
J. H. Stone Max Hirsch (E. Janss, Jr.)
LATEST WORKOUTS May 8 Bel 3f sly .38 bg May 4 Bel 5f fst 1.02 b May 2 Bel 3f fst .36 b Apr 29 Bel 5f fst 1.02⅗ b

Fast Cycle — B. f (1965–Ky), by Nadir—Amber Moon, by Ambiorix — 119 — 1967 0 M 0 0 —
J. Yonker R. P. Lake (Elmendorf Farm)
LATEST WORKOUTS May 2 Aqu 5f fst 1.04⅘ b Apr 29 Aqu 3f gd .38 bg Apr 20 Aqu 4f gd .54⅘ b Apr 15 Aqu 4f gd .50⅕ b

Indian Love Call — B. f. (1965–Md), by Jaipur-Scarlet Letter, by Native Dancer — 119 — 1967 0 M 0 0 —
A. G. Vanderbilt W. C. Freeman (A. G. Vanderbilt)
LATEST WORKOUTS May 9 Aqu 3f sl .37 b May 5 Aqu 5f fst 1.05 b May 1 Aqu 3f fst .36 h Apr 26 Aqu 4f fst .50 bg

Yes Sir — Dk. b. or br. f (1965-Ky), by Sir Gaylord—Fun House, by The Doge — 119 — 1967 0 M 0 0 —
C. V. Whitney I. G. Balding (C. V. Whitney)
LATEST WORKOUTS May 9 Bel tr.t. 3f gd .38 b May 4 Bel 4f fst .47 h May 2 Bel tr.t. 3f fst .38⅗ b Apr 29 Bel 4f fst .46⅘ h

Silk Step — Ch. f (1965–Ky), by Watch Your Step—Silk Velvet, by Mahmoud — 119 — 1967 2 M 0 0 —
E. M. O'Brien E. M. O'Brien (Danada Farm)
12Apr67-3Aqu fst 5f .24 .48⅖1.01 f-MdSpWt 9 7 53½ 86½101210¹⁴ MVenezia 119 46.10 66–21 Zoomalong 1191½ Tiegoon 119no Gay Matelda 119½ Fell far back 10
29Mar67-3Aqu my 5f .24⅕ .49⅕1.01⅗ f-MdSpWt 6 7 711 713 716 619 MVenezia 119 5.10 58–33 Pleasantness 1192 Worklamp 1198 Tiegoon 1192½ Never close 7
LATEST WORKOUTS Apr 29 Bel 4f fst .49 b Apr 21 Bel tr.t. 3f fst .37⅖ h Apr 8 Bel tr.t. 4f gd .51 b Mar 28 Bel tr.t. 3f sl .38 b

Wish Well — Dk. b. or br. f (1965–Ky), by Hail to Reason—Fingerling, by Fisherman — 119 — 1967 0 M 0 0 —
I. Bieber H. Jacobs (Bieber-Jacobs Stables)
LATEST WORKOUTS May 6 Aqu 4f gd .48⅗ h Apr 30 Aqu 5f fst 1.01⅖ h Apr 26 Aqu 4f fst .49 hg Apr 23 Aqu 4f fst .49⅘ d

Cherry Wine — B. f (1965–Ky), by Hillsborough—Cherry Puddin', by One Hitter — 119 — 1967 0 M 0 0 —
Little M Farm W. A. Kelley (Patrina Corp.)
LATEST WORKOUTS May 2 Aqu 4f fst .51 bg Apr 26 Aqu 5f fst 1.04 bg Apr 22 Aqu 5f fst 1.04 b Apr 18 Aqu 3f sly .41 b

Magnetism — B. f (1965–Ky), by Bold Ruler—Magneto, by Ambiorix — 119 — 1967 0 M 0 0 —
Wheatley Stable E. A. Neloy (Wheatly Stable)
LATEST WORKOUTS May 9 Bel 3f gd .35⅖ hg May 4 Bel 4f fst .49 bg Apr 30 Bel 5f fst 1.02⅕ b Apr 26 Bel 4f fst .48⅘ h

Best In Show — Ch. f (1965–Ky), by Traffic Judge–Stolen Hour, by Mr. Busher — 119 — 1967 0 M 0 0 —
Clearview Stable J. H. Skirvin (P. Connors)
LATEST WORKOUTS May 9 Bel 3f gd .36 h May 6 Bel 5f fst 1.01⅘ h May 2 Bel 4f fst .47 hg Apr 29 Bel 4f fst .50 bg

Horses Shown Below Are on the "Also Eligible" List and Are Not Listed in Order of Post Positions.

Silver Coin — Dk. b. or br. f (1965–Ky), by Never Bend—Silver Spoon, by Citation — 119 — 1967 0 M 0 0 —
C. V. Whitney I. G. Balding (C. V. Whitney)
LATEST WORKOUTS May 9 Bel tr.t. 3f gd .36⅖ h May 4 Bel 4f fst .47 h Apr 29 Bel 4f fst .46⅗ h Apr 24 Bel 4f fst .48⅖ b

Sewickley Heights Ro. f (1965-Pa), by Native Dancer—Rich Relation, by Midas 119 1967 2 M 1 0 $1,300
Buckland Farm T. M. Waller (Mrs. J. O. Burgwin)
3May67-4Aqu fst 5f .23⅖ .47⅘1.00⅘ f-MdSpWt 5 2 2½ 21½ 23 25 RTurcotte 119 10.50 76-21 Disco 1195 Sewickley Heights 1192½ Beauty Secret 1191 Fair try 10
26Apr67-3Aqu fst 5f .22⅘ .47⅕1.00⅗ f-MdSpWt 8 8 75½ 43 44½ 45 MYcaza 119 9.40e 77-17 Blitzed Eagle 1192½ General Store 1192 Set A Thief 119½ Greenly 10
LATEST WORKOUTS May 2 Bel tr.t. 3f fst .37 h Apr 24 Bel tr.t. 4f fst .49⅗ h Apr 20 Bel m.t. 3f fst .36 b Apr 15 Bel tr.t. 4f fst .49⅘ h

Many Veils: Jimmy Picou's well-bred filly broke slowly in its debut but showed some run in the final stages. A serious question must be raised about the month's delay between races. Also, the switch from Laffit Pincay to Bill Boland does not inspire great confidence. Boland, one of the greatest stretch riders of modern times, is at his best in longer races when the fast start is less important. Many Veils might do better under an Ussery or a Blum. NO BET.

Silk Step: Eddie O'Brien has not yet coaxed any speed out of this one. NO BET.

Sewickley Heights: Raced greenly, but well enough to finish fourth in a ten-horse field on April 26, only two weeks ago. Came back last week and ran an easy second to the highly regarded Disco, after staying close to the pace all the way. The recent action, the two quite good races, and the well-known ability of Tom Waller to get the money in any crowd make it impossible to bet against this filly. One might rate her more highly if she had managed to earn speed ratings in the eighties, but the competitive edge makes her a fair bet. CONTENDER.

The Running of the Race

THE ARISTOCRATIC BREEDING and impressive workouts of C. V. Whitney's Silver Coin made her the favorite. She ran a nice race, but, like so many first-time starters, was not yet ready. Bill Boland got Many Veils out of the gate promptly and saved ground with her all the way, but Many Veils was no match for the Waller filly. The good mutuel payoff on Sewickley Heights can be accepted as a lesson: regardless of what newspaper selectors, tipsheets, and the tote board say, it is foolish to discount the chances of a well-bred, well-handled previous starter that has showed some inclination to try.

FOURTH RACE 5 FURLONGS. (Bazaar, June 6, 1963, .57, 2, 122.)
Aqu - 31076 Maidens. Special weight. Purse $5,200. Fillies. 2-year-olds. Weight 119 lbs.
May 10, 1967
Value to winner $3,380, second $1,040, third $520, fourth $260. Mutuel pool $311,993.

Index	Horse	Eqt	A	Wt	PP	St	3/16	3/8	Str	Fin	Jockey	Owner	Odds $1
31022Aqu2	—Sew'ley Heights		2	119	9	1	11½	11	12	13½	R Turcotte	Buckland Farm	7.70
30739Aqu4	—Many Veils	b	2	119	1	2	2h	34	31	2¾	W Boland	J W Schiffer	5.10
	—Wish Well		2	119	5	8	81	81	62	3½	R Ussery	I Bieber	15.30
	—Silver Coin		2	119	10	3	34	2h	2h	4¾	H Gustines	C V Whitney	1.90
	—Magnetism		2	119	7	9	71½	4h	41	53½	B Baeza	Wheatley Stable	4.90
	—Indian Love Call		2	119	3	5	5h	5½	51½	62	E Belmonte	A G Vanderbilt	4.50
	—Best In Show		2	119	8	10	10	10	81	7no	L Gilligan	Clearview Stable	16.30
	—Wiggins		2	119	2	7	92	9h	10	82	J L Rotz	J H Stone	13.60
	—Cherry Wine		2	119	6	6	6h	62	7½	9h	R Morgan	Little M Farm	83.60
30739Aqu10	—Silk Step		2	119	4	4	4h	71	9h	10	M Venezia	E M O'Brien	55.70

Time .23⅖, .47⅗, 1.00⅖. Track fast.

$2 Mutuel Prices:			
9-SEWICKLEY HEIGHTS	17.40	7.20	4.40
1-MANY VEILS		6.60	4.00
5-WISH WELL			6.20

Ro. f, by Native Dancer—Rich Relation, by Midas. Trainer T. M. Waller. Bred by Mrs. J. O. Burgwin (Pa.).
IN GATE AT 3.04. OFF AT 3.04 EASTERN DAYLIGHT TIME. Start good. Won driving.
SEWICKLEY HEIGHTS broke in stride, opened up a clear lead and retained it throughout under vigorous handling. MANY VEILS raced close up along the inside, was unable to threaten the winner late but held well to save the place. WISH WELL began sluggishly, responded well through the stretch and finished fastest of all. SILVER COIN was hustled up on the outside to gain close contention then lacked a late response. MAGNETISM raced greenly. INDIAN LOVE CALL was never a serious factor.
Scratched—Fast Cycle, Yes Sir.

3. THIRD AT MONMOUTH, JUNE 12, 1967—Track Fast

Some maiden-special-weights races for three- and four-year-olds include good horses whose careers have been retarded by minor health problems. The quality of the field usually can be gauged by the amount of space its past-performance records occupy in the racing paper. If most of the animals are lightly raced and, indeed, show little or no action as two-year-olds, the quality is invariably higher than if most have run, and failed, a dozen times.

This particular field is a good one and is made more interesting by the presence of a first-starting Carry Back gelding from the formidable Woodside Stud string trained by J. Bowes Bond.

3rd Monmouth

Start — 6 FURLONGS — MONMOUTH PARK — Finish

6 FURLONGS (Chute). (Decathlon, June 11, 1957, 1.08⅗, 4, 130.)
Maidens. Special weights. Purse $4,300. Colts and geldings. 3- and 4-year-olds. Weights, 3-year-olds 115 lbs., 4-year-olds 122 lbs.

In Belief — Dk. b. or br. c (1964–Fla), by Promethee—Isa, by Eight Thirty — **115** — 1967 4 M 2 1 $2,065
Brookfield Farm E. I. Kelly (Brookfield Farm) — 1966 0 M 0 0
17May67-2GS fst 1$\frac{1}{16}$ .48⅖1.13⅕1.46⅗ Md Sp Wt 11 1 2^{1} $2^{1\frac{1}{2}}$ 6^{6} $7^{7\frac{1}{2}}$ JVelasquez b 115 3.70 64–18 Kummel 121^{nk} Victory String 112$^{1\frac{3}{4}}$ Acquitted 115$^{\frac{3}{4}}$ Speed, tired 12
5May67-4GS fst 1^{70} .46⅖1.11⅖1.42⅗ Md Sp Wt 6 1 1^{1} $1^{\frac{1}{2}}$ 2^{4} 3^{8} RBroussard b 116 3.70 73–20 Pebble Drive 115^{4} Victory String 112^{4} In Belief 116$^{2\frac{1}{2}}$ Tired 8
5Apr67-3GP fst 6f .22⅘ .46⅕1.11⅖ Md Sp Wt 5 6 $3^{\frac{1}{2}}$ 2^{2} 2^{3} 2^{6} DHidalgo b 120 *2.50 81–18 Orange Flower 115^{6} In Belief 120^{4} Le Parans 115^{3} Fair try 12
27Mar67-4GP fst 6f .22⅕ .45⅗1.12 Md Sp Wt 11 2 2^{h} $2^{2\frac{1}{2}}$ 2^{5} 2^{4} KKnapp b 120 16.80 80–18 Glimmer Girl 115^{4} In Belief 120^{1} Regal Count 120$^{1\frac{1}{2}}$ Gamely 12
LATEST WORKOUTS Jun 10 Mth 4f fst .50 b — Jun 6 Mth 6f fst 1.17 b — Jun 2 Mth 4f fst .48 h — May 25 GS 3f fst .36 h

Carry Away — B. g (1964–Fla), by Carry Back—Galamier, by Daumier — **115** — 1967 0 M 0 0 —
Woodside Stud J. B. Bond (C. F. Kieser) — 1966 0 M 0 0 —
LATEST WORKOUTS Jun 10 Mth 4f fst .47 hg — Jun 6 Mth 6f fst 1.15⅗ b — May 19 Lrl 6f fst 1.18⅖ b — May 13 Lrl 5f fst 1.02⅗ b

***Poilu II** — Dk. b. or br. c (1963), by Toreador—Infanteria, by Requiebro — **122** — 1967 1 M 0 0 —
Mrs. C. F. Parker D. Dodson (Urbano Arias) (Arg.) — 1966 0 M 0 0 ----
5Jun67-2Mth fst 6f .22⅕ .45⅕1.11⅖ Md Sp Wt 6 11 11^{10} 12^{19} 11^{21} 11^{26} JLeonard b 122 30.30 69–14 Fiddler's Green 115^{2} A Latin Spin 115^{5} Mafioso 115^{2} No speed 12
LATEST WORKOUTS Jun 3 Mth 6f fst 1.20 b — May 6 GS 6f fst 1.15 b — Apr 29 GS 5f gd 1.05 b — Apr 20 GP 4f fst .49⅘ bg

Olympia You — B. g (1964–Ala), by Olympia—You For Me, by Royal Charger — **115** — 1967 6 M 1 0 $1,230
F. W. Hooper A. J. Bardaro (F. W. Hooper) — 1966 0 M 0 0 ----
5Jun67-2Mth fst 6f .22⅕ .45⅕1.11⅖ Md Sp Wt 11 10 10^{5} 4^{9} $6^{7\frac{1}{2}}$ 6^{13} JVelasquez 115 *2.70 72–14 Fiddler's Green 115^{2} A Latin Spin 115^{5} Mafioso 115^{2} No rally 12
19May67-1Aqu fst 7f .23 .45⅗1.24 Md Sp Wt 5 3 $2^{\frac{1}{2}}$ 2^{h} 4^{4} 4^{8} ACorderoJr 114 9.20 78–18 Minnesota Mac 114no Sound Box 107^{3} Chronological 117^{5} Weakened 9
12May67-4GS gd 6f .22⅘ .46⅘1.12⅕ Md Sp Wt 4 6 $2^{\frac{1}{2}}$ 3^{3} 2^{3} 2^{6} JVelasquez 116 3.30 77–21 Battle Plan 116^{6} Olympia You 116$^{\frac{1}{2}}$ Acquitted 116$^{\frac{1}{2}}$ Held second 12
20Mar67-3GP fst 6f .22⅗ .46⅕1.11⅗ Md Sp Wt 11 2 3^{2} $3^{3\frac{1}{2}}$ 3^{3} $4^{3\frac{1}{4}}$ JVelasquez 120 13.20 83–15 Wifes Objectron 120^{nk} Pebble Drive 120^{3} Stockpile 120^{h} Tired 12
13Mar67-3GP fst 7f .22⅕ .45⅕1.24⅘ Md Sp Wt 1 12 12^{17} 12^{16} 7^{14} $6^{8\frac{1}{2}}$ JVelasquez 120 10.10 76–15 Self Mastery 120^{5} Golden Skates 120^{1} Sea Frost 120^{2} Slow start 12
23Feb67-4Hia gd 6f .22⅘ .46⅘1.12⅕ Md Sp Wt 5 9 10^{11} 10^{17} 9^{14} 7^{18} BMoreira 118 5.70 65–20 Romatan 118$^{4\frac{1}{2}}$ Chorus 118$^{3\frac{1}{2}}$ On The Right 118^{6} Never a threat 12
LATEST WORKOUTS Jun 1 Mth 5f fst 1.01 h — May 26 GS 3f fst .39 b — May 11 GS 3f fst .35⅖ h — May 7 GS 5f sly 1.04 b

Amerigo Hill — Ch. c (1964–Fla), by Amerigo—Lavender Hill, by Flushing II — **115** — 1967 7 M 1 0 $1,460
Grosse-Point Stock Farm A. Gauthier (C. Silvers–L. Bandel) — 1966 0 M 0 0 ----
7Jun67-3Mth fst 1^{70} .48 1.12⅖1.43 Md Sp Wt 5 1 1^{2} 1^{h} 2^{h} 2^{3} BThornburg b 115 2.10 83–13 EnchantedEaster 115^{3} AmerigoHill 115^{9} CountryDay 110^{10} Weak'n'd 7
29May67-5GS fst 1$\frac{1}{16}$ .48⅕1.13⅕1.46 Md Sp Wt 5 2 2^{h} 1^{h} $2^{1\frac{1}{2}}$ $4^{6\frac{1}{4}}$ WGavidia b 115 8.60 69–22 Acquitted 115$^{2\frac{3}{4}}$ Victory String 112^{3} Amber Wave 115$^{\frac{1}{2}}$ Tired 10
17May67-2GS fst 1$\frac{1}{16}$ .48⅖1.13⅕1.46⅗ Md Sp Wt 10 6 $4^{2\frac{1}{2}}$ $3^{1\frac{1}{2}}$ 3^{2} $4^{2\frac{3}{4}}$ WGavidia b 115 29.80 69–18 Kummel 121^{nk} Victory String 112$^{1\frac{3}{4}}$ Acquitted 115$^{\frac{3}{4}}$ Hung at end 12
12May67-4GS gd 6f .22⅘ .46⅘1.12⅕ Md Sp Wt 7 9 $10^{7\frac{1}{2}}$ 8^{9} 6^{8} $6^{8\frac{3}{4}}$ WGavidia b 116 102.70 74–21 Battle Plan 116^{6} Olympia You 116$^{\frac{1}{2}}$ Acquitted 116$^{\frac{1}{2}}$ No factor 12
28Apr67-2GS gd 6f .23⅖ .47⅖1.14 Md Sp Wt 4 7 $7^{6\frac{1}{4}}$ 8^{12} 7^{10} $7^{6\frac{1}{2}}$ WGavidia b 115 43.00 67–27 Famous Dancer 115no Pebble Drive 115^{3} Muskwin 115$^{\frac{1}{2}}$ No threat 10
5Apr67-3GP fst 6f .22⅘ .46⅕1.11⅖ Md Sp Wt 10 3 $8^{4\frac{3}{4}}$ 9^{12} 9^{18} 9^{23} JLynch b 120 5,20 64–18 Orange Flower 115^{6} In Belief 120^{4} Le Parans 115^{3} Tired 12
LATEST WORKOUTS Jun 4 Mth 4f fst .48⅖ h — May 25 GS 3f fst .38⅖ b — May 5 GS 4f fst .50⅗ b — Apr 22 GS 4f fst .50⅖ b

Cotuit — Dk. b. or br. g (1964–Va), by Hasty Road—Arctica, by Arctic Prince — **115** — 1967 2 M 0 0 $215
Elcee-H Stable L. Laurin (Mrs. J. P. Mills) — 1966 0 M 0 0 ----
5Jun67-2Mth fst 6f .22⅕ .45⅕1.11⅖ Md Sp Wt 8 2 5^{2} 5^{9} 5^{6} 4^{9} DBrumfield 115 23.70 76–14 Fiddler's Green 115^{2} A Latin Spin 115^{5} Mafioso 115^{2} No threat 12
17Feb67-3SA fst 6f .22⅖ .45⅘1.10⅘ Md 10000 7 5 $6^{5\frac{1}{2}}$ 8^{8} 11^{11} 11^{16} WMahorney 118 2.10 73–13 PrinceDarning 118^{6} Duke'sStrings 118^{3} LodgeMagic 118$^{\frac{3}{4}}$ Hesitated 12
LATEST WORKOUTS Jun 10 Mth 5f fst 1.04⅗ b — May 30 Bel tr.t. 4f fst .50⅕ h — May 24 Bel 6f fst 1.13⅗ hg — May 18 Bel tr.t. 3f fst .38 b

Beaulark — B. c (1964–Va), by Beauchef—Ree Lee, by Doswell — **115** — 1967 1 M 0 0 —
R. M. Ring R. M. Ring (R. M. Ring) — 1966 0 M 0 0 —
24May67-2GS fst 6f .22⅗ .47 1.12⅖ Md Sp Wt 3 5 $4^{2\frac{1}{2}}$ 10^{13} 10^{20} 10^{25} VMauro 116 63.90 57–14 Quibu's Comet 116$^{2\frac{3}{4}}$ Nawab 11 115$^{2\frac{3}{4}}$ Bay Guinea 116$^{2\frac{1}{2}}$ Brief factor 10
LATEST WORKOUTS Jun 6 Del 5f fst 1.02⅖ b — May 17 Lrl 6f gd 1.21 bg — May 16 Lrl 3f my .39⅗ bg — May 10 Lrl 6f gd 1.18 b

Mafioso — Ch c (1964–Mass), by Backbone—In Content, by Greek Song — **115** — 1967 2 M 0 1 $710
F. L. Pollara C. W. Auwarter (Dr. L. Pollara) — 1966 1 M 0 0 ----
5Jun67-2Mth fst 6f .22⅕ .45⅕1.11⅖ Md Sp Wt 10 1 3^{2} 3^{7} 3^{5} 3^{7} JCulmone 115 13.10 78–14 Fiddler's Green 115^{2} A Latin Spin 115^{5} Mafioso 115^{2} Evenly 12
24May67-2GS fst 6f .22⅗ .47 1.12⅖ Md Sp Wt 1 3 1^{h} $1^{1\frac{1}{2}}$ 2^{4} 4^{8} SBrooks 116 15.20 74–14 Quibu's Comet 116$^{2\frac{3}{4}}$ Nawab II 115$^{2\frac{3}{4}}$ Bay Guinea 116$^{2\frac{1}{2}}$ Used early 10
8Jly 66-5Mth fst 5½f .22⅗ .47 1.06⅖ Md Sp Wt 4 3 2^{1} 6^{5} 8^{8} 8^{12} RBroussard 118 19.30 73–17 Broker John 118^{h} Pointsman 118^{3} Winslow Homer 118^{h} Brief speed 9
LATEST WORKOUTS May 21 GS 4f fst .49 b — May 17 GS 6f fst 1.14⅕ h — May 10 GS 5f gd 1.03⅕ h — May 5 GS 5f fst 1.03 bg

Shipwise — Dk. b. or br. g (1964–Va), by Sky Ship—Worldly Wise, by Bimelech — M. Ritzenberg — J. Byer — (North Hill Farm) — **115**

1967	1	M	0	0	——
1966	6	M	0	1	\$420

5Jun67–2Mth	fst 6f	.22⅕	.45⅕	1.11⅖	Md Sp Wt	7	7	$8^{4\frac{3}{4}}$	11^{19}	12^{27}	12^{40}	CBaltzar	b 115	16.90	45–14	Fiddler's Green 115^{2} A Latin Spin 115^{5} Mafioso 115^{2}	Unruly 12
12Oct66–3Aqu	fst 7f	.23	.46⅗	1.25⅖	Md Sp Wt	7	5	3½	2^{2}	$10^{8\frac{1}{2}}$	10^{18}	LGilligan	b 122	32.90	61–18	Shah $122^{1\frac{1}{2}}$ Quiet Town 122^{2} Shadow Brook 122^{4}	Speed, tired 14
27Sep66–3Aqu	fst 6f	.23	.47	1.12⅖	Md 15500	4	4	3^{nk}	2^{h}	3^{1}	$3^{5\frac{1}{4}}$	JRuane	b 120	17.10	76–21	Choir Loft 118^{5} Shah 122^{nk} Shipwise 120^{h}	Well up, hung 10
21Sep66–4Aqu	sly 6f	.23⅕	.47⅖	1.13	Md Sp Wt	5	2	2^{h}	2^{h}	$4^{3\frac{1}{2}}$	$6^{8\frac{1}{2}}$	JRuane	b 122	27.30	69–24	Fort Marcy 122^{4} Quiet Town $122^{1\frac{1}{2}}$ George Arnold 122½	Weakened 8
22Jly66–5Aqu	fst 5½f	.22⅖	.46	1.05⅘	Md Sp Wt	6	4	$4^{1\frac{1}{2}}$	3^{4}	4^{7}	10^{11}	JRuane	b 122	101.00	73–19	Monitor $122^{4\frac{1}{2}}$ Duke Cannon 122^{h} Fort Marcy $122^{1\frac{1}{2}}$	Dropped back 12
15Jly66–3Aqu	fst 5½f	.22⅘	.46⅘	1.05	Md Sp Wt	4	9	9^{6}	$9^{7\frac{1}{4}}$	9^{14}	9^{21}	JRuane	122	72.20	67–20	Dr. Fager 117^{7} Lift Off 122^{4} Rising Market 122½	Never close 11
8Jly66–5Aqu	fst 5½f	.22⅗	.46⅘	1.06⅖	Md Sp Wt	5	8	$10^{5\frac{1}{2}}$	$10^{8\frac{1}{2}}$	$10^{6\frac{3}{4}}$	9^{12}	JRuane	122	73.00	69–21	Puntador 122½ London Jet 122^{3} One Gem 122^{4}	Raced greenly 10

LATEST WORKOUTS May 30 Bel tr.t. 4f fst .48⅘ h May 22 Bel t.c. 5f fm 1.01⅖ h May 20 Bel tr.t. 3f fst .38 b May 16 Bel 4f sly .49 hg

In Belief: Eddie Kelly has been trying to leg up this colt in longer races after watching him tire in the stretch in his first two efforts. Unfortunately he seems still unable to hold together for as much as six furlongs, even in the slower going of longer races. Moreover, he has been idle for almost a month. NO BET.

Carry Away: The smashing workout from the gate on June 10 entitles this one to further consideration just in case the more experienced animals in the race look empty. CONTENDER.

Poilu II: No sign of anything yet. NO BET.

Olympia You: The main characteristic of this one is inability to stay close to the pace without tiring in the stretch. If it had revealed an inclination to take the lead at any stage of any of its six starts, one might concede it a chance to get its feet under it today. But it looks like a slow learning late bloomer that needs more experience. NO BET.

Amerigo Hill: After three sprints in which it showed no speed, Gauthier tried this one at longer distances, and it began to come to hand. It got to the front in both its latest efforts and held on fairly well before weakening. The presumption must be that it has improved since its first three starts, is suited to today's six-furlong test, and should have more than enough zip left for the stretch run at the shorter distance. CONTENDER.

Cotuit: The June 5 race was a distinct improvement over the Santa Anita debut, but Laurin's gelding has not yet hinted that it has learned to run farther than the first quarter-mile. NO BET.

Beaulark: Nothing yet. NO BET.

Mafioso: Steve Brooks got early speed out of this colt on May 24 but had no horse left for the final stages. Joe Culmone tried to rate the animal a week ago and was able to get show money with him. The problem is how to rate him and persuade him to speed up toward the end. CONTENDER.

Shipwise: The veteran Jake Byer almost won a maiden claimer with this at Aqueduct, but has been unable to make it run in the final stages of better races. NO BET.

The contenders are Carry Away, Amerigo Hill, and Mafioso. With so many fainthearted or feeble legged quitters in the race, a come-from-behinder like Carry Away's daddy would have a romp. But it asks a little too much of the unraced Carry Away to come from out of the pack and beat the more experienced and apparently fit Amerigo Hill, which figures to challenge the leaders along about the quarter pole and seems to have no serious rival as a stretch runner. The horse to beat is probably Mafioso, which may finally achieve the proper blend of early speed and finishing kick. But the handicapper is obliged to assume that the presence of so many other speed horses in the race will do the Culmone mount no good. Amerigo Hill is, therefore, a logical choice.

The Running of the Race

WHERE DO RACETRACK CROWDS get their horses? One of America's most astute handicappers, Howard Rowe, tells me that fewer than 10 percent of Aqueduct patrons buy a *Telegraph* or *Form* from track vendors. Assuming that three times that number buy the paper and try to do some handicapping before reaching the track, one concludes that four out of five members of the most sophisticated racing crowd in the country do their "figuring" from scratch sheets, tipsheets, newspaper selection pages, the tote board, and hot tips.

The quality of the advice on which racegoers rely is good enough to produce one winning favorite in every three attempts. But careful, personal handicapping is so much better! This race, a really easy one to handicap, is a prime example.

The Monmouth crowd, possibly mistaking Amerigo Hill for a quitter racing against quitters, made Carry Away the favorite. It preferred In Belief as second choice, disregarding In Belief's lengthy layoff and the fact that Amerigo Hill had shown much more speed and stamina.

The green Carry Away was scarcely in the race at all. Mafioso tried to run, carried his early speed farther than usual, but faltered. Amerigo Hill was miles the best and won by five lengths even after the faltering Mafioso forced it to run wide. Note also that In Belief confirmed the pre-race analysis by showing no run in the stretch.

THIRD RACE
Mth - 31375
June 12, 1967

6 FURLONGS (Chute). (Decathlon, June 11, 1957, 1.08$\frac{2}{5}$, 4, 130.) Maidens. Special weights. Purse \$4,300. Colts and geldings. 3- and 4-year-olds. Weights, 3-year-olds 115 lbs., 4-year-olds 122 lbs.

Value to winner \$2,795, second \$860, third \$430, fourth \$215. Mutuel pool \$129,495.

Index	Horse	Eqt	A	Wt	PP	St	¼	½	Str	Fin	Jockey	Owner	Odds $1
$31339Mth^{2}$	—Amerigo Hill	b	3	115	5	6	$6^{\frac{1}{2}}$	$4^{1\frac{1}{2}}$	$1^{\frac{1}{2}}$	1^{5}	B Thornburg	Grosse-Point Stk Farm	4.60
$31320Mth^{6}$	—Olympia You		3	115	4	4	7^{h}	6^{4}	$4^{\frac{1}{2}}$	2no	J Velasquez	F W Hooper	6.10
$31320Mth^{3}$	—Mafioso		3	115	8	1	2^{2}	$1^{1\frac{1}{2}}$	2^{h}	3^{4}	J Culmone	F L Pollara	4.40
$31101GS^{7}$	—In Belief	b	3	115	1	8	$4^{\frac{1}{2}}$	3^{h}	3^{2}	4^{1}	K Knapp	Brookfield Farm	3.60
$31320Mth^{12}$	-Shipwise	b	3	115	9	3	$3^{\frac{1}{2}}$	5^{4}	5^{2}	5^{5}	D Kassen	M Ritzenberg	60.80
$31320Mth^{4}$	—Cotuit		3	115	6	2	1^{h}	2^{h}	6^{4}	$6^{1\frac{1}{2}}$	D Brumfield	Elcee-H Stable	8.20
$31146GS^{10}$	—Beaulark		3	115	7	5	8^{8}	8^{10}	8^{10}	$7^{1\frac{1}{2}}$	P Romero	R M Ring	127.00
	—Carry Away		3	115	2	7	5^{h}	7^{1}	$7^{\frac{1}{2}}$	8^{12}	C Baltazar	Woodside Stud	2.20
$31320Mth^{11}$	-Poilu II		4	122	3	9	9	9	9	9	J Leonard	Mrs C F Parker	49.10

Time .22$\frac{1}{5}$, .45$\frac{3}{5}$, 1.11$\frac{2}{5}$. Track fast.

\$2 Mutuel Prices:

5–AMERIGO HILL	11.20	5.00	3.60
4–OLYMPIA YOU		6.60	4.40
8–MAFIOSO			4.00

Ch. c, by Amerigo—Lavender Hill, by Flushing II. Trainer A. Gauthier. Bred by C. Silvers-L. Bandel (Fla.).

IN GATE AT 3.01. OFF AT 3.01 EASTERN DAYLIGHT TIME. Start good for all but POILU II. Won driving.

AMERIGO HILL lodged his bid from the outside nearing the stretch, was carried out to the middle of the track by MAFIOSO, put that one away and drew out to the wire. OLYMPIA YOU rallied to mid-stretch and hung. MAFIOSA gained command from the outside leaving the backstretch, drifted out into the lane and faltered. IN BELIEF saved ground to become a factor in upper stretch and faltered. COTUIT vied for the early lead and tired. CARRY AWAY showed nothing. POILU II was off poorly.

4. FIRST AT AQUEDUCT, NOVEMBER 29, 1966—Track Muddy

A STANDARD RULE among handicappers is that four-year-olds seldom are worth backing against three-year-olds in maiden races. The rule holds up. An animal that has reached age four without a victory is extremely unlikely to have victory in him. The more races he has run, the slimmer his chances become. The rule holds up, as I have said, but exceptional occasions arise on which lightly raced four-year-old maidens become logical choices.

This particular race, at the fag end of the long New York season, contains more than its share of equine derelicts—three- and four-year-old maidens entered to be claimed for $4,000 to $5,000. A field of this kind is usually so woeful that no reasonable choice materializes. The only hope is to see if anything has a single redeeming feature among all the blemishes.

1st Race Aqueduct

Start — 6 FURLONGS — AQUEDUCT — Finish

6 FURLONGS. (Near Man, July 17, 1963, 108⅗, 3, 112.)
Maidens. Claiming. Purse $3,500. 3-year-olds and upward. Weights, 3-year-olds 122 lbs., older 124 lbs. Claiming price, $5,000. 2 lbs. for each $500 to $4,000.

Private Plane $4,000 — Ch. c (1962), by Piet—Dublin Miss, by Solar Slipper — L. C. Ostrer — S. Cardile — (W. T. Markey) — **113⁷**
1966 7 M 0 0 —
1965 4 M 0 0 —

22Nov66-1Aqu fst 6f .23 .47⅖1.13⅖ Md 3500 1 8 52¾ 78 1015 1211 ACordero b 120 31.30f 65-23 Hunt Staff 118no Fiesta Day 115½ Burny Bee 111½ Fell back early 13
15Nov66-1Aqu fst 1 .47⅘1.14⅘1.39⅘ Md 3500 9 6 1417 1429 1439 1445 HGustines b 119 30.10 —— Wheyface 117½ Gracious 1133 Safety Switch 116½ No speed 14
26Oct66-2Aqu fst 1⅛.48⅗1.14⅖1.54 Md 3500 1 1 11 67½ 716 720 RRoland7 b 112 28.90 46-19 Count Nasrulla 1151 Wheyface 116½ Warrior Blue 1122 Used up 8
11Oct66-1Aqu fst 1⅛.47⅖1.12⅘1.54⅕ Md 3500 7 4 48 914 926 937 RRoland7 b 112 20.30 28-21 Weary Traveler 1102 Beau Star 1152 Wheyface 1161½ Fell back 9
27Sep66-1Aqu fst 1⅛.48⅕1.13⅗1.55 Md 3500 3 1 12 1½ 1h 77¼ RRoland7 b 113 59.60 54-21 Third Party 1152 Count Nasrulla 1152 Warrior Blue 1181½ Used up 12
16Sep66-1Aqu fst 1 .48⅕1 14 1.40⅗ Md 4000 4 12 116¾ 1416 1322 1326 RRoland7 b 112 21.60f 39-25 Florida Magic 1143 FleetImpelled115no Triton'sTrust1193 No factor 14
7Sep66-1Aqu fst 6f .23⅗ 48⅖1.14⅕ Md 3500 7 4 62¼ 911 1015 101[illegible] DChamberlin5 b 119 18.[illegible] 57-30 LightIntentions1205CountNasrulla120¾YankeeBrahmin120½ No f'ct'r 11
15Feb65-1Hia fst 6f .22⅘ .45⅘1.13 Clm 5000 12 3 52¼ 32 57 86 SHernandez b 114 60.00 73-17 Vietato 1061¼ The Flicks 1142½ Peewee's Joy 1151¾ Early speed 12
22Jan65-1Hia fst 6f .22⅖ .46 1.12⅖ Clm 6000 4 10 98¼ 813 1120 1120 SHernandez b 112 48.50 62-18 Captain Russ 1164 Landy's Lark 1121½ Knight's Note 109h No speed 12
13Jan65-2TrP fst 6f .22⅗ .45⅘1.12 Clm 5000 11 4 46 69 611 68¾ SHernandez b 114 8.60 73-16 Peewee's Joy 114½ Nodlac 1141 Family Feud 1154 No mishap 12
4Jan65-4TrP fst 6f .22⅗ .46 1.11⅘ Clm 5500 5 4 55½ 58½ 813 813 SHernandez 114 10.50 70-14 Family Feud 1111½ Rib Tickler 114nk Mr. Pat 1144 Fell back early 9
1Dec64-1Aqu fst 7f .23⅗ .47⅘1.26⅗ Md 9000 7 4 107½ 1010 1017 920 EBelmonte b 118 44.70 53-22 Ground Cover 118¾ Lou O'Neill 118½ Stoner Hill 118no Far back 10
16Nov64-3Aqu fst 6f .22⅘ .47 1.13⅖ Md 9000 1 14 105½ 107 118¼ 119¼ SHernandez b 118 9.80f 67-20 Prince Graff 122h Palmyran 1131½ Galvin 1221 Could not keep up 14
LATEST WORKOUTS Nov 21 Bel tr.t. 3f fst .39 b Oct 25 Bel tr.t. 4f fst .53 b

***Sean Mor** $4,000 — Dk. b. or br. c (1963), by Tamerlane—Ensign Rouge, by Magic Red — J. F. Dorrian — A. A. Fiore — (Woodpark Ltd.). (Ire.) — **118**
1966 4 M 0 0 —
1965 1 M 0 0 —

22Nov66-3Aqu fst 7f .22⅘ .47 1.25⅘ Md 6500 8 1 13 11½ 816 826 RUssery b 118 16.80 51-23 Big Shot 118½ Miss Mop 1141½ Pacifist 1226 Stopped badly 8
10Nov66-6Aqu fst 6f .22⅖ .46⅕1.11⅘ Md Sp Wt 2 1 13 2½ 67 1013 RTurcotte b 122 78.40 71-20 Solemn Nation 117¾ Vocalist 1221 Soldier's Story 1221 Stopped 12
20Oct66-4GS gd 6f .23⅕ .47⅕1.13⅗ Md Sp Wt 5 2 44 812 813 712 NReagan b 118 36.60 64-23 Lord Lionel 118nk Kanhurie 115no Change Maker 1183½ Fell back 10
21Jan66-3Hia fst 6f .21⅘ .45⅕1.11⅘ Md Sp Wt 6 5 34 36½ 1016 1123 DBrumfield b 118 52.20 62-22 Taravari 118nk Roving Satellite 118¾ Sales Pitch 11810 Stopped 12
20Dec65-6TrP sl 6f .22⅗ .46⅗1.12⅘ Allowance 1 11 75½ 87¼ 1015 1013 JParsons b 114 78.90 65-27 B. Golden 112nk Shannon Power 1151 Bullyampa 1081½ Fell back 11
LATEST WORKOUTS Nov 18 Bel tr.t. 5f fst 1.03 h Oct 17 GS 5f fst 1.03⅗ bg Oct 12 GS 4f fst .49 b Oct 3 Atl 4f gd .50⅖ b

Australian Sky * $4,000 — Ch. g (1963-Ky), by Australian Star—Turn to Gold, by Turn-to — R. Titus — T. J. Gullo — (Mrs. F. C. Rand, Jr.) — **118**
1966 9 M 2 0 $1,615
1965 3 M 1 0 $720

22Nov66-1Aqu fst 6f .23 .47⅖1.13⅖ Md 3500 3 10 99¼ 1214 1217 99½ HWoodhouse b 118 6.40 66-23 Hunt Staff 118no Fiesta Day 115½ Burny Bee 111½ Far off pace 13
25Oct66-1Aqu fst 6f .23 .47⅖1.13⅕ Md 5000 1 6 65 99½ 914 912 JLRotz b 121 *2.10 65-18 Yankee Brahmin 117h Photo Bob 1212½ Sum Farce 117nk Dull try 13
6Oct66-1Aqu fst 6f .23 .48⅕1.14⅕ Md 5000 7 12 1411 910 75¼ 46½ JLRotz b 121 *1.00 65-24 Fleet Impelled 1183 Yankee Brahmin 1171½ Bombax 1212 Broke slow 14
28Sep66-1Aqu fst 6f .22⅖ .46⅖1.12⅕ Md 6000 1 1 1h 1½ 2h 24 JLRotz b 116 *2.60 78-19 Don't Walk 1204 Australian Sky 116nk Burny Bee 116½ Gamely 14
9Sep66-4Aqu fst 6f .23 .47 1.13⅖ Md 6000 8 2 2½ 21½ 23 23½ JLRotz b 116 11.10 72-25 Yamamoto 1163½ Australian Sky 1161 Burny Bee 1164 Went well 12
13Jun66-1Aqu fst 6f .22⅘ .47⅕1.13⅕ Md 7500 2 4 46 55 117¼ 1110 BFeliciano b 115 28.50 67-21 Dans-Le Vent 115no Amanuensis 1152½ Don't Walk 108½ Tired 12
6Jun66-3Aqu fst 6f .22⅕ .45⅗1.11⅖ Md 7500 2 2 2h 44 46½ 59 BFeliciano b 115 9.40 77-20 Full Size 1042 Tamalpais 1151½ Don't Walk 1104 Well up, tired 14
26May66-1Aqu fst 7f .23 .46⅘1.25⅖ Md 12500 8 2 13 1½ 51¾ 810 BFeliciano b 114 9.00 69-19 Hobe Sound 110h Arpino 1243 Irish Kelly 120½ Speed, tired badly 8
11May66-1Aqu fst 6f .22⅖ .45⅘1.11⅘ Md Sp Wt 6 5 33 68¼ 811 916 BFeliciano b 114 61.60 68-19 Banquet Hall 1078 Eton Tie 114no Highly Pleased 1152 Brief sp'd 13
2Sep65-3Aqu fst 6f .23 47⅘1.13⅖ Md Sp Wt 4 4 21½ 22 45½ 613 MYcaza b 122 16.60 63-26 Sense of Rhythm 1224 Rehabilitate 1156 Fact Seeker 1221 Weakened 10
25Aug65-5Sar fst 6f .22⅗ .46⅗1.11⅗ M c-12500 5 8 62¼ 1114 108½ 1122 ACordero b 122 3.90 68-10 Freeway 1226 Golden Gala 1224 Ocean Game 1201 Fell far back 14
LATEST WORKOUTS Nov 8 Bel tr.t. 3f gd .39 b Nov 2 Bel tr.t. 4f fst .49⅖ h Oct 30 Bel tr.t. 5f fst 1.04⅗ b Oct 21 Bel tr.t. 4f gd .52 b

Bold Fool $4,000 — B. c (1963-Fla), by Tom's Lark—Mary Sheila, by Challedon — E. M. O'Brien — E. M. O'Brien — (Dr. W. O. Reed) — **118**
1966 6 M 1 0 $600
1965 0 M 0 0 —

22Nov66-1Aqu fst 6f .23 .47⅖1.13⅖ Md 3500 8 5 75¼ 810 814 76¾ JJMartin7 111 11.80 69-23 Hunt Staff 118no Fiesta Day 115½ Burny Bee 111½ Not a factor 13
1Nov66-2GS fst 6f .22⅕ .46 1.12⅗ Md 4000 8 3 77¼ 59½ 59 25 MVenezia 118 6.90 76-18 Hamorton 1075 Bold Fool 118¾ Backrullah 1151 Forced out 10
25Oct66-1Aqu fst 6f .23 .47⅖1.13⅕ Md 4500 12 2 11 42½ 1220 1218 MVenezia b 119 20.20 59-18 Yankee Brahmin 117h Photo Bob 1212½ Sum Farce 117nk Used up 13
6Oct66-1Aqu fst 6f .23 .48⅕1.14⅕ Md 4000 14 1 13 12 55 1012 MVenezia b 117 15.60 60-24 Fleet Impelled 1183 Yankee Brahmin 1171½ Bombax 1212 Stopped 14
29Mar66-3Aqu fst 1 .46⅘1.12⅖1.38⅖ Md 10000 7 3 45½ 615 721 732 TKelly10 103 42.30 44-25 Galanteador 11210 Midstater 112½ Major Planet 119½ Fell back 8
17Mar66-3Aqu fst 6f .23⅕ .46⅘1.12⅗ Md Sp Wt 4 5 52½ 79¼ 713 718 MVenezia 122 7.50 62-25 Yale Fence 1227 Prince Timmy 1223 Sanity 1226 Bore out late 7
LATEST WORKOUTS Oct 22 Bel tr.t. 3f fst .37⅗ h Oct 12 Bel tr.t. 3f fst .38 b Oct 17 Bel tr.t. 3f fst .38⅖ b Oct 4 Bel tr.t. 4f fst .51 b

Billie's Lassie $4,000 Dk. b. or br. f (1963–Ky), by King Hairan—Billie, by Bimelech 108⁷ 1966 11 M 0 0 $350
Grandview Stable T. A. Ecklund (Grandview Stables) 1965 1 M 0 1 $350
22Nov66–1Aqu fst 6f .23 .47⅖1.13⅖ Md 3500 5 9 1012 1113 915 66 TCordero7 109 31.30f 70–23 Hunt Staff 118no Fiesta Day 115½ Burny Bee 111½ Not a factor 13
11Aug66–1Sar fst 6f .22⅗ .46⅕1.12 Md 3500 4 10 1216 1219 1220 1224 JJMartin7 103 62.20 64–13 BeLively 1241 BlackRod 1143 BurnyBee 1151½ Raced far back 12
28Jly 66–1Aqu fst 1 .46⅗1.12⅘1.39⅘ Md 3500 10 9 97 107¾ 1013 911 DHidalgo5 105 44.50 60–21 Roy D. Jr. 115¾ Bold Milargo 103¾ Florida Magic 115no Raced wide 12
14Jly 66–1Aqu fst 6f .22⅘ .47 1.12⅗ f–Md 4000 8 7 1211 1015 912 916 ECardone5 107 28.60 64–12 Runnin' Rose 1162 The Chained Lady 1123 Tara's Girl 1161 No speed 14
5Jly 66–3Aqu fst 1 .47⅕1.13⅕1.41⅕ Md 3500 1 4 31 53½ 54½ 45½ JJMartin5 105 9.90 57–20 Irish Tract 110¾ Garth's Choice 1083 Florida Magic 1121½ Tired 6
1Jly 66–3Aqu fst 6f .22⅘ .46⅕1.12⅗ f–Md 3500 2 3 76½ 714 514 412 DChamberlin5 109 33.10 68–19 SimplicityPlus 1148 Joanna'sJolt 1142 TheChainedLady 1141½ Wide 8
20Jun66–1Aqu fst 6f .22⅗ .46⅗1.13⅘ f–Md 3500 2 4 87¼ 1014 713 914 RTurcotte b 114 22.60 60–21 NeverADoubt1091½d–BoldMilargo1074SimplicityPlus114h No factor 11
28Apr66–1Aqu my 7f .23⅕ .47⅕1.26⅗ f–Md 3500 9 1 64¾ 77¾ 917 723 GMineau5 106 40.20 50–24 Titaness 114½ Inspiring 1148 Express Purpose 1052½ Wide 10
14Apr66–2Aqu fst 6f .23⅕ .47⅗1.13⅘ f– 3500 2 6 53½ 74¼ 1012 1011 RTurcotte b 113 45.10 63–17 Fairly Fast 1142 Cool That 1132 Heads I Win 1081 Far back 10
30Mar66–1Aqu fst 6f .22⅘ .47⅕1.13⅘ f–Md 5500 6 3 88½ 917 913 920 AValenzuela b 117 16.30e 54–20 Thoughty 121¾ Titaness 1173½ Takes the Cake 1212½ No speed 10
18Mar66–1Aqu fst 6f .22⅘ .47⅕1.13⅘ f–Md 6500 7 2 76¼ 1017 1023 1025 AValenzuela 113 14.90 49–22 Norma Mathews 1075 Rita Marie 1143 Bold Milargo 103nk No speed 11
LATEST WORKOUTS Nov 21 Aqu 3f fst .37 b Nov 18 Aqu 4f fst .51 b Nov 14 Aqu 4f gd .51⅖ b Nov 9 Aqu 6f fst 1.16 h

Youngs Road $4,000 Ch. g (1963–NC), by My Hour II—Battling Hannah, by Hannibal 118 1966 1 M 0 0 —
Mrs. E. H. Hogan M. G. Walsh (E. H. Hogan) 1965 0 M 0 0 —
22Nov66–1Aqu fst 6f .23 .47⅖1.13⅖ Md 3500 2 13 1112 66 69½ 89½ WBlum b 118 28.40 67–23 Hunt Staff 118no Fiesta Day 115½ Burny Bee 111½ Far off pace 13
LATEST WORKOUTS Nov 17 Bel tr.t. 4f fst .49⅗ h Nov 11 Bel tr.t. 3f sly .38 b Oct 26 Bel m.t. 4f fst .48⅖ hg Oct 11 Bel tr.t. 5f fst 1.05 b

Marie W. $5,000 B. f (1962), by Prince John—Your Letta, by Your Reward 121 1966 4 M 0 0 $225
Claybrook Stable F. E. McMillan (O. Wilmot) 1965 0 M 0 0 —
26Oct66–7Kee fst 6½f.22⅗ .45⅕1.18⅘ f– Allow 1 8 75½ 77½ 78½ 811 WAPeake 116 57.60 73–19 Hurricane Liz 117¾ Hoop's Sis 1171 Strawshy 1174 No factor 9
20Oct66–5Kee sl 6½f.22⅗ .45⅘1.21⅕ f–MdSpWt 3 2 44½ 56 44 46¾ WAPeake 118 9.00 65–27 Starlight Eve 115¾ Dalam Day 1152 Indian Moccasin 1154 Evenly 6
15Jun66–1Suf fst 6f .22⅕ .45⅕1.11⅗ Md Sp Wt 5 8 76¼ 811 815 711 EDonnally 117 14.20 79–13 Miss High Hopes1082 Merry Flight109nk Interstate1132½ No speed 12
8Jun66–2Suf sl 6f .23 .47⅖1.13⅖ Md Sp Wt 9 9 54 44½ 49½ 516 EDonnally 117 6.50 63–26 Joe the Barber 1133½ Sir Grady 11310 Ameri Sonnet 112h No mishap 10
LATEST WORKOUTS Nov 26 Bel m.t. 5f fst 1.03 b Nov 22 Bel m.t. 5f fst 1.03⅖ b Nov 19 Bel m.t. 4f fst .51 b

Calizon $5,000 Ch. c (1962), by Barbizon—Jacalu, by Princequillo 124 1966 2 M 1 0 $1,015
T. C. Quisenberry H. A. Luro (W. L. Jones, Jr.) 1964 1 M 0 0 —
21Nov66–4Lrl fst 6f .23⅘ .49 1.15 Md Allow 5 1 31½ 32½ 34½ 22 CRogers 116 2.90 75–21 Kyrenia 1152 Calizon 116no Gold Fever 1146 Gave game effort 6
11Aug66–1Sar fst 6f .22⅗ .46⅕1.12 Md 4500 5 3 42½ 45 56½ 45½ HGustines 124 5.20 82–13 BeLively 1241 BlackRod 1143 BurnyBee 1151½ Drifted out stretch 12
17Aug64–3AP fst 6f .22⅘ .46 1.12⅘ Md Sp Wt 3 6 87¾ 816 611 68¾ KKnapp 118 18.00 72–13 Royal Stamp 1181½ Prime Minister 1183 Dusky Link 1131 No speed 12
LATEST WORKOUTS Nov 13 Lrl 4f fst .51⅗ b Nov 9 Lrl 5f fst 1.06 b

Najecam $4,000 Ro. f (1962), by Cochise—Summer Song, by Greek Song 117 1966 1 M 0 0 —
J. Siegel J. Rigione (J. N. Fletcher) 1965 3 M 1 0 $600
22Nov66–1Aqu fst 6f .23 .47⅖1.13⅖ Md 3500 11 4 3nk 33 713 1010 RStovall b 117 35.80 66–23 Hunt Staff 118no Fiesta Day 115½ Burny Bee 111½ Early foot, tired 13
28Jun65–1Mth fst 6f .22⅗ .46⅕1.13⅗ f–Md 6500 5 8 41½ 45 711 712 EMonacelli 115 *2.70 62–25 Miss Niagara 1102½ Big Treat 123nk Amber Flower 115¾ Taken up 10
24Jun65–1Mth fst 6f .22⅗ .46⅕1.13⅘ f–Md 5000 10 1 21½ 23 47½ 59¾ CGonzalez 115 *2.20 63–27 Sister Boma 1152 Rubicon 115nk Moonorama 1155 Weakened 12
11Jun65–3Mth fst 6f .22⅕ .46 1.13⅕ f– 3500 5 2 1h 11 11½ 2½ PKallai 113 3.00 75–19 Popcel 112½ Najecam 1131½ Angela Mia 112nk Failed to last 8
2Jly 64–3Mth fst 5½f.22⅕ .45⅗1.05⅘ f–Md 8000 7 7 31 56½ 1013 917 PKallai 113 6.40 73–15 Conference 1174 Clown Around 1174 Char Lady 110h Tired 12
LATEST WORKOUTS Nov 12 Bel tr.t. 4f my .50 h Nov 12 Bel tr.t. 4f my .50 h Nov 3 GS 3f sly .38⅘ b Oct 31 GS 3f fst .37⅗ bg

***Polly Bell** $5,000 Ch. f (1963), by Ballymoss—Poll-O-Mine, by Double Jay 119 1966 6 M 0 0 $150
F. J. Viggiani J. Evans (J. McShain) (Eng.) 1965 0 M 0 0 —
21Oct66–2GS fst 6f .22⅗ .46 1.11⅘ f– 6250 9 4 1016 Pulled up HHinojosa b 116 54.10 —— Infinita 1202¾ General Note 118½ Beau Mink 1181½ Bad step 10
12Aug66–3Atl fst 6f .22 .45⅘1.12⅕ Md 7500 8 4 66½ 614 611 57¾ GPatterson b 112 7.50 73–20 General Note 1074 Cheeky Carol 112nk May Wonder 1152 No factor 9
5Aug66–2Mth fst 6f .22⅘ .45⅗1.11⅘ Md 10000 10 4 78½ 69 56½ 46½ GPatterson b 112 66.80 76–17 Arabian Legend 117h Market Value 1134 Tejuela 1132½ No threat 10
29Jly 66–2Mth my 6f .22⅘ .46⅘1.13⅕ f–MdSpWt 5 4 54½ 58 59 515 NReagan b 115 56.10 61–25 Sarolsa 1152½ My Charlotte 1154 Connie S. N. 1152½ Never close 10
14Jly 66–6Mth fst 6f .22⅕ .45⅗1.12⅗ f–MdSpWt 11 10 106½ 711 812 99¾ CStone b 115 56.20 70–17 Shimmering 1152 New Love 115nk Saucy Susan 1151 Showed noth'g 12
26May66–1GS sly 6f .22⅘ .47 1.14⅘ f–M c–5000 3 11 1121 1018 919 714 JVelasquez 117 8.40 56–24 Pearl T. 1103½ Acean Love 117½ Last Act 1174 Broke in tangle 12
LATEST WORKOUTS Nov 19 Pim 4f fst .52⅘ b Nov 10 GS 6f fst 1.15⅘ b Nov 7 GS 3f fst .36 h Oct 12 GS 5f fst 1.03 bg

Fiesta Day $4,000 B. g, (1963–Ky), by Johns Joy—Seville, by Unbreakable 113⁵ 1966 12 M 2 0 $1,575
J. E. Smith N. Caton (Mereworth Farm) 1965 0 M 0 0 —
22Nov66–1Aqu fst 6f .23 .47⅖1.13⅖ Md 4000 13 7 63¾ 44½ 32 2no ECardone5 b 115 *1.90 76–23 Hunt Staff 118no Fiesta Day 115½ Burny Bee 111½ Closed gamely 13
15Nov66–1Aqu fst 1 .47⅘1.14⅘1.39⅘ Md 3500 1 1 11½ 1h 53 56 LGilligan b 116 4.60 63–22 Wheyface 117½ Gracious 1133 Safety Switch 116½ Used up 14
4Nov66–1Aqu fst 7f .22⅘ .46⅕1.25⅘ Md 3500 4 4 1½ 1h 3½ 2nk LGilligan b 118 9.90 79–20 Pippin 118nk Fiesta Day 1181½ Safety Switch 1181 Gamely 14
25Oct66–1Aqu fst 6f .23 .47⅕1.13⅕ Md 4000 2 8 44 32 34 42¾ LGilligan b 117 48.80 74–18 Yankee Brahmin 117h Photo Bob 1212½ Sum Farce 117nk No rally 13
6Oct66–1Aqu fst 6f .23 .48⅕1.14⅕ Md 4000 3 5 33 32 43 56½ BFeliciano b 117 54.60 65–24 Fleet Impelled 1183 Yankee Brahmin 1171½ Bombax 1212 Hung 14
27Sep66–1Aqu fst 1⅛.48⅕1.13⅗1.55 Md 3500 10 2 22 2½ 109 1015 WBlum b 115 13.40e 46–21 Third Party 1152 Count Nasrulla 1152 Warrior Blue 1181½ Fell back 12
16Sep66–1Aqu fst 1 .48⅕1.14 1.40⅗ Md 4000 9 1 2½ 53 79 811 WBlum b 114 11.50 54–25 Florida Magic 1143 Fleet Impelled 115no Triton's Trust 1193 Tired 14
9Sep66–4Aqu fst 6f .23 .47 1.13⅗ Md 6000 10 6 66½ 79 89½ 511 HGustines b 116 5.90 65–25 Yamamoto 1163½ Australian Sky 1161 Burny Bee 1164 No mishap 12
11May66–3GS fst 170.46⅘1.11⅘1.43⅘ Md Sp Wt 4 5 53 53¾ 45 66 DBrumfield b 120 3.60 71–12 d–AdmiralTudor 120½ FlyingClear 120h MarketValue 1204 No mishap 9
4May66–1Aqu fst 6f .23⅘ .47⅖1.12⅘ Md Sp Wt 6 2 21 55 54 56 ECardone7 b 106 44.00 75–20 Top to Bottom113½ Mincing Lane1133½ Robertsville115½ Weakened 10
13Apr66–4Aqu fst 6f .23 .46⅘1.11⅘ Md Sp Wt 9 2 33 57 916 921 WShoemaker 112 12.40 66–16 King's Jest 1125 d–Top to Bottom 1122 Solemn Nation 1123 Tired 10
5Apr66–2Aqu fst 6f .22⅘ .47 1.12⅘ Md Sp Wt 6 3 44½ 47½ 57 511 WShoemaker 113 10.60 69–23 Fact Seeker 1152 Dance Contest 1133½ It's Blitz 1135 Fell back 8
LATEST WORKOUTS Oct 22 Aqu 4f fst .50 b Oct 15 Aqu 4f fst .52 b

John Toppa Jr. $4,000 Dk. b. or br. g (1963–Pa), by Pied d'Or—Kay Phalanx, by Phalanx 118 1965 2 M 0 0 —
J. M. Toppa, Jr. N. Combest (C. Heckman)
13Sep65–4Nar sly 6f .24⅘ .49⅕1.16⅕ Md Sp Wt 8 5 62½ 64½ 1016 1017 RStovall 120 74.10 48–34 KimberleyPrince 120½ MaxKase 1203 Clear the Court 1204½ Fell b'k 11
31Aug65–6Rkm fst 6f .22⅕ .45⅘1.11 Allowance 2 9 97½ 98¾ 911 911 RStovall 112 60.30 78–14 Counselor S. 1192¾ Jet Formation 1161 Salute Ric 1191 No speed 10
LATEST WORKOUTS Nov 14 Nar 5f fst 1.03⅗ h Nov 5 Nar 4f fst .49⅕ hg Nov 2 Nar 6f fst 1.16⅘ b Oct 30 Nar 4f fst .50⅖ h

Kymry $4,000 B. c (1963–NY), by Nizami Blue—Edna Jane, by Hasteville 118 1966 4 M 0 0 —
Florence C. Lange H. Walker (Miss D. Charlson) 1965 0 M 0 0 —
22Nov66–1Aqu fst 6f .23 .47⅖1.13⅖ Md 3500 7 3 2h 1012 1322 1317 JRuane 118 31.30f 59–23 Hunt Staff 118no Fiesta Day 115½ Burny Bee 111½ Fell back early 13
15Nov66–1Aqu fst 1 .47⅘1.14⅘1.39⅘ Md 3500 2 2 21½ 1215 1329 1330 DChamberlin 118 91.80 39–22 Wheyface 117½ Gracious 1133 Safety Switch 116½ Stopped 14
4Nov66–1Aqu fst 7f .22⅘ .46⅕1.25⅘ Md 3500 12 2 32 78 1119 1326 DChamberlin 118 22.40f 53–20 Pippin 118nk Fiesta Day 1181½ Safety Switch 1181 Stopped 14
29Oct66–2Aqu fst 6f .23 .47 1.12⅕ Clm 5000 9 5 87 76½ 1114 1121 DChamberlain 116 65.80 61–21 C. U. Later 119½ Festival King 1191 Colonel Bay 1143 Far back 11
LATEST WORKOUTS Nov 21 Bel tr.t. 3f fst .37⅗ h Nov 13 Bel m.t. 4f sly .49⅖ h Nov 2 Bel tr.t. 3f fst .38 b Oct 26 Bel tr.t. 4f fst .50⅖ h

Beau Star $4,000 B. c (1963–Conn), by Dandy Ron—Etoile du Nord, by Northern Star 113⁵ 1966 17 M 1 1 $1,685
J. Shanbrom J. Lipari (J. Shanbrom) 1965 0 M 0 0 —
22Nov66–1Aqu fst 6f .23 .47⅖1.13⅖ Md 3500 4 12 1213 912 56½ 56 RUssery b 118 13.40 75–23 Hunt Staff 118no Fiesta Day 115½ Burny Bee 111½ Stride late 13
15Nov66–1Aqu fst 1 .47⅘1.14⅘1.39⅘ Md 3500 6 7 32 53¾ 816 1021 RUssery b 116 6.60 48–22 Wheyface 117½ Gracious 1133 Safty Switch 116½ Fell back 14
4Nov66–1Aqu fst 7f .22⅘ .46⅕1.25⅘ Md 3500 1 11 77½ 67½ 54½ 53 BBaeza b 118 *2.60 76–20 Pippin 118nk Fiesta Day 1181½ Safety Switch 1181 No threat 14
26Oct66–2Aqu fst 1⅛.48⅗1.14⅖1.54 Md 3500 5 2 21 1h 21 43½ BBaeza b 115 *1.30 62–19 Count Nasrulla 1151 Wheyface 116½ Warrior Blue 1122 Tired 8
20Oct66–2Aqu sl 1 .47⅘1.14⅖1.41 Clm 3500•11 1 33 44½ 54¾ 78 LLoughry b 113 7.80 55–23 Styrullah 1191½ On the Throne 116h Sudden Light 1192 Gave way 11
11Oct66–1Aqu fst 1⅛.47⅖1.12⅘1.54⅘ Md 3500 4 2 22 2h 12 22 LLoughry b 115 8.00 63–21 Weary Traveler 1102 Beau Star 1152 Wheyface 1161½ Good try 9
4Oct66–9Aqu fst 1⅛.47⅕1.13 1.53⅘ Clm 3500 2 1 1½ 12 21½ 48 LLoughry b 109 27.50 60–17 Royal Magician 1082 Porky 1086 Golden Mike 113h Tired 9
27Sep66–1Aqu fst 1⅛.48⅕1.13⅗1.55 Md 3500 11 4 46½ 4½ 2h 45½ LLoughry b 115 20.20 55–21 Third Party 1152 Count Nasrulla 1152 Warrior Blue 1181½ Tired 12
16Sep66–1Aqu fst 1 .48⅕1.14 1.40⅗ Md 4000 6 6 93¾ 65 56½ 67 LLoughry 114 21.60f 58–25 Florida Magic 1143 FleetImpelled115no Triton'sTrust1193 In close 14
8Sep66–9Aqu fst 1 .48⅗1.14⅗1.41 Clm 3500 10 2 3nk 31 53 55 DChamberlin 112 73.00 58–29 Inhand 112no Pinchers Pride 115no Space Control 1151½ Weakened 10
31Aug66–1Aqu fst 7f .23 .46⅗1.27⅕ Md 4000 5 14 910 1111 79½ 75½ HGustines 115 36.60 65–20 Black Rod 114¾ Florida Magic 1152 Russwin 112½ Slow start 14
24Aug66–1Sar gd 7f .22⅗ .45⅗1.26 Md 6500 11 2 89½ 79 87¾ 711 ACordero 115 19.00 69–17 First Port 1152 Captain's Mast 1242 Black Rod 110¾ No factor 11

Private Plane: Sam Cardile keeps entering this four-year-old without earning a dime back. And now it is stepping up in class after running twelfth to the poorest possible field—a $3,500 maiden race. NO BET.

Sean Mor: In the last nineteen days this one has shown distinct early speed against better maidens, quitting horribly each time. Often a horse holds its speed better when entered against cheaper animals than have been intimidating it. Sean Mor may have a chance. CONTENDER.

Australian Sky: In September it looked like Tommy Gullo might finally squeeze a victory out of this gelding, but it foundered in its most recent starts. NO BET.

Bold Fool: Ran too badly against this kind to merit support today. NO BET.

Billie's Lassie: Can't beat even $3,500 maiden fillies. NO BET.

Youngs Road: An unpromising debut last week. NO BET.

Marie W.: First race here, and unraced for more than a month. And a filly, besides. Has faced better and may make a showing today, but is not worth an investment. NO BET.

Calizon: After a two-year absence, this Horatio Luro colt ran a respectable race against Saratoga company similar to today's. Last week, against some of Laurel's better maidens, showed a good deal of run at a well-backed 2.90–1. Luro, a past master at shipping horses for spot victories, seems to have drawn a bead on today's cheap field and may have a good chance. CONTENDER.

Najecam: A filly with early speed and nothing else. NO BET.

Polly Bell: A filly that hurt herself while running against winners more than a month ago. Probably needs a race. NO BET.

Fiesta Day: Has been running well against the cheapest maidens in New York, but never well enough to win. Might win some day, but is scarcely a candidate for support against $5,000 stock. NO BET.

John Toppa Jr.: First claiming effort for something that has not run in more than two months, has not even worked out over the track, and has yet to show a lick of speed. NO BET.

Kymry: In four races during the last month has been whipped by a total of ninety-four lengths, beating exactly two of the fifty horses it faced. NO BET.

Beau Star: Chronic also-ran may do better at longer distance. NO BET.

The contenders are Sean Mor and Calizon. Rated off the Saratoga race, when he ended a two-year layoff by running faster than any horse in today's field has ever run, Calizon seems by far the better choice. Gustines now knows the colt's ways and will help, as will that sharp effort in Maryland five days ago. The possibility that Sean Mor might carry its early speed farther than usual is not overwhelming. If it quit to $6,500 maidens, it could quit to $5,000 ones. Its chances would seem brighter if that last race had been in better company and just a touch braver.

The Running of the Race

SENOR LURO'S MANEUVERS with the Barbizon colt were lost on the Aqueduct throng, which put most of its money on Fiesta Day. The smart dough went to Calizon, however, and he became the second choice at an incredibly liberal 6.90–1. Gustines was left at the post, but had enough horse to eat up everything in sight, muddy track or no muddy track. With a better start, the horse could have won by twelve lengths. It is interesting that Gustines seemed to realize this and did not punish the horse in the backstretch, allowing him to catch up on his own superior class and courage. If ever there was one, here was a case of a four-year-old maiden incomparably superior in class and condition to any of the three-year-old non-winners in his race.

FIRST RACE | **6 FURLONGS. (Near Man, July 17, 1963, 108⅗, 3, 112.)**

Aqu - 29417
November 29, 1966

Maidens. Claiming. Purse $3,500. 3-year-olds and upward. Weights, 3-year-olds 122 lbs., older 124 lbs. Claiming price, $5,000. 2 lbs. for each $500 to $4,000.

Value to winner $2,275, second $700, third $350, fourth $175. Mutuel pool $107,707.

Index	Horse	Eqt A Wt	PP	St	¼	½	Str	Fin	Jockey	Cl'g Pr	Owner	Odds $1
29330Lrl2	—Calizon	4 124	8	14	12¹¹½	8²	2²	1½	H Gustines	5000	T C Quisenberry	6.90
29363Aqu2	—Fiesta Day	b 3 113	11	1	3½	1¹½	1³	2²½	E Cardone5	4000	J E Smith	1.30
29363Aqu9	—Australian Sky	b 3 118	3	8	9h	6¹	5³	3¹	R Ferraro	4C00	R Titus	12.00
29019Kee8	—Marie W.	4 121	7	7	7²	7¹	3³	4½	R Turcotte	5000	Claybrook Stable	30.90
28965GS	—Polly Bell	b 3 119	10	10	8¹½	9¹½	4¹	5⁴	M Sorr'ntino	5000	F J Viggiani	48.10
29363Aqu5	—Beau Star	b 3 118	14	13	13⁵	12³	7²	6nk	J Ruane‡	40C0	J Shanbrom	10.90
25041Nar10	—John Toppa Jr.	3 118	12	9	11h	11¹	6¹	7¹½	J Combest	4000	J M Toppa Jr	9.90
29363Aqu6	—Billie's Lassie	3 108	5	12	14	13²	9²	8³	F Font7	4000	Grandview Stable	51.80
29363Aqu7	—Bold Fool	3 118	4	3	4¹	5³	10¹	9¹½	E Belmonte	4000	E M O'Brien	7.90
29365Aqu8	—Sean Mor	b 3 118	2	4	1¹½	2h	8h	10¹½	A Cordero	4000	J F Dorrian	10.90
29363Aqu12	—Private Plane	b 4 115	1	11	10½	14	13³	11h	R Morgan5†	4000	L C Ostrer	f-9.40
29363Aqu10	—Najecam	b 4 117	9	5	2h	3¹	11½	12nk	R Stovall	4000	Jan Siegel	49.50
29363Aqu13	—Kymry	b 3 118	13	2	5½	4¹½12½	13⁴		O Rosado	4000	Florence Lange	f-9.40
29363Aqu8	—Youngs Road	b 3 118	6	6	6⁴	10²	14	14	L Gilligan	4000	Mrs E H Hogan	f-9.40

f-Mutuel field. †Two pounds apprentice allowance waived. ‡Five pounds.

Time .22⅖, .47⅕, 1.13⅘ (with wind in backstretch). Track muddy.

Official Program Numbers ↘

$2 Mutuel Prices:

6-CALIZON	15.80	5.60	4.00
9-FIESTA DAY		3.00	2.60
2-AUSTRALIAN SKY			6.20

Ch. g, by Barbizon—Jacalu, by Princequillo. Trainer H. A. Luro. Bred by W. L. Jones Jr.

IN GATE AT 12.00. OFF AT 12.00½ EASTERN STANDARD TIME. Start good. Won driving.

CALIZON, away sluggishly and unhurried through run down backstretch, commenced to advance from between horses on rounding turn and wore down FIESTA DAY in closing stages. The latter, never far back, moved to fore when ready from outside midway of turn, drew well clear in upper stretch and just failed to last. AUSTRALIAN SKY found his best stride too late. MARIE W. loomed menacingly in upper stretch but could not sustain her bid. BOLD FOOL could not keep pace. SEAN MOR stopped badly. NAJECAM showed good early speed.
MOR stopped badly. NAJECAM showed good early speed.

Scratched—29363Aqu3 Burny Bee, 29264GS2 Gout, 29372Aqu1 Surely B. Kind.

---

5. THIRD AT AQUEDUCT, NOVEMBER 18, 1966—Track Fast

SPEED IS the chief factor in handicapping the shorter sprints programed for two-year-olds during spring and summer. But when the youngsters begin running six furlongs, pace becomes important. The two-year-old with the fastest previous final time at the distance is by no means a cinch in a race at six furlongs or beyond.

At a quick glance we recognize that this is a good maiden race. Most of the entrants have had very few starts and have not yet established themselves as duds. Several are from outstanding barns. Many are products of topnotch sires.

3d Race Aqueduct

▼Start — 6 FURLONGS — AQUEDUCT — ▲Finish

6 FURLONGS. (Near Man, July 17, 1963, 1.08⅗, 3, 112.)
Maidens. Special weight. Purse $4,200. Fillies. 2-year-olds. Weight 119 lbs.

Stormy Love — Ch. f (1964–Ky), by Promised Land—Michael's Angel, by Goya II — **119** — 1966 2 M 0 0 —
I. Bieber H. Jacobs (Bieber-Jacobs Stables)
11Nov66-4Aqu sly 7f .23 .46⅘1.26 f-MdSpWt 10 1 810 911 88 52¾ LPincayJr 119 43.50 73–17 Imanative 119no Forty Merry's 1192 Prejudice 119¾ Late foot 10
4Nov66-5Aqu fst 6f .22⅗ .46⅘1.12⅖ f-MdSpWt 7 10 1210 1191½ 1214 1213 WBlum 119 45.90 68–20 Sports Event 1192 Allofthem 119½ Helpful 1193 Never close 13
LATEST WORKOUTS Nov 8 Aqu 4f fst .48⅗ h Oct 31 Aqu 4f fst .49 b Oct 27 Aqu 6f fst 1.17 bg Oct 24 Aqu 5f fst 1.03 bg

What a Heart — Ch. f (1964–Fla), by Arrogate—Slideness, by Cable — **119** — 1966 1 M 0 0 —
Pepper Patch Farm N. Walker (Mrs. E. Marienhoff)
4Nov66-5Aqu fst 6f .22⅗ .46⅘1.12⅖ f-MdSpWt 2 5 108¾ 98¾ 910 911 LGilligan 119 79.90 70–20 Sports Event 1192 Allofthem 119½ Helpful 1193 Never close 13
LATEST WORKOUTS Nov 14 Bel m.t. 4f gd .50 b Nov 10 Bel m.t. 5f fst 1.01⅗ h Oct 29 Bel m.t. 5f fst 1.03⅗ h Oct 24 Bel m.t. 5f fst 1.02⅕ h

Royal Dispatch — Ch. f (1964–Ky), by Princequillo—The Runner, by Olympia — **119** — 1966 0 M 0 0 —
High Tide Stable L. S. Barrera (E. G. Burke)
LATEST WORKOUTS Nov 12 Bel tr.t. 3f my .36⅗ h Nov 5 Bel m.t. 7f fst 1.28 h Oct 28 Bel m.t. 6f fst 1.15⅖ hg Oct 24 Bel m.t. 3f fst .36⅕ bg

Secret Practice — Gr. f (1964–Md), by Native Dancer—Home-Made, by Occupy — **119** — 1966 1 M 0 0 —
A. G. Vanderbilt W. C. Freeman (A. G. Vanderbilt)
4Nov66-5Aqu fst 6f .22⅗ .46⅘1.12⅖ f-MdSpWt 9 11 98¾ 1210 1114 1112 HGustines 119 17.40 69–20 Sports Event 1192 Allofthem 119½ Helpful 1193 Never close 13
LATEST WORKOUTS Nov 15 Aqu 4f fst .48⅘ h Nov 10 Aqu 4f fst .50⅖ b Nov 3 Aqu 3f sly .37 b Oct 30 Aqu 6f fst 1.18⅗ b

Yirrkala — Ch. f (1964–Ky), by Gallant Man—Riverina, by Princequillo — **119** — 1966 2 M 0 0 —
King Ranch Max Hirsch (King Ranch)
8Nov66-5Aqu fst 6f .22⅕ .45⅗1.12⅖ f- Allow 8 8 914 813 812 64¾ JRuane 112 50.90 76–18 Sweet Laura 112¾ Pays to Sing 1072½ Murmuring 1161½ Late bid 9
14Oct66-5Aqu fst 7f .23 .46⅕1.26⅖ f-MdSpWt 12 8 1310 1112 1112 118½ DHidalgo 119 19.00 65–19 Harem Lady 119h Heladi 119no Vertical 119½ Never close 14
LATEST WORKOUTS Nov 15 Bel m.t. 6f fst 1.18 b Nov 12 Bel m.t. 3f my .35⅗ hg Nov 3 Bel m.t. 3f sly .40 b Oct 31 Bel m.t. 6f fst 1.17 b

Convertible Deb — B. f (1964–Ky), by Sunglow—Harvey's Delight, by Papa Redbird — **119** — 1966 1 M 0 0 —
Mrs. J. Grabosky E. W. King (C. W. Hayes, Jr.)
11Nov66-1GS sly 6f .22⅘ .47⅕1.13⅗ Md 5000 2 9 97½ 1015 1016 1119 LSantos b 116 64.70 57–22 Island Hop 107¾ Fuel King 117no Colossal Dream 1172 No speed 12
LATEST WORKOUTS Nov 5 GS 4f fst .51⅖ b Nov 2 GS 5f fst 1.06 b Oct 26 GS 4f fst .52 b

Dana's Flight — Ch. f (1964–Va), by Misty Flight—Babadana, by Flushing II — **119** — 1966 6 M 1 2 $1,765
D. H. Ingalls W. B. Cocks (Mrs. F. Ingalls)
14Oct66-5Aqu fst 7f .23 .46⅕1.26⅖ f-MdSpWt 13 2 21 3½ 1h 63¾ JCruguet 119 23.00 70–19 Harem Lady 119h Heladi 119no Vertical 119½ Short lead, tired 14
26Sep66-4Atl fst 6f .22⅗ .47⅖1.13⅗ f-MdSpWt 9 1 3nk 41½ 43½ 411 ENelson 117 5.70 63–29 Guinevere 1176 Gusher 1174 Anna Vertex 117½ Vied for lead, tired 12
19Sep66-4Atl fst 6f .22⅖ .46 1.11 f-MdSpWt 1 7 72½ 77¼ 23 26 ENelson 117 8.50 81–12 SillySession 1176 Dana'sFlight 1171 AnnaVertex 117nk Second best 12
5Sep66-1Atl fst 6f .22⅘ .46⅗1.13⅕ f-MdSpWt 10 4 51¼ 45 45¼ 34¾ SBrooks 117 5.00 71–17 Tumble Clara 117nk Jo Marel 1174½ Dana's Flight 117no Rallied 12
15Aug66-5Atl sly 6f .22⅘ .46⅘1.13⅘ f-MdSpWt 6 5 52 31 32½ 33½ SBrooks 117 62.20 69–24 Salad Bowl 1172½ Gusher 1171 Dana's Flight 1174 Went well 10
3Aug66-5Mth fst 6f .22⅘ .46⅗1.12⅗ f-MdSpWt 10 11 117½ 1112 913 911 SBrooks 117 17.30 68–19 Game Maid 117nk La Chunga 1171½ Miss C. 1172 Far off pace 12
LATEST WORKOUTS Nov 16 Lrl 3f fst .36⅖ h Nov 10 Lrl 5f fst 1.01⅗ h Nov 5 Lrl 5f fst 1.02⅖ b Oct 23 Bel tr.t. 3f fst .37⅖ b

Dance for Joy — B. f (1964–Ky), by Johns Joy—Hasty Act, by Hasty Road — **119** — 1966 5 M 0 0 —
Mrs. W. Gilroy K. E. Jensen (W. Gilroy)
4Nov66-5Aqu fst 6f .22⅗ .46⅘1.12⅖ f-MdSpWt 3 2 2h 109 1013 1318 MSorrentino 119 46.70 63–20 Sports Event 1192 Allofthem 119½ Helpful 1193 Speed, stopped 13
28Oct66-4Aqu fst 7f .23 .46⅖1.26⅕ f-MdSpWt 7 4 11½ 11½ 1419 1414 WBlum 119 42.00e 61–18 Jester's Belle 1191 Imanative 119nk Sumtex 119h Stopped 14
19Aug66-4Sar fst 6f .22⅗ .46⅕1.12⅘ f-MdSpWt 9 1 1½ 21 815 819 MVenezia 119 38.80 65–13 ChantillyJewel 1191½ She'sBeautiful 1195 PureHoney 114no Used up 9
6Jly 66-6Aqu fst 5½f.22⅘ .46⅘1.06⅕ f-MdSpWt 8 7 31½ 54½ 817 828 WBoland 119 59.90 54–20 Gay Gobha 1192½ Needles Lady 1194 Imanative 1192 Tired 9
29Jun66-3Aqu fst 5½f.22⅗ .46⅗1.06⅘ f-MdSpWt 2 8 77 68¾ 98 1011 JLRotz 119 44.10 68–17 ShirleyHeights119nk NeedlesLady119no ♦On the Carpet1193½ No f't'r 12
LATEST WORKOUTS Nov 17 Bel tr.t. 3f fst .37⅗ b Oct 27 Bel tr.t. 3f fst .37 h Oct 22 Bel m.t. 4f fst .50 bg Oct 15 Bel tr.t. 6f fst 1.16 h

Sumtex — B. f (1964–Ky), by Vertex—Miss Summons, by Helioscope — **119** — 1966 4 M 1 2 $1,435
E. M. O'Brien E. M. O'Brien (B. P. Walden)
28Oct66-4Aqu fst 7f .23 .46⅖1.26⅕ f-MdSpWt 5 8 43 21½ 44½ 31¼ MVenezia 119 13.30 74–18 Jester's Belle 1191 Imanative 119nk Sumtex 119h No mishap 14
3Aug66-5Mth fst 6f .22⅘ .46⅗1.12⅗ f-MdSpWt 7 3 74¼ 77¼ 57 55¼ SBoulmetis 117 *1.50 74–19 Game Maid 117nk La Chunga 1171½ Miss C. 1172 Had no mishap 12
12Jly 66-5Mth fst 5½f.22⅘ .47⅕1.06⅘ f-MdSpWt 7 12 74¾ 55½ 44 24 RFerraro 117 3.40 79–18 La Meme Chose 1174 Sumtex 117¾ Game Maid 117¾ Dwelt at start 12
29Jun66-3Aqu fst 5½f.22⅗ .46⅗1.06⅘ f-MdSpWt 4 9 98 79¾ 66 3nk RFerraro 119 ♦12.00 79–17 ShirleyHeights119nk NeedlesLady119no ♦On the Carpet1193½ Rallied 12
27Jun66—♦-Dead heat.
LATEST WORKOUTS Nov 16 Bel tr.t. 3f fst .37⅖ b Oct 24 Bel tr.t. 4f fst .50 h Oct 17 Bel tr.t. 5f fst 1.03⅖ b Oct 12 Bel m.t. 4f fst .49 b

Stormy Love: A slow starter, came on nicely toward the finish of a seven-furlong race last week. Needs more ground to show what she can do. NO BET.

What A Heart: Showed nothing in her debut. NO BET.

Royal Dispatch: Well-bred newcomer has been working nicely, if not spectacularly. Will have to be granted a chance if everything else in the race proves as unpromising as the first two we looked at. CONTENDER.

Secret Practice: The Vanderbilt filly has not been working well enough to suggest great improvement over that bad first outing. NO BET.

Yirrkala: Max Hirsch started this one in a seven-furlong maiden race and came back with it against allowance horses. After a dismal start, it showed a good deal of pep in the final stages. The November 12 workout and the switch to a top gate boy, Walter Blum, indicate that Hirsch is doing what he can to get this thing into the running earlier than usual. CONTENDER.

Convertible Deb: That dismal effort against cheap maidens in New Jersey slams the door here. NO BET.

Dana's Flight. On October 14 ran well enough through the first three-quarter-mile of a seven-furlong race. The layoff of more than a month is, however, a black mark. When ready to win, horses are given the chance to try—unless something is wrong. NO BET.

Dance For Joy: Has been stopping too badly. NO BET.

Sumtex: The October 28 effort was a lulu. Running close to the pace at the half mile, the filly apparently was pinched off, losing three additional lengths by midstretch. Yet she roared back to within a few leaps of the winner. Her ability to stay reasonably close to the early pace of a six-furlong race and get up in time to contest for the jackpot was strongly indicated in her two Monmouth starts at a shorter distance. That O'Brien will be trying is evident in the fact that he already has tried and come close with what obviously is an honest, improving filly. Furthermore, he has switched to Bill Boland, a marvel at getting the maximum in a stretch run. CONTENDER.

With Yirrkala and Sumtex as contenders, we can eliminate the debutante, Royal Dispatch. Yirrkala seems to be such a slow beginner that the race looks tailor-made for Sumtex. The possibility that Dana's Flight may steal the race seems unlikely, considering the filly's lengthy absence, plus the front-running tendencies of Dance for Joy. The latter should tire Dana's Flight sufficiently to make the late running easy for Sumtex.

The Running of the Race

O'BRIEN'S FILLY was the kind of standout that usually goes to the Aqueduct post at even money or worse. The reason she was allowed to go off at 2.10–1 may be that she had set no speed records in earlier races. But she had shown more speed than anything else in the race, especially when viewed with the pace factor in mind. Dana's Flight was second choice, and Yirrkala was held only a few pennies more cheaply.

We were right about the outcome, but not about the pace. Sumtex, extremely sharp, improved far more than expected. She captured the lead right away, held it with utmost ease and would have won by thirty lengths if Boland had not restrained her.

THIRD RACE   **6 FURLONGS. (Near Man, July 17, 1963, 1.08⅗, 3, 112.)**

Aqu - 29338   Maidens. Special weight. Purse $4,200. Fillies 2-year-olds. Weight 119 lbs.

November 18, 1966

Value to winner $2,730, second $840, third $420, fourth $210. Mutuel pool $241,401.

Index	Horse	Eqt A Wt	PP	St	¼	½	Str	Fin	Jockey	Owner	Odds $1
29111Aqu³	Sumtex	2 119	9	3	1³	1²	1⁷	1⁸	W Boland	E M O'Brien	2.10
29004Aqu⁶	Dana's Flight	2 119	7	1	3ʰ	4½	2¹	2²½	B Baeza	D H Ingalls	3.20
	Royal Dispatch	2 119	3	5	2½	2²	3²	3¹	E Belmonte	High Tide Stable	5.50
29259Aqu⁶	Yirrkala	2 119	5	9	8³	8⁶	7¹⁰	4ⁿᵒ	W Blum	King Ranch	3.70
29285Aqu⁵	Stormy Love	2 119	1	6	5½	7ʰ	6½	5²½	L Pincay Jr	I Bieber	6.30
29232Aqu⁹	What a Heart	2 119	2	2	5¹	5¹	4ʰ	6ʰ	L Gilligan	Pepper Patch Farm	44.60
29232Aqu¹¹	Secret Pract'e b	2 119	4	7	6³	3ʰ	5²	7¹⁴	H Gustines	A G Vanderbilt	12.90
29232Aqu¹³	Dance for Joy	2 119	8	4	4¹½	6¹	8⁵	8²½	M Sorrentino	Mrs W Gilroy	44.20
29273GS¹¹	Con'tible Deb b	2 119	6	8	9	9	9	9	R Ferraro	Mrs J Grabosky	117.00

Time .22⅗, .46⅕, 1.11⅕ (with wind in bacsktretch). Track fast.

$2 Mutuel Prices:
9-SUMTEX	6.20	3.20	2.40
7-DANA'S FLIGHT		4.00	2.80
3-ROYAL DISPATCH			3.60

B. f, by Vertex—Miss Summons, by Helioscope. Trainer E. M. O'Brien. Bred by B. P. Walden (Ky.).

IN GATE AT 1.03. OFF AT 1.03 EASTERN STANDARD TIME. Start good. Won easily.

SUMTEX moved to a commanding lead at once, saved ground to increase her advantage at will on entering stretch and won pulled up. DANA'S FLIGHT pasesd only tiring horses. ROYAL DISPATCH tired badly after prompting the issue to top of stretch. YIRRKALA and STORMY LOVE were without speed in dull performances. DANCE FOR JOY stopped badly.

6. FOURTH AT DELAWARE, JUNE 28, 1967—Track Fast

HERE'S A SNUG little middle-distance event that should inspire any player who likes money. While it has one fairly unusual feature, it does arrange itself with complete logic when the fundamentals of handicapping are applied.

The preliminary glance shows that the field includes some highly regarded maidens, as a race of this kind should. The owners include Harbor View and C. V. Whitney. Of the eight entrants, six are owned by the original breeders. On the other hand, several have run rather more often than speaks well for an expensive maiden. In general, the handicapper favors maidens which have not yet become accustomed to losing.

4th Race Delaware

1 1-16 MILES
DELAWARE PARK
▲Start ▲Finish

1 1-16 MILES. (Lady's Maid, June 11, 1960, 1.41⅘, 3, 106.)
Maidens. Special weights. Purse $3,700. 3-year-olds and upward. Weights 3-year-olds 114 lbs., older 122 lbs.

Duke Cannon — Ch. c (1964-Fla), by Alicibiades II—Polly Toogood, by Darius — Harbor View Farm — I. H. Parke — (Harbor View Farm) — **114**
1967 6 M 1 0 $965
1966 9 M 3 0 $2,940

15Jun67-3Del fm*1½ Hurdles 2.45 Md Sp Wt 7 5 66 31½ 21½ 2¾ CMoore 145 3.30 ---- Blockbuster 145¾ Duke Cannon 1457 Fiddler 1455 Gamely 8
5May67-5Aqu fst 7f .22⅖ .45⅕1.25⅖ Md 12500 1 13 1315 1213 77½ 77¾ JLRotz b 114 8.10 72-19 Participant120¾ Plymouth Pilgrim1141½ Brazen Blue114nk No thr't 14
22Apr67-5Aqu fst 6f .22⅕ .45⅗1.10⅘ Clm 16000 8 10 1014 1014 1019 1025 HGustines b 116 85.00 64-16 Babar 1163 Quaker City 116nk Popsie Doodle 1163 Slow start 10
31Mar67-6Aqu fst 6f .22⅗ .46⅕1.11⅗ Clm 20000 4 9 811 88¼ 912 1015 HGustines b 116 55.20 70-23 Dandy Steal 1162 Quaker City 105no Popsie Doodle 1155 No speed 10
7Mar67-8GP fst 6f .22⅕ .45 1.10⅖ Clm 20000 1 9 610 613 611 69 LMoyers b 116 24.00 83-17 Black Fleet 1164½ S'Cool 112¾ Besieger 114¾ Never a contender 9
19Jan67-5Hia fst 6f .22⅖ .45⅘1.12 Clm 16000 10 11 912 811 78½ 42¼ JVasquez b 116 21.40 82-17 Quaich 112h Burning Bridges 1112 Unexpected 116nk Late foot 11
24Oct66-5Aqu fst 1 .47⅗1.13⅕1.38⅘ Md Sp Wt 8 9 74¾ 88¼ 99 108¼ EFires b 122 *3.50 66-22 Savin Rock 122no Quiet Town 122no Vinces Choice 1121 Dull 13
12Oct66-3Aqu fst 7f .23 .46⅗1.25⅖ Md Sp Wt 5 11 95½ 88¼ 54½ 47½ JLRotz b 122 *2.80 71-18 Shah 1221½ Quiet Town 1222 Shadow Brook 1224 In close late 14
2Aug66-6Sar fst 5½f.22⅗ .47⅖1.06⅗ Md Sp Wt 11 11 98 86¼ 21½ 22 KKnapp b 122 6.10 82-14 Stamp Act 1222 Duke Cannon 122'½ Balouf 1222½ Wide, slow start 11
22Jly66-5Aqu fst 5½f.22⅖ .46 1.05⅘ Md Sp Wt 3 7 76½ 56 35 24½ BBaeza b 122 4.30 79-19 Monitor 1224½ Duke Cannon 122h Fort Marcy 1221½ Finished well 12
14Jly66-4Aqu fst 5½f.22⅘ .46⅕1.05⅗ Md 18000 5 6 54½ 54 34½ 21 KKnapp b 118 17.20 84-12 Unexpected 1181 Duke Cannon 118½ Big House 1185 Closed fast 10
7Jly66-4Aqu fst 5½f.22⅖ .46⅗1.06⅖ Md 18000 9 11 1218 1217 1217 1011 WBlum 122 25.40 70-15 Sun Seeker 1201½ Go To It 1202½ Pipes O'Pan 122¾ Bore out 12
23Jun66-4Aqu fst 5½f.22⅗ .46⅗1.06⅕ Md 18000 6 8 610 59 52½ 510 HGustines 118 17.60 72-17 Excathedra 122no SunSeeker 1186 SunStream 1203 Raced wide 8
LATEST WORKOUTS Jun 27 Bel tr.t. 4f fst .49⅖ h Jun 23 Bel 7f sly 1.29⅗ h Jun 13 Bel tr.t. 5f fst 1.02⅕ h Jun 12 Bel tr.t. 4f fst .49⅖ h

Sky Epic — Ch. g (1964-Va), by Western Sky II—Odyssey, by Orestes II — Mrs. W. Whittaker — N. L. Haymaker — (Mrs. H. C. Whittaker) — **114**
1967 3 M 0 1 $400
1966 0 M 0 0

20Jun67-5Del sf 1 Ⓣ 1.42 Md Sp Wt 3 5 58 511 512 38¾ RLAdams b 114 17.80 56-26 Victory Step 1142¾ Fool's Paint 1236 Sky Epic 114½ Rallied 8
5Jun67-4Del fst 6f .22⅗ .46 1.11⅖ Md Sp Wt 5 9 99 913 811 612 RKimball 113 56.20 76-14 Noah's Ark 1131½ Piercer 1062½ Meravis 113½ Not a threat 9
10May67-3Pim fst 6f .23⅗ .47⅘1.13⅖ Md Sp Wt 9 12 1215 1114 1011 1011 ORosado 113 97.70 72-17 High Kicker 113no Piercer 1061 ♦Uncle Blair 1221½ No speed 12
LATEST WORKOUTS Jun 15 Del 7f fst 1.30⅖ bg Jun 10 Del t.c. 7f fm 1.31⅘ b May 26 Del 6f fst 1.15⅗ h May 16 Lrl 5f my 1.04 b

Dunmore — Dk. b. or br. f (1964-Ky), by One-Eyed King—Efficient, by Princequillo — A. S. Bowman, Jr. — C. V. B. Cushman, Jr. — (Miss M. Rumsey) — **109**
1967 7 M 2 1 $2,000
1966 1 M 0 0 ——

8Jun67-9Del fm 1 Ⓣ 1.37⅘ Md Sp Wt 5 5 59¼ 27 28 49 RSurrency5 b 106 10.50 77-13 Loopstitch 1144 Jayette 1143 Victory Step 1142 Weakened 11
1Jun67-4Del fst 6f .22⅕ .46 1.12⅗ f-MdSpWt 5 12 1012 912 915 59 WJPassmore b 112 8.80 73-19 Steel Time 112½ Nosoca Joy 1135 Turn White 1132 Slow start 12
12May67-5Pim fst 6f .24 .48⅗1.14⅘ f-MdSpWt 3 5 46 44 52½ 63¼ WJPassmore b 120 3.80 73-15 Sharpness 113no Steel Time 120no Eagle Cloud 1202½ Lacked rally 12
28Apr67-4Pim gd 6f .24 .48⅕1.13 f-MdSpWt 2 6 55 45 26 27 WJPassmore b 120 3.90 78-17 Double Virtue 1207 Dunmore 1207 Tactful 120nk Best of others 7
12Apr67-5Pim fst 6f .23⅘ .48 1.14 f-MdSpWt 2 11 114½ 1112 83¾ 21½ WJPassmore b 120 29.60 78-17 Georgena Terry 1201½ Dunmore 120nk Never Too Far 1201½ Gamely 12
9Mar67-5Pim gd 6f .23⅘ .47⅘1.14 f-MdSpWt 5 12 1211 1017 108¼ 77¾ EMcIvor 120 14.90 72-22 Miss Big Shot 1202 Catty Corner 120no Li'l Foolish 120h Slow st. 12
3Feb67-3Bow fst 6f .23⅗ .47⅗1.13 f-MdSpWt 3 4 33 35 37 39¾ EBelville 120 7.40e 72-23 Missy Royal 1136 Lotis 1203¾ Dunmore 1201½ Lacked late rally 12
9Dec66-5Lrl fst 1 .47⅗1.14 1.40⅕ f-MdSpWt 6 2 21 33 910 1216 OTorres 117 23.80 64-18 Chriscinca 1172 Double Virtue 1172½ Cagey Lady 112½ Stopped 12
LATEST WORKOUTS Jun 27 Del 3f fst .36 h Jun 23 Del 5f sly 1.02⅕ b May 31 Del 3f fst .37⅗ b May 25 Del 3f fst .35⅘ h

Concordant — B. c (1964-Va), by Celtic Ash—Close Harmony, by Ardan — J. E. Hughes — G. L. Ballenger — (J. E. Hughes) — **114**
1967 6 M 0 1 $515
1966 0 M 0 0 ——

20Jun67-5Del sf 1 Ⓣ 1.42 Md Sp Wt 8 7 812 713 612 59¼ RKotenko 114 16.90 56-26 Victory Step 1142¾ Fool's Paint 1236 Sky Epic 114½ No threat 8
8Jun67-9Del fm 1 Ⓣ 1.37⅘ Md Sp Wt 7 10 1016 916 719 716 RKotenko7 b 107 10.70 70-13 Loopstitch 1144 Jayette 1143 Victory Step 1142 No speed 11
2Jun67-9Del fst 170 .47⅘1.13⅕1.43⅘ Md 7500 5 11 1110 68½ 48½ 35¾ RKotenko7 b 105 12.80 75-15 Morningside 112¾ Double Social 1125 Concordant 105no Rallied 11
17May67-4Pim fst 1 1/16 .48⅕1.13⅗1.46⅗ Md Sp Wt 4 11 1111 1113 77 79¼ RKotenko7 b 113 11.40 68-15 Castletown 1205 Classic Charcoal 120no Triumphus 120nk No speed 11
5May67-3Pim fst 1 1/16 .49⅕1.14⅖1.47 Md Sp Wt 3 8 815 89¾ 714 66¾ RKotenko7 b 113 5.50 68-18 Sandigan 1204 AltesseRoyale 109h ClassicCharcoal 1201½ Dull try 8
17Apr67-5Pim sly 6f .23⅖ .48 1.14⅗ Md 7500 9 11 1116 1116 99¼ 46½ RKotenko7 b 113 37.10 70-21 Come On George 120¾ Ed's Pro 120¾ Boondoggle 1185 Mild rally 11
LATEST WORKOUTS Jun 26 Del 4f gd .51 b Jun 16 Del 6f fst 1.16⅕ b Jun 13 Del 4f fst .49⅖ bg Jun 7 Del 5f fst 1.02 b

Never Too Far — Dk. b. or br. f (1964-Ky), by Ambiorix—Farullah, by Nasrullah — Rockburn Farm — C. Wahler — (H. B. Phipps) — **109**
1967 5 M 0 1 $535
1966 6 M 0 1 $645

17Jun67-3Del fst 6f .22⅖ .45⅘1.11⅕ Md Sp Wt 12 3 85¼ 88½ 811 49 RRincon 108 17.90 80-13 King's Palace 1135 I'm Nobody's Fool 1133 Rag Time 1131 No thr't 12
7Jun67-3Del fst 6f .22 .45⅗1.11⅘ f-MdSpWt 10 4 83 66 76¾ 65¾ DDSmith b 111 25.50 80-15 Christata 112¾ Gusher 1132 Cornish Girl 111no No threat 12
1Jun67-4Del fst 6f .22⅕ .46 1.12⅗ f-MdSpWt 7 11 1112 1114 1118 1122 RKimball b 111 10.40 60-19 Steel Time 112½ Nosoca Joy 1135 Turn White 1132 Unruly in gate 12
28Apr67-6Pim gd 6f .24 .48 1.13⅗ f-MdSpWt 8 5 5¾ 66½ 510 58½ NShuk b 120 4.70 73-17 Scottish Heath 113no Ranunculus 1203 Steel Time 1204½ Wide 8
12Apr67-5Pim fst 6f .23⅘ .48 1.14 f-MdSpWt 9 6 61¾ 53¾ 72¾ 31¾ RRincon b 120 21.10 78-17 Georgena Terry 1201½ Dunmore 120nk Never Too Far 1201½ Hung 12
17Nov66-3Lrl fst 1 .48⅕1.14⅗1.41 f-MdSpWt 5 3 31½ 32½ 33½ 511 RRincon b 117 15.00 65-18 Ein Prosit 117¾ Chriscinca 1176 Miss Dilly Dally 1171 Tired 12
10Nov66-5Lrl gd 6f .23⅖ .47⅘1.13⅘ f-MdSpWt 4 8 63½ 55½ 47 39½ RRincon b 117 2.80 74-14 Rocaille 1178 Spring 1121½ Never Too Far 1172½ Even effort 12
2Nov66-2GS fst 6f .22⅗ .46⅘1.12⅖ f-MdSpWt 5 6 3½ 73¾ 64 57 RRincon b 116 8.30 75-17 Kay's Valentine 116no Chriscinca 1165 Hills Best 117½ In close 12
14Oct66-2GS fst 6f .22⅖ .45⅘1.11⅗ f-MdSpWt / 4 51½ 23 23 42¾ HHinojosa h 116 17.50 83-13 ChampagneToni 1161½ Kay'sValentine116nk Chriscinca1161 We'k'n'd 12
LATEST WORKOUTS Jun 25 Del 7f fst 1.31⅗ b Jun 12 Del 4f fst .49⅗ b May 30 Del 4f sl .48⅖ h May 26 Del 3f fst .37⅘ b

```
Pouting              B. c (1964–Pa), by Cat Bridge—Po' Gal, by Valdina Orphan   114  1967 5 M 2 1 $1,750
                     Mrs. G. Watkins    C. D. Gilpin     (G. R. Watkins)             1966 1 M 0 0   $175
16Jun67-1Del  fst 6f .22⅗ .46⅕1.12⅗ Md 6000 12 12 108¼108¾ 44½ 2no ORosado 113 *3.40 82-16 Clover Prince 113no Pouting 113h Sheilas Spotlite 108¹½ Sharp 12
20Mar67-3Pim  fst 6f .23⅗ .47 1.11⅘ Md Sp Wt 1 8 63¾ 45½ 34½ 36 RKotenko7 113 6.90 87-12 Road At Sea 120³ Crack Ruler 120³ Pouting 113² Lacked late rally 9
13Mar67-3Pim  fst 6f .23⅖ .47⅗1.12⅖ Md Sp Wt 7 11 1112 fog 512 26 RKotenko7 113 ♦21.30 82-14 Lynch 120⁶ ♦World's Fairest 120no ♦Pouting 113no Rallied 11
  13Mar67—♦-Dead heat.
10Feb67-3Bow  fst 6f .23⅕ .47⅖1.12⅖ Md Sp Wt 10 9 76¼ 62¾ 46 67¼ AAgnello7 113 *4.50 78-20 Northern Bull 120²½ Make It Platinum 120¹½ Ima Lad 113³ Dull 12
  Jan67-8Bow  fst 7f .23⅕ .46⅘1.26⅕ Allowance 8 3 64¼ 57½ 46½ 45½ EMaple5 108 32.40 76-29 Hail's Image 113³ Grand Todd 120¹ Draw Fast 117¹½ No mishap 10
21Dec66-5Lrl  sly 6f .23⅖ .48⅗1.15⅖ Md Sp Wt 1 9 910 511 47½ 45 EMaple5 113 34.90 70-25 Ballsbridge 118¹½ Secret Ceremony 118³½ Mag Roth 118h No mishap 12
  LATEST WORKOUTS  Jun 27 Del 3f fst .39⅗ b   Jun 13 Del 4f fst .50 b   Jun 7 Del 5f fst 1.03 bg   Jun 3 Del 4f fst .50 b

Big Barb             Ch. c (1964–Ky), by Barbizon—Moonsight, by Mahmoud          114  1967 4 M 1 0 $600
                     C. V. Whitney    I. G. Balding      (C. V. Whitney)             1966 0 M 0 0 ——
14Jun67-4Del  fst 170.47⅘1.13⅕1.43⅘ Md Sp Wt 1 1 3nk 21 22 23½ ORosado 113 6.60 77-15 Jayette 113³½ Big Barb 113¹ Lady Tudor 108³½ Best of rest 8
 8Jun67-2Del  fm 1 Ⓣ 1.37⅖ Md Sp Wt 3 9 915 816 816 811 TLee 114 5.60 77-13 Goguerre 114no Atrevido 123³½ Fool's Paint 123no Dull try 11
31May67-6Del  fst 6f .22⅘ .47⅕1.13⅖ Md Sp Wt 5 9 117¼105¾ 711 57 TLee 113 40.30 71-20 Mighty Nimrod 113¹½ Piercer 106h Jayette 113½ Forced race wide 12
19Apr67-5Aqu  gd 6f .23 .47⅘1.13⅘ Md Sp Wt 10 7 99¾ 912 913 916 WTichenor10 105 66.00 58-26 Tote'm Home 114½ Chorus 114³ Battle Plan 114⁴ Tired 10
  LATEST WORKOUTS  Jun 27 Del 3f fst .37 bg   Jun 21 Del 6f fst 1.16 b   Jun 13 Del 3f fst .35⅘ h   May 29 Del 5f fst 1.03 b

Rag Time             Dk. b. or br. g (1964–Md), by Piano Jim—Tribulation, by Escadru   114  1967 9 M 1 3 $3,749
                     D. Christmas    D. Christmas    (Mr.–Mrs. D. Christmas)         1966 2 M 0 0 ——
17Jun67-3Del  fst 6f .22⅖ .45⅘1.11⅕ Md Sp Wt 6 10 74¼ 56½ 58 38 FLovato b 113 3.80 81-13 King's Palace 113⁵ I'm Nobody's Fool 113³ Rag Time 113¹ No thr't 12
31May67-6Del  fst 6f .22⅘ .47⅕1.13⅖ Md Sp Wt 8 5 84¼ 72¾ 35½ 42 BPulido b 113 *3.10 76-20 Mighty Nimrod 113¹½ Piercer 106h Jayette 113½ Rallied belatedly 12
10May67-3Pim  fst 6f .23⅗ .47⅘1.13⅖ Md Sp Wt 8 8 76½ 65 42½ 31 JKratz b 113 ♦3.50 82-17 High Kicker 113no Piercer 106¹ ♦Uncle Blair 122¹½ Rallied 12
  10May67—♦-Dead heat.
26Apr67-4Pim  gd 6f .24 .47 1.12⅘ Md Sp Wt 1 7 42 43½ 21 2no JKratz b 120 3.00 86-12 Highland Reel 115no Rag Time 120² Piercer 113⁴½ Held on well 8
18Mar67-8Pim  fst 1 1/16 .46⅖1.11⅕1.43 Challedon 5 4 46½ 59 512 416 ACannon 110 22.80 79-12 Gala Performance 119⁴½ Misty Cloud 122⁸ Irish Stile 112³ Bore out 6
 9Mar67-9Pim  fst 1 1/16 .47⅖1.11⅗1.45⅗ Allowance 6 5 58½ 616 614 513 RKimball 112 37.80 69-22 Misty Cloud 119h Corn Caster 105⁴ Irish Stile 112⁶ No factor 7
22Feb67-8Bow  gd 1 1/16 .49 1.14 1.45⅘ Pr.Georges 8 9 88½ 613 717 520 RKimball 110 24.40 64-24 GalaPerformance 113nk MistyCloud 119¹⁰ IrishStile 110¹ No fact'r 9
18Jan67-8Bow  fst 7f .23 .46 1.25⅕ Annapolis 1 5 57¼ 58½ 49 49¾ RKimball 112 69.60 77-26 MistyCloud 122nk GalaPerformance 116⁷ AirGeneral 113²½ No fact. 7
13Jan67-3Bow  fst 6f .23⅘ .47⅘1.14⅗ Md Sp Wt 1 7 42¾ 45 32½ 33¾ RKimball 120 8.80 70-29 Devrex 113³ Make It Platinum 12C¾ Rag Time 120¹½ No mishap 12
12Dec66-5Lrl  gd 1 .48⅖1.15⅕1.40⅗ Md Sp Wt 5 10 96 83¾ 79½ 512 TLe? 118 4.30 66-18 Royal Concert 118³ Big House 118no Thor III 111⁸ Far back 11
29Nov66-3Lrl  my 6f .23⅕ .47⅘1.14⅕ Md Sp Wt 8 11 1014 817 611 55½ SBrooks 118 16.70 76-17 Al's Birthday 118² Badge of Merit 118²½ Ameriverse 115½ Late foot 12
  LATEST WORKOUTS  Jun 27 Del 3f fst .37 b   Jun 21 Del 3f fst .37⅖ b   Jun 14 Del 4f fst .50⅘ b   Jun 10 Del 4f fst .53 b
```

Duke Cannon: Ivan Parke tried to unload this one in claimers last year, found no takers, got a surprisingly good race out of it, and moved it back into maiden-specials. It ran second three times in succession, turned dull, and was rested for three months. This year, after failing dismally against previous winners in claiming company, it lost when entered against maiden claimers. Its only presentable race was thirteen days ago, over the jumps. Even a good stable contains washouts, and this looks like one. NO BET.

Sky Epic: The fair performance on grass after two failures on dirt could mean that this one has tender feet. Or else is a grass horse. NO BET.

Dunmore: A filly that cannot beat fillies cannot beat colts. NO BET.

Concordant: The presumption must be that a horse which races unsuccessfully against $7,500 maidens will be outclassed by several of its rivals in a maiden-special. NO BET.

Never Too Far: Another filly, and with eleven consecutive losses besides. NO BET.

Pouting: This one has shown a great deal of willingness in the stretch of shorter races and may like the mile-and-one-sixteenth. But it rarely makes sense to risk money on a claiming animal in a maiden-special. NO BET.

Big Barb: After three indifferent attempts, the Whitney colt came awake two weeks ago. With breeding and management of this quality, it is reasonable to expect improvement today. CONTENDER.

Rag Time. I said that this race has an unusual feature. This gelding is it. Its eleven winless efforts include starts in three stakes races and an allowance.

It beat three horses in the Annapolis, four in the Prince Georges, and two in the Challedon. It never got really close to the classy leaders in those races or even in the allowance race, but it was racing. Does this mean that it has class? Not necessarily. If it had shown any run at any stage of any of those races, it would have to be credited with some quality. But its mere physical presence in the races does not make a stakes horse of it or even an allowance horse. It has been doing better since moving back into the maiden ranks, but not well enough to win. Its rallies in the two May outings imply that it might like today's distance. CONTENDER.

Big Barb was on the improve last time. Rag Time was not. Big Barb is a lightly raced Barbizon colt from the stables of C. V. Whitney. Rag Time is not. Big Barb is as logical a choice as one ever finds in a race of this calibre. The only kind of animal to bet on against him is the kind that is missing from this race—another lightly raced, influentially sponsored maiden that has been running swiftly and gamely.

The Running of the Race

BEMUSED BY Rag Time's "stakes credentials," the crowd made it a lukewarm favorite. Big Barb got the smart money and second favoritism, with Duke Cannon only slightly less enthusiastically supported.

Ossie Rosado ran into trouble from Duke Cannon at the eighth pole and had to slow down to avoid a collision. But he had enough horse to win going away. Sky Epic ran well, but his suspect underpinnings betrayed him and he bore out when set down for the final drive. Rag Time tried to run on the pace but was unable to stay there.

FOURTH RACE **1 1-16 MILES. (Lady's Maid, June 11, 1960, 1.41⅘, 3, 106.)**

Del - 31511 Maidens. Special weights. Purse $3,700. 3-year-olds and upward. Weights 3-year-olds 114 lbs., older 122 lbs.

June 28, 1967

Value to winner $2,405, second $740, third $270, fourth $185. Mutuel pool $80,185.

Index	Horse	Eqt	A	Wt	PP	St	¼	½	¾	Str	Fin	Jockey	Owner	Odds $1
31403Del^{2}	Big Barb	b	3	114	7	5	5^{2}	$4^{\frac{1}{2}}$	4^{1}	3^{h}	1^{1}	O Rosado	C V Whitney	3.00
31449Del^{3}	Sky Epic	b	3	114	2	2	2^{h}	$2^{\frac{1}{2}}$	2^{1}	$2^{1\frac{1}{2}}$	2no	R L Adams	Mrs W Whittaker	19.90
31411Del^{2}	Duke Cannon	b	3	114	1	7	7^{4}	6^{h}	5^{1}	$4^{\frac{1}{2}}$	$3^{1\frac{1}{2}}$	A Cordero Jr	Harbor View Farm	3.40
31429Del^{4}	Never Too Far	b	3	109	5	1	$1^{1\frac{1}{2}}$	$1^{2\frac{1}{2}}$	$1^{1\frac{1}{2}}$	$1^{\frac{1}{2}}$	4^{1}	R Rincon	Rockburn Farm	11.20
31418Del^{2}	Pouting		3	114	6	4	$6^{2\frac{1}{2}}$	7^{5}	$6^{\frac{1}{2}}$	5^{3}	$5^{3\frac{1}{2}}$	S Brooks	Mrs G R Watkins	4.10
31449Del^{5}	Concordant		3	114	4	8	8	8	8	7^{4}	$6^{1\frac{1}{2}}$	R Kotenko	J E Hughes	22.90
31429Del^{3}	Rag Time	b	3	114	8	6	3^{h}	3^{1}	3^{1}	$6^{\frac{1}{2}}$	$7^{3\frac{1}{2}}$	G Patterson	D Christmas	2.90
31363Del^{4}	Dunmore	b	3	109	3	3	4^{2}	5^{3}	7^{5}	8	8	T Lee	A S Bowman Jr	13.20

Time .23⅘, .47⅘, 1.12⅗, 1.39⅖, 1.45⅗. Track fast.

$2 Mutuel Prices:			
7-BIG BARB	8.00	4.80	3.20
2-SKY EPIC		13.60	7.80
1-DUKE CANNON			3.80

Ch. c, by Barbison—Moonsight, by Mahmoud. Trainer I. G. Balding. Bred by C. V. Whitney (Ky.).

IN GATE AT 3.03. OFF AT 3.03 EASTERN DAYLIGHT TIME. Start good. Won driving.

BIG BARB saved ground reaching contention, coasted a few yards when threatened by interference from DUKE CANNON a furlong out, but then responded gamely to punishment and won going away. SKY EPIC dropped back, steadied behind NEVER TOO FAR around the first turn, remained in closest attendance to the pace, and continued well despite drifting to the middle of the track in the drive. DUKE CANNON, taken back at the start, was urged forwardly after three furlongs, changed course abruptly when blocked by SKY EPIC passing the final furlong marker and then hung. NEVER TOO FAR dropped over to the rail when clear at the first turn, easily set the pace but weakened in the stretch drive. POUTING, reserved for more than a half-mile, circled extremely wide rallying into the stretch and hung. CONCORDANT was sluggish early. RAG TIME was hustled to have a forward placing early and weakened. DUNMORE was steadied behind NEVER TOO FAR around the first turn, then tired.

PART THREE

Handicapping Claiming Races

THE CENTRAL QUESTION about every horse in every claiming race is: "What is the animal doing in this race?"

Translation: "What is the trainer trying to accomplish?"

The handicapper saves much time and effort by studying the record of each horse with a view to answering that question. In process, he settles questions about the distance, class, and condition factors. He may also dispose of the jockey factor at that point, although he often prefers to save that part of the study for later, along with his analysis of pace and weights.

This is by no means the only way to study a race, as readers of my earlier books are fully aware. However, for someone reasonably familiar with what makes the wheels spin in racing, the effort to understand *why the animal is in the race* is the quickest, easiest means to separate legitimate contenders from also-rans.

1. NINTH AT AQUEDUCT, OCTOBER 13, 1966—Track Fast

THE CONDITIONS of this typical New York claimer give weight concessions to animals that have not won recently at a distance, unless the victories were scored in cheap company.

9th Race Aqueduct

1⅛ MILES
AQUEDUCT
Start | Finish

1 1-8 MILES (Sinatra, December 7, 1964, 1.47⅕, 5, 111.)
Claiming. Purse $4,200. 3-year-olds and upward. Weights, 3-year-olds 119 lbs., older 123 lbs. Non-winners of a race at a mile and a furlong or over since Aug. 27 allowed 3 lbs., of a race at a mile or over since then, 5 lbs. Claiming price, $5,000. 2 lbs. allowed for each $500 to $4,000. (Races when entered to be claimed for $3,500 or less not considered.)

```
*Tulyaric            $4,000    B. c (1962), by Branding—Lady Tulyar, by Tulyar              114   1966 16 2 3 0 $1,514
                               J. C. Toomey   J. E. Rich      (Haras El Pelado) (Arg.)           1965  5 1 1 2   $900
 6Oct66-9Aqu  fst 1⅛.47  1.12⅗1.53⅘ Clm   5000  6  4  58½ 46 610 611 HWoodhouse  b 118 18.70 55-24 Get the Point 116nk Express Stop 116¾ El Gordo 1162½   Tired 8
29Sep66-9Aqu  fst 1⅛.48⅖1.13⅘1.51⅗ Clm   5000  1  3  3nk 2h 23 49   HWoodhouse  b 118 49.20 69-18 Aerie 1185 Get the Point 1184 Inhand 115no   Well up, tired 8
24Sep66-1Aqu  fst 6f .23⅕ .47⅖1.13⅖ Clm   5000  5  5  54 76 78 79½   ECardone5   b 112 24.90 66-18 Pinkie Chollie 119½ Tempalado 1171 Donner Pass 117¾   No factor 8
12Sep66-1Aqu  fst 6f .22⅘ .46⅗1.13⅕ Cl  c-4000 10 13  1112 1113 1012 98½ HGustines   117 30.10 68-21 Bull and Bear 114no Chaleur Bay 1171½ Rio Coreo 1192½   No speed 13
 5Sep66-1Aqu  fst 6f .23    .47  1.13⅕ Clm  3500  8  7  66 57 811 88¾ JLRotz       117  5.50 68-25 Petite Milagro 1173½ Rio Coreo 124½ Royal Magician 1122½   Wide 13
27Aug66-4Atl  fst 1⅛.47  1.12⅕1.52⅖ Clm   4000  5  2  2½ 42 77 911  CGonzalez    114 39.50 65-17 Barterville 114no Alibhai Lane 1171 Blue Nahar 1142   Early speed 11
23Aug66-9Atl  sf*1⅛ Ⓣ        2.05⅗ Clm   5000 11  8  812 810 711 513 DBrumfield  113 76.30 ---- d-Disuelto 112¾ Golden Bugles 1155 Admiral Zip 1127   No threat 11
16Aug66-9Atl  gd 1⅛.48⅕1.13⅕1.52⅘ Clm    5000  5  7  812 713 814 822 DBrumfield  116 25.50 52-22 Balanced Budget 1111¼ Mapache II 1179 Seven Hills 1131½   No sp'd 9
11Aug66-5Atl  fst 7f .22⅘ .45  1.24⅕ Clm  7500  5  7  715 714 714 713 DBrumfield  116 23.40 69-23 Chronicie 114h Prince Chris 1184½ Babs' Brother 118¾   Trailed 7
22May66-Rosario (Arg.)  —*6f  1.12⅗ Allowance     6 ———          117 ——  ——  Missing data not available   6
 8May66-Rosario (Arg.)  —*6f  1.12   Allowance     2 ———          126 ——  ——   4
   LATEST WORKOUTS   Oct 11 Bel tr.t. 3f fst .36⅘ h   Oct 4 Bel tr.t. 4f fst .51 b   Sep 17 Be m.t. 3f fst .37 bg

Latin Artist         $5,000    Ch. h (1960), by Tenerani—Nenuphar, by Blue Peter            113⁵  1966 16 1 3 4 $8,035
                               J. Perricone   H. Jacobson     (Bell-Gardiner)                    1965 16 2 0 0 $9,145
 6Oct66-9Aqu  fst 1⅛.47  1.12⅗1.53⅘ Clm   5000  8  8  818 711 45 43½ ECardone5     111  4.10 62-24 Get the Point 116nk Express Stop 116¾ El Gordo 1162½   Rallied 8
16Sep66-9Aqu  fst 1⅛.48⅕1.13⅗1.53⅖ Clm   6250  6  4  39 57½ 49 47½  ECardone5     109  5.80 61-25 Daddy Hains 113h Main Count 1065 Duke's Liberty 1122½   No mis'p 6
 9Sep66-9Aqu  fst 1⅛.49  1.14  1.53  Clm   6250  2  6  611 57 55½ 55½ ECardone5     111  4.40 65-25 Mr. Spinelli 114h Daddy Hains 1132 Ibetu 1181   No mishap 8
 1Sep66-9Aqu  fst 1⅛.48⅗1.14  1.53⅘ Cl  c-5000  6  8  79½ 66 45 35½  LAdams        116  3.90 61-25 Hy-Nat 120½ Motor 1235 Latin Artist 1164   Finished willingly 8
29Jly66-9Aqu  fst 1⅛.49  1.14  1.52⅗ Clm   6500  4  5  714 713 711 511 HWoodhouse   118  6.80 62-17 Ski Dancer 1181½ Rao Raja 1183 Hy-Nat 1163½   Never a threat 7
15Jly66-9Aqu  fst 1⅛.47⅕1.12⅕1.53⅕ Clm   6500  4 10  917 811 52 21½  RTurcotte     118  5.80 68-20 Tobir 1161½ Latin Artist 1182 Hy-Nat 114h   Led between calls 11
 8Jly66-9Aqu  fst 1⅛.48⅖1.13  1.53⅗ Clm   6500  2  4  611 611 25 22½  RTurcotte     118  9.20 65-21 Main Count 1162½ Latin Artist 1186 Del Coronado 113½   Gamely 8
 1Jly66-9Aqu  fst 1⅛.48  1.13⅕1.52⅘ Clm   6500  5  5  612 58 58 511   RTurcotte     118  8.10 61-19 Tobir 111¾ No Kidding 1133 Hy-Nat 1161   Checked in early going 6
    1Jly66—Placed fourth through disqualification.
27May66-9Aqu  fst 1⅛.48⅗1.13⅗1.52⅗ Cl  c-6000  8  8  89 42 96¼ 912  MVenezia      112  7.40 61-18 Aberrant 1142 Street Fair 1162½ Egocentrical 1053   Stopped 9
29Apr66-9Aqu  my 1⅛.48⅘1.13⅕1.52⅖ Clm    6250  6  3  33½ 58 510 612  RUssery       115 *1.60 62-16 Ski Dancer 1111 Go Overboard 1143 Ruperto 1143   Brief speed 6
22Apr66-9Aqu  fst 1⅛.48⅕1.12⅘1.51⅘ Clm   6250  2  2  3½ 41½ 1h 3nk  RUssery     b 115 *1.70 77-14 Street Fair 116nk Nick J. G. 112h Latin Artist 1155   No excuse 6
   LATEST WORKOUTS   Oct 3 Aqu 3f gd .37 b   Aug 27 Bel tr.t. 1m fst 1.48 b

Get the Point ×      $5,000    Ch. g, (1962), by Sword Dancer—Not That, by Devil Diver      123   1966 20 3 3 2 $11,060
                               A. J. Bertilloti   F. Martin   (A. G. Vanderbilt)                 1965 14 M 1 0  $1,260
 6Oct66-9Aqu  fst 1⅛.47  1.12⅗1.53⅘ Clm   5000  5  5  48½ 56 31 1nk   BBaeza      b 116 *2.40 66-24 Get the Point 116nk Express Stop 116¾ El Gordo 1162½   Driving 8
29Sep66-9Aqu  fst 1⅛.48⅖1.13⅘1.51⅗ Clm   5000  5  6  73¾ 73¼ 58 25   BBaeza      b 118  9.70 73-18 Aerie 1185 Get the Point 1184 Inhand 115no   Finished well 8
20Sep66-9Aqu  fst 1⅛.49  1.14⅗1.54  Cl  c-4000  6  3  32½ 42½ 89 810 WBlum       b 116  3.50 56-22 No Problem 113h Andros Isle 1101 Clavero 1201   Early speed 9
 8Sep66-8Aqu  fst 1⅛.48⅖1.14⅘1.54⅘ Clm   5000  3  7  88 78 55½ 54½  DChamb'lin5 b 113 35.40 57-29 Ranchero 1181½ Old Bailey II 1202 Kalapur 118¾   Began slowly 10
 1Sep66-9Aqu  fst 1⅛.48⅗1.14  1.53⅘ Clm   5000  4  5  56 55 610 616  HGustines   b 116 13.30 51-25 Hy-Nat 120½ Motor 1235 Latin Artist 1164   No real threat 8
27Aug66-2Sar  fst 7f .23   .45⅗1.23⅗ Clm   6000  8  2  89¼ 814 712 413 HGustines   b 113 10.20e 79- 8 Gay Orchid 1175 Flannel 1077 Kalapur 115¾   Not a factor 8
20Aug66-9Sar  fst 1⅛.47⅘1.12⅗1.52⅗ Hcp  3500s  8  8  79 712 75¼ 617 HGustines   b 111 20.20 65-10 Aberrant 1223½ Kalonji 114h Motor 1114½   Never a contender 8
21Jun66-9Aqu  fst 1⅛.49  1.14⅖1.54⅘ Cl  c-3500  3  3  36 33 21½ 1½  JLRotz      b 120  4.40 62-24 Get the Point 120½ Peruginoll 1181½ OzarkJet 120no   Strong handling 8
16Jun66-9Aqu  fst 1  .46⅘1.12⅕1.39⅗ Clm   3500  7  6  56 55½ 32½ 2nk RTurcotte   b 120  4.00 70-21 William E. 112nk Get the Point 120¾ Te 1171   Made strong finish 9
11Jun66-1Mth  fst 1 1/16.48⅕1.13⅗1.46⅗ Clm 3750  2 10  1016 87½ 55¼ 56 WZakoor    119 18.50 66-21 Arctic Queen 1102 Joysjon 108½ Dulalet 1152½   Stumbled at start 10
21May66-4Aqu  fst 6f .22⅕ .45⅖1.11⅕ Clm   4500  3  7  715 714 713 79¼ JCombest      115 53.10 78-15 Gay Orchid 1215 Charge Hill 1191½ Oribi 117½   Trailed field 7
14May66-2Aqu  fst 7f .23   .46⅖1.24⅖ Clm   4500  7  2  88¼ 99 916 921 HGustines     115 13.80 63-13 King Salmon 1177 Hindoo II 1173½ William E. 108no   Far back 9
   LATEST WORKOUTS   Sep 28 Bel tr.t. 4f fst .51 b   Sep 18 Bel m.t. 6f fst 1.17 b

Inhand               $4,500    Dk. b or br. c (1963-Fla), by Like Magic—Lowestoff, by Annapolis  114  1966 23 3 4 4 $12,620
                               Mrs. S. Westfall   R. B. Murray   (W. O. Peterson)                 1965 13 2 2 2  $5,455
 6Oct66-9Aqu  fst 1⅛.47  1.12⅗1.53⅘ Clm   5000  2  6  611 610 814 815 JLRotz        116  9.90 51-24 Get the Point 116nk Express Stop 116¾ El Gordo 1162½   No speed 8
29Sep66-9Aqu  fst 1⅛.48⅖1.13⅘1.51⅗ Clm   5000  4  5  52¼ 52½ 47 39   JLRotz        115  5.40 69-18 Aerie 1185 Get the Point 1184 Inhand 115no   Made fair try 8
21Sep66-1Aqu  sly 6f .23   .46⅘1.12⅗ Clm   5000  5  8  85¼ 78 610 59½  ECardone5     114  6.10 70-24 Son of Roman 1145 Hip Shooter 116h Dance Contest 1122½   No threat 10
 8Sep66-9Aqu  fst 1  .48⅗1.14⅗1.41   Cl  c-4000  7  6  51¾ 42 32 1no   CMcPeek5      112 *2.10 63-29 Inhand 112no Pinchers Pride 115no Space Control 1151½   Just up 10
30Aug66-8Aqu  fst 1  .46⅕1.11⅗1.39⅕ Clm   5000  6  8  68½ 44 35 23½   CMcPeek5      112 *3.70 68-22 James A. P. 1163½ Inhand 1122½ Good Reputation 119h   Gamely 10
24Aug66-2Sar  gd 6f .22⅗ .46⅘1.13⅕ Clm    4500  1  5  64½ 52½ 42½ 42¾ DChamberlin5 117  4.80 79-17 Good Reputation 1192½ James A. P. 119h Burny Bee 108h   No mish'p 6
 1Jly66-8Aqu  fst 1  .46⅕1.11⅘1.38⅗ Cl  c-5000  7  5  43¼ 22 21 1½   LAdams        116  2.20 75-19 Inhand 116½ Pinchers Pride 112no Tigris River 1193½   Driving 8
24Jun66-9Aqu  fst 1⅛.47⅘1.13⅘1.54  Clm    5000  6  4  43 2h 1½ 21½    LAdams        112  6.80 64-21 Victaray 1131½ Inhand 1122½ Egocentrical 118¾   Second best 7
17Jun66-8Aqu  fst 1  .46⅕1.12  1.40⅕ Clm   5000  5  5  57½ 58 49 33½   LAdams        117  3.00 63-22 Venetian Music 1121½ Lt. Lynn 1072 Inhand 117nk   Strong finish 6
 4Jun66-9Aqu  fst 1⅛.48  1.12⅖1.52⅕ Hcp  5000s  5  5  69 915 914 916  LLoughry      107  5.20e 59-14 Mebs Last 118½ Sparkling Earth 113nk Ruperto 1125   Far back 10
31May66-2Aqu  fst 1  .45⅖1.10⅘1.38⅗ Clm   5000  5  6  68¼ 56 44½ 31¾  LAdams      b 116  4.40 73-22 Tigris River 1161 Twilight Love 113¾ Inhand 1161½   Finished fast 8
24May66-2Aqu  fst 7f .22⅗ .45⅘1.25⅕ Clm   5000  6  9  86¾ 75¼ 45 25   LAdams      b 116 12.20 75-20 Roma Deck 1135 Inhand 116¾ Flight Tracer 105nk   Made game effort 9
   LATEST WORKOUTS   Aug 20 Sar tr.t. 5f fst 1.04⅗ b
```

***Clavero ×** $4,500 B. h (1959) by Timor—Claveta, by Claro 111⁵ 1966 20 5 2 5 $16,745
Louise Horan F. J. Horan (Haras Don Santiago)(Arg.) 1965 21 6 7 2 $22,323
27Sep66-9Aqu fst 1⅛.48⅗1.13⅗1.52⅗ Cl c-3500 7 2 2½ 1h 34 410 HWoodhouse 123 7.90 63-21 Express Stop 1203 Golden Mike 1163 Kalapur 1114 Used up 12
20Sep66-9Aqu fst 1⅛.49 1.14⅗1.54 Clm 3500 2 1 12 11 2½ 31 HWoodhouse 120 3.70 65-22 No Problem 113h Andros Isle 1101 Clavero 1201 Much used 9
6Sep66-9Aqu fst 1⅛.49⅕1.15 1.56 Clm 3500 1 1 13 13 13 1nk HWoodhouse 119 5.10 56-28 Clavero 119nk North Channel 113no Halloween 113½ Hard drive 6
30Aug66-9Aqu fst 1⅛.48⅖1.14⅕1.54⅖ Clm 3500 1 1 1h 1½ 47 414 DChamberlin5 118 d 1.70 50-22 Never Wrong 12310 North Channel 1173½ Carino 112nk Bore out 6
30Aug66—d-Disqualified and placed last.
23Aug66-9Sar sly 1⅛.47 1.12⅕1.54⅕ Clm 3500 1 1 11½ 14 11 11 HWoodhouse 116 *0.60 74-15 Clavero 1161 Carino 1118 Supply 1066 Bore out driving 6
16Aug66-9Sar fst 1⅛.47⅖1.13 1.54⅕ Clm 3500 6 2 1½ 12 1½ 2¾ HWoodhouse 116 3.60 73-16 Never Wrong 116¾ Clavero 1162½ Motor 1238 Made game effort 10
9Aug66-9Sar fst 1⅛.48⅖1.13⅘1.54⅖ Clm 3500 2 4 64½ 45 33½ 34½ ECardone5 110 *2.00 68-17 Motor 1174 Carino 115½ Clavero 1104 Wide early, evenly 8
21Jly 66-9Aqu fst 1⅛.48 1.13⅕1.53⅗ Clm 4500 1 1 15 12 32½ 54½ WBlum 118 5.80 63-21 Old Bailey II 1201 Hy-Nat 123½ Daddy Hains 1113 Used early 7
28Jun66-9Aqu fst 1⅛.49⅗1.14⅖1.53⅖ Cl c-3500 7 1 11 2h 33 38 EBelmonte 123 8.20 61-19 Showell's Best 1183 Perugino II 1185 Clavero 1231½ Tired 11
21Jun66-5Aqu fst 7f .23⅖ .47⅕1.25⅗ Clm 4000 2 7 72¾ 76¼ 86¾ 811 ACordero 117 5.70 67-24 William E. 110¾ Bobandit 1161½ New Recruit 119½ No mishap 12
14Jun66-9Aqu fst 1⅛.48⅘1.14⅖1.54⅗ Clm 3500 7 1 13 11½ 1h 31¾ RUssery 120 3.00 61-19 Bobandit 111¾ Filisteo II 1181 Clavero 120¾ Used setting pace 7
LATEST WORKOUTS Oct 11 Bel tr.t. 4f fst .51 b Sep 14 Aqu 4f fst .51⅗ b

Space Control $4,500 Ch c (1963-Tex), by Zenith—Great Weapon, by Brazado 114 1966 18 6 0 2 $15,085
S. Friedfertig T. J. Gullo (King Ranch) 1965 5 M 0 0 ——
24Sep66-9Aqu fst 1 .48⅘1.15⅕1.42 Clm 4000 5 8 86¼ 52½ 3½ 11 ACordero b 117 *3.20 58-18 Space Control 1171 Barricado 115h Start Dancing 1151 Driving 8
17Sep66-1Aqu fst 7f .22⅘ .46⅖1.26⅘ Clm 3500 1 7 75¼ 77 1½ 12½ ACordero 115 *2.50 72-18 Space Control 1152½ Enchanter 115½ Validated 117½ Ridden out 11
8Sep66-9Aqu fst 1 .48⅗1.14⅗1.41 Clm 3500 8 7 4¾ 21 21 3h MYcaza b 115 5.10 63-29 Inhand 112no Pinchers Pride 115no Space Control 1151½ Game 10
30Aug66-1Aqu fst 6f .22⅘ .47 1.13⅗ Clm 3500 8 9 108½ 99¼ 711 67¾ ACordero b 122 4.20 67-22 Son of Roman 117h Lakythra 1122½ Dark Doings 115nk Wide late 10
30Jly 66-1Aqu fst 6f .23⅗ .47⅗1.13⅕ Clm 3500 8 7 63 44½ 31 11 ACordero b 119 4.00 77-22 Space Control 1191 James A. P. 117¾ Black Rod 110½ Driving 8
22Jly 66-2Aqu fst 7f .23 .46⅕1.26⅕ Clm 3500 5 4 77½ 710 67½ 55½ ORosado3 b 119 *1.70 69-19 Enchanter 1124 Irish Tract 1121 Validated 115½ No threat 7
15Jly 66-2Aqu fst 6f .23 .46⅘1.13⅘ Clm 3500 7 6 65½ 68½ 63½ 4nk ORosado3 b 116 2.50 74-20 Robin Oh 114h Enchanter 109nk Lakythra 114no Stumbled start 7
9Jun66-2Aqu fst 1 .46⅗1.11⅕1.38 Cl c-3500 6 1 2h 23 21 1no RUssery b 119 6.50 78-17 Space Control 119no On the Throne 115h Bluemat 1105 All out 7
24May66-2Aqu fst 7f .22⅗ .45⅘1.25⅕ Clm 4500 1 1 54¼ 85¾ 710 713 RUssery b 117 4.20 67-20 Roma Deck 1135 Inhand 116¾ Flight Tracer 105nk Fell far back 9
6May66-7Pim sf 1 Ⓣ .48⅘1.40⅗ Clm 7500 2 8 119¾ 1214 1224 1227 TLee b 119 12.00 55-14 King Olay 1132½ Aereal Spin 1221½ Bev Gladd 108¾ Never close 12
20Apr66-2Aqu fst 7f .23 .46⅘1.26 Clm 4000 6 1 41½ 11 13 12 GMineau5 b 110 *1.40e 76-16 Space Control 1102 Long Charlie 1061½ Deducts 113½ Easily 9
LATEST WORKOUTS Aug 22 Bel tr.t. 5f fst 1.05 b

***Meteoro** $4,500 Dk. b. or br. h (1961), by Candaules—Margarita Maria, by Faubourg 116 1966 2 0 0 0 ——
M. M. Garren G. Puentes (Haras Santa Eladia) (Chile) 1965 11 0 1 0 $782
8Oct66-2Aqu fst 6f .22⅖ .46 1.12⅕ Clm 4500 8 7 77¼ 911 912 916 HGustines 115 59.30 66-17 Count Bell 117¾ Sgraffio 1141½ Donner Pass 115nk No speed 9
26Sep66-2Aqu fst 6f .23⅕ .47 1.12⅖ Cl c-3500 8 1 53½ 910 915 927 JRuane 114 12.00 54-18 Royal Magician 1093 Te 1141 Bull and Bear 121no Brief speed 9
14Oct65-2Aqu fst 6f .23 .47 1.11⅖ Clm 7500 2 3 21 31½ 47 413 LOlah 117 11.50 73-17 Canal 214 Du Noir 1173 Tanteo 1156 Early speed, gave way 6
9Oct65-5Aqu fst 6f .22 .45 1.11⅗ Allowance 2 2 55¼ 810 914 915 ACordero 117 37.80 —— Pinkie Chollie 1141 Weighmaster 114¾ Timurid 1172 Tired 9
7Sep65-8Aqu fm 1$\frac{1}{16}$ TC 1.43⅖ Allowance 10 1 1h 43½ 1010 1014 GMineau7 109 25.40 75-11 Buckles 1161½ Annette's Ark 1121½ Account Balanced 116h Stopped 10
30Aug65-3Aqu fm 1$\frac{1}{16}$ TC 1.42⅗ Allowance 1 1 12 11 4¾ 711 WBlum 117 10.80 82- 7 Ram's Horn 1153 Island Stream 1121 Annette'sArk1122½ Stopped 7
23Aug65-6Sar fm 1⅛ TC 1.50⅗ Allowance 4 1 11 1h 2h 66½ LOlah 117 31.70 74-20 Mostar117no Ganelon II 119no Tabeeb1141½ Much used setting pace 7
14Aug65-4Sar fst 6f .22⅘ .45⅗1.10⅗ Allowance 7 7 65¼ 78 811 918 LOlah 117 74.00 77- 6 Understudy 1196 Timurid 117no Double Liar 119½ Showed nothing 9
9Aug65-8Sar my 7f .22⅘ .45⅘1.22⅗ Clm 12500 7 2 53 55¼ 612 726 GMineau7 112 18.00 71-12 Buffington 11915 No Ransom 119no Irish Lit 1124 Brief foot 7
29Jly 65-7Mth hd 5f TC .58⅘ Allowance 3 8 73¾ 75¼ 53½ 42½ LOlah 113 12.40 93- 8 Customs Officer 114nk Buddleia 1062 Erin Boy 119nk Went well 8
24Jly 65-5Aqu fst 6f .22⅗ .45⅗1.11 Allowance 2 1 22 45 68 611 LOlah 117 36.00 77-10 Big Darby 1121½ Double Liar 1171½ Tunnel Hill 1173½ Brief speed 6
21Feb65-Hipodromo (Chile) fst*6f 1.11⅖ Ciudad d'Santiago Esp. Hcp. 7 OCastillo 110 12.00 —— Ras Paddock 130½ Servicial 1041¾ Dadivoso 1101 10
LATEST WORKOUTS Oct 4 Bel tr.t. 5f fst 1.03⅘ b Sep 24 Bel tr.t. 5f fst 1.03⅖ b Sep 20 Bel tr.t. 5f fst 1.03⅗ b Sep 13 Bel m.t. 4f fst .49⅗ b

Express Stop * $5,000 Ch. c (1962) by Piatter—Nova Luna, by New Moon 118 1966 14 2 3 3 $9,320
Pond's Edge Stable E. Bishop (Nova Scotia Stud) 1965 32 1 1 2 $4,425
6Oct66-9Aqu fst 1⅛.47 1.12⅗1.53⅘ Clm 5000 1 3 34½ 23 2½ 2nk RTurcotte b 116 4.70 66-24 Get the Point 116nk Express Stop 116¾ El Gordo 1162½ Sharp 8
27Sep66-9Aqu fst 1⅛.48⅗1.13⅗1.52⅗ Cl c-3500 4 3 31½ 3nk 12 13 BBaeza b 120 3.80 73-21 Express Stop 1203 Golden Mike 1163 Kalapur 1114 Driving 12
22Sep66-9Aqu gd 1⅛.48 1.13⅕1.53⅗ Clm 4000 1 3 32 32 36½ 46½ HWoodhouse b 113 6.30 61-23 Double Dash 1172½ Del Coronado 1122 Mr. Spinelli 1072 Weakened 7
13Sep66-9Aqu fst 1⅛.49⅘1.14⅗1.54 Clm 3500 3 1 11 1½ 21 24 HWoodhouse b 116 2.80 62-22 Sir Rodolph 1164 Express Stop 1163 Halloween 1162½ Second best 8
5Sep66-4Aqu fst 7f .22⅘ .46⅖1.26⅘ Clm 6000 9 11 119 119¾ 1110 1113 HWoodhouse b 113 48.50 59-25 Brimer Pass 112¾ Jovial Twist 1104 Jay Roger 1122½ No speed 12
20Aug66-9Sar fst 1⅛.47⅘1.12⅗1.52⅗ Hcp 3500s 4 3 31½ 35 52¼ 516 HWoodhouse b 112 10.20 63-10 Aberrant 1223½ Kalonii 114h Motor 1114½ Couldn't keep up 8
12Aug66-9Sar gd 1⅛.47⅗1.12⅖1.52⅕ Clm 6000 3 2 23 21½ 23 26 HWoodhouse b 114 8.70 78-16 Mr. Elwood W. 1156 Express Stop 1142 Rao Raja 1183½ Gamely 7
6Aug66-9Sar fst 1⅛.47⅗1.12⅘1.53⅖ Hcp 3500s 6 3 33 31 2h 33¼ HWoodhouse b 110 15.30 75-12 Atlantic 120¾ Kalonii 1122½ Express Stop 110½ Bid, weakened 8
26Jly 66-9Aqu fst 1⅛.47⅖1.13 1.53⅗ Clm 3500 2 4 45½ 21½ 14 15 HWoodhouse b 115 6.60 68-19 Express Stop 1155 Motor 1172 Law Partner 1181 Easy score 8
19Jly 66-9Aqu fst 1⅛.48⅖1.13⅖1.55 Clm 3500 3 3 32 31 4nk 52¼ HWoodhouse b 116 5.40 59-19 Ozark Jet 1161 Empey Rullah 113h Lou O'Neill 109½ Used up 6
12Jly 66-9Aqu fst 1⅛.48⅖1.13⅖1.53⅖ Clm 3500 1 3 31½ 31½ 31½ 33 EGuerin b 115 12.30 66-19 Motor 118no Empey Rullah 1103 Express Stop 1154 Held on well 9
1Jly 66-2Aqu fst 1 .46 1.10⅗1.36⅘ Clm 3500 3 4 35 48 39 310 HWoodhouse b 118 26.70 74-19 [illegible] Fue 11810 Espartaco II 118nk Express Stop 1182½ Evenly 7
LATEST WORKOUTS Sep 19 Bel tr.t. 5f fst 1.04⅖ b Sep 11 Bel tr.t. 4f fst .54 b Sep 4 Bel tr.t. 3f fst .39 b Aug 18 Sar tr.t. 4f fst .50 h

---

Tulyaric: Since arriving in the United States has showed insufficient speed for sprints and not enough stamina for routes. Barring sudden improvement, its only hope would seem to be in slower, cheaper company. NO BET.

Latin Artist: Always seems to be gaining in the stretch, but never gets there in time. Presumably Buddy Jacobson will not put up with this sort of thing forever and has ideas about trying to correct the weakness today. In deference to Jacobson and to Ernie Cardone, the hottest rider in New York, we had better not eliminate this one yet. CONTENDER.

Get The Point: A winning favorite, but narrowly, when ridden by the great Braulio Baeza on October 6, Pancho Martin's gelding is now being asked to carry 123 pounds and the relatively inexperienced David Hidalgo. The weight would be burdensome even with Baeza. Note that this horse requires highly expert handling. Its only good races were under Baeza, Rotz, and Turcotte. NO BET.

Inhand: Looked awful in the October 6 race won by Get the Point and has never seemed to like to go farther than a mile. NO BET.

Clavero: This seven-year-old is a real speedster in cheap company. By waiving the apprentice allowance to ride Ussery, Horan indicates that he's shooting for the moon. It's probably too far away. Routers worth $5,000 are so much better than the $3,500 kind that the conditions of this race specifically exact no penalty on a horse whose wins have been in the $3,500 bracket. Clavero will be out there winging, but the record insists that he won't have enough quality to beat off a challenge in the final stages. NO BET.

Space Control: Looks like more horse than Clavero, but has never tried to go more than a mile. Has been soundly whipped every time he tried to run with horses worth more than $4,000. NO BET.

Meteoro: In two 1966 tries has failed to finish ahead of a single horse. NO BET.

Express Stop: Last August this colt ran well against a better field than he faces today. Last week he almost caught Get the Point at the wire. Is apparently in excellent trim. CONTENDER.

The contenders are Latin Artist and Express Stop. Conceding Buddy Jacobson the ability to improve Latin Artist's performance by showing Cardone how to start running sooner, one has to favor Express Stop anyhow. The horse is invariably on or close to the pace and, when in shape, has something left at the finish. Latin Artist may be coming in a hurry at the end, as usual, but Express Stop has every prospect of winning.

The Running of the Race

BETTING ON JACOBSON and Cardone, the crowd made Latin Artist a tepid favorite. The second favorite was Express Stop. Third choice was Clavero, the cheap speed.

Ussery busted out of the gate on top and held Clavero together until midstretch, when Express Stop came alongside, looked the aging cheapster in the eye, and drew away. Latin Artist broke more quickly than usual but dawdled until the final stages and could not come close to catching the winner. Get the Point tried but succumbed to fatigue, possibly because of the extra weight.

NINTH RACE
Aqu - 28999
October 13, 1966

1 1-8 MILES (Sinatra, December 7, 1964, 1.47$\frac{1}{5}$, 5, 111.)
Claiming. Purse $4,200. 3-year-olds and upward. Weights, 3-year-olds 119 lbs., older 123 lbs. Non-winners of a race at a mile and a furlong or over since Aug. 27 allowed 3 lbs., of a race at a mile or over since then, 5 lbs. Claiming price, $5,000. 2 lbs. allowed for each $500 to $4,000. (Races when entered to be claimed for $3,500 or less not considered.)

Value to winner $2,730, second $840, third $420, fourth $210. Mutuel pool $249,024.

Index	Horse	Eqt	A	Wt	PP	St	¼	½	¾	Str	Fin	Jockey	Cl'g Pr	Owner	Odds $1
28945Aqu^{2}	Express Stop	b	4	118	8	3	7^{3}	$6\frac{1}{2}$	6^{2}	$2\frac{1}{2}$	1^{2}	R Turcotte	5000	Pond's Edge Stable	3.10
28945Aqu^{4}	Latin Artist		6	113	2	2	6^{2}	7^{3}	$7\frac{1}{2}$	6^{1}	2^{2}	E Cardone^{5}	5000	J Perricone	2.40
28789Aqu^{1}	Space Control	b	3	114	6	8	8	8	8	5^{1}	3^{h}	A Cordero	4500	S Freidfertig	5.30
28807Aqu^{4}	Clavero		7	116	5	1	1^{h}	$1\frac{1}{2}$	$1\frac{1}{2}$	$1\frac{1}{2}$	4no	R Ussery†	4500	L M Horan	4.80
28945Aqu^{6}	Tulyaric	b	4	114	1	4	3^{4}	3^{3}	4^{1}	3^{2}	$5\frac{1}{2}$	H Woodh'use	4000	J C Toomey	12.10
28945Aqu^{1}	Get the Point	b	4	123	3	7	$4\frac{1}{2}$	5^{4}	5^{h}	4^{h}	6^{6}	D Hidalgo	5000	A J Bertolotti	6.40
28945Aqu^{8}	Inhand		3	114	4	6	5^{1}	4^{h}	3^{h}	7^{8}	7^{15}	J L Rotz	4500	Mrs S Westfal	13.00
28956Aqu^{9}	Meteoro		5	116	7	5	2^{3}	2^{2}	$2\frac{1}{2}$	8	8	E Belmonte	4500	M M Garren	25.80

†Five pounds apprentice allowance waived.

Time .$23\frac{4}{5}$, .$47\frac{3}{5}$, 1.$13\frac{2}{5}$, 1.$40\frac{2}{5}$, 1.$53\frac{2}{5}$ (with wind in the backstretch). Track fast.

$2 Mutuel Prices:

8-EXPRESS STOP	8.20	4.00	2.80
2-LATIN ARTIST		3.60	2.80
6-SPACE CONTROL			3.60

Ch. c, by Platter—Nova Luna, by New Moon. Trainer E. Bishop. Bred by Nova Scotia Stud.

IN GATE AT 5.30. OFF AT 5.30 EASTERN DAYLIGHT TIME. Start good. Won driving.

EXPRESS STOP overcame interference at the first turn and was steadied until near the stretch, responded to strong handling during the drive and after taking command from CLAVERO, retained a clear margin. LATIN ARTIST outrun until reaching the stretch, finished fast. SPACE CONTROL in trouble at the initial turn, was outrun for three-quarters and could not get to the leaders when set down through the stretch. CLAVERO saved ground and set the pace until inside the last eighth but faltered when challenged by EXPRESS STOP. TULYARIC tired during the final furlong. GET THE POINT weakened after making a mild bid in the upper stretch. INHAND made a bold bid approaching the stretch but had nothing left. METEORO engaged CLAVERO until near the final turn and stopped.

Get The Point was claimed by J. H. Moses, trainer L. C. Cavalaris, Jr. Express Stop was claimed by J. Shanbrom, trainer J. Lipari.

2. FIFTH AT BOWIE, FEBRUARY 2, 1967—Track Fast

Now COMES a real skull-buster. After the choice is made and the result revealed, the logic of it all will seem beyond challenge. But the trick is to see the logic *before* the race. And the way to do that, I insist, is to scrutinize the record of each horse in an effort to figure out what the trainer is doing, and why, and how the horse is likely to react to what the trainer is doing.

The conditions of this race identify it as a middle-distance jaunt for mature, high-priced claimers. Severe weight disadvantages are imposed on entrants that have been winning at the distance or thereabouts.

5th Race Bowie

1 1-16 MILES BOWIE START FINISH

1 1-16 MILES. (Social Outcast, April 9, 1955, 1.42⅗, 5, 125.)
Claiming. Purse $5,500. 4-year-olds and upward. Weights, 4-year-olds 121 lbs., older 122 lbs. Non-winners of two races at one mile or over in 1967 allowed 3 lbs., of one such race, 5 lbs., of any race since Dec. 19, 7 lbs. Claiming price, $13,000. 1 lb. allowed for each $1,000 to $11,000. (Races where entered for $9,500 or less not considered.)

Gasmegas * $13,000 B. g (1961), by Joe Price—Kissme, by Don Jose II
H. Queen R. W. Fitzgerald, Jr. (L. A. Gibson) **122** 1967 2 2 0 0 $7,150 / 1966 20 5 3 0 $12,883
14Jan67-6Bow gd 1 1/16 .49⅕ 1.15 1.49⅖ Clm 10000 6 12 1015 64½ 2½ 1nk FLovato b 117 3.10 66-27 Gasmegas 117nk Great Depths 1151½ Sirius II 108¾ Up final strides 12
7Jan67-4Bow fst 1 1/16 .50⅗ 1.16⅗ 1.48⅘ Clm 10500 3 6 42½ 52½ 2½ 14 FLovato b 119 6.40 69-27 Gasmegas 1194 Local Gossip 1082½ Sirius II 1083½ Ridden out 8
26Dec66-7Lrl sly 1⅛ .50⅘ 1.17⅕ 1.58⅘ Clm 10000 6 9 914 913 714 720 WChambers b 119 4.50 33-41 Sudanese 117nk Sirius II 1097 Gallant Scot 115nk Never a contender 9
12Dec66-6Lrl gd 1 3/16 .49⅖ 1.15 2.00⅗ Clm 10000 2 7 63¾ 32 32½ 2¾ FLovato b 119 5.30 92-18 Musical Night 107¾ Gasmegas 1192½ Curator 1191½ Bore in, brushed 7
3Dec66-9Lrl fm 1⅛ Ⓣ 1.53⅗ Clm 7500 8 9 85 31½ 3nk 1½ FLovato b 115 13.70 69-26 Gasmegas 115½ Sacred River 119¾ Shorty's Pride 1195 Driving 11
26Nov66-9Lrl fm 1⅛ Ⓣ 1.50 Clm 7500 11 11 1116 1114 812 78½ JKratz b 115 65.10 78-11 Red Dog 1171¾ Footprint 108¾ The Gent 1151½ Dwelt at start 12
24Sep66-9Haw fm 1 3/16 Ⓣ 1.13⅖ 1.57⅖ Handicap 2 12 1216 1217 1214 1216 HVicra b 114 46.70 81- 9 Triumvirate 1184½ Istmo 120nk Alnbil 116½ Trailed field 12
17Sep66-9Haw fm 1 Ⓣ .47⅗ 1.33⅖ Handicap 3 10 1015 1116 1212 129½ RNono b 119 20.00 74- 9 Istmo 118h Count Dormal 1201½ Island Beau 119¾ Raced far back 12
24Aug66-9Tim fst 1 .49⅖ 1.15⅘ 1.42⅖ Allowance 7 8 813 612 611 64¾ RFitzgerald b 120 6.30 77-20 Realism 113h Jezibel A. 1102½ George Jolson 113½ Never close 8
LATEST WORKOUTS Jan 28 Pim 4f my .51⅗ b Jan 23 Pim 4f fst .52⅖ b Dec 23 Pim 4f fst .50⅖ b Dec 18 Pim 4f fst .52 b

Swing Rex $11,000 Br. g (1961), by Bold Ruler—Harmonica, by Snark
Don-Don Stable W. Terrill (Hartland Farm) **113** 1967 3 0 0 2 $550 / 1966 3 0 0 0 $160
24Jan67-8Bow fst 7f .23⅕ .46⅗ 1.26⅕ Allowance 11 2 79¾ 915 1114 1111 AAgnello7 106 14.40 71-26 Regal Prince 118nk Steel Trap 1211½ Scotch Light 116¾ No factor 12
11Jan67-8TrP fst 1 1/16 .46⅖ 1.11⅕ 1.43⅗ Clm 12500 2 3 23 23 2½ 3nk RSurrency5 112 18.60 84-14 Prince Graff 119h Doubting Thomas 111h Swing Rex 112¾ Sharp try 9
2Jan67-5TrP fst 6f .21⅘ .44⅕ 1.09⅖ Cl c-10000 2 4 31 44½ 33½ 33 LAdams 117 6.70 92-10 New Ballot 114nk Hy Sonny 1222¾ Swing Rex 1171 Showed even try 8
26Dec66-8TrP fst 6f .21⅘ .44⅗ 1.10⅕ Clm 10000 7 3 44 33½ 54½ 4nk LAdams b 115 30.90 91- 9 Mt. Stromboli 115no TurfParade 122no AlhambraPal 113h Rallied 8
14Dec66-6TrP fst 6f .22 .44⅘ 1.10⅖ Clm 12000 2 5 65¾ 1015 1018 1023 JNoble b 109 50.30 67-17 Timely Note 1132¾ Fearless Lee 122½ Romanrig 118no Tired 10
29Oct66-5Kee fst 6f .22 .45⅘ 1.11 Allowance 3 1 77 710 711 712 LWGrubb 110 56.70 76-15 Solazo 116½ d-Dempsey 1192 d-Slade 1131 Never a factor 8
4Nov65-8CD fst 7f .22⅖ .45⅘ 1.25⅖ Allowance 5 5 56 45 33½ 1½ KKnapp b 120 5.90 80-16 Swing Rex 120½ Hurry Up Dear 118½ Winamac 1136 Strong urging 9
19Oct65-2Kee fst 6f .22⅗ .46⅖ 1.11⅘ Md Sp Wt 6 3 1h 11½ 11½ 12 KKnapp 120 *2.90 84-13 Swing Rex 1202 Sempre Diritto 1171½ Gap 1145 Under hard drive 10
9Sep65-5AP gd 7f .23⅕ .45⅗ 1.24⅖ Md Sp Wt 9 1 2½ 24 25 37½ EFires5 b 115 4.50e 77-12 Mer-Met 1156 Gallant Rogue 1151½ Swing Rex 115¾ Held well 9
LATEST WORKOUTS Jan 1 GP 3f fst .37 b Dec 23 GP 6f fst 1.16 b Dec 20 GP 4f fst .49 b Dec 12 GP 3f sly .38⅖ b

Beauante * $11,000 B. m (1960), by Beau Busher—Antebabe, by Sir Damion
Dane Hill Acres J. C. Meyer (J. L. Paddock) **103 5** 1967 2 0 0 1 $550 / 1966 22 1 1 6 $7,430
23Jan67-6Bow fst 7f .23⅕ .46⅗ 1.25⅗ f- 11500 1 10 1013 1011 714 59¾ FLovato b 115 *3.40 75-24 Scairt 1176 Miltreb Hazard 1131 Who Cabled 1142 Dull 12
3Jan67-9Bow hy 1 1/16 .51 1.17⅕ 1.53⅖ Clm 11500 3 4 53¾ 54½ 47 32 PKallai b 113 6.80 44-46 Two Up 115no Sirius II 1062 Beauante 113h Closed well 6
7Dec66-8Aqu fst 6f .22⅗ .46 1.12⅖ f- 15000 3 5 710 812 711 76 RTurcotte b 118 3.70 75-24 Equador II 1111¼ Bushy Tail 112no Italiana 1182 Dull effort 8
16Nov66-7Grd fst 1 3/16 .49⅗ 1.15 2.00 f-TatlingH 4 2 22 41½ 31 2nk HDittfach b 116 18.00 90-15 SpeedyLament 121nk Beauante 1162¾ d-Hinemoa 1172 Gain'g at end 6
9Nov66-7Grd sly 1 1/16 .48⅘ 1.15⅖ 1.50⅘ f- Allow 4 3 2h 22 34 34 HDittfach b 118 2.45 61-38 Speedy Lament 1192 Cosmic Grey 1092 Beauante 1185¼ Sp'd, weak'd 6
20Oct66-7WO gd 1 Ⓣ .49 1.39⅘ Allowance 5 4 22½ 2h 2nk 14¾ HDittfach b 114 •21.60 80-15 •Hempeter 1234¾ •Beauante 1144¾ Concession 123no Driving 8
20Oct66—•-Dead heat.
4Oct66-7Det fst 170 .47 1.11⅕ 1.42⅕ Allowance 3 1 1h 1h 3nk 33 EMaple5 b 106 16.90 89-20 Merano 122no New Crack 1193 Beauante 106½ Used in pace 6
24Sep66-8Det fst 170 .46⅖ 1.11 1.41⅘ Allowance 6 2 23 44½ 42½ 64½ EMaple5 b 106 15.90e 89-16 Grand Stand 115h County Chairman 1141¾ Jet Charger 117no Tired 11
LATEST WORKOUTS Jan 20 Bow 1m fst 1.47 b Jan 14 Bow 4f gd .49 b

True Blue $13,000 B. m (1962), by Jester—Blue Grail, by Blue Larkspur
Mrs. M. Flynn M. Flynn (Erdenheim Farms Co.) **110** 1967 3 0 0 0 $500 / 1966 21 1 3 2 $9,345
28Jan67-7Bow gd 1 1/16 .49⅗ 1.14⅘ 1.49⅖ Allowance 1 6 68 66 59 47½ WJPassmore 111 12.20 58-22 Navy Admiral 1171 Faultless Light 1193 Big Shot 1083½ No factor 7
24Jan67-8Bow fst 7f .23⅕ .46⅗ 1.26⅕ Allowance 1 4 69½ 910 911 84¾ WJPassmore 112 18.20 76-30 Regal Prince 118nk Steel Trap 1211½ Scotch Light 116¾ No factor 12
6Jan67-8Bow gd 7f .23⅕ .46⅘ 1.26⅖ Allowance 10 1 1013 1119 1012 1010 RMikkonen 108 78.90 72-26 Tulmar 1161 Steel Trap 1161¼ Fairy Queen 104½ Never close 10
31Dec66-8Lrl sl 6f .23⅕ .48⅖ 1.15⅕ Allowance 4 5 57½ 56 65½ 41½ DGorman 113 16.20 74-30 Knave's Delight 111no Thanks Doc 106h Hy Frost 1181½ Closed well 7
26Dec66-8Lrl sly 6f .22⅘ .48⅕ 1.16⅘ Allowance 1 4 57½ 713 63¾ 55¾ DGorman 113 47.40 62-41 Shelard 112h Cosimo 1171¾ Linear B 1153 Had no mishap 9
8Dec66-8Lrl fm*1 1/16 Ⓣ 1.49⅘ f- Allow 2 6 67½ 65¾ 68 57¼ TLee 112 3.30 67-19 Barletta 1221¾ Carolyn's World 1123 Glen Arm 1122½ Dull effort 6
30Nov66-8Lrl gd 1 .47⅗ 1.13⅘ 1.39⅗ f- Allow 6 4 43½ 22 32 21 TLee 112 7.50 82-15 Honor Bright 1161 True Blue 112½ La Picada 1125 Sharp try 7
19Nov66-4Aqu fst 6f .23 .47⅗ 1.12⅘ f- Allow 4 10 1214 1217 1014 95¼ JLRotz 116 26.60 74-19 Through theMist 1211¼ Song ofRome 113½ ShipShoal 118nk No sp'd 12
5Nov66-8Aqu fm 1 1/16 Ⓣ 1.46⅗ f- Allow 4 4 48 46½ 36½ 26 LAdams 116 5.00 67-27 River Lady 1136 True Blue 1161 Maggie Fast Step 1163 Rallied 8
LATEST WORKOUTS Dec 6 Lrl 4f fst .50 b

Fairy Queen × $13,000 Dk. ch. f (1963-Md), by Bobbie—Knot Lator, by Undulator or Sun Egret **102**7 1967 3 0 0 1 $850 / 1966 23 3 2 2 $11,445
Mrs. M. G. Heron M. G. Heron (Mrs. M. G. Heron)

26Jan67-7Bow fst 6f .24 .48⅕1.13⅖ f- Allow 10 8 76¾ 87¾ 75½ 75¼ RLAdams b 116 9.90 75-25 Teetotaler106no BankBookSadye117¾ d-Phyl'sDestiny107¾ Dull try 11
12Jan67-8Bow fst 7f .23⅘ .47⅕1.27 Allowance 8 5 31 31½ 33 4½ AAgnello7 b 104 5.30 77-35 Pretko 114no Soldier's Story 112h Nannie's Boy 110½ No rally 9
6Jan67-8Bow gd 7f .23⅕ .43⅘1.26⅖ Allowance 8 7 79½ 46 47½ 32¼ AAgnello7 b 104 19.30 79-30 Tulmar 1161 Steel Trap 1161¼ Fairy Queen 104½ Stride late 10
31Dec66-7Lrl sl 6f .24 .49⅕1.15 Clm 7500 7 2 1½ 14 13 13½ AAgnello7 b 105 28.80 77-30 Fairy Queen 1053½ Magellan 1151 Quick Post 1072¾ Driving 7
8Dec66-6Lrl fst 1 .47⅕1.13 1.39 Clm 10000 5 6 74½ 79½ 710 715 RMikkonen b 112 44.20 71-21 Over Roger 1154 Uptick 1122 Here He Goes 115¾ Not a contender 8
24Nov66-9Lrl fm 1⅛ Ⓣ 1.51⅕ Clm 10000 8 8 89½ 87¼ 73¾ 63¾ JCruguet 112 22.60 77-10 Bannisseur 116½ Jet Code 114½ Borealis 1171¼ Never close 8
14Nov66-7Lrl fst 1 .48⅖1.14⅕1.40⅖ f- Allow 1 3 63¼ 78 64½ 64½ RMikkonen 121 48.40 74-26 High Bluff 1181½ Wagon Lit 114½ Tacaro Landing 118no No factor 7
29Oct66-6Lrl fst 7f .23⅕ .47⅕1.25⅗ f- Allow 8 5 53 713 819 1017 JCruguet 112 108.50 74-16 Manya 1131½ Tempt Me Not 1154 Holly-O 122½ Gave way badly 12
19Oct66-8Mar sly 170.50⅖1.16⅖1.48⅖ f- Allow 1 2 2h 31 510 516 LReynolds b 121 10.80 —— Shiralee 1215 Tacaro Landing 1111½ Two Wings 1186 Tired badly 6
LATEST WORKOUTS Jan 3 Pim 4f my .51 b

Irish Gypsy $13,000 Dk. b. or br. c (1963-Va), by Sea O Erin—Greek Belle, by Gr'k Ship **107**7 1967 2 0 2 0 $1,800 / 1966 15 4 5 3 $14,535
North Lane Stable D. C. Le Vine (Dr. F. A. Howard)

14Jan67-9Bow gd 1⅛.48⅘1.14⅖1.55⅕ Hcp 5000s 1 2 26 26 23½ 33¼ PKallai b 118 3.50 75-27 d-Royal Decision 1251¾ Welcome Call 1151½ IrishGypsy1183 Impeded 8
14Jan67—Placed second thtrough disqualification.
7Jan67-5Bow fst 1 1/16.48⅗1.15 1.48⅗ Hcp 5000s 5 4 47 33 2h 23 PKallai b 119 *2.80 67-27 Royal Decision 1223 Irish Gypsy 1192 Sudanese 1187 Gamely 10
19Dec66-5Lrl sl 7f .23⅕ .47⅗1.28 Clm 12500 5 6 64½ 21 3½ 3¾ PKallai b 114 7.00 78-32 Rex de Plumbum 109¾ Linear B. 115h Irish Gypsy 1144 Went well 7
2Dec66-6Lrl gd 1 .47 1.13⅕1.39⅘ Clm 10000 3 4 41 21 1h 1nk PKallai b 113 9.00 82-24 Irish Gypsy 113nk Count Bell 1132 Sudanese 1191¾ Hard drive 12
23Nov66-9Lrl fm*1 Ⓣ .47⅗1.38⅘ Allowance 8 3 42½ 33 35 45¾ PKallai b 115 3.60 90- 4 Regal Prince 1155 Sarita 116nk O Lady O 110½ Lacked rally 10
16Nov66-6Lrl fm*1 Ⓣ .48⅗1.40⅗ Allowance 1 3 22 2h 2h 3nk PKallai b 114 2.50 87-12 Whey 114nk Regal Prince 115h Irish Gypsy 1146 Held on gamely 7
.Nov66-9GS fst 1 1/16.47⅖1.12⅗1.46⅕ Clm 10000 1 2 2h 1½ 2h 22 HHinojosa b 116 6.70 72-26 Canaanite 1122 Irish Gypsy 1161¼ Jet Code 1171 Gamely 9
28Oct66-9GS fst 1 1/16.46⅗1.12 1.46⅕ Clm 9500 5 2 26 21 1h 31½ HHinojosa b 112 3.80 72-19 Jet Code 115nk Harmony Again 1181¼ Irish Gypsy 112h Bid, tired 8
LATEST WORKOUTS Jan 12 Bow 6f fst 1.16 b Jan 6 Bow 3f fst .36 h Dec 12 Lrl 4f gd .51⅖ b Dec 8 Lrl 6f fst 1.21 b

Two Up $13,000 Dk. b. g (1961), by Double Jay—Up Early, by Sun Again **119** 1967 2 1 0 0 $3,575 / 1966 26 1 5 3 $9,955
T. A. Bruder H. F. Bowyer (Bull Run Stud)

18Jan67-7Bow fst 6f .22⅗ .46 1.12 Clm 14000 6 7 78 714 714 713 JBrockleb'k b 118 28.60 74-26 Get Gettin 1152 Five Rogues 1141 Star Spin 1081 Never close 8
3Jan67-9Bow hy 1 1/16.51 1.17⅕1.53⅖ Clm 12500 2 2 23 23 2h 1no JBrockleb'nk b 115 8.00 46-46 Two Up 115no Sirius II 1062 Beauante 113h Hard drive 6
27Dec66-3Lrl sly 7f .23⅘ .48⅗1.28⅘ Allowance 5 5 53 54¼ 44½ 38¾ JBrockleb'nk b 113 34.10 66-34 Hessian 1224 Pretko 1144¾ Two Up 1131½ Gave even effort 7
9Nov66-8GS fst 1 1/16.47⅖1.11⅕1.43 Allowance 1 1 2h 410 714 715 SHernandez b 113 22.80 75-17 Munden Point 1132¼ Fibran 1133½ Do Sparkle 1192¾ Used early 7
22Oct66-9GS fst 1 1/16.47⅘1.12⅕1.44⅗ Clm 14000 1 1 1h 1h 21½ 22¾ SHernandez b 116 5.20 79-20 Bama Day 1162¾ Two Up 1165 Beauport 116¾ Best of others 6
15Oct66-7GS fst 1 1/16.48⅗1.12⅖1.43⅘ Allowance 6 2 22 21 45 76 SHernandez b 113 72.40 80-15 Tronado 1161¼ Intercepted 1171 Tetanus 116no Used forcing pace 8
17Sep66-9Atl fm 1 Ⓣ 1.38⅘ Clm 13000 8 7 73¾ 53½ 67 59¾ JVelasquez b 113 5.60 64-24 Happy Highway 1134½ Tosinisbad 1115 Indian Relic 112nk Mild bid 8
10Sep66-9Atl fm*1 1/16 Ⓣ 1.46⅘ Clm 14000 5 5 44 34 43½ 55¾ DBrumfield b 114 16.70 89- 5 Red Dog 1163 The Gent 119¾ Island Stream 1141½ Bid, tired 9
8Aug66-6Atl fst 6f .22⅘ .46 1.11⅕ Clm 14000 2 9 912 916 813 811 DKassen b 114 8.60e 75-17 Tilmar 1162 ♦High Stool 1111½ ♦Vastland 1141½ Showed nothing 9
LATEST WORKOUTS Jan 31 Lrl 3f gd .38 b Jan 28 Lrl 6f my 1.18 b Jan 25 Lrl 3f fst .38 b Jan 17 Lrl 3f gd .38 b

Gasmegas: Consistent six-year-old gelding is being asked to carry 122 pounds after two successive victories at the distance on this track. The last one was a real squeaker which undoubtedly did nothing to help the old horse's condition. The high weight, the strain of the last race, and the rise in claiming price to a level that may be too tough are all black marks. But until we survey the remainder of the field, we had better not discard this one. CONTENDER.

Swing Rex: Hasn't won a race in more than a year. Broke its maiden at age four, then won an allowance race and laid off for a full year. Came to hand at Tropical Park slightly more than a month ago with a couple of genuinely swift efforts in sprints. Terrill claimed the gelding for $10,000 and got a magnificent effort out of it at today's distance against a field that should have been at least as good as today's. Interesting. Ordinarily, horsemen do not pay $10,000 for geldings that have not been racing and winning. Truth is that they *never* pay that kind of money unless reasonably confident that the animal can bring a profit in fast company. Swing Rex did not win its January 11 race but came close. It would undoubtedly have done better with a more experienced rider. Next move was the January 24 canter here, again with an apprentice aboard. Since it was the gelding's first outing here, and against allowance horses, the chances are that no great effort was made to flog it into a real run. The purpose more likely was to give it a nice, easy workout preparatory to more serious business. Could today be the day when Terrill tries to get some of his money back? Seems possible. The horse will be ridden by Chuck Baltazar, one of the country's best. CONTENDER.

Beauante: Seven-year-old mare ran well in Canada last fall but was very much out of sorts on January 23 when she went as favorite in a race against females. Having been well-prepared for that race and having failed, she does not figure to improve enough to beat males today. NO BET.

True Blue: This mare looks like the kind that will not see the winner's circle until her management lowers the sights a bit. Off recent form, today's claiming price is too high. NO BET.

Fairy Queen: Four-year-old fillies are at a grave disadvantage against older males early in the year, especially at longer distances on a slow track like this one, and even more especially when entered against relatively high-class stock. Note also that the filly has never shown anything at a mile or beyond. NO BET.

Irish Gypsy: Why in the world would Don LeVine switch this colt from the strong Paul Kallai to the green apprentice, Dick Morgan? Plainest reason seems to be the weight. The colt has never once carried his speed all the way to the finish of a race this long but has come fairly close to turning the trick under 116 pounds and, more recently, under 119. But there is a real question whether Morgan is experienced enough to take full advantage of the light weight. There also is a question about the colt's physical condition. He had four tough races between December 2 and January 14 and has been entirely idle since. Not even a workout. I would hate to risk money on his chances, but hesitate to eliminate him as yet. CONTENDER.

Two Up: On January 3, this gelding won a race similar to today's but in disastrously slow time, even considering the heavy track on which it ran. The record of only one victory in twenty-six starts last year, plus the turf races and the tiring performance last October 22, gives rise to suspicion that this one has gam trouble and dislikes a dry footing. Whether that is true or not, today's 119 pounds will not be any help. NO BET.

The contenders are Gasmegas, Swing Rex, and Irish Gypsy. I now eliminate Gasmegas for reasons mentioned earlier—weight, class, and possible lack of current sharpness. Swing Rex, whose people are certain to be cracking down today, should have all the speed in the race and seems perfectly able to hold it to the finish wire, particularly with the canny Baltazar in the saddle. Irish Gypsy should be close to the pace, if in shape, but may be outmaneuvered in the riding department. I like Swing Rex.

The Running of the Race

ONE PROBABLY SHOULD not criticize the Bowie audience for making Irish Gypsy the favorite, although some of the factors we have discussed might possibly have attracted more play to Swing Rex. Irish Gypsy turned out to be in excellent condition, as a matter of fact, and almost took the marbles. The margin, I believe, was Baltazar, who managed to save exactly enough horse to win by a neck. Gasmegas ran a nice race, but tired under the weight.

I believe that the only reason I spotted Swing Rex in this race was that I noticed the unusual circumstance of the $10,000 claim in January. Having noticed it, I became attentive to everything else about the horse, especially the maneuvering by its stable. It is impossible to catch decisive angles of this kind unless you are patient enough to read the horse's biography in its record. To do that you must read and interpret the whole record. To look at the last race or two is simply not enough.

Naturally, the expenditure of $10,000 on a losing horse does not guarantee that the animal will be transformed into a winner. No approach to the game is sillier than one which assumes that trainers always know precisely what they are doing. Trainers are as fallible as other men. Regardless of any trainer's previous accomplishments, the wise player refuses to bet a dime unless the record shows that the horse is a horse.

FIFTH RACE
Bow - 30114
February 2, 1967

1 1-16 MILES. (Social Outcast, April 9, 1955, 1.42⅗, 5, 125.)
Claiming. Purse $5,500. 4-year-olds and upward. Weights, 4-year-olds 121 lbs., older 122 lbs. Non-winners of two races at one mile or over in 1967 allowed 3 lbs., of one such race, 5 lbs., of any race since Dec. 19, 7 lbs. Claiming price, $13,000. 1 lb. allowed for each $1,000 to $11,000. (Races where entered for $9,500 or less not considered.)
Value to winner $3,575, second $1,100, third $550, fourth $275. Mutuel pool $80,721.

Index	Horse	Eqt A Wt	PP	St	¼	½	¾	Str	Fin	Jockey	Cl'g Pr	Owner	Odds $1
29952Bow[1]	Swing Rex	6 113	2	1	1[1]	1[2]	1[h]	1[2]	1[nk]	C Baltazar	11000	Don Don Stable	7.00
29890Bow[2]	Irish Gypsy	b 4 109	6	6	3[1½]	3[1½]	3[2]	3[h]	2[1½]	R Morgan[5]†	13000	North Lane Stable	1.80
29887Bow[1]	Gasmegas	b 6 122	1	4	4[h]	5[½]	4[h]	4[3]	3[1½]	F Lovato	13000	H Queen	4.30
29969Bow[7]	Fairy Queen	b 4 102	5	5	2[1]	2[½]	2[2]	2[2]	4[3½]	A Agnello[7]	13000	Mrs M G Heron	9.50
29941Bow[5]	Beauante	b 7 104	3	2	6[½]	6[1]	5[h]	5[h]	5[h]	A Cannon[5]	11000	Dane Hill Acres	5.10
29915Bow[7]	Two Up	b 6 119	7	7	7	4[h]	6[2½]	6[2½]	6[2]	J Brockle'k	13000	T A Bruder	6.30
29987Bow[4]	True Blue	5 112	4	3	5[1]	7	7	7	7	W J Pass're	13000	Mrs M Flynn	9.50

†Two pounds apprentice allowance waived.

Time .25, .50⅗, 1.15⅖, 1.41⅗, 1.48⅕. Track fast.

$2 Mutuel Prices:

2—SWING REX	16.00	5.20	3.80
6—IRISH GYPSY		3.00	2.40
1—GASMEGAS			3.00

Br. g, by Bold Ruler—Harmonica, by Snark. Trainer W. Terrill. Bred by Hartland Farm.
IN GATE AT 3.05. OFF AT 3.05 EASTERN STANDARD TIME. Start good. Won driving.

SWING REX assumed command at once, set the pace under snug restraint into the far turn, repulsed a bid from FAIRY QUEEN entering the stretch and held IRISH GYPSY safe in the drive. The latter, raced in close attendance to the leaders for three-quarters, moved outside the leaders for the drive and was getting to the winner in the final sixteenth. GASMEGAS, unhurried and saving ground for three-quarters, lacked sufficient response when set down for the drive. FAIRY QUEEN prompted the pace from soon after the start, lodged a bid for the lead on the far turn and gradually weakened when repulsed. BEAUANTE never entered contention. TRUE BLUE showed a poor effort.

Overweights—Beauante 1 pound, True Blue 2.
True Blue was claimed by P. Fuller, trainer J. C. Meyer.

Before handicapping more races, let's get some extra practice in reading the biographies of horses.

Cherokee Mary

ONE OF THE CUTEST ANGLES in the business is to enter a hard-knocking filly against colts and geldings. This races her into good condition while getting her soundly trounced. When she finally runs with her own kind, she is likely to be underrated by the crowd. She wins at a far better price than would otherwise be possible.

Cherokee Mary is an amusing example of this. Amusing, because her record shows that Al Scotti, a leading New York trainer, recognized that the filly was better than her record. Like all able horsemen, Scotti is a keen student of the past-performance lines. When he haltered Cherokee Mary for $8,500 on September 3, 1966, he knew exactly what he was doing.

Cherokee Mary ✻	$10 000						B. f (1963–Md), by Piano Jim—After Seven, by Adaris			116					
							M. Guerrieri A. A. Scotti	(C. A. Petrillo)			1966 18 3 3 3 $12,500				
											1965 0 M 0 0				
22Oct66–5Aqu	fst 7f	.22$\frac{4}{5}$ .45$\frac{3}{5}$ 1.24$\frac{2}{5}$ f–	Allow	6	3	3^2 $32\frac{1}{2}$ $31\frac{1}{2}$ $22\frac{1}{2}$	RTurcotte	b 114	6.20	81–16	Cherimoya 114$2\frac{1}{2}$ Cherokee Mary 114$1\frac{1}{2}$ Vie Eye 112$2\frac{1}{2}$				Gamely 9
10Oct66–8Aqu	fst 7f	.23 .46$\frac{2}{5}$ 1.25$\frac{3}{5}$ f–	7000	7	1	$32\frac{1}{2}$ 22 11 $12\frac{1}{2}$	BBaeza	b 116	9.60	78–20	Cherokee Mary 116$\frac{1}{2}$ Miss Mop 107^{nk} Fleet Impelled 112$\frac{3}{4}$				Rid'n out 8
3Sep66–5Aqu	fst 7f	.23$\frac{1}{5}$ .45$\frac{3}{5}$ 1.25$\frac{4}{5}$ Cl	c–8500	3	4	$42\frac{1}{4}$ 43 9^{12} 9^{19}	KKnapp	b 108	19.10	58–22	Your Day 116$2\frac{1}{2}$ Stamp Around 111$\frac{1}{2}$ Hobe Sound 114$1$				Stopped 9
25Aug66–8Atl	fst 6f	.22$\frac{1}{5}$ .46 1.11$\frac{3}{5}$ f–	8500	6	5	$56\frac{1}{2}$ 43 $43\frac{1}{2}$ 2^5	DFrench	b 115	17.90	80–17	Infinita 108^5 Cherokee Mary 115^{nk} Catharpin 115^{nk}				Second best 8
10Aug66–7Atl	fst 6f	.22$\frac{1}{5}$ .45$\frac{2}{5}$ 1.11$\frac{1}{5}$ Clm	8500	4	10	$10^{16}10^{24}10^{20}10^{19}$	DFrench	b 112	16.50	67–19	Background 116$1\frac{1}{2}$ Scairt 106$1\frac{1}{2}$ Ginnygem 111$\frac{1}{2}$				Raced far back 10
1Aug66–9Mth	fst 1⁷⁰.46$\frac{3}{5}$1.10$\frac{4}{5}$1.41$\frac{4}{5}$ Clm		8000	8	4	$54\frac{1}{2}$ 36 37 38	MMiceli[7]	b 105	22.60	84–17	Precious Cargo 101^8 Background 117^h Cherokee Mary 105^6				Evenly 11
21Jly66–5Mth	fst 6f	.22$\frac{3}{5}$ .46 1.12 Clm	8500	1	5	54 $45\frac{1}{4}$ $41\frac{3}{4}$ $45\frac{1}{4}$	CMcPeek	b 111	8.90	77–20	Behaving Bee 113^1 Always There 112$1\frac{1}{4}$ Infinita 105^3				Mild bid 7
9Jly66–4Mth	fst 6f	.22 .45$\frac{1}{5}$1.10$\frac{4}{5}$ f–	Allow	7	3	$54\frac{1}{4}$ 56 54 $45\frac{3}{4}$	SBoulmetis	b 116	8.40	82–18	Cute Sweetie 116^{nk} Tangle 116^3 Miss Kentuckian 116$2\frac{1}{2}$				No rally 7
24Jun66–6Mth	fst 6f	.22$\frac{4}{5}$ .46$\frac{2}{5}$1.12$\frac{3}{5}$ f–	7500	2	6	$52\frac{3}{4}$ $33\frac{1}{2}$ $31\frac{1}{2}$ $11\frac{1}{2}$	SBoulmetis	b 113	*3.20	79–20	Cherokee Mary 113$1\frac{1}{2}$ General Note 109$1\frac{1}{2}$ Sound Tract 113^3				Driving 8
15Jun66–8Aqu	fst 7f	.23 .46 1.25$\frac{1}{5}$ Clm	7500	11	4	$52\frac{1}{4}$ 43 $52\frac{3}{4}$ 5^3	JLRotz	b 113	9.20	77–16	Mt. Stromboli 116^{nk} Midstater 114^2 Child Prodigy 119no				No mishap 12
28May66–4Aqu	sly 6f	.22$\frac{3}{5}$ .46$\frac{2}{5}$1.12$\frac{4}{5}$ f–	10000	6	5	$74\frac{1}{4}$ 57 $31\frac{1}{2}$ $41\frac{1}{2}$	JLRotz	b 116	10.70	78–18	Three of Akind 118$\frac{1}{2}$ Bozanga 106$2\frac{3}{4}$ Nice Question 111^h				Wide 7
LATEST WORKOUTS		Nov 2 Bel tr.t. 3f fst .38 b					Oct 29 Bel tr.t. 5f fst 1.03$\frac{4}{5}$ b			Oct 8 Bel tr.t. 4f fst .49$\frac{3}{5}$ h			Oct 1 Bel tr.t. 4f fst .49$\frac{2}{5}$ h		

The filly's record begins with the May 28 race, when she runs a close fourth against $10,000 fillies, demonstrating that she was far from outclassed in such company. Next she goes with $7,500 males, finishing fifth. On June 24 the scene shifts to Monmouth Park. There, because of the weak race against $7,500 colts and geldings, she is allowed to pay better than 3–1 in a race against the kind of females she could whip on three legs.

On July 9 she is boosted into allowance company and suffers a predictable defeat. Then come three races against males, including a tenth-place finish on August 10. Presumably she is now in dreadful form, and no sensible punter will touch her.

On August 25 she turns up in a filly race at a whopping price—18–1, and runs second. You can't win 'em all. Back to Aqueduct she goes, against $8,500 males for a nineteen-length loss. But Al Scotti is there, waiting to pounce. And pounce he does, leading the filly to his barn after the race.

Scotti coddles her for five-and-a-half weeks and then cashes in on the information contained in the animal's biography. Knowing that she can whip $7,500 fillies and is probably not outclassed by $10,000 ones, he runs her for $7,000 and has the foresight to put Braulio Baeza aboard. She pays a ridiculous $21.20.

Good to begin with, and greatly improved by Scotti's expert handling, Cherokee Mary runs a spanking good race against authentic allowance company on October 22, finishing second behind Max Hirsch's hot Cherimoya. This, friends, is horse training. Especially the aspects of training that have to do with handicapping!

Athen's Gem

HERE IS ANOTHER EXAMPLE of the kind of intelligent manipulation that made Cherokee Mary good news for attentive readers of the past-performance records.

Athen's Gem **$14,000** B. f (1963–Ky), by Free America or High Bandit—Atheneum, by Bull Dandy **117** 1967 10 3 1 2 $11,075; 1966 23 7 4 3 $19,225

Rosemary Maziarz J. F. Plett (P. W. Salmen, Jr.)

16May67–7GS	fst 6f	.22⅖	.46⅗1.11⅗	Clm	15000	5	3	2h	1h	2h	21½	GPatterson	b 111	15.60	84–18	Joe The Barber 1111½ Athen's Gem 111nk Cuetip 1161½	Game try	8
6May67–7GS	sly 6f	.23⅕	.47⅕1.13	f–	Allow	1	2	61¾	67¼	77¾	79	JLeonard	b 112	12.60	70–23	Tangle 112½ I'm All Ready 115½ Queen Narda 1121½	Fell back	9
26Apr67–8Suf	fst 6f	.22	.44⅖1.09⅘	Clm	15000	3	7	41½	33	33½	35½	LMoyers	b 112	3.50	86–15	Flying Hat 1142 Rex De Plumbum 1143½ Athen's Gem 1122	Held on	7
13Apr67–5Aqu	fst 6f	.22⅖	.45⅗1.10⅘	Clm	15500	7	1	1½	1h	32½	36¾	RUssery	b 116	3.50	82–16	Two Stelle 121¾ Cuetip 1176 Athen's Gem 116no	Set pace, tired	7
22Mar67–5GP	fst 6f	.22⅖	.45⅖1.10⅗	Clm	13000	9	1	12	2½	21	1½	LMoyers	b 113	9.70	91–19	Athen's Gem 113½ Bwana Peacha 1163½ Mahjubill 116¾	Hard drive	9
15Mar67–7GP	fst 7f	.22⅘	.45⅗1.23⅘	f–	Allow	10	2	22	42	912	810	LMoyers	b 116	42.00	80–18	Nature 1222 Rose Court 1141 Boiseana 114¾	Failed to stay	12
27Feb67–8Hia	fst 6f	.22⅕	.45⅘1.10⅘	f–	Allow	6	2	1h	11	1½	1nk	LMoyers	b 112	7.20	90–14	Athen's Gem 112nk Mandioca 1133½ Foreign Fable 107nk	Lasted	12
1Feb67–7Hia	fm 1 1/16 Ⓣ		1.45⅖	Clm	14000	6	1	12	1h	86	119½	LMoyers	b 113	8.80	68–28	Brant 114no The Clown 1162 Bursun 1161½	Bore out badly	12
18Jan67–2Hia	fst 6f	.22⅖	.45⅘1.11⅗	f–	13000	1	5	12	13	13	11¾	LMoyers	b 116	7.10	86–12	Athen's Gem 1161¾ Naga 1121½ Get A Lot 1161½	Under hard drive	12
7Jan67–6TrP	fst 6f	.21⅘	.44⅖1.09⅗	Clm	12500	3	4	33	54	55	53¾	LMoyers	b 110	21.50	90–20	Blinking Star 114nk Cap'n Shorty 1171¼ New Ballot 1111¼	No mishap	8
29Dec66–8TrP	fst 6f	.22	.44⅗1.09	Allowance		3	4	21	43½	57	610	JGiovanni	b 112	22.80	87–11	The Cheat 1174¾ Call Me Fritz 117½ Roman John 115nk	Tired	12

LATEST WORKOUTS May 14 GS 3f fst .36 b May 14 GS 3f fst .36 b Apr 10 Bel tr.t. 4f gd .49⅘ b Apr 2 Hia 4f fst .49 b

Note the consistency of Athen's Gem. During 1966 she won seven races in twenty-three starts, was in the money a total of fourteen times, and earned almost $900 per outing. On December 29 she is nowhere against male allowance horses at Tropical. Nine days later, again facing males, she finishes less than four lengths back, in excellent time, at 20–1. The January 18 race is a much easier proposition—against fillies. She pays $16.20. A gift.

Now comes a workout against males, at the wrong distance and on the turf course, followed by a $16.40 mutuel against members of her own sex, at the right distance on the dirt! The crowd has not yet recognized the trainer's methods.

After testing her early speed against topflight allowance fillies (note the 42–1 odds), Athen's Gem next pays a stout $21.40, beating males!

Barlie Ann B.

SEE HOW K. T. Leatherbury recognized this diamond in the rough, bought it cheap, and put some polish on it. On March 7 the filly beat $3,000 males in the Pimlico mud for the first victory of her life. In fact, it was the first race of her life. Unraced at two and unpromising at three, she had simply been offered for sale in a cheap race. But she showed quality. She came from off the pace in that thick Maryland goo and won going away.

Barlie Ann B. * **$10,000** Ro. f (1964–NJ), by Veloz II—Gioconda, by The Rhymer **110⁷** 1967 9 3 1 0 $8,235; 1966 0 M 0 0 —

W. Page K. T. Leatherbury (J. P. Brunning)

11May67–7Pim	sly 5f	.22⅕	.46⅖ .59⅘	f–	Allow	8	4	1h	2h	31	21	RKotenko7	b 106	8.10	94–19	Banting 1101 Barlie Ann B. 1061½ Yemen's Dotter 1101	Gamely	11
4May67–6Pim	fst 6f	.23⅖	.46⅕1.12⅕	Clm	11500	5	1	2h	33½	34	45½	ACannon	b 114	2.60	83–16	Decacean 115½ Tin Ear 1153½ Pretty Music 1081½	Failed to stay	7
25Apr67–7Pim	fst 6f	.23⅗	.47 1.12⅖	Clm	9000	2	1	2½	1h	11	11½	AAgnello5	b 105	3.40	88–14	Barlie Ann B. 1051½ Cite The Nurse 107nk Whiskey 1151½	Drew clear	8
14Apr67–8Pim	fst 6f	.23⅕	.46⅗1.11⅘	f–	Allow	1	6	2h	21½	21	64¾	ACannon	b 103	15.30	86–14	Family Gallery 110½ Dana's Flight 1102½ Yemen's Dotter 1081	Tired	12
5Apr67–6Pim	fst 6f	.23⅖	.46⅖1.12⅗	Clm	6000	9	7	11½	13	14	14	ORosado	b 108	88.80	87–18	Barlie Ann B. 1084 Laurel Mark 115½ Verdant Shores 113h	Mild dr.	12
28Mar67–7Pim	fst 6f	.23⅖	.47⅕1.13⅕	f–	7000	1	12	1215	1217	1114	109	GPatterson	b 113	87.80	75–18	Cut And Comb 115½ Banting 1151 Royal Frolic 1081½	No speed	12
17Mar67–6Pim	my 6f	.24	.48⅗1.13⅗	Clm	6000	3	1	1h	44	54¾	811	GPatterson	b 110	13.70	71–24	Rogo 1134 Dark Ocean 1142½ Verdant Shores 1121	Brief speed	8
15Mar67–6Pim	sly 6f	.23⅘	.48⅕1.15	Cl	c–4750	2	6	3nk	511	38	56¼	RKimball	b 112	5.50	69–27	Ratio 1155 Minstrel Band 115no Lantern Hill 115nk	Fell back	11
7Mar67–1Pim	my 6f	.24⅖	.49⅗1.16⅖	Clm	3000	3	8	43½	35	32	12	RKimball	112	12.40	68–29	Barlie Ann B. 1122 Borla 1081½ Plum Pie 1131	Was going away	11

LATEST WORKOUTS Jun 3 Del t.c. 5f fm 1.05⅗ b

Eight days later the claiming price was $4,750 and Leatherbury bought. He wasted no time. Put her into a $6,000 race two days later and then into a $7,000 one. On April 5 she was ready. With Osvaldo Rosado and a scant 108 pounds, she whipped $6,000 males like a 2–1 shot. But she paid $179.60 for a $2 ticket. Was it an upset? For sure. But was it an accident? Not a bit of it.

After a splendid race against good allowance fillies, she came back against $9,000 males on April 25 and won impressively.

After the narrow loss to Banting in extremely fast time on May 11, the stewards might well have asked whether this was the same animal that had been entered for $3,000 barely two months earlier. The reply would have been obvious: The previous owners had failed to appreciate the filly's potential. The new owners capitalized on it. I hope the reader enjoys noticing that Leatherbury's methods with this filly are contrary to the normal procedure. He outmatches her against females and whales the whey out of the boys.

Hepzibah

A FINAL EXAMPLE of manipulation with fillies is provided by Skippy Shapoff.

Hepzibah * **$8,500** **Dk. b. or br. f (1964–Ky), by Count Amber—Fullopep, by Bernborough** **120**
A. Weiss M. Padovani (J. V. Martin)

1967	9	3	1	0	$8,115
1966	7	M	2	2	$2,200

5Jly 67–5Aqu	gd 7f	.23	.47	1.26⅕	f–	8500	9	6	6^{6}	6^{5}	11^{12}	13^{16}	LGilligan	b 116	17.10	59–21	Beth Gee 116¾ Fulcrum's Lass 111^{3} High Hairan $106^{2½}$	Tired	13
21Jun67–8Aqu	gd 1	.46⅖	1.12⅕	1.38⅘	f–	c–6500	7	5	$7^{6½}$	$6^{3¼}$	1½	1^{nk}	ECardone	b 118	5.50	74–21	Hepzibah 118^{nk} Little Mert 116^{h} Cheese Souffle 116^{6}	Driving	9
7Jun67–4Aqu	fst 1	.45⅖	1.10⅕	1.37⅘	f–	7500	2	8	6^{9}	$6^{9½}$	$6^{7½}$	5^{5}	ACordero7	b 109	3.40	74–16	Frostyanna 118^{2} Overcome 118^{nk} Fulcrum's Lass 112¾	Wide	8
23May67–7Suf	fst 6f	.22⅘	.46	1.11⅗	Clm	7500	3	12	11^{10}	11^{11}	$6^{5½}$	2^{h}	MCarrozzella	b 115	*2.10	83–20	Head High 115^{h} Hepzibah 115^{1} Dark Crusader 118½	Sharp try	12
12May67–8Suf	gd 6f	.23	.46⅗	1.11⅗	Clm	9500	5	3	4^{6}	$5^{5½}$	5^{8}	$4^{5¾}$	DKelly5	b 108	15.50	77–27	Cheerful Chap 114¾ Defensive Team $112^{2½}$ Pic Ship $120^{2¼}$	No mishap	8
20Apr67–6Suf	gd 6f	.23	.47⅕	1.13⅗	Clm	6250	7	8	$7^{6¾}$	$6^{4¾}$	$3^{3½}$	1½	DKelly5	b 108	2.50	73–23	Hepzibah 108½ Calico Cuffs $114^{1½}$ Ironman Mark $118^{1¼}$	Driving	10
7Apr67–10GP	fst 1 1/16	.48⅗	1.13⅖	1.46⅖	Clm	6500	2	3	3^{3}	2^{2}	5^{12}	5^{14}	RSurrency5	b 108	2.90	62–15	Impy Ash $109^{3½}$ Bold Ship 111^{nk} Ocean Grey 107^{8}	Tired	8
31Mar67–5GP	gd 7f	.23⅗	.46⅗	1.25	Clm	6000	1	1	3^{3}	3^{3}	3^{2}	1½	RSurrency5	b 105	17.80	84–18	Hepzibah 105½ Bold Felia $116^{1½}$ Back Home 116½	Up final strides	12
23Mar67–2GP	fst 6f	.22⅗	.45⅕	1.11⅘	Clm	6500	9	11	12^{19}	12^{21}	9^{17}	7^{11}	MSolomone	114	27.30	74–16	Little Who Who 106^{1} Quillostar $117^{3½}$ Back Home $116^{2½}$	No speed	12
25Aug66–1Sar	fst 6f	.22⅘	.47⅖	1.12⅗	f–Md	6500	4	5	$6^{2¾}$	$4^{2½}$	3^{5}	4^{12}	JLRotz	b 115	2.80	73–19	Dance Dress 119no Phenom 119^{12} Cheese Souffle 119no	Drifted out	9

LATEST WORKOUTS Jun 29 Aqu 4f fst .49 b Jun 17 Bel tr.t. 3f fst .37 b Jun 3 Bel 4f fst .49⅖ h May 19 Suf 3f fst .36 h

After seven unsuccessful tries with this one on the New York circuit during 1966, he broke her maiden with an interesting win against $6,000 males at Gulfstream on March 31, 1967. The $37.60 payoff was rather modest in the circumstances, and one may presume that a certain amount of smart money was on the lass that day, the intelligentsia having decided that she was finally ready to run.

The three Suffolk races reveal much. A solid victory against boys when entered for $6,250, then a fair effort in which she beat half the field when priced at $9,500, and finally a powerful move against $7,500 males on May 23. Next came the reacclimation race at Aqueduct, entered at the wrong distance under a raw apprentice, Tony Cordero. Two weeks later, facing $6,500 fillies and with clever Ernie Cardone in the irons, she went to the post at $5.50–1. Yet she was a standout—the only filly in the field that had run well at higher claiming prices and against males. The odds should have been no higher than 3–1.

3. EIGHTH AT FAIR GROUNDS, FEBRUARY 17, 1967 —Track Fast

MANY PLAYERS begin their study of a race by "trying to beat" the favorite. The past performances or the track's morning line tells them which horse is likely to be the favorite. They look for holes in the animal's record, hoping to establish in advance that it is a false favorite. If they find the holes, they hunt elsewhere in the field for something likely to win at a price.

My own preference is to let the favorites fall where they may. I look for the likeliest horse in the race, regardless of odds. And the way I find it is by drawing myself a detailed profile of each animal.

The race we are about to study is one in which the probable favorite is immediately obvious—and is full of holes. Longshot fanciers of the "beat the favorite" school will have no difficulty recognizing the horse and its flaws. Whether all of them will spot the eventual winner is another question, although I believe the winner was a standout, and I think I can demonstrate it.

This race is for $12,500 animals, but the purse of $3,000 is less than major tracks award to $3,500 stock. In other words, let us not get the idea that we are dealing with really good claiming racers. These beasts would bring nothing like $12,500 in a major-league market. Anyone who pays the inflated prices affixed to horses on the Louisiana-Illinois-Michigan circuits is either a prime sucker or an extraordinarily resourceful horseman capable of winning it all back in a hurry—perhaps by betting.

8th Fair Grounds

START ▾ 6 FURLONGS FAIR GROUNDS ▴ FINISH

6 FURLONGS. (Mike's Red, February 11, 1967, 1.10, 5, 117.)
Claiming. Purse $3,000. 4-year-olds and upward. Weights, 4-year-olds, 121 lbs., older 122 lbs. Non-winners of three races since Nov. 17 allowed 3 lbs., two races, 5 lbs., a race 8 lbs. (Races for a claiming price of $9,500 or less not considered.) Claiming price $12,500. If entered for $11,250 allowed 2 lbs.

Big Brigade $11,500 — B. g (1961), by Blue Prince—Police Society, by War Admiral
Mr.-Mrs. R. F. Roberts — R. Warren — (Dr. C. E. Hagyard) — **112**
1967 2 1 0 1 $2,040
1966 13 1 7 1 $33,325

25Jan67-8FG	fst 6f	.22⅖	.45⅘	1.10⅗	Allowance	1	5	4^{7}	4^{7}	4^{7}	3^{12}	RRincon	117	3.10	86-13	Prince Glory 114^{8} Bill Denton 116^{4} Big Brigade 117^{5}	Fair try	6
9Jan67-7FG	hy 6f	.23⅕	.47⅘	1.14⅕	Clm 8000	3	7	6^{6}	$5^{5\frac{1}{2}}$	$2^{1\frac{1}{2}}$	$1^{3\frac{1}{2}}$	GOverton	114	2.50	80-31	Big Brigade $114^{3\frac{1}{2}}$ Batsto 109^{2} Seven Circles 113^{nk}	Easily	8
21Dec66-6FG	fst 6f	.22⅘	.47	1.11⅖	Clm 10000	4	3	$4^{1\frac{1}{4}}$	$4^{1\frac{1}{4}}$	$5^{2\frac{1}{2}}$	6^{6}	GOverton	114	5.10	87-15	Shield ofValor114^{3}SensibleSon117^{nk}King ofOlympian114^{nk}	Checked	6
25Nov66-8FG	fst 6f	.23⅖	.47⅖	1.12⅕	Allowance	2	5	$3^{1\frac{1}{2}}$	4^{2}	7^{8}	8^{18}	GOverton	117	*1.50	72-21	Dixie Special $115^{2\frac{1}{2}}$ Whiz A Lot $110^{2\frac{1}{2}}$ Doctor Brocato $114^{3\frac{1}{2}}$	Tired	8
14May66-8CD	gd $1\frac{1}{16}$	.47	1.11⅗	1.43⅘	Louisv'leH	2	5	$5^{9\frac{1}{2}}$	$3^{4\frac{1}{2}}$	2^{2}	$3^{2\frac{3}{4}}$	JNichols	b 116	*1.30	90-13	Tartan Man $113^{\frac{3}{4}}$ I Owe 116^{2} Big Brigade 116^{nk}	Showed even effort	6
5May66-8CD	fst 7f	.22⅕	.44⅗	1.22	ChurchillH	5	3	4^{7}	4^{5}	2^{3}	2^{2}	DBrumfield	b 117	3.50	95-13	Bay Phantom 125^{2} Big Brigade 117^{1} Mr. Pak 110^{nk}	Game try	5
23Apr66-6Kee	fst $1\frac{1}{16}$	.47⅖	1.11⅕	1.42⅘	BenAliH	3	3	2^{2}	1^{2}	$2^{\frac{1}{2}}$	$2^{3\frac{1}{2}}$	JNichols	b 117	2.00	88-13	Swift Ruler $124^{3\frac{1}{2}}$ Big Brigade $117^{\frac{1}{2}}$ Charolero 114^{h}	2nd best	6
9Apr66-6Kee	fst 6f	.22	.44⅘	1.10	PhoenixH	5	3	$4^{2\frac{1}{2}}$	2^{2}	$2^{2\frac{1}{2}}$	2^{2}	DBrumfield	b 117	1.50e	91-14	Bay Phantom 124^{2} Big Brigade $117^{4\frac{1}{2}}$ Valiant Marbo $108^{\frac{1}{2}}$	Wide	6
26Mar66-9OP	fst $1\frac{1}{16}$	.45⅗	1.09⅘	1.42⅖	OaklawnH	13	3	3^{4}	$2^{1\frac{1}{2}}$	3^{nk}	$2^{\frac{3}{4}}$	JNichols	b 119	11.70	95-10	Swift Ruler $123^{\frac{3}{4}}$ Big Brigade 119^{h} Old Coin 111^{h}	Held on gamely	13
19Mar66-8OP	fst 6f	.22⅗	.46	1.10⅖	Allowance	1	4	3^{3}	2^{h}	1^{3}	1^{4}	LSnyder	b 122	*1.20	97- 9	Big Brigade 122^{4} Early Clan 110^{nk} Bad Luk Bil 119^{1}	Easy score	7

LATEST WORKOUTS Feb 12 FG 4f fst .53⅕ b

Dr. Jazz × $12,500 — B. g (1961), by Dr. Reed—Smarty Ann, by Can't Wait
H. Peltier — J. O. Meaux — (L. B. Ryan) — **114**
1967 3 0 1 1 $1,225
1966 30 9 5 5 $24,380

7Feb67-9FG	sl 6f	.23	.47⅗	1.13	Allowance	1	2	$3^{1\frac{1}{2}}$	$3^{2\frac{1}{2}}$	3^{4}	$4^{4\frac{3}{4}}$	LSnyder	114	*1.40	81-25	Ryder'sRequest114^{4} RoyalFranklin$114^{\frac{1}{2}}$ MagicRealm114^{nk}	No exc'se	6
18Jan67-8FG	fst 6f	.22⅘	.46⅕	1.11⅗	Allowance	4	1	2^{1}	$3^{1\frac{1}{2}}$	$4^{1\frac{1}{2}}$	3^{3}	LSnyder	114	5.30	90-20	Mike's Red 117^{1} Prince Glory 114^{2} Dr. Jazz $114^{\frac{1}{2}}$	Good effort	8
4Jan67-8FG	sl 6f	.23⅕	.48	1.13⅗	Allowance	1	2	3^{3}	3^{4}	2^{3}	2^{3}	LSnyder	114	*1.00	80-29	Turf Editor 114^{3} Dr. Jazz 114^{6} Scale Rule 113^{2}	No excuse	6
23Dec66-7FG	fst 6f	.22⅗	.46⅖	1.12	Clm 12500	3	3	$5^{4\frac{1}{2}}$	4^{3}	4^{2}	2^{h}	JPBowlds	114	4.60	88-14	Blue Struggle 117^{h} Dr. Jazz 114no ♦Wolf Hands $110^{1\frac{1}{2}}$	Gamely	7
9Dec66-8FG	my 6f	.23	.48	1.14⅕	Clm 12500	2	3	2^{2}	3^{3}	2^{1}	2^{2}	LSnyder	114	2.60	78-30	Enlightenment 122^{2} Dr. Jazz 114^{2} Odahmin 117no	Gamely	6
25Nov66-7FG	fst 6f	.22⅕	.47	1.13⅕	Clm 12500	3	2	3^{5}	$4^{4\frac{1}{2}}$	4^{5}	4^{2}	JLopez	114	2.60	83-21	Enlightenm't$119^{\frac{3}{4}}$CountyChairman114^{nk}King of Olym'n114^{1}	No mis'p	7
17Oct66-6Haw	fst 6f	.22⅘	.45⅗	1.10⅖	Clm 12500	3	7	7^{7}	$6^{9\frac{1}{2}}$	$6^{4\frac{1}{2}}$	$3^{3\frac{1}{2}}$	MHeath	118	5.70	91-15	Oh My Darling $113^{\frac{1}{2}}$ Sensible Son 114^{3} Dr. Jazz 118no	Finished well	9
10Oct66-7Haw	fst 6f	.22	.45⅕	1.10⅕	Clm 12500	2	5	$5^{4\frac{1}{2}}$	4^{5}	4^{4}	$3^{4\frac{1}{4}}$	MHeath	116	6.00	91-16	China Marine 122^{4} Oh My Darling 113^{nk} Dr. Jazz $116^{\frac{3}{4}}$	Rallied	10
20Sep66-7Haw	fst 6f	.22	.45⅖	1.10⅘	Clm 12500	3	5	3^{6}	3^{6}	3^{4}	$3^{4\frac{1}{2}}$	MHeath	120	9.30	88-12	Stay Up $118^{2\frac{1}{2}}$ Hard Track 116^{2} Dr. Jazz $120^{1\frac{1}{4}}$	No mishap	9
3Sep66-6AP	fst $6\frac{1}{2}$f	.22⅘	.46	1.16⅘	Clm 12500	9	9	$8^{5\frac{1}{2}}$	8^{10}	$8^{9\frac{1}{4}}$	$7^{9\frac{3}{4}}$	LMoyers	117	8.60	82-12	Cachito 115^{3} Island Beau 112^{1} Beau Masque $115^{2\frac{1}{4}}$	No speed	10

LATEST WORKOUTS Feb 15 FG 4f fst .52 b — Feb 4 FG 3f fst .38⅗ b — Jan 14 FG 3f my .38 b — Dec 31 FG 3f my .36⅗ h

Jimmerson $12,500 Dk. b. or br. h (1962), by Jimmer—Cheery Morn, by Johns Joy **119** 1967 2 2 0 0 $4,030
J. DeFee A. H. Johnston (Mrs. G. S. Mayer) 1966 18 2 3 3 $8,335
26Jan67-8FG fst 6f .22⅘ .46⅘1.11⅗ Allowance 4 3 3²½ 2¹ 3ⁿᵏ 1¹½ HRomero⁵ b 109 *0.80 93-16 Jimmerson 109¹½ Worthylouk 118ʰ Aweigh My Lads 117⁶ In time 6
20Jan67-7FG fst 6f .22⅕ .46 1.11⅗ Clm 12500 1 7 1½ 1¹ 2¹ 1ⁿᵒ HRomero⁵ b 109 3.50 94-13 Jimmerson 109ⁿᵒ Mr. Swoon 112ⁿᵏ Whiz A Lot 108² All out, lasted 8
23Dec66-7FG fst 6f .22⅗ .46⅖1.12 Clm 12500 6 2 4⁵ 5³½ 5³ 3ʰ DRichard b 114 ♦2.60 88-14 Blue Struggle 117ʰ Dr. Jazz 114ⁿᵒ ♦Wolf Hands 110¹½ Wide 7
23Dec66—♦-Dead heat.
14Dec66-7FG fst 6f .22⅕ .45⅘1.11⅖ Clm 9000 5 1 2³ 2³ 2² 1¹ DRichard b 112 9.00 94-15 Jimmerson 112¹ Bandera Beau 115¹ Shield of Valor 114² Driving 6
5Dec66-7FG fst 6f .21⅘ .45⅗1.12⅘ Clm 8000 3 2 5⁶ 5⁵½ 5⁶½ 2² LBroussard⁵ b 109 8.40 85-21 Ryder's Request 117² Jimmerson 109³½ Splash Splash 114² Rallied 8
28Nov66-8FG fst 6f .22⅘ .47⅗1.12⅕ Clm 8000 3 2 3¹½ 3¹½ 3⁴½ 2⁵ DRichard b 114 13.40 85-22 Brilliant Dunce 112⁵ Jimmerson 114¹ Bandera Beau 113¾ Gamely 6
22Sep66-7Haw fm 7f Ⓣ .47 1.24⅖ Clm 10000 3 5 2² 3³½ 8¹⁵ 8¹² IValenzuela b 118 12.60 82- 6 Bold Buck 118ⁿᵏ True Sue 115² High On'a 118¹¼ Early speed, tired 10
7Sep66-2AP fst 6f .23 .46 1.10⅘ Clm 10000 9 2 3³½ 3⁶ 6⁶¾ 9⁷¼ WHartack b 115 3.50 81-13 Trops Bob 115¹¾ Come on Jackie 112¹ Score King 115¹ Tired 10
31Aug66-6AP fst 6f .22⅗ .45⅕1.10⅖ Clm 10000 6 2 4³½ 3⁵½ 3⁴ 4² MSolomone b 117 12.60 89-12 Mr. Kish 115¾ Trops Bob 115¹ Road Grade 119ⁿᵏ Fairly even race 7
6Aug66-5AP fst 6f .22⅗ .45⅖1.10⅕ Clm 12500 3 8 8⁵½ 7⁵¾10⁹ 10⁸¼ NShuk b 117 21.80 84- 9 Fort Ringgold 115ʰ Shawnee Lady 110ⁿᵒ Pertinax 115²¼ Far back 12
LATEST WORKOUTS Feb 7 FG 3f my .37⅖ b

Odahmin $12,500 Ch. h (1961), by Saggy—Square Cut, by Jack High **114** 1967 4 0 2 0 $1,335
J. G. Ferrara J. G. Ferrara (J. C. Dudley-B. M. Heath) 1966 23 3 1 4 $15,015
6Feb67-7FG sly 1⁴⁰.48⅕1.14⅗1.44⅕ Cl c-10000 4 3 3¹½ 2ʰ 2¹ 2²½ RGallimore b 114 *1.90 71-22 Hero's Gift 109²½ Odahmin 114¹½ High On'a 117² Game effort 7
28Jan67-8FG fst 6f .22⅗ .46⅕1.10⅗ Allowance 2 6 2¹ 3¹½ 5⁶ 5⁹¼ LKunitake b 114 7.40 89-11 Diamond Beau 113³ I Owe 114³ Tartan Man 114²½ Speed, tired 9
18Jan67-8FG fst 6f .22⅘ .46⅕1.11⅗ Allowance 5 6 6³ 5³½ 5²½ 4³½ RGallimore b 117 4.10 89-20 Mike's Red 117¹ Prince Glory 114² Dr. Jazz 114½ Finished well 8
4Jan67-7FG sl 6f .23⅕ .47⅕1.13⅘ Cl c-10000 3 5 3² 2³ 2³ 2² RGallimore b 117 2.30 80-29 Bandera Beau 116² Odahmin 117¾ Ryder's Request 117½ Gamely 7
21Dec66-8FG fst 6f .22⅘ .46⅗1.11 Allowance 6 5 3² 3¹ 4³½ 3²½ RWinant b 117 6.20 93-15 Brilliant Dunce 113³ Glassell B. 122ⁿᵏ Odahmin 117ⁿᵒ Good effort 8
9Dec66-8FG my 6f .23 .48 1.14⅕ Clm 12500 3 2 4²½ 2² 4⁴½ 3⁴ GOverton b 117 3.20 76-30 Enlightenment 122² Dr. Jazz 114² Odahmin 117ⁿᵒ Weakened 6
1Dec66-8FG fst 6f .22⅖ .46⅘1.12⅖ Allowance 4 6 5³ 5³½ 1ʰ 3ⁿᵏ RGallimore b 114 17.90 89-18 County Chairman 114ⁿᵏ Viclemen 112ⁿᵒ Odahmin 114½ Faltered 8
19Nov66-7Spt fst 6½f.22⅗ .45⅘1.17⅗ Clm 12500 8 7 7⁴¾ 8⁷¼ 8⁶¼ 6⁴½ JLopez b 118 *1.90e 86-11 Chestnut Park 114ʰ Shield of Valor 108¹½ Grace Good 113¾ Dull 9
LATEST WORKOUTS Feb 15 FG 4f fst .48⅘ h Jan 1 FG 5f my 1.07⅗ b

Hero's Gift × $12,500 B. g (1961), by Noble Hero—Her Gift, by Halcyon Gift **117** 1967 4 1 0 0 $1,950
Arlene V. Soper G. H. Horstmann 3d (E. B. Carpenter) 1966 18 1 1 1 $7,214
6Feb67-7FG sly 1⁴⁰.48⅕1.14⅗1.44⅕ Clm 10000 1 4 4³ 4¹½ 1¹ 1²½ KAGaddis⁵ b 109 11.80 74-22 Hero's Gift 109²½ Odahmin 114¹½ High On'a 117² Mild drive 7
3Feb67-8FG fst 1⁴⁰.48⅕1.13⅘1.41⅗ Allowance 1 2 2ʰ 4¹½ 8⁸ 8¹² KAGaddis⁵ b 109 51.70 75-19 I Owe 114½ Wonder Dancer 113ⁿᵏ Viclemen 114³ Used early 9
13Jan67-8FG hy 6f .22⅘ .46⅘1.13⅗ Allowance 4 6 7¹⁰ 7¹³ 7¹³ 7¹⁶ LTauzin b 114 31.80 67-32 Sails Pride 116¹ Mike's Red 114⁵ Bill Denton 113¹ No speed 7
3Jan67-8FG hy 1$\frac{1}{16}$.49⅕1.15⅖1.48⅘ Allowance 2 6 5¹² 5¹² 5¹² 5¹⁷ RGCook b 117 19.40 54-37 Confiscation 114⁴½ Enlightenment 114¹ Viclemen 116³ No speed 6
27Dec66-8FG gd 1$\frac{1}{16}$.47⅘1.13⅕1.45⅘ Allowance 1 3 3² 3³ 3⁴½ 3⁶ KAGaddis⁵ b 112 22.30 80-23 Zeppelin 114¹ Confiscation 117⁵ Hero's Gift 112ⁿᵏ Evenly 6
23Dec66-7FG fst 6f .22⅗ .46⅖1.12 Clm 12500 7 7 7⁹½ 7⁸ 7⁷½ 7⁶¼ KAGaddis⁵ b 109 52.90 81-14 Blue Struggle 117ʰ Dr. Jazz 114ⁿᵒ ♦Wolf Hands 110¹½ Off slowly 7
8Dec66-8FG fst 6f .22⅕ .46⅖1.12 Allowance 4 1 5⁵ 6⁸½ 6¹¹ 6¹¹ RGCook b 117 37.40 80-19 Roger's Joy 114¾ Great Battle 117¹½ Glassell B. 119½ No factor 6
27Oct66-7Det fst 1⁷⁰.46⅖1.11 1.41 Clm 12500 1 2 2²½ 4⁴½ 5⁷ 5⁶½ JSluss b 114 9.60 92-15 Merano 119² Coralies Boy 115¹¾ Blue Struggle 112² Tired 5
21Oct66-7Det fst 1⁷⁰.46⅖1.11⅕1.42⅗ Clm 12500 6 7 6⁸½ 6⁸½ 6⁷ 5⁷ EJKnapp b 114 7.50 83-22 Merano 119²½ Blue Struggle 112¹¼ Grace Good 109¹½ No factor 6
LATEST WORKOUTS Feb 16 FG 3f fst .38 b Feb 1 FG 3f fst .38⅖ b Dec 21 FG 3f fst .38 bg

Blue Struggle ✻ $12,500 Ch. g (1962), by Blue Gay—Struggle II, by Combat **117** 1967 2 0 0 0 ——
Holiday Stable J. R. Smith (G. Goff) 1966 25 5 4 2 $18,364
20Jan67-7FG fst 6f .22⅕ .46 1.11⅗ Clm 12500 4 5 5⁴½ 5⁵ 7⁵½ 7⁵½ RNono b 117 8.30 88-13 Jimmerson 109ⁿᵒ Mr. Swoon 112ⁿᵏ Whiz A Lot 108² Unruly pre-race 8
6Jan67-8FG fst 6f .22⅗ .46⅘1.12⅘ Clm 12500 6 3 5⁵ 5⁵ 5⁵ 5²¾ DHolmes b 119 8.50 86-17 Chestnut Park 116ʰ King Of Olympian 114ⁿᵒ McGun 117ⁿᵒ No mis'p 6
23Dec66-7FG fst 6f .22⅗ .46⅖1.12 Clm 12500 4 6 6⁴½ 6⁴ 3² 1ʰ DHolmes b 117 13.00 88-14 Blue Struggle 117ʰ Dr. Jazz 114ⁿᵒ ♦Wolf Hands 110¹½ Driving 7
9Dec66-8FG my 6f .23 .48 1.14⅕ Clm 12500 4 6 6⁵½ 6⁶½ 6⁵½ 4⁴ JPBowlds b 117 11.70 76-30 Enlightenment 122² Dr. Jazz 114² Odahmin 117ⁿᵒ Rallied 6
25Nov66-7FG fst 6f .22⅕ .47 1.13⅕ Clm 12500 6 7 7⁷½ 6⁵½ 5⁷ 5⁴ RNono b 117 5.00 81-21 Enlightenm't119¾CountyChairman114ⁿᵏKing of Olym'n114¹ No sp'd 7
27Oct66-7Det fst 1⁷⁰.46⅖1.11 1.41 Clm 12500 2 1 1²½ 1¹ 2³ 3³¾ AGaddis⁵ b 112 2.70 94-15 Merano 119² Coralies Boy 115¹¾ Blue Struggle 112² Tired 5
21Oct66-7Det fst 1⁷⁰.46⅖1.11⅕1.42⅗ Clm 12500 2 2 1¹ 1³ 1ʰ 2²¼ AGaddis⁵ b 112 8.50 88-22 Merano 119²¼ Blue Struggle 112¹¼ Grace Good 109¹½ Couldn't last 8
7Oct66-7Det fst 1⁷⁰.47 1.11⅘1.43⅗ Clm 11500 3 1 1½ 1¹ 1¹ 1ⁿᵏ DHolmes b 114 5.20 85-19 Blue Struggle 114ⁿᵏ Billy Mike 114ⁿᵏ Confiscation 106¹ All out 6
27Sep66-7Det fst 1⁷⁰.47 1.11⅖1.42 Clm c10000 1 2 3½ 2¹½ 4²½ 5³¾ DHolmes 117 4.40 89-16 Merano 114² Irish Bull 114¹¼ Confiscation 107ⁿᵏ Early speed 6
14Sep66-8Det fst 1⁷⁰.46⅖1.12⅖1.42⅕ Clm 10000 1 1 1³ 1ʰ 2ʰ 2½ DHolmes b 117 5.00 91-20 Billy Mike 115½ Blue Struggle 117³ Merano 114ⁿᵏ Clear lead, failed 7
5Sep66-8Det fst 1⁷⁰.46⅕1.13⅗1.43 Allowance 1 2 2⁴ 4⁵½ 8¹⁷ 8¹² JPBowlds b 117 11.60 76-16 Great Battle 109¾ The Nutts 109¹ County Chairman 117¾ Tired 8
LATEST WORKOUTS Feb 15 FG 3f fst .39 b Feb 12 FG 4f fst .52⅕ b Feb 9 FG 4f fst .49⅗ b Feb 5 FG 4f fst .48⅘ h

Whiz A Lot $12,500 Dk. b. or br. c (1963-Tenn), byGee Whiz—Little Tweeny, by Cond'nt **108⁵** 1967 1 0 0 1 $300
Mrs. J. M. Branham O. Clelland (Mrs. J. M. Branham) 1966 15 3 2 2 $8,300
20Jan67-7FG fst 6f .22⅕ .46 1.11⅗ Clm 12500 5 6 4⁴½ 4¹ 3¹½ 3ⁿᵏ STheall⁵ b 108 19.10 94-13 Jimmerson 109ⁿᵒ Mr. Swoon 112ⁿᵏ Whiz A Lot 108² Game effort 8
6Dec66-8FG hy 6f .23 .48⅕1.14 Allowance 7 5 5⁴ 6⁵¾ 7⁷ 8⁹ STheall⁵ b 117 9.70 72-35 Tenzing II 114¹ Brilliant Dunce 119½ Estalight 114¹ Tired 9
1Dec66-8FG fst 6f .22⅖ .46⅘1.12⅖ Allowance 5 7 7⁵ 7⁵ 7⁴¾ 6⁵¼ STheall⁵ b 107 6.00 84-18 County Chairman 114ⁿᵏ Viclemen 112ⁿᵒ Odahmin 114½ Broke slowly 8
25Nov66-8FG fst 6f .23⅗ .47⅗1.12⅘ Allowance 6 1 1ʰ 1ʰ 1ʰ 2²¼ STheall⁵ b 110 26.00 87-21 Dixie Special 115²¼ Whiz A Lot 110²½ DoctorBrocato 114³¾ 2nd best 8
20Oct66-7GS fst 6f .22⅖ .46⅕1.12 Clm 13000 1 6 6⁶ 5⁶½ 4³½ 3²½ JGiovanni b 112 9.90 81-23 Fearless Lee 114²½ He Can Deal 112ⁿᵒ Whiz A Lot 112ⁿᵏ Rallied 7
13Oct66-5GS fst 6f .22⅕ .45⅕1.09⅘ Allowance 5 3 6⁵ 7⁷½ 7⁷¾ 7¹² STheall⁵ b 107 25.30 83-13 Trish M. 118¹½ Conchy Joe 108²½ Gary G. 112ⁿᵒ Fell back early 7
22Sep66-8Nar sly 6f .23⅕ .46⅗1.12⅗ Allowance 6 4 4³½ 3⁴ 2³ 3⁵¾ DMadden b 119 1.90 77-27 Lane 119⁵ Fuel Carrier 112¾ Whiz A Lot 119ⁿᵏ Bid, tired 6
22Aug66-7Rkm gd 6f .22⅗ .45⅗1.12⅗ Allowance 2 8 7⁹½ 8¹¹ 8¹² 8¹¹ DMadden b 112 8.40 76-20 Nike Point 119²½ Lane 108¹ Missy's Double 111² Raced far back 8
18Jun66-8Suf fst 6f .22⅗ .45⅗1.10⅗ Handicap 4 3 4¹½ 5¹½ 4ⁿᵏ 5²¼ DMadden b 113 3.60 92-12 Flame Tree 124ⁿᵏ It's Blitz 109¹ Mister Westgate 113¾ In close 7
11Jun66-8Suf gd 6f .22⅘ .46⅖1.11⅘ Allowance 1 6 6⁵¾ 5⁴¼ 4⁴½ 4⁴¾ DMadden b 118 3.00 85-18 d-Buddy's Choice 116ⁿᵒ Sandoval 122²½ Tick Tack 118² Evenly 7
LATEST WORKOUTS Feb 14 FG 6f fst 1.18 b Feb 10 FG 5f fst 1.04 b Feb 6 FG 5f sly 1.06⅖ b Jan 27 FG 5f fst 1.05 b

Chestnut Park $12,500 Ch. g (1963-Okla), by Good and Plenty—Nupi's Comet, by Teddy's Comet **118** 1967 5 1 0 1 $2,630
M. O. Savoie S. Parise (T. Yochum) 1966 18 6 0 1 $14,332
2Feb67-8FG fst 6f .21⅘ .45⅕1.11⅘ Allowance 4 7 5¹¹ 5⁶½ 4¹½ 4⁸ JAValdez b 113 5.10 84-15 Enlightenment 114⁴ Worthylouk 113² AweighMy Lads114² Weak'n'd 7
28Jan67-8FG fst 6f .22⅗ .46⅕1.10⅗ Allowance 7 8 5²½ 2¹½ 2⁵ 4⁸½ JAValdez b 114 38.70 89-11 Diamond Beau 113³ I Owe 114³ Tartan Man 114²½ Speed, tired 9
25Jan67-8FG fst 6f .22⅗ .45⅘1.10⅗ Allowance 4 1 1¹ 2² 3⁵ 5²⁰ RGallimore b 114 5.20 78-13 Prince Glory 114⁸ Bill Denton 116⁴ Big Brigade 117⁵ Used up 6
6Jan67-8FG fst 6f .22⅗ .46⅘1.12⅘ Clm 12500 1 5 3³ 3²½ 3½ 1ʰ GOverton b 116 9.10 89-17 Chestnut Park 116ʰ King Of Olympian 114ⁿᵒ McGun 117ⁿᵒ Just up 6
2Jan67-7FG my 6f .23⅕ .48⅕1.14⅗ Allowance 6 6 5⁸ 5⁴ 3³ 3⁶½ LSnyder b 113 8.00 71-31 Sir Gaybrook 111²½ No Moniker 114⁴ Chestnut Park 113⁴ No rally 6
24Dec66-7FG fst 6f .22⅕ .45⅕1.11⅘ Allowance 8 6 5⁸½ 5⁵½ 4⁵ 5⁶½ RGallimore b 117 2.30 87-10 Stellar Choice 119½ Hurricane Liz 116² Viclemen 117³ No mishap 8
20Dec66-8FG fst 6f .22⅘ .46 1.11⅘ Allowance 6 5 3³½ 2¹ 1½ 5²¼ RWinant b 120 1.90 89-13 Bill Denton 120ⁿᵏ Silver Beauty 109² Estalight 120ⁿᵒ Tired 7
10Dec66-6FG sl 6f .23 .47⅘1.13⅗ Allowance 10 9 12¹⁴12¹⁵10¹⁶10¹⁶ RBaldwin b 117 8.00 67-25 Kornekopie 117²½ Tenzing II 119ⁿᵏ Lee David 117ⁿᵒ Lacked speed 12
19Nov66-7Spt fst 6½f.22⅗ .45⅘1.17⅗ Clm 12500 7 8 9⁶¾ 9⁸¾ 7⁵¾ 1ʰ SLeJeune b 114 *1.90e 91-11 Chestnut Park 114ʰ Shield of Valor 108¹½ Grace Good 113¾ Driving 9
17Nov66-8Spt fst 6½f.22⅕ .46 1.18 Clm 8500 1 3 3³ 1² 1³ 1⁵ DWhited b 113 8.30 88-16 Chestnut Park 113⁵ Swami 115¹½ Nervous George 112² Mild drive 6
LATEST WORKOUTS Feb 15 FG 5f fst 1.02⅗ b Feb 11 FG 5f fst 1.02⅘ b Jan 19 FG 5f fst 1.06 b Jan 11 FG 3f hy .38⅗ b

Big Brigade: This gelding ran brilliantly in legitimate stakes races during 1966, then caved in. After a six-month vacation, it materialized in New Orleans, where it has been sparingly raced and has worked out scarcely at all. The easy win in an $8,000 claimer becomes less impressive when the handicapper notices that the animal was unraced for sixteen days thereafter and has now been idle for twenty-three more. Furthermore, the horse must be in obvious distress, or else someone should have claimed it for $8,000 on January 9. NO BET.

Dr. Jazz: Would be odds-on against $10,000 claimers but seems unable to beat the kind it faces today. Its only chance, as far as the record shows, is in slow company. Until we see whether today's company is fast, however, we had better not eliminate this gamester. CONTENDER.

Jimmerson: If this horse isn't the favorite today, I'll eat my program. Winner of two out of two this year, and in corking time. And the last outing was an allowance race! Ah, but there are holes. Big ones. First, the allowance race was a cheapie for non-winners of two. Secondly, both of Jimmerson's races this year have been terribly taxing efforts in which he had to run as fast as he ever had in his career, under hard drives. Thirdly, he has not raced in twenty-two days, indicating that the last outing drained him and that his people were more concerned with giving him a needed rest than with trying to cash in on what amateurs might assume to be his sharp form. Fourthly, he is being required to tote 119 pounds today, yet has never (as far as the record shows) won under more than 112. The minor tracks are full of animals whose breaking point is 112 or 114, and Jimmerson looks like one. NO BET.

Odahmin: Showed some speed under Winant in an allowance last December 21 and ran a game second to the hard-knocking Bandera Beau on January 4 when somebody claimed him for $10,000. Claimed a six-year-old son of Saggy for $10,000 at Fair Grounds! Ran fairly well behind Dr. Jazz on January 18, but less well ten days later. And then, when entered again for $10,000 on February 6 at a clearly unsuitable distance, ran quite a good race and was claimed by Ferrara for $10,000. Two claims in a month? What does Ferrara see in this animal? I don't know, but I see something in Ferrara. By no means the busiest horseman in the world, he makes his animals produce. During 1966 he was in only twenty-eight races, but won five of them and got some of the money in five more, collecting almost $1,000 per start. That's fancy going for this circuit. Can this horse beat $12,500 ones today? I can't rule it out. One thing is for sure: Ferrara has a ready animal and wants his money back. CONTENDER.

Hero's Gift: Comfortable winner of the race from which Ferrara claimed Odahmin, this gelding is no part of a six-furlong horse and does not like to carry 117 pounds. NO BET.

Blue Struggle: The December 23 victory seems to have blunted this gelding's edge. It was a terribly taxing drive, and the layoff since January 17 was undoubtedly necessary. Chances are the horse will need today's race, although the recent and frequent workouts suggest that it will run fairly well. I might consider it a contender if the record did not suggest that it needs seven furlongs to show its best. NO BET.

Whiz A Lot: This colt looked mighty sharp in his first race of the year after a six-week layoff. Why, then, has he not raced for an additional four weeks? A careful reading of the dates on which he has raced since June, 1966, shows that the colt does quite well after a layoff, but that Clelland also has made serious attempts to win with him after intervals of only a week. In other words, the horse is given these fresheners because he has problems of some kind, not because he runs better after a vacation. This horse may win, but not with my support. NO BET.

Chestnut Park: Since arriving from Sportsman's Park last November, this four-year-old squeaked to victory in the one claimer it entered, but showed a distressing tendency to collapse in the stretch of its other races. Its main function today, regardless of any hopes its handlers might have, will be to help pickle Jimmerson and Dr. Jazz—and itself—during an early speed duel. NO BET.

The contenders in this tight race seem to be Dr. Jazz and Odahmin, although others are not far behind. With Jimmerson definitely out of the picture and unlikely to approach his previous high speed, the highest pace rating in the field goes to Whiz A Lot. But I doubt he will approach that figure today. Odahmin, on the other hand, rates only a tick behind Whiz A Lot in the pace department. Off that nice tune-up of February 6, the horse can be expected to run back to his good performance of December 21. Because of the flaws in the competition, and out of respect for the judgment of the unusually consistent Ferrara, I consider Odahmin worth playing.

The Running of the Race

JIMMERSON'S FAILINGS eluded the throng, which made him a flabbergasting underlay at 1.80–1. Whiz A Lot, perhaps a more logical choice, was second favorite, and Dr. Jazz got the third most support. Odahmin was 6.60–1, probably because of the increase in claiming price. Yet the animal's credentials as a $12,500 runner were well established on December 9 and were verified by the claims entered for him every time he ran at a lower price!

Jimmerson ran a much better race than I expected, but Odahmin caught him by a short nose and would have beaten him by daylight had the race been 100 yards longer. Poor Whiz A Lot confirmed my suspicions by swerving all over the place, refusing to heed the rider.

EIGHTH RACE
FG 30238
February 17, 1967

6 FURLONGS. (Mike's Red, Feb. 11, 1967, 1:10, 5, 117.)
Claiming. Purse $3,000. 4-year-olds and upward. 4-year-olds, 121 lbs.; older, 122 lbs. Non-winners of three races since Nov. 17 allowed 3 lbs.; two races since then, 5 lbs.; a race since then, 8 lbs. Claiming price, $12,500; if for $11,250, allowed 2 lbs. (Races for a claiming price of $9,500 or less not considered.)
Value to winner $1,950; second, $600; third, $300; fourth, $150. Mutuel Pool, $62,296.

Index	Horses	Eq't A Wt PP St	¼	½	Str Fin	Jockeys	Cl'g Pr.	Owners	Odds to $1
30144FG²	Odahmin	b 6 114 4 5	5¹	5²	2½ 1ⁿᵒ	R Winant	12500	J G Ferrara	6.60
30001FG¹	Jimmerson	b 5 119 3 2	1½	1¹	1½ 2³½	M Venezia	12500	J Defee	1.80
29954FG⁷	Blue Struggle	b 5 117 6 4	6³	6²	5² 3ⁿᵏ	D Holmes	12500	Holiday Stable	12.50
29954FG³	Whiz A Lot	b 4 108 7 3	4¹	4½	4½ 4¹	S Theall⁵	12500	Mrs J M Branham	3.00
30156FG⁴	Dr. Jazz	6 114 2 1	2½	2ⁿ	3½ 5⁴	L Snyder	12500	H Peltier	4.70
29992FG³	Big Brigade	6 112 1 6	7²	7⁴	6¹ 6²½	J R Lopez	11250	Mr Mrs R F Roberts	6.50
30117FG⁴	Chestnut Park	b 4 118 8 8	3ʰ	3¹	7³ 7¹	G Overton	12500	M O Savoie	13.40
30144FG¹	Hero's Gift	b 6 117 5 7	8	8	8 8	L Tauzin	12500	Mrs A V Soper	38.10

Time, :23, :47⅕, 1:12⅕. Track fast.

$2 Mutuel Prices:

4-ODAHMIN	15.20	6.40	4.60
3-JIMMERSON		3.80	3.00
6-BLUE STRUGGLE			6.20

Ch. h, by Saggy—Square Cut, by Jack High. Trainer, J. G. Ferrara. Bred by J. C. Dudley and B. M. Heath.
IN GATE—4:43. OFF AT 4:43 CENTRAL STANDARD TIME. Start good. Won driving.
ODAHMIN, well handled, raced evenly for a half mile and, responding to brisk urging during the stretch run, won from JIMMERSON in the last strides. JIMMERSON went to the front early and held on gamely during the drive and just missed while easily second best. BLUE STRUGGLE, outrun for a half mile, finished determinedly. WHIZ A LOT, rank during the race, swerved repeatedly and the rider was unable to do his mount complete justice. DR. JAZZ, prominent until inside the stretch, failed to stay. BIG BRIGADE was never dangerous. CHESTNUT PARK had early speed and was tiring when bothered by WHIZ A LOT at the stretch turn. HERO'S GIFT, never close, had no mishap.

4. NINTH AT TROPICAL, JANUARY 13, 1967—Track Fast

PLAYERS WHO UNDERSTAND that horses sometimes run too well for their own good will have no trouble locating the winner of this race. But confusion awaits those who persist in the superstition that a good race last time means a good race today.

For reasons beyond my ken, most racegoers have not yet grasped the truth about the Thoroughbred form cycle. Most horses, particularly claiming animals, are raced into shape. They then win or run close. In so doing, they race themselves right out of shape. The older the horse, the more misleading its good last race is likely to be. If the race was too fast, and if it came soon after a strenuous drive in a previous race, it very likely ruined the beast's condition. Watch for this factor in the race that now faces us. It is the key to the outcome.

The conditions specify older sprinters worth $10,000 to $12,000.

9th Race Tropical

START ▾ 6 FURLONGS TROPICAL PARK ▴ FINISH

6 FURLONGS (Chute). (Sikkim, January 2, 1967, 1.07⅗, 4, 127.)
Claiming. Purse $3,200. 4-year-olds and upward. Weights 4-year-olds 120 lbs., older 121 lbs. Non-winners of two races since November 15 allowed 3 lbs., of a race since that date, 5 lbs., of a race since October 1, 5 lbs. Claiming price $12,000. 2 lbs. allowed for each $1,000 to $10,000. (Races for a claiming price of $8,500 or less not considered.)

Parawolf * **$12,000**
Lt. b. g (1962). by Parador—Wolf's Baby, by Heliopolis
S. Goldberg F. Calcagni (Mr.-Mrs. A. Winick) **114**
1967 1 0 0 0 —
1966 26 2 4 3 $7,330

9Jan67-9TrP	fst	6f	.22	.45	1.10⅕	Clm	10000	11	1	1½	31½	42	66¼	ATCordero	b 114	30.80	85-17	Sage Jamie 115nk Vastland 116½ Cut A Melon 1103¼	Gave way	12
29Dec66-6TrP	fst	6f	.21⅘	.44⅘	1.09⅘	Clm	12500	1	1	2h	32	57½	913	ACordero	b 113	38.80	80-11	Rome Express 1153¼ Your Day 102h Cap'n Shorty 1152¼	Speed, tired	9
17Dec66-6TrP	fst	6f	.22	.45	1.10⅗	Allowance		3	2	42½	88½	817	821	GKotenko	b 115	84.10	68-17	Papa W. 113nk George Raft 115¾ Conchy Joe 1101	Tired	8
26Nov66-8TrP	fst	6f	.21⅘	.44⅗	1.10	Allowance		4	3	46	812	819	823	GGlassner	b 116	105.80	69-11	Conchy Joe 1121 U. Bearcat 122no Valiant Bull 1221	Never close	8
5Nov66-8Tdn	sly	6f	.23	.46⅘	1.13⅕	Handicap		6	1	1h	33	722	726	DSanchez	b 113	13.60	57-28	Giftwrap 1201 Paul M. 1162½ Runforme 1182	Stopped to a walk	7
8Oct66-8Tdn	fst	5f	.22⅕	.46⅕	.58⅖	Allowance		7	2	47	69½	815	920	AAnderson	119	9.00	78-21	Chess Pie 122no Dual Exhausts 1167 Eternal Delight 114nk	Fell back	9
10Oct66-7Tdn	gd	4½f	.22⅗	.46⅖	.52⅗	Allowance		5	8		45	57	68	AAnderson	b 119	3.00	90- 2	Chess Pie 122no Eternal Delight 1141 Ice House Street 1112½	Tired	8
24Sep66-9Tdn	fst	6f	.22⅘	.46⅖	1.12	Cleveland		6	2	11½	1h	22	45¼	AAnderson	b 115	27.50	84-23	Dual Exhausts 1151¾ Busy Cycle 115½ Paul M. 1153	Used in pace	11
19Sep66-8Haw	fst	6f	.22	.45⅖	1.10	Allowance		7	1	54	55	611	619	WCox	115	10.50	78-10	Brainerd 115no Ol Dave 1195 Ramant 1156	Dropped back early	7

LATEST WORKOUTS Jan 3 TrP 3f fst .36 h Dec 12 TrP 4f fst .49⅕ h

Ambarmar **$11,000**
B g (1959), by Ambiorix—Polnettie, by Polynesian
R. J. Sabrinske H. Hoffman (N. W. Brent) **112**
1967 2 0 0 0 —
1965 15 2 3 3 $15,765

7Jan67-6TrP	fst	6f	.21⅘	.44⅖	1.09⅗	Clm	11500	2	7	68¼	66	66½	64½	DBrumfield	113	7.10	89-20	Blinking Star 114nk Cap'n Shorty 1171¼ New Ballot 1111¼	No threat	8
2Jan67-5TrP	fst	6f	.21⅘	.44⅕	1.09⅖	Clm	10000	1	7	72¾	66	66½	66¼	DBrumfield	117	14.30	89-10	New Ballot 114nk Hy Sonny 1222¾ Swing Rex 1171	Had no mishap	8
25Sep65-7Haw	fst	6f	.22⅖	.45⅗	1.11⅕	Allowance		1	6	612	515	515	611	MGonzalez	119	21.30	80-24	Sclazo 1212½ Killoqua 1241¼ Vertex Record 1196	No threat	8
11Aug65-8AP	fst	7f	.22⅗	.45⅕	1.21⅘	W.WrightH		7	8	811	812	77¾	88½	HHinojosa	116	32.50	89-13	Gallant Romeo 1262½ Tronado 1241½ Take Over 115h	Never close	10
21Jly65-6AP	fst	1	.47⅘	1.12	1.36	Allowance		5	2	22	2h	1h	11½	HHinojosa	119	1.80	89-11	Ambarmar 1191½ Stephen Foster 122¾ Hokum Pokum 1173½	Hard dr.	6
16Jly65-7AP	fst	7f	.22⅗	.45⅕	1.23⅖	Allowance		2	7	65½	54¾	21	1¾	RBroussard	116	*1.00	90-14	Ambarmar 116¾ Odahmin 1183 Pocholi 1155	Was up in time	7
7Jly65-8AP	fst	7f	.22⅘	.45⅕	1.23	Handicap		4	6	64¼	53	2½	21½	HHinojosa	113	5.90	90-15	Bold Velvet 1111½ Ambarmar 1133½ Rub Down 1123	Made game eff't	7

LATEST WORKOUTS Dec 27 Hia 4f fst .47⅗ b Dec 22 Hia 4f fst .49 b Dec 14 Hia 4f fst .48⅗ h Dec 10 Hia 3f fst .35⅘ h

Dance Contest **$10,000**
Gr. g (1963-Md). by Native Dancer—Try Hard, by Endeavour II
H. Bartell F. Martin (A. G. Vanderbilt) **109**
1967 1 0 0 0 —
1966 19 3 2 4 $10,500

2Jan67-5TrP	fst	6f	.21⅘	.44⅕	1.09⅖	Clm	9000	4	5	2½	21½	44	713	EMonacelli	114	10.50	82-10	New Ballot 114nk Hy Sonny 1222¾ Swing Rex 1171	Well placed, tired	8
24Nov66-5Aqu	fst	6f	.22⅘	.46⅗	1.12	Clm	8500	9	2	41¼	3½	2h	2h	BBaeza	116	4.00e	83-21	Your Day 116h Dance Contest 1162½ Swiss Bank 111½	Sharp try	11
17Nov66-5Aqu	fst	6f	.22	.45	1.11⅖	Clm	8500	2	2	12½	13	2½	53½	BBaeza	b 116	4.60	82-20	Farmer Snooty 116no Your Day 1161¼ Snow Dales 1091½	Used up	8
2Nov66-8Aqu	fst	7f	.22⅗	.44⅘	1.25⅕	Cl	c-6500	9	2	15	110	14	1013	FFont7	b 109	5.80	67-19	d-Taravari116nk PinchersPride1161½ WillowCreek1162	Stopped	11
19Oct66-2Aqu	sly	6f	.22⅖	.45⅗	1.12	Cl	c-5000	2	2	13	14	14	32½	RUssery	b 119	2.10	80-19	Validated 1162½ Pinchers Pride 116h Dance Contest 119nk	Tired	8
5Oct66-1Aqu	gd	6f	.22⅖	.45⅘	1.12⅗	Clm	5000	2	3	13	16	15	13	RUssery	b 116	*1.20	80-22	Dance Contest 1163 Lou Michaels 116no Validated 111nk	Mild drive	13
27Sep66-2Aqu	fst	6f	.22⅖	.45⅖	1.12⅖	Cl	c-3500	6	1	14	15	16	13½	HWoodhouse	b 115	*1.60	81-21	Dance Contest 1153½ Lakythra 1151 Wrong Intentions 1071½	Handily	10
21Sep66-1Aqu	sly	6f	.23	.46⅘	1.12⅗	Clm	4000	6	4	21½	21½	21½	35	HWoodhouse	b 112	*1.90	75-24	Son of Roman 1145 Hip Shooter 116h Dance Contest 1122½	No exc.	10
13Sep66-2Aqu	fst	6f	.22⅕	.45⅖	1.13⅗	Clm	4000	12	1	14	16	16	31¼	WBlum	b 113	*2.10e	74-22	Black Rod 112¾ Barricado 112½ Dance Contest 1132½	Used up	12
13Aug66-2Sar	fst	6f	.22⅖	.46⅖	1.12	Clm	6500	7	2	13	12	921	923	MVenezia	b 112	4.60	55- 9	Mt. Stromboli 1161½ Little Bullfrog 1196 Measure 114nk	Used up	9
4Aug66-1Sar	fst	6f	.22⅗	.45⅘	1.12	Clm	7500	5	2	12	14	13	55½	KKnapp	b 112	12.40	82-13	Hobe Sound 1113 Steve's Vow 1161½ Royal Decision 1161	Weakened	10

LATEST WORKOUTS Jan 8 Hia 5f fst 1.00 h Dec 31 Hia 4f fst .47 h Dec 26 Hia 3f. fst .35 h Nov 22 Bel tr.t. 3f fst .38⅗ b

Washita King **$10,000**
B. g (1960), by Olympian King—Exmae, by Excite
T. J. Sims D. Ruth (V. Shields) **105⁵**
1966 19 7 2 2 $11,146
1965 19 7 1 4 $6,267

26Dec66-6TrP	fst	6f	.22⅕	.45	1.09⅗	Clm	6000	9	1	11½	13	14	13½	RSurrency5	b 108	3.30	94- 9	Washita King 1083½ Winkie 120h •Everullah 1161¼	Kept driving	9
12Dec66-4TrP	fst	6f	.22⅘	.45⅘	1.11	Clm	5500	1	6	3nk	11½	11½	2h	RSurrency5	b 108	5.80	87-14	Out of Pocket 113h Washita King 1081 Windy Hill 1131¾	Missed	8
3Dec66-4TrP	fst	6f	.22⅖	.45⅖	1.10⅕	Clm	5500	10	3	1h	2h	2½	43½	BPearl	b 116	73.[illegible]0	87-10	Mr. Kish 1181¾ Porkchopper 118½ Mickey C. 1181¼	Weakened	10
26Nov66-5TrP	fst	6f	.22⅖	.45⅖	1.10⅕	Clm	6000	12	1	85	109	1113	1115	BPearl	b 111	66.90	76-11	Will Dance 118nk Turf Parade 1183¾ Mickey C. 114¾	No speed	12
5Oct66-3CD	fst	7f	.23⅘	.47	1.25⅗	Cl	c-4250	6	3	2h	2½	22	53¼	SClark	b 117	*2.60	76-17	•Choice T. 117nk •Ever Near 117nk Gee M Gee 1171½	Tired in drive	6
1Oct66-4CD	my	7f	.23⅗	.47⅕	1.26⅖	Clm	5000	5	5	33½	43½	67	710	SClark	b 114	5.30	65-22	Navy Jack 1151¼ Colonel Combat 1161¼ Orderly 1163	Failed to stay	8
24Sep66-5CD	fst	6f	.22⅕	.46	1.12	Clm	5000	4	8	66½	64¾	32	3¾	MManganello	b 116	6.20	85-14	Long Sunset 116nk Sharon A. 116½ Washita King 1162	Held on well	10
9Aug66-6Ran	fst	6½f	.23⅘	.47⅕	1.18⅘	Cl	c-3500	4	1	1h	12	13	17	FSaumell	b 122	*1.20	87-26	Washita King 1227 Marcumba Way 112no Grey Majesty 1161	Handily	8
2Aug66-5Det	gd	6f	.22⅘	.46⅘	1.12⅕	Clm	5000	6	7	65¾	65¾	68	67	JLopez	b 122	25.00	72-23	Royal Script 1222 Beacon Hill 115¾ Turkey inth Hay 1072½	No factor	10

LATEST WORKOUTS Nov 25 TrP 3f fst .36⅖ h

Hy Sonny $12,000 B. g (1961), by Shine Again—Loycee Dear, by Dust By
M. D. Kort N. J. Moran (I. Kort) **118**
1967 1 0 1 0 $640
1966 13 1 2 5 $6,010

2Jan67-5TrP fst 6f .21⅘ .44⅕1.09⅖ Clm 10000 5 1 1½ 1½ 1½ 2nk RCox b 122 12.70 95-10 New Ballot 114nk Hy Sonny 1222¾ Swing Rex 1171 Failed to last 8
CDec66-5TrP fst 6f .22 .44⅗1.09⅗ Clm 8000 9 1 11 11 1½ 1¾ RCox b 115 13.20 94-11 Hy-Sonny 115¾ Good Business 113nk Mr. Kish 1194½ Hard ridden 10
2Nov66-8TrP fst 6f .22⅕ .45⅕1.10⅕ Clm 10000 1 6 55 78¼ 712 89¾ RCox b 115 33.00 81-15 Measure 1131 Escobar II 122h Number One Son 1152½ No factor 12
5Nov66-6GS fst 6f .22⅕ .45⅗1.11⅕ Clm 9500 4 1 1h 21 23 34¼ MLukas7 b 107 9.90 84-23 Escobar II 1142½ Reneger 1142 Hy Sonny 107¾ Held for placing 9
2Sep66-6Atl sly 6f .22⅗ .46⅗1.12⅘ Clm 10000 7 1 43½ 53 74¼ 64½ DFrench b 115 13.90 72-28 Tiffany II 113nk Riot Squad 119¾ Prose King 115no No mishap 8
4Sep66-7Atl fst 6f .22⅗ .46⅘1.11⅘ Clm 10000 6 1 22 21½ 22½ 33 DFrench b 114 7.40 80-23 Speedy Admiral 1142 Tiffany II 1121 Hy Sonny 114h Bid, hung 8
3Sep66-4Atl fst 6f .22⅖ .45⅘1.11⅗ Clm 8500 2 2 11 13 13 3nk DBrumfield b 115 *3.10 85-17 Jimmy Miller 111nk Irish Charger 107h Hy Sonny 1154 Held well 8
6Aug66-5Atl gd 6f .22⅖ .46⅕1.11⅘ Clm 9000 4 4 51½ 44 45 34½ DBrumfield b 114 7.20 78-22 Transvaal 1162½ Speedy Admiral 1162 Hy Sonny 114h Even race 6
7Jly 66-4Del gd 6f .22 .46⅕1.12⅗ Clm 8000 1 1 2h 44 45 24½ CRogers b 115 3.10 77-15 Winged Step 1194½ Hy Sonny 115no Lightning Miss 1061½ 2nd best 6
3Jun66-8Del fst 6f .22⅕ .45⅗1.11⅗ Clm 10000 6 4 43½ 45½ 42½ 62½ CRogers b 115 9.30 86-13 Teetotaler 112h Count Mara 117h Winged Step 115no Tired 7
1Jun66-3Del gd 6f .23 .47⅗1.12⅗ Clm 11500 3 1 2h 2½ 45½ 611 CRogers b 118 5.70 71-22 Prose King 1126 Speedy Admiral 1191 Fieroval 1131 Early speed 8
LATEST WORKOUTS Dec 29 Hia 5f fst 1.01⅗h Dec 22 Hia 6f fst 1.16⅘b Dec 17 Hia 3f gd .39 b Dec 5 GP 4f fst .52 b

***Hercules II** $12,000 Ch. h (1962), by Solito—Teodolinda, by Adalid
S. Lazzarin E. Navarro (Haras La Quebrada-Tres Pinos) (Arg.) **114**
1966 14 4 1 1 $7,721
1965 11 2 3 2 $5,216
(Formerly named Tanger)

1Dec66-6TrP fst 6f .22⅖ .45⅗1.10⅗ Clm 10000 5 4 62½ 63¼ 66½ 56½ JVasquez 117 15.10 82-15 He's My Partner 112½ Someticco 112¾ Mr. Kish 1145 Early foot 8
2Jly 66-Monterrico (Peru) fst*5f .57⅖ Open Handicap 34 STrevilcock 121 7.00 —— Terron 1073¼ Pershing 110¾ Hercules 1211¼ 10
9Jun66-Monterrico (Peru) fst*6f 1.12 Open Handicap 7 STrevilcock 121 6.00 —— Pershing 1045 Divino Sol 107¾ Temblor 112nk 8
9Jun66-Monterrico (Peru) fst*5f .58⅖ Gran Premio America 11 SRuiz 128 13.00e —— Dardanus 130nk Bloody Mary 1237 Rubencito 1301½ 13
4Jun65-Monterrico (Peru) fst*5f .56⅘ Clasico Jky Club d'Montevideo 58½ SRuiz 129 3.00e —— Antojo 1012½ Aristeo 1201¼ Taumaturgo 1203¼ 5
7May66-Monterrico (Peru) fst*5f .57⅘ Premio Especial (Alw) 1no SRuiz 127 5.35 —— Hercules 127no Niquelita 1131¾ Macao 127no 12
2May66-Monterrico (Peru) fst*6f 1.12⅗ Allowance 1h JFreyre 118 4.40 —— Hercules 118h Bismark 112¾ Tibbles 119½ 6
LATEST WORKOUTS Jan 7 GP 4f fst .50 b Jan 3 GP 1m fst 1.45 b Dec 17 GP 6f fst 1.17 b Dec 12 GP 3f sly .36⅗ b

Your Day $11,000 Dk. b. or br. c (1963-Ky), by Day Court—Your Letta, by Your Reward
Windham Farm E. W. King (O. Wilmot) **111**
1967 1 0 0 0 $165
1966 33 4 7 5 $20,880

7Jan67-6TrP fst 6f .21⅘ .44⅖1.09⅗ Clm 10500 6 3 53½ 43 44½ 42¾ GMora5 b 104 6.90 91-20 Blinking Star 114nk Cap'n Shorty 1171¼ New Ballot 1111½ No mishap 8
9Dec66-6TrP fst 6f .21⅘ .44⅗1.09⅘ Clm 10500 2 7 64¾ 43½ 33½ 23¼ GMora5 b 102 14.60 90-11 Rome Express 1153½ Your Day 102h Cap'n Shorty 1152¼ Game try 9
2Dec66-9TrP fst 6f .22 .44⅗1.09⅕ Clm 12000 5 6 64¼ 78½ 815 613 BMoreira b 108 13.60 83-14 Fearless Lee 116nk Bwana Peacha 1075½ Romanrig 1141 No mishap 8
9Dec66-6Aqu fst 7f .22⅖ .45⅘1.23⅘ Clm 16000 5 8 64¾ 66 814 816 HGustines b 114 10.30 71-20 The Cheat 1141 There Goes Sam 118h Royal Harbinger 1192 Tired 8
CNov66-6Aqu gd 6f .22⅖ .46 1.12 Clm 14000 5 7 64½ 65¼ 22 2h EBelmonte b 112 9.00 82-22 Royal Harbinger 119h Your Day 112¾ Lane 1161½ Wide, gaining 8
4Nov66-5Aqu fst 6f .22⅘ .46⅗1.12 Cl c-8500 6 3 21 2h 1h 1h RUssery b 116 *1.40 83-21 Your Day 116h Dance Contest 1162½ Swiss Bank 111½ Hard urged 11
7Nov66-5Aqu fst 6f .22 .45 1.11⅗ Clm 8500 8 6 49½ 410 34½ 2no RUssery b 116 *1.50 86-20 Farmer Snooty 116no Your Day 1161¼ Snow Dales 1091½ Slow st. 8
9Nov66-9Aqu fst 7f .22⅗ .45⅕1.23⅗ Clm 12500 10 1 67½ 58 1016 1014 HWoodhouse 116 9.20 74-18 The Cheat 1162½ Cool Oasis 1091½ Gourmand 116no Far off pace 11
10ct66-8Aqu fst 6f .22⅗ .46 1.10⅘ Clm 13000 2 5 52½ 87¾ 88½ 87 JLRotz 115 10.00 82-16 Simpleton 119¾ It's Blitz 1084 Sole Support 117¾ Fell back 10
2Oct66-4Aqu fst 6f .22⅘ .47 1.11⅗ Clm 12500 6 4 52½ 32 31 32½ ACordero 116 3.50 82-18 Simpleton 1162½ Sole Support 116no Your Day 1165 Hung 7
LATEST WORKOUTS Dec 27 Hia 4f fst .47⅗ h Dec 20 Hia 3f fst .37⅖ b Dec 17 Hia 4f gd .50 b Dec 5 Bel tr.t. 4f fst .48⅗ h

New Ballot $10,000 B. g (1963-Ky), by Nilo—Meadow Flower, by Bull Lea
A. J. Mesler H. A. Jerkens (Danada Farm) **113**
1967 2 1 0 1 $2,410
1966 10 2 0 0 $5,320

7Jan67-6TrP fst 6f .21⅘ .44⅖1.09⅗ Clm 10500 7 2 43 32 33½ 31½ ECardone b 111 *1.00 92-20 Blinking Star 114nk Cap'n Shorty 1171¼ New Ballot 1111½ No mishap 8
2Jan67-5TrP fst 6f .21⅘ .44⅕1.09⅖ Clm 9000 7 2 41 32½ 21½ 1nk ECardone5 b 114 4.70 95-10 New Ballot 114nk Hy Sonny 1222¾ Swing Rex 1171 Up final strides 8
8Dec66-6TrP fst 6f .22⅕ .45⅕1.10⅕ Clm 6500 3 5 42½ 42 1½ 13¾ ECardone5 b 108 *1.50 91-14 New Ballot 1083¾ Bama Bear 113½ Nemah Sea 1173¼ Driving 9
9Dec66-8Aqu fst 7f .23 .46⅕1.25⅕ Clm 8500 7 3 1½ 2h 2½ 52¼ ECardone5 113 *2.80 77-20 Goyamo Lad 116½ Alhambra Pal 1211½ Tickled Silly 118¾ Faltered 11
3Dec66-9Aqu fst 6f .23⅗ .47⅘1.12⅖ Clm 9500 2 3 2½ 31 43½ 45 ECardone5 b 110 *2.40 76-20 Mr. C. H. 1192½ Background 1172 Joe Di Rosa 119½ Well up, tired 7
21Nov66-8Aqu fst 6f .22⅘ .46⅗1.11⅗ Clm 12500 6 2 31 42 45 45 ECardone5 b 114 12.70 81-20 Lord Birchfield 1173½ Loop the Loop 117h Hasty Mine 1131½ Tired 8
0Nov66-7GS fst 6f .22⅕ .45⅕1.10⅕ Allowance 2 4 43½ 64½ 56 59¾ GPatterson 112 9.30 83-15 Roving Satellite 1107 Cherrybrook 1101½ Rivoli 112½ Tired 8
2Nov66-6GS fst 6f .22⅖ .45⅗1.10⅘ Allowance 2 4 61¼ 66¾ 54½ 55½ JVasquez 112 22.60 84-17 Johnny'sForm1132 RovingSatellite112h AweighMyLads1122½ No m'p 11
7Sep66-7Haw fst 6f .22⅕ .45⅖1.10⅕ Allowance 7 1 32 57 56½ 410 LPincayJr 119 7.60 86-12 Box Man 1156 Five Rogues 1151½ Uncle Adolph 1192½ Fell back 9
7Sep66-5AP fst 6f .23⅗ .47 1.11⅗ Allowance 1 4 11½ 1h 2½ 11 LPincayJr 113 10.80 85-13 New Ballot 1131 Proxy Fight 113h Celeb X. 1201½ Going away 8
30Jun66-7AP fst 6f .22⅕ .45⅕1.10⅖ Allowance 2 5 54½ 610 816 816 HMoreno 111 16.80 75-15 Fusilier Boy 1101¾ Satin Son 1142½ Feudal Lord 1124 Fell back 8
LATEST WORKOUTS Dec 16 Hia 3f fst .37 b Dec 2 Bel m.t. 3f fst .38⅖ b Nov 19 Bel m.t. 4f fst .49⅗ b

Doll Smasher $10,000 Ch. g (1963-Va), by Gate Smasher—Lester's Doll, by Warlaine
P. McIntosh P. McIntosh (P. A. Triplett) **109**
1967 0 M 0 0 —
1966 0 M 0 0 —
LATEST WORKOUTS Jan 7 GP 5f fst 1.05⅘ b Jan 2 GP 5f fst 1.05⅗ b Dec 28 GP 4f fst .50⅖ b

Parawolf: This one could get nothing at Thistledown. I am unimpressed by its show of early speed on January 9 after being lowered in class three consecutive times. Sometimes early speed indicates the imminent return to form. But not in this case. The horse also showed early speed on December 29. Its problem seems to be that it can't run farther than five furlongs and will not begin to win until it faces cheaper horses. NO BET.

Ambarmar: Absent throughout 1966, this eight-year-old is apparently in good physical condition as evidenced by its two recent races within five days. Its December 27 workout suggests that it may have a bit of speed left, too. But it has not yet done any real running in competition, and cannot be expected to beat a field like today's. NO BET.

Dance Contest: This fast quitter belongs with cheaper horses. NO BET.

Washita King: The consistent—but cheap—seven-year-old ran a blazing race eighteen days ago but has not been seen since. Not even on the training track. I doubt it can beat this field anyhow. NO BET.

Hy Sonny: The 122 pounds may have defeated this six-year-old on January 2. It had been rested (sensibly), after its previous hard effort, but then —under all that weight—ran the fastest race in its record, losing after a suicidal drive. It is inconceivable to me that a horse of this kind, which has not been consistent in the past, can come back today and run its third brilliant race in succession. More likely, it will show the effects of its last effort and will lose decisively. NO BET.

Hercules II: That wasn't a bad try on December 21, but Peruvian horses usually need much more time to get adjusted to North American racing. NO BET.

Your Day: The good Aqueduct race of November 30 shows that Everett King's four-year-old is by no means outclassed today. His two latests races here were stern enough to bring him to top form. The switch to Angel Cordero will help. CONTENDER.

New Ballot: Allen Jerkens' gelding ran a spectacular six furlongs to defeat Hy Sonny on January 2. Five days later Cardone had it right on the pace but did not kill it in the stretch. It figures to be in good fettle today. CONTENDER.

Doll Smasher: First-time starters don't beat this kind of field. NO BET.

The contenders are Your Day and New Ballot. The former seems ready for a good effort. The other, in splendid shape, figures to crack down more rigorously this time than last and should run about as well as on January 2. I doubt Your Day can catch the Jerkens gelding on any afternoon that finds each of them at its best. New Ballot has the edge in early speed, plus the class to pursue even speedier sprinters like Hy Sonny and Dance Contest and beat them in the stretch. As an additional factor on New Ballot's side, I notice that it usually has run rather well in better company than today's. But Your Day's only good race in better company was his unsuccessful stretch run on November 30 against the notorious quitter, Royal Harbinger. Finally, I find it significant that the only victory in Your Day's recent record came after a race in which he showed much more finishing power than he has yet displayed at Tropical. Thus, the colt possibly is not yet at peak—which gives New Ballot an even better chance.

The Running of the Race

NEW BALLOT and Hy Sonny went to the post as co-favorites. The 2.90–1 on New Ballot was a huge overlay. The same odds on Hy Sonny were an underlay, considering the truth about its form. Your Day was held at 3.80–1, which seemed sensible.

New Ballot ran over Parawolf in the early stages and had no difficulty remaining on top the rest of the way. Your Day made a brave effort but was outgunned.

Hy Sonny, while best of the others, was well below its recent form and tired toward the end.

To me, the key element in this example is not the decision to pick New Ballot over Your Day. Far more important is the decision to eliminate Hy Sonny as a contender. The player should learn to recognize when apparently hot horses are actually on the downgrade.

NINTH RACE **6 FURLONGS (Chute). (Sikkim, January 2, 1967, 1.07⅗, 4, 127.)**

TrP - 29909
January 13, 1967

Claiming. Purse $3,200. 4-year-olds and upward. Weights 4-year-olds 120 lbs., older 121 lbs. Non-winners of two races since November 15 allowed 3 lbs., of a race since that date, 5 lbs., of a race since October 1, 7 lbs. Claiming price $12,000. 2 lbs. allowed for each $1,000 to $10,000. (Races for a claiming price of $8,500 or less not considered.)
Value to winner $2,080, second $640, third $320, fourth $160. Mutuel pool $96,811.

Index	Horse	Eqt A Wt	PP	St	¼	½	Str	Fin	Jockey	Cl'g Pr	Owner	Odds $1
29856TrP3	New Ballot	b 4 113	7	1	3^h	1^1	1^1	1^3	E Cardone	10000	A J Mesler	2.90
29856TrP4	Your Day	b 4 111	6	5	4^3	$2^{1\frac{1}{2}}$	2^h	$2^{2\frac{1}{2}}$	A T Cordero	11000	Windham Farm	3.80
29805TrP2	Hy Sonny	b 6 118	4	2	2^h	$3^{1\frac{1}{2}}$	$3^{1\frac{1}{2}}$	3^3	R Cox	12000	M D Kort	2.90
29856TrP6	Ambarmar	8 113	2	8	6^2	6^6	5^5	$4^{3\frac{1}{4}}$	D Brumfield	11000	R J Sabinske	5.20
29805TrP7	Dance Contest	4 109	3	6	$5^{\frac{1}{2}}$	4^2	4^3	5^7	H Gustines	10000	H Bartell	9.20
29869TrP6	Parawolf	b 5 114	1	4	1^h	$5^{\frac{1}{2}}$	6^6	6^{10}	F Iannelii	12000	S Goldberg	26.90
29676TrP5	Hercules II	5 114	5	7	7^3	7^{10}	7	7	J Velasquez	12000	S Lazzarin	5.20
	Doll Smasher	b 4 113	8	3	8	8	Outdist'd		K Korte	10000	P McIntosh	75.30

Time .22⅕, .44⅘, 1.09⅘. Track fast.

$2 Mutuel Prices:			
7-NEW BALLOT	7.80	4.00	2.80
6-YOUR DAY		4.80	3.00
4-HY SONNY			2.80

B. g, by Nilo—Meadow Flower, by Bull Lea. Trainer H. A. Jerkens. Bred by Danada Farm. (Ky.)
IN GATE AT 4.52. OFF AT 4.52 EASTERN STANDARD TIME. Start good. Won driving.

NEW BALLOT, prominent from the outset, wrested command while racing well out in the track on the turn and drew away under steady handling. YOUR DAY moved with NEW BALLOT rounding the turn but was no match for that one. HY SONNY saved ground to remain a factor to the final furlong and flattened out. AMBARMAR failed to menace. DANCE CONTEST made a mild bid leaving the turn but had nothing left. PARAWOLF had brief speed. HERCULES II was always outrun. DOLL SMASHER was a distant trailer.
Scratched—29716TrP1 Washita King. Overweights—Ambarmar 1 pound, Doll Smasher 4.

5. THIRD AT AQUEDUCT, NOVEMBER 14, 1966—Track Good

HERE IS ANOTHER toughie, the winner of which might elude a careless player. Just for fun, study the past-performance records briefly and see how many of the following questions you can answer without taking another peek at the records:

1. Only two horses in the race were entered for $10,000 claiming prices in their last starts. Which two?
2. Only one horse in the race was a beaten favorite in its last start. Name it.
3. Today's claiming price is $8,500. Have any of the entrants ever been claimed at that price or higher?
4. One of the horses has been the favorite in four of its starts, indicating that the smart guys like it and its barn. Which horse?
5. Which four horses in today's race ran against each other five days ago?
6. Are any first-time starters entered?
7. Have any of the entrants been away from competition for three weeks or more?
8. Two horses run as an entry. Which two? Who is the trainer?
9. Which two horses have the advantage of having run two races in the past two weeks?
10. How old are the horses?

If you were able to answer four or five of those questions without peeking, you are an able handicapper who takes in a great deal of information and sorts it out effectively. Not all the questions dealt with absolute fundamentals, but the answer to each one has some bearing on a proper analysis of the race.

The race is for two-year-olds of less than middling quality. Each has demonstrated that it can't run with allowance horses or topnotch claimers.

3d Race Aqueduct

Start — 6 FURLONGS — AQUEDUCT — Finish

6 FURLONGS. (Near Man, July 17, 1963, 1.08⅗, 3, 112.)
Claiming. Purse $3,800. 2-year-olds. Weight, 122 lbs. Non-winners of three races allowed 3 lbs., of two races, 6 lbs. Claiming price, $8,500. 2 lbs. allowed for each $500 to $7,500.

(3rd Aqu)—Coupled—Rooms and Hail's Image.

Gem Richmond $8,500 — Ch. c (1964-Ky), by Royal Gem II—Dainty Joy, by Johns Joy — S. Sommer F. Martin (E. W. Richmond) — **116** — 1966 9 1 2 0 $3,825

9Nov66-3Aqu	fst 1	.45⅘1.11⅗1.38⅗	Clm	10000	10	1	$4^{1\frac{1}{4}}$	3^{1}	9^{11}	9^{11}	IValenzuela	b 119	*3.40	64-18	Key to Success 120¾ Genuine 117^{3} Out the Window 116½	Stopped	11
1Nov66-3Aqu	fst 7f	.22⅗ .45⅖1.23	Clm	16000	5	1	4^{3}	$4^{3\frac{1}{2}}$	5^{12}	6^{16}	FAlvarez	b 118	9.40	75-19	Primo Theo 122^{2} Broker John 122^{5} Army Game 114$^{2\frac{1}{2}}$	Fell back	7
18Oct66-4Aqu	fst 1	.47⅖1.12⅗1.38⅖	Md	8000	5	1	$1^{1\frac{1}{2}}$	$1^{1\frac{1}{2}}$	1^{3}	1^{8}	BBaeza	b 120	*2.10	76-24	GemRichmond120^{8} OurBabuRuler118$^{1\frac{1}{2}}$ Col.Pyncheon113¾	Easily	11
13Oct66-1Aqu	fst 6f	.23 .46⅘1.12⅘	Md	6500	3	3	3^{1}	3^{2}	$3^{\frac{1}{2}}$	$2^{\frac{1}{2}}$	BBaeza	b 122	*0.90	78-20	Quick Stepper 117½ Gem Richmond 122^{4} Go Go Joe 118^{4}	Gamely	14
26Sep66-4Aqu	fst 7f	.23⅕ .46⅘1.26	Md	10000	4	7	$7^{3\frac{1}{4}}$	3^{4}	$6^{5\frac{1}{2}}$	$5^{8\frac{1}{2}}$	BBaeza	122	4.90	67-18	Irish Dude 122$^{3\frac{1}{2}}$ Star Hitter 122^{3} Genuine 122no	Bid, tired	13
28Apr66-3Aqu	my 5f	.23 .46⅗ .59⅕	Md	15000	1	6	$6^{7\frac{1}{2}}$	$6^{5\frac{1}{2}}$	$5^{7\frac{1}{2}}$	8^{11}	HGustines	b 115	4.30	78-24	Hermogenes 115½ Ted's Pick 116^{5} Star Hitter 115½	Close quarters	9
18Apr66-3Aqu	fst 5f	.22⅘ .46⅘ .59⅕	Md	c-8500	5	2	$1^{\frac{1}{2}}$	$1^{1\frac{1}{2}}$	$1^{\frac{1}{2}}$	2^{5}	JCombest	b 122	*1.70	84-17	AIG.Specialist118^{5} GemRichmond 122$^{1\frac{1}{2}}$ WilliamJ.Ross122^{5}	2d best	9
31Mar66-4Aqu	fst 5f	.23⅖ .47⅗1.00⅗	Md	12500	9	9	6^{6}	$6^{8\frac{1}{2}}$	$8^{8\frac{1}{4}}$	8^{13}	KKnapp	b 122	3.10	69-24	BrooklynWillie118$^{1\frac{1}{2}}$ Tillyard122^{2} Smuggler'sNotch118$^{2\frac{1}{2}}$	No factor	10

LATEST WORKOUTS **Oct 25 Bel tr.t. 5f fst 1.06 b** **Oct 7 Bel tr.t. 5f fst 1.03⅖ b** **Oct 3 Bel tr.t. 3f fst .37 h** **Sep 21 Bel tr.t. 7f sly 1.33 b**

Scotch Corner $8,500 — B. f (1964-Ky), by Cohoes—Skye, by Blue Peter — D. Shaer F. L. Moore (E. B. Ryan) — **116** — 1966 11 2) 0 $5,270

9Nov66-3Aqu	fst 1	.45⅘1.11⅗1.38⅗	Clm	9500	4	3	$8^{5\frac{1}{2}}$	9^{7}	10^{12}	10^{12}	JRuane	b 116	33.50	63-18	Key to Success 120¾ Genuine 117^{3} Out the Window 116½	No factor	11
26Oct66-1Aqu	fst 7f	.23 .47⅕1.26⅗	f-	8500	12	1	1^{2}	1^{3}	1^{h}	$1^{\frac{3}{4}}$	JRuane	b 116	13.10	73-19	Scotch Corner 116¾ Greek Glory 121½ Nice Princess 116^{3}	Driving	12
17Oct66-5Aqu	fst 6f	.23 .48 1.14	t-	10000	12	9	$12^{7\frac{1}{4}}$	14^{11}	14^{18}	14^{16}	WShoemaker	b 116	18.40	57-19	Recall 116^{1} Bright Beauty 116^{nk} Nice Princess 117^{nk}	No factor	14
26Sep66-5Aqu	fst 6½f	.23⅕ .46⅘1.18⅗	t-	14000	5	7	$6^{6\frac{1}{2}}$	$7^{8\frac{1}{2}}$	$7^{9\frac{3}{4}}$	6^{13}	ACordero	b 112	66.50	74-18	Native Joy 114^{2} Ethical 113^{3} Recall 114^{h}	Not a contender	8
16Sep66-2Aqu	fst 6f	.23 .47⅖1.14	f-	14000	4	4	$5^{4\frac{3}{4}}$	$6^{6\frac{1}{2}}$	7^{11}	7^{13}	WShoemaker	b 114	18.80	60-25	Ethical 109¾ Bittern 118^{1} Sweeping Wing 111^{h}	Tired	8
3Sep66-3Aqu	fst 6f	.22⅘ .47 1.13⅗	f-	15000	5	3	$4^{2\frac{1}{2}}$	4^{2}	6^{6}	8^{11}	JRuane	b 112	13.70	64-22	Greek Song's Get 111no Dance Dress 112^{5} Native Joy 113½	Wide	8
10Aug66-5Sar	fst 5½f	,22⅘ .47⅕1.07⅗	f-Md	13000	5	3	2^{1}	$2^{1\frac{1}{2}}$	2^{1}	1^{1}	JRuane	b 115	7.80	79-15	Scotch Corner 115^{1} Nursemaid 117^{nk} Princess Jupon 115^{1}	Driving	12
3Aug66-5Sar	fst 5½f	.22⅖ .46⅘1.06⅗	f-Md	12500	10	7	$9^{9\frac{3}{4}}$	8^{5}	7^{8}	4^{6}	EBelmonte	b 119	31.50	78-12	AvantiGirl 119^{4} Count theWays119^{1} ArabianCountess115^{1}	No mish'p	12
13Jly66-5Aqu	fst 5½f	.22⅕ .46⅕1.05⅘	f-MdSpWt		4	9	Propped				HWoodhouse	b 119	60.90	——	On theCarpet 119^{nk} She'sBeautiful 119^{4} Arrangement 114½	Eased up	12
14Jun66-4Aqu	fst 5½f	.22⅘ .47 1.07⅖	f-mc-12500		6	2	1^{h}	$3^{\frac{1}{2}}$	3^{1}	$5^{4\frac{1}{4}}$	DChambe'lin^{7}	b 112	9.50	72-19	My Ego 115½ Corullah 119^{nk} Dirnacia 115^{3}	Short lead, tired	8

LATEST WORKOUTS **Nov 8 Bel m.t. 3f gd .36 h** **Nov 5 Bel 6f fst 1.14⅘ h** **Nov 3 Bel m.t. 4f sly .51 b** **Oct 23 Bel m.t. 4f fst .47⅗ h**

Rooms $7,500 Dk. b. or br. g (1964-Md), by Barbizon—Abeyance Lass, by Ambiorix **107⁵** 1966 8 1 0 1 $2,810
S. J. LeFrak H. Jacobson (Mr.-Mrs. H. J. O'Donovan)

21Oct66-1Aqu fst 6f .22⅘ .47 1.13⅘ Md 7500 5 7 76½ 64¾ 33½ 1½ JLRotz b 122 3.50 74-16 Rooms 122½ Go Go Joe 113½ Dollar Sign 115nk Up final strides 14
6Oct66-4Aqu fst 6½f.23⅗ .48⅕1.21 Md 7500 13 1 43½ 24 37 39 JLRotz b 122 3.70 66-24 Bold Fella 1207 Heliotropic 1182 Rooms 1225 Well up, hung 14
12Sep66-4Aqu fst 6f .22⅘ .46⅘1.13 Md 10500 10 10 1114111510121015 JLRotz b 118 21.90 63-21 Second Encounter 1192½ Willup 1222 Salmon River 120nk No speed 12
8Sep66-1Aqu fst 6f .23⅘ .48 1.13⅘ Md 7500 3 6 62¾ 66 48 48¾ JLRotz b 122 3.70 65-29 Starstitch 1226 Fire Escape 1172½ Royal Regent 122nk No rally 14
29Aug66-3Aqu fst 6f .23 .47⅕1.13⅘ Md 10500 3 7 43 54½ 67 78¾ MVenezia b 118 72.50 66-13 Young Noble 113h Quaich 1225 Royal Concert 122h Tired 12
17Aug66-4Sar fst 6f .22⅘ .46⅘1.14⅕ Md 14000 1 11 1011119¾ 86½1111 JLRotz b 118 16.80 66-14 Especially You 118¾ Willup 118h Chorus 1203 Not a factor 12
1Apr66-5Aqu fst 5f .23⅕ .47 1.00 Md Sp Wt 10 7 76½ 96¾1018 1020 JLRotz b 122 35.30 65-22 Quaker City 1223½ S'Cool 1226½ Tom's Favor 122nk Never a factor 10
16Mar66-4Aqu fst 5f .23⅘ .47 .59⅘ Md Sp Wt 3 2 810 921 927 926 JLRotz 122 15.80 62-25 Tumiga 1229 Quaker City 1221 Golden Singer 122nk No factor 10
LATEST WORKOUTS **Nov 12 Aqu 3f sly .39 b** **Nov 8 Aqu 3f fst .38⅘ b** **Nov 4 Aqu 3f fst .38⅘ b** **Oct 25 Bel m.t. 4f fst .48⅗ h**

Mr. Hal F. $8,500 Ch. c (1964-NM), by Social Hour—Glory Locks, by Ike's Glory **116** 1966 18 1 2 2 $2,605
J. C. Lawrence J. C. Lawrence (Foester-Heatley Farms, Inc.)

3Nov66-2Aqu sly 6f .22⅘ .46⅗1.13 Clm 7500 4 2 1¹ 1³ 1h 22½ WBlum 113 7.70 75-21 Quick Stepper 1172½ Mr. Hal F. 1136 Gromlech 112¾ Couldn't last 7
19Oct66-1Aqu sly 6f .22⅘ .46⅗1.13 Clm 7500 1 6 11½ 1n 45 515 ORosado b 112 29.20 67-20 Quick Stepper 117no Mighty John W. 116½ RentedTux1202½ Tired 12
14Oct66-1GS fst 6f .22⅕ .46 1.11⅘ Clm 7000 9 5 3½ 45 44½ 55½ ORosado b 116 21.40 72-19 Laurel Mark 1134 Best Brandy 109h Ativon 113no Never close 12
10Oct66-5Aqu fst 7f .23⅕ .46⅗1.24⅘ Clm 10500 4 6 79 87¾ 88¾ 86¾ RTurcotte b 116 31.20 75-19 Broker John 1143½ Star Hitter 1118 Sing a Bit 112½ Used up 8
3Oct66-2Aqu fst 6f .22⅕ .46⅕1.12⅕ Clm 10000 11 6 86 77½ 811 67½ SBoulmetis b 114 8.50 77-13 Star Hitter 111h Gaelic Reply 1163½ Acceloro 118½ Never close 9
29Sep66-2Aqu fst 7f .23⅕ .46⅘1.24⅘ Clm 10500 4 4 22 43 37 412 RTurcotte b 112 12.70 70-18 Royal Speed 1197 Albear Road 1162½ Sing A Bit 1142 Tired 8
19Sep66-2Aqu fst 6f .22⅘ .46⅕1.12⅗ Clm 10000 1 6 34 45 54½ 57½ LAdams b 116 8.40 73-20 Tillyard 1163½ Steve the Boss 1172 Starstitch 1161 Tired 10
3Sep66-1Aqu fst 6f .23⅘ .47⅖1.14⅖ Clm 10000 1 2 41 23 22 31½ ORosado b 122 12.90 70-22 Young Noble 115nk Star 1191 Mr. Hal F. 1222½ Showed good effort 9
24Aug66-4FL fst 5f .23 .47⅕1.00⅗ Md Sp Wt 6 2 12 15 16 110 JOlivares b 118 *0.60 97- 9 Mr. Hal F. 11810 Nuzzle In 1152 Dotty's Beau 1154 Easy score 7
17Aug66-4Sar fst 6f .22⅘ .46⅘1.14⅕ Md 14000 7 2 32½ 33 42½ 65 HW'dhouse b 118 15.80 72-14 Especially You 118¾ Willup 118h Chorus 1203 Well up, tired 12
29Jly 66-4Aqu fst 5½f.23 .47⅕1.05⅘ Md Sp Wt 7 1 53 62¾ 97½ 914 HWoodhouse 122 •32.60 70-17 One Gem 1225 Fort Marcy 1221 Rising Market 122½ Dropped back 11
LATEST WORKOUTS **Nov 12 Bel m.t. 4f my .49⅗ b** **Nov 2 Bel m.t. 3f fst .36 h** **Oct 27 Bel m.t. 5f fst 1.02⅘ b** **Oct 24 Bel m.t. 5f fst 1.03⅕ b**

May Be Lucky $8,500 Ch. c (1964-Fla), by Sid's Gambol—Danish Pastry, by Turn-to **111⁵** 1966 0 M 0 0 —
Anne Jerkens H. A. Jerkens (Mmes. C. Leonard-H. A. Jerkens)
LATEST WORKOUTS **Nov 12 Bel tr.t. 5f my 1.03 h** **Nov 9 Bel m.t. 6f fst 1.16⅗ b** **Nov 5 Bel m.t. 4f fst .50 bg** **Nov 1 Bel m.t. 3f fst .37⅕ bg**

Mighty John W. × $7,500 B. g (1964-Ky.), by Royal Sting—Just-A-Coin, by Nirgal **112** 1966 10 1 5 2 $6,180
J. W. Mecom E. Nelson (E. A.-T. E. Bischoff)

19Oct66-1Aqu sly 6f .22⅘ .46⅗1.13 Clm 7500 2 2 1½ 1¹ 1h 2no JRuane 116 3.20 78-19 Quick Stepper 117no Mighty John W. 116½ Rented Tux 1202½ Sharp 12
7Oct66-1Aqu fst 6f .22⅘ .46⅘1.13 Clm 6500 1 4 2h 2h 2h 21½ JRuane b 116 *2.70 77-18 Key to Success 1191½ Mighty John W. 1161 RentedTux122h Gamely14
30Sep66-1Aqu fst 7f .22⅗ .46 1.25⅗ Clm 7500 3 4 1h 1h 31½ 56½ JRuane b 116 10.40 71-19 Rented Tux 114h Col. Pyncheon 107no Fire Escape 1166 Used up 10
15Aug66-3Sar fst 6f .23⅕ .47⅗1.14⅕ Md 6500 8 3 2¹ 2h 1² 13½ JRuane b 118 3.30 77-17 MightyJohnW.1183½ Rock of Gibraltar1201 RoyalRegent1133 Easily 13
6Aug66-1Mth fst 6f .22⅘ .46⅖1.13 Md 6000 11 4 3nk 11½ 11½ 21½ CBaltazar b 114 3.40 76-12 Matjan 1181½ Mighty John W. 1141½ Jaldi Jaldi 1187 Second best 11
5May66-1CD fst 4½f.22⅘ .46⅗ .53⅘ Md c-5000 5 5 42½ 23 21 BPhelps b 120 3.40 91- 8 Catignani 1201 Mighty John W. 1206 Roman Lover 1122½ Sharp 12
26Apr66-2Kee fst 4½f.23 .46⅗ .52⅘ Clm 6000 8 2 2h 1h 3½ BPhelps 115 9.30 94- 5 Idol Affair 115nk Catignani 115nk Mighty John W. 1151½ Bumped 10
LATEST WORKOUTS **Nov 8 Bel tr.t. 5f gd 1.05 b** **Nov 5 Bel tr.t 4f fst .50⅘ b** **Nov 1 Bel tr.t. 4f fst .50 h** **Oct 26 Bel tr.t. 4f fst .49 h**

Hail's Image $8,000 Dk. b. or br. c (1964-Fla), by Hail to Reason—Rosebloc, by Tudor Minstrel **109⁵** 1966 17 1 1 1 $3,465
Sugartown Stable H. Jacobson (Harbor View Farm)

9Nov66-3Aqu fst 1 .45⅘1.11⅗1.38⅗ Clm 9000 2 2 1h 1h 31½ 54½ ECardone5 b 107 5.00 70-18 Key to Success 120¾ Genuine 1173 Out the Window 116½ Used up 11
2Nov66-5Aqu fst 6f .22⅘ .45⅘1.11⅘ Clm 11500 4 7 56½ 67 68 55¾ ECardone5 b 109 7.80 80-19 CalypsoJim 1163½ SalmonRiver 116½ WithoutAPaddle 116¾ No m'ch'f 10
22Oct66-1Aqu fst 6f .22⅕ .45⅗1.11⅘ Clm 12500 4 4 65¾ 48½ 67¾ 64¾ JSellers b 116 14.50 79-16 Brooklyn Willie 105h Broker John 1192½ Amstel 112nk No mishap 10
10Oct66-5Aqu fst 7f .23⅕ .46⅗1.24⅘ Clm 12500 6 2 2½ 2h 34½ 412 RUssery b 116 4.40 70-20 Broker John 1143½ Star Hitter 1118 Sing a Bit 112½ Used up 8
1Oct66-5Aqu sly 7f .23⅕ .47 1.26⅕ Allowance 2 7 65½ 67¾ 916 916 WHartack b 116 30.50 59-24 IrishRebellion1174 FortMarcy122no GalaPerformance122½ No speed 12
24Sep66-5Aqu fst 6½f.22⅘ .46⅘1.18⅘ Allowance 7 6 97½ 86 12151213 ECardone5 b 110 17.60 74-18 Sun Seeker 115h Rising Market 1222½ Proviso 1221 Far back 14
9Aug66-8Rkm fst 6f .22⅘ .45⅗1.10⅘ Allowance 5 6 64½ 65½ 46 310 HWajda 117 *1.60 80-19 Lowboy 1157 Land to Port 1173 Hail's Image 117no Even effort 9
29Jly 66-2Aqu fst 5½f.23 .47⅕1.05⅕ Cl c-18000 4 5 62¾ 62¾ 31½ 22½ KKhapp 116 3.30 84-17 Misty Cloud 1142½ Hail's Image 1163½ Unexpected 116¾ Game 8
19Jly 66-5Aqu fst 5½f.22⅘ .45⅘1.05⅗ Clm 25000 8 5 53 75¾ 73¾ 65¾ JRuane 116 32.20 80-19 Golden Singer 1163 Gay Youth 105½ Biller 1191 Never close 10
9Jly 66-3Mth fst 5½f.22⅘ .46⅕1.05⅘ Allowance 3 4 53½ 44½ 43½ 44½ DBrumfield 115 7.50 86-18 Silencer 117¾ Rhiwin 1171½ Lord Robert 1172 Mild rally, hung 7
LATEST WORKOUTS **Oct 30 Aqu 3f fst .38⅕ b** **Oct 18 Aqu 4f fst .50 b** **Oct 8 Aqu 3f fst .38 b** **Sep 21 Aqu 4f sly .49 b**

Star Hitter $8,500 B. c (1964-Fla), by Hitter—Creep Mousie, by Bimelech **111⁵** 1966 16 1 4 4 $7,785
Birchfield Farm N. Combest (C. Block)

9Nov66-3Aqu fst 1 .45⅘1.11⅗1.38⅗ Clm 10000 7 10 1011 85½ 77 68½ JCombest b 119 11.20 66-18 Key to Success 120¾ Genuine 1173 Out the Window 116½ No factor 11
22Oct66-1Aqu fst 6f .22⅕ .45⅗1.11⅘ Clm 11500 3 6 55½ 611 79¾ 77¾ JJMartin7 b 110 11.70 76-16 Brooklyn Willie 105h Broker John 1192½ Amstel 112nk Tired 10
10Oct66-5Aqu fst 7f .23⅕ .46⅗1.24⅘ Clm 12500 7 3 42½ 31 11½ 23½ ECardone5 b 111 *1.70 78-20 Broker John 1143½ Star Hitter 1118 Sing a Bit 112½ Second best 8
3Oct66-2Aqu fst 6f .22⅕ .46⅕1.12⅕ Clm 10000 5 5 45½ 33 21 1h ECardone5 b 111 3.30 82-19 Star Hitter 111h Gaelic Reply 1163½ Acceloro 118½ Hard drive 9
26Sep66-4Aqu fst 7f .23⅕ .46⅘1.26 Md 10000 3 6 3½ 2h 2h 23½ JCombest b 122 *1.40 72-18 Irish Dude 1223½ Star Hitter 1223 Genuine 122no Went well 13
20Sep66-4Aqu fst 6f .23 .47⅖1.12⅗ Md 14000 8 3 31½ 52 54½ 54½ JCombest b 118 9.30 76-22 Court Service 122¾ Ted's Pick 1221½ d-Vinces Choice 1122 Crowded 14
20Sep66—Placed fourth through disqualification.
22Aug66-5Sar sly 6f .22⅘ .47⅕1.13⅕ Md 10000 8 3 31½ 22 23 2no JCombest b 122 *3.60 82-17 William J. Ross 118no Star Hitter 12210 Van Curler 118½ Gamely12
8Aug66-4Sar fst 5½f.23⅕ .47⅗1.06⅗ Md 10000 7 4 21 13 1h 35½ JCombest b 122 *3.20 78-13 Flying Plaid 117½ Young Noble 1225 Star Hitter 1224 Tired 12
2Aug66-6Sar fst 5½f.22⅗ .47⅖1.06⅗ Md Sp Wt 4 10 109 1010 73¾ 712 JCombest b 122 22.00 72-14 Stamp Act 1222 Duke Cannon 1221½ Balouf 1222½ Never a factor 11
28Jly 66-3Aqu fst 5½f.23 .47⅘1.07 Md 12500 7 3 1h 11 2½ 44½ JCombest b 122 5.10 73-21 Star 1183 Starstitch 122no Greek Luck 1201½ Set pace, tired 9
LATEST WORKOUTS **Nov 5 Aqu 5f fst 1.01⅕ h** **Oct 28 Aqu 5f fst 1.02 h** **Oct 18 Aqu 5f fst 1.04 b** **Oct 15 Aqu 4f fst .53 b**

Some King × $7,500 Ch. c (1964-Ky), by Festival King—Fortune Chaser, by Eternal Bull **115** 1966 15 2 0 2 $4,175
P. Utman P. Utman (Marshall Lands, Inc.)

3Nov66-4Aqu sly 6f .22⅕ .46 1.12⅕ Clm 7500 1 3 2h 3nk 32 66½ JRuane b 112 9.60 75-21 RovingAmbassador115½ Acceloro1123 SpartanChief1161½ Weakened 7
30Oct66-7Suf fst 6f .22⅘ .46⅕1.12 Clm 8000 6 1 32 33 56½ 57¾ DGorman b 117 8.70 73-20 Oloron 117nk Roving Ambassador 117½ Trolley Car 1163 Early speed 7
26Sep66-9Suf fst 6f .22⅘ .46⅗1.12⅗ Clm 8250 6 2 11½ 1½ 3½ 63½ DGorman b 119 11.80 74-19 •GoNavy1141½ •Pete'sSister1131½ RovingAmbassador1191½ Used up 8
3Sep66-5Rkm sl 6f .22⅘ .46⅗1.13⅗ Clm 9500 8 2 21 21 32 WShoemaker b 115 5.50 75-16 Righteous Teddy 1121½ River Road 112nk Some King 1153 Bore in 8
26Aug66-5Rkm fst 6f .22⅘ .46⅖1.13 Clm 8000 6 1 45 55 65½ 57¾ EMerlano5 b 112 3.60 71-23 RovingAmbassador1171½WeeWillie1171½Right'sTeddy1143½ No thr't 8
20Aug66-5Rkm fst 6f .22⅕ .45⅘1.12⅘ Clm 9500 5 2 3nk 32 32 42½ JKurtz b 114 8.60 79-17 Acceloro 116h War Devil 1171½ Sunny Voyage 109½ Lacked rally 7
11Aug66-6Rkm fst 6f .22⅘ .46 1.13 Clm 6500 3 2 2h 31 11½ 13¾ PRubbicco5 b 110 8.60 79-22 SomeKing 1103¾ MotorTrail 1191½ MaryLib 1141¾ Drew clear driv'g 8
29Jly 66-7Rkm gd 5½f.23 .48⅕1.08⅕ Clm 7500 7 4 51½ 52¾ 65¾ 77¾ DGorman b 116 7.10e 73-24 Bold Copy 1081½ Black Adaris 114½ Bow Chile 115½ Tired 8
11Jly 66-6Rkm fst 5½f.22⅘ .47 1.06⅘ Allowance 4 7 78¾ 811 817 913 Flannelli b 115 38.60 77-18 Spanish Cone 115h Win Isle 1172½ Lowboy 115h Not a factor 9
30May66-8Suf fst 5f .23⅕ .47⅕1.00⅘ Allowance 7 6 52 54½ 56½ 56¾ DMadden b 115 3.90e 82-20 Misak's Gal 112½ Our Flyer 1122½ Spanish Cone 1153¾ No threat 9
21May66-4Suf fst 4½f.23⅕ .47⅗ .53⅘ Allowance 5 3 31 43 44¾ DMadden b 115 *0.80e 85-10 Famous Line 1183 Our Flyer 115no River Road 1181½ Lacked rally 9
14May66-3Suf fst 4½f.23 .46⅕ .53⅕ Allowance 1 2 22 21½ 3½ DMadden b 115 4.50e 92- 7 Magic Bud 113½ Our Flyer 115no Some King 1151½ Fin'd willingly 10
LATEST WORKOUTS **Oct 31 Aqu 5f fst 1.06 b** **Oct 17 Nar 5f fst 1.02⅗ h** **Sep 24 Nar 5f gd 1.01⅘ h**

Gem Richmond: After two good but unsuccessful efforts to break his maiden when running as a favorite, Pancho Martin's colt got the job done under Braulio Baeza in a mile race on October 18. On November 1 he was outclassed by $16,000 horses. Five days ago, he tried the mile again, this time as favorite in a field of $10,000 winners. He was beaten by a fast early pace which found him traveling six furlongs a full second faster than ever before. Against today's undoubtedly easier company, he has the advantage of that superb six-furlong effort on November 9, plus the upgrading effects of the November 1 race, plus the services of Baeza. Barring the presence of a live, improving horse, this one stands a chance today. CONTENDER.

Scotch Corner: Frankie Moore is one of the real shrewdies in racing. If today's sprint were for $9,000 fillies, this one would be a threat. But not against boys. NO BET.

Rooms: Buddy Jacobson gets fifteen pounds off this one by switching from Rotz to Apprentice Cardone. The feather might help, but the animal's victory in a cheap maiden race was not decisive enough to suggest that it has really come to hand. It would have to improve greatly to merit support in a race like today's. NO BET.

Mr. Hal F.: Unable to hold its early speed in cheaper company and unable to catch better horses. NO BET.

May Be Lucky: Scratched.

Mighty John W.: This gelding has been running honestly for Eddie Nelson. I would regard it as a dangerous contender if it had been racing recently. After that good race on October 19, it should have been back in a week or ten days. That it needed a layoff of almost a month is not a good sign, regardless of the four very ordinary workouts it has had in that period. In view of this problem, I am not inclined to give the horse the right to step up in class, as it is doing today. NO BET.

Hail's Image: The other half of the Jacobson entry has been skidding down the class ladder ever since October 1 when Buddy made his third vain attempt to cadge an allowance purse and begin earning some of the $18,000 he paid for the beast in July. Is Hail's Image an $8,500 horse? The pace-setting effort on November 9 against Gem Richmond and Scotch Corner hints that the colt might do well in a six-furlong race against the same animals. If Jacobson were to use Cardone today, he could run Hail's Image with the 109 pounds permitted by the apprentice rule. But having switched Cardone to the other half of the entry, he puts Ussery on this one, and the impost increases to 115— including a pound of overweight. I find it noteworthy that this horse has never yet shown any real early lick in a sprint. But I suppose that the swift early fractions on November 9 could mean a change of style or improved condition or both. The post position near the outside will help, especially with the fast-breaking Ussery in the driver's seat. On balance, we had better take a closer look at this horse's prospects. CONTENDER.

Star Hitter: A potential threat, but scratched.

Some King: Can handle $6,500 stock at Rockingham. NO BET.

The contenders are Gem Richmond and Hail's Image. The Jacobson entry is sure to be favored. The crowd loves Jacobson and loves entries. It probably will be optimistic about Rooms with the hot Cardone aboard. And it is sure to think that Hail's Image is the strong horse in the race, considering those good early fractions of five days ago plus the drop in class.

Our pick, however, is Gem Richmond. The reasons are numerous:

1. He was only a length behind the speeding Hail's Image at the three-quarters call of the November 9 race, yet was carrying 119 pounds against the other's 107. Today he totes only 116, while Hail's Image goes to 115. Imposts in the 115-pound range are seldom burdensome to horses of this calibre, but an eleven-pound weight shift (three off Gem Richmond and eight on Hail's Image) can be significant—especially since Hail's Image has never displayed early speed when carrying anything like today's weight. Gem Richmond, on the other hand, has usually been quite close to the pace when carrying 118, 119, 120, and 122.

2. Gem Richmond's status as a beaten favorite dropping in class is an important plus value. The Aqueduct crowd, far from infallible, is the smartest in the land. If the New Yorkers preferred Gem Richmond and 119 pounds to Hail's Image and 107, they probably had some good reasons at the time. In any case, a well-conditioned beaten favorite is always a threat when its people drop it in class.

3. The switch from Valenzuela to Baeza is tremendously important. Martin wants the best rider in the country, because today is the day for all-out effort. And Baeza apparently regards the animal as ready to run for him as it has in the past.

4. One need not be worried because Hail's Image finished fifth in the eleven-horse field on November 9, whereas Gem Richmond wound up ninth. Valenzuela obviously eased Gem Richmond rather than punish him. Fernando Alvarez did the same thing with Gem Richmond in his previous race when he was even more badly overmatched. Handling of that kind by the two experienced riders is evidence that Trainer Martin thinks highly of the two-year-old and is not willing to abuse him in an attempt to get third or fourth money. The fact that Cardone persevered with Hail's Image after setting the early pace on November 9 indicates that Jacobson has decided that there is no further sense in coddling his disappointing $18,000 purchase.

The Running of the Race

THE JACOBSON ENTRY was a 6–5 favorite. Gem Richmond was second choice. After putting away Scotch Corner, Baeza won in a gallop. Hail's Image was never really close and conked out when Ussery tried to set him down in the stretch. Mighty John W. ran another honest race but was not good enough.

THIRD RACE **6 FURLONGS. (Near Man, July 17, 1963, 1.08$\frac{3}{5}$, 3, 112.)**

Aqu - 29302

November 14, 1966

Claiming. Purse $3,800. 2-year-olds. Weight, 122 lbs. Non-winners of three races allowed 3 lbs., of two races, 6 lbs. Claiming price, $8,500. 2 lbs. allowed for each $500 to $7,500.

Value to winner $2,470, second $760, third $380, fourth $190. Mutuel pool $243,968.

Index	Horse	Eqt	A	Wt	PP	St	¼	½	Str	Fin	Jockey	Cl'g Pr	Owner	Odds $1
29266Aqu^{9}	Gem Richmond	b	2	116	1	4	3^h	$1\frac{1}{2}$	1^3	1^6	B Baeza	8500	S Sommer	3.10
29036Aqu^{2}	M'hty J'hn W.	b	2	112	5	6	4^2	3^2	2^3	2^4	H W'dhouse	7050	J W Mecom	3.40
29266Aqu^{10}	Scotch Corner	b	2	116	2	3	$1^{1\frac{1}{2}}$	$2\frac{1}{2}$	4^1	$3\frac{3}{4}$	J Ruane	8500	D Shaer	19.10
29054Aqu^{1}	Rooms	b	2	107	3	7	5^h	4^h	$3^{1\frac{1}{2}}$	4^1	E Cardone^5	7500	S J LeFrak	a-1.20
29220Aqu^{2}	Mr. Hal F.		2	116	4	2	2^h	$6^{1\frac{1}{2}}$	6^h	$5\frac{3}{4}$	W Blum	8500	J C Lawrence	9.80
29266Aqu^{5}	Hail's Image	b	2	115	6	1	$6^{1\frac{1}{2}}$	5^h	$5^{1\frac{1}{2}}$	$6\frac{1}{2}$	R Ussery†	8000	Sugartown Stable	a-1.20
29222Aqu^{6}	Some King	b	2	115	7	5	7	7	7	7	L Pincay Jr	7500	P Utman	7.40

a-Coupled—Rooms and Hail's Image. **†Five pounds apprentice allowance waived.**

Time .22$\frac{4}{5}$. .47, 1.12 (no wind in backstretch). Track good.

$2 Mutuel Prices:			
2-GEM RICHMOND	8.20	5.00	4.60
6-MIGHTY JOHN W.		4.40	4.00
3-SCOTCH CORNER			6.60

Ch. c, by Royal Gem II—Dainty Joy, by Johns Joy. Trainer F. Martin. Bred by E. W. Richmond (Ky.).

IN GATE AT 1.03. OFF AT 1.03 EASTERN STANDARD TIME. Start good. Won easily.

GEM RICHMOND followed in close pursuit of early pacemaker, continued along inside to take command on final bend, drew off at once and won with something left. MIGHTY JOHN W. raced wide to be best of others. SCOTCH CORNER succumbed suddenly. ROOMS was through early. HAIL'S IMAGE tired badly in closing drive. SOME KING was without speed.

Scratched—May Be Lucky, 29266Aqu^{6} Star Hitter. Overweight—Hail's Image 1 pound.

Hail's Image was claimed by J. Basta, trainer D. McCoy.

---

6. FIFTH AT MONMOUTH, JUNE 19, 1967—Track Sloppy

EXPENSIVE THREE-YEAR-OLD claimers, some of them overpriced.

5th Monmouth

6 FURLONGS
MONMOUTH PARK
Start
Finish

6 FURLONGS (Chute). (Decathlon, June 11, 1957, 1.08⅖, 4, 130.)
Claiming. Purse $5,000. 3-year-olds. Weight, 122 lbs. Non-winners of two races since May 12 allowed 3 lbs., a race, 5 lbs., a race since April 21, 7 lbs. Claiming price, $13,000. 1 lb. for each $500 to $11,000. (Races where entered for $9,000 or less not considered.)

Fiddler's Green $13,000 B. c (1964–Fla), by Stella Aurata—Lovely Ann, by Flaming Fleet **119** 1967 3 1 1 0 $3,695
J. L. Frost K. Noe, Sr. (R. Williams) 1966 5 M 0 1 $/00
5Jun67-2Mth fst 6f .22⅕ .45⅕1.11⅖ Md Sp Wt 12 9 42½ 22 2h 12 BThornburg b 115 3.60 85–14 Fiddler's Green 115² A Latin Spin 115⁵ Mafioso 115² Driving 12
23May67-4GS fst 6f .22⅖ .45⅘1.11⅖ Md 9000 2 8 43½ 46 26 25 JVasquez b 116 *1.40 82–16 Safari Guide 116⁵ Fiddler's Green 116¾ Beau Ben 111³ Gamely 9
12May67-4GS gd 6f .22⅘ .46⅘1.12⅕ Md Sp Wt 11 3 3½ 21½ 45 57¾ FLovato b 116 7.50 75–21 Battle Plan 116⁶ Olympia You 116½ Acquitted 116½ Speed, tired 12
15Jly 66-4Mth sl 5½f.22⅘ .46⅖1.05⅘ Md Sp Wt 3 1 2h 1h 2½ 44½ CBaltazar b 118 6.20 83–19 Make It 118nk Columnist 118³ Pointsman 1181¼ Used up early 9
8Jly 66-2Mth fst 5½f.22⅖ .46⅕1.05⅗ Md Sp Wt 9 2 31½ 3½ 54½ 56¾ BPhelps b 118 9.90 82–17 Gay Lord Flynn 118nk Fastpack 118² Bye Bye Bird 118no Tired 10
1Jly 66-5Mth fst 5½f.22⅕ .45⅗1.05⅖ Md Sp Wt 8 9 89¾ 613 59 38½ BPhelps h 118 *3.10 81–15 In Reality 118⁸ Broker John 118½ Fiddler's Green 118¾ Rallied 12
17Jun66-4Mth fst 5f .22⅘ .46⅗ .59⅕ Md Sp Wt 5 9 74¾ 67 46½ 44¾ BPhelps b 118 7.90 89–22 Rhiwin 1181½ By the Numbers 118³ Joey Lubas 118nk Mild bid 12
7May66-3GS fst 5f .22 .45⅘ .58⅕ Md Sp Wt 12 12 1111 1115 1015 1211 KKnapp 117 *2.60 87–10 Bold Point1171½ Milady's Man117no Royal Malabar1172½ Dull try 12
LATEST WORKOUTS Jun 14 Mth 3f fst .36⅖ b Jun 3 Mth 4f fst .48⅗ h May 9 GS 5f sly 1.03⅕ b

Regal Dancer ✻ $11,500 Gr. g (1964–Can), by Grey Monarch—Natalma, by Native Dancer **112** 1967 3 0 1 0 $900
Windfield Farm G. T. Poole (E. P. Taylor) 1966 7 2 1 1 $4,610
3Jun67-4Mth fst 6f .21⅘ .45 1.11⅕ Clm 9500 5 4 12 13 13 2½ DBrumfield b 113 6.70 85–15 Famous Dancer 114½ Regal Dancer 113½ Destigate 114³ Gamely 10
25May67-5GS fst 6f .22⅕ .46⅕1.12⅗ Clm 9000 5 5 15 16 1h 55¼ JVasquez b 116 4.20 76–25 Mrs. Jay 116no Destigate 118nk Question Moore 113⁴ Gave way 9
11May67-7GS sly 6f .22⅖ .46 1.12⅗ Allowance 4 4 2h 23 510 616 JLeonard b 113 14.20 65–19 Taradash 1131½ Royal Rhythm 113³ Mr. Scipio 113¹ Speed, tired 6
11Nov66-7Grd my 7f .23⅖ .48⅕1.30⅘ Allowance 2 2 2nk 23 1nk 1h AGomez b 119 2.80 68–39 RegalDancer 119h PageRoyal 1223¼ VictoriaFleetest 1172¾ Driving 7
1Nov66-6Grd fst 7f .23⅘ .47⅕1.26⅘ Allowance 7 6 21½ 1h 1½ 4nk AGomez b 117 *0.95e 88–18 JamesBay 117h GreenStinger 117h SixBits 110no Necked blanket fin. 8
17Oct66-7WO gd 6f .22⅖ .46⅕1.12⅖ Allowance 9 2 22 21½ 31 24½ AGomez b 122 *0.75 78–21 Sir Trio 1154½ Regal Dancer 122no Never Delay 117² Game try 10
30Sep66-3WO gd 6f .22⅖ .46⅕1.13⅘ Md Sp Wt 1 6 1nk 12 11½ 1nk AGomez b 116 *0.80 76–26 Regal Dancer 116nk Sir Trio 1154¾ Roman Trooper 120¾ Driving 12
16Aug66-4Sar fst 6f .22⅘ .46⅘1.13⅖ Md Sp Wt 10 1 12 12 1h 31½ BBaeza 122 *2.20 79–16 Happy Lark 122no Doug Oswald 1221½ Regal Dancer 122² Weakened 12
9Aug66-6Sar fst 5½f.22⅗ .46⅗1.06⅗ Md Sp Wt 2 1 12 13 13 41 BBaeza 122 2.60 83–17 Richroband 122nk Magic Beat 122½ Hornbeam 122nk Weakened 12
2Aug66-4Sar fst 5½f.22⅘ .47 1.06 Md Sp Wt 3 1 12 12 1h 45¼ CFarmer 122 2.90 82–14 Nanak 1223½ Hornbeam 122¹ Quiet Town 122¾ Set pace, tired 11
LATEST WORKOUTS Jun 10 Mth 5f fst 1.02 b Jun 1 Mth 4f fst .48⅖ h May 24 GS 3f fst .35⅘ h May 20 GS 5f sly 1.03⅖ b

Tom's Brother ✻ $13,000 B. g (1964–Md), by Yes You Will—Gentle Slam, by Grand Slam **115** 1967 5 1 1 1 $3,750
P. Bongarzone P. Bongarzone (Dr. J. B. Cloran) 1966 0 M 0 0 ——
12Jun67-5Mth fm*5f (T) .59⅗ Clm 13000 5 4 31 Bolted WGavidia 113 22.00 —— Barrie B. 111¾ No Note 102nk Bit Of Dash 112¹ Bolted on turn 10
3Jun67-4Mth fst 6f .21⅘ .45 1.11⅕ Cl c-10000 9 3 32 23 34 54¼ TBove 114 4.90 82–15 Famous Dancer 114½ Regal Dancer 113½ Destigate 114³ Tired 10
18May67-6GS fst 6f .22 .45⅕1.11 Clm 10000 4 6 51¾ 32½ 35 27 TBove 116 8.10 82–20 Holly War 112⁷ Tom's Brother 1161½ Greek Music 116h Fair try 9
11May67-6GS sly 6f .22⅖ .46⅖1.12⅗ Clm 9500 7 1 810 88 76¾ 36¾ TBove 114 4.60 74–19 Minnie Baby 112¾ Destigate 120⁶ Tom's Brother 114no Mild rally 8
2May67-2GS fst 6f .22⅖ .46⅕1.12 Md 5000 9 3 21½ 11 14 15 TBove 115 22.60 84–18 Tom's Brother 115⁵ Telafilly 109½ Tired Stork 113¾ Easily 12
LATEST WORKOUTS Jun 10 Mth 4f fst .50 b Jun 9 Mth t.c. 3f fm .36⅗ b May 17 GS 3f fst .38⅗ b Apr 27 GS 4f sly .53⅘ b

Fuel King ✻ $13,000 B. c (1964–Fla), by Bolinas Boy—Oil Show, by Ponder **115** 1967 12 1 2 0 $3,455
P. Q. Wilson L. W. Jennings (Farnsworth Farm) 1966 12 1 1 2 $3,210
24May67-6GS fst 6f .22⅖ .45⅘1.11⅗ Clm 12500 3 5 711 713 612 56½ JLeonard b 116 7.80 79–14 Holly War 116no Wee Willie 118³ Famous Dancer 116h Late foot 7
10May67-8GS fst 170.47⅖1.12⅖1.42⅗ Allowance 2 3 42 43 66½ 613 JLeonard b 112 17.70 68–24 Last Cry 112⁶ Flotage 1213½ Run Fool Run 115no Speed, tired 6
26Apr67-7GS fst 170.46⅘1.12⅕1.43 Allowance 1 7 62¾ 62¾ 57¼ 57 GPatterson b 113 6.70 72–19 Courant d'Air 113½ Sky Switch 113no Mauve Decade113⁴ No threat 8
10Apr67-9GP fm 1 (T) .46⅖1.35⅘ Allowance 4 4 45½ 33 2½ 21 WBlum b 114 ♦9.80 94–10 I'm Smiley 112¹ ♦Fuel King 1141½ ♦Derby Sam 1121½ Game try 7
10Apr67—♦—Dead heat.
1Apr67-5GP fst 6f .22⅖ .46 1.11⅕ Clm 18000 9 8 95½ 94 64 53¾ KKnapp b 113 14.60 84–15 Golden Cap113nk Royal De Fur116² By The Numbers1161½ No mish'p 9
18Mar67-3GP fst 7f .23⅕ .46⅖1.24⅘ Clm 13000 4 8 78 67 33½ 22 JVelasquez b 116 2.20 85–14 Golden Cap 116² Fuel King 1162½ Ile D'Levant 107½ Best of others 8
7Mar67-8GP fst 6f .22⅕ .45 1.10⅖ Clm 20000 7 6 916 717 714 79 JVelasquez b 116 6.80 83–17 Black Fleet 1164½ S'Cool 112¾ Besieger 114¾ Never a contender 9
11Feb67-7Hia fst 7f .23⅖ .46⅖1.23 Allowance 9 3 54 56 56 612 JVelasquez b 112 15.40 82–20 Ask The Fare1143½ Wedgedale116no Sun Seeker115⁴ Fell back 12
4Feb67-4Hia fst 6f .22⅖ .46 1.11⅖ Allowance 7 10 1212 119½ 75½ 64½ JVelasquez b 112 15.50 82–13 Air Rights 115² Royal De Fur 112¹ Hornbeam 115h Closed gap 12
25Jan67-5Hia gd 7f .22⅘ .46⅕1.25 Allowance 4 7 914 98 79 75¼ JVelasquez b 112 23.60 79–15 Sir Winzalot 1121½ Royal Malabar 118no Comfrey 121nk No factor 9
LATEST WORKOUTS Jun 11 Mth 5f fst 1.04 b

Rupin $13,000 Ch. g (1964–Ky), by Royal Coinage—Duchess Peg, by Whirlaway **115** 1967 5 0 0 0 ——
Calumet Farm H. Forrest (Calumet Farm) 1966 11 2 1 1 $5.540
12Jun67-5Mth fm*5f (T) .59⅗ Clm 14000 7 10 96¼ 812 68 52¼ DBrumfield b 115 33.80 96– 3 Barrie B. 111¾ No Note 102nk Bit Of Dash 112¹ In close, rallied 10
7Mar67-8GP fst 6f .22⅕ .45 1.10⅖ Clm 20000 5 7 712 921 Bled RBroussard b 116 15.00 —— Black Fleet 1164½ S'Cool 112¾ Besieger 114¾ Was eased up 9
11Feb67-7Hia fst 7f .23⅖ .46⅖1.23 Allowance 8 7 64½ 67½ 1121 1227 JVasquez b 113 46.90 67–20 Ask The Fare1143½ Wedgedale116no Sun Seeker115⁴ Far back 12
4Feb67-4Hia fst 6f .22⅖ .46 1.11⅖ Allowance 4 3 42 31½ 97 98¾ JVasquez b 112 46.10 78–13 Air Rights 115² Royal De Fur 112¹ Hornbeam 115h Factor, tired 12
7Jan67-3TrP fst 6f .22⅕ .44⅗1.09⅗ Allowance 9 9 84½ 78½ 915 916 KKnapp b 118 28.20 78–20 Salishan 121h Thong 116¾ More Scents 117⁵ Never a factor 10
12Oct66-5GS fst 6f .22⅗ .46⅖1.11⅖ Allowance 4 10 910 811 77¼ 68½ DGorman b 113 8.70 78–16 Steel City 117no Woozem 1174½ High Hat 120¹ No factor 10
5Oct66-6Atl sly 7f .21⅘ .45 1.26⅕ Allowance 8 6 79½ 69 66 53½ HHinojosa b 117 5.50 68–27 Jim J. 117nk More Scents 1131½ High Hat 117nk No apparent mishap 8
28Sep66-6Atl sl 6f .22⅗ .46⅗1.13⅕ Allowance 2 8 78 77 68¼ 57½ HHinojosa b 117 *1.40 68–28 Cosmic Pick 115nk Taradash 117² More Scents 113¾ No mishap 9
10Sep66-8Atl fst 7f .22⅗ .45⅖1.23⅕ Playground 6 9 116 76½ 510 516 JVelasquez b 115 5.70 71–24 Dr. Fager 115¹² Glengary 1153½ Pointsman 115h Not a factor 11
27Aug66-6Atl fst 6f .22⅖ .46⅖1.11⅘ Allowance 10 2 88 73½ 11 13 RBroussard b 117 3.40 83–17 Rupin 117³ Pointsman 1153½ By the Numbers 115no Ridden out 10
5Aug66-3Mth fst 6f .22 .45⅗1.11⅖ Md Sp Wt 8 10 1112 97¾ 53½ 11½ ADeSpirito b 118 5.60 85–17 Rupin 1181½ Farbizon 118h Pointsman 118h Bumped, driving 12
29Jly 66-5Mth gd 5½f.23⅖ .48 1.06⅘ Md Sp Wt 5 1 53½ 31½ 22 2½ ADeSpirito b 118 3.20 82–26 Air General 118½ Rupin 118⁹ Mister G. R. 118no Gave game try 8
LATEST WORKOUTS Jun 17 Mth 3f fst .37⅖ b Jun 9 Mth 4f fst .49 hg Jun 5 Bel 5f fst 1.04⅕ b May 31 Bel 4f fst .48 bg

Namay × $13,000 B. c (1964–Md), by Nade—Flymay, by Devil Diver 117 1967 11 2 2 4 $10,720
M. Polinger B. P. Hacker (M. Polinger) 1966 6 2 0 1 $6,065
12Jun67-5Mth fm*5f Ⓣ .59⅗ Clm 14000 10 3 43 47 57 63¾ JJohnson 118 *2.60 94- 3 Barrie B. 111¾ No Note 102nk Bit Of Dash 1121 Well up, tired 10
6Jun67-5Mth fst 6f .22⅖ .45⅖1.10⅘ Clm 15000 7 2 1h 2h 3nk 32 JJohnson 118 6.40 86-16 La Chunga 105h Wee Willie 1182 Namay 1181½ Speed, weakened 7
17May67-8Pim fst 6f .23⅖ .46⅘1.12 Allowance 1 4 2h 1h 31 31¾ CGonzalez 110 3.50 88-15 Priam's Joker 113nk Devrex 1121½ Namay 1103 Held on gamely 12
25Apr67-8Pim fst 6f .23⅘ .46⅗1.12⅖ Allowance 1 2 15 17 16 1¾ CGonzalez 108 9.30 88-14 Namay 108¾ Native Uprising 112h Telepathy 1171½ Scored easily 8
13Apr67-6Pim fst 6f .22⅗ .45⅘1.12 Clm 15500 3 4 45 43½ 31½ 21½ GPatterson 113 3.80 88-16 Ponwood 1091½ Namay 1131¼ Lucky Roman 1151½ Best of others 6
6Apr67-6Pim gd 6f .23⅕ .46⅗1.12⅘ Clm 14500 5 1 22 32½ 31½ 32 CRogers 114 *2.20 84-14 Ted's Pick 1151½ Dancing Beauty 112¾ Namay 1142 Impeded 6
22Mar67-7Pim sly 6f .23⅖ .47 1.12⅗ Allowance 1 4 32 24 21½ 21¼ CRogers 115 ♦5.80 86-20 Calwood 1151¼ ♦Namay 1151½ ♦Roman Away 1221½ Gamely 7
22Mar67—♦–Triple Dead Heat.
8Mar67-7Pim gd 6f .23⅗ .47⅖1.13⅘ Clm 10000 8 1 32 2h 1h 1¾ CRogers 115 *1.30 81-23 Namay 115¾ Regal Foot 113¾ Rodema 1152½ Strong urging 9
22Feb67-7Bow gd 6f .23⅕ .47 1.12⅕ Allowance 1 3 1h 2h 31½ 43½ CRogers 115 2.30 82-24 Charles Elliott 115h St. Mawr 1142¼ Quaker City 1121¼ Used up 7
10Feb67-7Bow fst 6f .22⅘ .46⅗1.11⅗ Allowance 10 2 63¼ 63 23 33 CRogers 119 4.40 86-20 Lagoon Girl 1132¼ Burnished Gold 119¾ Namay 119nk Bid, hung 12
23Jan67-7Bow fst 6f .23⅕ .46⅘1.12⅘ Allowance 6 5 44 44 2h 41 WChambers 119 8.20 82-24 Last Cry 115½ Quaker City 112½ Young Sam 119h Bid, tired 10
10Dec66-6Lrl fst 6f .23⅕ .47⅖1.13 Allowance 8 2 2h 43¼ 44¼ 41¼ WChambers 119 4.10 86-14 Crowned King 117h Sky Count 1191 Fairhill Drive 122h Weakened 10
LATEST WORKOUTS May 14 Pim 3f fst .35 h

Battle Plan $13,000 Ch. c (1964–Ky), by Prince John–Battle Eve, by Battlefield 117 1967 7 1 0 1 $3,430
Elmendorf V. J. Nickerson (Elmendorf Farm) 1966 0 M 0 0 ——
8Jun67-7Mth fst 6f .21⅗ .44⅘1.11 Allowance 4 5 33 43½ 511 512 JLeonard 113 8.30 75-17 First And Finest 1157 Self Mastery 1111½ MerryMaster 1203 Weak'd 10
23May67-7Aqu fst 6f .22 .45⅖1.11⅗ Allowance 10 2 11½ 12 53 87¾ LGilligan 114 5.30 77-20 Puntador 113½ Tolk 109no Tartan Dance 119¾ Wide upper turn 10
12May67-4GS gd 6f .22⅘ .46⅘1.12⅕ Md Sp Wt 1 8 1½ 11½ 13 16 JVasquez 116 *1.20 83-21 Battle Plan 1166 Olympia You 116½ Acquitted 116½ Easily best 12
1May67-1Aqu fst 1⅛.46⅘1.11⅗1.52⅘ Md Sp Wt 7 1 16 15 53 817 ADeSpirito 114 5.40 55-20 Firestitch 1134½ Round Tower 1121½ Chronological 123¾ Used up 10
26Apr67-1Aqu fst 6f .22⅕ .45⅖1.10⅘ Md Sp Wt 6 2 31 22 26 49¾ EBelmonte b 122 8.30 79-17 Mr. Washington 1227 Minnesota Mac 122nk IcedCoffee1222½ Tired 14
19Apr67-5Aqu gd 6f .23 .47⅘1.13⅘ Md Sp Wt 5 1 14 14 11 33¾ WShoemaker b 114 2.50 70-26 Tote'm Home 114¾ Chorus 1143 Battle Plan 1144 Bore out 10
12Apr67-1Aqu fst 6f .22⅘ .46⅘1.12⅕ Md Sp Wt 1 5 1h 11 22 47¼ RUssery b 122 5.00 75-21 Velvet Flash 1225½ Prinkipo 122nk Royal Comedian 1221¼ Gave way 14
LATEST WORKOUTS Jun 6 Mth 4f fst .48 h May 21 Aqu 3f fst .39 b May. 10 Aqu 4f fst .51⅗ b

Famous Dancer $12,000 Ch. g (1964–Ky), by Native Dancer—Acantha, by Bossuet 117 1967 8 2 0 1 $6,290
Warner Stable R. Metcalf (Mrs. G. Proskauer) 1966 1 M 0 0 ——
12Jun67-5Mth fm*5f Ⓣ .59⅗ Clm 12000 3 9 84¾ 57 46½ 42 BThornburg b 116 8.40 96- 3 Barrie B. 111¾ No Note 102nk Bit Of Dash 1121 Closed willingly 10
3Jun67-4Mth fst 6f .21⅘ .45 1.11⅕ Clm 10000 7 7 53½ 44½ 23 1½ BThornburg b 114 4.20 86-15 Famous Dancer 114½ Regal Dancer 113½ Destigate 1143 Driving 10
24May67-6GS fst 6f .22⅖ .45⅘1.11⅗ Clm 12500 7 2 1½ 2½ 23 33 JVelasquez b 116 16.90 83-14 Holly War 116no Wee Willie 1183 Famous Dancer 116h Went well 7
19May67-8GS fst 6f .22 .45⅕1.11⅘ Allowance 5 2 31½ 35 59 713 JVelasquez b 116 11.50 72-20 St. Mawr 113½ Andrews Bridge 1131 Robert Kope 1137 Fell back 7
6May67-6GS sly 6f .22⅘ .46⅕1.12⅕ Allowance 3 6 64¼ 711 713 722 SHernandez b 112 23.20 61-23 All At Sea 1132 Dark Eagle 112h More Scents 1123 No factor 7
28Apr67-2GS gd 6f .23⅖ .47⅖1.14 Md Sp Wt 6 2 1h 13 14 1no JVelasquez b 115 14.80 74-27 Famous Dancer 115no Pebble Drive 1153 Muskwin 115½ All out 10
8Apr67-6GP fst 6f .22⅖ .46 1.11⅖ Allowance 8 9 97¾ 912 918 919 BMoreira b 114 84.20 68-14 Newshawk 117no PartyBoy 1173 DustyMan 1173½ Trailed the field 9
20Mar67-3GP fst 6f .22⅗ .46⅕1.11⅗ Md Sp Wt 8 9 98 69 69¼ 712 BMoreira b 120 100.40 74-15 Wifes Objection 120nk Pebble Drive 1203 Stockpile 120h No speed 12
24Sep66-2Atl fst 6f .22⅘ .47⅕1.13⅕ Md Sp Wt 10 10 62½ 79½ 1217 1225 JVelasquez b 118 10.90 51-26 Tangelo 1182½ Wedgedale 1183½ Regal Count 1181¼ Far off pace 12
LATEST WORKOUTS May 15 GS 3f fst .37⅖ b May 11 GS 5f fst 1.04 b Apr 24 GS 5f my 1.06 b Apr 20 GS 5f gd 1.02⅘ b

Deepsprings ✻ $13,000 B. f (1964–Ky), by Barbizon—Swooning, by The Doge 105⁵ 1967 7 0 3 2 $4,625
Mrs. D. W. Evans E. Yowell (E. G. Drake) 1966 10 2 1 1 $5,945
23May67-6GS fst 6f .22 .46 1.11⅗ f- 14000 6 2 57 43½ 42½ 32 MMiceli5 b 106 3.60 84-16 Athen's Gem 117½ Minnie Baby 1121½ Deepsprings 106¾ No mishap 7
9May67-8GS my 6f .22⅖ .46⅖1.12⅘ f- Allow 5 5 63¼ 57 42¼ 22½ MMiceli5 b 107 12.60 77-24 Regal Hostess 1182½ Deepsprings 1071 Momma Pierre 1121 Rallied 6
22Apr67-6GS fst 6f .22 .45⅗1.11⅘ f- Allow 7 4 44 36½ 33 49 RTurcotte b 113 7.20 76-20 Lori Mac 1132 She's Very Ultra 1137 Barrie B. 116h Weakened 9
27Feb67-7Hia fst 7f .22⅘ .46⅕1.25⅕ f- 14000 3 4 2½ 31 14 22 SHernandez b 116 6.60 81-14 Dancing Dale 1142 Deepsprings 116no Cast Your Fate 1162 Faltered 10
15Feb67-6Hia fst 6f .22⅕ .45⅗1.12⅕ f- 15000 11 6 2½ 13 12 31 KKnapp b 118 *2.90 82-16 d-Lady Avalon 112h Ethical 1161 Deepsprings 1182½ No excuse 12
23Jan67-6Hia sly 6f .22⅘ .46⅕1.12⅘ f- 14000 7 1 3½ 13 13 2no KKnapp b 114 3.80 76-19 Minnie Baby114no Deepsprings1143½ Duchess Nancy1121½ Gamely 11
19Jan67-7Hia fst 6f .22⅗ .46⅖1.12⅕ f- Allow 5 7 42½ 42¼ 1013 1010 RFerraro b 112 9.00e 73-17 Lady Ebony 112nk Shirley Heights 1152½ Betoken 115½ Speed 4 fur. 12
30Dec66-7TrP fst 6f .22 .45⅕1.10⅖ Allowance 1 4 1h 11 12 1½ SHernandez b 112 3.80 90-12 Deepsprings 112½ Miss Vertex 1122½ Debbie's Tam 1123½ Driving 11
6Dec66-7TrP fst 6f .21⅘ .45⅕1.10⅘ Allowance 9 2 1½ 1h 21½ 35 SHernandez b 115 3.70 83-14 Game Maid 1151¼ Debbie's Tam 1113¾ Deepsprings 1151¼ Tired 12
9Nov66-6GS fst 6f .22⅖ .46 1.11⅘ Allowance 2 3 11½ 1h 1h 2h SHernandez b 112 39.30 85-17 La Meme Chose 112h Deepsprings 112no Quaker City 1183 Sharp 7
2Sep66-2Atl fst 6f .22⅗ .47 1.13⅖ f- c-7500 1 4 1h 11 13 45½ CBaltazar b 117 5.70 69-22 Ricos Spy 1174 Hestra 1191 Je Ne Sais Quoi 113½ Used in lead 12
LATEST WORKOUTS Jun 14 Mth 5f fst 1.04 b Jun 10 Mth 4f fst .53 b Jun 6 Mth 3f fst .38⅖ b Jun 2 Mth 3f fst .36⅘ b

---

Fiddler's Green: Unable to beat $9,000 maidens on May 23, and unclaimed from that race, this colt improved sharply two weeks ago and could conceivably have a chance if the rest of this field were of the same dubious quality. Since the field is not all that bad, out goes Fiddler's Green. NO BET.

Regal Dancer: Tremendous early speed against cheaper horses, but no sign of the stamina needed to lead from wire to wire against $13,000 stock. NO BET.

Tom's Brother: Claimed for $10,000 earlier this month, the gelding is required by racing law to run at $12,500 or higher for thirty days. Which is the only reason it is in this race. NO BET.

Fuel King: Scratched.

Rupin: Promising last year, went to seed early this year and was rested for three months. It also was rested for three months last fall and winter. These vacations may have been on doctor's orders, as the bleeding of March 7 suggests. Could surprise today, I suppose, but not for my money. NO BET.

Namay: Speedy, but no great shakes in the final stages, this one is sure to be in the running and might take it all. CONTENDER.

Battle Plan: The only entrant that has never run in a claimer, Lefty Nickerson's colt would be a threat for that reason alone. The switch from Leonard to the hottest rider in the country, Jorge Velasquez, is a proclamation that Lefty is shooting for the money. CONTENDER.

Famous Dancer: A threat, but scratched.

Deepsprings: A nice little filly which probably is in here for a tightener after being away for almost a month. Off her best May form on this circuit, she would not figure to beat the kind of males she meets today. NO BET.

The contenders are Namay and Battle Plan. Battle Plan's Svengali, Lefty Nickerson, has not been getting much lately with the Elmendorf stock, but the stable remains potent and Lefty is one of the foremost manipulators in the sport. It is entirely unlikely that despair explains the Nickerson decision to run Battle Plan in a claimer. The race he got out of the horse on May 12 was against maidens but was an authentically powerful showing on an off track. It was the logical result (for a good colt) of Nickerson's deliberate effort to leg up the animal by making him run nine furlongs on May 1. Nickerson very evidently knows this horse and how to get some run from him. The high odds against Battle Plan on May 23 at Aqueduct and June 8 here were warranted by the toughness of the competition. But the colt showed enough speed in the Aqueduct effort to convince me that he can rule the early pace here today. Since the track is sloppy, Valasquez can expect some advantage over off-pace horses after he gets the lead. Namay appears to offer no danger in a duel of early speed, because of his susceptibility to discouragement when something else runs with him. Regal Dancer might also vie for the lead, but lacks the class to hang in there. Namay's main hope lies in Jim Johnson snugging him off the pace, as Garth Patterson did in a comparable race at Pimlico on April 13. Then, if Battle Plan tires, Namay will have some run left for the final furlong.

Knowing Nickerson and being confident that he knows his horse, I am not fearful that Battle Plan will conk out. The two recent allowance races were partly hopeful experiments but mainly were preparations for a real crackdown. With Velasquez in the driver's seat, today is the day, and the sloppy track will help no end.

The Running of the Race

NAMAY WAS FAVORED on grounds of recent form. The crowd quite sensibly ignored his poor performance on the grass but noted that he had been close to the front end in more expensive races than this one. Battle Plan was a wholesome 3.40–1, with Deepsprings rated third at the mutuel windows.

Velasquez laughed his way to the wire. Johnson rated Namay off the pace, but the horse cooperated too enthusiastically and came into the stretch much too far out of it to catch Battle Plan.

Take it as a rule of thumb that you should respect a lightly raced three-year-old that has demonstrated some speed, if its record shows distance and/or class maneuvers by the trainer, and if the trainer is a major leaguer, and if the horse finally is dropped into a claimer for the first time in its life. Horses of this kind do not always win their first claiming races, but must—repeat *must*—be conceded a chance and should never be ruled out until you have studied the situation carefully.

FIFTH RACE
Mth - 31431
June 19, 1967

6 FURLONGS (Chute). (Decathlon, June 11, 1957, 1.08⅖, 4, 130.)
Claiming. Purse $5,000. 3-year-olds. Weight, 122 lbs. Non-winners of two races since May 12 allowed 3 lbs., a race. 5 lbs., a race since April 21, 7 lbs. Claiming price, $13,000. 1 lb. for each $500 to $11,000. (Races where entered for $9,000 or less not considered.)
Value to winner $3,250, second $1,000, third $500, fourth $250. Mutuel pool $138,726.

Index	Horse	Eqt	A	Wt	PP	St	¼	½	Str	Fin	Jockey	Cl'g Pr	Owner	Odds $1
31352Mth^{5}	—Battle Plan		3	117	6	1	2^{h}	$1\frac{1}{2}$	1^{5}	1^{9}	J Velasquez	13000	Elmendorf	3.40
31377Mth^{6}	—Namay		3	117	5	3	6^{5}	6^{4}	$4\frac{1}{2}$	$2^{1\frac{1}{4}}$	J Johnson	13000	M Polinger	2.80
31141GS^{3}	—Deepsprings	b	3	105	7	2	4^{1}	4^{1}	3^{h}	3^{3}	M Miceli^{5}	13000	Mrs D W Evans	3.50
31377Mth^{5}	—Rupin	b	3	115	4	6	$5\frac{1}{2}$	5^{3}	5^{2}	4^{nk}	K Knapp	13000	Calumet Farm	6.50
31313Mth^{2}	—Regal Dancer		3	113	2	4	1^{1}	2^{4}	$2^{1\frac{1}{2}}$	5^{nk}	D Brumfield	11500	Winfields Farm	5.70
31320Mth^{1}	—Fiddler's Gr'n	b	3	119	1	7	7	7	7	6^{6}	J Vasquez	13000	J L Frost	9.80
31377Mth	—Tom's Brother		3	115	3	5	3^{4}	3^{h}	6^{3}	7	P Kallai	13000	P. Bongarzone	9.50

Time .22, .45⅘, 1.11⅗. Track sloppy.

$2 Mutuel Prices:

6–BATTLE PLAN	8.80	5.00	3.00
5–NAMAY		4.00	2.80
8–DEEPSPRINGS			2.80

Ch. c, by Prince John—Battle Eve, by Battlefield. Trainer V. J. Nickerson. Bred by Elmendorf Farm (Ky.).

IN GATE AT 3.49. OFF AT 3.49 EASTERN DAYLIGHT TIME. Start good for all but FIDDLER'S GREEN. Won ridden out.

BATTLE PLAN, away alertly, was sent up to relieve REGAL DANCER of command nearing the stretch, drew well out and won while kept to intermittent pressure to the end. NAMAY outfinished the others for place. DEEPSPRINGS was never a factor. RUPIN failed to menace. REGAL DANCER set the pace for the three furlongs and faltered.. FIDDLER'S GREEN broke in a tangle. TOM'S BROTHER fell back leaving the backstretch.

Scratched—31150GS^{5} Fuel King, 31377Mth^{4} Famous Dancer. Overweight—Regal Dancer 1 pound.
Namay was claimed by Meadow Ridge Stable, trainer B. Lepman.

---

7. FIFTH AT GARDEN STATE, MAY 4, 1967—Track Fast

THE FIRST FEW WEEKS of the Florida, Illinois, New York, and New Jersey racing seasons offer stern challenges to the patience and resourcefulness of the expert player. Horses arrive on the grounds from all over the country. Until they have raced a time or two, it is difficult to know much about their condition. The wise handicapper avoids play. He keeps his wallet buttoned until the animals have had time to sort themselves out.

Yet opportunities sometimes arise during the confused early days of the season. The player can exploit these opportunities if he is alert to certain angles—factors which arise frequently throughout the year yet are of special significance early in the season.

This sprint, we see, is for $12,500 fillies and mares. Slightly on the cheap side of allowance quality, but considerably better than the $5,000–$7,500 stock that is the staple of big-time racing.

5th Race Garden — 6 FURLONGS GARDEN STATE (Start / Finish)

6 FURLONGS (Chute). (I Appeal, May 21, 1955, 1.08⅘, 4, 112.)
Claiming. Purse $5,000. Fillies and mares. 3-year-olds and upward. Weights, 3-year-olds, 115 lbs.; older, 121 lbs. Non-winners of two races since April 2, allowed 2 lbs.; two races since March 4, 4 lbs.; a race since April 15, 6 lbs. Claiming price $12,500; 2 lbs. allowed for each $1,000 to $10,500. (Races where entered for $9,000 or less not considered.)

Navy Heroine ✕ $11,500 — B. m (1962), by Jutland—Blueblend, by Blue Swords — Crown Stable — B. Lepman — (J. E. Hughes) — **113** — 1967 10 1 3 1 $5,485 — 1966 17 4 4 1 $14,303

2Apr67-6GP fm 1 1/16 Ⓣ 1.11⅕1.42⅘ Clm 12500 5 2 25 33½ 32½ 54 WGavidia 111 14.40 86–15 Argosy 114no Toro Charger 1163½ Officer Sweeneyl 114½ Speed, tired 9
4Apr67-8GP fst 7f .22⅘ .46 1.24 f– 12500 4 6 85½ 89¼ 47 46¾ WGavidia 118 6.00 82–15 Manta H. 111¾ Greek Princess 1165 Naga 1161 Had no mishap 9
2Mar67-5GP fst 6f .22⅖ .45⅖1.10⅗ Clm 13000 8 4 89½ 99½ 79½ 67¼ MMiceli5 106 3.70e 84–19 Athen's Gem 113½ Bwana Peacha 1163½ Mahjubill 116¾ No threat 9
8Mar67-4GP fst 7f .22⅘ .45⅖1.23 f– c-10000 4 3 55 23 2½ 1½ BMoreira 115 2.50 94–11 NavyHeroine 115½ ColorMeGone 1151½ GreekPrincess 1152 Driving 7
2Mar67-4Hia fst 7f .23⅖ .46⅖1.24⅖ f– 11500 6 4 44 43½ 41 21¼ BMoreira 114 5.90 86–13 Bakery Babe 1181¼ Navy Heroine 1143 Nix 111nk Made game try 9
2Feb67-5Hia sly 7f .23⅕ .46⅕1.24 f– 13000 4 3 77½ 912 7:½ 76½ WHartack 116 7.20 82–17 Blended White 1123 High Bluff 1161 Color Me Gone 112½ No factor 10
4Feb67-4Hia fst 7f .23⅕ .46⅕1.24 f– 10000 1 6 32½ 58 35 25 BMoreira 116 *1.90 84–13 Bakery Babe 1165 Navy Heroine 1163½ Greek Princess 1163 Gamely 11
1Jan67-5Hia fst 7f .23⅕ .46⅖1.24⅗ f– 11000 3 5 42 43 42 2¾ BMoreira 112 12.40 85–16 Ship Shoal 116¾ Navy Heroine 112¾ Native Twin 1163 Wide 12
23Jan67-7Hia sly 7f .23⅘ .47⅕1.25⅘ f– 13000 5 3 85¼ 88 52 54¼ BMoreira 112 7.10 76–19 Needles Sword 117nk Zeesa Adelle 1121 Admiral's Gift 1122 No thr't 11
3Jan67-9TrP fst 170.45⅖1.10 1.40⅕ Clm 10000 3 4 58¾ 44½ 32 33¼ BMoreira 111 5.50 93–13 Florida Scheme 1201¾ Tulran 1141½ Navy Heroine 1115 Rallied 8
1Dec66-10TrP fst 1 1/16.46⅕1.11 1.43⅖ Clm 12500 6 6 66½ 57 56½ 57 BMoreira 111 3.90 78–15 Cash Customer 118no Count Dormal 1135 The Clown 1142 Evenly 8
LATEST WORKOUTS Apr 19 GP 5f fst 1.00⅖ h Apr 12 GP 5f fst 1.03 b Apr 1 GP 4f gd .50 b

Swiss Maid $10,500 — B. f (1964–Ky), by Dotted Swiss—Winter Garden, by Windfields — Craig–Menarde — T. J. Arkinson — (J. D. Drymon–H. V. Greenslit) — **111** — 1966 14 2 4 1 $7,582

10Oct66-1GS fst 6f .22⅕ .46⅕1.12⅘ f– 8000 2 12 1210 99½ 88½ 43½ BThornburg b 116 5.70 76–16 Rodarap 1162 Trolley Car 1141 Better or Worse 114½ Rallied 12
4Oct66-5GS fst 6f .22⅖ .45⅗1.11⅕ f– Allow 10 8 96¾ 95¼ 66½ 68 BThornburg b 114 14.30 80–13 La Chunga 114h Captivating Lady 1146 Ponwood 114¾ No threat 11
4Oct66-5Atl fst 6f .23 .46⅖1.12⅘ f– 7000 7 2 2½ 15 14 16 BThornburg b 116 3.40 78–24 Swiss Maid 1166 Royal Frolic 114h Seventh Street 120no Easily 9
0Sep66-1Atl sly 6f .22⅖ .46⅗1.12⅗ Cl c-5500 5 7 69½ 49 24 23½ JCulmone 115 *2.40 75–28 Carpet Slipper 1153½ Swiss Maid 1152½ Royal Frolic 1141½ Gamely 10
0Sep66-3Atl fst 6f .22⅖ .47⅕1.15 Clm 5500 9 8 77½ 66¾ 44¼ 22 JCulmone b 115 *2.00 65–24 Carpet Slipper 1152 Swiss Maid 115½ Cameron 115h Rallied 9
0Aug66-5Atl fst 6f .22⅕ .46⅕1.12⅘ Clm 5500 6 4 33½ 32 31½ 23 CMcPeek5 b 109 *1.80 75–19 Corby Dot 1113 Swiss Maid 109½ Second Show 1142 Went well 9
9Jly 66-3Del gd 5½f.22⅕ .46⅗1.05⅘ Clm 6500 10 8 84¾ 45 28 27 JVasquez b 117 4.40 84–17 Special Bonus 1077 Swiss Maid 1174 Charm Dancer 1161 2nd best 11
1Jly 66-3Del fst 5½f.22⅕ .47⅖1.07 f– 6000 4 5 55 48½ 23 1¾ GReeder5 b 111 4.90 85–18 Swiss Maid 111¾ Special Bonus 1166 Missy Rose 116¾ Driving 12
5Jly 66-1Del fst 5½f.22⅕ .47 1.06⅕ Clm 6000 10 6 56½ 37½ 49 511 SBrooks b 113 10.90 78–16 Pieces of Change1205½ Lord Gregory1163½ Royal Frolic1171 No thr't 11
6Jly 66-3Del fst 5½f.22 .46⅖1.06⅖ Md 7500 8 9 78¼ 710 56¾ 47 SBrooks b 117 7.20 81–14 Pieces of Change 1206 To the Day 117nk Special Bonus 117¾ Wide 9
LATEST WORKOUTS Apr 20 GS 3f gd .39⅗ b Apr 14 GS 4f fst .49⅗ b

Bakery Babe $12,500 — B. f (1963–Ill), by Jet Colonel—Tasty, by Oil Capitol — Carolyn K. Stable — J. C. Wozneski — (Lucky Seven Farm) — **115** — 1967 6 2 1 0 $6,975 — 1966 15 2 2 2 $7,039

5Mar67-10GP fm 1 1/16 Ⓣ 1.11⅕1.42⅗ Clm 14000 9 1 11 55½ 914 917 JVelasquez b 113 6.40 74– 3 Brant 1201 Yar 1162 Capotillo 1161½ Hard used early 10
2Mar67-4Hia fst 7f .23⅖ .46⅖1.24⅖ f– 12500 3 3 1½ 1½ 1½ 11¼ RUssery b 118 *1.10 87–13 Bakery Babe 1181¼ Navy Heroine 1143 Nix 111nk Under hard drive 9
2Feb67-5Hia sly 7f .23⅕ .46⅕1.24 f– 14000 1 6 21½ 32½ 33½ 55¼ JSellers b 114 3.20 84–17 Blended White 1123 High Bluff 1161 Color Me Gone 112½ Tired 10
4Feb67-4Hia fst 7f .23⅕ .46⅕1.24 f– c-10000 6 4 2½ 12 15 15 JSellers b 116 2.10 89–13 Bakery Babe 1165 Navy Heroine 1163½ Greek Princess 1163 Easily 11
6Feb67-5Hia fst 6f .22⅖ .45⅖1.11⅕ f– 10000 2 4 62¾ 54½ 44 2½ LMoyers b 114 6.00 87–14 Blended White 112½ Bakery Babe 114h Color Me Gone 1164½ Wide 12
8Jan67-2Hia fst 6f .22⅖ .45⅘1.11⅗ f– 12000 10 8 912 814 810 44¾ JChoquette b 114 7.10 81–12 Athen's Gem 1161¾ Naga 1121½ Get A Lot 1161½ Found stride late 12
9Dec66-8TrP fst 6f .22 .44⅗1.09 Allowance 9 5 52 75¼1010 913 LMoyers b 112 32.10 84–11 The Cheat 1174¾ Call Me Fritz 117½ Roman John 115nk Tired 12
9Dec66-7TrP gd 6f .22⅕ .45⅗1.11⅖ Clm 10000 1 6 45½ 44 23 2nk LMoyers b 108 11.70 85–19 Judy's Whiz 113nk Bakery Babe 1086 Misty Bandit 116h Sharp 7
6Nov66-4TrP fst 6f .22⅕ .45⅕1.10⅗ Clm 10000 3 7 54½ 65¼ 67¼ 84¼ JRuybali b 111 11.70 85–11 Athen's Gem 1132 Tenor 114½ Naga 111no Lacked a response 12
10Oct66-6Haw fst 6f .22⅕ .45⅖1.11 Allowance 1 7 67 710 88½ 63¼ IValenzuela b 113 *2.50 89– 9 Wolf Hands 109½ Miss Pry 1112 Better Bee Best 109½ No excuses 8
LATEST WORKOUTS May 1 GS 6f fst 1.15⅖ h Apr 21 GS 4f gd .50 b Apr 16 GS 5f gd 1.03 b Apr 8 TrP 4f fst .53 b

Cute Sweetie $12,500 B. f (1963–Ky), by Nantallah—Ragtime Band, by Johnstown **115** 1967 2 0 0 0 $360
Mrs. I. Friedman L. Laurin (Edw. B. Benjamin) 1966 12 2 2 1 $9,925

28Apr67–6Aqu	sl 6f	.23	.47⅕1.12⅖	f–	15000	7	6	54½	54½	56	45½	BFeliciano	b 116	8.20	75–26	Bubbles O'Tudor 116h Zayer Naytik 1125 Ship Shoal 109½	Wide	7
31Mar67–7Aqu	fst 6f	.22⅘	.46 1.11⅗	f–	Allow	6	1	611	612	611	610	BFeliciano	b 118	26.70	75–23	Arrangement 108nk Kate's Intent 1085 Ship Shoal 118½	No speed	6
22Sep66–8Aqu	gd 7f	.22⅖	.45⅗1.25⅖	f–	15000	4	3	68	57½	23	13	RUssery	b 115	4.20e	79–23	Cute Sweetie 1153 Speedy Lady 1095 Buffet Dinner 1141	Easily	8
16Sep66–6Aqu	fst 7f	.22⅘	.46⅖1.25⅖	f–	15000	4	4	55½	43½	45½	55½	BFeliciano	b 112	4.60	73–25	Ski Dancer 112½ Speedy Lady 1073 Windswept 118no	No mishap	7
8Sep66–7Aqu	fst 7f	.23⅕	.47⅕1.25⅕	f–	Allow	4	4	77½	44	44½	45	EBelmonte	b 116	14.00e	75–29	Air Whirl 1192 Terrific Traffic 1192 River Lady 1151	No mishap	9
15Aug66–6Sar	fst 7f	.23	.46 1.24⅘	f–	Allow	4	4	23	23	23	62½	BFeliciano	b 118	13.20	83–17	Fatal Step 113nk Darlin Phyllis 113no Miss Flirt 106½	Hung	9
3Aug66–8Sar	fm 1 1/16 Ⓣ		1.41⅕	f–	Allow	6	3	3nk	34	43½	49½	BFeliciano	b 113	34.10	89– 1	Snow Queen 1166 Silver Bright 1061 Our Dear Ruth 1122½	Tired	9
29Jly 66–5Aqu	fst 6f	.23	.46⅖1.11	f–	Allow	3	2	44½	47	45	34½	KKnapp	b 116	2.40	83–17	Streamer 1162½ Home Lass 1062 Cute Sweetie 1162½	Mild rally	6
22Jly 66–6Aqu	fst 6f	.22⅘	.45 1.11⅕	f–	Allow	4	2	25	24	24	22	BFeliciano	b 116	3.40	85–19	Lucky Eagle 1052 Cute Sweetie 1162 Tomeen 1131	Second best	6
9Jly 66–4Mth	fst 6f	.22	.45⅕1.10⅘	f–	Allow	4	3	33½	31½	1h	1nk	JVelasquez	b 116	*1.30	88–18	Cute Sweetie 116nk Tangle 1163 Miss Kentuckian 1162½	Driving	7
1Jly 66–6Mth	fst 6f	.22⅕	.45 1.10⅘	f–	Allow	7	2	21½	32½	32	2½	JVelasquez	b 118	6.50	87–15	Spring Dream 116½ Cute Sweetie 118½ Miss Kentuckian 1166	Gamely	7

LATEST WORKOUTS Apr 25 Bel tr.t. 4f gd .49⅘ h Apr 20 Bel tr.t. 4f fst .50 h Apr 15 Bel tr.t. 5f fst 1.03⅗ h Mar 30 Bel tr.t. 3f my .41 b

***Nix** $10,500 Dk. b. or br. m (1962), by Niquel—Morronga, by Selim Hassan **111** 1967 8 1 0 2 $3,100
F. P Dyer G. Zateslo (Haras Santana) (Peru) 1966 16 2 0 4 $8,922
(Eligible for racing purposes only.)

24Apr67–8GP	fm 1 Ⓣ	.47	1.36⅘	f	Allow	6	2	25	24	46	57	MMiceli5	b 117	21.00	83–14	Funny Valentine 1125 Pituca 112no Camerola 1131½	Gave way	6
4Apr67–8GP	fst 7f	.22⅘	.46 1.24	f–	12500	7	4	2½	32½	813	813	RBroussard	b 118	3.40	76–15	Manta H. 111¾ Greek Princess 1165 Naga 1161	Early speed, tired	9
27Mar67–5GP	fst 6f	.22⅗	.45⅘1.11⅕	f–	9000	1	6	32	2h	12	13	WBlum	b 113	2.40	88–18	Nix 1133 Manta H. 116h Come On Jackie 1122¾	Won going away	7
15Mar67–4GP	fst 6f	.22⅘	.46⅖1.11⅕	f–	7500	3	5	2h	11½	2½	31¾	MMiceli5	b 111	4.40	86–18	Get A Lot 1161½ Lovely Bolero 118nk Nix 1112	Clear lead, tired	9
2Mar67–4Hia	fst 7f	.23⅗	.46⅖1.24⅖	f–	12500	2	2	32	32	2½	34¼	MMiceli5	b 111	34.30	83–13	Bakery Babe 1181¼ Navy Heroine 1143 Nix 111nk	Bold bid, tired	9
9Feb67–5Hia	gd 6f	.22⅗	.46⅕1.11⅘	f–	c-9500	7	7	74	78½	811	810	RCox	b 116	28.70	75–16	Dulat's Twin 1181½ Color Me Gone 1162 My Marion 1112½	No factor	10
2Feb67–2Hia	fst 6f	.22⅕	.45⅗1.11⅗	Cl	c-7000	9	10	74¾	86¼	78½	64½	MMiceli5	b 102	16.50	81–14	Erin Boy 114½ Grand Marais 114½ Judy's Whiz 1141½	Wide	12
6Jan67–5TrP	fst 6f	.22	.44⅘1.09⅘	f–	7500	7	9	95¼	98¾	811	710	LMoyers	b 116	9.50	83–12	Primfear 1143 My Marion 1161½ Vie Eye 113h	Never close	10
23Dec66–4TrP	fst 6f	.21⅘	.44⅗1.10⅖	Clm	8500	8	6	87¼	78¾	67½	55½	MMiceli5	b 108	17.20	84–11	Runagate 106nk Measure 1103 Primfear 1111¼	Not a contender	10
9Dec66–8TrP	gd 6f	.22	.45⅗1.11	f–	Allow	5	5	59½	611	713	615	MMiceli5	b 115	67.80	72–19	Codorniz 1202¼ Neat 'n Sweet 1112 Zamilu 1132¾	Bad start	8
24Nov66–7Lrl	fst 7f	.23	.47⅕1.25⅘	f–	Allow	7	4	41	78¾	78¾	715	JKratz5	b 111	22.10	75–17	TemptMeNot 1101½ Bunch of Daisies 1191½ Teetotaler 1192	Fell back	8

LATEST WORKOUTS Apr 22 GP 4f fst .50⅘ b Apr 16 GP 3f fst .37 b Mar 24 GP 3f fst .37⅖ b Mar 10 GP t.c. 4f fm .51⅗ b

McCoy $12,500 B. f (1963–Ky), Hillsdale—Attica, by Mr. Trouble **115** 1967 3 0 0 0 ——
Circle M. Farm J. Long (Mrs. R. W. Bell) 1966 13 1 3 1 $8,087

27Apr67–5Kee	fst 6f	.21⅘	.45⅗1.11	f–	Allow	3	6	56½	48½	410	511	DKassen	b 117	41.20	77–17	Prim Lady 1056 Miss Boyd 1144½ Caryl Kay 108no	Had no mishap	9
11Jan67–7TrP	fst 6f	.22⅕	.45 1.09⅕		Allowance	4	6	77	610	613	514	DKassen	b 114	47.70	82–14	Jet Avenger 1144 Rome Express 113½ Wesley Ashcraft 1215	No fact.	7
4Jan67–4TrP	fst 6f	.22⅖	.46 1.11⅕		Allowance	10	9	88½	79	89	79½	DKassen	b 114	10.50	76–17	Round Table Pet 111nk Uncle Adolph 1143 High Stool 1134	Wide	11
4Aug66–5Sar	fst 6f	.22⅖	.46 1.12⅕	f–	Allow	2	6	23	24	34½	65½	LAdams	b 115	14.90	81–13	Lucky Eagle 110½ Smoky Dale 1161½ Rose Court 1112	Drifted out	9
12Jly 66–7Mth	fst 6f	.22⅕	.45⅘1.11⅗	f–	Allow	6	1	32	32	21½	1nk	DKassen	b 113	2.10	84–18	McCoy 113nk River Lady 1143½ Summer Mark 116h	Hard drive	7
27Jun66–8Mth	fst 6f	.22	.44⅘1.10⅘	f–	Allow	4	3	3nk	1½	11½	21½	DKassen	b 114	27.80	86–16	Telepathy 1181½ McCoy 114no Chavalon 1143½	Gave game effort	7
20Jun66–7Mth	fst 6f	.21⅘	.44⅗1.11⅕	f–	Allow	3	4	44	511	612	617	DBrumfield	b 113	7.00	69–18	Royalene 109½ Summer Mark 116½ Home Lass 1166	Dropped back	6
28Apr66–6GS	sly 6f	.22⅘	.47 1.13	f–	Allow	5	1	21½	22	43½	49	SBoulmetis	b 113	5.20	70–27	Horn Quarter 1134½ Royalene 1071½ Nasa 1133	Early factor, tired	7
21Apr66–8GS	fst 6f	.22⅖	.45⅗1.10⅖	f–	Allow	4	4	31½	21½	21	32¼	DBrumfield	b 113	7.60	90–17	Ways to Win 113nk Royalene 1072 McCoy 1135	Well up, weakened	9
10Mar66–8GP	fst 6f	.22⅕	.45⅖1.10⅗	f–	Allow	2	7	44½	58½	712	910	DBrumfield	b 116	7.50	81–12	Stealaway 114¾ Sport Queen 1142 Tulip Tree 1092½	Fell back	10
1Mar66–7Hia	fst 6f	.22⅕	.45⅖1.11⅗	f–	Allow	5	6	64	55½	55½	47¾	EFires5	b 107 ♦	3.50	79–15	Squeeze 1151 Stealaway 1124 Miss Foxcroft 1072½	Raced wide	8

LATEST WORKOUTS Apr 26 Kee 3f sly .37⅖ b Apr 23 Kee 5f fst 1.03⅗ b Apr 19 Kee 4f fst .49 b Apr 12 Kee 4f fst .50 b

Scairt $11,500 B. f (1963–Ky), by Barbizon—Big Fright, by Phalanx **113** 1967 7 2 0 2 $7,615
P. D. De Paul C. L. Robbins (W. L. Jones, Jr.) 1966 12 0 2 0 $2,145

11Apr67–6Pim	fst 6f	.23⅖	.46⅘1.12	Clm	13500	7	3	62¾	64¾	77½	55	AAgnello5	b 105	11.20	85–18	Jeannie'sRuler1152½ FiveRogues1161 d-Knave'sDelight115h	No mis'p	7
11Apr67—Placed fourth through disqualification.																		
16Mar67–4Pim	sl 6f	.23⅕	.47⅕1.13	Clm	11500	3	4	43	33½	32½	3¾	ACannon5	b 106	6.40	84–25	♦Five Rogues 115¾ ♦Arctic Swirl 117¾ Scairt 1064	Good try	6
21Feb67–7Bow	sl 7f	.22⅘	.45⅖1.25⅖	Clm	12500	1	2	12	1h	86½	89½	JJohnson	b 113	7.50	76–30	Well To Do 114¾ Arctic Swirl 117nk Two Up 117h	Used up	9
14Feb67–8Bow	fst 6f	.22⅘	.45⅘1.11⅘	f–	Allow	1	6	22½	24	33½	105¾	JJohnson	b 114	3.90	82–23	FlashyShot 1141 d-DoveHunt 110nk CherokeeMary 112nk	Stopped	11
31Jan67–8Bow	fst 7f	.23⅖	.47⅕1.25⅗		Allowance	6	1	12	1½	2h	33½	JJohnson	b 112	*1.40	81–21	Double Strings 1151 Tudor Mistress 1072½ Scairt 1121½	Tired	7
23Jan67–6Bow	fst 7f	.23⅕	.46⅗1.25⅗	f–	11000	11	1	12½	13½	15	16	JJohnson	b 117	4.40	85–24	Scairt 1176 Miltreb Hazard 1131 Who Cabled 1142	Easily	12
7Jan67–6Bow	fst 6f	.22⅘	.46⅘1.13⅘	Clm	10000	8	5	34½	33	42½	21¼	JJohnson	b 113	94.10	77–27	d-Five Rogues 1181¼ Scairt 113nk Star Spin 108½	Made game try	12
7Jan66—Placed first through disqualification.																		
10Nov66–5GS	fst 6f	.21⅘	.44⅘1.10⅗		Allowance	4	4	45	48	45½	47½	JVelasquez	b 112	12.80	83–15	Fleet Admiral 114h Fearless Lee 1133½ Hul A Hul 1224	Evenly	7
12Oct66–6GS	fst 6f	.22⅖	.46 1.11	f–	Allow	8	6	65¾	810	87	78¼	RLStevenson	b 114	54.80	81–16	Double Switch 1151 Jungle Beat 1181½ Rose Court 118¾	No speed	8
6Oct66–8Atl	fst 6f	.22⅕	.46⅗1.13	f–	Allow	5	6	66½	67½	46½	57¼	RLStevens'n	b 114	48.70	70–28	d-Welshwyn 115½ Juanita 1223½ Enchanting Miss 117nk	No threat	7

LATEST WORKOUTS Apr 29 GS 4f gd .51⅖ b Apr 26 GS 3f fst .37 b Apr 21 GS 5f gd 1.02 b Apr 1 Pim 5f fst 1.01⅗ h

Navy Heroine: This mare needs at least a furlong more ground than today's three quarters of a mile. The lack of workouts since her arrival from Gulfstream is another deterrent. Horsemen know better than to sell Bud Lepman short; he is a master strategist. But Navy Heroine doesn't really fit this race. NO BET.

Swiss Maid: Unraced since last October and, on the record, seriously short of the necessary class. NO BET.

Bakery Babe: Idle for more than seven weeks, the filly is entered at the right claiming price but, like Navy Heroine, might want more distance. NO BET.

Cute Sweetie: A bona fide $15,000 item in New York, this filly runs today against the easiest field of her career after a nice tightener only six days ago at Aqueduct. It was no disgrace for the filly to lose her second outing of the year, when the opposition included the likes of Bubbles O'Tudor and Zayer Naytik. I note with interest that the race was on a slow, holding track and that Feliciano took the scenic route, yards wide of the inner rail. Yet the horse was loping as close to the winner at the end as at the beginning. The strong implication of good form, the drop in class, and the switch to the money rider, Jorge Velasquez, make Cute Sweetie very much the horse to beat. CONTENDER.

Nix: If this one had been working or racing here, she still would not menace Cute Sweetie. NO BET.

McCoy: Returned to the races at Tropical Park in January and was entered for conditioning purposes in two races against males. Evidently something went awry because another three-month layoff followed. If the filly were in any kind of shape, she would be dangerous in this, her first claiming race. But the 1967 record is not promising. NO BET.

Scairt: You have to get up mighty early in the morning to beat Charlie Robbins. An index to this filly's quality is its 1967 earnings record—better than $1,000 a start. The detailed past performances are less impressive until you notice that most of the races have been against males. The January 23 victory suggests the true class of the horse. CONTENDER.

Cute Sweetie versus Scairt. Laurin's animal is a fully established $15,000 New York article, shipped into Jersey with malice aforethought—to take a purse from the cheapest field of its career. Robbins' *may* be a $15,000 horse but has not yet demonstrated it. And she *may* be in sharp condition after her absence of more than three weeks. But Cute Sweetie is almost positively sharp. And Jorge Velasquez rates a big edge this season over the veteran Steve Brooks. Cute Sweetie by a comfortable margin.

The Running of the Race

THE LAURIN operation was so obvious to the crowd that Cute Sweetie went off at less than 2–1 and was an overlay at the price. Navy Heroine ran an excellent race. Scairt showed early foot but lacked the condition to stay with it.

FIFTH RACE
GS - 31023
May 4, 1967

6 FURLONGS (Chute). (I Appeal, May 21, 1955, 1.08⅘, 4, 112.)
Claiming. Purse $5,000. Fillies and mares. 3-year-olds and upward. Weights, 3-year-olds, 115 lbs.; older, 121 lbs. Non-winners of two races since April 2, allowed 2 lbs.; two races since March 4, 4 lbs.; a race since April 15, 6 lbs. Claiming price $12,500; 2 lbs. allowed for each $1,000 to $10,500. (Races where entered for $9,000 or less not considered.)

Value to winner $3,000, second $1,000, third $650, fourth $350. Mutuel pool $168,279.

Index	Horse	Eqt A Wt	PP	St	¼	½	Str	Fin	Jockey	Cl'g Pr	Owner	Odds $1
30868Aqu4	—Cute Sweetie	b 4 115	4	2	4¹	2½	1¹½	1³	J Velasquez	12500	Mrs Irish Friedman	1.90
30886GP5	—Navy Heroine	5 113	1	6	2h	5h	4¹½	2h	W Gavidia	11500	Crown Stable	11.20
30500GP9	—Bakery Babe	b 4 115	3	5	5½	6¹½	5½	3¾	J Vasquez	12500	Carolyn K Stable	3.10
30778Pim4	—Scairt	b 4 113	7	1	1h	3²	2¹½	4½	S Brooks	11500	P Depaul	4.90
30898GP5	—Nix	b 5 114	5	3	7	7	6³	5³	W Blum	10500	F P Dyer	7.10
30809Kee5	—McCoy	b 4 115	6	4	6h	4½	7	6²	B Thornburg	12500	Circle M Farm	5.60
28964GS4	—Swiss Maid	b 3 111	2	7	3h	1h	3h	7	F Lovato	10500	Craig-Menarde	14.40

Time .22⅖, .46, 1.12⅕. Track fast.

$2 Mutuel Prices:

4-CUTE SWEETIE	5.80	3.60	2.40
1-NAVY HEROINE		7.00	3.60
3-BAKERY BABE			2.80

B. f, by Nantallah—Ragtime Band, by Johnstown. Trainer L. Laurin. Bred by Edw. B. Benjamin (Ky.).
IN GATE AT 4.01. OFF AT 4.01 EASTERN DAYLIGHT TIME. Start good. Won handily.

CUTE SWEETIE remained with the pace as the leaders bunched shortly after the start raced between rivals gained command into the stretch, drew off and won in hand. NAVY HEROINE, gave some ground after racing in tight quarters early came again through the stretch to edge BAKERY BABE. The latter wore down tiring rivals. SCAIRT, much used dueling for the lead had little in the drive. NIX raced without mishap. McCOY raced on the outside and did not threaten. SWISS MAID, saved ground throughout, raced forwardly to the stretch and flattened out

Overweight—Nix 3 pounds.
Cute Sweetie was claimed by Red Oak Stable, trainer J. Kulina.

---

8. FOURTH AT AQUEDUCT, MAY 12, 1967—Track Slow

I GUARANTEE you fun with this one. It is a grab-bag of handicapping fundamentals, garnished with angles and more than one surprise.

The distance and the high claiming price mean that the horse likeliest to win is one that has shown something at the route when running in good company. A horse without credentials at the distance is likely to be a poor risk unless favored by some quirk of pace.

4th Race Aqueduct

1⅛ MILES
AQUEDUCT
Start ▸ | ◂ Finish

1 1-8 MILES (Sinatra, December 7, 1964, 1.47⅕, 5, 111.)
Claiming. Purse $8,000. 4-year-olds and upward. Weight 122 lbs. Non-winners of a race at a mile and a furlong or over since March 12 allowed 3 lbs., of a race at a mile or over since then, 6 lbs. Claiming price $15,000. 2 lbs. allowed for each $500 to $14,000. (Races when entered to be claimed for $12,000 or less not considered.)

(4th Aqu)—Coupled—Participant and Your Prince.

Sir Sanford $14,500 Ch. g (1962), by Royal Warrior—Miss Boodle, by Mr. Busher
S. Nadler W. R. Corbellini (M. W. Smith) **114** 1967 3 0 1 0 $1,30 / 1966 14 2 5 2 $13,82
3May67-8Aqu fst 1 .46⅘1.12 1.38 Clm 15000 5 5 78½ 68½ 66 63¼ GMora7 109 1.80e 75-21 Demigod 114¾ Needles' Count 1171½ Koh-I-Noor 122½ Dull effort
17Apr67-4Aqu sly 7f .23 .46⅕1.23⅘ Cl c-11500 5 3 54½ 44½ 33½ 45¼ JLRotz 115 4.00 82-23 Lou Michaels 117¾ Poggibonsi 1194 Direct Action 115½ No rally
1Apr67-5Aqu fst 7f .23⅖ .46⅖1.23 Clm 11500 8 2 65½ 43½ 25 210 JLRotz b 115 15.80 81-15 Koh-I-Noor 12410 Sir Sanford 115nk Syncope 113¾ Raced wide
7Dec66-7Aqu fst 1⅛.49⅗1.14 1.52⅗ Allowance 4 5 51¼ 43 34 54¾ ACordero 118 3.00 68-24 Solemn Nation 115¾ Royal Decision 1154 Aerie 123h Lacked rally
29Nov66-6Aqu my 1⅛.50⅕1.14⅘1.54 Allowance 2 4 52¼ 42½ 5¾ 63½ ACordero 116 *0.90 62-28 Base Leg 113nk Big Shot 1132½ Royal Decision 113no Bid, hung
23Nov66-9Aqu fst 1⅛.47⅖1.12⅗1.52⅖ Clm 8500 8 9 911 43½ 12 2½ LPincayJr 120 *2.00 73-17 Bent Spur 112½ Sir Sanford 1203 Grandioso 116½ Gamely 1
2Nov66-9Aqu fst 1⅛.47⅘1.13 1.51⅖ Clm 10000 2 1 Fog 23 23½ JLRotz 123 *1.80 75-19 Nashaweena 1083½ Sir Sanford 123nk Barbagris 1165 Gamely
25Oct66-6Aqu fst 1⅛.48 1.13⅗1.51⅕ Clm 9500 5 5 47 31 23 25 JLRotz 123 *2.10 75-18 EnfantTerrible 1235 SirSanford 1232 Listen toReason 1164 2nd best
19Oct66-9Aqu sly 1⅛.46⅘1.12⅕1.53 Clm 14000 7 3 36 23 22 57¾ DChamberlin 114 10.50 63-19 Why Lie 1183½ Gallant Scot 120¾ Demigod 119no Bid, tired
21Sep66-9Aqu sly 1⅛.47⅖1.12⅗1.53⅘ Clm 12500 6 5 47½ 45½ 33½ 512 JLRotz 123 4.60 55-24 Nashwood 1133 Mt. Greenery 1185 Bent Spur 1201½ Never close
LATEST WORKOUTS May 9 Bel tr.t. 5f gd 1.02 b Apr 29 Bel tr.t. 5f fst 1.06 b Apr 24 Bel tr.t. 5f fst 1.05 b Apr 14 Bel tr.t. 3f fst .35⅘ h

Participant $14,000 B. c (1963-Ky), by Ben Lomond—Maharani, by Tenerani
Elmendorf V. J. Nickerson (Elmendorf Farm) **112** 1967 3 1 0 0 $3,25 / 1966 1 M 0 0 —
5May67-5Aqu fst 7f .22⅘ .45⅕1.25⅖ Md 10500 5 9 96 54½ 2½ 1¾ RFerraro b 120 25.80 79-19 Participant120¾ Plymouth Pilgrim1141½ Brazen Blue114nk Driving 1
17Apr67-1Aqu fst 7f .22⅘ .46⅖1.25 Md 9000 10 6 1010108½ 910 711 LPincayJr 120 *2.20e 70-14 Admiral Gene 1142½ Brazen Blue 1133½ Mt. Jungle 1152 No speed 1
11Apr67-5Aqu fst 1 .49 1.15 1.40⅖ Md Sp Wt 2 6 83½ 62½ 45¼ 611 ADeSpirito 124 25.30 55-27 Wowzer 1132¼ Best Example 113no Firestitch 1168 No mishap 1
20Jly 66-1Aqu fst 6f .23 .47 1.12⅗ Md Sp Wt 6 12 121111141111111 RFerraro 117 33.00 69-23 Big Rapids 110¾ As You Like 1121 Golden Gala 1123 No speed 1
17Sep65-4Haw fst 6½f.22⅘ .46⅖1.17⅗ Md Sp Wt 1 8 76¼ 811 Bled WMahorney 120 2.60 —— Eltiempo 120no Go It Alone 1202 Hamlet Jr. 120no Far back, bled
6Sep65-4AP fst 6f .22⅘ .46⅖1.11⅘ Md Sp Wt 4 11 87 78 56½ 21¼ WMahorney 118 11.40 83-11 Jesterson 1181¼ Participant 1181¼ Extra Power 118nk Rallied 1
3Sep65-4AP fst 6f .22⅘ .45⅘1.1 Md Sp Wt 9 Lost rider WShoemaker 118 6.90 —— Lake Forest 1183½ Uncle Adolph1181¼ d-BloomingHills115½ St'mbl'd 1
27Aug65-4AP fst 6f .22⅘ .46⅕1.12 Md Sp Wt 9 9 99¾ 78½ 58½ 57 HHinojosa b 118 8.60 76-15 Doitforme 118h Lake Forest 1181 d-Hamlet Jr. 1182½ Evenly 1
20Aug65-5AP fst 6f .22⅘ .46⅕1.11⅘ Md Sp Wt 9 12 1112 916 717 412 RBroussard 118 10.60 72-22 Demon Dyno 1186 Jesterson 1182½ Sidate 1183 Passed tired ones 1
3Jly 65-3Aqu fst 5½f.22⅕ .45⅘1.05⅖ Md Sp Wt 8 7 79½ 58 59½ 36½ DPierce 122 11.35 79-13 Bold Tactics 1222½ Total Talent 1224 Participant 122¾ Rallied
18Jun65-4Aqu fst 5½f.22⅘ .46 1.04⅖ Md Sp Wt 2 6 53¾ 66¾ 66½ 514 IValenzuela 122 22.85 77-16 Alexville 12210 Bobillard 1221½ Pointed Remark 122½ No mishap 1
LATEST WORKOUTS May 11 Aqu 3f fst .37⅖ b May 4 Aqu 3f fst .37 b Apr 29 Aqu 1m gd 1.45 b Apr 26 Aqu 3f fst .36⅖ b

Your Prince $14,000 B. h (1962), by Prince John—Your Stocking, by Our Boots
A. Wohl V. J. Nickerson (W. C. Partee) **112** 1967 2 0 0 0 — / 1966 8 2 1 0 $9,77
3May67-8Aqu fst 1 .46⅘1.12 1.38 Clm 14000 6 2 24 23 54½ 53¼ EBelmonte b 112 6.60 75-21 Demigod 114¾ Needles' Count 1171½ Koh-I-Noor 122½ No mishaps
21Apr67-7Aqu fst 7f .22⅘ .45⅖1.23⅕ Allowance 1 6 613 614 617 621 EBelmonte b 121 26.90 69-22 Mincing Lane 1191 Road At Sea 114no Golden Buttons 1213 Trailed
8Aug66-9Sar fm 1⅛ Ⓣ 1.47⅕ Clm 22500 5 9 129 118 109¾ 914 EBelmonte b 118 7.20 83- 3 Clatterbox 1168 Rochefort 118½ Service Ace 118½ No speed 1
7Jly 66-9Aqu hd 1⅛ Ⓣ 1.48⅘ Allowance 4 6 512 58½ 4¾ 1¾ EBelmonte b 118 5.80 91-13 Your Prince 118¾ Hardihood 1202½ Annette's Ark 1184 Driving
27May66-5Aqu fst 1 .45⅘1.10⅖1.36⅖ Clm 18000 4 4 23 31 31 42½ MVenezia b 115 2.50 83-18 Demigod 112¾ Africanus 1161 Hail the King 119¾ Bore out
13Apr66-6Aqu fst 1⅛.48⅖1.13⅕1.50⅗ Allowance 6 6 73½ 63 1h 2no MVenezia b 123 22.60 83-16 Throne Room 113no Your Prince 1234 Sea Castle 1122½ Sharp
7Apr66-5Aqu fst 1 .47⅖1.11 1.36⅕ Allowance 5 5 53¾ 59 46 44¾ ORosado5 b 118 11.40 82-17 Buffle 113¾ Michigan Avenue 1151 Portfolio 1203 Wide late
23Mar66-4Aqu fst 1 .47⅕1.13 1.39 Allowance 6 6 65½ 4¾ 2½ 12 MVenezia b 119 *1.70 73-25 Your Prince 1192 Port Royal 115h Much More 1152½ Bore out, up
16Mar66-6Aqu fst 7f .23⅗ .47⅗1.26⅕ Allowance 2 8 87¼ 44 L't rider MVenezia b 115 *1.10e —— Noon Rock 1105 Port Royal 118¾ Yucatan 1133½ Bolted turn
1Mar66-5Hia fst 7f .23⅕ .46⅖1.24⅘ Allowance 3 7 77 44 76 78¼ MVenezia b 115 14.20 77-15 Vail Pass 1154 Jim Dooley 112h Spinsome 110¾ Fell back early
5Aug65-9Sar fst 6f .22⅖ .45⅘1.11⅕ Clm 15000 4 8 69 610 43½ 2¾ RTurcotte b 114 24.90 91-12 Bargain Counter 107¾ Your Prince 1142 Ping 106nk Rallied
LATEST WORKOUTS May 10 Aqu 4f fst .51 b Apr 29 Aqu 6f gd 1.20 b Apr 9 Aqu 4f sl .51 b Apr 5 Aqu 4f fst .52 b

Needles' Count * $15,000 Br. g (1962), by Needles—Countess Tecla, by Count Fleet
Aisco Stable F. H. Merrill (J. C. Dudley-B. M. Heath) **114[5]** 1967 7 2 1 2 $9,85 / 1966 15 2 1 2 $10,61
3May67-8Aqu fst 1 .46⅘1.12 1.38 Clm 15000 2 6 45 44 1½ 2¾ RSurrency5 117 6.40 77-21 Demigod 114¾ Needles' Count 1171½ Koh-I-Noor 122½ Couldn't last
25Apr67-6Aqu sl 1 .47⅖1.12⅘1.38 Clm 16000 5 7 66 55½ 57½ 46½ RTurcotte 116 3.10 71-28 Koh-I-Noor 116nk Emerald Lake 1166 Demigod 113nk No mishap
27Mar67-6Aqu sl 1 .47⅗1.13⅕1.38⅖ Clm 18000 2 7 711 56½ 47½ 36½ RTurcotte 112 6.70 69-31 Sheet Anchor 1164½ Off The Top 1122 Needles' Count 112no Rallied
14Mar67-6Aqu fst 1 .46⅗1.12⅕1.37⅗ Clm 12500 5 5 614 46 1h 11¼ RTurcotte 119 6.70 80-22 Needles' Count 1191¼ Naturalist 1141½ Rocky Ford 1143½ Driving
4Mar67-4GP fst 1 1/16.47⅗1.11⅘1.44⅗ Clm 12500 2 3 34½ 23 23 32½ FToro 118 2.90 82-10 Red Redeemer 1122¼ Uncle Beau 116no Needles' Count 1183½ Hung
23Feb67-5Hia gd 1 1/16.47⅕1.11⅘1.43⅗ Clm 15500 8 4 56½ 65¾ 45 48¼ FToro 114 17.20 77-20 One Night Stand 1164¾ Count Bell 1162¾ The Clown 114¾ Evenly
9Feb67-10Hia sly1⅛.46⅘1.12⅕1.51⅘Clm 10000 3 4 45½ 31½ 11½ 1nk FToro 116 *2.10 76-17 Needles' Count 116nk Pinchers Pride 1165 Tulran 1163 Driving
24Nov66-6TrP fst 170.46⅗1.11 1.40⅘ Clm 10000 1 8 64 53½ 54¼ 65¾ FToro 119 *1.90 87- 9 Skeg 1142¼ Coralies Boy 1192¼ Popetrenea 114¾ Lacked response 1
19Nov66-8TrP fst 170.46⅗1.12 1.42⅕ Allowance 11 7 1110106½ 53½ 76¼ MNGonzalez 122 5.80 80-14 Clatterbox 119no Saeharf 1142½ Jet Charger 1171½ Never close 1
2Nov66-8Spt fst 1⅛.47⅘1.13⅗1.51⅗ Allowance 4 3 32 31 12 12 FToro 117 4.60 90-15 Needles' Count 1172 Chickasaw 1143 The Dancer 114h Under drive
LATEST WORKOUTS May 11 Bel tr.t. 3f fst .36 h May 2 Bel tr.t. 3f fst .37 h Apr 21 Bel tr.t. 7f fst 1.33⅘ b Apr 17 Bel tr.t. 4f gd .50⅖ b

```
Demigod *                    $14,000   B. g (1961), by Gallant Man—Plotter, by Double Jay             115   1967  7  1 0 1  $6,250
                                       J. R. Daly   P. A. Healy   (L. Combs 2d–Mrs. J. M. Olin)             1966 24  4 2 3 $22,975
May67-8Aqu  fst 1   .46⅘1.12  1.38   Clm 14500 7 3 34 33 32½ 1¾ WBoland 114 9.00 78-21 Demigod 114¾ Needles' Count 1171½ Koh-I-Noor 122½ Brisk drive 7
Apr67-6Aqu  sl 1    .47⅖1.12⅘1.38    Clm 15000 3 8 77 66½ 47 36¼ WBoland 113 8.50 72-28 Koh-I-Noor 116nk Emerald Lake 1166 Demigod 113nk Mild bid 8
Mar67-8Aqu  my 1    .49⅕1.15⅗1.41⅖   Clm 14000 10 9 107 54 43½ 42¾ ATCordero 112 17.20 58-33 Corredor II 117¾ Emerald Lake 111½ Direct Action 1121½ Rallied 10
Feb67-10Hia fm*1 3/16 (T)   2.01     Clm 11500 12 12 1227 1224 1221 1225 MCarrozzella 114 136.30 52-21 Officer Sweeney 1161½ Punisher 109½ Concession 1075 No speed 12
Feb67-7Hia  fm 1 1/16 (T)  1.45⅖     Clm 13000 11 12 1225 1227 1228 1227 MCarrozzella 114 78.60 51-28 Brant 114no The Clown 1162 Bursun 1161½ Trailed thruout 12
Jan67-10Hia my 1⅛ .47⅗1.12⅗1.51⅗   Clm 12500 2 10 1028 924 818 820 MCarrozzella 116 10.10 57-20 CountDormal 1163½ ListenToReason 1183½ CoolOasis 116½ No speed 10
Jan67-5Hia  fst 7f  .23⅗ .46⅗1.24⅕  Clm 15000 9 11 1118 1119 1020 1018 BBaeza 114 16.80 70-12 O Lady O 107¾ Inclusive 1174 Prince Graff 1223 Never close 11
Dec66-9Aqu  fst 1⅛  .47⅗1.12⅗1.51⅘ Clm 16000 5 9 919 917 817 712 LPincayJr 114 6.80 65-19 Big Shot 1112½ Fleet Musketeer 1162½ High Bluff 105½ No speed 9
Nov66-9Aqu  fst 1⅛  .48⅕1.12⅘1.50⅘ Clm 15000 3 7 714 715 715 616 LPincayJr 118 5.90 66-20 Nashaweena 1044 Enfant Terrible 1161¼ Cool Oasis 1064 No speed 7
Nov66-8Aqu  fst 1⅛  .49⅘1.13⅘1.51⅘ Clm 18000 2 4 45½ 67½ 4¾ 33 LPincayJr 112 6.80 74-22 Dark Alloy 1141½ Naturalist 1161½ Demigod 112no Mild bid 6
LATEST WORKOUTS   May 10 Bel tr.t. 6f fst 1.19 b   Apr 19 Bel m.t. 3f my .37⅖ b   Apr 12 Bel tr.t. 1m fst 1.44 h   Apr 8 Bel tr.t. 7f gd 1.31 h

Emerald Lake *               $15,000   Dk. b. or br. c (1963–Fla), by Beau Gar—Lake Garda, by Turn-to  116   1967  7  0 3 0  $4,200
                                       L. Silver   T. J. Gullo   (Hobeau Farm, Inc.)                        1966 16  2 2 3 $10,745
May67-8Aqu  fst 1   .46⅘1.12  1.38   Clm 15000 4 4 56 58 42½ 42¾ BBaeza 116 *1.30 75-21 Demigod 114¾ Needles' Count 1171½ Koh-I-Noor 122½ Bid, hung 7
Apr67-6Aqu  sl 1    .47⅖1.12⅘1.38    Clm 16000 1 6 55 44 22 2nk BBaeza 116 2.80 78-28 Koh-I-Noor 116nk Emerald Lake 1166 Demigod 113nk Sharp try 8
Mar67-8Aqu  my 1    .49⅕1.15⅗1.41⅖   Clm 15000 4 5 2½ 3½ 21 2¾ MCariglio5 111 6.60 60-33 Corredor II 117¾ Emerald Lake 111½ Direct Action 1121½ Sharp 10
Mar67-8Aqu  my 6f   .23⅕ .48⅖1.14    Allowance 3 7 714 715 615 58½ MCariglio5 118 12.10 64-35 Mister Pitt's Kid 1132½ Dandy Steal 1123 Disembark 121no Slow st. 7
Mar67-6GP   fm 1 1/16 (T) 1.11 1.41⅘ Clm 18000 2 6 612 67 714 714 LMoyers 116 8.40 81-11 VoluntarioIII112¾ FlamingTriumph1122½ AdmiralClove1163 No sp'd 9
Feb67-10Hia fm 1⅛ (T)      1.50⅕    Clm 18000 5 8 811 74½ 54½ 24½ ECardone 112 13.20 86-10 Top Victory 1164½ Emerald Lake 112h Loopy Loop 1163½ Rallied 8
Jan67-9Hia  sly 7f  .23⅗ .47  1.25⅕  Allowance 4 3 31½ 32 69½ 713 WBoland 119 *0.90e 70-19 Saeharf 118½ Beau Legs 113no Wondrascope 1132 Brief foot 7
Dec66-6Aqu  fst 7f  .22⅖ .45⅘1.23⅘  Clm 18000 1 3 22 45 69 56½ ECardone5 115 *0.80e 80-20 The Cheat 1141 There Goes Sam 118h Royal Harbinger 1192 Tired 8
Dec66-6Aqu  fst 7f  .23  .46  1.24⅖  Allowance 7 1 43¼ 41½ 1h 2no JRuane 122 1.90e 84-23 It's Blitz 117no Emerald Lake 1223 ♦Solemn Nation 1153 Wide 7
Nov66-8Aqu  fst 6f  .22⅗ .45⅘1.10⅘  Allowance 1 3 32½ 45 47 34¼ EBelmonte 122 9.20 85-21 Second Venture 1151¼ Holly Man 1153 Emerald Lake 122nk Mild bid 9
LATEST WORKOUTS   Apr 12 Bel tr.t. 3f fst .38⅖ b   Apr 4 Bel tr.t. 3f fst .38 b

Nashwood *                   $14,000   B. c (1963–Ky), by Nashua—Querida, by Alibhai                   112   1967 10  1 3 0  $6,855
                                       Halbed Stable   P. G. Johnson   (L. Combs 2d, J. W. Hanes–            1966 25  2 1 0 $10,025
                                                                        Walmac Farm)
May67-8Aqu  fst 6f  .22⅗ .46  1.10⅘  Clm 12500 6 6 32 44½ 67 610 GMora7 110 12.60 79-18 Lochoir 117h Last Chain 1135 Beaustone 117½ Fell back early 8
Apr67-4Aqu  fst 6f  .22⅗ .46⅕1.11⅘  Cl c-10000 3 11 43 65 109½ 1011 RUssery 117 *2.20 73-16 Poggibonsi 113¾ Last Chain 115nk McGun 1172½ Slow start, tired 12
Mar67-2Aqu  hy 1    .46⅕1.11⅗1.39⅕  Clm 7500 6 1 13 16 110 17 RUssery b 116 *1.10 72-33 Nashwood 1167 Bigamo 1228 Came To Play 116½ Speed to spare 7
Mar67-6Aqu  my 1    .48⅕1.15⅗1.43⅗  Clm 8500 4 1 1½ 12 1½ 2½ RUssery 116 *1.20 49-40 Cool Oasis 116½ Nashwood 116nk Winter Joy 116½ Held well 8
Mar67-6Aqu  fst 1   .46⅗1.12⅕1.37⅗  Clm 11500 8 1 15 13½ 31 46¼ ATCordero 114 10.60 74-22 Needles' Count 1191¼ Naturalist 1141½ Rocky Ford 1143½ Used up 8
Feb67-6Bow  fst 1 1/16 .47⅖1.12⅗1.47 Clm 9000 2 1 15 14 1h 43 AAgnello7 106 3.30 75-18 Tide Mill 1152½ Great Depths 115½ Welcome Call 122h Used up 8
Feb67-6Bow  fst 7f  .23⅕ .46⅘1.26⅕  Clm 8000 8 2 11½ 11½ 1h 1h ORosado 114 d*0.80 82-29 d-Nashwood 114h Well To Do 1175 Sun Native 113h Bore out 8
   6Feb67—d-Disqualified and placed second.
Jan67-5Bow  gd 7f   .22⅗ .45⅗1.26    Clm 10000 5 4 44½ 68 43 41 TLee 114 2.90 82-22 Grandioso 108½ Dolington Road 113no Arctic Swirl 115½ Late foot 10
Jan67-6Bow  fst 1 1/16 .49⅖1.14⅖1.47⅘ Clm 10000 3 1 1h 2h 2h 2nk TLee 114 9.50 74-22 Magellan 107nk Nashwood 1144½ Great Depths 1154½ Sharp, missed 10
Jan67-6Bow  gd 1 1/16 .49⅕1.15 1.49⅖ Clm 10000 3 1 3½ 1½ 41 65¾ TLee 114 5.50 60-27 Gasmegas 117nk Great Depths 1151½ Sirius II 108¾ Used in lead 12
LATEST WORKOUTS   May 10 Aqu 3f fst .37 b   Apr 29 Aqu 7f gd 1.31 b   Apr 22 Aqu 6f fst 1.14 h   Apr 10 Bel tr.t. 3f gd .36 h
```

Sir Sanford: Bill Corbellini has emerged from the shadows this year. He has won more races during the young season than any other New York trainer. His recently claimed gelding is a bona fide nine-furlong horse but, barring remarkable improvement, is outclassed in $15,000 company. The switch to jockey Cordero signifies that Corbellini wants this purse and may have a chance. If the rest of the field is that bad, I want no part of the action. NO BET.

Participant: Scratched.

Your Prince: Scratched.

Needles' Count: Can go the distance, especially in $10,000 circles and under a seasoned rider like Fernando Toro. But with a green apprentice in the saddle is likely to run into pace problems just as it did on May 3. If the horse had ever showed real early speed, the choice of rider might be less important. But the record makes plain that a strong, crafty rider is needed to keep the gelding close enough to the pace without exhausting it. NO BET.

Demigod: Winner of a mile race over Needles' Count and Sir Sanford only nine days ago, this sluggish old plater is well-suited to today's distance, as the November 14 race implies and as it showed in earlier races no longer itemized in the record. After a miserable Florida season, the Gallant Man offspring began to race into form. Its powerful last effort at the most taxing of distances—one mile around only one turn—not only demonstrated real sharpness but spoke well for its ability to handle the more leisurely pace of today's longer race. CONTENDER.

Emerald Lake: Roundly beaten by the improving Demigod on May 3, Tommy Gullo's colt now tries a longer route against almost exactly the same field. He may do better at a mile and one-eighth than at shorter distances, but the record gives no evidence to that effect. The time for Emerald Lake to win was on May 3, off the strong race he ran on April 25. Perhaps that race was *too* strong. The animal's form seemed to suffer rather than improve from the exertion. Can improvement be expected today? I doubt it, although there is a slim possibility that Baeza may be able to steal the race by grabbing the early lead. CONTENDER.

Nashwood: Cheap speed and not a contender. But will be moving swiftly enough in the first half mile to wreck any plans Tommy Gullo might have about a wire-to-wire victory for Emerald Lake. NO BET.

The contenders are Demigod and Emerald Lake. Except that Emerald Lake's best chance to win is nullified by the early speed of Nashwood. Suppose, however, that Emerald Lake is in better form than his last race suggests. I still like Demigod, which is at or near peak, is more clearly suited to today's distance and is a more consistent money-winner when fit.

The Running of the Race

THE CROWD made Demigod its third choice. This is hard to believe. It can be explained on only one basis: The newspaper selectors ascribe almost magical powers to Braulio Baeza. And many of them think that beaten favorites are marvelous bets, regardless of class, form, or distance. So Emerald Lake was a short-priced favorite and again ran fourth. Needles' Count was second favorite, apparently because of the improvement it showed the last time it lost to Demigod.

FOURTH RACE
Aqu - 31094
May 12, 1967

1 1-8 MILES (Sinatra, December 7, 1964, 1.47⅕, 5, 111.)
Claiming. Purse $8,000. 4–year–olds and upward. Weight 122 lbs. Non–winners of a race at a mile and a furlong or over since March 12 allowed 3 lbs., of a race at a mile or over since then, 6 lbs. Claiming price $15.000. 2 lbs. allowed for each $500 to $14,000. (Races when entered to be claimed for $12.000 or less not considered.)
Value to winner $5,200, second $1,600, third $800, fourth $400. Mutuel pool $293,617.

Index	Horse	Eqt	A	Wt	PP	St	¼	½	¾	Str	Fin	Jockey	Cl'g Pr	Owner	Odds $1
31026Aqu1	Demigod		6	115	3	5	5	5	$2^{\frac{1}{2}}$	$1^{\frac{1}{2}}$	$1^{\frac{3}{4}}$	W Boland	14000	J R Daly	3.00
31026Aqu2	Needles' Count		5	114	2	2	4^{4}	4^{2}	$4^{\frac{1}{2}}$	3^{5}	2^{5}	R Surrency5	15000	Aisco Stable	2.90
31026Aqu6	Sir Sanford		5	114	1	1	3^{6}	$2^{\frac{1}{2}}$	$1^{\frac{1}{2}}$	$2^{1\frac{1}{2}}$	3^{10}	A Cordero Jr	14500	S Nadler	6.80
31026Aqu4	Emerald Lake	b	4	116	4	3	2^{h}	3^{5}	5	4^{5}	4^{8}	B Baeza	15000	L Silver	1.40
31017Aqu6	Nashwood		4	112	5	4	1^{2}	$1^{1\frac{1}{2}}$	$3^{\frac{1}{2}}$	5	5	R Turcotte	14000	Halbed Stable	5.70

Time .23⅖, .47⅖, 1.13⅕, 1.39, 1.52 (against wind in backstretch). Track slow.

$2 Mutuel Prices:			
4–DEMIGOD	8.00	3.80	2.60
3–NEEDLES' COUNT		3.80	2.40
1–SIR SANFORD			3.00

B. g, by Gallant Man—Plotter, by Double Jay. Trainer P. A. Healy. Bred by L. Combs 2d-Mrs. J. M. Olin.
IN GATE AT 2.58. OFF AT 2.58 EASTERN DAYLIGHT TIME. Start good. Won driving.

DEMIGOD saved ground while outrun early but moved up fast on the outside approaching the stretch and, after taking command from SIR SANFORD, retained a safe margin while under brisk urging. NEEDLES' COUNT saved ground after beginning alertly and responded readily when set down through the stretch but but could not overtake the winner while easily second best. SIR SANFORD prominent until inside the stretch gave way when challenged by DEMIGOD. EMERALD LAKE was finishd early. NASHWOOD set the pace for five–eighths and stopped.

Scratched—31026Aqu5 Your Prince, 31041Aqu1 Participent.

9. NINTH AT AQUEDUCT, MARCH 30, 1967—Track Slow

I BELIEVE that this one should be easy for any handicapper. Note that it is at nine furlongs for older girls in the $3,500–$4,500 price range. Note also that this is a peculiar price range. Nothing cheaper than $3,500 ever runs in New York. Yet $4,500 horses often compete against $5,000 and $5,500 ones. We had better watch for concealed signs of superior class in some animal. But we also had better remember that this is a route race in which the safest bet is a horse able to cover the ground without dying in the final yards.

9th Race Aqueduct — 1⅛ MILES AQUEDUCT (Start→ ←Finish)

1 1-8 MILES (Sinatra, December 7, 1964, 1.47⅕, 5, 111.)
Claiming. Purse $4,200. Fillies and mares. 4-year-olds and upward. Weight 123 lbs. Non-winners of a race at a mile and a furlong or over since January 16 allowed 3 lbs., a race at a mile or over since October 29, 5 lbs., two races at any distance since August 27, 7 lbs. Claiming price $4,500. 2 lbs. for each $500 to $3,500.

Andros Isle × $4,500 — B. f (1963-Md), by Midnight Sun—Bloomin Alibi, by Alibhai — Sunwood Stable — A. J. Danko — (J. L. Reynolds-O'Brien Bros.) — **118**5 — 1967 7 2 0 1 $5,405 — 1966 28 2 3 3 $8,830
Andros Isle entered in Wednesday's 9th race.
16Mar67-9Aqu sly 1⅛.49⅕1.15⅕1.56⅖ f- 4000 2 3 36 35 2h 12½ RMorgan5 115 *1.20 54-33 Andros Isle 1152½ Change Of Mind 1135 Orbity Anna 1175 Driving 5
23Feb67-4Bow fst 6f .22⅘ .45⅘1.12⅖ f- 5000 2 9 911 818 819 713 MAristone b 116 29.70 72-22 Yang Imp 116h Deep Clover 1122 Lucky Shirl 1142 No mishap 9
6Feb67-5Bow fst 1 1/16.49⅕1.14⅖1.47⅖ f- 5000 6 8 811 513 49 39 MAristone 118 11.70 67-29 Matchless Monte 1144 Another Spin 1195 Andros Isle 118no Rallied 10
28Jan67-3Bow sl 1 1/16.50⅕1.16⅘1.52⅗ f- 4000 4 4 47 54¾ 21 11 MAristone 114 7.50 50-32 Andros Isle 1141 Duby Cat 1155 Gay Staddie 110nk Drew out 12
23Jan67-5Bow fst 1 1/16.49⅖1.15⅘1.49⅕ f- 5000 9 11 1124 1016 819 723 MAristone 112 19.40 44-24 Arctic Queen 1164½ Another Spin 1135 Two Wings 1121 No speed 11
13Jan67-5Bow fst 1 1/16.50⅖1.16⅖1.50⅘ f- 5000 5 11 117¾ 65¼ 41½ 62¼ MAristone 116 22.50 57-29 Wheyface 114½ Matchless Monte 107½ Noureige 115½ Bid, tired 12
3Jan67-4Bow hy 1 1/16.50⅕1.16⅘1.54 Clm 5000 8 11 1123 1123 1119 1022 MAristone 111 31.70 —— Hellenic Royal 1141¼ Michael J. Toppa 1127 Navy Jack 1131 No sp'd 12
10Dec66-9Aqu fst 1 3/16.49⅗1.14⅗2.00⅖ Hcp 3500s 2 3 fog 912 911 RStovall 111 84.20 66-21 Ambi Enshalah 1131 Canadian Tudor 1161 Kalonji 116¾ Far back 12
LATEST WORKOUTS Feb 19 Bow 3f gd .38 b Feb 2 Bow 3f fst .37 b

Change of Mind $3,500 — Ch. m (1962), by Stymie—Dizzy Lady, by Shannon II — J. Trisolini — E. W. King — (Bieber-Jacobs Stables) — **112** — 1967 7 0 2 1 $1,890 — 1966 31 1 4 1 $7,252
25Mar67-3Aqu my 1 .49 1.16⅖1.43⅕ Clm 3500 6 4 44½ 47½ 49 46½ ECardone b 107 9.00 45-35 Gracious 112½ That's Hew 110h Spruce Up 1196 No late rally 8
16Mar67-9Aqu sly 1⅛.49⅕1.15⅕1.56⅖ f- 3500 3 2 1h 12 1h 22½ ECardone b 113 2.90 51-33 Andros Isle 1152½ Change Of Mind 1135 Orbity Anna 1175 Gamely 5
14Mar67-2Aqu fst 1 .47⅘1.13⅕1.39⅕ Clm 3500 6 7 714 812 813 57¼ TBove b 110 13.00 65-22 Blakstep 1224½ Have Integrity 115¾ Chamango 1171 Far back 8
21Feb67-10Hia fm*1⅛ Ⓣ 1.53 f- 5000 6 12 1220 1113 912 74¼ ATCordero b 112 21.60e 75-12 Want A Cracker 1132½ Snow Tears 112nk Jay Flight 112nk No mish'p 12
5Feb67-1Hia fst 1⅛.47⅗1.13 1.52⅗ f- 3500 2 11 99¾ 55½ 34 34¼ ATCordero b 112 13.10 68-16 Joanette 112¾ Dozens O'Cousins 1153½ Change Of Mind 1123 Rallied 12
26Jan67-5Hia my 1⅛.48 1.12⅘1.54⅘ f- 3500 9 10 913 917 818 717 ATCordero b 112 7.00 44-29 Mia Mello 1076 Chance Bet 1072 Gabby Abby 1151½ Not a factor 12
11Jan67-2TrP fst 1 1/16.47⅕1.12⅖1.45⅖ Clm 3500 9 9 94¼ 64¾ 43½ 2¾ GMora5 b 102 32.30 74-14 Lolidora 113¾ Change Of Mind 102½ Fayui 118h Gaining 12
10Dec66-1Aqu fst 7f .22⅖ .46 1.26⅘ f- 3500 11 13 1317 1317 119½ 84¼ JJHealy b 116 25.00 68-21 Playampa 120½ Doran Darcy 116¾ •Summer Sunshine 118h No threat 14
3Dec66-3Aqu fst 1 .47⅘1.13 1.39⅖ f- 4000 4 2 26 27 27 26 ACordero b 118 16.10 65-20 In the Sun 1186 Change of Mind 1182 Doran Darcy 1183½ Sec'd best 6
26Nov66-1Aqu gd 7f .23⅖ .47⅘1.27⅕ f- 3500 12 12 1217 1217 1114 1010 LGilligan b 116 25.30f 60-20 Summer Sunshine 116no Orbity Anna 111¾ Pragmatic 1163½ No sp'd 13
21Nov66-4Aqu fst 7f .23⅗ .47⅕1.26⅖ f- 3500 1 8 811 911 817 711 RFerraro 112 91.40 63-20 Cheeky Carol 1181½ Pragmatic 1133 Yang Imp 1161½ No factor 9
12Nov66-2GS sly 170.48⅗1.14⅖1.45 Clm 3000 9 7 77 611 611 617 SHernandez b 112 15.40 52-29 Encantado 1152 Revistero 1176 Eibar 1151½ No factor 10
LATEST WORKOUTS Mar 12 Bel tr.t. 5f fst 1.07 b Feb 11 Hia 6f fst 1.17 b

Judy Mann $4,500 — Ch. f (1963-Ky), by Catapult—Davidann, by Mount Marcy — Clara L. Ostriker — E. Jacobs — (Mrs. A. J. Ostriker) — **116** — 1967 2 0 0 1 $400 — 1966 19 2 1 3 $6,695
20Mar67-4Aqu my 7f .23⅗ .48⅕1.29⅗ f- 4000 4 7 79 77 56½ 33 ECardone b 112 26.40 55-39 Princess Nuks 1143 Long Nell 116no Judy Mann 1122½ Rallied 7
15Mar67-2Aqu gd 6f .23⅗ .48 1.13⅖ f- 3500 9 11 1110 1110 1112 1111 HGustines b 114 16.50 65-21 d-PrincessNuks 120nk Joela 114no That'sHew 114¾ Showed nothing 12
1Jly 66-5Mth fst 1 1/16.48⅖1.14 1.47⅗ Clm 5000 9 9 96½ 910 75¾ 57 JVelasquez b 110 4.40 60-19 Quick Post 1152½ Gov't. Cut 1172 Michael J. Toppa 115½ Slow start 9
1Jly 66-9Mth fm 1 1/16 Ⓣ 1.47 Clm 5750 2 8 75¾ 63¼ 56 46¾ JVelasquez b 109 11.30 72-17 Cap'n Shorty 1141½ Timbro 1184 Lesfear 1131¼ No mishap 10
23Jun66-9Aqu fst 1 .46⅕1.11⅖1.38⅘ Clm 6500 6 5 513 513 58½ 59¼ JLRotz b 114 10.00 65-17 Green Gusher 1171 Venetian Music 122¾ Tigris River 1176 No sp'd 6
16Jun66-5Aqu fst 1 .47 1.12 1.38⅖ f- 6500 9 5 64½ 78½ 78 67¼ JJMartin7 b 107 13.70 69-21 Inspiring 116¾ Pink Rose 1165 Jimmerette 105nk No factor 9
10Jun66-6Mth fst 170.46⅗1.12⅖1.44 Clm 7500 2 7 812rain 816 816 RBroussard b 116 12.50 65-21 Best Award 1163½ Gary Lee 1182½ Timbro 116½ Never a factor 10
1Jun66-8Aqu fst 1 .46⅗1.12⅕1.39⅖ Clm 7500 10 8 89¾ 99½ 912 88½ HWoodhouse b 111 25.20 62-19 BlewBy 107¾ Wyoming 1162½ MidMontana 116h Never in contention 12
23May66-3Aqu fst 1 .46⅖1.11⅘1.38⅘ f- 7000 5 8 87¼ 75¾ 75¼ 65 ACordero b 117 3.30 69-20 Moon Ray 1182 Cool That 111h Trijugate 1161½ Dull performance 8
10May66-9GS fst 1 1/16.47 1.12⅗1.45⅗ Clm 7500 3 4 54½ 52¼ 2h 1nk JVelasquez b 111 *1.90 77-13 Judy Mann 111nk Vermeil 116¾ Sir Devil 1162¾ Up final strides 6
5May66-4Aqu fst 1 .45⅗1.11 1.39⅖ f- 7000 10 10 98¾ 53¾ 21 2½ ACordero b 112 d23.90 70-20 Five Handicap 116½ d-Judy Mann 112¾ Miss Remaid 1051 Swerved 10
5May66--d-Disqualified and placed last.
LATEST WORKOUTS Mar 13 Aqu 3f fst .38 bg Feb 14 Hia 6f fst 1.19 b Feb 9 Hia 6f gd 1.17⅗ h Feb 5 Hia 5f fst 1.05 b

Muskoka $4,500 — Br. m (1961), by Nearctic—Mythical II, by My Babu — M. Sadlier — J. C. Meyer — (E. P. Taylor) — **116** — 1967 5 0 0 0 $350 — 1964 19 2 0 2 $4,465
1Mar67-4Pim fst 1 1/16.47⅘1.13 1.46⅗ f- 3750 8 1 11 1½ 32 48¾ RTurcotte b 114 37.10 68-16 Tooglo 1191¼ Flower Dance 1151½ Icon 1126 Used in pace 8
20Feb67-4Bow fst 1 1/16.49⅕1.14⅗1.48⅘ f- 3750 9 8 812 87 813 818 PIGrimm b 114 6.20e 51-17 Icon 1112½ Duby Cat 119no Matchless Monte 1162 Far back 9
22Feb67-5Bow gd 6f .23⅕ .47⅖1.13⅕ f- 3750 4 10 96½ 88½ 58½ 47½ NTurcotte b 114 11.50 73-24 Miles Miss 1141 Infinita 1115 Milk And Honey 1141½ No mishap 12
10Feb67-6Bow fst 7f .23⅖ .47 1.25⅖ f- 4750 5 10 97 88 75½ 66¼ NTurcotte 113 26.70e 75-20 Daisy Klauber 1062 Opellette 1142 Eager Sis 119no No threat 12
3Feb67-4Bow fst 6f .23⅗ .47⅗1.12⅖ f- 5000 2 11 1113 1114 1013 1012 JCulmone 115 49.30 68-23 Winning Tune 109no Joela 1151 Lucky Shirl 1141¼ Never close 12
20Nov64-6Grd sl 1 .49⅕1.14⅖1.40⅖ Allowance 2 1 21 68½ 615 627 WParsons5 107 21.15 —— Fast Answer 1144½ Mixed Colors 1148¾ Ice Jam 1162¼ Brief factor 8
6Nov64-6Grd fst 1 1/16.47⅗1.12⅗1.45⅗ f-Allow 2 4 43 55¼ 511 514 WHarris5 108 21.95 —— Avec Vous 1122¾ Forest Rover 1144 Belarctic 1132¾ Fell back 6
30Oct64-6Grd sl 7f .24⅘ .49 1.28⅕ Allowance 3 7 76 76¼ 616 622 JFitzsimmons 116 8.80e —— Plain John 1166½ PrinceAnthony 119h MixedColors 1174¾ No factor 7
23Oct64-7WO sf*1 Ⓣ .49⅗1.44 f-Allow 4 4 32 32 23½ 33½ KRobinson 109 9.40 —— Royal Spirit 1191¼ Free Trial 1142¼ Muskoka 1092½ Hung in drive 7
14Oct64-6WO fst 6f .21⅘ .44⅖1.09⅖ f-Allow 7 1 41 42½ 47¼ 711 PRemillard 110 42.50 —— Belarctic 110no Famous Road 1126¾ Apache Dancer 112¾ Gave way 7

That's Hew $4,500 — Ch. f (1963-Ky), by Traffic Judge—Poule d'Eau, by Bimelech — E. Konoski — E. P. Jenks — (W. P. Little) — **116**

1967	7	0	2	1	$1,850
1966	20	1	1	1	$3,500

25Mar67-3Aqu	my 1	.49	1.16⅖	1.43⅕	Clm	4000	7	6	$5^{6\frac12}$	3^6	3^4	$2^{\frac12}$	RStovall	110	5.10	51-35	Gracious $112^{\frac12}$ That's Hew 110^h Spruce Up 119^6	Bore in badly	8
20Mar67-2Aqu	my 6f	.23	.48⅗	1.16	f-	3500	9	9	$8^{9\frac14}$	$7^{5\frac34}$	$2^{1\frac12}$	$2^{\frac12}$	RStovall	114	5.20	62-39	Una Luca $114^{\frac12}$ That's Hew 114^4 Jungle Bunny II $114^{1\frac12}$	Bore in	9
15Mar67-2Aqu	gd 6f	.23⅗	.48	1.13⅘	f-	3500	12	10	$10^{8\frac14}$	8^4	$5^{1\frac12}$	3^{nk}	RStovall	114	58.00	76-21	d-PrincessNuks 120^{nk} Joela 114no That'sHew $114^{\frac34}$	Finished gamely	12
4Mar67-3Bow	fst 7f	.23⅖	.47	1.25⅘	Clm	3500	5	5	$6^{2\frac14}$	$10^{9\frac14}$	12^{15}	12^{18}	RStovall	110	58.50	68-16	Hamlet 115^1 Best Award $115^{\frac12}$ Debedeavon 115^4	Far back	12
22Feb67-3Bow	gd 6f	.23⅕	.47	1.13⅗	f-	3500	8	3	10^7	10^8	$9^{7\frac12}$	$8^{3\frac12}$	RStovall	112	70.80	75-24	Shuswap Sal 115^h River Sty 113^h Scotch Charmer $107^{\frac34}$	No mishap	12
1Feb67-2Bow	fst 1$\frac{1}{16}$	.49⅕	1.15⅖	1.49⅘	f-	3000	11	11	12^{18}	11^{13}	6^{10}	$6^{8\frac14}$	RStovall	113	18.00	56-22	Tooglo 113^4 Muldoon's Lassie 113no Coral Rock 115no	No factor	12
30Jan67-9Bow	fst 1$\frac{1}{16}$	.49⅗	1.15	1.48⅖	f-	5000	5	8	8^{18}	7^{12}	6^{13}	6^{14}	RStovall	112	33.60	57-22	Another Spin 113^h Madel 115^4 Two Wings 113^4	Never a factor	8
31Dec66-1Lrl	sl 6f	.24⅕	.49⅘	1.17	Clm	3500	12	11	12^{14}	10^{12}	11^{13}	$11^{9\frac12}$	RStovall	113	44.50	57-30	Pied D'Allas 103no Bar of Tales $116^{\frac12}$ Tisamour $110^{1\frac34}$	No speed	12
19Dec66-9Lrl	sl 1⅛	.49⅘	1.16⅘	1.59	Clm	3000	8	8	8^8	7^{11}	4^7	$5^{3\frac12}$	RStovall	b 111	10.30	48-32	Drag Pit $112^{\frac34}$ Yankee Brahmin 107^{nk} Roy D. Jr. $112^{1\frac12}$	Late foot	9
8Dec66-2Aqu	fst 6f	.22⅘	.46⅗	1.13⅗	Clm	3500	6	10	9^{10}	9^{10}	6^{11}	$6^{5\frac14}$	RFerraro	b 116	43.00	70-22	On the $Throne122^1$ $DelawareFlash115^{no}$ Fair n' $Breezy112^{nk}$	Broke sl.	11
1Dec66-2Aqu	fst 6f	.22⅘	.47	1.13⅖	Clm	3500	1	4	$8^{4\frac14}$	$7^{7\frac14}$	7^{13}	$9^{8\frac14}$	$RMorgan^5$	b 112	31.60	68-23	Stormy Outlook $118^{\frac12}$ Oversleep $118^{\frac34}$ Boffo $118^{3\frac12}$	No factor	11
26Nov66-1Aqu	gd 7f	.23⅖	.47⅘	1.27⅕	f-	3500	10	4	11^{15}	11^{14}	$6^{5\frac12}$	$6^{4\frac12}$	$RMorgan^5$	113	25.30f	65-20	Summer Sunshine 116no Orbity Anna $111^{\frac34}$ Pragmatic $116^{3\frac12}$	L'te bid	13

LATEST WORKOUTS Mar 13 Bel tr t. 4f fst .52⅖ b

Gracious × $4,500 — Dk. b. or br. f (1963-Va), by Tennyson II—Noorarda, by Noor — N. B. Trittipoe — K. E. Jensen — (Whitehead Stud) — **120**

1967	2	1	0	0	$2,790
1966	8	1	1	1	$3,515

25Mar67-3Aqu	my 1	.49	1.16⅖	1.43⅕	Clm	4000	2	3	$2^{\frac12}$	2^2	$2^{\frac12}$	$1^{\frac12}$	ATCordero	b 112	10.20	52-35	Gracious $112^{\frac12}$ That's Hew 110^h Spruce Up 119^6	Swerved, lasted	8
1[illegible]Mar67-8Aqu	sly 1	.47⅗	1.14⅕	1.41⅕	Clm	4000	5	4	4^6	$4^{8\frac12}$	4^{11}	4^{10}	JRuane	b 111	3.60	52-33	Petite Milagro $116^{3\frac12}$ Keep Knockin' $122^{3\frac12}$ Sudden Storm 119^3	Slip'd	6
8Dec66-1Aqu	fst 1	.46⅗	1.12⅘	1.39⅕	Md	4000	9	6	5^6	2^h	1^5	1^6	ACordero	b 117	3.70	72-22	Gracious 117^6 Warrior Blue $117^{4\frac12}$ John Toppa Jr. 117^h	Mild drive	10
15Nov66-1Aqu	fst 1	.47⅘	1.14⅘	1.39⅘	Md	3500	11	11	$9^{7\frac14}$	2^h	1^h	$2^{\frac12}$	ACordero	b 113	9.40e	68-22	Wheyface $117^{\frac12}$ Gracious 113^3 Safety Switch $116^{\frac12}$	Game try	14
8Nov66-1GS	fst 170	.48⅖	1.13⅗	1.45⅗	Md	4500	9	8	9^3	6^9	$5^{7\frac12}$	$3^{4\frac34}$	BThornburg	b 115	11.90	61-20	Grand Banks $118^{1\frac34}$ Miss Larchwood 111^3 Gracious 115^1	Rallied	11
21Oct66-2Aqu	fst 7f	.22⅗	.45⅘	1.26	f-	3500	7	12	12^{15}	11^{16}	10^{16}	7^7	ACordero	b 114	60.00	69-16	Yang Imp $114^{\frac12}$ d-My Emmy 114^{nk} Cool That 114^3	No factor	12
11Oct66-1Aqu	fst 1⅛	.47⅖	1.12⅘	1.54⅕	Md	4500	8	7	7^{10}	$7^{7\frac14}$	7^{12}	7^{11}	MSorrentino	b 116	34.00	54-21	Weary Traveler 110^2 Beau Star 115^2 Wheyface $116^{1\frac12}$	Never close	9
16Sep66-1Aqu	fst 1	.48⅕	1.14	1.40⅗	Md	5000	10	11	$12^{7\frac14}$	11^{13}	11^{15}	11^{15}	MSorrentino	115	21.60f	50-25	Florida Magic 114^3 $FleetImpelled115^{no}$ $Triton'sTrust119^3$	No factor	14
22Aug66-4Sar	sly 1	.47⅗	1.13	1.38⅖	f-MdSpWt		6	6	6^{11}	6^{18}	6^{22}	6^{38}	MSorrentino	115	18.20	44-17	$SandBuggy115^{2\frac12}$ $TwoKeys110^{15}$ Seeds $ofWar110^{10}$	Disliked the slop	6
29Jly66-1Aqu	fst 6f	.22⅖	.46⅗	1.12⅗	f-MdSpWt		7	13	13^{17}	13^{16}	13^{15}	13^{26}	MSorrentino	116	65.70	54-17	Wise Lady 116^1 Lobelia $116^{\frac34}$ Jane's Joy $116^{2\frac12}$	Trailed far back	13

LATEST WORKOUTS Mar 15 Bel tr.t. 4f fst .51⅗ b — Feb 11 TrP 4f fst .50 h

---

Andros Isle: Beat a similar field at today's distance on an allegedly sloppy but (as the figures show) unusually slow track two weeks ago. A Thoroughbred that runs so powerful a race can usually be counted on to repeat the performance if she gets a chance within two weeks. While I usually mistrust apprentice riders in races around two turns, it is impossible to fault young Dick Morgan. He has proved that he can bring this filly off the pace and win at the distance. CONTENDER.

Change of Mind: Has never won at today's distance and is invariably worse than usual on a holding track. NO BET.

Judy Mann: Something went haywire with this miss during the summer of 1966 and she did not race again until fifteen days ago. On March 20 she gave strong evidence of a return to form. She could jump up and win at nine furlongs for the first time in her life, especially if favored by an early pace that allows her to have everything her own way—on the lead. CONTENDER.

Muskoka: Bye-bye Judy Mann. This mare lacks the class to beat today's field but is a cinch to be out there winging at the start, making life entirely too difficult for anything else that hopes to win in pace-setting fashion. NO BET.

That's Hew: Any horse that bears in badly in its two most recent races and goes to the post with the same rider today is a horse that simply cannot help bearing in. In other words, a horse with physical difficulties. NO BET.

Gracious: A gaining win over males only five days ago establishes this filly as a form horse. Can she go today's distance? Perhaps we can overlook the race of last October 11, which took place before the animal was in decent trim. But can we also overlook today's impost of 120 pounds? That's a lot of weight for a filly to carry over a distance that she has never negotiated before. Can we also overlook the fact that Gracious swerved in the stretch last time and had footing trouble the time before? Taken alone, none of these doubts is strong enough to wash out the Kay Jensen girl. But taken together, they add up to a superabundance of doubt. NO BET.

The contenders are Andros Isle and Judy Mann. But Judy Mann's predictable early speed in a race of this kind will get her nowhere, with Muskoka contesting the pace. Cardone might try to snug Judy back and bring her on in the stretch, as Velasquez did in a slightly shorter race against a better field last May 10. But I doubt the filly is in sharp enough shape to carry off that kind of a gaining win today. Her only hope is to get a big lead and hope that nobody catches her at the wire. And that hope, as we have seen, is dead. Andros Isle looks to have everything her own way.

The Running of the Race

THE AUDIENCE went for Gracious, having failed to notice the several dubious aspects of her credentials. Andros Isle won in a walk as second favorite. Judy Mann turned out to be in even better condition than I expected, running not far behind Muskoka and catching that one at the end.

The official result chart contains a rare typographical error. The index number and name of Judy Mann were put where the index number and name of Andros Isle should have been. And vice versa. The remainder of each line, from Equipment through Odds, is correct as printed.

NINTH RACE
Aqu - 30508
March 30, 1967

1 1-8 MILES (Sinatra, December 7, 1964, 1.47⅕, 5, 111.)
Claiming. Purse $4,200. Fillies and mares. 4-year-olds and upward. Weight 123 lbs. Non-winners of a race at a mile and a furlong or over since January 16 allowed 3 lbs., a race at a mile or over since October 29. 5 lbs., two races at any distance since August 27, 7 lbs. Claiming price $4,500. 2 lbs. for each $500 to $3,500.
Value to winner $2,730, second $840, third $420, fourth $210. Mutuel pool $254,345.

Index	Horse	Eqt	A	Wt	PP	St	¼	½	¾	Str	Fin	Jockey	Cl'g Pr	Owner	Odds $1
30440Aqu3	Judy Mann	b	4	116	3	1	3^h	$5^{1\frac{1}{2}}$	3^h	1^3	1^7	R Morgan5	4500	Sunwood Stable	2.70
30436Aqu1	Andros Isle		4	118	1	3	$2^{1\frac{1}{2}}$	3^h	$4^{\frac{1}{2}}$	$3^{\frac{1}{2}}$	2^{nk}	E Cardone	4500	Clara L Ostriker	8.20
30449Pim4	Muskoka	b	6	116	4	2	1^3	$1^{1\frac{1}{2}}$	1^h	$2^{1\frac{1}{2}}$	3^h	R Turcotte	4500	Maxine Sadlier	12.60
30466Aqu1	Gracious	b	4	120	6	6	6	4^h	$5^{1\frac{1}{2}}$	5^4	4^3	A T Cordero	4500	Narrie B Trittipoe	2.50
30466Aqu4	Ch'ge Of Mind	b	5	112	2	4	$4^{1\frac{1}{2}}$	2^2	2^2	4^1	5^8	W Boland	3500	J Trisolini	6.30
30466Aqu2	That's Hew		4	116	5	5	5^h	6	6	6	6	R Stovall	4500	E Konoski	4.60

Time .25⅕, .50⅗, 1.16⅗, 1.43⅖, 1.56⅖ (with wind in backstretch). Track slow.

$2 Mutuel Prices:			
1-ANDROS ISLE	7.40	4.20	2.40
3-JUDY MANN		4.60	3.20
4-MUSKOKA			4.80

B. f, by Midnight Sun—Bloomin Alibi, by Alibhai. Trainer A. J. Danko. Bred by J. L. Reynolds-O'Brien Bros. (Md.).

IN GATE AT 5.29. OFF AT 5.29 EASTERN STANDARD TIME. Start good. Won easily.

ANDROS ISLE, handled alertly at the start, was taken under wraps and saved ground within striking distance, found an opening to take command while still under restraining in the upper stretch and, after one tap of the whip, drew out on her own courage. JUDY MANN was well placed along the outside under intermittent restraint, lost ground entering the stretch and finished well to best the others. MUSOKA was snugly rated for a slow pace and lacked a response for the final run. GRACIOUS, in hand early, failed to respond. CHANGE OF MIND weakened under pressure. THAT'S HEW was under wraps early and could not be properly handled when the saddle slipped after a half-mile.

Gracious was claimed by J. Maccatroni, trainer H. Jacobson.

10. NINTH AT AQUEDUCT, JUNE 1, 1967—Track Fast

To SHOW HOW things happen in Thoroughbred racing and how the attentive handicapper manages to stay a hop and a skip ahead of certain things that happen, we now renew acquaintances with Emerald Lake. A few pages ago we saw Tommy Gullo's Beau Gar colt go off as an undeserving favorite. Today's race is different.

It is for four-year-olds and upward, at nine furlongs, for horses with price tags ranging from $10,500 to $12,500.

9th Race Aqueduct

1⅛ MILES AQUEDUCT Start▸ ◂Finish

1 1-8 MILES (Sinatra, December 7, 1964, 1.47⅘, 5, 111.)
Claiming. Purse $7,700. 4-year-olds and upward. Weight, 122 lbs. Non-winners of two races at a mile and a furlong or over since March 11 allowed 3 lbs., of two races at a mile or over since then, 6 lbs. Claiming price, $12,500. 2 lbs. allowed for each $1,000 to $10,500. (Races when entered to be claimed for $8,500 or less not considered.)

Spartanburg * $11,500 Ch. g (1961), by Third Brother—Chance's School, by Greek Star (Mrs. E. B. Dent) D. Sorantino E. W. King **114** 1967 15 4 2 2 $17,175 / 1966 28 3 1 1 $13,000
26May67-6Aqu my 1 .47⅗1.13 1.37⅘ Clm 14000 6 6 612 615 618 528 MYcaza b 116 10.60 51-26 Koh-I-Noor 1182 Needles' Count 1194 Ganelon II 1101½ No speed 6
17May67-9Aqu fst 1⅛.48⅖1.13 1.51⅖ Clm 11500 4 6 65½ 42½ 23 34 JLRotz b 120 4.80 75-16 Koh-I-Noor 1192 Artist's Award 1202 Spartanburg 1203 Hung 7
9May67-9Aqu gd 1⅛.48 1.12⅘1.52⅗ Cl c-9000 1 4 45½ 54 43½ 2½ RTurcotte b 115 *3.10 72-25 Pomidoro 117½ Spartanburg 115¾ Artist's Award 192½ Sharp try 6
27Apr67-9Aqu sly 1⅛.49⅖1.14⅘1.54⅘ Clm 9000 7 7 712 79 46 47 MVenezia b 118 5.00 55-34 Nike Site 116h Bigamo 1144 Winter Joy 1143 Began very slowly 7
22Apr67-9Aqu fst 1⅛.46⅖1.11 1.52 Hcp 5000s 8 8 720 817 77½ 66¼ RUssery b 122 7.80 70-16 Primo Theo 1103 Cormier 1151½ Lou Michaels 117¾ No speed 9
11Apr67-9Aqu fst 1⅛.47 1.12⅘1.53⅕ Clm 12500 8 10 1020 912 911 58¼ HGustines b 122 5.30 62-27 Ganelon II 109nk Cormier 1144 Listen To Reason 1161½ No threat 10
25Mar67-9Aqu my 1⅛.49⅗1.17 1.58 Hcp 5000s 1 5 618 45½ 1½ 1nk HGustines b 122 2.40 46-35 Spartanburg 122nk Count Bell 1203 Mr. Spinelli 1218 Driving 6
14Mar67-6Aqu fst 1 .46⅗1.12⅕1.37⅗ Clm 12500 6 7 716 611 66 58¾ BBaeza b 122 6.50 71-22 Needles' Count 1191¼ Naturalist 1141½ Rocky Ford 1143½ No factor 8
17Feb67-10Hia fst1⅛.46⅖1.11⅗1.50⅖ Cl c-10000 5 5 56½ 44½ 2h 1nk JLRotz b 118 *1.80 83-16 Spartanburg 118nk Yar 1164 Artist's Award 112¾ Just up 12
11Feb67-10Hia fst1⅛.47⅘1.12 1.49⅘Clm 10000 2 3 45 43½ 21½ 23 RUssery b 122 *1.50e 83-20 Koh-I-Noor 1163 Spartanburg 1226 Board Buster 1123 Gamely 10
8Feb67-10Hia sly 1⅛.46 1.10⅖1.49 Clm 13000 6 8 820 716 612 613 RUssery b 120 8.00 77-12 Count Dormal 118nk Count Bell 1175 Ni Modo 112½ Dull perform'ce 10
26Jan67-7Hia my 1⅛.49 1.13⅗1.53⅕ Clm 10000 9 8 65 67½ 31½ 11 RUssery b 120 4.80 69-29 Spartanburg 1201 Handy Helper 114h Ni Modo 1122 Closing strides 10
14Jan67-4TrP fst*1¼ 2.02 Hcp 5000s 8 8 917 79 66 32 HGrant b 122 *1.30 94-13 Mr.Spinelli 115½ Posey's Special 1171½ Spartanburg 1221½ Broke sl. 10
LATEST WORKOUTS May 24 Bel 6f fst 1.14⅗ h Apr 21 Bel tr.t. 3f fst .37 h Apr 10 Bel m.t. 5f fst 1.03⅕ h

Winter Joy * $11,500 B. g (1962), by Our Joy—Snowy, by Bold Venture (C. C. Boshamer) D. Shaer F. L. Moore **114** 1967 10 0 1 4 $3,900 / 1966 15 4 3 1 $11,575
16May67-9Aqu gd 1⅛.46⅘1.11⅘1.52⅖ Cl c-8500 2 8 817 712 57 36 BBaeza 116 *2.10 68-22 Birdsofafeather 1161 Bent Spur 1165 Winter Joy 1161 Rallied 8
27Apr67-9Aqu sly 1⅛.49⅖1.14⅘1.54⅘ Clm 9500 6 6 612 68½ 34½ 34 ADeSpirito 114 5.30 58-34 Nike Site 116h Bigamo 1144 Winter Joy 1143 Lacked early foot 7
20Apr67-8Aqu fst 1⅛.47⅘1.13⅖1.53 Clm 10000 2 4 711 98¼ 75 32 BBaeza 116 6.30 69-26 Artist's Award 115no Bigamo 1122 Winter Joy 116h Rallied 10
11Apr67-9Aqu fst 1⅛.47 1.12⅘1.53⅕ Clm 10500 9 8 919 1013 1013 914 MVenezia 112 5.10 56-27 Ganelon II 109nk Cormier 1144 Listen To Reason 1161½ No speed 10
28Mar67-9Aqu gd 1⅛.49⅘1.14⅗1.55⅕ Clm 9500 7 7 712 57¾ 55 2½ MVenezia 114 5.70 59-26 Mr. Spinelli 107½ Winter Joy 114h Listen To Reason 116h Sharp 7
21Mar67-6Aqu my 1 .48⅕1.15⅗1.43⅗ Clm 8500 6 8 818 614 59½ 3¾ MVenezia 116 13.50 49-40 Cool Oasis 116½ Nashwood 116nk Winter Joy 116½ Closed fast 8
14Mar67-6Aqu fst 1 .46⅗1.12⅕1.37⅗ Clm 10500 7 3 512 714 710 713 MVenezia 112 35.50 67-22 Needles' Count 1191¼ Naturalist 1141½ Rocky Ford 1143½ Fell back 8
11Feb67-10Hia fst1⅛.47⅘1.12 1.49⅘Cl c-10000 7 5 68 813 914 919 FToro 116 2.90 67-20 Koh-I-Noor 1163 Spartanburg 1226 Board Buster 1123 Dull try 10
28Jan67-5Hia gd 7f .23 .46⅕1.25⅗ Clm 12000 8 11 1020 1023 917 69½ FToro 113 5.30 71-26 Count Bell 1073 Why Lie 1145 Bargain Counter 1181 Slow start 11
19Jan67-6Hia fst 6f .22 .45⅘1.10⅘ Clm 13000 2 12 1220 1216 1014 66½ FToro 113 44.40 83-17 LordBirchfield 112nk Farmer'sSon 1163 Cap'nShorty 1142 Slow start 12
21Sep66-7BB fst 170 1.43⅘ Allowance 1 3 311 411 210 28 CLedezma 119 1.50e 85-22 Doubting Thomas 1128 Winter Joy 1193 Bengal 1131½ Gamely 6
11Sep66-6BB fst 1 1/16.48⅕1.13⅕1.46⅕ Allowance 4 4 48½ 48 26 13 CLedezma 119 *0.65 86-16 Winter Joy 1193 Teardrop Lane 1111½ Bengal 1141½ Drew clear 5
LATEST WORKOUTS May 28 Bel 4f fst .49 b May 15 Bel tr.t. 3f fst .37 h

Daily Reminder * $12,500 B. g (1962), by Arrogate—Forgot, by Stymie (Ocala Stud Farms, Inc.) F. S. Fiore P. P. Mosconi **116** 1967 3 0 1 0 $1,320 / 1966 9 0 1 2 $2,700
27May67-8Aqu fst 6f .22⅖ .45⅗1.11⅕ Clm 12500 3 8 89 811 85¾ 77 BBaeza 117 8.40 80-15 Prospect Street 117¾ Santo Domingo 1171 Big Rapids 113½ No thr't 10
6May67-4Aqu sly 7f .24⅕ .48 1.27 Cl c-10000 6 3 5¾ 33 41¼ 21¼ ATCordero 117 4.00 70-27 Syncope 1171¼ Daily Reminder 1171½ Lash Back 1213 Game try 6
15Apr67-2SoP hd*7f Ⓣ 1.25⅖ Clm 03500 11 7 64½ 55¼ 52¾ 42¼ TWalsh s 147 ——e —— Principio II 147¾ Willup 1441½ DiMonza 137h Evenly 15
7Sep66-9Aqu fst 1⅛.49⅖1.14⅗1.53⅘ Clm 12500 6 7 69 46½ 35 24 KKnapp b 118 10.00 63-30 Sir Sanford 1184 Daily Reminder 1183 Rocky Ford 1182½ Second best 7
11Aug66-8Sar sly 1⅛.48⅗1.13⅕1.52⅕ Clm 14000 4 6 611 614 76 58¼ KKnapp b 114 21.90 76-16 Demigod 1141 Round Table Pet 1186 King Trece 114¾ Never close 8
3Aug66-9Sar fst 1 .47 1.12⅖1.37⅘ Clm 14000 3 7 713 54 74 66¼ KKnapp 114 19.20 79-12 Rocky Ford 118¾ Round Table Pet 116½ Dark Alloy 1131½ No mishap 8
5Jly 66-9Aqu fst 1 .45⅘1.10⅘1.36⅘ Clm 15000 5 7 65½ 63¾ 57½ 35 KKnapp 114 6.30 79-20 Upset Victory 1142½ Vail Pass 1182½ Daily Reminder 114nk Raillied 8
30Jun66-8Aqu fst 6f .22⅖ .45⅕1.10⅗ Clm 15000 1 8 916 912 89¼ 46½ KKnapp 115 ♦26.90 83-20 ♦Ways to Learn 1075 ♦New Leader 1155 Yucatan 1141½ Late foot 9
30Jun66—♦-Dead heat.
23Jun66-5Aqu fst 7f .22⅘ .45⅘1.23⅗ Clm 18000 5 6 78 511 47½ 46¼ LLoughry5 110 14.30 82-17 Solid Mike 1155 Corredor II 115½ Jovial Jeff 108¾ Mild rally 9
4Jun66-5Aqu fst 7f .22⅕ .44⅗1.22⅘ Allowance 2 8 813 811 86½ 66¾ DChamberlin5 116 105.40 85-14 Aforethought 1072½ Woodford 114h Ringing Appeal 1121½ No factor 9
26Apr66-7Kee sly 6½f.22⅗ .46 1.18⅕ Allowance 4 7 713 713 59½ 59¼ EFires 123 5.70 78-19 Council Town 1132¾ Yonder 1153½ Valiant Marbo 1231 No factor 7
LATEST WORKOUTS May 26 Bel tr.t. 3f sly .38 b Apr 7 Bel tr.t. 5f gd 1.04⅗ b May 3 Bel tr.t. 5f fst 1.01⅖ b

Emerald Lake * $12,500 Dk. b. or br. c (1963–Fla), by Beau Gar—Lake Garda, by Turn-to (Hobeau Farm, Inc.) L. Silver T. J. Gullo **116** 1967 9 0 3 0 $4,600 / 1966 16 2 2 3 $10,745
26May67-6Aqu my 1 .47⅗1.13 1.37⅘ Clm 14000 5 1 33 511 516 628 JGiovanni b 112 4.50 51-26 Koh-I-Noor 1182 Needles' Count 1194 Ganelon II 1101½ Stopped 6
12May67-4Aqu sl 1⅛.47⅖1.13⅕1.52 Clm 15000 4 2 32 52 47 416 BBaeza b 116 *1.40 60-26 Demigod 115¾ Needles' Count 1145 Sir Sanford 11410 No excuse 5
3May67-8Aqu fst 1 .46⅘1.12 1.38 Clm 15000 4 4 56 58 42½ 42¾ BBaeza 116 *1.30 75-21 Demigod 114¾ Needles' Count 1171½ Koh-I-Noor 122½ Bid, hung 7
25Apr67-6Aqu sl 1 .47⅖1.12⅘1.38 Clm 16000 1 6 55 44 22 2nk BBaeza 116 2.80 78-28 Koh-I-Noor 116nk Emerald Lake 1166 Demigod 113nk Sharp try 8
29Mar67-8Aqu my 1 .49⅕1.15⅗1.41⅖ Clm 15000 4 5 2½ 3½ 21 2¾ MCariglio5 111 6.60 60-33 Corredor II 117¾ Emerald Lake 111½ Direct Action 1121½ Sharp 10
25Mar67-8Aqu my 6f .23⅕ .48⅖1.14 Allowance 3 7 714 715 615 58½ MCariglio5 118 12.10 64-35 Mister Pitt's Kid 1132½ Dandy Steal 1123 Disembark 121no Slow st. 7
11Mar67-6GP fm 1 1/16 Ⓣ 1.11 1.41⅘ Clm 18000 2 6 612 67 714 714 LMoyers 116 8.40 81-11 VoluntarioIII112¾ FlamingTriumph1122½ AdmiralClove1163 No sp'd 9
27Feb67-10Hia fm 1⅛ Ⓣ 1.50⅕ Clm 18000 5 8 811 74½ 54½ 24½ ECardone 112 13.20 86-10 Top Victory 1164½ Emerald Lake 112h Loopy Loop 1163½ Rallied 8
23Jan67-9Hia sly 7f .23⅗ .47 1.25⅕ Allowance 4 3 31½ 32 69½ 713 WBoland 119 *0.90e 70-19 Saeharf 118½ Beau Legs 113no Wondrascope 1132 Brief foot 7
9Dec66-6Aqu fst 7f .22⅖ .45⅘1.23⅘ Clm 18000 1 3 22 45 69 56½ ECardone5 115 *0.80e 80-20 The Cheat 1141 There Goes Sam 118h Royal Harbinger 1192 Tired 8
1Dec66-6Aqu fst 7f .23 .46 1.24⅖ Allowance 7 1 43¼ 41½ 1h 2no JRuane 122 1.90e 84-23 It's Blitz 117no Emerald Lake 1223 ♦Solemn Nation 1153 Wide 7
LATEST WORKOUTS May 23 Bel tr.t. 4f fst .49⅗ h May 18 Bel tr.t. 4f fst .48⅗ h Apr 12 Bel tr.t. 3f fst .38⅖ b Apr 4 Bel tr.t. 3f fst .38 b

Your Prince $12,500 B. h (1962), by Prince John—Your Stocking, by Our Boots
A. Wohl V. J. Nickerson (W. C. Partee) **116**

1967	3	0	0	0	——
1966	8	2	1	0	$9,775

19May67-8Aqu	fst 1⅛	.47⅗ 1.11 1.49⅖	Clm 18000	3	4	4^{10}	4^{10}	5^{11}	5^{17}	WBoland	b 113	3.90	72-18	Beau Legs 116^{10} Macherio $116^{1\frac{1}{2}}$ Snow Cap II $116^{1\frac{1}{2}}$	Away sluggishly	5
3May67-8Aqu	fst 1	.46⅘ 1.12 1.38	Clm 14000	6	2	2^{4}	2^{3}	$5^{4\frac{1}{2}}$	$5^{3\frac{1}{4}}$	EBelmonte	b 112	6.60	75-21	Demigod $114^{\frac{3}{4}}$ Needles Count $117^{1\frac{1}{2}}$ Koh-I-Noor $122^{\frac{1}{2}}$	No mishaps	7
21Apr67-7Aqu	fst 7f	.22⅘ .45⅖ 1.23⅕	Allowance	1	6	6^{13}	6^{14}	6^{17}	6^{21}	EBelmonte	b 121	26.90	69-22	Mincing Lane 119^{1} Road At Sea 114no Golden Buttons 121^{3}	Trailed	6
8Aug66-9Sar	fm 1⅛ Ⓣ	1.47⅕	Clm 22500	5	9	12^{9}	11^{8}	$10^{9\frac{3}{4}}$	9^{14}	EBelmonte	b 118	7.20	83- 3	Clatterbox 116^{8} Rochefort $118^{\frac{1}{2}}$ Service Ace $118^{\frac{1}{2}}$	No speed	12
7Jly 66-9Aqu	hd 1⅛ Ⓣ	1.48⅘	Allowance	4	6	5^{12}	$5^{8\frac{1}{2}}$	$4^{\frac{3}{4}}$	$1^{\frac{3}{4}}$	EBelmonte	b 118	5.80	91-13	Your Prince $118^{\frac{3}{4}}$ Hardihood $120^{2\frac{1}{2}}$ Annette's Ark 118^{4}	Driving	9
27May66-5Aqu	fst 1	.45⅘ 1.10⅖ 1.36⅖	Clm 18000	4	4	2^{3}	3^{1}	3^{1}	$4^{2\frac{1}{2}}$	MVenezia	b 115	2.50	83-18	Demigod $112^{\frac{3}{4}}$ Africanus 116^{1} Hail the King $119^{\frac{3}{4}}$	Bore out	6
13Apr66-6Aqu	fst 1⅛	.48⅖ 1.13⅕ 1.50⅗	Allowance	6	6	$7^{3\frac{1}{2}}$	6^{3}	1^{h}	2no	MVenezia	b 123	22.60	83-16	Throne Room 113no Your Prince 123^{4} Sea Castle $112^{2\frac{1}{2}}$	Sharp	8
7Apr66-5Aqu	fst 1	.47⅖ 1.11 1.36⅕	Allowance	5	5	$5^{3\frac{3}{4}}$	5^{9}	4^{6}	$4^{4\frac{3}{4}}$	ORosado5	b 118	11.40	82-17	Buffle $113^{\frac{3}{4}}$ Michigan Avenue 115^{1} Portfolio 120^{3}	Wide late	5
23Mar66-4Aqu	fst 1	.47⅕ 1.13 1.39	Allowance	6	6	$6^{5\frac{1}{2}}$	$4^{\frac{3}{4}}$	$2^{\frac{1}{2}}$	1^{2}	MVenezia	b 119	*1.70	73-25	Your Prince 119^{2} Port Royal 115^{h} Much More $115^{2\frac{1}{2}}$	Bore out, up	6
16Mar66-6Aqu	fst 7f	.23⅗ .47⅗ 1.26⅕	Allowance	2	8	$8^{7\frac{1}{4}}$	4^{4}	L't rider		MVenezia	b 115	*1.10e	——	Noon Rock 110^{5} Port Royal $118^{\frac{3}{4}}$ Yucatan $113^{3\frac{1}{2}}$	Bolted turn	8
1Mar66-5Hia	fst 7f	.23⅕ .46⅖ 1.24⅘	Allowance	3	7	7^{7}	4^{4}	7^{6}	$7^{8\frac{1}{4}}$	MVenezia	b 115	14.20	77-15	Vail Pass 115^{4} Jim Dooley 112^{h} Spinsome $110^{\frac{3}{4}}$	Fell back early	8

LATEST WORKOUTS May 29 Aqu 4f fst .50 b May 24 Aqu 5f fst 1.02 h May 15 Aqu 5f fst 1.05⅘ b May 10 Aqu 4f fst .51 b

Artist's Award $12,500 Ch. g (1962), by John Constable—Claque, by Alibhai
J. I. Nischan N. Gonzalez (P. Mellon) **116**

1967	11	2	2	3	$11,035
1966	22	0	4	3	$5,250

17May67-9Aqu	fst 1⅛	.48⅖ 1.13 1.51⅖	Clm 11500	7	7	7^{6}	$7^{4\frac{1}{2}}$	3^{3}	2^{2}	LAdams	b 120	9.00	77-16	Koh-I-Noor 119^{2} Artist's Award 120^{2} Spartanburg 120^{3}	Rallied	7
9May67-9Aqu	gd 1⅛	.48 1.12⅘ 1.52⅗	Clm 10000	2	6	$6^{5\frac{3}{4}}$	3^{2}	$3^{2\frac{1}{2}}$	$3^{1\frac{1}{4}}$	LAdams	b 119	8.00	72-25	Pomidoro $117^{\frac{1}{2}}$ Spartanburg $115^{\frac{3}{4}}$ Artist's Award $19^{2\frac{1}{2}}$	Rallied	6
20Apr67-8Aqu	fst 1⅛	.47⅘ 1.13⅖ 1.53	Clm 9500	6	7	$5^{6\frac{1}{2}}$	$5^{1\frac{3}{4}}$	2^{2}	1no	MYcaza	b 115	20.40	71-26	Artist's Award 115no Bigamo 112^{2} Winter Joy 116^{h}	Just up	10
8Mar67-10GP	fm 1 1/16 Ⓣ	1.12 1.43⅗	Clm 10000	1	4	3^{2}	3^{2}	$4^{2\frac{1}{2}}$	$3^{2\frac{1}{2}}$	BMoreira	b 118	4.40	83- 8	Sage Jamie $118^{2\frac{1}{2}}$ Mt. Greenery 112no Artist's Award 118no	Wide	11
25Feb67-10Hia	fm 1 3/16 Ⓣ	1.56⅖	Clm 9000	1	4	$5^{2\frac{1}{4}}$	2^{h}	$1^{\frac{1}{2}}$	$2^{1\frac{1}{2}}$	ATCordero	b 112	13.70	85- 9	MaggieFastStep$113^{1\frac{1}{2}}$Artist'sAward112^{nk}Shorty'sPride$116^{\frac{3}{4}}$	Gamely	11
17Feb67-10Hia	fst 1⅛	.46⅖ 1.11⅗ 1.50⅖	Clm 9000	7	9	8^{11}	6^{8}	4^{6}	$3^{4\frac{1}{4}}$	ATCordero	b 112	26.10	79-16	Spartanburg 118^{nk} Yar 116^{4} Artist's Award $112^{\frac{3}{4}}$	Rallied	12
11Feb67-10Hia	fst 1⅛	.47⅘ 1.12 1.49⅘	Clm 9500	3	4	3^{2}	$3^{1\frac{1}{2}}$	6^{7}	5^{12}	JVasquez	b 114	7.20	74-20	Koh-I-Noor 116^{3} Spartanburg 122^{6} Board Buster 112^{3}	Bid, tired	10
2Feb67-10Hia	fst 1⅛	.46⅖ 1.11⅗ 1.50⅗	Clm 10000	1	8	$5^{7\frac{1}{2}}$	$4^{3\frac{1}{2}}$	4^{5}	5^{8}	HViera	b 118	10.70	74-14	Ni Modo $114^{\frac{1}{2}}$ Pinchers Pride 112^{3} Punisher 118^{3}	Bid, tired	12
21Jan67-10Hia	my 1⅛	.47⅗ 1.12⅗ 1.51⅗	Clm 11500	9	7	$7^{8\frac{1}{2}}$	7^{13}	7^{14}	7^{18}	HGustines	b 114	14.50	59-20	CountDormal $116^{3\frac{1}{2}}$ ListenToReason $118^{3\frac{1}{2}}$ CoolOasis $116^{\frac{1}{2}}$	No speed	10
16Jan67-8TrP	my 1 1/16	.47⅗ 1.12⅘ 1.45⅖	Clm 12500	5	8	4^{6}	4^{7}	4^{12}	4^{18}	HGustines	b 121	11.70	57-26	DoubtingThomas$114^{7\frac{1}{2}}$CountDormal 113^{3}ListenToReason121^{7}	Sl. st't	8
6Jan67-7TrP	fst 1 1/16	.47⅖ 1.11⅗ 1.43⅗	Clm 9000	5	1	1^{2}	1^{2}	1^{3}	1^{7}	HGustines	b 115	*2.50	84-12	Artist's Award 115^{7} Fact Seeker 116^{1} Bucklin 113^{nk}	Handily	7
31Dec66-6TrP	fst 1 1/16	.46⅗ 1.11 1.43⅗	Clm 8500	3	5	$4^{3\frac{1}{2}}$	3^{3}	$3^{2\frac{1}{2}}$	2^{3}	HGustines	b 115	8.80	81-16	Count Bell 115^{3} Artist's Award $115^{2\frac{1}{2}}$ Man of Note $113^{3\frac{1}{2}}$	Gamely	8

LATEST WORKOUTS May 26 Bel 3f sly .37 b Apr 11 Bel tr.t. 4f fst .51 b

Spartanburg: Likes the distance. Seems best suited to $10,000 company but was far from disgraced when carrying 120 pounds against a field like today's on May 17. Came back six days ago and took a dreadful whipping in the mud (which it likes) at a mile (which is too short). Everett King usually cracks down with claimed horses as soon as he can. Allowing for the distinct possibility that this animal is in about as good form as ever, we have to award it a fair chance today—especially if a couple of speed horses pave the way by tiring each other out. CONTENDER.

Winter Joy: Looks overmatched. NO BET.

Daily Reminder: When Pete Mosconi claimed this for $10,000 last month, he knew very well that it had shown a bit of run against $12,500 animals at today's distance in a race last September. He works wonders with claimed animals but can't get blood out of a turnip. Until Daily Reminder proves otherwise, we are compelled to assume that it belongs in cheaper races. NO BET.

Emerald Lake: Steps down another notch after disappointing as a favorite on May 3 and 12 and running a terrible mile in the mud on May 27. The two May workouts over the slow Belmont training track indicate, however, that the horse has all his speed and needs simply to find the right spot. His record is that of a miler that begins his final drive too tardily to beat top-grade claiming horses at that distance. Gullo's insistence on entering him at a longer route, as on May 12 and today, must be taken as evidence that the colt might benefit from a race in which he has the early pace all his own way. Assuming he can get on top in a hurry and is subjected to no serious challenge by anything else, he probably could win at the longer distance. If Gullo were Joe Blow, I would not go along with this reasoning, but Gullo happens to be an ace operative on the toughest, smartest racing circuit in the country. In deference to him and his way with horses, I conclude that Emerald Lake is sure to be speedier than most routers and can win in today's relatively low class, if allowed to set the pace. CONTENDER.

Your Prince: Raced and worked out frequently enough in May to establish its fitness for competition. But has not yet offered a single clue as to the class of horses it can beat after its long vacation. The last outing was so bad —fifth by seventeen lengths in a five-horse field—that winning seems out of the question tody, even in this easier race. NO BET.

Artist's Award: Three good stretch drives in succession—the last two against horses like today's—figure to take the edge off this five-year-old. Is very consistent about getting into the money, but beats only cheaper fields. NO BET.

The contenders are Spartanburg, with solid credentials, and Emerald Lake, favored by the absence of any other early speed. Because of the way Gullo has been handling the colt, I have to assume that he will prove ready to take full advantage of the soft spot.

The Running of the Race

AN OPTIMISTIC CROWD sent Your Prince (the "class horse") at 2.10–1, with Artist's Award (the "form horse") as second favorite, and Spartanburg next. Emerald Lake's pace advantage was overlooked, and he exploited the situation beautifully, extending his lead at the finish. Spartanburg came on to beat the others with authority.

I think this race deserves extra-close study. It reveals how an intelligent trainer, without necessarily trying to conceal the form of a horse, can find an easy touch for him at a long mutuel—after he has disappointed the chalk players by flubbing more difficult assignments.

NINTH RACE Aqu - 31309 June 1, 1967

1 1-8 MILES (Sinatra, December 7, 1964, 1.47$\frac{1}{5}$, 5, 111.)

Claiming. Purse $7,700. 4-year-olds and upward. Weight, 122 lbs. Non-winners of two races at a mile and a furlong or over since March 11 allowed 3 lbs., of two races at a mile or over since then, 6 lbs. Claiming price, $12,500. 2 lbs. allowed for each $1,000 to $10,500. (Races when entered to be claimed for $8,500 or less not considered.)

Value to winner 05,005, second 01,540, third $770, fourth $385. Mutuel pool $308,116.

Index	Horse	Eqt	A	Wt	PP	St	¼	½	¾	Str	Fin	Jockey	Cl'g Pr	Owner	Odds $1
31204Aqu^{6}	Emerald Lake		4	116	4	3	1^{2}	1^{3}	1^{3}	1^{3}	$1^{3\frac{1}{2}}$	J Giovanni	12500	L Silver	6.40
31204Aqu^{5}	Spartanburg	b	6	114	1	1	5^{3}	4^{1}	4^{1}	$3^{\frac{1}{2}}$	$2^{2\frac{1}{2}}$	R Turcotte	11500	D Sorantino	3.90
31152Aqu^{5}	Your Prince	b	5	116	5	5	3^{h}	$2^{\frac{1}{2}}$	$3^{1\frac{1}{2}}$	$4^{\frac{1}{2}}$	3^{nk}	E Belmonte	12500	A Wohl	2.10
31135Aqu^{2}	Artist'sAward	b	5	116	6	6	6	6	5^{4}	5^{6}	4^{h}	L Adams	12500	J I Nischan	3.00
31215Aqu^{7}	Daily Reminder		5	116	3	4	4^{1}	3^{1}	2^{h}	$2^{\frac{1}{2}}$	5^{8}	A Cordero Jr	12500	F J Fiore	4.70
31126Aqu^{3}	Winter Joy		5	114	2	2	$2^{1\frac{1}{2}}$	5^{2}	6	6	6	B Baeza	11500	D Shaer	9.20

Time :24$\frac{4}{5}$, .49$\frac{1}{5}$, 1.13$\frac{1}{5}$, 1.38$\frac{1}{5}$, 1.50$\frac{4}{5}$. (with wind in backstretch) Track fast.

$2 Mutuel Prices:

4-EMERALD LAKE	14.80	8.40	5.80
1-SPARTANBURG		5.40	3.40
5-YOUR PRINCE			3.40

Dk. b. or br c, by Beau Gar—Lake Garda, by Turn-to. Trainer T. J. Gullo. Bred by Hobeau Farm, Inc. (Fla.).

IN GATE AT 5.33. OFF AT 5.33$\frac{1}{2}$ EASTERN DAYLIGHT TIME. Start good for all but ARTIST'S AWARD. Won easily.

EMERALD LAKE, hustled to the front early, saved ground while making the pace under steady rating and, responding readily when shaken up entering the stretch, retained a clear margin. SPARTANBURG outrun early but saving ground, finished determined next to the inner rail. YOUR PRINCE had no mishap in a game effort. ARTIST'S AWARD began poorly. DAILY REMINDER tired after making a good bid in the upper stretch. WINTER JOY gave way after showing brief speed.

---

11. FOURTH AT AQUEDUCT, JUNE 9, 1967—Track Fast

AND NOW FOR a final visit with our contrary friend, Emerald Lake, and his resourceful trainer, Tom Gullo. This time the claiming price is $15,000, and the horse seeks his second consecutive victory at a mile and an eighth.

4th Race Aqueduct

1⅛ MILES
AQUEDUCT
Start ▸ ◂ Finish

1 1-8 MILES (Sinatra, December 7, 1964, 1.47⅘, 5, 111.)
Claiming. Purse $8,500. 3-year-olds and upward. Weights 3-year-olds 114 lbs., older 123 lbs. Non-winners of a race at a mile and a furlong or over since April 20 allowed 3 lbs. Claiming price $15,000. 2 lbs. allowed for each $500 to $14,000. (Races when entered to be claimed for $12,000 or less not considered.)

(4th Aqu)—Coupled—Solemn Nation and Birdsofafeather.

Solemn Nation * **$15,000** Dk. b. or br. g (1963–Ky), by Stymie—Tweet Fleet, by Count Fleet **120** 1967 10 0 2 2 $5,365
Windham Farm E. W. King (Dr. C. E. Hagyard) 1966 12 2 3 4 $12,420
1Jun67-6Aqu fm 1 1/16 Ⓣ 1.43⅕ Clm 18000 9 6 68 43 23 25 EBelmonte b 116 7.00 85-10 Koh-I-Noor 1165 Solemn Nation 116½ Shady Living 1202 Hung 9
25May67-6Aqu sl 1⅛.49⅖1.14⅕1.51 Allowance 3 4 45 710 715 718 ADeSpirito 123 25.90 63-24 Prinkipo 1132½ Royal Comedian 1132 Fort Marcy 1102 Checked 8
18May67-7Aqu fst 7f .22⅗ .45⅕1.22⅘ Allowance 1 6 33½ 56½ 59½ 514 BBaeza 115 3.20 78-20 Walk Out 1152½ Eagle Lair 1086 Big Red Rocket 1154 Tired 8
11May67-6Aqu sly 1⅛.46⅘1.13⅖1.53⅖ Allowance 7 6 621 610 44½ 210 EBelmonte 123 12.20 59-24 Blast'gCharge11310SolemnNation123noRuffledFeathers1144 Fair try 7
4May67-4Aqu fst 1⅛.49⅘1.13⅗1.51⅗ Allowance 4 2 2½ 43½ 34½ 57 EBelmonte 123 15.00 71-20 Dunderhead 1233 Blasting Charge 1102 Trade In 120½ Tired 7
27Apr67-6Aqu sly 1⅛.48 1.14⅘1.54⅗ Allowance 4 3 511 33 31 32¾ EBelmonte 123 10.00 60-34 Wowzer 1132 Tom Poker 113¾ Solemn Nation 1232 Rallied, hung 7
22Apr67-4Aqu fst 6f .22⅕ .45⅗1.11 Allowance 1 6 67½ 45½ 46½ 43½ EBelmonte 121 10.80 84-16 Smooth Seas 1211 Velvet Flash 1132½ Irish Dude 113h Sluggish early 6
18Apr67-6Aqu my 7f .28⅖ .46⅘1.25 Cl c-14000 5 2 32 33 44½ 37 WShoemaker 117 ♦ 2.50 74-25 Counsellor 1192 Well To Do 1215 ♦Beaustone 1154 Weakened 5
18Apr67—♦Dead heat.
13Apr67-5Aqu fst 6f .22⅖ .45⅗1.10⅘ Clm 16000 6 6 65½ 54 44 56¾ JTartaglia10 111 9.70 82-16 Two Stelle 121¾ Cuetip 1176 Athen's Gem 116no Began slowly 7
7Jan67-7TrP TT 1 .46⅘1.11 1.35⅖ Handicap 5 7 98¼104¼ 94½ 85½ RFerraro 117 7.10 —— Thermoject 113no Wiggins Fork 114¾ Wondrascope 1181 No factor 10
LATEST WORKOUTS May 31 Bel 3f fst .36⅖ hg Apr 12 Aqu 3f fst .36 h

***Ganelon II** **$14,000** Ch. h (1961), by Tatan—Elite, by Seductor **116** 1967 6 1 1 1 $6,725
Mrs. A. Fiore A. A. Fiore (Haras Comalal) (Arg.) 1966 4 0 0 0 ——
26May67-6Aqu my 1 .47⅗1.13 1.37⅘ Clm 14000 1 4 44 33 44 36 GMora5 b 110 19.70 73-26 Koh-I-Noor 1182 Needles' Count 1194 Ganelon II 1101½ Evenly 6
11Apr67-9Aqu fst 1⅛.47 1.12⅘1.53⅕ Clm 12500 7 7 713 56 55 1nk GMora7 b 109 33.10 70-27 Ganelon II 109nk Cormier 1144 Listen To Reason 1161½ Just up 10
11Mar67-6GP fm 1 1/16 Ⓣ 1.11 1.41⅘ Clm 16000 1 4 410 56½ 59 46¼ MCarr'zzella b 112 18.90 89-11 VoluntarioIII112¾ FlamingTriumph1122½ AdmiralClove1163 No mis'p 9
8Mar67-10GP fm 1 1/16 Ⓣ 1.12 1.43⅗ Clm 10000 10 7 89 811 65 42½ JVelasquez b 116 *3.00 83- 8 Sage Jamie 1182½ Mt. Greenery 112no Artist's Award 118no Wide 11
28Feb67-10Hia fm 1⅛ Ⓣ 1.50⅕ Clm 12500 8 4 46½ 45½ 42½ 21 HGustines b 112 26.90 90-10 DoubtingThomas 1161 GanelonII 112½ OfficerSweeney 1181 Gamely 11
16Feb67-10Hia fm*1 3/16 Ⓣ 2.01 Clm 11500 5 7 711 1112 910 715 MYcaza b 114 28.30 62-21 Officer Sweeney 1161½ Punisher 109½ Concession 1075 No speed 12
7Jly 66-9Aqu hd 1⅛ Ⓣ 1.48⅘ Allowance 3 7 814 819 55¾ 512 MYcaza b 123 12.20 79-13 Your Prince 118¾ Hardihood 1202½ Annette's Ark 1184 No speed 9
1Jly 66-7WO fst 1⅛.46⅕1.10⅖1.48⅘ DomDayH 4 6 611 413 515 518 SMcComb b 114 24.85 81-12 Victorian Era 1263 E. Day 1169¼ Chancero 1154½ Raced evenly 6
22Jun66-8Del fm 1 Ⓣ 1.38⅕ Allowance 8 10 1013 94¾ 87½ 69½ RMikkonen b 124 17.00 74-16 Tout Royal 124¾ Island Stream 124h Final Approach 1147 No threat 10
16Jun66-8Aqu fm 1⅛ Ⓣ 1.50⅗ Allowance 11 9 1120 1120 97½ 107 MYcaza b 118 9.30 75-18 Fleet Musketeer 1201 Nashwood 1062 Annette's Ark 118h Off slow 12
4Sep65-7FE fm 1⅜ TC 1.13 2.20 NiagaraHp 5 7 713 56½ 411 57¼ JLeBlanc b 116 11.75 78-15 Quick Pitch 120h Blue Sol 1113¾ Uncle Blue 1133½ Never prominent 9
23Aug65-6Sar fm 1⅛ TC 1.50⅗ Allowance 6 6 54½ 63½ 61¾ 2no BBaeza b 119 3.40 80-20 Mostar117no Ganelon II 119no Tabeeb1141½ In close, just missed 7
16Aug65-8Sar fm 1⅛ TC 1.49 Allowance 7 7 64 57½ 43½ 32¾ BBaeza b 119 9.70e 85-12 Lancastrian 117¾ Burned Up 1222 Ganelon II 119nk Closed fast 9
LATEST WORKOUTS Jun 7 Bel 4f fst .50⅕ b May 11 Bel tr.t. 4f fst .52⅖ b

Emerald Lake * **$14,500** Dk. b. or br. c (1963–Fla), by Beau Gar—Lake Garda, by Turn-to **118** 1967 10 1 3 0 $9,605
L. Silver T. J. Gullo (Hobeau Farm, Inc.) 1966 16 2 2 3 $10,745
1Jun67-9Aqu fst 1⅛.49⅕1.13⅕1.50⅘ Clm 12500 4 1 13 13 13 13½ JGiovanni 116 6.40 82-15 Emerald Lake 1163½ Spartanburg 1142½ Your Prince 116nk Easily 6
26May67-6Aqu my 1 .47⅗1.13 1.37⅘ Clm 14000 5 1 33 511 516 628 JGiovanni b 112 4.50 51-26 Koh-I-Noor 1182 Needles' Count 1194 Ganelon II 1101½ Stopped 6
12May67-4Aqu sl 1⅛.47⅖1.13⅕1.52 Clm 15000 4 2 32 52 47 416 BBaeza b 116 *1.40 60-26 Demigod 115¾ Needles' Count 1145 Sir Sanford 11410 No excuse 5
3May67-8Aqu fst 1 .46⅘1.12 1.38 Clm 15000 4 4 56 58 42½ 42¾ BBaeza 116 *1.30 75-21 Demigod 114¾ Needles' Count 1171½ Koh-I-Noor 122½ Bid, hung 7
25Apr67-6Aqu sl 1 .47⅖1.12⅘1.38 Clm 16000 1 6 55 44 22 2nk BBaeza 116 2.80 78-28 Koh-I-Noor 116nk Emerald Lake 1166 Demigod 113nk Sharp try 8
29Mar67-8Aqu my 1 .49⅕1.15⅗1.41⅖ Clm 15000 4 5 2½ 3½ 21 2¾ MCariglio5 111 6.60 60-33 Corredor II 117¾ Emerald Lake 111½ Direct Action 1121½ Sharp 10
25Mar67-8Aqu my 6f .23⅕ .48⅖1.14 Allowance 3 7 714 715 615 58½ MCariglio5 118 12.10 64-35 Mister Pitt's Kid 1132½ Dandy Steal 1123 Disembark 121no Slow st. 7
11Mar67-6GP fm 1 1/16 Ⓣ 1.11 1.41⅘ Clm 18000 2 6 612 67 714 714 LMoyers 116 8.40 81-11 VoluntarioIII112¾ FlamingTriumph1122½ AdmiralClove1163 No sp'd 9
27Feb67-10Hia fm 1⅛ Ⓣ 1.50⅕ Clm 18000 5 8 811 74½ 54½ 24½ ECardone 112 13.20 86-10 Top Victory 1164½ Emerald Lake 112h Loopy Loop 1163½ Rallied 8
23Jan67-9Hia sly 7f .23⅗ .47 1.25⅕ Allowance 4 3 31½ 32 69½ 713 WBoland 119 *0.90e 70-19 Saeharf 118½ Beau Legs 113no Wondrascope 1132 Brief foot 7
9Dec66-6Aqu fst 7f .22⅖ .45⅘1.23⅘ Clm 18000 1 3 22 45 69 56½ ECardone5 115 *0.80e 80-20 The Cheat 1141 There Goes Sam 118h Royal Harbinger 1192 Tired 8
1Dec66-6Aqu fst 7f .23 .46 1.24⅖ Allowance 7 1 43¼ 41½ 1h 2no JRuane 122 1.90e 84-23 It's Blitz 117no Emerald Lake 1223 ♦Solemn Nation 1153 Wide 7
LATEST WORKOUTS May 23 Bel tr.t. 4f fst .49⅗ h May 18 Bel tr.t. 4f fst .48⅗ h Apr 12 Bel tr.t. 3f fst .38⅖ b

Demigod * **$14,000** B. g (1961), by Gallant Man—Plotter, by Double Jay **116** 1967 9 2 0 1 $11,450
J. R. Daly P. A. Healy (L. Combs 2d-Mrs. J. M. Olin) 1966 24 4 2 3 $22,975
1Jun67-8Aqu fm 1 1/16 Ⓣ 1.43⅕ Clm 18000 9 10 1020 1017 1015 1021 WBoland 116 5.00 69-10 Primarosa II 1151 Cleareye 116nk Good Ore 111nk Not a contender 10
12May67-4Aqu sl 1⅛.47⅖1.13⅕1.52 Clm 14000 3 5 59 2½ 1½ 1¾ WBoland 115 3.00 76-26 Demigod 115¾ Needles' Count 1145 Sir Sanford 11410 Driving 5
3May67-8Aqu fst 1 .46⅘1.12 1.38 Clm 14500 7 3 34 33 32½ 1¾ WBoland 114 9.00 78-21 Demigod 114¾ Needles' Count 1171½ Koh-I-Noor 122½ Brisk drive 7
25Apr67-6Aqu sl 1 .47⅖1.12⅘1.38 Clm 15000 3 8 77 66½ 47 36¼ WBoland 113 8.50 72-28 Koh-I-Noor 116nk Emerald Lake 1166 Demigod 113nk Mild bid 8
29Mar67-8Aqu my 1 .49⅕1.15⅗1.41⅖ Clm 14000 10 9 107 54 43½ 42¾ ATCordero 112 17.20 58-33 Corredor II 117¾ Emerald Lake 111½ Direct Action 1121½ Rallied 10
16Feb67-10Hia fm*1 3/16 Ⓣ 2.01 Clm 11500 12 12 1227 1224 1221 1225 MCarrozzella 114 136.30 52-21 Officer Sweeney 1161½ Punisher 109½ Concession 1075 No speed 12
1Feb67-7Hia fm 1 1/16 Ⓣ 1.45⅗ Clm 13000 11 12 1225 1227 1228 1227 MCarrozzella 114 78.60 51-28 Brant 114no The Clown 1162 Bursun 1161½ Trailed thruout 12
21Jan67-10Hia my 1⅛.47⅗1.12⅗1.51⅗ Clm 12500 2 10 1028 924 818 820 MCarrozzella 116 10.10 57-20 CountDormal 1163½ ListenToReason 1183½ CoolOasis 116½ No speed 10
18Jan67-5Hia fst 7f .23⅗ .46⅗1.24⅕ Clm 15000 9 11 1118 1119 1020 1018 BBaeza 114 16.80 70-12 O Lady O 107¾ Inclusive 1174 Prince Graff 1223 Never close 11
5Dec66-9Aqu fst 1⅛.47⅗1.12⅗1.51⅘ Clm 16000 5 9 919 917 817 712 LPincayJr 114 6.80 65-19 Big Shot 1112½ Fleet Musketeer 1162½ High Bluff 105½ No speed 9
21Nov66-9Aqu fst 1⅛.48⅕1.12⅘1.50⅘ Clm 15000 3 7 714 715 715 616 LPincayJr 118 5.90 66-20 Nashaweena 1044 Enfant Terrible 1161¼ Cool Oasis 1064 No speed 7
14Nov66-8Aqu fst 1⅛.49⅘1.13⅘1.51⅘ Clm 18000 2 4 45½ 67½ 4¾ 33 LPincayJr 112 6.80 74-22 Dark Alloy 1141½ Naturalist 1161½ Demigod 112no Mild bid 6
LATEST WORKOUTS Jun 8 Bel tr.t. 4f fst .49⅖ h May 30 Bel tr.t. 5f fst 1.02⅗ b May 20 Bel tr.t. 4f fst .50 h May 10 Bel tr.t. 6f fst 1.19 b

Wondrascope **$15,000** Dk. b. or br. h (1962), by Helioscope—Native Sarong, by Native Dancer **120**
De Cap Stable R. Desmarais (Helis Stock Farm)

1967	16	0	0	5	$3,500
1966	13	2	3	0	$6,840

1Jun67-6Aqu	fm	1 1/16 Ⓣ	1.43⅕	Clm	18000	8	9	9^{11}	$7^{5\frac14}$	$6^{5\frac14}$	$5^{7\frac12}$	BFeliciano	b 116	9.20	82–10	Koh-I-Noor 116^{5} Solemn Nation $116^{\frac12}$ Shady Living 120^{2}	No threat 9
25May67-6Aqu	sl	1⅛	.49⅖ 1.14⅕ 1.51	Allowance		2	5	$7^{7\frac12}$	8^{11}	8^{15}	8^{19}	BFeliciano	b 120	56.30	62–24	Prinkipo $113^{2\frac12}$ Royal Comedian 113^{2} Fort Marcy 110^{2}	Far back 8
2May67-7Aqu	fst	1⅛	.48⅕ 1.12⅘ 1.49⅘	Allowance		6	3	3^{5}	$3^{4\frac12}$	$5^{7\frac12}$	5^{16}	BFeliciano	b 115	56.50	71–18	Sette Bello 116^{7} Bol 'N Jac $122^{4\frac12}$ Fast Count 115^{3}	Weakened 9
27Apr67-6Aqu	sly	1⅛	.48 1.14⅘ 1.54⅗	Allowance		5	6	6^{14}	7^{13}	7^{16}	7^{20}	HGustines	b 120	13.20	43–34	Wowzer 113^{2} Tom Poker $113^{\frac34}$ Solemn Nation 123^{2}	Never close 7
22Apr67-8Suf	gd	1	.46⅗ 1.11⅕ 1.37⅕	Allowance		5	9	9^{14}	9^{12}	7^{7}	6^{12}	TDunlavy	b 113	6.20	79–17	Rabbit's Foot 119^{h} Richmond Grays $112^{1\frac14}$ Fusion III 112^{6}	Slow start 9
4Apr67-6Aqu	fst	7f	.23 .46 1.23⅘	Clm	c35000	1	6	7^{13}	6^{13}	6^{17}	6^{21}	ATCordero	b 117	33.40	66–21	It's Blitz $115^{1\frac12}$ Auric $113^{\frac34}$ Sheet Anchor $115^{\frac34}$	Forced up 7
30Mar67-7Aqu	sl	1	.47⅖ 1.12⅖ 1.38⅖	Allowance		3	5	$5^{4\frac12}$	6^{10}	6^{13}	5^{10}	JLRotz	b 121	13.90	66–33	Primo Theo 115^{2} Tom Poker $121^{\frac12}$ Fort Marcy 110^{7}	No mishap 6
24Mar67-8Aqu	my	7f	.24 .48⅖ 1.28⅕	Allowance		3	5	$5^{8\frac12}$	6^{16}	6^{19}	6^{19}	JLRotz	b 121	6.30	46–46	Mimado II $123^{\frac34}$ Tom Poker $121^{1\frac12}$ Air Rights 112^{10}	Far back 6
1Mar67-7Hia	fm	1 1/16 Ⓣ	1.42⅗	Clm	40000	12	9	10^{15}	8^{9}	$6^{6\frac12}$	3^{nk}	JLRotz	b 114	41.40	92–14	Tom Poker 112no Round Table Pet 113^{nk} Wondrascope $114^{1\frac14}$	Gaining 12
24Feb67-7Hia	fst	7f	.23⅕ .46⅕ 1.23⅖	Allowance		7	4	$6^{7\frac14}$	6^{8}	$5^{8\frac14}$	$3^{9\frac14}$	HGustines	b 113	49.90	83–15	Irongate $121^{1\frac14}$ Tom Poker 113^{8} Wondrascope $113^{1\frac12}$	Rallied 12

LATEST WORKOUTS Jun 8 Aqu 3f fst .37⅕ b Jun 3 Mth 5f fst 1.03⅗ bg May 31 Aqu 3f fst .37⅘ b May 24 Aqu 3f fst .37 b

Birdsofafeather **$14,000** B. g (1963-Ky), by Nadir—Sunny Liege, by Heliopolis **116**
Windham Farm E. W. King (Danada Farm)

1967	12	2	2	2	$12,395
1966	6	1	0	2	$3,570

31May67-8Aqu	fst	1⅛	.47⅘ 1.12⅘ 1.51⅗	Cl	c-8500	1	1	$1^{\frac12}$	$2^{\frac12}$	2^{1}	2^{h}	RUssery	b 119	*1.50	78–19	Sir Sanford 119^{h} Birdsofafeather 119^{5} Razonable $116^{\frac12}$	Came again 8
24May67-9Aqu	fst	1⅛	.47⅘ 1.12⅗ 1.51⅖	Clm	9000	3	1	$1^{\frac12}$	$2^{1\frac12}$	$3^{1\frac12}$	$2^{\frac12}$	HGustines	b 115	♦5.40	78–18	Sir Sanford $116^{\frac12}$ ♦Birdsofafeather 115^{4} ♦Bent Spur 116^{4}	Gamely 7
24May67—♦-Dead heat.																	
16May67-9Aqu	gd	1⅛	.46⅘ 1.11⅘ 1.52⅖	Clm	8250	6	1	$1^{\frac12}$	$1^{\frac12}$	1^{2}	1^{1}	RUssery	b 116	4.60	74–22	Birdsofafeather 116^{1} Bent Spur 116^{5} Winter Joy 116^{1}	Driving 8
11May67-3Aqu	fst	1⅛	.48⅖ 1.12⅗ 1.52⅕	Cl	c-6500	1	1	$1^{\frac12}$	1^{2}	1^{2}	$1^{1\frac12}$	JLRotz	b 116	4.20	75–21	Birdsofafeather $116^{1\frac12}$ Ruperto $114^{1\frac12}$ Sudden Storm $109^{\frac34}$	Driving 8
3May67-9Aqu	fst	1⅛	.48 1.12⅘ 1.51	Clm	8000	8	2	2^{2}	$5^{4\frac12}$	5^{9}	5^{17}	JLRotz	b 116	22.70	64–21	Pomidoro $116^{1\frac12}$ Gray Prince $114^{\frac12}$ Portfolio 117^{12}	Fell back 9
26Apr67-2Aqu	fst	1	.45⅘ 1.11⅕ 1.38⅕	Clm	8500	6	2	$3^{2\frac12}$	$4^{2\frac12}$	$3^{1\frac12}$	$4^{4\frac12}$	RTurcotte	b 116	3.50	72–17	Ronnie's Rebel 112^{1} Florida Scheme 118^{3} Sum Farce $122^{\frac12}$	Weak'd 8
17Apr67-2Aqu	fst	6f	.22⅗ .45⅖ 1.11	Clm	8000	1	3	$4^{5\frac12}$	$4^{6\frac12}$	3^{6}	$3^{4\frac12}$	RTurcotte	b 117	9.00	83–14	MasterCoosaw 117^{2} MisterJudge $119^{2\frac12}$ Birdsofafeather 117^{4}	Evenly 7
11Apr67-8Aqu	fst	6f	.23⅖ .47⅗ 1.12⅘	Clm	6500	4	6	7^{7}	6^{8}	$6^{7\frac12}$	3^{6}	RTurcotte	b 117	5.40	73–27	Hamorton $115^{2\frac12}$ Raider Radka $117^{3\frac12}$ Birdsofafeather 117^{1}	Rallied 11
11Feb67-2SA	fst	6f	.22 .45⅕ 1.10⅗	Clm	9000	6	8	$9^{6\frac34}$	$8^{6\frac12}$	$7^{9\frac12}$	$7^{8\frac34}$	WBlum	b 113	27.40	80–12	Rulark 116no Dear Bill 122no SquadLeader $117^{3\frac12}$	No apparent mishap 12
28Jan67-2SA	fst	6f	.22⅕ .45⅗ 1.11	Clm	10000	2	12	$11^{9\frac14}$	11^{11}	11^{10}	$9^{8\frac14}$	MValenzuela	117	25.10	79–15	Spy Fox 113^{3} Knight Prowler $118^{\frac12}$ Royal French 117^{h}	No speed 12
18Jan67-7SA	fm	1⅛ Ⓣ	1.11 1.48	Allowance		1	3	$5^{2\frac12}$	12^{11}	12^{17}	12^{19}	MValenzuela	113	237.10	74– 7	♦Flit-To 119^{7} ♦Model Fool 115^{7} Traveling Dust 116^{2}	Tired 12
10Jan67-9SA	fst	1 1/16	.47 1.11⅗ 1.43⅗	Clm	17500	7	5	$6^{6\frac12}$	12^{11}	12^{14}	12^{13}	BBaeza	b 116	27.90	72–16	Grand Slam Mike 115^{h} Off The Top 122no Beau Masque 122^{4}	No sp'd 12

LATEST WORKOUTS Jun 6 Bel tr.t. 5f fst 1.06 b Jun 3 Bel tr.t. 4f fst .50 h Apr 25 Bel tr.t. 3f gd .36⅖ h

Needles' Count * **$15,000** Br. g (1962), by Needles—Countess Tecla, by Count Fleet **120**
Aisco Stable F. H. Merrill (J. C. Dudley-B. M. Heath)

1967	9	2	3	2	$13,050
1966	15	2	1	2	$10,615

26May67-6Aqu	my	1	.47⅗ 1.13 1.37⅘	Clm	15000	3	5	5^{7}	$4^{4\frac12}$	3^{3}	2^{2}	RTurcotte	119	2.30	77–26	Koh-I-Noor 118^{2} Needles' Count 119^{4} Ganelon II $110^{1\frac12}$	Gamely 6
12May67-4Aqu	sl	1⅛	.47⅖ 1.13⅕ 1.52	Clm	15000	2	4	4^{7}	$4^{1\frac12}$	3^{2}	$2^{\frac34}$	RSurrency5	114	2.90	75–26	Demigod $115^{\frac34}$ Needles' Count 114^{5} Sir Sanford 114^{10}	Gamely 5
3May67-8Aqu	fst	1	.46⅘ 1.12 1.38	Clm	15000	2	6	4^{5}	4^{4}	$1^{\frac12}$	$2^{\frac34}$	RSurrency5	117	6.40	77–21	Demigod $114^{\frac34}$ Needles' Count $117^{1\frac12}$ Koh-I-Noor $122^{\frac12}$	Couldn't last 7
25Apr67-6Aqu	sl	1	.47⅖ 1.12⅘ 1.38	Clm	16000	5	7	6^{6}	$5^{5\frac12}$	$5^{7\frac12}$	$4^{6\frac12}$	RTurcotte	116	3.10	71–28	Koh-I-Noor 116^{nk} Emerald Lake 116^{6} Demigod 113^{nk}	No mishap 8
27Mar67-6Aqu	sl	1	.47⅗ 1.13⅕ 1.38⅖	Clm	18000	2	7	7^{11}	$5^{6\frac12}$	$4^{7\frac12}$	$3^{6\frac12}$	RTurcotte	112	6.70	69–31	Sheet Anchor $116^{4\frac12}$ Off The Top 112^{2} Needles' Count 112no	Rallied 7
14Mar67-6Aqu	fst	1	.46⅗ 1.12⅕ 1.37⅗	Clm	12500	5	5	6^{14}	4^{6}	1^{h}	$1^{1\frac14}$	RTurcotte	119	6.70	80–22	Needles' Count $119^{1\frac14}$ Naturalist $114^{1\frac12}$ Rocky Ford $114^{3\frac12}$	Driving 8
4Mar67-4GP	fst	1 1/16	.47⅗ 1.11⅘ 1.44⅗	Clm	12500	2	3	$3^{4\frac12}$	2^{3}	2^{3}	$3^{2\frac12}$	FToro	118	2.90	82–10	Red Redeemer $112^{2\frac12}$ Uncle Beau 116no Needles' Count $118^{3\frac12}$	Hung 8
23Feb67-5Hia	gd	1 1/16	.47⅕ 1.11⅘ 1.43⅗	Clm	15500	8	4	$5^{6\frac12}$	$6^{5\frac34}$	4^{5}	$4^{8\frac14}$	FToro	114	17.20	77–20	One Night Stand $116^{4\frac34}$ Count Bell $116^{2\frac34}$ The Clown $114^{\frac34}$	Evenly 8
9Feb67-10Hia	sly	1⅛	.46⅘ 1.12⅕ 1.51⅘	Clm	10000	3	4	$4^{5\frac12}$	$3^{1\frac12}$	$1^{1\frac12}$	1^{nk}	FToro	116	*2.10	76–17	Needles' Count 116^{nk} Pinchers Pride 116^{5} Tulran 116^{3}	Driving 8
24Nov66-6TrP	fst	170	.46⅗ 1.11 1.40⅘	Clm	10000	1	8	6^{4}	$5^{3\frac12}$	$5^{4\frac14}$	$6^{5\frac34}$	FToro	119	*1.90	87– 9	Skeg $114^{2\frac14}$ Coralies Boy $119^{2\frac14}$ Popetrenea $114^{\frac34}$	Lacked response 10
19Nov66-8TrP	fst	170	.46⅗ 1.12 1.42⅕	Allowance		11	7	11^{10}	$10^{6\frac12}$	$5^{3\frac12}$	$7^{6\frac14}$	MNGonzalez	122	5.80	80–14	Clatterbox 119no Saeharf $114^{2\frac12}$ Jet Charger $117^{1\frac12}$	Never close 12
2Nov66-8Spt	fst	1⅛	.47⅘ 1.13⅗ 1.51⅗	Allowance		4	3	3^{2}	3^{1}	1^{2}	1^{2}	FToro	117	4.60	90–15	Needles' Count 117^{2} Chickasaw 114^{3} The Dancer 114^{h}	Under drive 5

LATEST WORKOUTS Jun 2 Bel tr.t. 1m fst 1.45 h May 25 Bel tr.t. 3f fst .39⅖ b May 20 Bel 1m fst 1.44 b May 11 Bel tr.t. 3f fst .36 h

Solemn Nation: Moves down another notch after a respectable try on the grass eight days ago. On May 2, ran second in a slow allowance race at today's distance on a sloppy track. The entire record is of a horse that can't take a hard track. Needs mud or slop or grass. If the feet hurt in allowance company, they will feel no better at a $15,000 claiming price, and the horse's lack of early speed will hamper it as much here as in the better races. NO BET.

Ganelon II: A longshot winner at this distance in April, after being on the shelf for a month, this six-year-old then returned to idleness for an additional six weeks. Its last effort, in mud, was not at all bad, but was not surprising for a confirmed grass runner. Suspicions about the animal's ability to hold up in fast company on a fast track is not really dispelled by the one narrow victory under 109 pounds. NO BET.

Emerald Lake: Here we go again. Ran off and hid on June 1, racing exactly as the figures predicted. Should do equally well today—but only if the pace is favorable again. CONTENDER.

Demigod. This is the one that beat Emerald Lake on May 12. Healy put it into a turf race on June 1, probably for laughs, because the gelding always finishes last on the grass. The fresh air, sunshine, and mild exercise of that race, combined with three workouts since the May 12 triumph, should have left the horse in good trim. CONTENDER.

Wondrascope: Has been running poor races against good horses. Today's drop in class is long overdue, but I see no reason to expect a victory. For all anyone knows, the horse may be unable to beat $10,000 ones. Until it shows a flash of speed in a race, we'll never know where it belongs. NO BET.

Birdsofafeather: Stablemate of Solemn Nation is far out of its class today but is bound to uncork enough early speed to guarantee problems for Emerald Lake and victory for a horse that comes on in the stretch. NO BET.

Needles' Count: A nice, steady sort, as its earnings show. In shape, it would have a good chance against today's field. But I prefer to downgrade it on grounds of form. Those tough stretch drives in its three latest races must have taken something out of the animal. NO BET.

The contenders are Emerald Lake and Demigod. The early speed of Birdsofafeather practically guarantees that Emerald Lake will have less than the necessary energy for the stretch drive. Demigod looks as close to a mortal cinch as one finds at a race track.

The Running of the Race

THE CROWD made Demigod a 2–1 favorite probably because of the recent victory over Emerald Lake and the slight but apparent edge in class. Emerald Lake had his supporters, however, and went at slightly better than 5–2. The race followed the blueprint, with Emerald Lake trying to catch Birdsofafeather and succeeding, but being overtaken and outfooted by the fast-closing Demigod. Ganelon and Needles' Count were both catching Emerald Lake at the wire.

FOURTH RACE 1 1-8 MILES (Sinatra, December 7, 1964, 1.47⅕, 5, 111.)

Aqu - 31367
June 9 1967

Claiming. Purse $8,500. 3-year-olds and upward. Weights 3-year-olds 114 lbs., older 123 lbs. Non-winners of a race at a mile and a furlong or over since April 20 allowed 3 lbs. Claiming price $15,000. 2 lbs. allowed for each $500 to $14,000. (Races when entered to be claimed for $12,000 or less not considered.)

Value to winner $5,525, second $1,700, third two $637.50 each. Mutuel pool $319,935.

Index	Horse	Eqt	A	Wt	PP	St	¼	½	¾	Str	Fin	Jockey	Cl'g Pr	Owner	Odds $1
31308Aqu^{10}	Demigod		6	116	4	6	5^{2}	5^{4}	4^{1}	1^{h}	$1^{1\frac{1}{2}}$	W Boland	14000	J R Daly	2.00
31309Aqu^{1}	Emerald Lake		4	118	3	2	2^{4}	2^{1}	2^{3}	$2^{\frac{1}{2}}$	2^{nk}	J Giovanni	14500	L Silver	2.70
31204Aqu^{3}	DH Ganelon II	b	6	116	2	4	4^{4}	3^{2}	$3^{\frac{1}{2}}$	$3^{\frac{1}{2}}$	3	A Cordero Jr	14000	Mrs A A Fiore	DH-9.20
31204Aqu^{2}	DH N'dles' Count		5	120	7	7	6^{2}	6^{h}	6^{1}	5^{2}	3^{4}	R Turcotte	15000	Aisco Stable	DH-3.90
31242Aqu^{2}	Birdsofaf'ther	b	4	116	6	3	1^{3}	$1^{\frac{1}{2}}$	$1^{\frac{1}{2}}$	4^{3}	5^{1}	A DeSpirito	14000	Windham Farm	a-3.20
31306Aqu^{2}	Solemn Nation	b	4	120	1	1	3^{1}	4^{1}	5^{3}	6^{2}	$6^{2\frac{1}{2}}$	E Belmonte	15000	Windham Farm	a-3.20
31306Aqu^{5}	Wondrascope	b	5	120	5	5	7	7	7	7	7	B Feliciano	15000	Decap Stable	16.80

a-Coupled, Birdsofafeather and Solemn Nation. DH Dead heat.

Time .24⅕, .48⅖, 1.12⅕, 1.38, 1.51⅗ (with wind in backstretch). Track fast.

$2 Mutuel Prices:

4-DEMIGOD	6.00	3.40	2.40
3-EMERALD LAKE		4.20	2.60
2 DH-GANELON II			2.40
6 DH-NEEDLES' COUNT			2.20

B. g, by Gallant Man—Plotter, by Double Jay. Trainer P. A. Healy. Bred by L. Combs 2d–Mrs. J. M. Olin.

IN GATE AT 3.06. OFF AT 3.06 EASTERN DAYLIGHT TIME. Start good. Won driving.

DEMIGOD, in hand until near the stretch, took command before reaching midstretch and retained a safe margin while under brisk handling. EMERALD LAKE, well placed from the start, reached the front between calls in the upper stretch but was unable to stay with DEMIGOD. GANELON II saved ground and had no mishap but was under pressure during the late stages to dead heat with NEEDLES' COUNT for third. NEEDLES' COUNT outrun for three-quarters closed gamely and finished on equal terms with GANELON II. BIRDSOFAFEATHER set the pace until reaching the stretch and weakened. SOLEMN NATION was finished early. WONDRASCOPE showed nothing.

Needles' Count was claimed by Mrs. C. D. Morgan, trainer V. J. Cincotta.

12. SECOND AT AQUEDUCT, JULY 21, 1967—Track Fast

ANYBODY WHO DOESN'T zero in on the contenders in this sprint has not been paying attention. It is for fillies and mares whose owners think they are worth from $7,000 to $8,000.

2nd Race Aqueduct — 6 FURLONGS AQUEDUCT (Start / Finish)

6 FURLONGS. (Near Man, July 17, 1963, 1.08⅗, 3, 112.)
Claiming. Purse $5,800. Fillies and mares. 3-year-olds and upward. Weights, 3-year-olds 116 lbs., older 123 lbs. Non-winners of two races since May 31 allowed 3 lbs., of a race since July 1, 5 lbs. Claiming price, $8,000. 2 lbs. allowed for each $500 to $7,000. (Races when entered to be claimed for $6,000 or less not considered.)

***Tejuela *** $8,000 Ch. f (1963), by Branding—Rejuela, by Rustic
B. C. Brittingham W. H. Dixon (Haras El Pelado) (Arg) **118** 1967 11 2 4 2 $9,930 / 1966 19 1 1 6 $6,190
10Jly 67-3Del fst 6f .22⅖ .46 1.11⅘ Clm 8000 4 4 42 54¾ 54 23 FToro 112 2.80 83-16 Ariel Road 1153 Tejuela 1121½ Tabitha 117¾ Best of rest 7
26Jun67-6Del fst 6f .22⅕ .46⅕1.12⅖ Clm 9250 4 2 51¾ 32 21½ 31½ ORosado b 111 5.30 81-22 Bellagio 119½ Warming Up 1161 Tejuela 1115 Well up, hung 7
13Jun67-7Del fst 6f .23⅕ .46⅗1.12 Clm 8500 5 4 32 23 24½ 35 ORosado b 116 *1.40 80-20 Little Blackjack 1173½ Warming Up 1151½ Tejuela 1161½ Bid, tired 7
23May67-6Aqu fst 6f .22⅖ .46⅕1.12 f- 8500 4 10 54½ 53 3½ 2no ACorderoJr b 116 11.20 83-20 Storm Brewing 118no Tejuela 116h Trinket 1111 Nosed out 11
15May67-5Aqu fst 6f .22⅕ .45⅗1.11⅕ f- 9000 2 fog 57 511 ACorderoJr b 112 4.60 76-13 Fennel 1164 Storm Brewing 116h Trinket 1051½ No rally 10
4Apr67-8Aqu fst 6f .22⅖ .46 1.12⅕ f- c-6750 6 7 83¾ 64 31 21½ MYcaza b 121 *2.00 80-21 Deep Clover 1071½ Tejuela 121¾ Lucky Shirl 1131 Game try 10
28Mar67-2Aqu gd 6f .23⅕ .47⅗1.13⅕ f- 7000 7 3 11 11 1h 2nk MYcaza b 118 *1.40 77-26 BushyTail 116nk Tejuela1185½ NormaMathews1164 Bumped, crowded 7
24Mar67-3Aqu my 6f .23⅗ .49⅖1.17⅕ f- 6250 6 2 2h 14 15 14 MYcaza b 116 *1.50 57-46 Tejuela 1164 Sea Moon 1162 Fleet Impelled 1182½ Handily 6
15Mar67-3Aqu gd 6f .23⅖ .47⅘1.13 f- 5000 5 6 52½ 3½ 12 12½ MYcaza b 116 3.00 78-21 Tejuela 1162½ Infinita 113½ Noureige 1164 Under mild drive 7
LATEST WORKOUTS Jly 18 Del 4f fst .49 b Jly 8 Del 4f fst .50 b Jly 4 Del 4f fst .51 b Jun 23 Del 6f sly 1.20 b

Yankeenesian $8,000 Dk. b. or br. f (1963-Del), by Boston Doge—Deanesian, by Polynesian
J. J. Amriati R. P. Lake (Marydel Farm) **108**10 1967 1 0 0 0 $275 / 1966 21 3 7 1 $18.040
14Jly 67-9Aqu fst 6f .22⅖ .45⅘1.11⅗ f- 6250 8 2 3nk 2½ 2½ 45¼ ECardone b 118 16.00 80-20 Kitty Quick 1183½ Wiltare 1111½ Everything Roses 116nk Tired 13
21Oct66-2GS fst 6f .22⅗ .46 1.11⅘ f- 6250 2 7 45¼ 37 55¾ 67¼ EFires b 116 *1.60 78-16 Infinita 1202¾ General Note 118½ Beau Mink 1181½ Dull effort 10
14Oct66-4GS fst 6f .22⅖ .45⅗1.11⅖ f- 6ᴇ00 3 3 32 24 22 22 RCox b 111 2.50 85-13 John's Nell 1162 Yankeenesian 111nk General Note 1091 Gamely 9
15Sep66-5Aqu gd 6f .23 .47⅖1.14⅖ f- 10500 3 3 22½ 21½ 22 57¾ EFires b 117 13.20 63-30 d-Stowe 116no Gem's Reward 118nk Court Hostess 1145 Used up 6
1Sep66-3Aqu fst 7f .23⅗ .47⅗1.26 f- c-7500 6 5 54½ 33 33 58½ CMcPeek5 b 116 2.90 67-25 Fancy Bolero 1167 Career Lady 113no Her Grace 1121 Weakened 8
18Aug66-6Sar fst 6f .22⅗ .46⅗1.12⅖ f- 9000 2 6 64¾ 65¾ 74 35 ECardone5 b 114 *2.50 81-16 Air Whirl 1165 Runnin' Rose 114no Yankeenesian 114h Rallied 9
5Aug66-3Sar fst 6f .22⅘ .46⅘1.12⅘ f- 10000 2 6 54 51½ 2h 1h ECardone5 b 116 7.00 84-12 Yankeenesian 116h Federal Princess 1072 Stowe 116no Just up 8
29Jly 66-8Aqu fst 6f .22⅘ .46⅖1.12 f- 9000 8 7 65¼ 43½ 22 1nk ECardone5 b 109 9.30 83-17 Yankeenesian 109nk Trinket 1143½ Sweep Past 1182 Driving 9
21Jly 66-6Aqu fst 6f .22⅘ .45⅘1.11⅖ f- 12500 9 6 63 64¾ 75½ 710 ECardone5 b 113 9.30 76-21 Whiglet 1191½ Last Act 118h Stowe 111½ Not a contender 9
LATEST WORKOUTS Jly 13 Aqu 3f fst .39⅘ b Jly 8 Aqu 6f fst 1.15 h Jly 3 Aqu 7f sly 1.33 bg Jun 28 Aqu 5f fst 1.05⅗ b

Native Twin $8,000 Ch. m (1962), by Alternative—Twinette, by Alerted
J. A. Bolha J. Lipari (A. P. Bovello) **118** 1967 3 1 0 2 $5.700 / 1966 24 4 4 2 $18,220
12Jly 67-5Aqu fst 7f .22⅗ .45⅘1.24⅕ f- 9500 1 12 86 78¼ 54 65 EBelmonte b 116 8.30 80-13 Her Favourite 114no Zeesa Adelle 114½ Nix 1133½ Sluggish start 13
5Jly 67-3Aqu gd 1 .47 1.12⅘1.38⅕ Clm 10000 4 1 3½ 3½ 34 58 LAdams b 113 7.80 69-21 Lochoir 1181 Bigamo 1143½ McGun 114½ Drifted out 8
28Jun67-8Aqu fst 7f .22⅘ .45⅘1.25⅕ f- 9500 3 3 41½ 56 66¾ 42¼ EBelmonte b 118 5.20 78-17 Nix 111¾ Her Favourite 114no Sound Tract 1181½ Unruly, mild rally 11
6Jun67-5Aqu fst 6f .22⅕ .46⅕1.11⅖ f- 10000 4 4 42½ 32 43 35 JLRotz b 120 6.80 81-14 Zayer Naytik 1163½ Savannalamar 1181½ Native Twin 120nk Evenly 9
4May67-8Aqu fst 7f .22⅖ .45 1.24⅗ f- 12500 8 4 55 68 65½ 44¾ EBelmonte b 120 5.40 78-20 Needles Sword 118¾ Sound Tract 1123 Savannalamar 1141 Wide 10
21Apr67-8Aqu fst 7f .22⅘ .45⅘1.25⅗ f- 10000 3 4 34½ 46 33½ 1½ EBelmonte b 118 *2.00 78-22 Native Twin 118½ Lucky Shirl 112¾ Andros Isle 1124 In time 7
31Jan67-5Hia fst 7f .23⅕ .46⅖1.24⅗ f- 13000 6 3 1½ 2½ 2½ 31½ BBaeza b 116 4.50 84-16 Ship Shoal 116¾ Navy Heroine 112¾ Native Twin 1163 Weakened 12
6Jan67-6TrP fst 6f .22⅕ .44⅗1.09 Allowance 2 3 42½ 55½ 68¾ 57½ ATCordero b 115 24.10 89-12 Zipperpedium 1202 Fleet Admiral 1155 Cleareye 115no Tired 8
28Dec66-8TrP fst 6f .22⅖ .45 1.10 f- Allow 5 9 83¾ 85 97 55 RSurrency5 b 115 14.30 87-14 Zamilu 113¾ Rare Feather 115h Fizzy 1132¾ Raced very wide 12
LATEST WORKOUTS Jun 27 Bel tr.t. 3f fst .35⅘ h Jun 3 Bel tr.t. 5f fst 1.03 h

Gem's Reward $8,000 B. f (1963-Ky), by Armageddon—Dot's Gem, by Royal Gem II
Mrs. J. C. Silverman S. R. Shapoff (Mrs. J. C. Silverman) **118** 1967 3 0 0 0 —— / 1966 19 2 0 2 $7,405
12Jly 67-5Aqu fst 7f .22⅗ .45⅘1.24⅕ f- 9000 13 1 11 1h 33 96½ ECardone b 114 33.60f 78-13 Her Favourite 114no Zeesa Adelle 114½ Nix 1133½ Used early 13
28Jun67-8Aqu fst 7f .22⅘ .45⅘1.25⅕ f- 10000 6 11 117 1111 1114 1111 MVenezia b 118 51.80 69-17 Nix 111¾ Her Favourite 114no Sound Tract 1181½ Trailed field 11
20Jun67-4Aqu sly 6f .23 .47⅗1.13⅕ f- 10500 2 4 35 45½ 47 57¾ MVenezia b 114 33.20 69-23 Zayer Naytik 118h Ship Shoal 1183½ Blended White 1144 Weakened 6
3Dec66-9Aqu fst 6f .23⅗ .47⅘1.12⅖ Clm 10000 5 6 77½ 79¼ 715 716 JRuane b 114 15.70 65-20 Mr. C. H. 1192½ Background 1172 Joe Di Rosa 119½ Trailed field 7
23Nov66-5Aqu fst 6f .22⅕ .46 1.11⅘ f- 10000 4 5 711 711 68 45 ECardone5 b 111 5.90 79-17 Farmer's Sweetie 1162½ Dulat's Twin 1132½ FlashyShot109h Late bid 7
3Nov66-8Aqu sly 6f .22⅗ .46⅕1.11⅘ f- 10000 7 1 54 32½ 32½ 33¾ WBlum b 116 7.10 80-21 Whiglet 1163 Bushy Tail 107¾ Gem's Reward 116¾ Held evenly 7
20Oct66-8Aqu sl 7f .23 .47 1.25⅗ f- 12500 10 1 35 810 68 57¼ WShoemaker b 120 16.80 71-23 Zeesa Adelle 1163½ Whiglet 1153 High Bluff 115nk No mishap 10
5Oct66-9Aqu gd 7f .23⅖ .47⅕1.26 f- 12500 6 1 12 11 66½ 811 WBlum b 121 13.20 65-22 Buffet Dinner 109h Fancy Bolero 114¾ High Bluff 1143 Used up 8
22Sep66-8Aqu gd 7f .22⅖ .45⅗1.25⅖ f- 14500 2 6 56 68½ 711 511 WBlum b 114 4.30 68-23 Cute Sweetie 1153 Speedy Lady 1095 Buffet Dinner 1141 No threat 8
LATEST WORKOUTS Jly 10 Bel tr.t. 3f fst .38⅗ b Jly 6 Bel 4f fst .49⅖ h Jun 16 Bel tr.t. 3f fst .37⅗ h Jun 14 Bel tr.t. 6f fst 1.20 b

Fleet Impelled $8,000 Dk. b. or br. f (1963-Cal), by Fleet Prince—Impelled, by Fanfare
Colonade Farm P. G. Johnson (P. Falkenstein) **118** 1967 17 1 1 3 $7,500 / 1966 15 2 5 2 $10,500
14Jly 67-9Aqu fst 6f .22⅖ .45⅘1.11⅗ f- c-6250 12 12 1310 1112 87¾ 55¼ HWoodhouse b 118 4.30 80-20 Kitty Quick 1183½ Wiltare 1111½ Everything Roses 116nk No threat 13
6Jly 67-5Aqu fst 1 .46⅗1.12⅖1.38⅗ f- 7000 6 8 76¾ 42 42½ 51¾ ACorderoJr b 116 4.10 73-20 Button My Shoe 118nk Overcome 113½ Lou's Hildy 116½ Bid, hung 9
29Jun67-4Aqu fst 6f .22⅘ .46⅖1.11⅘ f- 6500 4 11 109¾ 76 78 22½ ACorderoJr b 119 7.80 81-19 Clems Fairy Gold 1162½ Fleet Impelled 119h Sea Nail 1121 Rallied 11
12Jun67-4Aqu fst 6f .22⅗ .46⅕1.12⅕ f- 6500 8 6 812 78 75½ 4nk ACorderoJr b 120 5.30 82-18 PrincessNuks116nk EverythingRoses113no Discretion116no Gaining 8
3Jun67-4Aqu fst 7: .23⅕ .46⅗1.24⅘ f- 6500 2 10 108¾ 95¾ 56 44¾ ACorderoJr b 118 *2.40 77-15 Ginnygem 1052½ Lou's Hildy 112¾ Norma Mathews 1161½ Rallied 10
18May67-6Aqu fst 7f .22⅖ .45⅕1.25 f- 6500 2 10 1016 915 610 53¾ ACorderoJr b 120 7.00 77-20 Clem'sFairyGold1161 Trijugate112nk NormaMathews116h Stumbled 10
5May67-8Aqu fst 6f .22⅕ .45⅗1.12⅘ f- 6250 8 10 911 912 52¼ 1no ATCordero b 116 13.20 79-19 FleetImpelled116noClem'sFairyGold1163½PrincessNuks116no Just up 10
21Apr67-8Aqu fst 7f .22⅘ .45⅘1.25⅗ f- 10000 2 7 717 715 713 711 RUssery b 116 3.50 67-22 Native Twin 118½ Lucky Shirl 112¾ Andros Isle 1124 Dull try 7
12Apr67-5Aqu fst 7f .23⅖ .47⅖1.26⅖ f- 6500 5 9 915 811 56¼ 44½ RUssery b 116 *3.40 69-21 Lucky Shirl 1142 d-Wiltare 108½ Silvie 1182 Impeded, no chance 9
12Apr67—Placed third through disqualification.
LATEST WORKOUTS Jun 24 Bel tr.t. 4f my .49⅗ h

May Berry * $8,000 Ch. m (1962), by Esprit De France—Game Time, by Eight Thirty 111[7] 1967 8 1 1 1 $2,675
Mrs. F. H. Merrill F. H. Merrill (Mrs. M. K. Finlay) 1966 16 5 3 3 $10,209
12Jly 67-5Aqu fst 7f .22⅗ .45⅘1.24⅕ f- 10000 7 2 2¹ 3² 12¹³13¹³ MVenezia b 120 26.40 72-13 Her Favourite 114no Zeesa Adelle 114½ Nix 113³½ Speed, tired 13
17Jun67-5WO my 6f .22⅘ .46 1.11 Clm 9000 3 5 2¹½ 2h 1nk 1²½ HHinojosa b 113 4.75 90-23 May Berry 113²½ Chorr Beauty 109³¼ Land Office 115²¼ Handy score 6
27May67-4WO fst 6½f.23⅕ .46⅕1.17 Clm 9000 2 6 2¹ 2¹ 2³ 3³¼ RFerraro b 108 3.75 85-12 Satin Son 109³ Choir Beauty 106nk May Berry 108⁵ Well placed, tir. 6
15May67-4WO sf 1 Ⓣ .49⅘1.42⅘ Clm 9000 6 3 2¹ 2²½ 2⁴ 6¹⁰ JFitzsimmons b 108 6.15 60-34 Feast Or Famine 111³½ Carodana 113²¼ Purly Sark 114h Tired last ⅛ 8
28Apr67-5FE fst 6½f.23⅗ .46⅘1.18⅗ Clm 9000 5 3 1½ 1h 1¹ 2² JFitzsimmons b 108 4.60 88-16 MorninsMornin 119² MayBerry 108½ FeastOrFamine 111²½ Game try 6
21Apr67-7FE fst 6f .22⅕ .45⅘1.12⅗ Clm 12000 1 7 6⁹ 4⁹ 4⁷½ 6⁶¾ DBowcut 109 8.75 79-18 MorninsMornin 116¹¼ d-SatinSon 116¹¾ PresidentJim 106²¾ Far back 7
12Apr67-7Grd fst 6½f.23⅕ .47⅕1.18⅖ Allowance 7 5 4²¾ 5²¾ 5⁵¾ 5⁷¾ DBowcut 109 29.00 89-11 GrandGalop120nk SpeedyLament115¹¾HesASm'thie123⁴½ Early sp'd 7
31Mar67-6Grd fst 4½f.23⅕ .47 .53 Allowance 1 5 5²½ 3¹ 3² DBowcut 109 6.00 94- 9 Brief Attire 104nk Des Erables 114¹¾ May Berry 109³½ Even effort 5
14Nov66-6Grd sl 1 .49⅕1.15⅖1.43⅗ Clm 12000 2 1 1¹ 2½ .2h 3²¼ DBowcut b 110 9.00 61-40 Lord Saybrook 116¾ Mornins Mornin 113¹½ May Berry 110½ Used up 5
LATEST WORKOUTS Jly 19 Bel 3f fst .36⅖ b Jly 9 Bel tr.t. 4f fst .49 h

Kitty Quick * $8,000 B. m 1960), by Prince Quest—Kilchattan, by Rockefella 113[7] 1967 5 2 0 0 $7,065
Bar-Rox Farm D. Bentham (Cavanaugh-Associates, Inc.) 1966 21 3 0 2 $8,765
14Jly 67-9Aqu fst 6f .22⅖ .45⅘1.11⅗ f- 6250 7 1 1h 1½ 1¹½ 1³½ BBaeza b 118 3.80 85-20 Kitty Quick 118³½ Wiltare 111¹½ Everything Roses 116nk Easily 13
6Jly 67-5Aqu fst 1 .46⅗1.12⅖1.38⅗ f- 7000 7 1 2h 7⁷½ 8⁹½ 8¹¹ ACordero⁷ b 109 15.10 64-20 Button My Shoe 118nk Overcome 113½ Lou's Hildy 116½ Weakened 9
29Jun67-4Aqu fst 6f .22⅘ .46⅖1.11⅘ f- 7500 6 2 2h 1¹ 3²½ 5⁶ RUssery b 118 *1.30 78-19 Clems Fairy Gold 116²½ Fleet Impelled 119h Sea Nail 112¹ Tired 11
16Jun67-2Aqu fst 6f .22⅗ .45⅗1.11 f- 5000 5 1 1¹ 1¹ 1³ 1⁴ BBaeza b 118 3.30 88-14 Kitty Quick 118⁴ Floria II 116h Sea Moon 116h Easy score 9
7Jun67-9Aqu fst 6f .23 .45⅘1.13⅕ f- 5000 4 2 6⁵ 5⁵ 5⁴½ 4⁵ BBaeza b 116 8.90 72-16 Portico II 112² Joela 112¹ Galowo 112² Lacked early foot 7
15Nov66-4Aqu fst 6f .23 .47⅕1.12⅖ f- 6250 2 2 2¹½ 2h 11¹⁶11¹³ RUssery b 116 19.10 68-22 FleetImpelled116nk GayBlossom118½ ReluctantDragon111³ Stopped 11
1Nov66-8Aqu fst 6f .22⅖ .45⅘1.11⅘ f- 6500 10 1 2² 2⁵ 8¹⁶ 8¹¹ RTurcotte b 115 18.20 73-19 Reluctant Dragon110³ Helpful Hint115³ Runnin' Rose114h Fell back 11
12Oct66-9Aqu fst 6f .22⅘ .46⅘1.12⅗ Clm 6500 4 2 2½ 3¹½ 6¹⁰ 6¹¹ WShoemaker b 117 6.90 69-18 Gay Blossom 117h Vie Eye 120¾ Reluctant Dragon 108³½ Early speed 7
4Oct66-2Aqu fst 6f .22⅘ .46⅖1.12⅘ f- 5000 4 2 2h 1½ 1³ 1³½ RUssery b 116 3.60 79-17 Kitty Quick 116³½ Joela 116¾ Tehama 111¹ Drew out steadily 7
LATEST WORKOUTS Jly 19 Aqu 4f fst .49⅗ b Jly 11 Aqu 5f fst 1.02⅕ h Jun 25 Aqu 6f gd 1.19 b Jun 13 Aqu 4f fst .50 b

Best Secret $8,000 Dk. b. or br. f (1964-Fla); by Clandestine—Liked Best, by Fighting Frank 106[5] 1967 9 1 1 2 $5,745
Mrs. J. H. Leib A. A. Fiore (West Wind Ranch) 1966 7 2 0 2 $7,245
19Jun67-5Aqu sly 6f .22⅘ .47⅕1.13⅗ f- 9000 2 1 1³ 1³ 1² 3¹½ ECardone 112 4.60 73-26 Lady Lenore 118¹½ She Shawnee 116h Best Secret 112¹½ Faltered 10
8Jun67-4Aqu fst 6f .22 .45⅗1.12 f- 6500 4 1 1¹½ 1³ 1⁶ 1³ ACorderoJr 116 *1.50 83-16 Best Secret 116³ Little Mert 113¾ Anchored 112³ Easy score 11
29May67-2Aqu fst 6f .22⅖ .46 1.12⅖ f- 6500 8 1 1² 1⁴ 1⁵ 2¾ GMora⁵ 111 7.90 80-18 Overcome 116¾ Best Secret 111² Anchored 116³ Best of rest 11
11May67-8Aqu sly 6f .22⅗ .46⅗1.13⅘ f- 6000 10 6 3¹½ 3⁴ 3⁴½ 3⁶½ GMora⁷ 105 4.90 67-24 Tumble Clara 116²½ Must Be Glad 116⁴ Best Secret 105½ No mishap 10
19Apr67-9Aqu gd 6f .22⅘ .47⅘1.14⅘ f- 5000 6 1 1⁵ 1⁵ 1³ 5⁴½ ATCordero b 116 5.80 64-26 AnotherPrincess107nkTwiceAsRoyal 114nkP'padonna116³½ Tired 10
25Mar67-2Aqu my 6f .23 .49 1.16 f- 6500 3 5 1h 7⁴½ 9¹¹10¹³ GMora⁵ b 111 12.90 50-35 Driving Rain 116no Frostyanna 116nk Anchored 116²½ Brief speed 11
8Mar67-6GP fst 6f .22 .45⅖1.10⅕ Clm 7500 11 3 1h 1² 3⁵ 8¹³ GMora⁵ b 106 6.00 80-11 Galo 116⁸ Quillostar 116² Ruffled Bustle 111no Used up 12
23Feb67-2Hia gd 6f .22⅘ .46⅘1.13⅕ f- 10000 9 2 2¹ 3³ 5⁶ 8⁶¾ RUssery 116 *2.70 71-20 Scrollation 118nk Mrs. Jay 114no Golden Lamp 114nk Tired 12
9Feb67-1Hia gd 6f .22⅕ .45⅘1.12 f- 9000 9 3 2½ 2² 2³ 4⁶ RUssery 116 *1.70 78-16 Falconry 111¹ Lady Avalon 116⁴ Mrs. Jay 116¹ Well up, tired 12
LATEST WORKOUTS Jly 10 Bel tr.t. 4f fst .50 h Jun 28 Bel tr.t. 4f fst .48⅗ h May 22 Bel tr.t. 4f fst .49 h

Her Favourite * $8,000 B. m (1962), by Auditing—Dark Favorite, by Eight Thirty 123 1967 9 2 2 0 $11,025
S. Sommer F. Martin (W. Ewing) 1966 3 1 1 0 $4,500
12Jly 67-5Aqu fst 7f .22⅗ .45⅘1.24⅕ f- 9000 5 5 4⁴ 5⁴¼ 2h 1no BBaeza b 114 *2.50 85-13 Her Favourite 114no Zeesa Adelle 114½ Nix 113³½ Hard drive 13
28Jun67-8Aqu fst 7f .22⅘ .45⅘1.25⅕ f- 9000 5 4 2¹ 2h 1² 2¾ BFeliciano b 114 6.20 79-17 Nix 111¾ Her Favourite 114no Sound Tract 118¹½ Made game effort 11
23Jun67-8Aqu sly 6f .22⅗ .46⅗1.13⅕ f- 6250 7 3 2¹½ 1¹½ 1³ 1³½ BBaeza b 118 *1.90 77-25 HerFavourite 118³½ EverythingRoses 116² JungleBunnyII 114h Easily 8
17Jun67-4Aqu fst 6f .22⅕ .45⅕1.10⅘ f- 7500 5 3 5³½ 7⁷ 5⁷½ 2⁷ BBaeza b 118 4.10 82-15 Blended White 118⁷ Her Favourite 118no Court Hostess 116h Rallied 11
6Jun67-5Aqu fst 6f .22⅕ .46⅕1.11⅖ f- 10000 3 1 2² 2¹½ 2² 5⁵¾ BBaeza b 116 5.50 80-14 Zayer Naytik 116³½ Savannalamar 118¹½ Native Twin 120nk Tired 9
15May67-5Aqu fst 6f .22⅕ .45⅗1.11⅕ f- 10000 5 fog 4⁵ 4⁵½ JCamoretti b 116 23.70 81-13 Fennel 116⁴ Storm Brewing 116h Trinket 105¹½ Even try 10
LATEST WORKOUTS Jly 10 Bel tr.t. 4f fst .48⅗ h Jun 3 Bel tr.t. 5f fst 1.02⅖ h May 29 Bel tr.t. 4f fst .49 h

Savannalamar × $7,500 Ch. m (1961), by Thinking Cap—Man's Fancy, by Half Crown 116 1967 11 1 2 1 $6,105
Celeste Stable E. Giuffra (Christiana Stable) 1966 13 0 1 2 $2,100
12Jly 67-5Aqu fst 7f .22⅗ .45⅘1.24⅕ f- 9000 2 13 6⁵ 11¹¹11¹¹11⁹¾ GMora⁵ b 109 19.20 75-13 Her Favourite 114no Zeesa Adelle 114½ Nix 113³½ Slow start 13
28Jun67-8Aqu fst 7f .22⅘ .45⅘1.25⅕ f- 10000 11 2 1¹ 1h 2² 7³½ ECardone b 118 9.20 76-17 Nix 111¾ Her Favourite 114no Sound Tract 118¹½ Speed to stretch 11
21Jun67-9Aqu gd 1⅛.48 1.13⅕1.52⅖ Clm 10000 2 7 8⁸½ 8¹¹ 8¹⁶ 7²³ RC'ningham⁷ b 106 15.10 51-21 Kummel 118⁴ Daily Reminder 118¹½ Joe Di Rosa 118⁶ No threat 8
6Jun67-5Aqu fst 6f .22⅕ .46⅕1.11⅖ f- 10000 8 8 5⁴ 4³ 3²½ 2³½ ECardone b 118 10.70 82-14 Zayer Naytik 116³½ Savannalamar 118¹½ Native Twin 120nk Gamely 9
4May67-8Aqu fst 7f .22⅖ .45 1.24⅗ f- 11500 3 6 4³ 4⁵ 4² 3³¾ ECardone b 114 15.40 79-20 Needles Sword 118¾ Sound Tract 112³ Savannalamar 114¹ Good try 10
3Apr67-5Aqu fst 7f .24 .48⅕1.26⅖ f- 10000 1 4 1² 1h 2¹½ 2⁸ LPincayJr 120 2.30 66-25 Bushy Tail 112⁸ Savannalamar 120½ Fresh Colonel 116¹ Weakened 7
LATEST WORKOUTS Jly 20 Bel 3f fst .37⅕ h Jly 8 Bel tr.t. 5f fst 1.04 b Jun 17 Bel 7f fst 1.30 b Jun 5 Bel tr.t. 3f fst .38 b

---

Tejuela: Three fair races against males since June—but in Delaware. Horses from Delaware rarely duplicate their form when they arrive in New Jersey or New York. However, let us not be too hasty. This is not a Delaware horse. She is a New York horse. She simply went to Delaware for three races with boys. Before leaving, she did everything but win a sprint against Aqueduct females slightly better than those she meets today. Merits a closer look for that reason, plus her admirable in-the-money consistency, plus Dixon's curious insistence on running her against males in her last three starts. Was he trying to leg her up for something? CONTENDER.

Yankeenesian: This one looked adequate in her belated 1967 debut last week, but will have to prove that she can go all the way against $8,000 fillies. From July 5, 1966, to the present date (including nine months of undoubtedly enforced idleness), Ray Lake's charge has yet to gain an inch in the stretch of a race. NO BET.

Native Twin: A seven-furlong horse which has been deteriorating since its April victory. Note the comments on her last three races: "Unruly," "Drifted out," "Sluggish start." Each refers to the kind of behavior associated with an unsound, reluctant animal. Today's company may be the cheapest of her career, but the mare probably is in no shape to enjoy the opportunity. NO BET.

Gem's Reward: Before going into drydock for more than six months, this four-year-old looked as if she had insufficient speed for six furlongs and not enough stamina for seven. Her two bad races in June of this year were perhaps forgivable. The July 12 race was a distinct improvement in the early-speed department. But I foresee no win today. NO BET.

Fleet Impelled: Phil Johnson's newly acquired filly is over her head today. NO BET.

May Berry: Probably a useful mare, if the Canadian form in races against males can be credited. If she were a genuine speed horse, the switch to apprentice Ray Cunningham might help. But the mare is not really sudden out of the gate and young Cunningham will have his hands full in the traffic. The horse ought to improve over its July 14 debut here, but not enough to beat $8,000 stock. NO BET.

Kitty Quick: Scratched.

Best Secret: A three-year-old—the only one in the field. Has plenty of early run and should have a good deal to say about the early pace, but seems incapable of staying until the finish. For one thing, has been away for more than a month. Secondly, her performances against older horses (the races in which she carried extremely low weight) have been far from impressive. NO BET.

Her Favourite: After three excellent showings, involving two extremely hard stretch drives, this one steps down a peg and totes 123 pounds. I doubt that the ill effects of the mare's two last races are compensated by the drop in claiming price. Nor will the 123 pounds help. NO BET.

Savannalamar: They have tried seven furlongs and six and a mile-and-an-eighth and fillies and males. They have ridden Pincay, Cardone, Cunningham, and Mora, and today they have Turcotte. No soap. NO BET.

The only contender is Tejuela. All the others are riddled with holes. Can Tejuela overtake Best Secret and May Berry? No doubt. They will simply back up to her. And nothing else seems in condition to outfoot Tejuela in the stretch.

The Running of the Race

THE FAVORITE was Her Favourite because of the three good races in the past month. When will they ever learn? Best Secret, the speedy three-year-old, was second favorite, undoubtedly because she had the most early speed and was counted on to steal the race. Tejuela was third choice at a robust 5.60–1 and won without serious difficulty. Gem's Reward ran a superb race—better than anything on its past-performance list. Best Secret led everybody into the stretch and no farther. Her Favourite ran badly, like an overworked mare.

SECOND RACE
Aqu - 31755
July 21, 1967

6 FURLONGS. (Near Man, July 17, 1963, 1.08⅗, 3, 112.)
Claiming. Purse $5,800. Fillies and mares. 3-year-olds and upward. Weights, 3-year-olds 116 lbs., older 123 lbs. Non-winners of two races since May 31 allowed 3 lbs., of a race since July 1, 5 lbs. Claiming price, $8,000. 2 lbs. allowed for each $500 to $7,000. (Races when entered to be claimed for $6,000 or less not considered.)
Value to winner $3,770, second $1,160, third $580, fourth $290. Mutuel pool $210,202.

Index	Horse	Eqt	A	Wt	PP	St	¼	½	Str	Fin	Jockey	C'lg Pr	Owner	Odds $1
31666Del²	Tejuela		4	118	1	6	5½	5¹	3h	1¹	J L Rotz	8000	B C Brittingham	5.60
31686Aqu⁹	Gem's Reward	b	4	118	4	1	2¹	3½	4²	2¹	E Cardone	8000	Mrs J C Silverman	23.70
31440Aqu³	Best Secret		3	105	7	9	1½	1½	1h	3½	G Mora⁵	8000	Mrs J H Leib	3.40
31686Aqu¹³	May Berry	b	5	111	6	5	3½	2½	2½	4¹½	R Cun'gham⁷	8000	Mrs F H Merrill	11.10
31708Aqu⁴	Yankeenesian	b	4	118	2	3	7³	6³	6¹	5¹½	L Adams†	8000	J J Amriata	7.40
31708Aqu⁵	Fleet Impelled	b	4	118	5	8	9	7²	7³	6²	H Gustines	8000	Colonnade Farm	21.60
31686Aqu¹¹	Savanalamar	b	6	116	9	4	6½	8²	8¹	7½	R Turcotte	7500	Celeste Stable	13.40
31686Aqu⁶	Native Twin	b	5	118	3	7	8½	9	9	8¹	E Belmont	8000	J A Bolha	9.30
31686Aqu¹	Her Favourite	b	5	123	8	2	4¹	4¹	5½	9	B Baeza	8000	S Sommer	1.80

†Ten pounds apprentice allowance waived.

Time .22⅖, .45⅘, 1.11⅕ (with wind in backstretch). Track fast.

$2 Mutuel Prices:

1-TEJUELA	13.20	7.40	4.40
4-GEM'S REWARD		16.60	8.60
7-BEST SECRET			4.20

Ch. f, by Branding—Rejuela, by Rustic. Trainer W. H. Dixon. Bred by Haras El Pelado (Arg.).

IN GATE AT 1.59. OFF AT 1.59½ EASTERN DAYLIGHT TIME. Start good. Won driving.

TEJUELA saved ground while racing evenly for a half mile and. responding readily during the stretch run, disposed of the leaders inside the last eighth and retained a safe margin. GEM'S REWARD, prominent from the start, finished gamely in a good effort. BEST SECRET, hard hustled after beginning slowly, set the pace until reaching midstretch and faltered. MAY BERRY had no mishap. YANKEENESIAN was never dangerous. FLEET IMPELLED lacked early foot. SAVANNALAMAR dropped out of serious contention early. NATIVE TWIN showed nothing. HER FAVOURITE raced wide leaving the backstretch and, tiring badly after a half mile, lost her action and was beaten off.

Scratched—31708Aqu¹ Kitty Quick.

---

13. FOURTH AT MONMOUTH, JULY 19, 1967—Track Fast

IT MAY SEEM impossible to choose among the contenders in this race. Their records are quite similar. But the reader who is patient enough to check out all fundamentals of handicapping will finally discover that the similarity is more apparent than real. One of the contenders is a far better choice than the others.

The conditions are unremarkable. It is a run-of-the-mill sprint for fillies whose owners are willing to sell them for $6,500 to $7,500.

4th Monmouth

6 FURLONGS — MONMOUTH PARK — Start — Finish

6 FURLONGS (Chute). (Decathlon, June 11, 1957, 1.08⅖, 4, 130.) Claiming. Purse $4,300. Fillies. 3- and 4-year-olds. Weights, 3-year-olds 117 lbs., 4-year-olds 122 lbs. Non-winners of two races since June 9 allowed 3 lbs., a race, 6 lbs. Claiming price, $7,500. 1 lb. allowed for each $250 to $6,500. (Races where entered for $4,500 or less not considered.)

Swift Destiny $7,500 — Dk. b. or br. f (1964-Fla), by Ambehaving—Missus Beau, by Bolero — Frederica F. Emert — H. Paley — (Meadowbrook Farm, Inc.) — **114** — 1967 15 1 1 2 $6,355 — 1966 10 1 0 1 $2,785

12Jly 67-4Mth fst 6f .22⅕ .45⅘1.12⅖ Clm 7500 2 6 52½ 66¼ 56½ 32¼ WGavidia b 113 *2.40 78-17 Swiss Maid 1121¼ Mount Pelion 1181 Swift Destiny 1134½ Rallied 7
5Jly 67-2Mth my 6f .22⅗ .47 1.12⅗ Clm 7500 1 5 54¼ 45 53 44¾ WGavidia b 113 11.20 74-20 He's A Pip 1122½ Rogo 112nk Check The Deck 1142 No late rally 11
21Jun67-5Mth fst 6f .22⅖ .45⅘1.12⅖ Clm 7500 4 8 42 31 1½ 1h WGavidia b 112 5.00 80-21 Swift Destiny 112h Marlisa 1098 Cache Mobile 107½ Driving 10
17Jun67-5Mth fst 6f .22 .45⅖1.11⅗ Clm 10000 9 5 77¼ 67¼ 46½ 25 KKorte b 112 29.00 79-18 Destigate 1145 Swift Destiny 1123 Holly War 120½ Rallied 11
5Jun67-7Mth fst 6f .22⅖ .45⅘1.11⅘ f- Allow 6 6 106 76¾ 52¾ 42¾ KKorte b 112 39.50 80-14 Double Virtue 114½ Le Parans 1131¾ Double Destine 113½ Late foot 12
29May67-7GS gd 1 1/16 .47⅘1.13⅕1.46⅗ Clm 7500 6 7 75¾ 55¼ 33 46¾ KKorte b 113 5.20 65-22 Ile D'Levant 1171¾ Fair Page 1163½ Great Patriot 1131½ Tired 8
23May67-7GS fst 6f .22⅘ .46 1.11⅘ Clm 8000 11 3 87¼ 78 65¾ 31¾ KKorte b 113 54.20 83-16 Olympia Jo 116¾ Ethical 1171 Swift Destiny 113½ Closed well 12
11May67-6GS sly 6f .22⅖ .46⅖1.12⅗ Clm 10000 4 4 54¼ 65½ 89¾ 89 DHidalgo b 111 15.50 72-19 Minnie Baby 112¾ Destigate 1206 Tom's Brother 114no Brief factor 8
24Apr67-7GP fm 1 1/16 Ⓣ 1.12⅖1.44 Allowance 7 2 2½ 3½ 55½ 67 JChoquette b 113 16.30 77-14 Royal Esteem 1172½ Royal Intent 117½ Enough Talk 117h Used up 7
14Apr67-8GP fm 1 Ⓣ .47⅕1.37⅖ Allowance 4 4 31½ 33½ 54½ 47½ GGallitano5 b 107 6.70 79-18 Jester's Belle 1141 Pointsman 1175 Unexpected 1191½ Weakened 8
6Apr67-6GP fm 1 Ⓣ .47⅖1.37 Allowance 10 4 42 21½ 32 46 GGallitano5 b 107 86.90 83-14 Mauve Decade 1172 Dig In 1172½ Royal Intent 1171½ Weakened 12
LATEST WORKOUTS Jly 3 Mth 3f sl .38⅘ b — Jun 30 Mth 5f sly 1.04⅘ b — Jun 14 Mth 4f fst .49⅗ b

Meryl Ann $7,500 — Dk. b. or br. f (1964-Ky), by Paper Tiger—Davidann, by Mount Marcy — Clara L. Ostriker — A. Jacobs — (Mrs. C. L. Ostriker) — **111** — 1967 10 1 0 2 3,855 — 1966 2 M 0 0 —

6May67-8Aqu sly 7f .23⅗ .48 1.28⅘ f- 5000 1 7 54½ 45 32 47½ RSurrency5 113 6.70 54-27 Anchored 1162½ Irish Stout 1163 Amber River 1162 Bid, tired 7
2May67-9Aqu fst 1 .46⅖1.12 1.39⅗ f- 6500 6 8 77¼ 85 54 44 RSurrency5 107 24.60 63-18 Great Patriot 116½ Exotic Red 109no Driving Rain 1163½ Rallied 10
27Apr67-8Aqu sly 6f .23⅖ .48⅘1.14⅘ f- 6500 8 6 1013 87 87 814 MVenezia 116 8.50 55-34 Roaming Miss 1141 Tumble Clara 1163½ Fulcrum's Lass 113½ Far b'k 10
20Apr67-4Aqu fst 1 .47⅗1.13⅕1.39⅘ f- 6500 8 8 86½ 65 46½ 36¼ BBaeza 116 3.30 62-26 Salad Bowl 116nk Driving Rain 1166 Meryl Ann 1164½ Late bid 8
15Apr67-4Aqu fst 6f .23 .46⅘1.11⅕ f- 9000 12 7 1114 1113 919 818 WShoemaker 112 11.20 69-14 Linny Boob 1148½ Guicecca 1121 Lancerrae 1123 No speed 12
30Mar67-3Aqu hy 6f .22⅘ .48 1.15⅖ f-M 5000 10 9 812 57 11½ 15 BBaeza 121 *1.30 66-33 Meryl Ann 1215 Limey Mouse 1213 Scalene 121h Speed to spare 11
21Mar67-1Aqu my 6f .23⅖ .48⅗1.16 f-Md 6500 6 5 811 715 59½ 45¼ BBaeza 113 11.00 58-40 Dance For Joy 1131½ Fulcrum's Lass 109¾ Beau Cookie 1133 Rallied 9
16Mar67-1Aqu sly 6f .23⅖ .46⅘1.15⅖ f-Md 6000 5 4 57 49½ 45½ 37½ ECardone 121 5.10 58-33 Dust To Dust 1215 Honey's Li'l Mitts 1212½ Meryl Ann 1212½ Evenly 11
1Mar67-5Hia fst 6f .22⅖ .46 1.11⅕ Clm 9000 2 8 1112 1215 1217 1013 BMoreira 109 65.30 75-13 Keene Terra 116no Army Game 1162 Sweet Intent 1091¾ No speed 12
LATEST WORKOUTS Jly 17 Mth 3f sly .36⅗ b — Jly 12 Mth 4f fst .48⅘ h — Jly 7 Mth 6f fst 1.19 b — Jly 3 Mth 4f sl .50⅗ b

Tabitha $7,500 — B. f (1963-Va), by County Delight—Key Bridge, by Princequillo — Audley Farm Stable — J. B. Dodson — (P. Mellon) — **119** — 1967 7 2 0 2 $6,070 — 1966 13 0 2 1 $2,500

10Jly 67-3Del fst 6f .22⅖ .46 1.11⅘ Clm 8000 5 1 2h 2h 22 34½ ORosado b 117 5.60 81-16 Ariel Road 1153 Tejuela 1121½ Tabitha 117¾ Speed, tired 7
26Jun67-4Del fst 6f .23⅕ .46⅘1.12⅖ Clm 7000 6 1 21½ 13 12 13 ORosado b 114 9.60 83-22 Tabitha 1143 Brentwood Miss 1103½ Linear B. 1151 Mild drive 7
5Jun67-4Mth fst 6f .22⅗ .45⅘1.11⅘ Clm 7500 2 2 42 76½ 77 65 CGonzalez b 112 16.70 78-14 Second Breakfast 1132 Uxbridge 114h Rule Of Facts 1141½ Tired 8
17May67-6Pim fst 6f .23⅕ .47 1.13 f- 7500 3 2 3, 231½ 22 31¼ CGonzalez b 119 *1.60 84-15 Go Up 1131 Miles Miss 113nk Tabitha 119½ Tried to bear out 7
10May67-4Pim fst 6f — — 1.12⅗ f- 6500 10 2 3nk 11½ 11½ 11¾ CGonzalez b 115 10.70 87-17 Tabitha 1151¾ Compass Rose 114½ Lightning Miss 1154 Driving 11
1May67-4Pim fst 6f .23⅖ .46⅗1.12 f- 6000 8 4 1h 31 63¼ 54 CGonzalez b 115 14.20 86-12 Tuhela 1151½ Lightning Miss 115¾ Miles Miss 112¾ Brushed, tired 9
25Apr67-5Pim fst 6f .23⅗ .46⅖1.12 Clm 7500 7 5 53½ 56½ 713 712 CGonzalez b 107 16.20 78-14 Flashing Glass 117¾ Broken Needle 1041½ Jice 1153 Fell back 7
29Jly 66-8Aqu fst 6f .22⅘ .46⅖1.12 f- 9000 7 2 86¾ 810 917 913 DChamb'lin7 b 106 43.30 70-17 Yankeenesian 109nk Trinket 1143½ Sweep Past 1182 No factor 9
12Jly 66-4Aqu fst 6f .22⅗ .45⅗1.11⅘ f- 10000 6 4 64 56 610 612 DChambe'lin7 b 109 11.30 72-19 Stowe 107½ Federal Princess 111no Blooming Hills 1163 No threat 7
5Jly 66-5Aqu fst 6f .22⅗ .46⅗1.12⅘ f- 10500 2 2 56 54 2½ 21½ DChambe'lin7 b 106 22.10 77-20 Yankeenesian 1031½ Tabitha 107½ Last Act 1212½ Good effort 6
3Jun66-2Aqu fst 6f .22⅖ .45⅘1.11⅕ f- c-8000 5 6 54¼ 56½ 712 818 MVenezia b 107 18.60f 69-16 Omaha Beach 1138 Kitty Beale 120½ Happy Hummer 1152½ Fell b'k 9
LATEST WORKOUTS Jly 18 Mth 3f sl .39 b — Jly 7 Mth 3f fst .36⅗ b — Jun 16 Mth 6f fst 1.15⅖ b

Four Flats * $6,500 — Ch. f (1964-Ky), by Royal Note—Greek's Goldie, by Greek Song — F. P. Dyer — J. O'Brey, Sr. — (T. Wilson-J. Curry) — **105⁵** — 1967 7 1 3 0 $4,760 — 1966 0 M 0 0 —

8Jly 67-1Mth fst 6f .22⅕ .45⅗1.12 Cl c-4500 2 6 44½ 59½ 58½ 68 GGallitano7 b 105 3.50 74-18 Persian Mate 1155 Flying Fun 116½ Galo 115¾ Fell far back 10
28Jun67-3Mth fst 6f .22⅗ .46⅕1.13⅖ f- 5500 7 2 4¾ 41¼ 3nk 2no JVasquez b 115 3.10 75-19 Aqua Val 110no Four Flats 115no Great Darling 1152½ Sharp try 8
20Jun67-1Mth my 6f .22⅗ .47 1.14 Md 5000 12 1 23 11 16 12 JVasquez b 113 2.60 72-21 Four Flats 1132 Olympus II 1151½ Irish Gloss 1153 Mild drive 12
9Jun67-2Mth fst 6f .21⅗ .45⅕1.11⅘ Md 7000 12 4 25 24 23 45¾ MMiceli5 b 103 3.90 77-22 MountPelion 1155½ Fairminary 115no NeverNeverMiss 115nk Weak'd 12
25May67-2GS fst 6f .23 .47⅖1.13⅕ f-Md 5000 5 3 11½ 11½ 12 22¾ WGavidia b 115 *1.60 75-25 Great Darling 1152¾ Four Flats 1156 Nalodaya 1151¾ Weakened 12
18May67-1GS fst 6f .22⅗ .46⅖1.13 f-Md 7500 5 2 1h 1h 2h 21¾ JVelasquez b 115 *1.30 77-20 Hey Sug 1151¾ Four Flats 115½ Doesn't She 1131 Tired in drive 10
4May67-4GS fst 6f .22⅖ .46⅕1.13⅕ Md 9000 11 4 3nk 1h 89 86½ WBlum 114 5.60 71-16 Prime Facts 116½ Bay Guinea 1161 Zurk 109nk Early foot, tired 12
LATEST WORKOUTS Jly 15 Mth 5f gd 1.03⅘ b — Jun 16 Mth 4f fst .50 b — Jun 3 Mth 4f fst .48⅗ h

Foreign Fable $7,500 Dk. b. or br. f (1963–Ark), by Bagdad—Lush Lie, by Diamond Dick **111**5 1967 9 0 0 1 $550
L. Lear L. Lear (F. H. Lindsay) 1966 26 2 10 6 $14,305
11Jly 67–8Mth fst 6f .22 .45⅖1.11⅗ f– Allow 8 1 42 46 713 713 JLeonard b 112 15.40 71–20 Shae Maidle 1132 Who Cabled 114no Golden Hostess 116¾ Tired 8
15Jun67–7Mth fst 6f .22⅖ .46 1.12 f– 10000 5 1 53¾ 34½ 34 52¼ MMiceli5 b 111 10.50 80–22 Detente 1161¼ Nix 116no National Hookup 111½ Had no mishaps 8
26May67–7GS fst 6f .22⅗ .46⅗1.12⅕ f– 11000 5 3 1h 21 41½ 84¾ MMiceli5 b 111 5.10 78–20 Sweet Surcease 1141½ Nix 116¾ Detente 116no Used early part 11
18May67–8GS fst 6f .22 .45⅗1.11⅗ f– Allow 3 5 3½ 43½ 63¾ 55½ MMiceli5 b 110 49.10 80–20 PersianIntrigue1091¾HavaNiceDay115noLaMemeC'se111nk No mis'p 12
4Apr67–8GP fst 7f .22⅘ .46 1.24 f– 12500 1 5 4¾ 22 610 611 MMicelli5 b 111 7.40 78–15 Manta H. 111¾ Greek Princess 1165 Naga 1161 Early speed, tired 9
27Feb67–8Hia fst 6f .22⅕ .45⅘1.10⅘ f– Allow 10 6 98¼ 88 42½ 33¾ MMiceli5 b 107 27.90 86–14 Athen's Gem 112nk Mandioca 1133½ Foreign Fable 107nk Wide 12
9Feb67–9Hia sly 6f .22⅖ .46⅕1.11⅗ f– Allow 1 4 22 24 59 911 MMiceli5 b 107 29.00 75–17 Meadow Stream 1123½ Zamilu 1151½ Boiseana 112h Factor, tired 12
2Feb67–7Hia fst 5½f Ⓣ 1.05 f– Allow 2 5 31½ 54 33 62 MMiceli5 b 107 17.60 91–12 Mighty Happy 118½ Sun Play 1131 Manta H. 112no No late response 12
11Jan67–9TrP fst 6f .21⅘ .44⅗1.10 f–Handicap 3 7 75½ 66 56½ 99¼ MMiceli b 112 66.70 83–14 Little Portress 114¾ Welshwyn 1161¾ Bear Grass 1162½ No threat 11
30Dec66–8TrP fst 6f .22 .45⅕1.10⅗ Allowance 7 4 34 31½ 2h 11 MMiceli5 b 110 *2.00 89–12 Foreign Fable 1101 Paraphernalia 111no Toulousette 1152 In time 12
17Dec66–8TrP fst 6f .22⅕ .45⅖1.10⅘ f– Allow 4 5 1h 11 3nk 33 MMiceli5 b 107 *2.60 85–17 Fizzy 1072 Naga 1141 Foreign Fable 107¾ Set pace, tired 12
8Dec66–7TrP fst 6f .21⅗ .44⅗1.09⅘ Allowance 4 1 32 21½ 22 26 BMoreira b 112 *1.60 87–14 Call Me Fritz 1156 Foreign Fable 1122¼ Bust–On 1123¼ 2nd best 10
28Nov66–7TrP fst 6f .22⅗ .46⅖1.11⅗ f– Allow 3 3 1¼ 2h 11½ 3nk BMoreira b 109 *2.00 84–15 Angels Serenade 111nk Shade II 115no Foreign Fable 109nk Weak'n'd 7
LATEST WORKOUTS Jly 16 Mth 4f sly .53 b Jly 2 Mth 5f fst 1.02 b Jun 30 Mth 3f sly .39 b Jun 26 Mth 3f gd .38 b

Scairt $7,500 B. f (1963–Ky), by Barbizon—Big Fright, by Phalanx **116** 1967 14 2 0 3 $8,695
P. D. De Paul C. L. Robbins (W. L. Jones, Jr.) 1966 12 0 2 0 $2.145
14Jly 67–6Mth fst 6f .23 .46⅖1.12 Clm 7000 1 4 41½ 67½ 612 611 MMiceli5 b 106 9.50 71–19 Second Breakfast 119½ Your Day 1161¼ Miss Pry 1126 Tired 8
6Jly 67–5Aqu fst 1 .46⅗1.12⅖1.38⅗ f– 7500 2 2 1h 2h 2½ 41¼ RTanner10 b 108 24.90 74–20 Button My Shoe 118nk Overcome 113½ Lou's Hildy 116½ Used up 9
27Jun67–5Mth fst 6f .22⅖ .45⅖1.11⅕ Clm 7500 7 3 32½ 36 35½ 33¾ MMiceli5 b 105 9.80 82–19 Aweigh My Lads 1191¼ Your Day 1152½ Scairt 1051 Mild bid 7
17Jun67–4Aqu fst 6f .22⅕ .45⅕1.10⅘ f– 7500 10 4 43 45½ 47 69¼ MVenezia b 118 9.90 80–15 Blended White 1187 HerFavourite118no CourtHostess116h Tired 11
26May67–7GS fst 6f .22⅗ .46⅗1.12⅕ f– 10000 10 1 84½ 75¼109¼106 SHernandez b 114 25.50 77–20 Sweet Surcease 1141½ Nix 116¾ Detente 116no Fell back early 11
12May67–5GS gd 6f .23 .47⅖1.12⅗ f– 11500 6 1 22 32 66¾ 66¼ JJohnson b 116 4.40 75–21 Navy Heroine 116¾ Nix 1141 Saddle Song 1072 Early speed 7
4May67–5GS fst 6f .22⅖ .46 1.12⅕ f– 11500 7 1 1h 3½ 21½ 43¾ SBrooks b 113 4.90 79–16 Cute Sweetie 1153 Navy Heroine 113h Bakery Babe 115¾ Tired 7
11Apr67–6Pim fst 6f .23⅖ .46⅘1.12 Clm 13500 7 3 62¾ 64¾ 77½ 55 AAgnello5 b 105 11.20 85–18 Jeannie'sRuler1152½ FiveRogues1161 d–Knave'sDelight115h No mis'p 7
11Apr67—Placed fourth through disqualification.
16Mar67–4Pim sl 6f .23⅕ .47⅕1.13 Clm 11500 3 4 43 33½ 32½ 3¾ ACannon5 b 106 6.40 84–25 •Five Rogues 115¾ •Arctic Swirl 117¾ Scairt 1064 Good try 6
21Feb67–7Bow sl 7f .22⅘ .45⅖1.25⅖ Clm 12500 1 2 12 1h 86½ 89½ JJohnson b 113 7.50 76–30 Well To Do 114¾ Arctic Swirl 117nk Two Up 117h Used up 9
LATEST WORKOUTS Jun 24 Mth 3f sl .37 b Jun 8 Mth 5f fst 1.01⅗ h

Craigs Kam * $7,500 Dk. b or br. f (1964–Va), by Craigwood—Kamikaze, by Devil Diver **111** 1967 7 3 1 0 $7,725
J. V. Alexander J. V. Alexander (Audley Farm) 1966 8 2 2 0 $4.800
7Jly 67–2Mth fst 6f .22⅕ .46 1.13⅕ f– c–3500 2 3 11 13 14 13 SHernandez 116 *2.50 76–25 Craigs Kam 1163 Quiet Jennie 117nk Jetaleen 1146 Ridden out 12
30Jun67–2Mth sly 6f .22⅖ .46⅖1.12⅘ f– 3500 11 1 13 12 11½ 13½ SHernandez 115 *2.40 78–22 Craigs Kam 1153½ Andonine 1084 Orcinus 1132 Ridden out 12
23Jun67–3Mth sly 6f .22⅕ .45⅘1.12⅘ f– 3500 1 5 11 12 1½ 2½ CBaltazar 115 4.00 77–18 Andonine 108½ Craigs Kam 1151 Moodadir 1171¼ Game try 12
16Jun67–2Mth fst 6f .22⅘ .47 1.12⅘ f– 3500 2 6 11½ 22 714 914 CGonzalez 115 2.50 64–18 StarTreachery1171¾ Petare'sJewel1124 NonaMarianna114h Stopped 12
9Jun67–4Mth fst 6f .22 .45⅗1.13 f– 3500 10 1 12 14 12 12 CGonzalez 112 3.30 77–22 CraigsKam 1122 Tanner'sCreek 1121½ StarTreachery 1173½ Driving 12
2Jun67–2Mth fst 6f .22⅗ .46⅖1.13 f– 4000 2 3 13 2h 23 64¾ CGonzalez b 113 4.20 72–14 Quiet Jennie 106no Rulerina 113½ Gem–Wood Bell 1131¼ Used up 12
13May67–2Pim fst 6f .23 .46⅘1.13⅕ f– 5000 5 1 12 13 11 43¼ CGonzalez 113 11.10 81–14 Palmerette 1131½ Lady's Cite 1151½ Sweet Innocence 117nk Used up 12
7Oct66–4Atl fst 6f .22⅗ .47 1.12⅗ Clm 6500 9 2 21½ 65¼ 916 928 CGonzalez 114 13.40 51–23 Mushroom Cloud 1163 Count Gene 1173½ Godfather 1155 Brief speed 9
30Sep66–6Atl sl 6f .22⅕ .47 1.15⅗ f– 5500 9 1 12 11 1½ 11¼ CGonzalez 116 *1.70 64–30 Craigs Kam 1161¼ Cartling 1131 Sickle Moon 116¾ Driving 12
21Sep66–2Atl sly 6f .22⅗ .46⅗1.14⅕ f–Md 6000 10 1 11½ 14 13 1¾ CGonzalez 119 *1.70 71–26 Craigs Kam 119¾ Repair Scare 1102 Irate Doge 1191 Driving 12
15Sep66–2Atl sly 6f .22⅘ .47⅖1.15 Md 5500 4 4 1h 12 12 23 JVasquez 115 4.80 64–29 Second Show 1183 Craigs Kam 1151 Richie Easton 1181¼ Faltered 12
LATEST WORKOUTS Jly 6 Mth 3f gd .39 b Jun 15 Mth 3f fst .36⅕ b Jun 8 Mth 3f fst .37⅖ b

Ricos Spy $7,500 B. f (1964–Fla), by Rico Tesio—Wood Song, by Spy Song **111** 1967 6 0 0 1 $675
P. Cresci L. McDonald (P. Crespi) 1966 16 3 0 1 $7,870
14Jly 67–5Mth fst 6f .22⅗ .46⅕1.12⅕ f– 10500 6 6 73¾ 712 79½ 75¾ PKallai b 112 8.60 75–19 Bakery Babe 1151½ Lucy Bean 117½ Saddle Song 111h Dull try 8
7Jly 67–8Mth fm*1 Ⓣ 1.43 f– Allow 1 8 79¼ 811 810 712 JCombest b 113 11.90 74–14 Bright New Day 112h Chriscinca 1185 Island–Hop 112nk No speed 8
15Jun67–7Mth fst 6f .22⅖ .46 1.12 f– 10000 8 3 43½ 56 45 41¾ JCombest b 113 6.80 80–22 Detente 1161¼ Nix 116no National Hookup 111½ Finished willingly 8
6Jun67–4Mth fst 6f .22⅕ .45⅕1.11⅘ f– 10000 3 5 57¼ 58½ 47 32½ JCombest b 113 13.30 80–16 Saddle Song 113no Detente 1162½ Ricos Spy 113nk Closed well 6
23May67–6GS fst 6f .22 .46 1.11⅗ f– 14000 7 4 68 710 711 611 FLovato b 111 22.60 75–16 Athen's Gem 117½ Minnie Baby 1121½ Deepsprings 106¾ No speed 7
16May67–8GS fst 6f .22⅗ .46⅖1.12⅕ f– Allow 2 5 58 78 710 89½ NReagan b 113 34.60 73–18 Queens Waltz 1132 Double Destine 113½ Tudor Song 1131 No speed 8
16Dec66–7Lrl sly 6f .22⅘ .47⅕1.14 f– Allow 7 9 98¾ 811 76¾ 43¼ FLovato b 118 15.80 79–18 Solar Princess 1152 Dana's Flight 118½ Amy D. 116¾ Late foot 9
1Dec66–6Lrl gd 7f .22⅗ .46⅕1.25⅖ f– Allow 5 9 86½ 914 614 412 FLovato b 116 11.40 80–18 Lady Ebony 1186 Solar Princess 1161½ Dana's Flight 1184 Rallied 10
12Nov66–6GS sly 170.46⅗1.12⅘1.44⅖ Allowance 2 5 45½ 612 717 723 FLovato b 110 17.60 49–29 Mr. Scipio 1123 High Hat 1173 Sun Stream 1121 Fell back 8
4Nov66–4GS fst 6f .22⅗ .46⅖1.12⅘ f– 11000 9 2 53½ 43½ 31 1h FLovato b 116 7.40 80–26 Ricos Spy 116h Question Moore 1163½ Game Maid 1162¾ Driving 9

Trolley Car $6,500 B. f (1964–Fla), by Vox Pop—Funny Way, by Hilarious **107** 1967 7 0 0 1 $620
Rosemary Maziarz J. F. Plett (Hobeau Farm) 1966 17 4 6 4 $12,615
4Jly 67–4Aqu fst 7f .22⅗ .46⅕1.25⅘ Clm 6500 11 3 33 42½ 86¼1011 BFeliciano 111 17.00 66–17 Carrot Bird 115½ Sing A Bit 1142½ Hasty Hero 1142½ Speed, tired 13
21Jun67–5Mth fst 6f .22⅖ .45⅘1.12⅖ Clm 7500 8 2 52 57 58 58½ DBrumfield 113 17.70 71–21 Swift Destiny 112h Marlisa 1098 Cache Mobile 107½ No threat 10
1Jun67–7Suf fst 6f .22⅗ .46⅗1.12⅖ Clm 6250 5 2 21 1h 2½ 31¾ TDunlavy 112 4.50 77–19 Col. Boyd B. 1121 ¼Ironman Mark 120 Trolley Car 1121 Faltered 9
6Apr67–5GP fst 7f .22⅘ .45⅘1.25 f– 8000 2 12 105¼ 911 917 914 JGiovanni 116 12.80 70–17 Little Who Who 1181½ Mrs. Jay 116nk Policy Power 116h No speed 12
23Mar67–4GP fst 6f .22⅖ .45⅘1.11⅗ f– 11000 11 10 107 10151017 1014 LMoyers 116 16.00 72–16 Here's Neptune 113¾ Golden Lamp 1162½ Lady Goldie 116¾ No speed 12
27Feb67–7Hia fst 7f .22⅘ .45⅕1.25⅕ f– 14000 8 5 52½ 53¼ 99¼ 79 LMoyers 116 5.60 74–14 Dancing Dale 1142 Deepsprings 116no Cast Your Fate 1162 Tired 10
15Feb67–6Hia fst 6f .22⅕ .45⅗1.12⅕ f– 15000 4 5 31 56 56 43½ LMoyers 118 7.80 79–16 d–Lady Avalon 112h Ethical 1161 Deepsprings 1182½ Tired 12
31Dec66–9TrP fst 170.46⅕1.11⅕1.42⅕ C.MiamiH 7 4 42¼1213 1221 1222 LMoyers 112 31.70 64–16 Fort Drum 115h Biller 1181¾ Pepperwood 1212½ Stopped 12
22Dec66–7TrP fst 6f .22⅕ .45⅕1.10⅕ Alw 7500s 9 1 3nk 1½ 13 18 LMoyers 118 *1.70 91–14 Trolley Car 1188 Old Dudley 1181¾ Varsity Boy 111no Ridden out 12
12Dec66–9TrP fst 170.46⅕1.10⅘1.41⅗ Alw – – – s 5 1 13 12 2h 23½ JGiovanni 114 9.70 85–14 Crafty Look 1193½ Trolley Car 114½ Sunny Voyage 1154½ Gamely 8
5Dec66–4TrP fst 6f .22⅖ .45⅕1.10⅖ Clm 7000 11 1 2½ 11 11½ 13¼ JGiovanni 111 3.40 90–12 Trolley Car 1113¼ Pic Ship 1151¼ Oloron 113nk Cl'r under pressure 12
24Nov66–2TrP fst 6f .22⅖ .45⅕1.10⅗ Clm 6500 / 2 21 22 23 21¼ JGiovanni 110 *2.00 88– 9 Kelly A'Go Go 1101¼ Trolley Car 1104¾ Oloron 1153½ Game try 12
LATEST WORKOUTS Jly 1 Mth 3f my .37⅖ b Jun 17 Suf 3f fst .38 b Jun 12 Suf 5f fst 1.02⅖ h May 29 Suf 5f fst 1.02⅖ h

---

Swift Destiny: Has won only once since April, but has displayed plenty of determination against much tougher fields than she meets today. On June 21 she showed that six furlongs is a suitable distance for her, getting the lead well before the finish. CONTENDER.

Meryl Ann: Away for two and a half months and would be outclassed by this field even if she were in condition. NO BET.

Tabitha: Dodson had this one nice and sharp last May when she beat a field of today's general quality at Pimlico. Beat males in Delaware on June 26 at odds of almost 10–1. And now it looks as if Dodson hopes to find a soft touch against fillies. With this one's early speed, he might do it. CONTENDER.

Four Flats: Likes to get out in front, but has not yet been able to do it against winners. NO BET.

Foreign Fable: Moves down sharply today after an effort eight days ago in which the ill effects of recent inactivity were noticeable. That race probably helped, and so will today's softer field. CONTENDER.

Scairt: The June 27 race against males was good enough to assure the Charlie Robbins filly of careful consideration if he brought her back in a sprint against females of her own class. Instead, he sent her to New York where she made a gallant try at a mile. And then, five days ago, he pitted her against males again and she showed nothing. Can that dreary effort be overlooked? I doubt it, but Jorge Velasquez—who has become the winningest jockey in the country—rides today. And if Robbins is ever going to get a purse with this filly without lowering her claiming price to $6,000, this should be the day. Pending further scrutiny, we had better not eliminate this horse. CONTENDER.

Craigs Kam: Cheap speed. NO BET.

Ricos Spy: Her efforts this year indicate that she might do better at seven furlongs. She does not start running soon enough to catch $7,500 fillies. NO BET.

Trolley Car: Scratched.

The contenders are Swift Destiny, Tabitha, Foreign Fable, and Scairt, each of which is moving down the class ladder for today's race. The most impressive recent performances have been Swift Destiny's. Her June 21 victory here rates considerably higher than Tabitha's June 26 win at Delaware. Quite apart from the $500 difference in claiming price, the quality of competition at Monmouth is superior to that in Delaware. Furthermore, this is the first time Swift Destiny has run for a claiming price against females. Her claiming races have been against males—including the 11-horse field of $10,000 ones in which she finished a gaining second on June 17. Tabitha's front-running tendencies will be no asset today, with Craigs Kam and Four Flats trying to run her to earth in the early stages. She can now be eliminated as outclassed by Swift Destiny and as unlikely to last until the stretch drive after a ferocious early pace.

Which brings us to Foreign Fable. The raps against this one include a suspicion of unsoundness. She has been raced too sparingly since February. The horses that have been trouncing her would not have outclassed Swift Destiny. Eliminate Foreign Fable.

Scairt's June 27 race against males was faster than Swift Destiny's victory over a similar field on June 21. But I note that the Robbins horse was carrying only

105 pounds on that day. Today she carries 116. That is not much weight, perhaps, but is considerably more than the filly has taken anywhere all year. Swift Destiny, on the other hand, has been charging at males while carrying 112 and 113 but should not be overburdened with 114 against today's troop of fillies.

Because Scairt's condition is dubious and the weight apparently too much for her, we can cross her out. Only Swift Destiny is left. Will the pace suit her? Absolutely. Craigs Kam and Tabitha figure to wear each other out, allowing Swift Destiny to have things her own way in the final stages.

The Running of the Race

THE NEW JERSEY punters made Swift Destiny the favorite, ahead of Ricos Spy and Scairt. It was an intelligent choice. Craigs Kam and Tabitha ran according to the blueprint, cooking each other in the early going. Swift Destiny took over at the head of the home stretch and was so much the best that Bill Gavidia had his whip sheathed during the final yards. Foreign Fable ran swiftly and gamely but could not begin to catch the winner. Scairt also tried to win, under Velasquez's strenuous urging, but had to settle for third money.

FOURTH RACE **6 FURLONGS (Chute). (Decathlon, June 11, 1957, 1.08⅔, 4, 130.)**

Mth - 31739

July 19, 1967

Claiming. Purse $4,300. Fillies. 3- and 4-year-olds. Weights, 3-year-olds 117 lbs., 4-year-olds 122 lbs. Non-winners of two races since June 9 allowed 3 lbs., a race, 6 lbs. Claiming price, $7,500. 1 lb. allowed for each $250 to $6,500. (Races where entered for $4,500 or less not considered.)

Value to winner $2,795, second $860, third $430, fourth $215. Mutuel pool $212,297.

Index	Horse	Eqt A Wt	PP	St	¼	½	Str	Fin	Jockey	Cl'g Pr	Owner	Odds $1
31395Mth3	Swift Destiny	b 3 114	1	4	5³	4¹	1¹	1³	W Gavidia	7500	Frederica F Emert	2.20
31660Mth7	Foreign Fable	b 4 111	5	2	4¹	2¹½	2²	2¾	M Miceli5	7500	L Lear	6.30
31705Mth6	Scairt	b 4 116	6	5	6¹	6³	4h	3¹¼	J Velasquez	7500	P DePaul	4.50
31655Del3	Tabitha	b 4 119	3	3	2¹	3¹	5⁴	4²½	P Kallai	7500	Audley Farm Stable	4.60
31704Mth7	Ricos Spy	b 3 113	8	7	7½	7⁴	6¹	5²½	J Combest	7500	P Cresci	3.60
31647Mth1	Craigs Kam	3 111	7	1	1¹	1h	3h	6nk	M Lukas	7500	J V Alexander	13.30
31655Mth6	Four Flats	b 3 111	4	6	3h	5²	7³	7no	J K Daly†	6500	F P Dyer	22.90
31053Aqu4	Meryl Ann	3 113	2	8	8	8	8	8	D Brumfield	7500	Clara L Ostriker	25.00

†Five pounds apprentice allowance waived.

Time .22⅖, .45⅖, 1.11⅕. Track fast.

$2 Mutuel Prices:

1—SWIFT DESTINY	6.40	3.80	2.80
5—FOREIGN FABLE		5.60	3.80
6—SCAIRT			3.20

Dk. b. or br. f, by Ambehaving—Missus Beau, by Bolero. Trainer H. Paley. Bred by Meadowbrook Farm, Inc. (Fla.).

IN GATE AT 3.33. OFF AT 3.33 EASTERN DAYLIGHT TIME. Start good. Won ridden out.

SWIFT DESTINY was sent around the leaders to take command entering the stretch and drew out under intermittent encouragement. FOREIGN FABLE, never far back, gained command between calls in the upper stretch then was no match. SCAIRT rallied between horses in the drive but could not menace. TABITHA had speed to the stretch and weakened. RICOS SPY was never a factor. CRAIGS KAM set the pace to the stretch and tired from her efforts. FOUR FLATS was through early.

Scratched—31622Aqu10 Trolley Car. Overweights—Meryl Ann 2 pounds, Four Flats 1, Ricos Spy 2.

14. FIFTH AT TROPICAL, DECEMBER 12, 1966 —Track Fast

WHAT IS a playable race? Conservative racegoers tend to avoid fields which require a lot of digging below the surface of the past-performance records. They argue that one should not try to find a winner but should await the spots in which choice is unavoidable. This sounds nice, but it is often a camouflage for unwillingness or inability to do real handicapping. Too many self-styled conservative players pass any race in which the leading contender is not a standout at a short price. But I insist that it is much more fun and incomparably more rewarding to dig and dig and dig. Every year, hundreds upon hundreds of Thoroughbreds win at good odds over false favorites. Their victories are predictable. The forecast can be made by any good handicapper willing to spend a few minutes at the job.

Here is a typically mixed-up Tropical Park sprint for $4,500 and $5,000 stock. The winner is by no means a sure thing, but its outstanding chances are predictable. Therefore, the race is eminently playable.

5th Race Tropical

START ▼ 6 FURLONGS TROPICAL PARK ▲ FINISH

6 FURS. (Chute). (Roman Colonel, Dec. 12, 1959, 1.08⅖, 3, 122.)
Claiming. Purse $2,800. 3- and 4-year-olds. Weights, 3-year-olds, 118 lbs., older 120 lbs. Non-winners of two races since Oct. 1 allowed 3 lbs., of a race, 6 lbs. Claiming price $5,000. 3 lbs. allowed if entered for $4,500.

Pinuht's Way $5,000 Dk. ch. c (1962), by Mark the Way or Dulat—Pinutha, by Lochinvar. J.-Y. Stable B. Webb (Mrs. J. Schwartz) **109**5 1966 12 1 1 0 $2,810 1965 16 2 2 3 $6,0[illegible]

26Nov66-5TrP fst 6f .22⅘ .45⅘1.10⅕ Clm 6500 8 8 96½ 87 99¾ 910 CStone b 116 6.60 81-11 Will Dance 118nk Turf Parade 1183¾ Mickey C. 114¾ No speed 12
14Oct66-7Suf fst 6f .23 .46⅕1.10⅗ Clm 10000 4 1 2h 5¾ 58 58½ EMerlano5 b 112 7.50 79-23 Brockton Boy 1126 Mr. Hatfield 114h Terrible 1121½ Early speed 6
7Oct66-8Suf fst 170.46⅗1.11⅗1.42⅘ Cl c-8000 3 3 41¼ 54¾ 712 622 RBruno b 115 3.20 69-16 Cool Caution 1155 Miltreb Hazard 1111 Warriors Day 1124 Tired 7
28Sep66-6Suf fst 6f .21⅘ .45⅕1.10⅗ Allowance 1 1 33 31½ 2h 11½ RBruno b 117 7.10 88-15 Pinuht's Way 1171½ Jack Russell 1132 Smiling Irish 110nk Driving 8
12Sep66-6Nar fst 6f .22⅗ .45 1.09⅖ Clm 7750 5 6 64¾ 78 611 612 RBruno b 113 24.80 87-13 Shushan 1174½ Cimanyd 1172¼ Mr. Hatfield 113no Never a threat 8
21Jly 66-8Rkm fst 6f .22 .45⅖1.11 Allowance 2 6 47 57½ 613 611 RBruno b 112 6.00 78-21 Disdad 1064½ Nannie's Boy 1121½ Shop the Market 109no No factor 7
6Jly 66-8Rkm fst 6f .22⅖ .45⅗1.10⅗ Allowance 3 1 32½ 63¾ 64¾ 65½ RBruno b 115 3.70 85-15 Admiral J. B. 1192¾ Shoot Luke 1081¼ Poco Allegro 113h Brief sp'd 8
21Jun66-7Suf fst 6f .22⅖ .45⅖1.10⅘ Allowance 3 5 52½ 33 32 22 RBruno b 118 5.50 90-17 Lane 1092 Pinuht's Way 1181¼ Royal Ring 110¾ Made a game try 7
7Mar66-6GP fm 1 1/16 Ⓣ 1.12⅖1.44 Clm 7500 •2 2 3½ 64¾122412 23 RBruno b 116 17.10 61-12 Conjunto 1121¾ Mister Lumpus 1164 Eiffel II 1161½ Brief foot 12

Nerva Rullah $5,000 B. f (1962), by Colleoni—Nerve, by Charing Cross Francis Leon Stable H. R. Riley (O. Sledge) **114** 1966 16 4 2 2 $12,337 1965 22 5 4 1 $15,355

2Dec66-5TrP fst 6f .22⅗ .45⅗1.11 f- 5000 2 10 85¼ 54 52¾ 43½ RLawless 117 5.70 83-11 Perfect Lane 115½ Cyco Sal 1152½ Matchless Mark 115½ In close 12
24Oct66-6Det fst 6f .22⅗ .45⅖1.11 Clm 6500 8 3 32 32½ 2h 1no AGaddis5 106 3.50 85-20 Nerva Rullah 106no Launch Out 1142¼ Uppity 1141 Under hard drive 9
10Oct66-8Det sl 6f .22⅗ .45⅗1.11⅗ Clm 6500 6 8 52½ 32 23 24½ ACannon5 106 4.80 77-26 Pied Beauty 1174½ Nerva Rullah 1053½ Entangled 1151½ Game try 8
5Sep66-5Det fst 6f .22⅗ .45 1.11 Clm 08500 6 2 22 31½ 53½ 55 AGaddis5 109 7.10 83-16 Gem Line 117¾ Bee's Little Man 1102½ Skyeppona 112no Early speed 8
29Aug66-8Det fst 6f .22⅗ .44⅘1.10 Clm 8500 5 3 42 43 52½ 44 AGaddis5 112 3.40 86-13 Ryder's Request 1143 Skyepoona 114h Roads End 1171 No mishap 8
22Aug66-7Det gd 6f .22⅕ .45⅗1.11⅗ Clm 11500 2 6 610 610 74½ 64½ AGaddis5 104 8.20 78-22 Green Creek 114h The Nutts 1092½ By Jove 114¾ Lacked early foot 7
LATEST WORKOUTS Nov 27 TrP 7f fst 1.32⅗ b Nov 20 TrP 5f fst 1.04 b Nov 18 TrP 5f fst 1.08⅖ b

Counselor R. H. * $5,000 Dk. b. g (1962), by Condiment—No Story, by Hierocles F. Gomez E. T. Garcia (C. J. Pike) **117** 1966 20 4 2 3 $10,548 1965 19 4 3 1 $10,015

5Dec66-5TrP fst 6f .21⅘ .44⅗1.10⅖ Clm 5000 2 105912 101310 9 109 JVelasquez b 114 *1.10 81-12 Floridafair 114½ Tulran 114½ Nemah Sea 1114¾ Pinched back 11
1Dec66-6TrP fst 6f .22⅕ .45 1.10⅖ Clm 5000 4 6 53¼ 42½ 42½ 42½ BMoreira 116 6.10 87-13 Jingo 1182 Golden Phoenix 116no Cipango 118½ Even effort 12
26Nov66-5TrP fst 6f .22⅖ .45⅖1.10⅕ Clm 6500 3 6 41¼ 52½ 54¼ 67¾ CHMarquez5 110 33.20 83-11 Will Dance 118nk Turf Parade 1183¾ Mickey C. 114¾ Fell back 12
21Nov66-8TrP fst 6f .22⅗ .46 1.10⅗ Clm 7500 7 6 83¾ 76½ 712 912 FSaumell 114 36.60 77-16 Misty Bandit 1155½ Dicks Patrol 119½ Traffic Siren 113¾ Wide 12
13Oct66-6Det fst 6f .22⅖ .45 1.10⅗ Cl c-5000 2 5 42 2½ 2h 2nk DHolmes 117 2.80 87-19 Traffic Line 116nk Counselor R. H. 1174½ Capred 1122½ Gamely 8
30Sep66-8Det sl 6f .22⅗ .45⅗1.12 Clm 6500 2 5 43½ 32 44 43¼ JPBowlds 114 •12.00 77-27 Gem Line 1193 Port Royal 109nk Cosmigraph 1124 No mishap 8
30Sep66—•Dead heat.
21Sep66-6Det my 6f .23 .46⅗1.13⅘ Clm 5000 7 3 2h 2h 11½ 12 JPBowlds 114 *2.30e 71-32 Counselor R. H. 1142 Foot Hills 1142½ Capred 109no Kept to pres're 8
15Sep66-7Det fst 6f .22⅗ .45⅗1.11⅗ Clm 6500 6 5 62¼ 88 712 68¾ DHolmes 114 4.10 73-18 Launch Out 1171¾ Cosmigraph 1141 Dimension 1141 Showed nothing 8
6Sep66-8Det fst 6f .22⅘ .45⅗1.11 Clm 6500 5 4 32½ 41¾ 54 64¼ JPBowlds 114 7.40 81-20 Batsto 115nk Royal Script 117¾ My Pridden Joy 1221 Brief factor 9
LATEST WORKOUTS Nov 12 TrP 3f fst .37⅖ b

Matchless Mark $5,000

Ch. f (1962), by Attention Mark—Royal Freedom, by Four Freedoms
H. Chernia   G. J. Getz   (R. C. Howard, Sr.)   **111**   1966 9 0 1 1 $1,940
1955 15 3 3 0 $6,486

2Dec66–5TrP	fst 6f .22⅗ .45⅗1.11 f–	5000 8	6 4¹½ 2h 1h 3³ CStone b 115 7.20	Bore in 12
13Oct66–6Haw	sly 6f .22⅗ .46 1.11⅘ Clm	7500 8	8 8¹⁵ 8¹⁵ 7¹² 6¹¹ RWinant 113 23.60	No speed 8
30Jly66–9AP	fst*5½f ⓣ	1.07⅕ Clm 12500 7	5 4³½ 2² 68 88½ HMoreno b 111 21.70	Never a contender 10
6Jly66–7AP	fm*5½f ⓣ	1.06 Clm 12500 6	8 8⁷ 8⁷½ 7⁹½ 7⁶½ DWeiler b 112 14.20	Never a contender 10
21Jun66–7AP	fm 5½f ⓣ .47⅕1.05⅕ Clm	11000 1	7 7⁷½ 7⁷½ 6⁵ 4⁴½ DWeiler b 111 19.10	Late foot 9
4Jun66–7AP	fm 5½f ⓣ .45⅗1.03⅗ Clm	20000 6	1 4⁴½ 46 7¹¹ 6⁸¼ DWeiler b 110 33.30	Fell back 8

84–11 Perfect Lane 115¹ Cyco Sal 115²½ Matchless Mark 115½
77–14 Strong Salient 118² Girl of Honor 110¹ Gantlet 118¹½
76–17 Even Take 115¹ Trops Bob 115¹ Fort Ringgold 115¹½
83–11 McGun 117²¾ Gossiper 114h Trops Bob 117½
86– 6 Sensible Son 121¹ A. J.'s Winn 118nk Joyn's Rullah 118³
88– 6 Admiral Clove 117h Silver Joey 123¾ Loopy Loop 114²

Rocky Spring $5,000

B. g (1963–Ill), by Rocky Royale—Sycamore, by Billings
Daybreak Farm   P. L. Kelley   (L. C. Persch–H. Trotsek)   **112**   1966 14 2 0 1 $4,652
1955 5 2 1 0 $4,445

26Oct66–8Det	fst 6f .22⅗ .45⅕1.10⅗ Clm	o6500 3	5 4³½ 4³½ 43 55½ JPBowlds b 114 8.40	Had no mishap 8
12Oct66–6Det	fst 6f .22⅗ .44⅕1.10⅗ Clm	o6500 3	5 3²½ 34 44½ 46 WZakoor b 114 7.00	No mishap 10
4Oct66–6Det	fst 6f .22 .44⅕1.11⅗ Clm	7500 7	4 4² 42½ 34 46 RGallimore b 117 8.40	Had no mishap 9
27Sep66–8Det	fst 6f .22⅕ .45⅗1.11⅗ Clm	o6500 6	2 2¹½ 3¹½ 33½ 31½ RGallimore b 119 2.90	Evenly 8
21Sep66–7Det	my 6f .22⅗ .46 1.12⅕ Clm	75000 5	4 4nk 43½ 6¹¹ 7¹⁵ BWalt b 117 5.10	Tired 7

LATEST WORKOUTS   Dec 10 Hia 3f fst .37⅗b

81–17 Dripping Springs 114²½ Buress 109¹½ Balafib 111½
80–18 Bill Denton 114h Balafib 114³½ Duress 114²½
75–20 Tenor 117³½ Sassy Liz 114²½ Colonel Al 116¹
81–16 Mist o' Len 107nk Royal Discovery 119¹½ Rocky Spring 119³
61–32 RejectedTrouble117¹½ CharmingAlibi112² EastKentucky117²½

Dec 3 Hia 4f fst .49⅖b   Nov 30 Hia 5f fst 1.04 b   Nov 22 Hia 5f fst 1.02 b

Windy Pick $4,500

Ch. c (1963–Ky), by Windy City II—Picks Girl, by Bobs Girl
J. Zoberg   R. E. Dole   (J. B. White Estate)   **109**   1966 14 2 1 1 $6,620
1955 11 3 1 0 $8,355

7Dec66–2TrP	fst 6f .45⅗1.11 Clm	4000 10	2 2¹½ 1h 3½ 3³ MCamacho⁵ b 110 12.00	Bore out 12
28Nov66–1TrP	fst 6f .23 .46½1.10⅗ Clm	3500 2	5 1¹ 2½ 25 7¹⁴ MCamacho⁷ b 113 59.70	Used up 12
15Aug66–2Atl	sly 6f .22⅗ .47 1.13⅗ Clm	3500 1	5 5¹½ 44 44½ 7¹⁰ MCamacho⁷ b 108 18.20	Used up 10
27Jly66–6Mth	fst 6f .22⅗ .45⅕1.12 Clm	5500 7	3 6³½ 6⁷½ 6¹¹ 8²¹ SHernandez b 114 12.00	Factor, tired 10
15Jun66–2Mth	fst 6f .22 .45⅕1.12½ Clm	5000 1	6 1¹¹ 1¹½ 53¹¹ 10¹¹ SHernandez b 116 4.10	Fell far back 8
8Jun66–5Mth	fst 6f .22⅗ .45⅕1.14⅗ Clm	7000 4	1 1h 1½ 32½ 8¹³ SHernandez b 113 10.40	Used up 11
12May66–5Pim	fst 6f .22⅗ .45⅕1.13⅗ Clm	7500 4	2 2h 1¹ 2¹ 7⁹½ LGino b 116 3.40	Early speed, tired 11
22Apr66–8GP	fm 1 ⓣ 1.11⅗1.37 Clm	10500 4	4 5³½ 7¹² 8¹⁸ 8²⁵ FToro b 116 24.40	Tired when headed 8
11Apr66–5GP	fst 6f .22⅗ .45⅕1.12⅗ Clm	7000 1	6 3¹½ 2½ 1h 34 JSellers b 114 2.80	Brief speed 8
24Mar66–4GP	fst 6f .21⅗ .44⅕1.10⅗ Clm	9000 3	3 3³½ 5⁷ 8¹⁵ 9²⁰ SHernandez b 116 10.90	Faltered 8
8Mar66–6GP	fst 6f .22⅗ .45⅕1.11 Clm	10500 9	5 2¹½ 58¹²10¹⁸10²¹ BMoreira b 112 4.20	Tired 9

LATEST WORKOUTS   Nov 27 GP 3f fst .36⅗ b

84–13 Jr. Derby 117¹½ Windy Pick 110² Mesa Marie 113¹
75–15 Grand Marais 116¹⁰ Self Winder 116¹¾ La Vedette 111¹½
65–24 Rakish Lad 114² Peppy Sailor 117⁴½ Mr. Shine j151¼
He's My Partner 112½ Harmo 122¹½ No Proof 113⁶
70–16 Cap'n. Shorty 116²½ Harmo 119nº Count Melody 114¾
72–22 Rakish Lad 122¹ Longloc 119¹½ Eva Kin 113¹½
64–19 Kerensa 106³½ Sage Jamie 116nº Colonel Bob A. 116½
77–21 FlamingBull 112¹½ DeepWaterPoint 116²½ WindyPick 114²
72–17 Vale of Tears 116⁴ Cosmic Lane 111³ Harmony Again 122²
68–12 Nashua's Joy 116² Brawny John 116² Cosmic Lane 111¹½

Top Musketeer $5,000

B. g (1962), by Bolero U.—Flaming Belle, by Tiger Rebel
Mrs. E. Branch   R. C. Baker   (Mrs. B. T. Megibben)   **120**   1966 13 6 4 0 $10,990
1965 18 5 3 1 $8,980

3Dec66–2TrP	fst 6f .22⅗ .45⅗1.10⅕ Clm	3500 3	8 86½ 62½ 1½ 1¹ RBehrens b 118 7.90	Driving 12
29Oct66–2Det	fst 6f .22⅗ .45⅗1.10⅘ Clm	o2500 7	7 66½ 5² 21² 23½ VTartaglia b 117 3.90	Game try 9
22Oct66–4Det	fst 6f .22⅗ .44⅗1.11⅗ Clm	o2500 5	6 5²½ 63½ 24 32½ VTartaglia b 119 2.40	Finished well 8
	22Oct66—Awarded second purse money.		
8Oct66–3Det	fst 6f .22⅕ .44⅕1.10 Cl	c–2000 4	4 3²½ 3¹½ 2½ 1½ DAnderson⁵ b 114 2.90	Hard drive 8
28Sep66–8WO	fst 1¹⁄₁₆.47 1.11⅗1.45 Clm	3000 4	1 1²½ 1¹ 1½ 22½ BWerry⁵ b 118 *2.30	Couldn't last 8
20Sep66–8WO	fst 1¹⁄₁₆.47⅗1.12⅘1.46⅗ Clm	3000 6	1 1²½ 15 1⁶ 1²½ BWerry⁵ b 117 9.55	Mild dr. 8

91–8 Top Musketeer 118¹ Keller 116⁷ Innocence 113²½
82–23 Vita Brevis 107³½ Top Musketeer 117³ Larry R 116½
80–15 T. Bird 117¹½ Quarter Til 112¹ Top Musketeer 119³
90–13 Top Musketeer 114½ T Bird 122⁶ Voan 114²
78–18 Paraguyao 115²½ Top Musketeer 118¹ Uniprix 110²½
83–23 TopMusketeer117²½ RococoRogue117⁴d–GoldenBubble108¹½

Ken O. F. $4,500

B. c (1962), by Pry—Royal Fete, by Royal Charger
H. Trotsek   H. Trotsek   (B. Johnson)   **111**   1966 2 0 0 0 $160
1965 5 1 0 1 $1,990

5Dec66–5TrP	fst 6f .21⅘ .44⅗1.10⅘ Clm	5000 3	3 1¹¹ 3² 99 LHensman b 114 12.80	Hard used 11
13Jan66–6TrP	fst 6f .22 .44 1.10⅘ Clm	7500 9	1 14 13 1¹ 42¾ EFires⁵ 109 4.40	Used in pace 9
27Dec65–7TrP	fst 6f .22⅕ .45⅗1.10⅘ Clm	7000 4	5 52½ 1¹ 1¹ 3½ ECardone⁵ 114 24.50	Clear lead, tired 10
16Dec65–1TrP	fst 6f .22 .45 1.11⅘ Md	5000 10	1 1h 1³ 1³ 1h ECardone⁵ 115 27.60	All out to last 11
19Nov65–6CD	fst 6f .23 .46⅗1.13 Md Sp Wt	2	1 1¹ 1² 2¹½ 66½ RTurner⁵ 113 48.10	Much used in lead 11
2Oct65–1Haw	my 6½f.22⅗ .47⅕1.22½ Clm	2500 4	1 53 69 6¹⁰ 8¹² ECardone⁵ 108 24.30	Tired 10
15Oct65–5Haw	fst 6f .22⅕ .45⅗1.14⅘ Clm	3500 5	2 2h 1h 10¹²11¹¹⁷ ECardone⁵ 108 90.60	Stopped 12

LATEST WORKOUTS   Dec 4 Hia 3f fst .38 b

81–12 Floridafair 114½ Tulran 114½ Nemah Sea 111⁴½
85–17 Jet Fare 114¹½ Tanteo 114¹½ Nail's Gal 107nº
89–14 TrojanFleet 114h JamesB.W. 109¼ KenO.F. 107⁴
84–15 Ken O. F. 115h Boldbrook 120¹½ Norval 120¹½
75–19 Copra Girl 115³ Gap 115nk School Tie 118¹½
51–29 Mighty Venture 122⁶ Aunt Faye 107¹ Grand Garden 113¹
71–16 Sailing Chance 118² Federal Case 120nk Bless Frances 114²

First Warrior $5,000

Dk. b. or br. f (1963–Mont), by Sun Warrior—Lively Anne, by Marching Sir
C. Leitzel   J. H. Smith   (R. C. Forster)   **109**   1966 11 3 2 0 $3,597
1965 0 M 0 0

5Nov66–9Wat	sly 6f .23⅕ .47⅗1.14⅗ Allowance	5	1 1½ 1h 2h 74¾ SDesOrmeaux⁵ 111 16.90	Used up 9
19Oct66–8Wat	sly 6f .23⅗ .47⅗1.14⅗ Allowance	4	6 3¹½ 5¹¾ 64 6¹¹ SDesOrmeaux⁵ 107 4.90	Bad start 6
5Oct66–8Wat	fst 5½f.23⅗ .47 1.07⅗ Allowance	5	1 1² 1¹½ 1½ 2½ SDesOrm'x⁵ 107 5.60	Hard drive 8
18Aug66–9EvD	fst 6f .22 .46⅗ .58⅗ Allowance	6	4 64½ 66¾ 67½ 68 JManuel 109 20.80	Fell back 8
13Aug66–1EvD	fst 1¹⁄₁₆.47⅗1.13⅗1.50 Houston	2	7 67½ 56 43 54¼ DBaker 114 3.60	Evenly 7
6Aug66–8EvD	my 6½f.23⅗ .48⅕1.23 Allowance	2	1 3²½ 34 43½ 45½ JManuel 109 *2.10	No excuse 10
23Jly66–8EvD	gd 7f .22⅗ .46 1.26⅗ Allowance	1	2 1²½ 2¹ 2¹½ 2¹½ JManuel 109 4.50	Held on willingly 7

72–28 Taffy's Brother 116² Dr. Powder 113¾ Royal Gaiety 108¹
68–32 Rum Punch 112h Barton's Mistake 112¹½ Pat Santo 115²
79–29 First Warrior 107¹ Star Player 116³ Balsark 106nk
—— Moving Free 117²½ Irwin 119² Pixie Creek 107²½
—— Beebe's Fare Eve 109nº Boeble Coin 111½ Ed Turner 116¹
—— Retsev 117nk Rock Breaker 117h Tribe's Son 109⁵
—— Irwin 116¹½ First Warrior 109³½ Retsev 116²½

Nemah Sea $5,000

Ch. f (1962), by Nemah—Just Sea, by Plowshare
C. J.–P. T. Adwell   P. T. Adwell   (C. R. Roth)   **111**   1966 26 4 2 5 $10,757
1965 29 3 3 5 $9,135

5Dec66–5TrP	fst 6f .21⅗ .44⅗1.10⅘ Clm	5000 11	4 34 35 2h 3¹ WAPeake b 111 39.40	Sharp try 11
26Nov66–2TrP	fst 6f .22⅗ .46 1.10 f–	5000 2	4 2¹ 33 38 IValenzuela b 117 4.60	Weakened 12
24Oct66–5Spt	fst 6½f.22⅗ .46⅗1.18 Clm	4500 4	2 33½ 2¹ 2² 2² LSnyder b 117 3.30	Well placed, evenly 10
19Oct66–5Haw	gd 6f .22⅗ .45⅗1.12 f–	5000 6	8 8¹¹ 9¹² 77½ 46¹ MHeath b 122 *2.70e	Stride late 12
8Oct66–6Haw	fst 6½f.22⅗ .45⅗1.17⅕ Clm	4500 10	8 88½ 87³ 42½ 2nº MHeath b 117 9.20	Just missed 12
24Sep66–2Haw	fst 6½f.22⅗ .45⅗1.17⅕ Clm	3500 10	6 77½ 77½ 64 5¹ IValenzuela b 115 *7.80	Going away 11
16Sep66–2Haw	fst 6f .22⅗ .46 1.16⅘ Clm	3500 9	2 42 2¹ 2½ 51½ IValenzuela b 117 3.10	Weakened 9
30Aug66–6AP	fst 1 .45⅗1.10 1.36⅕ Clm	1500 12	3 53 44¼ 96¾ IValenzuela b 113 18.9¹	Early foot 12
23Aug66–5AP	fst 6f .22⅕ .45⅕1.11 f–	5000 1	9 65½ 46 56 IValenzuela b 117 5.00e	Closed well 12
13Aug66–4AP	fst 6½f.23⅗ .46⅗1.17⅘ Clm	5000 10	5 10 10⁹½ 8¹² 9⁸½ 85² RCox⁵ b 109 6.20	Never close 12

LATEST WORKOUTS   Dec 3 TrP 4f fst .50 b

89–12 Floridafair 114½ Tulran 114½ Nemah Sea 111⁴½
79–11 Brentwood Miss 112⁴½ Koala 112³½ Nemah Sea 117nº
86–12 Cipango 118¾ Nushka 116² Nemah Sea 112⁴
80–17 My Marion 122¹½ Tillie's Alibi 115⁴½ Chiclu 120¹
88–11 Crown Chief 122nº Nemah Sea 117¹ Cipango 122¾
88–12 Nemah Sea 115³ Troy Our Boy 112¹½ Troa 116½
88– 4 Overton Lane 122nk Better Hit 116nº Granitville 117¹½
78–12 Good Pacific 110² Flight Line 110nº Zagtoora 110³
85–14 Chiclu 113²½ My Marion 113nk Bay Maid 117½
81–19 Whiz Luke 119¹½ Bay Maid 114½ Fleet n' True 119nk

Shootin Rabbit $5,000

B. f (1963–Ky), by Gun Shot—Skid Row, by Shut Out
M. Level   M. Level   (H. Jones)   **109**   1966 13 0 0 2 $990
1965 10 1 0 2 $3,030

15Oct66–6Suf	fst 6f .22⅗ .46⅗1.12⅘ Clm	3500 10	8 74½ 95½ 72 43½ HWajda 111 5.70	Raced slightly wide 10
4Oct66–6Suf	fst 6f .22⅗ .45⅗1.13⅘ Clm	5000 7	2 76 68 79 78½ MCarrozz'la b 114 4.10	Bore in early 7
27Sep66–4Suf	fst 6f .22⅗ .45⅗1.11⅗ Clm	3500 7	6 54½ 44 22 22 MCarrozzella 111 23.80	Hung 8
24Sep66–3Suf	fst 6f .22⅗ .46⅗1.13⅗ Clm	3750 2	6 43½ 44½ 56½ 65½ TThorndike 107 11.50	Brief factor 8
9Sep66–2Aqu	fst 6f .22⅗ .46⅗1.14 Clm	3500 7	1 41½ 41½ 56½ 67 CMcPeek⁵ b 105 7.80	Tired 7
1Sep66–1Aqu	fst 7f .23 .47 1.27¹⁄₅ f–	3500 1	7 34 46 44½ 54¹ CMcPeek⁷ 107 45.70	No late response 12
25Aug66–9Sar	fst 6f .22⅗ .46⅗1.13⅘ f–	3500 4	6 85½ 87½ 87 87½ JCombest 114 29.40	No factor 9
16Aug66–2Sar	fst 1¹⁄₁₆.47⅗1.13 1.54¹⁄₅ Clm	3500 3	1 2½ 54 81⁶10³¾ JJMartin⁷ 99 27.50	Fell far back 10
9Aug66–2Sar	fst 6f .22⅕ .46⅗1.13⅘ f–	3500 4	6 54 68½ 78½ 8¹¹ JCombest 114 18.50	Brief foot, tired 10
21Jly66–1Aqu	fst 6f .22⅗ .46⅗1.13⅘ f–	3500 5	3 31½ 85½ 89 9¹⁰ JCombest 114 4.70	No factor 9
28Jun66–7Aqu	fst 6f .22⅗ .46⅕1.12⅘ Clm	4500 2	3 32 46½ 68½ 6¹¹ ECardone 111 *1.50	Could not keep up 8

LATEST WORKOUTS   Dec 1 TrP 5f fst 1.03 b

73–19 Kaladerma 107¹½ Kings Fool 117¹ Living In 111¹
74–21 Blakstep 117nk Area Code 114¹ Miss Saybrook 116²
83–17 Styrullah 120nº Jeepdolf 114½ Shootin Rabbit 111½
67–21 Ready Mix 113nk Predensa 112² Doctor Lucky 110¹
63–25 Validated 113² Enchanter 117⁵ Dark Doings 115¼
73–19 Perfect Shoe 118² Pear Shaped 112¹ Tara's Girl 112²½
41–16 Never Wrong 116³ Clavero 116²½ Motor 123⁸
41–16 Perfect Shoe 113³² Huleen 117½ That's Hew 114²½
66–21 Huleen 118³ Never a Doubt 111¹½ Syncom 114½
69–19 Aurous 118³½ Deducts 107¹ Early Moon 107³

Parkway North × $5,000 — B. g (1963-Ky), by North Cone—Our Carol, by Goya II — Iso Stable — J. F. Plett — (O. C. Rasch) — **112**

1966	19	1	1	4	$4,395
1965	4	M	1	1	$1,400

21Nov66-6TrP	fst	6f	.22⅗	.45⅖	1.10⅘	Clm	6500	9	10	1119	1222	1226	1226	LMoyers	b 115	58.30	62-16	Judy's Whiz 1195½ Mr. Joe A. 1171 Runagate 1152	Never close	12
10Sep66-5Ran	fst	6f	.23⅕	.47	1.12⅖	Allowance		8	7	75¾	78	45	33	RSterling	b 115	*1.30	83-21	Red Cone 1152 Zim 1151 Parkway North 115½	Lacked early foot	8
5Sep66-8Ran	gd	6½f	.23⅘	.47⅗	1.19⅗	Allowance		5	8	66	811	713	713	RSterling	b 112	84.20	70-27	Billispace 1191¼ Diamond Beau 122½ Arbitrary 1221	Showed nothing	9
26Aug66-6Ran	fst	6f	.22⅘	.47⅕	1.13	Allowance		6	4	51¾	4¾	2½	31¼	GRichards	b 119	3.30	82-23	Belle Musique 117½ Marshall Jay 122¾ Parkway North 1191½	In close	8
18Aug66-7Ran	fst	5½f	.23	.47⅕	1.06⅗	Allowance		4	1	32	23	22	35	GRichards	b 116	19.10	81-29	Ariel Road 116h Stake Sauce 1185 Parkway North 1162	Good effort	8
1Aug66-5Mth	fst	6f	.22⅕	.45⅗	1.11⅖	Allowance		8	6	66	815	813	716	RMcCurdy	115	20.10e	69-17	Quite an Accent 1141½ Conchy Joe 1065 Farmer's Son 1152	No sp'd	8
25Jly 66-7Mth	fst	6f	.22	.45⅕	1.10⅘	Allowance		1	7	76	812	812	815	CBaltazar	113	28.80	73-17	Tully, Jr. 1133½ Bon Voyageur 1153 Johnny's Form 116¾	Dull try	8
2Jly 66-4Mth	fm	1 1/16 (T)			1.44⅘	Clm	12000	1	1	3½	46	815	720	DBrumfield	113	21.20	71- 9	Silver Score 1143 Crimson Tide 1145 Proxy Fight 1162½	Used up	8
25Jun66-3Mth	fst	1 1/16	.47⅗	1.12	1.45	Clm	13000	4	8	812	713	711	512	RMcCurdy	112	26.40	68-13	Lanoma Sun 1072 Came to Play 114nk Tara Host 1162	Broke slowly	8
15Jun66-5Mth	fst	6f	.22⅘	.46⅖	1.12⅗	Cl	c-7000	6	4	51¼	54¼	77¼	87	GPatterson	b 116	7.20	72-16	Behaving Bee 1193½ South Creek 112¾ Sound Tract 113½	Tired	9
8Jun66-5Mth	fst	6f	.22⅕	.45⅕	1.11⅖	Clm	7500	11	6	/63¼	76½	75¼	712	JKDaly	b 115	10.50	73-11	Child Prodigy 1152 Boffo 1152½ Snap Back 1132	Forced to race wide	11
1Jun66-7Del	fst	6f	.22⅘	.47⅗	1.13⅖	Clm	7500	11	7	72¾	54	43½	34¼	KDaly	b 115	7.00	74-24	Longloc 1174 Cross the Sea 114nk Parkway North 1153	Went wide	11
17May66-7GS	sly	6f	.22⅗	.46⅗	1.12	Clm	11000	6	3	42	51¾	67½	710	GPatterson	b 112	19.10	74-23	WillContinue1164½RetreatingStar1161½LanomaSun1161¼	Wide	7

LATEST WORKOUTS Dec 6 TrP 5f fst 1.01⅖ bg

Horses Shown Below Are on the "Also Eligible" List and Are Not Listed in Order of Post Positions.

Perfect Lane × $5,000 — B. f (1963-Can), by Dutch Lane—Perfect Cee, by Roman Might — E. I. Mack — L. W. Jennings — (D. G. Kellough) — **115**

1966	20	5	5	3	$13,640
1965	12	2	1	2	$3,590

2Dec66-5TrP	fst	6f	.22⅗	.45⅗	1.11	f-	4500	11	2	52¾	42	3nk	1½	JVelasquez	115	*0.80	87-11	Perfect Lane 115½ Cyco Sal 1152½ Matchless Mark 115½	Driving	12
23Nov66-3TrP	fst	6f	.22⅗	.46	1.10⅘	f-	4000	2	4	44½	32	1½	16	JVelasquez	114	3.70	88-11	Perfect Lane 1146 Think Pretty 1141½ Merizon 1182¾	Ridden out	12
8Nov66-4GS	fst	6f	.22⅖	.46⅖	1.12⅘	f-	3500	2	2	84¾	53¾	54¾	56	JVelasquez	113	*1.40	74-20	Floral 113½ Ruddy-Dud 1204 Fair Flapper 113no	No response	12
24Aug66-6Atl	gd	7f	.23	.46⅖	1.25⅕	f-	5500	5	4	2h	2h	21½	83	MMiceli7	108	5.40	74-21	Who Cabled 113½ Unfair 115½ Lesfear 117¾	Well up, tired	12
16Aug66-3Atl	gd	6f	.22	.46⅕	1.13	f-	4500	7	2	25	23	1½	13	JVelasquez	112	*1.40	77-22	Perfect Lane 1123 Who Cabled 1121½ Arctic Aid 1052	Mild drive	7
7Jly 66-6Mth	fst	6f	.22⅗	.46⅕	1.12⅕	f-	6250	4	6	21	31	53	75¾	CBaltazar	111	8.90	75-20	Tennessee Iris 108nk Greek Princess 1091½ Infinita 1151½	Used up	10
24Jun66-6Mth	fst	6f	.22⅘	.46⅖	1.12⅗	f-	6750	8	2	42½	57½	67	68¾	CBaltazar	110	3.50	70-20	Cherokee Mary 1131¼ General Note 1091¾ Sound Tract 1133	Wide	8

LATEST WORKOUTS Dec 10 Hia 4f fst .50 b — Nov 19 Hia 4f sly .49⅕ h — Nov 5 GS 5f fst 1.02⅖ b — Oct 22 GS 4f fst .48⅘ h

Cissycidella $5 000 — Ch. f (1963-Ky), by Australian Star—Speed Trust, by On Trust — E. A. Dust — J. P. Mayberry — (C. Carmine) — **104⁵**

1966	6	M	0	0	$25
1965	6	M	1	0	$920

30Jly 66-7Rd	fm	7½f (T)			1.33⅖	Handicap		2	6	814	913	817	719	TJoseph	109	52.80	71-18	Miss Hill 1122¼ Little to Say 1131¼ Regal Denial 120nk	No speed	9
27Jun66-3RD	fst	6f	.22⅖	.46⅕	1.11⅘	Md Sp Wt		9	11	910	1014	78	78¾	TJoseph	b 106	8.80	78-16	Drill Master 1134 Josie's Gal 110h Greek Beau 114	Broke slowly	12
21Jun66-8RD	fst	170	.46⅘	1.12	1.42⅖	Allowance		5	5	31	53½	716	721	TJoseph5	b 107	25.50	67-14	UncleCooter 1134 Commoroman 1083 LikelyTale113nk	Stopped badly	7
9Jun66-3MP	fst	4½f	.22⅕	.46	.52⅗	f-MdSpWt		3	8		76¾	711	57½	LGRivera	b 112	11.60	87- 9	Tootie Belle 1153 Printable 1122½ Fast Living 1131	Bore out	8
19May66-7CD	fst	6f	.21⅗	.45⅕	1.11⅕	f-Allow		3	9	810	711	915	911	LWGrubb	108	42.80	79-12	Lisanninga 1121½ Casa Do Oir 112h I've Arrived 107½	Far back	10
26Apr66-4Kee	fst	6f	.22⅕	.45⅘	1.10⅗	Md Sp Wt		2	7	87½	1014	919	817	JYork	108	21.20f	73-13	Dominar 1127 Sam's Pacemaker 111h He's My Fella 111h	No speed	12

LATEST WORKOUTS Dec 9 GP 4f fst .48 hg — Dec 5 GP 5f fst 1.03 bg — Nov 28 GP 3f fst .36⅗ b — Nov 24 GP 6f fst 1.16 b

Pinuht's Way: Scratched.

Nerva Rullah: Scratched.

Counselor R.H.: After two preparatory efforts in November, this consistent minor-league winner was dropped into a race for $5,000 animals and showed a touch of run on December 1. Came back four days later as favorite under Velasquez and lost all chance when a slow start from the gate left the jockey without room in which to maneuver. Slow-breaking horses are at a terrible disadvantage here, as at most other tracks. Even if Counselor R.H. turns out to be the best horse in this race, I would not risk money on its chances. NO BET.

Matchless Mark: Getz went for broke in this filly's first Florida start ten days ago, dropping her into a race against $5,000 females and almost getting the winner's end. The emphasis on grass races during June and July, and the poor effort on the dirt in October combine with the latest drop in claiming price to imply that the animal has physical troubles. Finally, Matchless Mark would probably have won on December 2 if she had not ducked toward the rail in the stretch—another hint of unsoundness. NO BET.

Rocky Spring: Scratched.

Windy Pick: Scratched.

Top Musketeer: That was a good win in excellent time on December 3, but this honest horse is too cheap for serious consideration in a $5,000 field. It may surprise, but I would not want to venture a bet on its chances. NO BET.

Ken O.F.: Harry Trotsek kept this front-runner for almost eleven months before springing it on December 5. It showed enough of its former early speed to justify a prediction of improvement today. But even at its best in late 1965, it was the kind that gave up the ghost in the stretch. It gets a vote of no confidence from me, but can be expected to be in early contention. NO BET.

First Warrior: If this filly can't win five-furlong allowance races at Evangeline Downs, she can be discarded in her first start at Tropical. NO BET.

Nemah Sea: Gobbled up Ken O.F. a week ago and almost won a race exactly like today's. Her swift performance on that occasion can be taken as readiness to do even better today. Fears about her essential class are warranted but should not be exaggerated. In particular, one should not be put off by that $1,500 claiming price last August 30. The figure is a typographical error in the official past-performance record. Arlington Park does not run races for $1,500 horses. Chances are it was a $4,500 or $5,500 price tag, as the high odds suggest. The good closing effort against $4,500 males on October 24, the comfortable debut here on November 26, and the corking effort of last week make this filly a possibility. CONTENDER.

Shootin Rabbit: Scratched.

Parkway North: The drop in claiming price does not promise to help this horse, which has been on the downgrade since May and can't even win at Randall Park. NO BET.

Perfect Lane: Larry Jennings has won two-for-two here with this speedy, consistent miss, and now he tries her against the opposite sex. CONTENDER.

The contenders are both fillies—the four-year-old Nemah Sea and the younger Perfect Lane. Nemah Sea's last race was a decisively faster one than Perfect Lane's. Note the pace figures: .44% and 1.10% for the Nemah Sea race, as against .45% and 1.11 for Perfect Lane. Inasmuch as Nemah Sea has demonstrated her willingness to run against males and promises to improve over her last effort, she must be accorded a big edge over the Jennings entrant. Perfect Lane shows no races against males in her past performances and no speed comparable to Nemah Sea's.

The Running of the Race

THE CROWD seldom goes in for close analysis of pace. In this case it put most of its money on Perfect Lane and made Counsellor R.H. its second favorite. Nemah Sea was a pronounced overlay at 4.60–1.

Ken O.F. showed the usual early speed but, also as usual, was unable to stay in front. Counselor R.H. got off to its customary slow start and never reached true contention. Matchless Mark ran a splendid race, but Nemah Sea was too good, drawing away at the finish.

FIFTH RACE **6 FURLONGS (Chute).** **(Sikkim, December 10, 1966, 1.08, 3, 119.)**

TrP - 29595 Claiming. Purse $2,800. 3- and 4-year-olds. Weights, 3-year-olds, 118 lbs., older 120 lbs. Non-winners of two races since Oct. 1 allowed 3 lbs., of a race, 6 lbs. Claiming price $5,000. 3 lbs. allowed if entered for $4,500.

December 12, 1966

Value to winner $1,820, second $560, third $280, fourth $140. Mutuel pool $52,984.

Index	Horse	Eqt A Wt	PP	St	¼	½	Str	Fin	Jockey	Cl'g Pr	Owner	Odds $1
29535TrP^{3}	Nemah Sea	b 4 111	6	5	3^{1}	3^{2}	3^{4}	$1^{1\frac{1}{4}}$	W A Peake	5000	C J-P T Adwell	4.60
29515TrP^{3}	M'tchless M'rk	b 4 113	2	6	1^{h}	2^{3}	2^{h}	$2^{2\frac{1}{2}}$	C Stone	5000	H Chernin	6.70
29535TrP^{9}	Ken O. F.	b 4 111	4	1	2^{2}	$1^{1\frac{1}{2}}$	1^{h}	3no	L Hansman	4500	H Trotsek	5.70
29535TrP^{10}	C'nselor R. H.	b 4 114	1	7	5^{1}	4^{2}	4^{3}	4^{3}	A Cordero	5000	F Gomez	3.80
29522TrP^{1}	Top Musketeer	b 4 120	3	8	8	$7^{1\frac{1}{2}}$	5^{1}	$5^{2\frac{1}{4}}$	R Behrens	5000	Mrs E Branch	4.70
29216TrP^{12}	Parkway North	b 3 112	7	3	7^{2}	8	7^{1}	6^{h}	L Moyers	5000	Iso Stable	29.40
29515TrP^{1}	Perfect Lane	3 115	8	2	$6\frac{1}{2}$	6^{h}	6^{h}	$7^{3\frac{1}{4}}$	J Velasquez	5000	E I Mack	2.40
29246Wat^{7}	First Warrior	3 115	5	4	4^{1}	$5^{1\frac{1}{2}}$	8	8	L Hills	5000	G Leitzel	50.30

Time .22$\frac{3}{5}$, .45$\frac{2}{5}$, 1.11$\frac{1}{5}$. Track fast.

$2 Mutuel Prices:

6-NEMAH SEA	11.20	5.80	3.60
2-MATCHLESS MARK		9.00	5.60
4-KEN O. F.			5.20

Ch. f, by Nemah—Just Sea, by Plowshare. Trainer P. T. Adwell. Bred by C. R. Roth.

IN GATE AT 3.03. OFF AT 3.03 EASTERN STANDARD TIME. Start good. Won driving.

NEMAH SEA, never far back, was sent up along the inside to reach the leaders a furlong out and outfinished MATCHLESS MARK. The latter, hustled into contention along the inside leaving the chute, came outside to catch KEN O. F. entering the stretch and continued on with good energy. The latter opened a clear lead on the turn but failed to stay. COUNSELOR R. H. finished evenly. TOP MUSKETEER was always outrun. PERFECT LANE had no mishap. FIRST WARRIOR showed some early foot.

Scratched—29244TrP^{9} Pinuht's Way, 29514TrP^{4} Nerva Rullah, 29101Det^{5} Rocky Spring, 29552TrP^{2} Windy Pick, 29020Suf^{4} Shootin Rabbit, 28232RD^{7} Cissycidella.

Corrected weight—Counselor R. H. 114, First Warrior 115. Overweight—Matchless Work 2 pounds.

Nemah Sea was claimed by A. W. Bettman, trainer G. Gay. Perfect Lane was claimed by Bartlett-Ternes, trainer J. Bartlett.

---

15. FIFTH AT ROCKINGHAM, AUGUST 23, 1967—Track Fast

A SIX-FURLONG sprint for $5,000 and $5,500 two-year-olds. The final payoff is enormous, in view of the circumstances.

5th Rockingham

Start ▾ **6 FURLONGS** ROCKINGHAM PARK ▴Finish

6 FURS. (Chute). (Dandy Blitzen, Aug 29, 1959, 1.08⅘, 4, 116.) Claiming. Purse $3,000. 2-year-olds which have not won two races. Weight, 122 lbs. Non-winners since July 30, allowed 3 lbs., June 30, 6 lbs. Claiming price, $5,500, 2 lbs. allowed for each $250 to $5,000.

La Suena — $5,250

B. f (1965–Ark), by Cheiron—Donna Mon, by Easy Mon — B. Coffey, B. Coffey (B. Coffey) — **111** — 1967 11 1 0 0 $2,041

15Aug67–4Rkm	fst 6f	.22⅘ .47⅕ 1.13⅖	f–	4750	8	2	31½	32	41¾	42½	CBrinson	114	13.40	74–16	Velvet Sheen 107h Tache De Beaute 117¾ Tyche 1201¾	Weakened	8
8Aug67–5Rkm	fst 6f	.22 .46 1.13⅕	Clm	5500	4	4	35	45	45½	46	CBrinson	116	11.40	72–19	Fractious 1062¼ Su Neila T. 1112 Lin's Royal Dawn 1091¾	No threat	10
1Aug67–4Rkm	fst 6f	.22⅘ .47⅖ 1.13⅕	Clm	5000	8	3	21	33	48½	514	CBrinson	114	15.70	64–19	Not Too Modest 1151¼ Fractious 1055¼ Eddie'sBlaze1163½	Tired	8
18Jly 67–6Rkm	fst 5½f	.23⅕ .46⅖ 1.06⅖	f–	5000	7	4	73	815	819	721	CBrinson	114	5.50	69–18	Half Space 1097½ Fractious 112¾ Tache De Beaute 1102	Tired	8
29Jun67–4Aks	fst 5½f	.22⅗ .46⅕ 1.05⅖	Allowance		1	5	107¾	915	914	916	LCPeck	119	6.00f	73–13	Mama'sShadow1124How–Tum1142½Herm'sRoyal1093½	Lacked speed	12
20Jun67–3Aks	fst 5½f	.23⅕ .48 1.08⅗	Md Sp Wt		7	8	84¼	84½	41½	1h	LCPeck	b 115	15.40	74–19	La Suena 115h T. Model 118nk Cardinal Bird 118nk	Narrowly best	12
18May67–4Aks	fst 4½f	.23 .46⅘ .53	Clm	7500	12	12		107¾	910	86	RMundorf	111	31.10f	89– 5	Step In Space 1162 Oldport 114¾ Diron Star 117¾	Began slowly	12
5May67–3Spt	fst 4f	.22⅗ .46	f–MdSpWt		5	8		717	818	914	JCantu	120	14.10	84– 2	PalTotsy1207 HereSheGoes 1203 LikeReward 1202	Showed nothing	10
27Apr67–4Spt	fst 4f	.22⅖ .46⅘	Clm	5500	1	5		611	67¼	55½	JCantu	114	46.10	88– 6	Sun Jet 1122¼ Iron Spike 1163 Special Flame 112h	Not a threat	9
4Apr67–5OP	fst 4f	.23⅗ .47⅖	Ark. Fut'y		4	5		711	812	712	JEbardt	115	110.20	77–12	Etony 120½ Touch A Go Go 1201 Jeri Gift 1152½	Was never close	10

4Apr67—The Arkansas Futurity run in two divisions, 4th and 5th races.

LATEST WORKOUTS Aug 5 Rkm 6f sl 1.16 h — Jly 29 Rkm 4f gd .50 h — Jly 16 Rkm 3f fst .38⅘ b

Tache De Beaute — $5,000

B. f (1965–Fla), by Leslie Boy—Nancy H., by Manteau — B. A. Dario, W. A. LaRue (B. A. Dario) — **115** — 1967 14 1 4 2 $4,725

15Aug67–4Rkm	fst 6f	.22⅘ .47⅕ 1.13⅖	f–	4750	4	3	1½	1h	1h	2h	HWajda	b 117	4.70	77–16	Velvet Sheen 107h Tache De Beaute 117¾ Tyche 1201¾	Sharp	8
1Aug67–3Rkm	fst 5½f	.23⅕ .47⅘ 1.07⅘	Md	4000	1	3	13	12	11½	1nk	LMoyers	b 113	*1.80	83–19	TacheDeBeaute113nk Mr.Ararat120nk CapriciousSue1122¾	Driving	10
18Jly 67–6Rkm	fst 5½f	.23⅕ .46⅖ 1.06⅖	f–	4500	5	6	42¼	46½	48	38¼	LMoyers	b 110	*1.40	82–18	Half Space 1097½ Fractious 112¾ Tache De Beaute 1102	No excuse	8
12Jly 67–3Rkm	my 5½f	.22⅗ .46⅘ 1.06⅘	Md	5500	6	6	43	33	23	25¼	LMoyers	b 113	*1.30	83–18	MarryFreddy1175¼TacheDeBeaute1131¾Dooberg'sDare116h	No exc.	11
15Jun67–3Suf	fst 5f	.23⅕ .47⅘ 1.00⅗	Md	5500	2	5	41½	42	23	24	HWajda	b 115	*1.60	84–18	Quid's Glory 1144 Tache de Beaute 1152½ No Smoke 113no	No excuse	10
6Jun67–3Suf	fst 4½f	.23 .47⅗ .54⅕	Md	5500	9	7		33½	35	33½	HWajda	b 117	2.80	84–12	Su Neila T. 1173½ WhirlingAbility120no TacheDeBeaute1173	Evenly	10
9May67–3Suf	hy 4½f	.24 .49⅖ .56⅕	Md	7000	3	3		31½	66	69¼	CG'mbardella	b 112	3.00	69–22	d–All Magic 113nk Esquire House 1182½ I'm in Favor 118no	Tired	8
25Apr67–3Suf	sl 4½f	.23⅘ .48⅘ .55⅗	Md	7000	2	2		2½	2h	21¼	HWajda	b 111	4.40	80–19	Hot Chance 1141¼ Tache De Beaute 111nk Su Neila T. 1121	Gamely	9
31Mar67–3GP	gd 5f	.23 .47 1.00⅕	Md	10000	1	2	812	812	613	69½	HWajda	117	4.70	77–18	Bley's Queen 1173 Maquinarias 1203 New Listen 1171	No speed	12
10Mar67–3GP	fst 3f	.22⅖ .33⅘	f–MdSpWt		4	14			1316	75¼	HWajda	119	14.10f	88– 7	HilariousEvening119no SoArrogant1192 SomeWind119½	Squ'zed st.	14

LATEST WORKOUTS Aug 3 Rkm 5f gd 1.02 h — Jly 28 Rkm 4f fst .50⅘ b — Jly 11 Rkm 3f fst .37⅗ b — Jly 7 Rkm 3f fst .39 b

Not Scared — $5,500

Ch. g (1965–Ky), by No Fear—Lou's Girl, by Arilou — Mrs. J. C. Hauer, J. C. Hauer (Mr.–Mrs. J. C. Hauer) — **116.** — 1967 0 M 0 0 —

LATEST WORKOUTS Aug 16 Rkm 4f fst .49⅖ h — Aug 10 Rkm 4f gd .51⅖ b — Aug 8 Rkm 4f gd .49 h — Aug 2 Rkm 4f fst .50 hg

Su Neila T. * — $5,000

Ch. f (1965–Fla), by Stratmat—To–Neila, by Mr. Busher — A. DiMascio, M. Kamal (A. DiMascio) — **112** — 1967 17 1 4 1 $4,850

8Aug67–5Rkm	fst 6f	.22 .46 1.13⅕	Clm	5000	10	7	57¼	35	22½	22¼	LMoyers	b 111	3.30	76–19	Fractious 1062¼ Su Neila T. 1112 Lin's Royal Dawn 1091¾	Gamely	10
25Jly 67–5Rkm	my 5½f	.23⅕ .47⅖ 1.07⅖	Clm	5000	5	1	46½	46½	710	813	LMoyers	b 112	6.70	72–23	Skillsaw 1165½ Fractious 105nk Eddie's Blaze 1162½	Fell back	9
12Jly 67–5Rkm	my 5½f	.22⅘ .46⅗ 1.07	Clm	6000	3	3	55	57½	47	46¾	LMoyers	b 116	5.90	80–18	Blue Oak 1152½ All Magic 113nk Not Too Modest 1184	Even race	8
5Jly 67–6Rkm	sly 5½f	.23 .47⅖ 1.07⅘	Clm	5500	5	4	54½	88¾	85¼	75¼	MHole	b 116	4.00	78–19	Royal Supreme 1162 Not Too Modest 118¾ Sister Joan 1121	No thr't	9
21Jun67–3Suf	my 5f	.23⅘ .48⅕ 1.00⅘	Clm	7000	7	3	2½	11	13	2½	LMoyers	b 115	12.60	86–25	Natural Whig 118½ Su Neila T. 1157 Fractious 112h	Couldn't last	8
14Jun67–6Suf	fst 5f	.22⅗ .47⅕ 1.01	Clm	7000	10	8	75¾	89	86¾	84½	L Moyers	b 115	10.80	81–19	HighPrincess 110nk DiamondCharm 118½ TrailMate 113h	No thr't	11
6Jun67–3Suf	fst 4½f	.23 .47⅗ .54⅕	Md	5500	8	5		12½	14	13½	LMoyers	b 117	*2.70	88–12	Su Neila T. 1173½ WhirlingAbility120no TacheDeBeaute1173	Driving	10
26May67–3Suf	my 4½f	.24⅗ .49⅗ .56⅕	Md	5500	1	3		41¼	42¾	24	TSisum	b 115	d*2.20	74–22	Sister Joan 1124 d–Su Neila T. 1152 Brave Bid 115h	Bore in	9

26May67—d–Disqualified and placed last.

18May67–3Suf	fst 4½f	.23 .47⅕ .53⅖	Md	5500	4	5		52¾	33½	26	MHole	b 115	3.40	86– 8	Minmognovich 1116 SuNeilaT. 1153 Monlabow 1152½	Roughed start	9

LATEST WORKOUTS Jly 11 Rkm 4f fst .51 b — Jly 4 Rkm 3f my .39 b

Karate * — $5,500

Gr. c (1965–La), by Loukenmac—Tonadilla, by Westerlands Prince — C. L. Rutherford, J. E. Patterson (Dr. C. L. Rutherford) — **116** — 1967 7 1 0 1 $2,100

7Aug67–5Rkm	gd 6f	.22⅕ .46⅕ 1.12⅖	Allowance		4	6	87¼	87	813	819	TSisum	b 116	37.30	63–22	Amber Bead 11610 Iron Line 116nk Green For Go 1141¾	Far back	8
31Jly 67–5Rkm	sl 6f	.23⅗ .47⅕ 1.14	Allowance		1	6	2h	2h	74¼	67¼	MGordon	b 116	36.10	67–27	Matchless 114¾ Linden Road 116no Full O'Prunes 122no	Tired	8
24Jly 67–7Rkm	fst 5½f	.22⅘ .47⅖ 1.06⅘	Allowance		7	1	52¼	66¾	77½	711	TSisum	b 114	11.10	77–19	Policy Pete 1142 Sky Sailor 116no Sister Goodie 108¾	Gave way	7
4Jly 67–9Suf	fst 6f	.22⅗ .46 1.11	Mayflower		1	9	41¼	1114	1222	1229	JBrockleb'nk	b 113	70.40	57–19	Four Fingers 1171 Retail King 1151¾ Noted Scholar 111h	Steadied	13
24Jun67–7Suf	fst 5f	.22⅘ .47 1.00⅖	Allowance		8	5	43	44½	78¾	68¾	JBrockleb'nk	b 118	22.30	80–19	Fulcrum's Lad 118h Bright Ruffle 115h Mibeju 1182½	Tired	8
8May67–3Suf	my 4½f	.24 .49 .55⅘	Md Sp Wt		6	4		1h	2h	1½	JBrocklebank	118	*1.90	80–20	Karate 118½ Mill Pond 118¾ Mademore 118h	Long, hard drive	7
1May67–3Suf	fst 4½f	.23⅖ .47⅗ .54	Md Sp Wt		4	4		53¼	53	32½	JBrocklebank	118	22.80	86–11	Handy Bob 1181¾ Allegro Conbrio 118¾ Karate 118½	Lacked room	9

LATEST WORKOUTS Aug 22 Rkm 3f fst .37⅖ b — Aug 19 Rkm 5f fst 1.01⅖ h — Aug 8 Rkm 3f gd .37 h — Jly 22 Rkm 4f fst .49⅗ h

Eddie's Blaze		**$5,500**		B. c (1965–N Y), by Scottdale—Blaze of Glory, by Priam II									**116**	1967	11 M 2 3		$2,350	
				Mrs. E. M. Corbett F. Duncan (Mrs. E. Corbett)														
17Aug67–3Rkm	fst 6f .23	.47 1.13⅗	Md	5500	7	1	45	43½	21	21¾	TDunlavy	b 116	*1.40	75–15	Gray Lip 1161¾ Eddie's Blaze 1165¼ Miss Challenger 1132		Gamely	9
10Aug67–3Rkm	fst 6f .23	.47⅖1.13⅘	Md	5000	9	7	64¾	52¾	1h	2½	TDunlavy	b 116	3.50	74–20	Dr. Rainey 120½ Eddie's Blaze 1163¾ Himsjon 116no		Couldn't last	12
1Aug67–4Rkm	fst 6f .22⅘	.47⅖1.13⅕	Clm	5500	6	5	54½	53¼	35½	36½	TDunlavy	b 116	3.30	71–19	Not Too Modest 1151¼ Fractious 1055¼ Eddie'sBlaze1163½		No mis'p	8
25Jly 67–5Rkm	my 5½f.23⅕	.47⅖1.07⅖	Clm	5500	8	5	78¼	67	45½	35¾	TDunlavy	b 116	22.80	79–23	Skillsaw 1165½ Fractious 105nk Eddie's Blaze 1162½		Closed well	9
13Jly 67–4Mth	fst 5½f.22⅗	.46⅘1.07⅖	Md	6500	7	7	89½	813	812	76	KKnapp	b 118	17.20	74–21	Game Effort 1182 Crossfire 118¾ Hallucinaction 1182		No threat	12
4Jly 67–3Mth	fst 5½f.23⅖	.48 1.08⅘	Md	6500	3	7	63¾	813	48½	35¼	JVelasquez	b 118	13.50	68–24	Royal Senor 1181¼ Captain's Jade 1184 Eddie's Blaze 118h		Rallied	12
24Jun67–1Mth	gd 5f .23⅕	.48 1.01⅖	Md	6500	3	8	85¼	85¼	97¼	78	SHernandez	118	26.70	75–17	Swimmin' Hole 1181¾ Happy Will 1161¼ Open Throttle 118½		No rally	12
9May67–3GS	my 5f .23⅗	.48⅗1.01⅘	Md	7500	5	1	61¾	64¼	68½	88¼	SHernandez	115	8.50	72–24	Autumn Joy 115¾ Mark's Flash 115no Senor Irish 112nk		Crowded	12
27Apr67–2GS	sly 5f .24	.49⅗1.02⅖	Md	13000	8	6	63	57½	68¼	68	SHernandez	113	30.70	69–30	Trouble Rules 1161 Ben-Ham 116¾ Baruby 113¾		Never threat	9
10Apr67–3GP	fst 5f .22⅘	.46⅘ .59⅗	Md Sp Wt		1	11	1211	1220	1021	1018	AGonzalez	120	184.30	73–16	Waking Dawn 120¾ Silver 1202 Advance Party 1202½		Never close	12
LATEST WORKOUTS	Jly 24 Rkm 3f fst .38⅖ b			Jly 1 Mth 4f my .51⅖ bg														

Velvet Sheen		**$5,500**		Dk. b. or br. f (1965–Fla.), by Ambehaving—Myra R., by Royal Note									**114**5	1967	5 1 1 0		$2,500	
				Meadowbrook Farm B. Webb (Meadowbrook Farm, Inc.)														
15Aug67–4Rkm	fst 6f .22⅘	.47⅕1.13⅖	f–	4750	7	1	2½	2h	2h	1h	KMasters5	b 107	3.40	77–16	Velvet Sheen 107h Tache De Beaute 117¾ Tyche 1201¾		Driving	8
7Aug67–3Rkm	gd 6f .23	.47⅘1.15⅕	f–M	6000	9	1	4nk	4nk	2h	2½	KMasters5	b 109	4.70	67–22	Peeps 114½ Velvet Sheen 109h Teenie McKnight 1144½		Gamely	11
25Jly 67–3Rkm	my 5½f.22⅘	.47⅘1.07⅘	Md	4250	9	5	42½	33½	25	46¾	MGordon	b 115	9.10	76–23	Goody Jessie 1174¼ Schtarka 120nk Peeps 1172¼		Speed, tired	11
16May67–3GS	fst 5f .22⅘	.47⅕1.00	f–Md	7500	9	7	83½	69	615	614	JLeonard	b 115	48.50	75–18	Pendulous 1153½ Flow Gently 1152½ Chime Song 1153		No threat	12
28Apr67–3GS	gd 5f .23⅗	.49 1.01⅗	f–M	8500	2	6	79¾	715	714	718	JLeonard	113	14.40	63–27	Good Game 1135 Behoove 1132 Ships Singer 1163		Trailed field	7
LATEST WORKOUTS	Jly 20 Rkm 4f fst .48⅘ h			Jly 8 Mth 4f fst .50⅖ bg											Jun 26 Mth 3f gd .38 b			

Gray Lip		**$5,500**		B. g (1965–Ky), by I Will or Landman—Dart, by Be Fleet									**122**	1967	3 1 0 0		$1,650	
				W. C. Prickett M. F. Holman (J. L. Cleveland)														
17Aug67–3Rkm	fst 6f .23	.47 1.13⅗	Md	5500	9	2	66½	57	11	11¾	LMoyers	116	7.40	77–15	Gray Lip 1161¾ Eddie's Blaze 1165¼ Miss Challenger 1132		Driving	9
10Aug67–3Rkm	fst 6f .23	.47⅖1.13⅘	Md	5500	6	1	85	77¼	67¼	711	LMoyers	120	7.50	64–20	Dr. Rainey 120½ Eddie's Blaze 1163¾ Himsjon 116no		No threat	12
27Jly 67–3Rkm	fst 5½f.23	.47⅖1.07⅘	Md	6000	2	8	77	812	912	86	JTaylor	120	23.60	77–21	d-Aunt Louise 1171¼ Seamount 1201¾ SilverStandard113½		No threat	10
LATEST WORKOUTS	Aug 22 Rkm 3f fst .36⅗ h			Aug 16 Rkm 3f fst .36⅖ h											Jly 25 Rkm 5f sly 1.08 b		Jly 7 Rkm 3f fst .37⅗ bg	

La Suena: Has shown little since arriving from Ak-Sar-Ben, and showed little while there. NO BET.

Tache De Beaute: Eight days ago, this one failed against females, a softer assignment than today's. Seems to like to run on the front end, a style that pays off on this track. But will have to find the early pace entirely to her liking or will tire in the stretch, as her record proves. Pending a pace analysis, we had better concede the filly an outside chance. CONTENDER.

Not Scared: First-time starter without special distinction. NO BET.

Su Neila T.: After four races on off tracks against males, this filly ran a stout, gaining race on a fast track fifteen days ago. Seems to like two-week intervals between races. Pace analysis will tell whether chances are good. Class seems to be no problem. CONTENDER.

Karate: Drops far down in class, a move that seems long overdue in view of its miserable performances. If he had ever shown anything in the way of speed, we might have to worry about this colt today, but the record is too bad for further study. NO BET.

Eddie's Blaze: Floyd Duncan's colt is still a maiden and should be running in a maiden race. NO BET.

Velvet Sheen: After finishing second in a maiden race on August 7, this filly beat previous winners on August 15, and did it in powerful style. Worth an extra look. CONTENDER.

Gray Lip: A good win last out, plus a couple of recent workouts are omens of better things for this gelding. A pace analysis may help us to decide whether it has the class for today's competition. CONTENDER.

The contenders are Tache De Beaute, Su Neila T., Velvet Sheen, and Gray Lip. Su Neila T. not only is more experienced in relatively fast company but has a distinct edge in speed. Let us see why, beginning with Tache De Beaute. This one fades when forced to run as fast as .47⅕ for the first half-mile of a six-furlong race. But Su Neila T. ran faster than that on August 8—behind a leader who covered the half in .46—and was gaining ground in the stretch. Velvet Sheen nosed out Tache De Beaute in breaking her maiden but had a ten-pound weight advantage. Velvet Sheen looks like a game little filly, but Su Neila T. seems much the better in the pace department. Gray Lip displayed plenty of finishing kick while winning on August 17, but is a bit too slow in the early furlongs to catch Su Neila T. in the stretch. And the 122 pounds will not help.

It looks as if Su Neila T. will run Tache De Beaute into the ground and win going away. Like all other racing predictions, this one will be accurate only if (a) the horses are in the expected form and (b) no outsider shows surprising improvement.

The Running of the Race

KARATE, the supposed "allowance horse" that had never displayed allowance class, was sent to the post as favorite. Tache De Beaute, the alleged "speed horse," was second choice. Su Neila T. was a lovely 4.40–1.

Tache De Beaute broke on top and stayed there, with Su Neila T. in pursuit. The half-mile in .46⅘ was too much for the front-runner, however, and Su Neila T. took over in the stretch to win going away. Gray Lip made a big run from far back but could not quite catch the decelerating Tache De Beaute.

FIFTH RACE	6 FURS. (Chute). (Dandy Blitzen, Aug 29, 1959, 1.08⅘, 4, 116.)
Rkm - 32090	Claiming. Purse $3,000. 2-year-olds which have not won two races. Weight, 122 lbs. Non–winners since July 30, allowed 3 lbs., June 30, 6 lbs. Claiming price, $5,500, 2 lbs. allowed for each $250 to $5,000.
August 23, 1967	

Value to winner $1,750, second $675, third $350, fourth $175, fifth $50. Mutuel pool $89,217.

Index	Horse	Eqt A Wt	PP	St	¼	½	Str	Fin	Jockey	Cl'g Pr	Owner	Odds $1
31963Rkm²	Su Neila T.	b 2 112	4	3	2h	2¹	1½	12½	T Sisum	5000	A Dimascio	4.40
32020Rkm²	T'he De B'ute	b 2 115	2	1	1¹	1¹	2¹½	2nk	H Wajda	5000	B A Dario	3.40
32039Rkm¹	Gray Lip	2 122	8	4	7½	4h	45	3½	J Taylor	5500	W C Prickett	7.40
31953Rkm⁸	Karate	b 2 116	5	2	3⁴½	35	3¹	45	J Giovanni	5500	C L Rutherford	2.40
32020Rkm⁴	La Suena	2 114	1	6	5h	6½	5¹	5nk	C Brinson	5250	B Coffey	17.90
32039Rkm²	Eddie's Blaze	b 2 116	6	7	8	8	7²½	6²	T Dunlavy	5500	Mrs E M Corbeit	5.80
32020Rkm¹	Velvet Sheen	b 2 114	7	5	4¹	5¹½	6²	7³	K Masters⁵	5500	Meadowbrook Farm	7.50
	Not Scared	2 116	3	8	6¹	7¹½	8	8	D Hidalgo	5500	Mrs J C Hauer	22.50

Time .22⅘, .46⅘, 1.12⅘. Track fast.

$2 Mutuel Prices:

4–SU NEILA T.	10.80	5.40	4.00
2–TACHE DE BEAUTE		4.40	3.00
8–GRAY LIP			4.00

Ch. f, by Stratmat—To-Neila, by Mr. Busher. Trainer M. Kamal. Bred by A. DiMascio (Fla.).

IN GATE AT 3.57. OFF AT 3.57½ EASTERN DAYLIGHT TIME. Start good. Won driving.

SU NEILA T. raced nearest pacesetter, reached lead in early stretch and drew away. TACHE DE BEAUTE set pace for bit over half mile then could not stay with winner and lasted over GRAY LIP. The latter, taken under restraint after start, rallied steadily leaving backstretch and made up ground. KARATE tired in final quarter mile. LA SUENA was no threat.

Overweight—La Suena 3 pounds.

---

16. NINTH AT SARATOGA, AUGUST 24, 1967—Track Fast

IF GIVEN your choice, would you like a fairly consistent five-year-old facing the softest competition of its career? Or would you have more confidence in an eight-year-old whose only victory in its last nineteen starts came on a disqualification?

Put that way, the problem seems simple. But things never are simple at race tracks.

This race is for $4,000 to $5,000 routers.

9th Race Saratoga

1⅛ MILES
SARATOGA
Start Finish

1 1-8 MILES. (Stupendous, August 5, 1967, 1.48⅕, 4, 114)
Claiming. Purse $6,000. 3-year-olds and upward. Weights 3-year-olds 117 lbs., older 123 lbs. Non-winners of two races at a mile and a furlong or over since July 1 allowed 3 lbs., two races at a mile or over since then 5 lbs. (Races when entered to be claimed for $3,500 or less not considered.) Claiming price $5,000. 2 lbs. for each $500 to $4,000.

Marvina's Tusc * $5,000
Dk. b. or br. c (1963–Md), by Tuscany—Marvina K., by Beau Son — 120 — 1967 17 2 3 1 $9,765
Adele E. Pondfield W. J. Pascuma (J. F. Ambrose) — 1966 20 2 4 4 $11,110

11Aug67-9Sar fst 1⅛.47⅗1.12⅗1.52⅗ Clm 6250 6 5 68¼ 77½ 76 68½ LAdams 118 9.70 72-12 Plow 1182½ Abolengo II 1183 Cormier 118no Not a contender 8
29Jly 67-9Aqu sf 1 3/16 Ⓣ 1.59⅗ Hcp 5000s 6 7 95¾ 119 1014 812 JShufelt 114 17.50 60-27 Austral II 110nk Came To Play 1122 Sectario 119¾ Had no mishap 13
20Jly 67-9Aqu fst 1 3/16.48⅗1.13⅖1.58⅖ Cl c-5000 6 3 32½ 42¼ 2h 3nk GMora5 118 3.60 87-15 Bent Spur 118h Plow 118nk Marvina's Tusc 11810 Made sharp try 9
15Jly 67-2Aqu sly 1⅛.48⅖1.13⅕1.53⅗ Cl c-4000 6 3 31 31 1½ 12½ RTurcotte 120 3.20 68-18 Marvina's Tusc 1202½ Porky 1111 d-Talo 1133 Speed to spare 8
4Jly 67-1Aqu fst 7f .23 .46⅗1.25⅘ Clm 3500 9 1 79 55 32½ 11 LAdams 115 *1.70 77-17 Marvina's Tusc 1151 Speedy Admiral 115¾ Noureige 1051 Driving 9
19Jun67-9Mth sly 1 1/16.47⅖1.13⅖1.47⅘ Clm 5000 7 4 48 28 34 49½ CBaltazar 115 *2.40 66-17 Lord Saybrook 1193½ Fleet N' True 1116 Quine 115no No mishap 9
15Jun67-9Mth fm*1 1/16 Ⓣ 1.48⅗ Clm 5000 9 1 12 1h 3nk 46 CBaltazar 115 3.20 80-11 Nothing Left 112h Garlandeer 1204 Niso 1142 Hard used 9
10May67-7Pim sf 1 1/16 Ⓣ 1.16⅗1.50⅖ Clm 7000 5 3 41 41¾ 42½ 53 CBaltazar 113 8.00 60-35 Art Form 1051 Corsair II 1151½ Bayard Park 111nk Factor, tired 10
1May67-5Pim fm 1 Ⓣ .48⅖1.39⅘ Clm 7500 1 5 46 42½ 4½ 42 CBaltazar 114 *2.40 84-12 Sectario 115¾ Art Form 110½ Acceptance 105¾ No response 10
17Apr67-6Pim sly 1 1/16.47⅘1.13⅗1.46⅗ Clm 7000 1 1 1h 1½ 1h 21½ CBaltazar 115 4.60 75-21 Bayard Park 1131½ Marvina's Tusc 1157 Fine Kettle 1151½ Gamely 7
LATEST WORKOUTS Aug 5 Sar 4f sly .51 b Jly 28 Bel 3f fst .37⅕ b Jly 3 Bel Trt 3f sly .39⅘ b

Stay Away War $4,500
Ro. c (1963–Ky), by Warfare—Stay Smoochie, by Alquest — 116 — 1967 2 0 0 0 ——
Helen Lee H. Jacobson (Harbor View Farm) — 1966 25 2 3 4 $12,780

18Aug67-9Sar fst 1 .46⅖1.12⅗1.38⅖ Cl c-3500 7 7 78½ 810 813 627 DBrumfield b 116 8.30 55-12 Notes 1163½ Smoking 1163 Sir Rodolph 11616 Not a threat 9
26Jly 67-2Aqu gd 7f .22⅗ .46 1.24⅕ Clm 6000 6 4 711 1117 Eased up HGustines b 115 27.30 —— Direct Action 119nk Raider Radka 1192½ Last Chain 1171 Stopped 11
21Oct66-9Aqu fst 1⅛.48⅘1.13⅗1.52⅘ Cl c-6500 4 1 13 12 1½ 21 MYcaza b 114 *1.20 71-16 Never Wrong 1141 Stay Away War 1141½ Spartanburg 1182 Gamely 6
14Oct66-1Aqu fst 1 .46⅘1.11⅗1.37⅕ Clm 9000 9 9 95¾ 84¾ 53 42¼ MYcaza b 114 10.40 80-17 Florida Scheme 116nk Hobe Sound 114½ Robertsville 1121½ Rallied 11
30Sep66-9Aqu fst 1⅛.47⅘1.12⅘1.52 Clm 6500 1 2 21½ 2h 1h 21¼ MYcaza b 115 3.40 75-19 Del Coronado 1161¼ Stay Away War 1153 Never Wrong 1145 Bore in 8
23Sep66-6Aqu sf 1⅛ Ⓣ 1.53 Allowance 3 4 42½ 43½ 44½ 49 JRuane b 111 8.20 61-30 Glenrose 115½ Bold Stand 1114½ Flit-To 1114 No mishap 8
30Aug66-6Aqu fst 7f .22⅘ .45⅘1.23⅗ Clm 15000 5 5 64 86½ 813 716 JRuane b 116 42.30 72-22 Royal Harbinger 1142½ Royal Decision 112½ Hurry Khal 1168 Tired 9
22Aug66-6Sar sly 1 .46⅘1.12⅗1.39⅖ Allowance 6 5 53 43¼ 42½ 46 JRuane b 109 9.00 71-17 Beau Legs 1044½ Royal Decision 1111 Mt. Greenery 116½ Wide 6
13Aug66-8Sar fm 1 1/16 Ⓣ 1.43⅕ Allowance 5 6 712 69½ 58½ 510 ECardone b 105 *1.90 79-11 Pass the Brandy 1101½ Bold Stand 1113 Crying Towel 1102 Dull try 7
LATEST WORKOUTS Aug 14 Sar 4f fst .49⅗ b Aug 10 Sar tr.t. 1m fst 1.49⅗ b Jly 21 Bel 5f fst 1.06 b Jly 11 Bel tr.t. 3f fst .38 b

Florida Scheme * $5,000
B. g (1963–Fla), by Clandestine—M. Louise, by Sun Teddy — 118 — 1967 12 1 2 1 $5,540
S. J. Pace N. Combest (Ocala Stud Farms, Inc.) — 1966 25 2 0 3 $8,970

17Aug67-9Sar fst 1⅛.46⅗1.12 1.52⅕ Clm 5000 6 9 917 812 3½ 33 ADespirito 118 6.00 80- 9 d-Snow Dales 118no Ruperto 1113 Florida Scheme 1184 Rallied 10
4Aug67-9Sar sly 1⅛.48⅕1.13⅕1.52⅘ Clm 6500 6 8 812 914 916 931 WBoland 118 7.60 49-20 Sudden Storm 1148 Abolengo II 1164 Sir Sanford 1182½ Disliked slop 9
27Jly 67-8Aqu fst 7f .22⅖ .45⅖1.24⅕ Clm 7500 2 9 816 920 915 814 TMolter10 109 15.30 71-15 Spruce Up 1191½ Mr. Hal F. 1071½ Mornins' Mornin 1191 R'ced wide 9
31May67-8Aqu fst 1⅛.47⅘1.12⅘1.51⅗ Clm 8000 3 8 77¾ 88 47 45½ RTurcotte 114 14.80 72-19 Sir Sanford 119h Birdsofafeather 1195 Razonable 116½ Slow start 8
26Apr67-2Aqu fst 1 .45⅘1.11⅕1.38⅕ Cmn 7500 8 3 42½ 11 1½ 21 WBoland 118 23.00 76-17 Ronnie's Rebel 1121 Florida Scheme 1183 Sum Farce 122½ Wide 8
13Apr67-9Aqu fst 1⅛.47⅘1.12⅗1.52⅖ Clm 7500 2 5 510 44½ 611 612 WBoland 114 5.60 62-16 Golden Mike 118½ Pomidoro 116½ Cool Oasis 119nk Far back 6
25Feb67-4Hia fst 1⅛.46⅗1.12⅖1.51⅗ Clm 7500 10 10 1018 87¾ 55 44¾ GPatterson 118 7.50 72-20 Mr. Spinelli 116½ Beauport 112nk No Snakes 1124 Closed well 11
17Feb67-10Hia fst1⅛.46⅖1.11⅗1.50⅖ Clm 10000 8 12 1220 1013 69½ 57 HGrant 117 7.80 76-16 Spartanburg 118nk Yar 1164 Artist's Award 112¾ Late foot 12
2Feb67-10Hia fst1⅛.46⅖1.11⅗1.50⅗ Clm 10000 5 10 911 66 67½ 79½ JLRotz 118 *2.30e 72-14 Ni Modo 114½ Pinchers Pride 1123 Punisher 1183 Dull effort 12
LATEST WORKOUTS Jly 22 Aqu 4f fst .51 b

Sir Sanford $5,000
Ch. g (1962), by Royal Warrior—Miss Boodle, by Mr. Busher — 118 — 1967 14 2 1 2 $13,550
J. Hinkle S. J. Smith (M. W. Smith) — 1966 14 2 5 2 $13,825

11Aug67-9Sar fst 1⅛.47⅗1.12⅗1.52⅗ Clm 5750 7 6 56¼ 45 42 45½ EBelmonte 114 6.90 75-12 Plow 1182½ Abolengo II 1183 Cormier 118no Mild bid, tired 8
4Aug67-9Sar sly 1⅛.48⅕1.13⅕1.52⅘ Clm 6500 4 7 79½ 57½ 35½ 312 HGustines 118 5.60 68-20 Sudden Storm 1148 Abolengo II 1164 Sir Sanford 1182½ Held on 9
25Jly 67-9Aqu fst 1⅛.46⅘1.11 1.50⅘ Clm 9000 12 12 99 87¼ 87 1113 RStovall 114 45.20 69-11 Joe Di Rosa 1181½ Sectario 1162½ Daily Reminder 118h Slow start 12
21Jly 67-8Aqu fst 7f .22⅗ .45⅗1.23⅗ Allowance 6 6 77¼ 65¾ 64½ 69¼ HGustines 119 28.70 79-14 Kummel 1211½ Lucky Vertex 1141 Big Equipment 1174 No factor 7
28Jun67-9Aqu fst 1⅛.49 1.13⅗1.51⅘ Clm 11500 4 4 64¼ 56½ 54¾ 59½ RTurcotte 116 6.20 67-17 Pomidoro 118h Artist's Award 1205 Beaustone 1162½ No threat 6
21Jun67-9Aqu gd 1⅛.48 1.13⅕1.52⅖ Cl c-9000 3 5 45½ 31½ 45 412 ACorderoJr 119 4.10 62-21 Kummel 1184 Daily Reminder 1181½ Joe Di Rosa 1186 Speed, tired 8
14Jun67-9Aqu fst 1⅛.47⅗1.12 1.50⅗ Clm 10500 5 5 53 41¾ 31 53 ACorderoJr 116 2.80 80-14 Bombax 118no Spartanburg 118¾ Cormier 116nk Well up, hung 8
6Jun67-9Aqu fst 1⅛.48⅖1.13 1.52 Clm 10000 2 2 2h 2½ 3½ 41½ ACorderoJr 123 2.90 74-14 Artist's Award 1201½ Kummel 120no Gray Prince 118no Weakened 8
31May67-8Aqu fst 1⅛.47⅘1.12⅘1.51⅗ Clm 8500 6 2 2½ 1½ 11 1h ACorderoJr 119 2.60 78-19 Sir Sanford 119h Birdsofafeather 1195 Razonable 116½ Lasted 8
24May67-9Aqu fst 1⅛.47⅘1.12⅗1.51⅖ Clm 10000 4 3 34½ 32½ 1½ 1½ ACorderoJr 116 *1.90 79-18 Sir Sanford 116½ ♦Birdsofafeather 1154 ♦Bent Spur 1164 Driving 7
LATEST WORKOUTS Aug 1 Sar 5f fst 1.05 b Jly 31 Sar 3f fst .37⅘ b Jly 19 Bel 6f fst 1.15⅕ h Jly 18 Bel 3f fst .36 h

***Kalonji**			**$5,000**		**B. g (1961), by Tropique—King's Maid, by Mieuxce**									**118**	1967 21 1 4 1 $7,610			
					S. Caruso S. Caruso									(Haras Las Ninas) (Arg.)	1966 12 3 4 2 $13,000			
7Aug67-9Sar	fst 1⅛	.47⅘ 1.13⅕ 1.54	Cl	c-3500	1	4	33½	21½	11	13	JLRotz	115	*1.60	75-15	Kalonji 1153 Real Beat 1175 Royal Rick 1075	Much the best	9
31Jly 67-9Sar	fst 1⅛	.47⅘ 1.12⅗ 1.52⅕	Clm	3500	2	4	35	25	25	27	JLRotz	b 118	*1.70	76-12	Swing Rex 1187 Kalonji 11816 Rao Raja 118½	Best of others	7
24Jly 67-9Aqu	fst 1⅛	.47⅘ 1.12⅘ 1.52⅕	Clm	3500	6	4	42½	31	1h	2nk	JLRotz	b 115	4.90	75-17	Jimmy Miller 117nk Kalonji 1153 Willow Creek 1152	Sharp	8
15Jly 67-2Aqu	sly 1⅛	.48⅖ 1.13⅕ 1.53⅗	Clm	3500	5	2	2½	2½	33½	57	JRuane	b 115	18.00	61-18	Marvina's Tusc 1202½ Porky 1111 d-Talo 1133	Checked on turn	8
15Jly 67-Placed third through disqualifications.																	
24Jun67-2Aqu	gd 1⅛	.48⅘ 1.14⅕ 1.54⅕	Clm	3500	1	3	32½	34½	66½	712	LGilligan	b 115	5.30	53-18	Came To Play 118½ Crafty Trail 104½ Full Size 1156	Tired	8
19Jun67-9Aqu	sly 1⅛	.49 1.16 1.57⅖	Clm	3500	2	5	66½	55½	58	515	LGilligan	b 115	3.30	34-26	Jimmy Miller 1183½ MichaelJ.Toppa1152½ CornishLad1185	No threat	6
15Jun67-9Aqu	fst 1⅛	.46⅗ 1.11⅕ 1.51⅘	Clm	5000	6	4	49	35½	57½	57	LGilligan	b 118	5.00	70-13	d-Victaray 114¾ Real Beat 116¾ Campari II 118½	No rally	10
10Jun67-5Aqu	fst 6f	.22⅕ .45⅖ 1.11	Clm	5000	1	11	107¾	109	109	108	RStovall	b 117	28.40	80-12	Bullyampa 1174 Predicador 1171 Sum Farce 117no	Wide turn	13
29May67-9Aqu	fst 1⅛	.47⅘ 1.12⅖ 1.51⅖	Clm	4000	1	2	21½	2h	2h	2no	RUssery	b 116	4.10	79-18	Try Cash 116no Kalonji 1164 Scarlet Stone 1098	Sharp try	7
LATEST WORKOUTS		**Aug 23 Sar 3f fst .38⅕ b**						**Jly 30 Sar 3f fst .39⅕ b**						**Jly 23 Bel 3f fst .38 b**	**Jly 13 Bel tr.t 4f fst .52 b**		

***Ruperto**			**$5,000**		**Ch. h (1959), by Penny Post—Romanella, by Cairngorm**									**118**	1967 19 1 3 2 $8,925			
					Mrs. W. A. Kelley W. A. Kelley									(Haras El Moro) (Arg.)	1966 38 6 3 4 $26,820			
17Aug67-9Sar	fst 1⅛	.46⅗ 1.12 1.52⅕	Clm	5000	4	8	816	69	2h	2no	ALoguercio7	b 111	3.40	83- 9	d-Snow Dales 118no Ruperto 1113 Florida Scheme 1184	Impeded	10
17Aug67---Placed first through disqualification.																	
4Aug67-2Sar	fst 1⅛	.47⅗ 1.12⅖ 1.51⅕	Clm	5000	7	5	511	57½	31½	35¾	HGustines	b 118	11.60	82-10	Plow 1185½ Eight Up 118nk Ruperto 1185	Held for placing	7
29Jun67-9Aqu	fst 1⅛	.47⅕ 1.12⅕ 1.52⅘	Clm	5000	8	8	711	711	712	69¼	RTurcotte	b 118	5.90	63-19	Awesome 1204 Victaray 118nk Sir Rodolph 1181½	No speed	8
22Jun67-9Aqu	fst 1 3/16	.49⅘ 1.14⅕ 1.59⅘	Clm	5000	6	4	32½	32	32½	33½	WBoland	b 118	3.00	76-17	Awesome 1181½ Victaray 1182 Ruperto 1185	Evenly in drive	6
9Jun67-9Aqu	fst 1⅛	.47⅘ 1.12⅗ 1.52⅕	Clm	6000	2	3	411	47	46	67½	RTurcotte	b 114	7.20	67-17	Jo Di Rosa 1201½ Ronnie's Rebel 118¾ Hy-Nat 116nk	No threat	7
2Jun67-9Aqu	fst 1⅛	.47⅖ 1.12 1.52⅕	Clm	6250	7	9	917	913	89½	56¼	RTurcotte	b 116	40.50	69-18	Joe Di Rosa 118½ Ronnie's Rebel 1201½ Abolengo II 118nk	Late foot	9
19May67-9Aqu	fst 1⅛	.48⅕ 1.12⅘ 1.53⅗	Clm	6250	8	11	1112	86½	61	43	RTurcotte	b 114	4.10	65-18	d-Tulyaric 1161 Razonable 1162 Abolengo II 114h	Late foot	11
11May67-3Aqu	fst 1⅛	.48⅖ 1.12⅗ 1.52⅕	Clm	6250	6	4	41½	33	22	21½	RTurcotte	b 114	3.50	73-21	Birdsofafeather 1161½ Ruperto 1141½ Sudden Storm 109¾	Good try	8
21Apr67-3Aqu	fst 1⅛	.48⅗ 1.13⅕ 1.52⅕	Clm	6500	5	7	79½	66½	56½	45¾	RTurcotte	b 116	7.30	69-22	Parkway North 1151 Portfolio 1124 Flannel 116¾	Mild rally	8
14Apr67-9Aqu	fst 1⅛	.49⅗ 1.14⅖ 1.52⅘	Clm	6500	2	5	42¼	32	32½	42½	RTurcotte	b 116	8.50	69-18	Hy-Nat 112½ Ronnie's Rebel 1161 Plow 1131	No mishap	8
LATEST WORKOUTS		**Aug 8 Sar 4f fst .53 b**						**Jly 28 Aqu 1m fst 1.45⅖ b**						**Aug 3 Sar 3f fst .39⅗ b**	**Jly 23 Aqu 6f fst 1.18 b**		

Marvina's Tusc: Warren Pascuma's colt, if in shape, is positively able to beat $4,000 stock at today's distance. He may even be able to beat $5,000 animals. But he has shown no inclination to run since his three good July races. Moreover, aside from his good effort on a fast track at a freak distance on July 20, his record is that of an animal that prefers soft footing. NO BET.

Stay Away War: Buddy Jacobson usually knows what he's doing when he claims a horse, but the 1967 performances of this one do not inspire confidence in its ability to stay with the animals it faces today. NO BET.

Florida Scheme: This gelding has been dropping steadily down the claiming-price scale. Its third-place finish last week indicated that Nick Combest may finally have found a level at which the animal can function. However, I dislike the incredibly slow starts to which the horse is addicted—a severe disadvantage with an inner post position like today's. And I have yet to see any indication that the horse can get close to contention at today's distance without fading at the finish. NO BET.

Sir Sanford: Two fair efforts in its Saratoga starts, and this gelding now faces easier competition than ever. Is apparently no longer the $10,000 animal of last May, but is no cripple, either. Against today's cheapies, a bit of improvement seems likely. CONTENDER.

Kalonji: This firmly established $3,500 item might be granted a chance of beating $4,000 ones, after that good race 17 days ago, but hasn't a prayer against the likes of Sir Sanford. NO BET.

Ruperto: In its fourth attempt to beat a $5,000 field, the smart Walter Kelley's old-timer won on a disqualification last week. Will undoubtedly be running fastest of all in the stretch—as usual. But can it put together a winning race after that extraordinarily tough effort seven days ago? Aged claiming horses seldom can, except when they benefit from an unusual advantage in class or pace or both. Further analysis should tell the tale. CONTENDER.

The contenders are Sir Sanford and Ruperto. Sir Sanford has an edge in class and age. Considering Ruperto's difficult last race and the strain its extraordinarily fast time must have imposed, I believed that Sir Sanford probably has an advantage in condition as well. As to pace, if Stay Away War is in form at all like that of a year ago (which I doubt), it probably will get the early lead, with Sir Sanford and others close behind. On the assumption that Stay Away War will fade even if not pressed too strenuously by other horses, we can figure that Eddie Belmonte will be able to call the tune in the final furlongs, saving Sir Sanford's strength.

The Running of the Race

THE SARATOGA wise guys liked Ruperto best, allowing Sir Sanford to go at almost 3–1. The old horse made another gallant attempt, gaining five lengths in the stretch and almost catching Sir Sanford. But not quite. Favored by the failure of Stay Away War to hold its early speed (the poor thing went lame), Belmonte took over on the final turn and opened too big a lead to be caught.

Ruperto was the better horse, which I did not recognize in analyzing the past performances. But Sir Sanford was good enough to win over the surprisingly good veteran—as the class, form, and pace factors predicted.

NINTH RACE Sar 32089 August 24, 1967 — **1 1-8 MILES. (Stupendous, Aug. 5, 1967, 1:48⅕, 4, 114.)** Claiming. Purse $6,000. 3-year-olds and upward. 3-year-olds, 117 lbs.; older, 123 lbs. Non-winners of two races at one and one-eighth miles or over since July 1 allowed 3 lbs.; of two races at a mile or over since then, 5 lbs. Claiming price, $5,000; 2 lbs. for each $500 to $4,000. (Races when entered to be claimed for $3,500 or less not considered)

Value to winner $3,900; second, $1,200; third, $600; fourth, $300. Mutuel Pool, $147,576.

Index	Horses	Eq't	A	Wt	PP	St	¼	½	¾	Str	Fin	Jockeys	Cl'g Pr.	Owners	Odds to $1
31990Sar^4	—Sir Sanford		5	118	4	2	$2^{1/2}$	2^1	2^2	1^3	1^h	E Belmonte	5000	Joanne Hinkle	2.90
32035Sar^1	—Ruperto	b	8	118	6	5	$5^{1 1/2}$	6	6	$4^{1/2}$	2^1	R Turcotte	5000	Mrs W A Kelley	2.30
32035Sar^3	—Florida Scheme		4	118	3	6	6	5^1	$4^{1/2}$	3^2	$3^{2 1/2}$	W Boland	5000	S J Pace	3.90
31954Sar^1	—Kalonji	b	6	118	5	4	4^4	4^3	3^h	2^h	$4^{3 1/2}$	J L Rotz	5000	S Caruso	6.90
31990Sar^6	—Marvina's Tusc		4	118	1	1	$3^{1 1/2}$	3^h	5^4	5	5	A Cord'o Jr	5000	Adele E Pondfield	3.[illegible]0
32014Sar^6	—Stay Away War	b	4	116	2	3	1^3	1^2	$1^{1/2}$	Lame.		A DeSpirito	4500	Helen R Lee	15.00

Time, :24, :48⅕, 1:13⅕, 1:39, 1:52⅘ (crosswind in backstretch). Track fast.

$2 Mutuel Prices:			
4-SIR SANFORD	7.80	4.00	3.20
6-RUPERTO		3.20	2.60
3-FLORIDA SCHEME			2.80

Ch. g, by Royal Warrior—Miss Boodle, by Mr. Busher. Trainer, S. J. Smith. Bred by M. W. Smith.
IN GATE—6:16. OFF AT 6:16 EASTERN DAYLIGHT TIME. Start good. Won driving.
Corrected weight—Marvina's Tusc, 118.
Marvina's Tusc claimed by Mrs. W. H. Hochman, trainer S. Cardile. Sir Sanford claimed by Windham Farm, trainer E. W. King.

PART FOUR

Handicapping the Starter Handicaps

THE GAME is organized in such a way that the proprietor of a claiming horse risks losing the animal any time it is entered in a race that it can win. Such a race is one in which the claiming price is low enough to assure relatively soft competition. But if the price is that low, the horse itself is for sale cheap and may be grabbed by another barn.

Naturally, the horseman can protect himself against loss of the horse by running it at inflated claiming prices, thereby guaranteeing that it will be outclassed and unable to win enough purse money to pay its feed bill.

Out of sympathy with the desire of horsemen to send their claiming stock after good purses with no danger of a claim, tracks offer occasional races of a special nature. The most familiar is the optional claimer, which permits the barn to enter the horse at a claiming price or not, depending on preference. The ground rules which govern such races are hopelessly confusing. A horse that wins one when *not* entered to be claimed is credited with a victory in an allowance race and suffers weight penalties in future starts. Moreover, its people are not permitted to put it back in an optional claimer against its own kind for the rest of the season without entering it for claim.

Optional claimers have gone out of fashion on the New York circuit. To replace them, The Big Apple tracks offer a starter handicap every couple of weeks. The conditions are likely to say something like: Purse $8,500. For Three-Year-Olds and Upward which have started for a claiming price of $5,000 or less in the past year. One Mile and Three-Sixteenths.

The weights for a race of this kind are assigned by the track handicapper, just as if it were an authentic handicap race for top horses. The races themselves are delightful, especially at the cashier's window. Favorites seldom win, largely because ordinary handicapping procedures are ineffective. The crowd, and the tipsters who furnish the crowd with its dominant opinions, are caught off guard time and again.

The trainers of horses that win starter handicaps often prepare for the coups weeks and months in advance. The first step often is to take a $7,500 beast to Maryland and enter it for $3,500 on the first day of a meeting. Nobody is likely to claim the horse on that day, chiefly because nobody can claim any horse at any meeting until he has started a horse of his own at the same meeting. Opening day is therefore a day devoid of claims.

The animal's record of having run for $3,500 makes it eligible for a flock of starter handicaps in New York later in the year. Some of the opposition, but not much, will be furnished by lightly weighted $3,500 horses whose records show numerous efforts at that price. Other entrants are likely to be erstwhile $3,500 skates that have been climbing the class ladder and can now get the job done for $5,000 or $6,000.

Like as not, the ultimate winner is a creature whose lone $3,500 race took place so long ago that it no longer appears in the past-performance record. The horse is not now and never was a $3,500 horse. But it does not stick out like the famous sore thumb. Its recent record may be downright putrid.

Trainers seem unable to win ordinary claiming races with certain animals that repeatedly jump up and win these more lucrative starter handicaps. And there, perplexing though it may seem, is the key to picking the winners.

Forget form. Forget class. Forget weights. Forget jockeys. As matters stand in 1968, and as they have for several years, the only worthwhile bet in a New York starter handicap is a horse that has won a starter handicap in the past!

In 1962 the winners of twenty-one of the twenty-six starter handicaps in New York were horses that had won previous starter handicaps. As Charles Barrett disclosed in the March, 1965, issue of *American Turf Monthly,* betting favorites won only six of the races. Here are the 1962 results:

Date	Horse	Mutuel Price
March 27	Noble Sel	$ 7.00
April 2	Mr. General	5.20
April 7	Gateway	22.90
April 14	Refuting	7.70
April 21	Gateway	7.70
April 30	Ufo	8.70
May 12	Gateway	11.60
May 22	Noble Sel	8.70
May 30	Oscar Award	9.10
June 2	Noble Sel	10.30
June 9	Refuting	6.50
June 16	Oscar Award	9.60
June 23	Good Style	9.30
July 4	Good Style	6.60
July 21	Grand Quivera	13.10
July 28	Grand Quivera	5.30
August 4	Good Style	6.30
August 11	Graphs Pet	18.80
August 25	Doctor Bern	24.50
September 8	Chantalia	12.20
September 22	Good Style	7.20
October 6	Castelstone	7.40
October 13	Count Chuck	10.60
November 3	Count Chuck	5.90
November 24	Count Chuck	12.50
November 30	Chantalia	5.30

A player who had confined his bets on these races to previous winners would have cashed in on Gateway twice, Noble Sel twice, Refuting once, Good Style three times, Count Chuck twice, and Chantalia once. A total of twelve winning bets, against fourteen losses on winners that failed to repeat. Assuming a $20 bet on each horse, a net profit of $419 would have been returned—or about 80 cents per wagered dollar.

In 1963, the major New York tracks carded twenty-four starter handicaps. I shall not trouble you with the full list of winners. However, you may enjoy drooling over the nine animals that qualified for play because they had already won starter handicaps during the season:

Date	Horse	Mutuel Price
June 8	Young Chris	$13.10
June 15	Baldpate	6.40
June 22	Carbangel	9.50
June 29	Young Chris	8.70
July 4	Merry Will	14.30
July 19	Young Chris	6.80
Sept. 2	Merry Will	6.50
Sept. 14	Young Chris	10.10
Sept. 21	Young Chris	13.30

One of the least credible aspects of all this is that Young Chris could pay $13.30 on September 21 after having won five previous starter handicaps during the season.

Mechanical play, betting on all entrants with a previous win in this kind of race, on this circuit, this year, required twenty-eight bets. At $20 per ticket, the profit was $327—or 58 cents per wagered dollar.

In 1964, ten repeat winners yielded a profit of only 5 cents per dollar—principally because twenty-six other horses lost when trying to repeat. Charles Barrett, compiler of these materials, tells me that the rate of profit would have been much higher if the player had bet not on all previous winners in each race but on the *most recent* winner. This, of course, would have spoiled the idea by requiring the poor player to do some work. That is, he would have had to see which previous winner won most recently.

In 1965 and 1966 the New York tracks presented sixty-eight of these races. Favorites won twelve of them—an average of 18 percent, far below the one winner in three which can be expected in normal Thoroughbred racing.

But Street Fair won five starter handicaps in 1965, Lysander won three, Try Cash won five, Get Crackin won two. And Nike Site won four in 1966, Ruperto won four, Black Joy won three, Gypsy Baron won five, Atlantic won two, Aerie won two, and Mr. Spinelli won two. Seven horses won twenty of the season's thirty-six starter handicaps!

While the 1967 season was still in progress, I checked the result charts and found that Swing Rex had won four starter handicaps. Fuzzy King had won two, as had Austral II, Riot Squad, and Parkway North. Swing Rex had paid $11.60 in its fourth victory! Parkway North paid $17.20 for its second!

Quite plainly, the racegoer will do well to concentrate his attention on previous winners of starter handicaps, awarding preference to the one with the most recent triumph in such a race. The races are so peculiar that this kind of "handicapping" is absolutely certain to do at least as well as any other.

PART FIVE

Handicapping a Full Card

CLAIMING, ALLOWANCE, and maiden races offer the good handicapper abundant opportunity to pick a high percentage of winners at adequate mutuel prices. On certain circuits, gimmick races like starter handicaps provide extra bonanzas.

Stakes races, handicaps, races on the grass, and races over jumps are less rewarding. The difficulty of most stakes and handicap races is that they bring together evenly matched animals of high quality. The player may sometimes be able to make a choice on grounds of current condition or weights (or, in stakes sprints for two-year-olds, on grounds of speed or class), but the mutuel paid by the predictable winner of one of these affairs is usually low.

Turf races are popular among owners and trainers of Thoroughbreds with tender hoofs or freakish dispositions and a resultant preference for lawn running. The races also are popular among gamblers, because upsets are frequent and mutuel payoffs high. At most tracks they are a headache for the conscientious handicapper. Occasionally, the entire field has established its grass form and the player has a fair chance. Much more often, form fails to stand up or cannot be determined because several entrants have never raced on grass or have not tried it lately or are gimpy.

With regard to jump races, the less said the better. Racing luck plays far too important a role, and real class differences are far too difficult to recognize. The jumpers are lovely to watch, but lousy to bet on.

Rather than give examples of how stakes, handicaps, turf and jump races may sometimes be beaten, I shall content myself with the assertion that anyone able to beat claiming, allowance, and maiden races knows enough about the sport to recognize the opportunities that sometimes arise in other races.

Now I think the reader might profit from the experience of handicapping an entire card and deciding which of the races contain the brightest opportunities. For that purpose I have selected the greatest racing day in decades—Saturday, September 30, 1967, at Aqueduct. That was the program on which Buckpasser, Damascus, and Dr. Fager met in the $107,800 Woodward Stakes.

I shall approach this card of races as if the reader and I were at the track together, trying to decide what to bet on, or whether to bet at all.

Abracadabra. We are at Aqueduct before the first race on September 30, 1967, and you do not know yet whether any race on the program will offer a decent betting opportunity. I plan to bet on the big race because I follow the sport closely enough to know what Buckpasser, Damascus, and Dr. Fager can do. Or at least I think I know what each is likely to do today. When we get to that race—the seventh—I'll show you why I think one of the three famous Thoroughbreds is a good bet.

But I have no idea what is running in the other eight races on the program. Before looking into the records of the horses entered in the first, let's dispose of the problem of the daily double. I don't play it. I don't play it because I have a lot of trouble picking two winners in succession, especially in the inferior races on which daily doubles are based. Nevertheless, I often can locate the two or three or four likeliest contenders in each of the daily-double races. By "wheeling" them—buying tickets which pair each contender in the first race with each contender in the second—I can hit the double about four times out of ten. That is, buying between $18 and $24 worth of tickets, I am able to win daily doubles. But I do not do it because I would much rather bet the money on one solid horse at fair odds. Daily double odds are unknown until long after the tickets are bought and the first race has been run. Daily doubles, then, are a pig in a poke. So I shall not play the double on this day. If you want to, go ahead. Indeed, if I can find the contenders in the races, I'll point them out.

But don't expect to make any money on the double. During the twenty-five racing days of July, 1967—a perfectly representative month—only eight daily doubles paid $100 or more. Only eight, in other words, paid enough to reward the purchaser of $24 worth of tickets with 3–1 odds. Or the holder of $18 worth of tickets with slightly better than 4–1. On the other hand, eight of the July doubles paid less than $24 (they ranged from $13.80 to $21.80). And twelve of the doubles—just about half—paid less than $54. Why do I mention $54? Because a mutuel price of that amount is 2–1 odds for the player who bought $18 worth of doubles tickets. Pretty thin porridge for picking two winners.

THE FIRST RACE

THIS IS at six furlongs for maiden two-year-old fillies. Before taking another step, let's see whether any of them has run the distance before. Most of them have. Might be a play here.

Whose fillies are running? Look at the names of the owners and trainers. This might be a pretty good troop of horses. Among those represented are Harbor View, King Ranch, Cain Hoy, Alfred Vanderbilt, Rokeby. Some of the best trainers in the business are involved: Johnny Nerud, Ivan Parke, Max Hirsch, Roger Laurin, Mike Freeman, Elliott Burch, Laz Barrera.

1st Race Aqueduct  6 FURLONGS. (Near Man, July 17, 1963, 1.08⅗, 3, 112.)
Maidens. Special weight. Purse $5,500. Fillies. 2-year-olds. Weight, 119 lbs.

(1st Aqu)—Coupled—Alumbrada, Bast and Mertensia. Worklamp and Leanino.

Pronghorn
Dk. b. or br. f (1965-Ky), by Jaipur—Portage, by War Admiral 119 1967 0 M 0 0 —
J. M. Roebling J. A. Nerud (Harbourton Stud, Inc.)
LATEST WORKOUTS Sep 26 Bel 5f fst 1.02 h   Sep 20 Bel 3f fst .36⅕ bg   Sep 15 Bel 5f fst 1.03⅕ b   Sep 9 Bel 4f fst .48½ hg

Flip-Top-Tail
Ch, f (1965-Fla), by Francis S.—Mary Ellard, by Tudor Minstrel 119 1967 2 M 0 0 —
Harbor Veiw Farm I. H. Parke (Harbor View Farm)
1Sep67–5Aqu fst 6f .22⅘ .47 1.13⅕ f–MdSpWt 9 2 86¼111111151121 ACorderoJr 119 11.40 70–11 Eagle's Tryst 119no Mick B Quick 119nk Teddy's True 1194 No speed 14
24Aug67–3Sar fst 5½f.22⅖ .45⅘1.05⅕ f–MdSpWt 9 2 86¼111111151121 ACorderoJr 119 11.40 70–11 Kitty Standish 119³ Mick B Quick 119⁶ RunningCedar 119¹ Far back 12
LATEST WORKOUTS Sep 21 Bel 5f fst 1.01 bg   Sep 17 Bel t.r.t. 5f fst 1.05 b   Sep 13 Bel 4f fst .51 b   Sep 8 Bel 4f fst .48⅗ bg

Alumbrada
Dk. b. or br. f (1965-Ky), by Mamboreta—Beam, by Bimelech 119 1967 1 M 0 0 —
King Ranch Max Hirsch (King Ranch)
11Sep67–4Aqu fst 6f .23 .47⅕1.12⅗ f–MdSpWt 2 14 1414141914181422 JLRotz 119 25.50 58–21 Expectancy 119⁵ Bravissimo 119nk Bring Back 119h Slow start 14
LATEST WORKOUTS Sep 27 Bel 5f fst 1.03⅕ bg   Sep 24 Bel 4f fst .51 b   Sep 19 Bel 3f fst .36⅕ hg   Sep 16 Bel 3f fst .35⅖ hg

Worklamp *
Dk. b. or br. f (1965-Fla), by Stella Aurata—Needlework, by 119 1967 10 M 3 2 $3,850
H. T. Larkin J. E. Picou Needles (H. T. Larkin)
18Sep67–5Aqu fst 6½f.22⅘ .45⅘1.19¾ f–MdSpWt 11 1 32½ 2½ 12 22 ECardone b 119 11.20 81–15 Set A Thief 119² Worklamp 119³ Pointing West 119¹½ Gamely 13
2Aug67–4Sar gd 6f .46⅕1.05⅕ f–MdSpWt 2 1 1h 2h 63¾1018 ECardone b 119 8.50 73– 8 Polish Hop 119¹½ Beauty Kit 119³ ManyHappyReturns 119² Stopped 10
19Jly 67–3Aqu fst 5½f.22⅕ .46 1.05⅖ f–MdSpWt 2 1 51¾ 42 44½ 66½ EBelmonte 119 9.90 79–13 Full Of Laughs 109²½ Dark Mirage 119²½ Este Noche 119h Weak'n'd 12
22Jun67–4Aqu fst 5f .22⅘ .46⅘1.00⅕ f–MdSpWt 3 2 63¾ 55 33½ 32¾ ECardone 119 4.10 81–17 Just Muffy 119²½ Dragnetta 119nk Worklamp 119²½ Fair try 10
24May67–4Aqu fst 5f .23⅕ .46⅖ .59 f–MdSpWt 5 2 2h 2½ 2h 23 ACorderoJr b 119 4.30e 87–18 Wish Well 119³ Worklamp 119¹½ Set A Thief 119nk Best of others 10
26Apr67–3Aqu fst 5f .22⅘ .47⅕1.00⅗ f–MdSpWt 4 5 53½ 32½ 34½ 55 ATCordero 119 6.60e 77–17 Blitzed Eagle 119²¼ General Store 119² Set A Thief 119½ Tired 10
12Apr67–3Aqu fst 5f .24 .48⅖1.01 f–MdSpWt 8 5 2h 2½ 64 89½ RUssery b 119 *1.20e 71–21 Zoomalong 119¹½ Tiegoon 119no Gay Matelda 119½ Well up, tired 10
29Mar67–3Aqu my 5f .24⅕ .49⅕1.01¾ f–MdSpWt 2 2 42½ 3½ 2h 22 RUssery 119 *2.10 75–33 Pleasantness 119² Worklamp 119⁸ Tiegoon 119²½ Went well 7
23Feb67–3Hia gd 3f .22 .33⅖ f–MdSpWt 12 6 43½ 32½ EFires 119 14.90 93– 5 Ritura 116¹½ Snoopstep 116¹ Worklamp 116² Finished well 13
17Feb67–3Hia fst 3f .22⅖ .34⅕ f–MdSpWt 1 8 4⅜ 5² EFires 116 51.80 89– 9 Moon Chase 116no Lachette 116no Forward Press 116½ Tired 13
LATEST WORKOUTS Sep 28 Bel 4f fst .50 b   Sep 24 Bel 6f fst 1.19 b   Sept 14 Bel 3f fst .36 h   Sept 10 Bel 6f fst 1.17⅕ b

Teddy's True
Ch. f (1965-KY), by Jet Action—Darling Adelle, by Polynesian 119 1967 5 M 2 2 $3,525
M. Schneider J. Rigione (Maine Chance Farm)
25Sep67–1Aqu fst 7f .22⅘ .46⅕1.24⅘ f–MdSpWt 12 1 1¹ 13 11½ 2¾ WBoland b 119 8.10 81–21 Amadancer 119³ Teddy's True 119³½ Bast 119³ Sharp try 13
18Sep67–1Aqu fst 5½f.22⅘ .46⅖1.18⅘ f–MdSpWt 7 2 1½ 1½ 1h 2½ WBoland b 119 11.50 85–15 Polly N. 119½ Teddy's True 119h Bring Back 119h Game effort 14
1Sep67–5Aqu fst 6f .22⅘ .47 1.13⅕ f–MdSpWt 3 9 1h 1h 2h 3nk WBoland b 119 16.60f 77–21 Eagle's Tryst 119no Mick B Quick 119nk Teddy's True 119⁴ Weak'd 14
21Aug67–2Sar sly 5½f.22 .46⅕1.05⅜ f– 125C0 9 6 91¹113 96¾ 35½ WBoland 116 11.00 83–14 Gloriously Yours 116⁴ Follow 112²¼ Teddy's True 116² Stride late 11
31Jly 67–1Sar fst 5½f.22⅘ .46⅕1.05⅕ f– 12500 2 4 2¹½ 33½ 57¼ 410 WBoland 116 15.60 81–12 Dream Path 116¹⁰ Flustered 116nk Gem's Emerald 116h Tired 9
LATEST WORKOUTS Sep 23 Bel t.r.t. 4f fst .49 h   Sep 16 Bel t.r.t. 4f fst .49 h   Sep 10 Bel t.r.t. 3f fst .35⅖ h   Sep 6 Bel t.r.t. 4f fst .48⅗ h

Still
B. f (1965-Ky), by On-And-On—Little Sequoia, by Double Jay 119 1967 4 M 0 0 —
F. E. Dixon, Jr. J. S. Nash (S. Hancock—W. K. Taylor)
11Sep67–5Aqu fst 6f .22⅘ .46⅘1.11⅘ f–MdSpWt 4 12 138½1213 9¹² 8¹² BFeliciano b 119 36.80 72–21 Best InShow 119¹½ ManyHappyReturns 119²½ LoveTap 119¹ No thr't 14
2Aug67–6Sar fst 5½f.22⅘ .46⅕1.04⅗ f–MdSpWt 3 5 42 41½ 32 66¾ RFerraro b 119 21.70 87– 8 Dark Mirage 119⁴ Chenille 119no Best In Show 119¹ Weakened 11
15Jun67–3Aqu fst 5f .22⅘ .46⅕ .59 f–MdSpWt 3 8 811 814 712 814 ALdams b 119 7.00 76–13 Wiggins 119² Este Noche 119¹½ Karate Skill 119⁴ Far back 10
19Apr67–3Aqu gd 5f .23⅘ .48⅖1.00⅘ f–MdSpWt 3 3 32 55 45½ 69 RTurcotte 119 44.90 72–26 Syrian Sea 119h Disco 119²½ Chicago Flo 119⁶ Well up, tired 10
LATEST WORKOUTS Sep 29 Bel 3f sly .36⅕ h   Sep 20 Bel 6f fst 1.17 h   Sep 8 Bel t.r.t. 4f fst .50 h   Sep 4 Bel 4f fst .50 b

Turn To Waves
B. f (1965-Ky), by Turn-to—Dangerous Dame, by Nasrullah 119 1967 0 M 0 0 —
Cain Hoy Stable R. Laurin (H. F. Guggenheim)
LATEST WORKOUTS Sep 28 Bel 4f fst .51 h   Sep 23 Bel 4f fst .50 h   Sep 14 Bel 4f fst .48⅘ hg   Sep 10 Bel 5f fst 1.04⅗ b

Second The Motion
Ch. f (1965-Md), by Turn-to—Next Move, by Bull Lea 119 1967 3 M 0 0 —
A. G. Vanderbilt W. C. Freeman (A. G. Vanderbilt)
11Sep67–4Aqu fst 6f .23 .47⅕1.12⅗ f–MdSpWt 4 1 1½ 1h 3¹ 57½ RTurcotte b 119 24.50 73–21 Expectancy 119⁵ Bravissimo 119nk Bring Back 119h Used up 14
1Sep67–5Aqu fst 6f .22⅘ .47 1.13⅕ f–MdSpWt 9 4 3½ 62½ 99¼1111 JRuane b 119 60.30 66–26 Eagle's Tryst 119no Mick B Quick 119nk Teddy's True 119⁴ Tired 14
9Aug67–4Sar fst 5½f.22⅕ .45⅘1.05⅗ f–MdSpWt 10 12 121412121220 1220 RTurcotte 119 12.20 69–11 Marion Pride 119nk Kitty Standish 119h Silver Coin 119² Sluggish 12
LATEST WORKOUTS Sep 29 Aqu 3f sly .35⅕ h   Sep 25 Aqu 6f fst 1.15 b   Sep 21 Aqu 6f fst 1.16⅘ b   Sep 17 Aqu 3f fst .37 b

Silk Train Dk. b. or br. f (1965-Va), by Hasty Road—Lalana, by Swaps
Rokeby Stable E. Burch (F. E. Mars) **119** 1967 2 M 0 0 —
(Formely named Gull Foil).
11Sep67-5Aqu fst 6f .22⅖ .46⅘1.11⅘ f-MdSpWt 9 4 41½ 89 811 1015 RTurcotte 119 13.60 69-21 Best InShow 1191½ ManyHappyReturns 1192½ LoveTap 1191 Tired 14
24Aug67-4Sar fst 5½f.22⅘ .46⅕1.05⅔ f-MdSpWt 11 11 75½ 79½ 89¼ 613 RTurcotte 119 2.90 77-11 Dawn Of Tomorrow 1197 NativeTree 1192 ApplyFreely 1191 No thr't 12
LATEST WORKOUTS Sep 27 Bel 5f fst 1.01⅗ h Sep 22 Bel 4f fst .49⅗ h Sep 18 Bel 3f fst .35⅕ h Sep 9 Bel 3f fst .35⅘ hg

Bold Honor B. f (1965-Ky), by Bold Ruler—Her Honor, by Count Fleet
R. Lehman J. P. Conway (R. Lehman) **119** 1967 0 M 0 0 —
LATEST WORKOUTS Sep 27 Bel tr.t. 6f fst 1.17⅖ h Sep 23 Bel tr.t. 5f fst 1.03 b Sep 19 Bel 5f fst 1.06 b Sep 15 Bel 5f fst 1.05 b

Little Juanita Ch. f (1965-Ill), by Little Tytus—Giradilla, by Ghirlandaio
E. P. Bixer N. Combest (E. P. Bixer) **119** 1967 1 M 0 0 $275
11Sep67-4Aqu fst 6f .23 .47⅕1.12⅗ f-MdSpWt 8 11 64 2h 2½ 45¼ WBoland 119 9.20 75-21 Expectancy 1195 Bravissimo 119nk Bring Back 119h Faltered 14
LATEST WORKOUTS Sep 27 Aqu 5f fst 1.05 b Sep 23 Aqu 7f fst 1.29⅖ h Sep 2 Aqu 5f fst 1.00 h Aug 30 Aqu 5f fst 1.02⅘ b

Peach Sundae B. f (1965-Ky), by Estampido—Peach Fizz, by Phidias
M. F. Drinkhouse F. Dougherty (Southern Stud, Inc.) **119** 1967 4 M 0 0 —
11Sep67-4Aqu fst 6f .23 .47⅕1.12⅗ f-MdSpWt 1 13 1312 1011 1011 1015 JCruguet b 119 22.00f 65-21 Expectancy 1195 Bravissimo 119nk Bring Back 119h No speed 14
1Sep67-4Aqu fst 6f .22⅗ .46⅘1.12⅘ f-MdSpWt 8 14 1415 1314 1320 1317 JRuane b 119 76.00 62-21 Heartland 1192½ Best In Show 119¾ Bring Back 119h Checked 14
26Jly 67-5Aqu gd 5½f.22⅗ .46⅘1.05⅕ f-MdSpWt 8 9 1215 1111 1015 1022 EBelville 119 132.10 65-15 Mrs. Peterkin 1194½ Leanino 1192½ Miss Reason 1192½ No speed 12
19Jly 67-5Aqu fst 5½f.22⅘ .46⅕1.05⅘ f-MdSpWt 4 8 813 914 919 921 EBelville 119 45.10 64-13 Hawaiian Bubble 1191 Set A Thief 1191 Best In Show 1191½ No sp'd 12
LATEST WORKOUTS Aug 28 Aqu 6f my 1.20 b Aug 24 Aqu 5f fst 1.04 b Aug 20 Bel 4f fst .51 b Aug 16 Bel 3f fst .38⅖ b

Gosh A'Mighty Ch. f (1965-Va), by Amerigo—Jet Bright, by Jet Pilot
Hickory Tree Stable W. H. Turner, Jr. (M. Church 3d) **119** 1967 1 M 1 0 $700
13Jly 67-6Del fst 5½f.22⅘ .48⅕1.08⅘ f-MdSpWt 10 9 1011 98 63½ 2no ENelson 117 7.10 77-22 Noholme's Gal 117no Gosh A'Mighty 117½ Kurtera 117½ Alt'r'd c'rse 10
LATEST WORKOUTS Sep 29 Bel 3f sly .37⅘ b Sep 26 Bel 3f fst .38 b Sep 21 Bel 5f fst 1.02⅘ h Sep 18 Bel 5f fst 1.03⅕ b

Leanino Ch. f(1965-Fla), by Rico Tesio—Ninabalea, by Jet Action
D. L. Clark 3d J. E. Picou (E. J. Boysen-C. E. Nix, Jr.) **119** 1967 3 M 1 1 $1,650
2Aug67-7Sar fst 5½f.21⅘ .45 1.04⅗ f-Schyvlle 1 5 1110 1312 1213 1211 ECardone 112 60.30 83- 8 Idealistic 116no Copper Canyon 116nk Ave Valeque 116no No factor 13
26Jly 67-5Aqu gd 5½f.22⅗ .46⅘1.05⅕ f-MdSpWt 2 5 75½ 52 23 24½ ECardone 119 4.90 82-15 Mrs. Peterkin 1194½ Leanino 1192½ Miss Reason 1192½ Good try 12
15Jly 67-3Aqu sly 5f .22⅘ .46 .59 f-MdSpWt 3 7 55½ 45½ 47½ 35½ EBelmonte 119 5.90 84-18 Wildwook 1191½ A Pleasant Sort 1194 Leanino 119h Rallied 10
LATEST WORKOUTS Sep 22 Bel 4f fst .48 b Sep 18 Bel 6f fst 1.15⅖ b Sep 16 Bel 3f fst .37⅗ b Sep 10 Bel 3f fst .37⅗ b

Horses Shown Below Are on the "Also Eligible" List and Are Not Listed in Order of Post Positions.

Bast B. f, (1965-Ky), by Summer Tan—Polygamous, by Polynesian
J. H. Stone Max Hirsch (Mrs. J. H. Stone) **119** 1967 3 M 0 2 $920
25Sep67-1Aqu fst 7f .22⅗ .46⅕1.24⅗ f-MdSpWt 6 8 67½ 45 34½ 34¼ ADeSpirito 119 8.20e 78-21 Amadancer 119¾ Teddy's True 1193½ Bast 1193 Held gamely 13
2Jun67-6Del fst 5f .22⅕ .47⅗ .59⅗ f-MdSpWt 1 10 98½ 77 65½ 38½ RKimball 117 3.50 82-16 SingingRain 1173½ Nasrullah'sGlory 1175 Bast 117no Unrully at post 12
18May67-3Pim fst 5f .22⅗ .46⅕ .59⅗ f-MdSpWt 7 12 811 815 713 66 RKimball 118 4.10 91-13 Guest Room 118no Cease Fire 1182 Silk Hat II 1182½ Poor start 12
LATEST WORKOUTS Sep 29 Bel tr.t. 4f sly .49⅖ h Sep 23 Bel 4f fst .48⅖ bg Sep 20 Bel 4f fst .49 b Sep 16 Bel 7f fst 1.31 b

Chicago Flo Dk. b. or br. f (1965-Fla), by Clandestine—Flevo, by Hill Prince
J. B. Frisone W. R. Corbellini (J. M. O'Farrell-C. Wacker) **119** 1967 7 M 1 2 $1,870
14Sep67-3Aqu fst 6f .23 .47⅘1.13⅕ f-M 10000 10 9 98 74½ 54½ 32¼ ORosado b 119 7.90 75-17 d-Mix And Mingle 1192 Oldtown 110nk Chicago Flo 1193 Checked 13
14Sep67—Placed second through disqualification.
28Aug67-1Aqu sl 6f .23 .47⅗1.15⅗ f-M 10000 12 7 66 56½ 47 32½ ORosado b 119 9.70 63-31 Instomatic 115no Freesia 1192½ Chicago Flo 1194 Rallied 13
7Jun67-5Aqu fst 5f .22⅘ .46⅗ .59⅕ f-MdSpWt 5 10 910 810 812 713 MVenezia b 119 22.20 76-16 Mother Russia 1193 Round Pearl 119h Set A Thief 1191½ No threat 10
10May67-5Aqu fst 5f .22⅘ .46⅘ .59 f-MdSpWt 10 9 77½ 88¾ 79½ 719 ACorderoJr 119 6.00 71-21 QueenOfTheStage1199 MickB.Quick119½ FunnyMiss1193½ No threat 10
3May67-4Aqu fst 5f .23⅘ .47⅘1.00⅘ f-MdSpWt 9 6 63½ 55½ 48½ 711 ATCordero 119 5.90 70-21 Disco 1195 Sewickley Heights 1192½ Beauty Secret 1191 Tired 10
19Apr67-3Aqu gd 5f .23⅘ .48⅗1.00⅘ f-MdSpWt 2 1 21 23 22 32½ ATCordero 119 17.60 78-26 Syrian Sea 119h Disco 1192½ Chicago Flo 1196 Held on evenly 10
10Mar67-3GP fst 3f .22⅗ .33⅘ f-MdSpWt 11 10 87½ 1311 JGiovanni 119 14.10f 82- 7 HilariousEvening119no SoArrogant1192 SomeWind119½ No speed 14
LATEST WORKOUTS Sep 27 Bel 3f fst .37 b Sep 23 Bel 4f fst .50 b Sep 13 Bel 3f fst .38 b Sep 7 Bel 3f fst .37⅕ h

Mertensia Ch. f (1965-Ky), by T. V. Lark-Bluebility, by Blue Swords
Mereworth Farm Max Hirsch (Mereworth Farm) **119** 1967 2 M 0 0 —
25Sep67-5Aqu fst 7f .22⅘ .46⅘1.25⅕ f-MdSpWt 4 2 21 33½ 77½ 811 JLRotz b 119 3.70 69-21 Bravissimo 1193½ Hillca 1192 Love Tap 119no Early factor, tired 12
11Sep67-5Aqu fst 6f .22⅘ .46⅘1.11⅘ f-MdSpWt 6 2 3nk 32 67 68½ JLRotz b 119 8.80 76-21 Best InShow 1191½ ManyHappyReturns 1192½ LoveTap 1191 Tired 14
LATEST WORKOUTS Sep 24 Bel 3f fst .37 b Sep 21 Bel 3f fst .35⅕ hg Sep 18 Bel 4f fst .51 b Sep 15 Bel 5f fst 1.04 b

Warm Glow Ch. f (1965-Ky), by King of the Tudors—Golden Heels, by Heliopolis
Judith Burke L. S. Barrera (L. C. Ledyard-J. E. Ryan) **119** 1967 3 M 0 2 $1,100
1Sep67-5Aqu fst 6f .22⅘ .47 1.13⅕ f-MdSpWt 12 8 117 117½ 1010 98¾ EBelmonte b 119 3.10 68-21 Eagle's Tryst 119no Mick B Quick 119nk Teddy's True 1194 Wide 14
16Aug67-4Sar fst 6f .22⅘ .46⅗1.12⅘ f-MdSpWt 4 4 64½ 54 54 33½ ACorderoJr b 119 2.40 82- 8 Silver Coin 119½ Dawn Of Tomorrow 1193 Warm Glow 119h Bore out 11
9Aug67-6Sar fst 5½f.22⅘ .46⅗1.05⅘ f-MdSpWt 12 11 62½ 63½ 34 35 ACorderoJr b 119 *1.70 84-11 Chenille 1194 Mick B. Quick 1191 Warm Glow 1193½ Slow start, wide 12
LATEST WORKOUTS Sep 28 Bel tr.t. 5f fst 1.03 b Sep 23 Bel tr.t. 5f fst 1.02 b Sep 18 Bel tr.t. 4f fst .50⅘ h Aug 30 Bel tr.t. 4f fst .48 h

---

The program shows the following scratches: Turn To Waves, Little Juanita, Peach Sundae, Leanino, Bast, Warm Glow. And there are some jockey switches. Cordero isn't here today, and Parke has put Larry Gilligan on Flip-Flop Tail. Tony DeSpirito is on Alumbrada, with Johnny Rotz on the other half of Max Hirsch's entry, Mertensia. Ronnie Ferraro replaces Ben Feliciano on Still. Braulio Baeza gets Elliott Burch's Silk Train. Dave Hidalgo is on the first-time starter, Pronghorn, and Eric Guerin has come from New England to ride the other debutante, Jim Conway's Bold Honor, which has the breeding of a champion and the workouts of a mule.

We might as well go through the field with an axe and knock off all entrants that have showed no run in their recent performances.

We therefore cross out Flip-Flop Tail, Alumbrada, Still and Silk Train. And now we can kiss off the first-starters, because other entrants—notably Worklamp and Teddy's True—have been running well enough to beat green beginners.

We now are left with six horses: Worklamp, Teddy's True, Second The Motion, Gosh A'Mighty, Chicago Flo, and Mertensia. I see no reason to bother further with Chicago Flo, which has been running in maiden claimers. Or with Gosh A'Mighty, a Delaware import which has not raced since mid-July and has yet to break anyone's stopwatch. Likewise, the well-bred Second The Motion looks like a loser, having conked out after setting an extremely slow early pace in her last race. Nor would I bet a pfennig on Mertensia, another filly that has yet to generate any real speed.

Which leaves two contenders, in case you are thinking of playing the daily double.

Worklamp: Has not yet raced six furlongs, but showed fair speed at six-and-a-half less than two weeks ago. Is obviously primed for an all-out try, as that last race and the two subsequent workouts indicate. Quite aside from anything that a pace analysis might reveal about today's race, this filly should be comfortable at six furlongs, having run the first half-mile of her last race in excellent time, holding her energy until the final stages of that longer sprint.

Teddy's True: After this filly's brave showing in a claimer on August 21, Rigione moved it into the special-weights division and got three more all-out tries. That is quite a strenuous program for such a young filly, especially when interlarded with those four hard workouts.

Where are we? Worklamp has been trying to win from expensive maidens ever since February and has come fairly close five times. Teddy's True was unraced until July but has been as busy as a Shenandoah Downs five-year-old ever since and has been performing quite well.

Perhaps a pace analysis will reveal differences between the two fillies.

The best basis for comparison is the performance of each filly at six-and-a-half furlongs on September 18. Worklamp ran in the fifth race on that day. She was right on the heels of the leader at the half-mile call in .45⅘ before taking over the lead herself and holding it until the last sixteenth or so.

Teddy's True ran on the front end of her own race but took .46⅗ to get to the half-mile and was backing up at the eighth pole.

On this basis it seems clear that Worklamp could slow down to .46 or .46⅕ and annihilate Teddy's True, meanwhile saving more than enough juice for the stretch. Is there anything else in the race that might be able to keep pace with Worklamp? The fractional times and running lines of the past-performance records contain nothing remotely like Worklamp's last effort.

I think Worklamp is worth a bet in this race. But not in the daily double. If you want to play a double, perhaps you had better wheel Worklamp and Teddy's True with whatever you can find in the second race. Why go back to Teddy's True? Because Worklamp is by no means a gilt-edged cinch. The other filly has demonstrated real honesty. Even with all the exertion recently demanded of her, she might have enough quality to show improvement today.

The Running of the Race

THE CROWD went to Teddy's True, with Worklamp a distant second choice and Pronghorn—John Nerud's debutante—the third favorite.

Teddy's True and Second the Motion ran with each other on the head end for the first quarter-mile, but Worklamp ate them up before the half-mile call, drew out nicely in the stretch, and began to tire. Max Hirsch's surprising Mertensia almost caught our filly at the wire. But not quite.

FIRST RACE   **6 FURLONGS. (Near Man, July 17, 1963, 1.08⅗, 3, 112.)**
Aqu - 32426   Maidens. Special weight. Purse $5,500. Fillies. 2-year-olds. Weight, 119 lbs.
September 30, 1967
Value to winner $3,575, second $1,100, third $550, fourth $275. Mutuel pool $311,077.

Index	Horse	Eqt A Wt PP St	¼	½	Str	Fin	Jockey	Owner	Odds $1
32331Aqu[2]	—Worklamp	b 2 119 4 1	3^3	1^h	1^2	1^h	E Cardone	H T Larkin	5.20
32385Aqu[8]	—Mertensia	b 2 119 12 4	$5\frac{1}{2}$	4^4	3^3	$2^{3\frac{1}{2}}$	J L Rotz	Mereworth Farm	a-14.20
32381Aqu[2]	—Teddy's True	b 2 119 5 10	1^h	$2^{1\frac{1}{2}}$	$2^{1\frac{1}{2}}$	$3^{1\frac{3}{4}}$	W Boland	M Schneider	1.30
32302Aqu[2]	—Chicago Flo	b 2 119 11 8	$10^{1\frac{1}{2}}$	8^2	5^3	4^4	O Rosado	J B Frisone	13.70
32276Aqu[5]	—S'd T'e M't'n	b 2 119 7 2	2^h	3^3	4^3	5^1	R Turcotte	A G Vanderbilt	10.40
31696Del[2]	—Gosh A'mighty	2 119 10 1	11^3	9^h	$7\frac{1}{2}$	6^{nk}	E Nelson	Hickory Tree Stable	13.80
32277Aqu[8]	—Still	b 2 119 6 9	9^h	$10^{1\frac{1}{2}}$	10^2	$7\frac{1}{2}$	R Ferraro	F E Dixon Jr	59.10
32277Aqu[10]	—Silk Train	2 119 8 3	$7\frac{1}{2}$	11^4	11^4	8^1	B Baeza	Rokeby Stable	17.30
	—Pronghorn	2 119 1 11	4^h	$5\frac{1}{2}$	$6\frac{1}{2}$	9^1	D Hidalgo	J M Roebling	5.50
	—Bold Honor	b 2 119 9 6	$8^{1\frac{1}{2}}$	7^h	9^h	$10^{1\frac{1}{2}}$	E Guerin	R Lehman	14.70
32205Aqu[14]	—Flip-Top-Tail	2 119 2 5	6^2	$6\frac{1}{2}$	$8\frac{1}{2}$	11^4	L Gilligan	Harbor View Farm	46.30
32276Aqu[14]	—Alumbrada	2 119 3 12	12	12	12	12	A DeSpirito	King Ranch	a-14.20

a–Coupled, Martensia and Alumbrada.

Time .22⅕, .46, 1.12⅘ (with wind in backstretch). Track good.

Official Program Numbers

$2 Mutuel Prices:

4-WORKLAMP	....	12.40	6.40	3.60
12-MERTENSIA (a-entry)	....		12.80	5.00
5-TEDDY'S TRUE	....			2.40

Dk. b. or br. f, by Stella Aurata—Needlework, by Needles. Trainer J. E. Picou. Bred by H. T. Larkin (Fla.).

IN GATE AT 1.30. OFF AT 1.30 EASTERN DAYLIGHT TIME. Start good. Won driving.

WORKLAMP took command from TEDDY'S TRUE entering the stretch and, responding to strong handling, retained a safe advantage. MERTENSIA steadily worked her way forward and finished extremely fast. TEDDY'S TRUE had early speed but faltered after entering the stretch. CHICAGO FLO, racing well off the inner rail, lacked early foot. SECOND THE MOTION had early speed but failed to stay. GOSH A'MIGHTY, outrun for a half-mile, was unable to reach serious contention during the drive. STILL raced wide early and was never dangerous. SILK TRAIN drifted out through the stretch. PRONGHORN gave way after showing brief speed. BOLD HONOR was never dangerous. FLIP-TOP-TAIL bore out entering the stretch. ALUMBRADA raced greenly.

Scratched—Turn To Waves, 32276Aqu[4] Little Juanita, 32276Aqu[10] Peach Sundae, 31916Sar[12] Leanino, 32381Aqu[3] Bast, 32205Aqu[9] Warm Glow.

THE SECOND RACE

THIS IS a typical six-furlong affair for claimers in the $4,000–$5,000 range. We might as well run through the list and eliminate anything unsuited to the distance, obviously outclassed, out of shape, or scratched.

2nd Race Aqueduct

6 FURLONGS AQUEDUCT (Start / Finish)

6 FURLONGS. (Near Man, July 17, 1963, 1.08⅗, 3, 112.)
Claiming. Purse $5,000. 3-year-olds and upward. Weights, 3-year-olds, 120 lbs., older 124 lbs. Non-winners of four races since Mar. 11 allowed 3 lbs., of three races since then, 5 lbs., of two races since then, 7 lbs., of a race since then, 9 lbs. Claiming price $5,000. 2 lbs. allowed for each $500 to $4,000. (Races when entered to be claimed for $3,500 or less not considered.)

Speedy Admiral $4,500 — Ch. g (1961), by Ace Admiral—Kiki K., by Air Hero — M. Gilbert P. K. Yee (P. B. Fichera) **113** — 1967 18 1 3 2 $6,200 — 1966 23 3 7 4 $16,475

19Sep67-4Aqu fst 6f .22⅗ .46⅕1.11 Clm 5000 6 7 74¼ 68½ 98 88¼ AGarr'mone7 b 110 14.70 80–14 Cartabon 1124½ Mr. Elwood W. 1171 Fair Valley 116nk No threat 11
13Sep67-2Aqu fst 6f .22⅘ .46⅗1.12⅕ Cl c-3500 6 2 42¼ 24 34½ 55¾ BBaeza b 117 2.90 76–14 Match Wits 124no Colbert II 1123½Festival King 1141½ Weakened 9
30Aug67-2Aqu fst 6f .22⅘ .46⅕1.12 Clm 3500 4 2 2½ 2h 33 31½ LPincayJr b 117 5.50 81–18 Fair Valley 1171 Ash Blue 121½ Speedy Admiral 117h Gamely 14
29Jly 67-8Aqu fst 6f .22⅕ .45⅗1.11⅖ Clm 5000 4 2 31 43 67½ 63¼ JRuane b 119 4.90 83–14 Big Luxury 110½ Prevalent 108nk Rogo 112½ Could not keep up 8
22Jly 67-2Aqu fst 7f .22⅘ .45⅗1.24 Clm 3500 3 4 1½ 11½ 11½ 12 BBaeza b 117 *2.00 86–11 Speedy Admiral 1172 Don't Walk 1101 Party Giver 1125 In hand 10
12Jly 67-1Aqu fst 6f .22⅗ .46⅘1.12⅗ Clm 3500 4 3 21½ 33 42 22 JGiovanni b 117 *2.20 78–13 Suerte Fue 1172 Speedy Admiral 1171½ Don't Walk 117h Gamely 13
4Jly 67-1Aqu fst 7f .23 .46⅗1.25⅘ Clm 3500 2 6 21 2½ 11 21 JGiovanni b 115 *3.60 76–17 Marvina's Tusc 1151 Speedy Admiral 115¾ Noureige 1051 Gamely 9
28Jun67-2Aqu fst 6f .22⅘ .46⅕1.12⅕ Clm 3500 3 4 52¼ 56 66¾ 34½ JGiovanni b 117 5.90 77–17 Fair Valley 1173 Silly II 1101½ Speedy Admiral 117nk Mild bid 13
21Jun67-2Aqu gd 6f .22⅖ .46 1.11⅘ Clm 3500 6 6 69½ 59 69 47½ JGiovanni b 117 9.90 76–21 Match Wits 1193½ Party Giver 119h Pippin 1144 No threat 13
14Jun67-4Aqu fst 7f .22⅗ .45⅗1.24⅗ Clm 3500 8 3 3½ 64¼ 89½ 78 JGiovanni b 119 4.10 75–14 Pippin 121nk Flipaway 119nk Bold Fool 1192 Fell back early 14
7Jun67-2Aqu fst 6f .21⅘ .45⅕1.11⅘ Clm 3500 7 4 33 54 56½ 22 JGiovanni b 115 8.20 82–16 Festival King 1212 Speedy Admiral 115½ Poor Jud 1152 Gamely 14

Lash Back * $4,000 — B. g (1963–Va), by Cochise—Whipsaw, by Pilate — A. E. Kennedy J. R. Hastie (Renappi Corp.) **113** — 1967 12 1 0 2 $5,975 — 1966 10 2 1 1 $9,175

9Aug67-1Sar fst 6f .23⅕ .46⅘1.12 Clm 3500 2 10 86¼ 87½ 54½ 66½ RFerraro b 117 8.40 81–11 Ash Blue 121h Sum Farce 1153 Mister G. R. 1151½ Sluggishly 10
17Jun67-2Aqu fst 7f .23 .46⅕1.24⅘ Clm 5000 2 10 83½ 87 89 66¼ BFeliciano b 119 3.60 76–15 Predicador 1192 Blew By 1192½ Plow 117no Failed to rally 10
13Jun67-8Aqu fst 6f .22⅖ .45⅗1.11 Clm 7500 6 8 711 78½ 66½ 65¾ JLRotz b 119 11.90 82–14 Mister Judge 1174 Last Chain 117no Wiggins Fork 117nk Lame 8
20May67-4Aqu fst 6f .22 .45⅗1.11⅕ Clm 9000 6 11 1212 1216 914 98½ GMora7 b 108 15.20 78–14 Beaustone 117no Dior 1191½ Last Chain 115h Slow start 14
6May67-4Aqu sly 7f .24⅕ .48 1.27 Clm 10000 4 1 3nk 21 1h 32¾ JLRotz b 121 *1.60 68–27 Syncope 1171½ Daily Reminder 1171½ Lash Back 1213 Weakened 6
18Apr67-6Aqu my 7f .23⅖ .46⅘1.25 Clm 14000 4 1 42 43 55 511 ATCordero b 121 3.80 70–25 Counsellor 1192 Well To Do 1215 ♦Beaustone 1154 Bore out 5
27Mar67-6Aqu sl 1 .47⅗1.13⅕1.38⅖ Clm 18000 1 5 2½ 45½ 512 516 RFerraro b 112 11.20 60–31 Sheet Anchor 1164½ Off The Top 1122 Needles' Count 112no Tired 7
15Mar67-7Aqu sly 7f .23⅘ .48 1.26⅕ Allowance 6 3 32 2½ 11½ 14 RFerraro b 115 7.70 75–24 Lash Back 1154 Guy Zog 124¾ Yale Fence 1151 Steady hand ride 6
LATEST WORKOUTS Sep 24 Bel 6f fst 1.17 h — Sep 20 Bel 6f fst 1.18⅗ h — Sep 15 Bel 4f fst .51 h — Sep 4 Bel 4f fst .51 b

***Fair Valley** $5,000 — B. g (1961), by Set Fair—Perivale, by Persian Gulf — E. Rieser W. Terrill (P. R. Dunne) (Eng.) **115** — 1967 11 2 0 2 $6,685 — 1966 14 2 3 3 $6,275

19Sep67-4Aqu fst 6f .22⅗ .46⅕1.11 Clm 4500 3 6 64¼ 57½ 43 35½ RUssery b 116 4.30 82–14 Cartabon 1124½ Mr. Elwood W. 1171 Fair Valley 116nk Mild bid 11
6Sep67-1Aqu fst 6f .23 .46⅖1.11⅗ Clm 3500 3 6 64 56 43½ 41¼ EBelmonte b 124 *3.10 84–18 Big Luxury 121½ Don't Walk 114¾ Festival King 114h No mishap 14
30Aug67-2Aqu fst 6f .22⅘ .46⅕1.12 Clm 3500 9 3 3½ 3nk 1h 11 EBelmonte b 117 10.10 83–18 Fair Valley 1171 Ash Blue 121½ Speedy Admiral 117h Good try 14
2Aug67-2Mth fst 6f .22⅖ .46 1.11⅗ Clm 3500 6 4 1h 12 2h 44¼ CBaltazar b 115 5.40 80–15 Silver Monarch 1161¾ Fleet N' True 1152½ Pippin 115no Weakened 12
26Jly 67-4Aqu gd 6f .22⅗ .46⅘1.11⅗ Clm 3500 1 4 22 21½ 1h 46¼ ADeSpirito b 121 2.50 79–15 Pippin 1141 Party Giver 1165 Ash Blue 124nk Short lead, tired 9
19Jly 67-1Aqu fst 6f .22⅖ .45⅘1.11⅗ Clm 3500 6 3 2½ 2½ 3½ 32¾ ADeSpirito b 118 6.80 81–13 Lord Birchfield 1242½ Big Luxury 108nk Fair Valley 1182 In close 9
15Jly 67-4Aqu sly 6f .22 .46 1.12⅖ Clm 4500 9 4 43 63 66 69 ECardone b 117 27.80 72–18 Stormy Outlook 1092½ Lord Birchfield 114h Solid Mike 119nk Tired 9
6Jly 67-2Mth fst 6f .22⅗ .46⅘1.13⅕ Clm 4000 9 1 64½ 62½ 87 64 JLeonard b 119 5.80 72–26 Nash 1192 Craig Lynn 116nk Paddyland 116½ Had no mishap 11
28Jun67-2Aqu fst 6f .22⅘ .46⅕1.12⅕ Clm 3500 5 2 2h 14 13 13 RUssery b 117 5.10 82–17 Fair Valley 1173 Silly II 1101½ Speedy Admiral 117nk Mild drive 13
21Jun67-2Aqu gd 6f .22⅖ .46 1.11⅘ Clm 3500 7 8 710 1011 1014 1015 LGilligan b 117 *3.60e 69–21 Match Wits 1193½ Party Giver 119h Pippin 1144 No speed 13
LATEST WORKOUTS Sep 14 Bel tr.t. 3f fst .37 h — Aug 23 Bel 3f fst .38 b — Aug 16 Bel 5f fst 1.03 b — Aug 12 Bel 4f fst .49⅗ b

Open Sight $5,000 — Ch. g (1964–Ky), by Tompion—Fair Clarissa, by Fair Trial — J. Napolitano M. Wachs (Elmendorf Farm) **111** — 1967 3 M 0 0 — — 1966 2 M 0 0 —

31Aug67-1Aqu fst 1 .46⅘1.13 1.40⅕ Md 3500 5 5 54 53½ 54 66½ ACordero7 110 10.90 60–22 Conviction 1084 Eagle Nest 123h Marsh King 117h No mishap 13
23Aug67-1Sar fst 7f .23 .46⅘1.24⅗ Md 10000 10 5 73¾ 86¾ 911 925 RTurcotte 119 18.60 62–11 Anglican 119¾ Go To It 1158 Prestidigitator 1203½ Fell back 10
10Aug67-1Sar fst 6f .22⅘ .46⅗1.13⅖ Md 8500 7 7 1011 109½ 1011 97½ ALoguercio7 112 35.00 73–15 Swift Reward 1151 Stone Arabia 1171 Silver Shot 1081½ Wide 12
7Dec66-5Lrl fst 6f .23⅕ .47⅕1.13⅕ Md Sp Wt 1 7 74¾ 67½ 49 58¼ OTorres 118 10.40 78–18 Stu Agogo 1182½ Hopi 1184 Secret Ceremony 118nk No threat 12
21Nov66-5Lrl fst 6f .23⅕ .48 1.14⅖ Md Sp Wt 2 12 914 712 711 66 OTorres 118 4.30e 74–21 Sky Count 1182 Tigers Tune 118½ Tumbling Water 1182 Slow st. 12
LATEST WORKOUTS Sep 20 Aqu 5f fst 1.04 b — Sep 14 Aqu 5f fst 1.04 b — Sep 8 Aqu 4f fst .51⅖ b — Aug 29 Bel tr.t. 4f fst .52 b

Bethson $4,000 — B. c (1963–Ky), by Nasco—Irish Beth, by Macbeth — J. C. Toomey J. E. Rich (C. J. Wade) **111** — 1967 15 0 0 1 $810 — 1966 16 3 1 1 $9,590

20Sep67-2Aqu fst 7f .22⅘ .46⅕1.25⅖ Clm 3500 10 14 148½ 1416 127 127¼ ACaceres b 117 24.30f 72–14 Manga Reva 117nk Peace Offer 113¾ Colbert II 117½ No speed 14
9Sep67-1Aqu fst 7f .22⅖ .45⅕1.24⅕ Clm 4000 4 11 98 811 1011 1113 ACaceres b 113 90.40 72–16 Cartabon 1075 Blew By 117nk Eagle's Scream 1173 No factor 13
26Aug67-2Sar fst 7f .22⅘ .46 1.24⅖ Clm 4000 5 7 88½ 76½ 75 811 AGarram'e10 b 104 36.10 77– 7 Eiffel II 117¾ Chai Cha-Na 1172½ Hamorton 117½ Never close 9
2Aug67-5Sar fst 6f .22⅘ .45⅗1.10⅗ Clm 6000 1 7 915 912 914 921 LAdams b 113 56.50 74– 8 Chartist 1174 Credential 1031 Cartabon 116¾ Trailed field 9
1Jly 67-2Aqu my 7f .22⅖ .45⅗1.26⅕ Clm 5000 8 8 911 915 914 913 RStovall b 119 56.80 62–21 Match Wits 1192 Stormy Outlook 1091 Party Giver 1171½ No speed 10
20May67-9Aqu fst 7f .23 .45⅘1.24⅗ Clm 5000 10 2 77 1011 1116 1120 LAdams b 117 21.20 63–14 TV Dinner122nk Martial Owens1171½ Sir Rodolph1211 Far back 11
20Apr67-8GP fst 6f .22⅖ .45⅘1.10⅗ Clm 6000 4 10 116½ 1111 1114 913 RWinant b 112 39.40 78–14 Maktar 1147 Fuerza 112½ Free Game 112½ Never a contender 12
11Apr67-6GP fst 7f .22⅘ .45⅘1.23⅘ Clm 6000 6 5 52¼ 31 35 37 SBrooks b 114 42.80 83–14 Bust-On 1166 Tulran 1161 Bethson 1141½ Showed fair effort 11
4Apr67-6GP fst 7f .22⅗ .45⅗1.23⅗ Clm 6250 3 11 72¾ 63 57½ 46¾ SBrooks b 114 71.80 84–15 Windy Hill 1143½ Roads End 1161½ Tulran 1162 No mishap 12
28Mar67-4GP fst 7f .22⅗ .45⅗1.24 Clm 6250 2 12 1111 1114 1117 812 PMaxwell b 114 41.80 77–14 Rocky Spring 1121 Hi Hammy 113¾ Ninino 1132½ Never close 12
13Mar67-4GP fst 7f .23 .45⅘1.24⅕ Clm 6000 11 2 3½ 42½ 69 55¾ JVelasquez b 112 5.60 82–15 Ambarmar 1161 Arkangel 1162½ Winkie 116¾ Early factor, tired 12
LATEST WORKOUTS Sep 29 Bel tr.t. 3f sly .38 b — Sep 26 Bel tr.t. 4f fst .48⅗ h — Sep 18 Bel tr.t. 5f fst 1.06 b — Sep 14 Bel tr.t. 4f fst .49 h

Inflexible * $5,000
B. g (1961), by Jutland—Manchette, by Johnstown 115 1967 12 0 0 2 $1,680
Belle Karson W. P. King (J. E. Hughes) 1966 26 2 3 4 $11,230

19Sep67-4Aqu fst 6f .22⅗ .46⅕1.11 Clm 5000 8 8 86½ 89½ 55 45¾ ACaceres b 117 45.70 82-14 Cartabon 1124½ Mr. Elwood W. 1171 Fair Valley 116nk Wide 11
22Jly 67-4Aqu fst 7f .22⅘ .45⅘1.24 Clm 5000 8 1 42½ 54 79 710 JRuane b 119 41.30 76-11 Bold Fool 1191½ d-Cartabon 112nk Snow Dales 1195 Raced wide 8
8Jly 67-1Aqu fst 7f .22⅕ .45⅕1.24⅗ Clm 5000 8 5 47 68½ 712 812 ACaceres b 119 25.60 71-14 Match Wits 1241½ Cartabon 1125 Indiecito 119no Tired steadily 9
1Jly 67-2Aqu my 7f .22⅖ .45⅗1.26⅕ Clm 5000 9 9 88¾ 79½ 56½ 67¼ LGilligan b 119 19.40 67-21 Match Wits 1192 Stormy Outlook 1091 Party Giver 1171½ No threat 10
24Jun67-1Aqu gd 6f .22⅕ .45⅗1.11⅗ Clm 5000 4 6 56½ 57½ 47 411 ORosado b 119 14.80 74-18 Flipaway 1192 Match Wits 1175 Snow Dales 1193½ Wide 8
17Jun67-2Aqu fst 7f .23 .46⅕1.24⅘ Clm 5000 6 6 63½ 76 58 87½ ADeSpirito b 119 6.70 74-15 Predicador 1192 Blew By 1192½ Plow 117no Not a threat 10
10Jun67-5Aqu fst 6f .22⅕ .45⅖1.11 Clm 5000 12 6 72½ 63½ 55 55¾ RTurcotte b 117 6.90 82-12 Bullyampa 1174 Predicador 1171 Sum Farce 117no No rally 13
3Jun67-3Aqu fst 7f .23 .46 1.24⅗ Clm 5000 8 5 52½ 32½ 32½ 31¾ RTurcotte b 117 3.50 81-15 LocalTalent119nk Pike'sPeak1171½ Inflexible1171 Wide in stretch 8
27May67-3Aqu fst 6f .23 .47⅕1.12⅕ Clm 5000 2 12 98 85½ 42 43 RTurcotte b 117 38.30 79-15 Wrapped Up 1191 Wiggins Fork 117no Ambi Enshalah 1082 Hung 13
22Apr67-3Aqu fst 7f .22⅖ .45⅖1.24 Cl c-5000 2 10 89½1012101610 17 HGustines b 117 11.90 69-16 Farmer Snooty 1176 Bandy 1152½ Warriors Day 117nk Slow start 10
15Apr67-1Aqu fst 6f .22⅘ .45⅘1.10⅖ Clm 5000 4 8 56½ 57½ 36½ 312 HGustines b 117 *3.20e 79-14 Joe Di Rosa 1212 Stormy Outlook 11710 Inflexible 117½ Far back 10
3Apr67-2Aqu fst 6f .23 .47⅕1.12⅘ Clm 6000 8 7 73½ 68½ 59½ 611 HGustines b 113 6.30e 70-25 Master Coosaw 1171½ Mister Judge 1172½ Solid Mike 117h No mish'p 9
LATEST WORKOUTS Sep 3 Bel tr.t. 4f fst .50⅖ h Aug 19 Bel 4f fst .51⅖ b Aug 16 Bel 4f fst .54 b

School Tie * $4,500
Dk. b, g (1962), by Etonian—Winsome Woman, by Blandisher 108⁷ 1967 15 1 2 1 $4,925
Emmess Stable M. J. Hoey (H. A. Jones) 1966 4 1 0 0 $2,520

12Sep67-9Aqu fst 1 .45⅘1.09⅗1.36⅗ Cl c-3500 3 7 79 915 918 919 LGilligan 116 4.90 66-20 Big Luxury 1136 Manga Reva 1162 Willow Creek 1164 No speed 14
17Aug67-2Sar fst 6f .23⅘ .46⅕1.11 Clm 6250 1 5 79 66 53½ 54 JRuane 119 6.60 89- 9 Cretaceous 119½ Soldier's Story 1192 World Guide 1171 No threat 8
5Aug67-2Sar fst 6f .22⅕ .45⅖1.10⅘ Clm 8500 3 8 915 915 67 55½ LGilligan 117 28.10 88- 6 Get Gettin 1171 Age Of Reason 116nk Your Day 1154 No threat 9
19Jly 67-4Aqu fst 7f .22⅕ .45⅕1.23⅗ Clm 8500 7 6 1113 911119½ 66½ LAdams 118 18.80 81-13 Wiggins Fork 1162 Eagle's Scream 118no Oxidized 118½ Bore out 11
11Jly 67-8Aqu fst 7f .22⅘ .45⅘1.24⅖ Cl c-6500 5 5 67 67½ 41 32¼ LAdams 119 4.40 82-15 Evert 110¾ Eagle's Scream 1191½ School Tie 1192 In close late 7
29Jun67-8Aqu fst 1 .46⅗1.11⅗1.37⅖ Clm 8500 4 12 111311131015 1012 RFerraro 118 18.80f 69-19 Razonable 118½ Charlie Tooley 120h Mister Judge 120½ No speed 14
10Jun67-4Aqu fst 6f .23⅕ .46⅖1.10⅘ Clm 10500 4 5 68 68½ 69½ 611 LAdams 113 23.00 78-12 Farmer's Son 1171½ Mr.C.H.1151½ Big Rapids 1171 Never a factor 6
3Jun67-5Aqu fst 6f .22⅗ .45⅗1.11 Clm 10000 6 8 911 912 79 55½ PAnderson 117 43.20 82-15 Storm Crost 1212½ Mr.C.H.117½ Colbert II 1132½ Stride late 9
20May67-5Pim fst 1 1/16 .47⅖1.12⅖1.44⅗ Clm 10500 1 5 66½ 53½ 54 64¾ BBaeza 115 3.40 82-11 Sectario 115no Officer Sweeney 1151 Over Roger 1223½ No mishap 9
LATEST WORKOUTS Sep 28 Bel tr.t. 3f fst .40 b Sep 25 Bel tr.t. 3f fst .39⅖ b Sep 20 Hag 3f fst .37⅗ b Sep 9 Bel tr.t. 5f fst 1.03 b

Fire Escape * $5,000
Dk. b. or br. c (1964–NY), by Nizami Blue—Shady Cee, by Fort Salonga 108⁵ 1967 16 1 2 1 $6,950
J. Papsidero J. Papsidero (Triad Farm) 1966 10 1 2 2 $4,575

26Sep67-4Aqu fst 6f .22⅕ .44⅗1.11⅗ Clm 6000 11 6 76 1111 811 77 GMora7 b 107 25.70f 78-11 Past-President 109¾ Zurk 1071½ Compromising 120¾ Raced wide 13
18Sep67-8Aqu fst 7f .22⅖ .45⅖1.24⅘ Clm 6000 14 1 21 2½ 4¾ 65 GMora5 b 107 27.20 77-15 Hasty Hero 112nk Nailon 1121 Tom's Brother 1162 Speed, tired 14
7Sep67-8Aqu fst 7f .23 .46 1.24⅕ Clm 6000 9 3 910 91113171316 GMora5 b 104 15.30 69-17 Bullyampa 1212 Chai Cha-Na 1152½ Highly Pleased 117nk Far back 14
14Aug67-8Sar fst 6f .22⅘ .46⅕1.12⅗ Clm 5000 7 3 21½ 21 11 1½ ACorderoJr b 116 5.10 85-16 Fire Escape 116½ Ballsbridge 1162 Mister G. R. 114nk Driving 12
29Jly 67-8Aqu fst 6f .22⅕ .45⅗1.11⅗ Clm 5000 6 1 2½ 21½ 31½ 41½ GMora5 b 107 9.10 85-14 Big Luxury 110½ Prevalent 108nk Rogo 112½ Well placed, hung 8
25Jly 67-2Aqu fst 6f .22⅖ .46⅕1.12 Clm 5000 5 2 3½ 1h 21½ 32¼ MYcaza b 116 4.70 80-11 Zurk 119no Fleet Imp 1192½ Fire Escape 1164½ Tired in drive 8
20Jly 67-3Aqu fst 6f .22⅗ .46⅕1.11⅗ Clm 6000 2 3 43½ 44½ 45 69 LGilligan b 112 18.00 76-15 Mr. Hal F. 1075 Cock Robin 116¾ Sing A Bit 116nk Had no mishap 8
4Jly 67-4Aqu fst 7f .22⅗ .46⅕1.25⅘ Clm 6500 4 5 43½ 32 62½ 45½ LGilligan b 116 36.00 71-17 Carrot Bird 115½ Sing A Bit 1142½ Hasty Hero 1142½ Rough trip 13
19Jun67-8Aqu sly 7f .23⅗ .49 1.27⅕ Clm 6500 1 4 32½ 23 34½ 57¾ LGilligan b 117 17.30 62-26 Nailon 1202 My Character 1203½ Me Tarzan 1171½ Well up, tired 8
LATEST WORKOUTS Sep 24 Bel 4f fst .51 b Sep 15 Bel 5f fst 1.04 b Sep 12 Bel 4f fst .50⅕ h Sep 6 Bel 3f fst .37⅘ b

O'Calawise $5,000
B. g (1963–Fla), by Rough'n Tumble—Old Bess, by Vincentive 119 1967 19 6 0 0 $16,575
G. Maccheroni R. Jacobs (Ocala Stud Farms, Inc.) 1966 14 0 0 1 $480

14Sep67-9Aqu fst 1⅛ .47 1.12⅗1.52⅗ Clm 5000 3 4 46½ 32 53½ 510 RUssery b 118 3.70 63-17 Lucidus 118½ Eagle's Scream 1182 Florida Scheme 1113½ Bid, tired 7
6Sep67-1Aqu fst 6f .23 .45⅖1.11⅗ Cl c-3500 5 11 74 119 67½ 55½ ALoguercio7 b 112 5.50 80-18 Big Luxury 121½ Don't Walk 114¾ Festival King 114h Bore out 14
29Jly 67-8Aqu fst 6f .22⅕ .45⅗1.11⅗ Clm 4500 8 5 67 55 811 86½ RTurcotte b 119 6.20 80-14 Big Luxury 110½ Prevalent 108nk Rogo 112½ Never a factor 8
8Jly 67-9Aqu fst 1 3/16 .47⅘1.12⅗1.58⅗ Hcp 3500s 7 2 43½ 67½Eased ECardone b 117 22.10 —— Fuzzie King 1241 Encantado 1142 Awesome 1142½ Gave way badly 10
23Jun67-9Aqu sly 1⅛ .48⅖1.13⅘1.54⅕ Cl c-6500 1 3 44½ 54½ 511 618 ACorderoJr b 118 2.90 47-25 Sudden Storm 118h Bigamo 1186 Direct Action 1131 Fell back 7
13Jun67-9Aqu fst 1⅛ .48 1.12⅗1.51⅖ Clm 8000 8 6 33 44 34½ 57 ACorderoJr b 114 *2.30 72-14 Joe Di Rosa 1142½ Abolengo II 114h Razonable 118½ No excuses 8
8Jun67-9Aqu fst 1⅛ .47⅘1.12⅘1.52 Cl c-5000 4 3 32½ 31 14 15 ACorderoJr b 120 2.90 76-16 O'Calawise 1205 Yucal 121nk Sir Rodolph 120½ Easily best 8
2Jun67-2Aqu fst 1 .45 1.10⅕1.37⅖ Cl c-4000 1 7 56½ 64½ 2½ 12¼ ACorderoJr b 117 3.20 81-18 O'Calawise 1172¼ Sir Rodolph 1152½ Manga Reva 115nk Driving 10
30May67-1Aqu fst 6f .22 .46⅕1.11⅗ Clm 3500 7 4 56½ 44 21½ 12 BBaeza b 121 *2.00 85-13 O'Calawise 1212 Bullyampa 1152½ Festival King 1182½ Handily 10
LATEST WORKOUTS Sep 26 Aqu 4f fst .49 b Sep 2 Aqu 5f fst 1.01⅗ h Sep 2 Aqu 5f fst 1.01⅗ h Aug 25 Sar 5f fst 1.01⅘ h

Up All Hands $5,000
Dk. b. or br. c (1963–Ky), by All Hands—Source Sucree, by Admiral Drake 115 1967 5 0 0 0 ——
C. Petigrow H. Jacobson (H. F. Guggenheim) 1965 11 3 2 0 $11,445

16Sep67-2Aqu fst 6f .22⅘ .45⅘1.11⅗ Clm 8500 1 3 2h 21½ 913 920 WBoland 117 3.20 65-16 Bullyampa 1191½ Wiggins Fork 117¾ Last Chain 1101½ Brief foot 9
9Sep67-4Aqu fst 6f .22 .45⅕1.11 Clm 10000 1 4 42½ 42½ 45 65½ ALoguercio7 110 13.70 82-16 Dion 1171 Metairie Padre 117¾ World Report 117¾ Gave way 12
25Jly 67-4Aqu fst 6f .22 .44⅗1.09⅘ Clm 19000 3 6 2½ 9¾Pulled up RUssery 117 2.40e —— Rebellious 1142 Space Song 1172½ Simpleton 115h Stopped 9
17Jly 67-4Aqu gd 6f .22⅖ .45⅗1.11⅖ Cl c-15000 4 1 11½ 11 1h 53¼ BFeliciano b 114 4.90 83-15 Space Song 1171 At First Blush 1182 Simpleton 118nk Used up 5
12Jun67-8Mth fst 6f .22⅕ .45⅘1.10⅘ Allowance 6 2 1½ 2h 48 56½ JVelasquez 114 4.00 82-17 Twin Teddy 122h Swoonland 114nk Flowers Boy 1222½ Tired 6
8Dec65-7Aqu fst 7f .22⅗ .45⅗1.24⅗ Allowance 2 2 24 24 58½ 516 LAdams 122 2.10 67-25 FleetAdmiral 117hRoyalHarbinger112noDoubleHappy1174 Stopped 6
30Nov65-5Aqu fst 6f .23⅕ .47⅕1.11⅘ Allowance 1 2 1½ 1h 14 11½ LAdams 122 3.70 84-23 Up All Hands 1221½ Escalation 1226 Brand Royal 122nk Driving 7
10Nov65-8GS fst 170.46⅕1.11⅘1.42 Allowance 9 4 51¾ 87½11131014 MYcaza 115 6.80 70-18 Stands to Reason 1121 Prince Saim 1145 Defiant Son 113nk Tired 14
1Nov65-6Aqu fst 6f .22⅘ .46⅖1.11⅖ Allowance 3 3 42 42 4¾ 11½ WShoemaker 117 2.10 86-21 Up All Hands 1171½ Aforethought 117nk Brand Royal 1172 Driving 8
LATEST WORKOUTS Sep 28 Aqu 4f fst .52⅕ b Sept 8 Aqu 3f fst .39⅘ b Sept 5 Aqu 4f fst .51 b Sept 1 Aqu 3f fst .36⅖ b

Fighting Phantom $5,000
Gr. g (1962), by Gray Phantom—Black Disc, by Fighting Fox 105¹⁰ 1967 14 1 0 2 $4,065
Anita C. Heard T. H. Heard, Jr. (O R. Harrod) 1966 19 1 3 3 $5,945

22Jun67-9Aqu fst 1 3/16 .49⅘1.14⅕1.59⅘ Clm 4000 2 5 67 610 46½ 58¼ BBaeza b 114 *1.70 71-17 Awesome 1181½ Victaray 1182 Ruperto 1185 Showed nothing 6
15Jun67-9Aqu fst 1⅛ .46⅘1.11⅘1.51⅘ Clm 4500 4 5 513 47 35 42 BBaeza b 116 3.80e 75-13 d-Victaray 114¾ Real Beat 116¾ Campari II 118½ Impeded 10
15Jun67—Placed third through disqualification.
8Jun67-9Aqu fst 1⅛ .47⅘1.12⅘1.52 Clm 4500 5 6 67½ 76 76½ 56 BBaeza b 118 6.50 70-16 O'Calawise 1205 Yucal 121nk Sir Rodolph 120½ Lacked room 8
3Jun67-3Aqu fst 7f .23 .46 1.24⅗ Clm 5000 3 6 65½ 66½ 68 53¼ FPulizzi10 b 107 40.40 79-15 LocalTalent119nk Pike'sPeak1171½ Inflexible1171 Wide, late 8
3Apr67-9Aqu fst 1⅛ .49⅗1.15⅘1.55⅕ Cl c-3500 8 4 42½ 42½ 1½ 11 BBaeza b 112 *2.50 60-25 Fighting Phantom 1121 Latin Artist 1161½ Real Beat 119½ Driving 8
29Mar67-9Aqu my 1⅛ .49⅗1.15⅘1.55⅕ Clm 5000 2 5 68 57 59½ 411 HDittfach 116 7.10 49-33 Have Integrity 114no Yucal 1145 Keep Knockin' 1096 No rally 7
13Mar67-2Aqu fst 7f .23⅕ .46⅖1.25 Clm 6000 5 11 117¼ 911 711 77¾ HGustines 113 16.30f 73-18 Cormier 124½ Local Talent 117h Wrapped Up 114½ No factor 13
6Mar67-6Pim sly 1 1/16 .48⅖1.14⅘1.49 Clm 6500 11 7 77 76½ 88½1011 CBaltazar b 115 8.00 54-26 Quick Post 1153 Indian Relic 115no Helioroad 115no No factor 11
27Feb67-7Bow fst 1 1/16 .47⅘1.12⅗1.45 Clm 6500 8 6 611 59 58½ 56¾ CBaltazar b 115 11.60 81-12 Arctic Queen 105nk TV Dinner 1141 Great Lover 1153½ No rally 12
LATEST WORKOUTS Sep 29 Aqu 4f sly .50⅖ b Sep 25 Aqu 7f fst 1.31 b Sep 20 Aqu 6f fst 1.15⅖ h Sep 16 Aqu 5f fst 1.04 b

oters Guide $5,000 — B. g (1963-Va), by Assemblyman—Razzberry, by Wait A Bit — Hubie Stable — C. W. Parish — (Mr.-Mrs. W. E. Parke) — **115**

1967	8	0	0	0	——
1966	25	1	2	0	$5,510

ug67-1Sar	fst 7f	.22⅘	.45⅘	1.24⅕	Clm	6250	9	8	1113	109¼	1111	1113	AGarram'e10	b 105	13.40	76–11	Soldier's Story 117nk Hobe Sound 117¾ Snow Dales 1171½	Far back 11
ug67-2Sar	fst 6f	.23⅖	.46⅕	1.11	Clm	6000	6	7	66	55	74½	64½	MSorrentino	b 117	26.20	88– 9	Cretaceous 119½ Soldier's Story 1192 World Guide 1171	No threat 8
ug67-9Sar	fst 7f	.22⅘	.47⅕	1.25⅕	Clm	6500	5	11	105½	109½	98	78¾	MSorrentino	b 117	47.40	75–15	LightningStorm117nk WrappedUp1132 LordBirchfield113no	No mis'p 14
ly 67-2Aqu	fst 6f	.22⅖	.45⅘	1.11	Clm	6250	7	5	57	55½	54¼	55¼	MSorrentino	b 119	41.60	83–13	Defiant Son 1142½ Cretaceous 119¾ Match Wits 1191	No rally 9
ly 67-8Aqu	fst 7f	.22⅘	.45⅘	1.24⅖	Clm	6500	2	4	21½	22	53	57¼	HWoodhouse	b 119	6.90	77–15	Evert 110¾ Eagle's Scream 1191½ School Tie 1192	Failed to stay 7
ly 67-9Aqu	fst 1⅛	.47⅖	1.12⅗	1.52	Clm	8000	6	1	2h	33	820	826	MSorrentino	b 118	54.40	50–20	Nike Site 118½ Razonable 1203 Charlie Tooley 118½	Used up 8
lay67-5Aqu	fst 6f	.22⅕	.45⅖	1.10⅘	Clm	8500	6	10	1014	1015	1015	1019	JRuane	b 117	150.70	70–15	LordBirchfield 116no BuzOn 1171½ MisterJudge 1173	Never close 10
lay67-4Aqu	fst 6f	.22	.45⅗	1.11⅕	Clm	10000	12	9	1415	1419	1422	1419	HGustines	b 117	10 80f	68–14	Beaustone 117no Dicn 1191½ Last Chain 115h	No factor 14
ec66-8Aqu	fst 7f	.23	.46⅕	1.25⅕	Clm	8500	6	4	2½	1h	3½	42½	RStovall	b 118	35.80	77–20	Goyamo Lad 116½ Alhambra Pal 1211¼ Tickled Silly 118¾	Weakened 11

.ATEST WORKOUTS Sep 28 Bel tr.t. 5f fst 1.03⅖ b — Sep 19 Bel tr.t. 6f fst 1.17 h — Sep 10 Bel 7f fst 1.33 b — Aug 15 Sar tr.t. 5f fst 1.03⅗ b

latch Wits * $4,500 — Ch. rig (1960), by Swaps—Sweet Woman, by Roman — Jean M. Virga — W. R. Corbellini — (Mrs. E. S. Moore) — **112**[7]

1967	19	5	2	2	$17,850
1966	7	1	0	0	$3,250

Sep67-2Aqu	fst 6f	.22⅘	.46⅗	1.12⅕	Cl	c-3500	9	1	12	14	14	1no	RTurcotte	124	*1.70	82–14	Match Wits 124no Colbert II 1123½Festival King 1141½	All out 9
Aug67-3Sar	sly 6f	.22⅖	.46⅕	1.11⅗	Clm	8500	1	2	2h	21	1012	1120	JRuane	117	8.80	71–10	Bullyampa 113h Your Day 115nk Metaire Padre 1176½	Stopped 11
Aug67-2Sar	fst 6f	.22⅖	.45⅘	1.11⅕	Clm	9000	2	1	1½	21	21½	46½	JRuane	113	17.00	85–11	Get Gettin 119h Chartist 1135 Float Trip 1131½	Tired 7
Aug67-2Sar	fst 6f	.22⅕	.45⅖	1.10⅘	Clm	8500	2	1	11½	22	812	820	JRuane	117	9.00	74– 6	Get Gettin 1171 Age Of Reason 116nk Your Day 1154	Tired 9
Jly 67-2Aqu	fst 6f	.22⅖	.45⅘	1.11	Cl	c-6250	6	1	12	11	2h	33¼	MYcaza	119	*1.10	85–13	Defiant Son 1142½ Cretaceous 119¾ Match Wits 1191	Tired 9
Jly 67-1Aqu	fst 7f	.22⅕	.45⅕	1.24⅗	Clm	5000	6	1	14	13	13	11½	MYcaza	124	*2.80	83–14	Match Wits 1241½ Cartabon 1125 Indiecito 119no	Was ridden out o
ly 67-2Aqu	my 7f	.22⅖	.45⅗	1.26⅕	Clm	5000	7	1	13	13	13	12	ACorderoJr	119	4.30	75–21	Match Wits 1192 Stormy Outlook 1091 Party Giver 1171½	Mild drive 10
Jun67-1Aqu	gd 6f	.22⅕	.45⅗	1.11⅗	Cl	c-4000	5	1	13	12	12	22	RUssery	117	*1.00	83–18	Flipaway 1192 Match Wits 1175 Snow Dales 1193½	Tired 8
Jun67-2Aqu	gd 6f	.22⅖	.46	1.11⅘	Clm	3500	8	1	12	14	16	13½	RUssery	119	*3.60e	84–21	Match Wits 1193½ Party Giver 119h Pippin 1144	Easy score 13

ATEST WORKOUTS Sep 8 Bel tr.t. 4f fst .49 h — Sep 2 Bel tr.t. 3f fst .39 b — Aug 29 Bel tr.t. 3f fst .38 b — Aug 17 Sar 4f fst .47 h

east or Famine $5,000 — Dk. b. g (1962), by Endeavour II—Picnic Spread, by Feast — A. G. Smithers — F. H. Merrill — (Mrs. M. E. Tippett) — **117**

1967	8	2	0	2	$4,955
1966	19	1	0	1	$3,094

Sep67-4Aqu	fst 6f	.22⅗	.46⅕	1.11	Clm	5000	10	1	11½	13	1h	56	FToro	b 117	5.30e	82–14	Cartabon 1124½ Mr. Elwood W. 1171 Fair Valley 116nk	Tired 11
Jun67-5WO	my 6f	.22⅘	.46	1.11	Clm	9000	1	6	65	45½	56¾	59	JKelly5	b 113	8.20	81–23	May Berry 1132½ Choir Beauty 1093¼ LandOffice 1152¼	Showed little 6
Jun67-6WO	sl 170	.47⅕	1.12⅗	1.44⅖	Clm	9000	3	1	12	14	31½	57	JKelly5	b 117	2.10	76–23	Carodana 1191 Purly Sark 113½ Footprint 1162½	Long lead, tired 6
May67-4WO	sf 1	Ⓣ	1.49⅘	1.42⅘	Clm	9000	3	1	11	12½	14	13½	RGrubb7	b 111	*2.75e	70–34	Feast Or Famine 1113½ Carodana 1132¼ Purly Sark 114h	Easily best 8
Apr67-5FE	fst 6½f	.23⅗	.46⅘	1.18⅗	Clm	9000	6	1	2½	2h	31½	32½	JKelly5	b 111	3.20	87–16	Mornins Mornin 1192 May Berry 108½ FeastOrFamine 1112½	Fair try 6
Mar67-6GP	fst 6f	.22⅗	.46⅕	1.11⅗	Clm	7500	7	6	63¾	42¼	33½	33½	FToro	b 116	6.90	82–14	Strikeplate 1121½ San Sue 1122 Feast Or Famine 1162	Good try 12
Mar67-2Hia	fst 7f	.23⅗	.46⅘	1.24	Clm	7000	5	7	2h	12	13	1½	FToro	b 113	25.60	89–13	Feast Or Famine 113½ Windy Hill 1124½ Fuerza 1131½	Fully extended 12
Feb67-5Hia	fst 7f	.23⅕	.46	1.23⅘	Clm	7000	2	7	31	55½	57	79½	JGiovanni	b 112	53.30	80–13	Penny Sale 1124½ Big Swede 112nk Plow 112no	Brief speed, tired 12
Oct66-4Aqu	fst 6f	.22⅗	.46	1.12	Clm	5000	5	8	62¾	55½	97½	1117	JCombest	b 118	17.10	76–16	Gay Orchid 116nk Pinkie Chollie 1222½ Templado 1181	Tired 14
Oct66-9Aqu	fst 7f	.22⅖	.45⅕	1.25	Clm	6500	6	4	1h	1½	41½	911	EFires	b 117	9.80	70–18	Brimer Pass 119¾ Jovial Twist 1101½ Del Coronado 117½	Used up 12
Oct66-4Aqu	sly 6f	.23⅕	.47⅗	1.12⅘	Clm	8500	4	6	63¼	64½	87¼	713	RStovall	b 117	31.60	66–24	Lord Birchfield 1194½ Solid Mike 1151½ Alhambra Pal 1105	Far back 9

We promptly eliminate Speedy Admiral (outclassed), Lash Back (scratched), Fair Valley (scratched), Open Sight (a maiden), Bethson (form and distance), School Tie (form), Up All Hands (its record is that of a hospital case), Fighting Phantom (a router entered for exercise), Voters Guide (form), Match Wits (an elderly speedster unlikely to win here after almost losing to $3,500 stock), and Feast or Famine (another speed horse without the class to keep running when challenged).

The survivors are Inflexible, Fire Escape, and O'Calawise. The first two will have the same riders as in their last outings. O'Calawise switches from Bob Ussery to Eddie Belmonte. At second glance, something serious seems wrong with this horse. The bottom three races on its past-performance list were sensational: three powerful victories, each at a longer distance against stiffer competition. On July 8, however, it ran so badly that Ernie Cardone eased it. After another feeble effort it was rested for more than a month and entered for sale at $3,500. On that occasion it not only lost but bore out—a sign of aches and pains. The gelding really is no contender today.

Which leaves Inflexible and Fire Escape. Of these, Inflexible is the less impressive. It has almost no early speed and has not been as close as third in a six-furlong race since last April. It is a contender in this race only by process of elimination, but I would hate to bet on it.

As to Fire Escape, both his July 29 and August 14 races were swift enough to demolish the rest of today's field. He seems to dislike seven furlongs, so we can forgive his poor efforts of September 7 and 18. Nor is it compulsory to penalize the colt for racing wide four days ago. A race of that kind, in which the rider takes the scenic, overland route through choice or necessity, often is the prelude to dramatic improvement. I like the animal coming back after only four days after that nice, wide, invigorating canter. I am not crazy about the jockey, apprentice Gerry Mora, but I must admit that he has won a lot of races at New York this year and was on Fire Escape when the horse ran his good race on July 29. On the other hand, it took Angel Cordero to *win* with the horse. And the victory was against three-year-olds (as the weight indicates), whereas today's race is against older animals.

If Cordero or Baeza were up, I think Fire Escape might be a sound bet against the chaff he meets today. But I don't like the setup well enough to bet on him. If you are playing daily doubles, however, he must be one of the horses in your wheel. The others? Perhaps you'd better pick two among Match Wits (the likely favorite), Up All Hands (Buddy Jacobson), and Inflexible (process of elimination). In fact, since there are only two real contenders in the first race, and you probably will want to squander $16 on doubles tickets anyway, perhaps you will choose to wheel Worklamp and Teddy's True with Fire Escape, Match Wits, Up All Hands, and Inflexible.

The Running of the Race

MATCH WITS was a firm 9–5 favorite, with Up All Hands at 5–2 and the Canadian horse, Feast or Famine, at 5–1.

Fire Escape, 9–1, won like 1–9, seven lengths in front.

You may argue that I should have bet on Fire Escape because the handicapping put him on top. I disagree. It is possible to put something on top in any race, but I have found that it pays to bet only on horses which, beyond being the best in bad fields, have no outstanding flaws of their own. I was afraid that Mora was not strong enough to win with this horse. I was wrong. But I did not lose any money on the deal.

SECOND RACE
Aqu - 32427
September 30, 1967

6 FURLONGS. (Near Man, July 17, 1963, 1.08$\frac{3}{5}$, 3, 112.)
Claiming. Purse $5,000. 3-year-olds and upward. Weights, 3-year-olds, 120 lbs., older 124 lbs. Non-winners of four races since Mar. 11 allowed 3 lbs., of three races since then, 5 lbs., of two races since then, 7 lbs., of a race since then, 9 lbs. Claiming price $5,000. 2 lbs. allowed for each $500 to $4,000. (Races when entered to be claimed for $3,500 or less not considered.)

Value to winner $3,250, second $1,000, third $500, fourth $250. Mutuel pool $425,658.

Index	Horse	Eqt	A	Wt	PP	St	¼	½	Str	Fin	Jockey	Cl'g Pr	Owner	Odds $1
32393Aqu^7	—Fire Escape	b	3	108	6	3	3^1	2^3	1^2	1^7	G Mora^5	5000	J Papsidero	9.00
32339Aqu^4	—Inflexible	b	6	115	4	10	6^1	$6^{1\frac{1}{2}}$	3^3	2^3	A Caceres	5000	Belle Karson	20.80
32319Aqu^9	—Up All Hands	b	4	117	8	1	1^3	$1^{1\frac{1}{2}}$	2^4	3^1	R Ussery	5000	C Petigrow	2.50
32346Aqu^{12}	–Bethson	b	4	111	3	9	8^h	9^2	6^1	$4^{\frac{3}{4}}$	O Rosado	4000	J C Toomey	f-56.90
32339Aqu^8	—Sp'dy Admiral	b	6	113	1	8	5^2	5^2	4^1	5^1	A DeSpirito	4500	M Gilbert	35.40
32081Sar^{11}	–Voters Guide	b	4	115	10	6	9^3	$8^{\frac{1}{2}}$	7^1	6^1	D Hidalgo	5000	Hubie Stable	76.20
32308Aqu^5	—O'Calawise	b	4	119	7	11	$10^{\frac{1}{2}}$	10^2	9^1	7^{nk}	E Belmonte	5000	G Maccheroni	9.00
32290Aqu^9	—School Tie	b	5	108	5	12	11^5	11^3	10^2	8no	A Garra'ne^7	4500	Emmess Stable	15.20
32339Aqu^5	—F'st Or Famine	b	5	117	12	4	4^2	3^h	5^h	9^2	P Toro	5000	A G Smithers	5.00
31471Aqu^5	—Figh'g Ph'tom	b	5	105	9	7	12	12	12	10^h	F Pulizzi^{10}	5000	Anita C Heard	59.30
31928Aqu^6	—Open Sight	b	3	112	2	5	7^3	7^h	8^1	11^4	R Turcotte	5000	J Napolitano	f-56.90
32292Aqu^1	—Match Wits		7	112	11	2	2^h	4^h	$11^{\frac{1}{2}}$	12	R Tanner^7	4500	Jean M Virga	1.80

f-Mutuel field.

Time .22$\frac{2}{5}$, .46, 1.11$\frac{4}{5}$ (with wind in backstretch). Track good.

$2 Mutuel Prices:

5—FIRE ESCAPE	20.00	9.60	5.60
3—INFLEXIBLE		15.60	7.60
7—UP ALL HANDS			3.80

Dk. b. or br. c, by Nizama Blue—Shady Cee, by Fort Salonga. Trainer J. Papsidero. Bred by Triad Farm (N. Y.).

IN GATE AT 2.02. OFF AT 2.02 EASTERN DAYLIGHT TIME. Start good. Won easily.

FIRE ESCAPE, well placed early, took command from UP ALL HANDS before reaching midstretch and won with something left. INFLEXIBLE raced evenly for a half mile and finished willingly but could not threaten the winner while easily second best. UP ALL HANDS set the pace until challenged by FIRE ESCAPE and failed to stay. BETHSON lacked early foot. SPEEDY ADMIRAL saved ground but could not reach serious contention. VOTERS GUIDE was never dangerous. O'CALAWISE, slow to reach his best stride, was always far back. SCHOOL TIE began sluggishly. FEAST OR FAMINE was finished early. FIGHTING PHANTOM dropped out of serious contention immediately after the start. OPEN SIGHT gave way during the stretch run. MATCH WITS stopped after showing early speed.

Scratched—32339Aqu[3] Fair Valley, 31964Sar[6] Lash Back. Overweights—Open Sight 1 pound, Up All Hands 2.

Match Wits was claimed by A. B. Crain, trainer same. Fire Escape was claimed by J. Gallo, trainer R. Sanseverino.

As to the $151 daily double—a net profit of $135 to the purchaser of eight $2 tickets—I do not begrudge you the windfall. Just keep playing $16 wheels every day and I fear that you will be playing Parcheesi for jelly beans within six months.

THE THIRD RACE

THIS RACE fields a band of sprinters in the $7,500–$8,500 category. Let's run down the list and eliminate any animals that do not fit that description, are clearly out of form, or are scratched.

Last Chain * $8,500 Blk. g (1963-Md.), by Cornwall—Chain Miss, by Jacopo 117 1967 15 1 7 3 $11,122
Little M Farm W. A. Kelley (Mr.-Mrs. B. Christmas) 1966 22 4 2 6 $9,759
16Sep67-2Aqu fst 6f .22⅗ .45⅘1.11⅗ Clm 8500 9 1 1h 1½ 1½ 3²¼ ALoGuercio⁷ b 110 5.40 83-16 Bullyampa 119 1½ Wiggins Fork 117¾ Last Chain 110 1½ Weakened 9
31Aug67-4Aqu fst 6f .23⅕ .46⅘1.12⅕ Cl c-6500 3 3 1² 1½ 1½ 2¾ ACorderoJr b 119 *2.10 81-22 Cretaceous 119¾ Last Chain 119¾ Rogo 112½ Held on well 9
26Jly 67-2Aqu gd 7f .22⅗ .46 1.24⅕ Cl c-6250 7 3 1³ 1½ 1³ 3²¾ JRuane b 117 4.20 82-15 Direct Action 119nk Raider Radka 119 2½ Last Chain 117¹ Tired 11
19Jly 67-4Aqu fst 7f .22⅕ .45⅕1.23⅗ Clm 8500 10 1 3²½ 2¹ 2¹½ 7⁷ HDiaz⁷ b 111 31.80 81-13 Wiggins Fork 116² Eagle's Scream 118no Oxidized 118½ Weakened 11
8Jly 67-4Aqu fst 6f .22⅕ .45 1.10⅘ Clm 8500 8 3 2¹½ 2¹ 2¹½ 4⁶¾ ECardone b 119 10.40 82-14 Big Rapids 115¾ Spruce Up 115⁴ Your Day 119² Speed to stretch 10
20Jun67-8Aqu sly 6f .23 .46⅘1.12⅕ Cl c-6250 3 2 1h 1h 2½ 2⁴ RC'ningham⁷ b 112 1.90 78-23 Charlie Tooley 115⁴ Last Chain 112¹ Wrapped Up 119⁵ Bore in 7
13Jun67-8Aqu fst 6f .22⅗ .45⅗1.11 Clm 7000 4 1 1½ 1¹½ 1½ 2⁴ WBoland b 117 2.60 84-14 Mister Judge 117⁴ Last Chain 117no Wiggins Fork 117nk Gamely 8
27May67-5Aqu fst 6f .22⅕ .45⅖1.10⅘ Clm 8500 5 3 1½ 1h 2h 5⁵¼ BBaeza b 119 3.20 84-15 LordBirchfield 116no BuzOn 117 1½ MisterJudge 117³ Speed, tired 10
20May67-4Aqu fst 6f .22 .45⅗1.11⅕ Clm 9500 14 2 2½ 1³ 1³ 3¹¾ WBoland b 115 5.20 85-14 Beaustone 117no Dion 119 1½ Last Chain 115h Led, tired 14
LATEST WORKOUTS Sep 28 Aqu 4f fst .50 b Sep 23 Aqu 1m fst 1.48 b Sep 13 Aqu 4f fst .52⅗ b Sep 7 Aqu 6f fst 1.16 b

Prisoner's Base * $8,500 Dk. b. or br. g (1963-Ky), by Turn-to—Old Game, by Menow 117 1967 6 2 0 0 $6,025
Big Lion Stable H. Jacobson (Greentree Stud, Inc.) 1966 7 M 1 0 $760
9Sep67-3Aqu fst 7f .22⅘ .45⅘1.23⅘ Clm 12500 6 2 4³½ 6⁵½ 7⁸ 6¹¹ HGustines b 119 4.40 78-16 UpsetVictory 117³ OneNightStand 119¾ AtFirstBlush 115¾ Tired 7
18May67-7Aqu fst 7f .22⅗ .45⅕1.22⅘ Allowance 4 5 4⁴ 4⁵ 4⁸½ 4¹³ RUssery b 119 *2.00 79-20 Walk Out 115 2½ Eagle Lair 108⁶ Big Red Rocket 115⁴ No mishap 8
2May67-5Aqu fst 7f .23⅗ .46⅖1.23⅘ Clm 27500 5 5 5³½ 6³¾ 7⁷½ 6⁵½ WTichenor¹⁰ b 107 28.00 81-18 Yucatan 124 1½ Simpleton 117nk King's Jest 113h Raced wide 7
24Feb67-7Hia fst 7f .23⅕ .45⅗1.23⅗ Allowance 1¹ 2 4⁵ 4⁴ 6⁹½10¹⁴ WBoland b 121 4.80 78-15 Irongate 121 1½ Tom Poker 113⁸ Wondrascope 113 1½ Tired 12
16Feb67-7Hia fst 7f .22⅗ .45⅖1.23⅗ Allowance 4 5 3⁴ 2⁴ 1² 1² RUssery b 115 *2.30 91-12 Prisoner's Base 115² Yale Fence 115¹ Phantom Island 121¹ Handily 11
6Feb67-3Hia fst 7f .22⅘ .45⅗1.24⅖ Md Sp Wt 7 5 2⁴ 2² 1² 1⁶ BBaeza b 119 3.60 87-14 Prisoner's Base 119⁶ Two Keys 114 1½ Prestidigitator 119¹ Driving 12
2Nov66-1Aqu fst 7f .23⅕ .47 1.25⅘ Md Sp Wt 5 8 5¹½ 5²¾ 5³ 5⁶½ WTichener¹⁰ b 112 9.90 72-19 Sum Farce 122 2½ Right Reason 122no Solemn Nation 117 1½ No m'h'p 10
20Oct66-1Aqu sl 7f .23⅘ .48⅖1.27 Md 9000 2 6 6²¾ 4³½ 1h 2¹ HGustines b 117 7.80 70-23 Bombax 117¹ Prisoner's Base 117½ Bicarb Jr. 110 2½ Sharp try 9
14Oct66-2Aqu fst 6f .23 .46⅘1.11⅗ Md Sp Wt 5 1 3³ 3¹½ 4⁴½ 5⁷¾ HGustines b 121 16.50 77-17 Birdsofafeather 121⁵ Solemn Nation 121¹ Sharp 116nk Tired 7
6Oct66-5Aqu fst 6f .23⅘ .47⅕1.12⅖ Md Sp Wt 10 1 5⁵½ 6⁷¾ 6¹² 5¹⁸ WTichenor¹⁰ b 111 49.70 63-24 Sermon 121 11 Vocalist 121½ Birdsofafeather 121⁴ Fell back 10
LATEST WORKOUTS Sep 27 Aqu 4f fst .52⅗ b Sep 24 Aqu 4f fst .52 b Sep 6 Bel 6f fst 1.16⅖ b Sep 2 Bel 5f fst 1.02⅖ h

Wiggins Fork $8,500 Dk. b. or br. g (1963-Ky), by Double Jay—Point Pleasant, by Princequillo 117 1967 13 1 4 4 $12,150
1966 7 2 0 1 $6,005
S. Marciano R. Frankel (Harburton Stud, Inc.)
23Sep67-3Aqu fst 6f .22⅘ .46⅖1.11 Clm 9500 2 1 1¹ 1h 3½ 3²½ LGilligan b 115 9.70 85-13 Santo Domingo 117½ Bullyampa 113² Wiggins Fork 115² Tired 8
16Sep67-2Aqu fst 6f .22⅗ .45⅘1.11⅗ Clm 8500 4 2 3nk 3¹½ 3¹½ 2¹½ RUssery b 117 4.00 83-16 Bullyampa 119 1½ Wiggins Fork 117¾ Last Chain 110 1½ Good try 9
2Sep67-3Aqu fst 6f .23 .46⅗1.11⅗ Clm 8500 1 3 3⁴½ 4³ 3⁴½ 4⁶½ LGilligan b 119 7.20 78-16 Spruce Up 117 2½ Dion 117 3½ Bullyampa 119½ Well placed, hung 8
19Jly 67-4Aqu fst 7f .22⅕ .45⅕1.23⅗ Clm 8000 9 2 2² 3¹ 1¹½ 1² RUssery b 116 9.80 88-13 Wiggins Fork 116² Eagle's Scream 118no Oxidized 118½ Mild drive 11
8Jly 67-4Aqu fst 6f .22⅕ .45 1.10⅘ Clm 8500 1 7 7⁶ 6⁹ 7⁹ 5⁷½ MVenezia b 119 11.90 82-14 Big Rapids 115¾ Spruce Up 115⁴ Your Day 119² Not a contender 10
24Jun67-4Aqu gd 7f .23⅗ .46⅕1.24⅕ Clm 9000 3 2 2¹½ 1½ 3½ 3⁶ MVenezia b 115 5.70 79-18 Razonable 115no Mister Judge 117⁶ Wiggins Fork 115¹ Weakened 7
17Jun67-5Aqu fst 7f .22⅗ .44⅘1.23⅗ Clm 9000 7 3 1½ 1¹½ 1² 2⁴½ MVenezia b 115 16.00 83-15 MisterJudge115 4½ WigginsFork115 1½ DailyReminder119¹ Lost action 11
13Jun67-8Aqu fst 6f .22⅗ .45⅗1.11 Clm 7000 3 4 5⁶ 6⁷ 3³½ 3⁴ MVenezia 117 9.10 84-14 Mister Judge 117⁴ Last Chain 117no Wiggins Fork 117nk Hung 8
27May67-3Aqu fst 6f .23 .47⅕1.12⅕ Cl c-5000 3 4 3²½ 3² 1h 2¹ JLRotz 117 *1.80 81-15 Wrapped Up 119¹ Wiggins Fork 117no Ambi Enshalah 108² Gamely 13
LATEST WORKOUTS Sep 13 Bel tr.t. 4f fst .51 h Sep 9 Bel tr.t. 4f fst .50 h Aug 30 Bel tr.t. 4f fst .49⅘ h Aug 26 Bel tr.t. 5f my 1.06 b

Resolute King $8,500 B. g (1963-Cal), by Determine—Reticent, by Teddy's Comet 110⁷ 1967 13 0 0 1 $763
A. J. Crevolin G. E. Roberts (W. R. Hawn) 1966 29 3 3 2 $12,802
23Sep67-3Aqu fst 6f .22⅘ .46⅖1.11 Clm 9000 5 8 8⁹ 8⁹¾ 8¹⁴ 8¹² AGarramone⁷ b 106 38.80 76-13 Santo Domingo 117½ Bullyampa 113² Wiggins Fork 115² St'mbl'd st. 8
9Sep67-4Aqu fst 6f .22 .45⅕1.11 Clm 9000 10 8 9⁸¼10⁹½ 8¹¹ 7⁷ AGar'mone¹⁰ b 104 65.40 81-16 Dion 117¹ Metairie Padre 117¾ World Report 117¾ No threat 12
17Jun67-5Hol fst 6f .22⅕ .45⅕1.10⅘ Clm 10000 1 7 6⁷ 7¹⁰ 7¹¹ 7¹¹ DPierce b 116 22.50 76-22 Steele Blade 116¹ Royal Step 111½ Merry Road 113¹ Showed nothing 7
20May67-5Hol fst 1 .46⅕1.11⅖1.37⅘ Clm 12500 2 1 1h 4¹ 8⁶½ 9⁸ ARValenzuela b 113 35.80 69-16 Sir Captain 115no First Rating 111no Bond Ali 116½ Speed, tired 10
19Apr67-8GG my 6f .22⅘ .46⅕1.11⅕ Clm 12500 3 3 3¹ 8⁵¾ 8⁵¾ 6⁶¼ MCariglio⁵ b 108 12.90 77-26 Jet Patrol 113 2½ Galvin 115½ Herby II 116nk Some early foot 9
10Apr67-9GG sly 1 .46⅕1.12 1.39⅖ Clm 10000 9 2 2½ 1² 3³ 3¹½ MCariglio⁵ b 110 18.90 69-24 Columns Right 114 1½ Silent Trust 113no Resolute King 110h Good try 9
3Apr67-7GG fst 6f .22⅗ .45⅖1.09⅗ Clm 15000 8 2 1h 3¹½ 8⁶½ 8⁷ JCValenzuela b 117 58.70 84-12 Diomond D. 120 1½ Herby II 117½ Galvin 117½ Early speed, gave way 8
25Mar67-5GG fst 6f .22⅕ .45⅘1.10 Clm 12500 5 4 6² 7⁵¾ 8⁸¾ 8⁹¼ DPierce b 116 6.80 80-13 Diomond D. 116 1½ Wooden Soldier 113 1¼ Scott's Blue 116¾ Dull try 8
17Mar67-6GG gd 6f .22⅘ .46 1.10⅗ Clm 12500 3 5 3³ 3¹ 3² 4³½ IValenzuela b 115 12.50 82-22 Corporal Tige 122½ Lucky Bond 116 2½ Herby II 119½ Lacked rally 6
LATEST WORKOUTS Sep 21 Bel tr.t. 5f fst 1.04 b Sep 15 Bel t.c. 1m fm 1.41⅕ h Sept 8 Bel 3f fst .35⅗ h Sept 5 Bel tr.t. 6f fst 1.03 b

***Capitalino** $8,000 B. h (1962), by Cullanhall—Pelusilla, by At Home 115 1967 6 0 0 1 $529
S. A. Calder O. S. Barrera (Haras La Constancia) (Arg.) 1966 16 3 2 1 $6,112
16Sep67-2Aqu fst 6f .22⅗ .45⅘1.11⅗ Clm 8500 7 7 6⁸ 8¹² 8⁸¾ 8⁸ SHernandez 117 77.30 77-16 Bullyampa 119 1½ Wiggins Fork 117¾ Last Chain 110 1½ Never close 9
9Sep67-4Aqu fst 6f .22 .45⅕1.11 Clm 9500 5 10 12¹⁵21¹⁴12¹⁶10¹⁰ SHernandez 115 105.30 78-16 Dion 117¹ Metairie Padre 117¾ World Report 117¾ No speed 12
23Mar67-La Plata (Arg.) fst*6f 1.12⅘ Allowance 4 — 117 — —— Missing data not available 14
26Feb67-San Isidro (Arg.) fm*6f 1.10⅗ Ⓣ Clasico Ecuador Hcp. 7 JOrtiz 115 21.95 —— Bonirock 123 2½ Blasco 126¹ Chinazo 120 Never troubled leaders 8
7Feb67-San Isidro (Arg.) fm*5f .57⅘ Ⓣ Clasico Paraguay Hcp. 5 LCamoretti 127 21.75 —— Laconique 121¾ Barranga 137 1½ Amore 109 Could not keep pace 8
15Jan67-San Isidro (Arg.) fm*5f .59⅕ Ⓣ Premio The Curragh (Alw.) 3²½ DMagarino 110 15.00 —— Monticelli 122 1½ RodoPereira 118¹ Capitalino 127 Closed ground late 11
12Dec66-La Plata (Arg.) hy*7f 1.26 Premio Especial Hcp. 11 DMagarino 121 9.10 —— Arabe 129⁶ Chinazo 123¹ Rodo Pereira 126 11
25Nov66-La Plata (Arg.) fst*7f 1.26⅖ Pr. Moreno Especial (Alw.) 5 JOrtiz 129 4.15 —— Chinazo 121 1½ Ardido 117² Lautaro 127 12
LATEST WORKOUTS Sep 27 Bel tr.t. 4f fst .50 h Sep 14 Bel tr.t. 3f fst .37⅕ h Sept 5 Bel tr.t. 7f fst 1.33 b Aug 29 Bel tr.t. 5f fst 1.06 b

Caught Short * $8,000 Br. h (1962), by His Babu—French Fry, by Papa Redbird 117 1967 20 4 3 4 $14,945
D. Shaer F. L. Moore (E. W. Richmond) 1966 30 3 2 3 $10,125
18Sep67-7LD fst 7f .23⅗ .47⅘1.25⅗ Allowance 2 7 4¹ 5²¾ 7¹⁰ 7¹² TSisum b 122 8.20 82-17 Middletown Billy 114² Tara Host 122 2½ Admiral J. B. 119h Steadied 7
31Aug67-8Rkm gd 6f .23⅕ .46⅘1.12 Allowance 8 1 3¹ 2¹½ 2h 1³¾ LMoyers b 119 6.40 84-24 Caught Short 119 3¾ Ye Ye Prince 113³ Bucklin 112 3¾ Strong handl'g 8
17Aug67-6Rkm fst 6f .22⅘ .45⅗1.11 Clm 7500 5 6 5²¾ 5³¼ 5²¼ 5²¾ MHole b 116 10.70 86-15 Big Judge 112 1¼ World Report 116no Naw Sir 107¹ Hung in drive 8
10Aug67-7Rkm fst 6f .22⅘ .46⅖1.11⅗ Clm 7500 1 8 9⁶½ 8⁶½ 7⁸ 7⁷ MHole b 116 7.60 79-20 Half Stoned 115 3½ World Report 116³ Robins Joy 111nk No threat 12
1Aug67-7Rkm fst 6f .23⅕ .46 1.11 Cl c-6000 9 3 6¹½ 5⁴½ 4⁵½ 2⁴½ MHole b 115 *2.30 85-19 Half Stoned 115⁴½ Caught Short 115 1½ Me N'Jet 114 3½ Gamely 9
25Jly 67-7Rkm my 6f .22⅘ .46⅖1.12⅕ Clm 6000 2 4 4¹½ 4¹½ 4¾ 3¹½ MHole b 115 3.50 81-23 Tex Rullah 115¾ Half Stoned 115¾ Caught Short 115½ No mishap 8
3Jun67-8Suf fst 6f .22⅗ .45⅘1.11⅘ Clm 7500 8 8 6⁶¾ 6⁶ 5⁶ 6⁴½ MHole b 114 4.30 80-16 Scissor Tail 114¹ Tom's Dream 119no Fairway Ruler 114¹ Evenly 9
27May67-8Suf gd 6f .22⅘ .46⅕1.11⅘ Clm 7500 7 1 2¹ 2¹½ 2³½ 3¹¾ WMayorga b 114 3.30 80-20 Buddys Choice 114nk Tom's Dream 117 1½ Caught Short 114¹ Hung 8
20May67-6Suf fst 6f .22⅗ .45⅗1.11 Clm 7500 1 3 1h 2h 2h 2½ WMayorga b 114 3.90 85-15 Tom's Dream 120½ Caught Short 114⁴ Half Stoned 117 1¾ Gamely 9
9May67-8Suf sl 170.48⅕1.14⅗1.47 Clm 10000 3 1 1h 5⁵ 6¹⁴ 5²³ WMayorga b 114 4.70 42-37 Bucklin 114¹ Handy Helper 112⁸ Achill Island 112½ Used up 6
3May67-9Suf my 6f .23⅕ .47 1.12⅗ Clm 13000 2 5 5⁵ 5⁸ 6⁸ 5¹⁵ WMayorga b 112 6.90 63-29 Hi Luke 115⁹ Fighting Steve 117 2½ Do Easy 112¹ Never a threat 7
LATEST WORKOUTS Sep 29 Nar 3f sly .39 b Sep 25 LD 5f fst 1.02⅗ h Sep 17 LD 3f fst .37⅘ h Sep 8 LD 3f fst .38 b

---

We knock out Wondrascope (a router), Cabay (class), Cretaceous (scratched), Olympia Jo (class and form), Last Chain (class), Prisoner's Base (a suspiciously drastic drop in class, plus apparent preference for more distance), Resolute King (form), Capitalino (form), Caught Short (outclassed shipper).

The contenders seem to be World Report, which gets John Rotz today, and

Wiggins Fork, with Braulio Baeza. I don't like either of them. World Report, a front-runner which backed up in the late stages against New England fields inferior to the one it meets today, will be run ragged by Last Chain, another speed horse. Baeza undoubtedly will try to rate Wiggins Fork off the pace and come on in the late stages. But the gelding has not shown enough genuine finishing kick to be a good bet. Anything can win this race. I shall sit it out.

The Running of the Race

WIGGINS FORK was the favorite at 9–5. World Report was slightly less than 5–2, with Prisoner's Base almost 11–2.

The race itself was a fiasco. World Report put Last Chain away in the early going but had nothing left after the turn for home. Cabay was all over the track, bumping Resolute King into Wiggins Fork and forcing Baeza to apply the brakes. After the melee, the Panamanian was unable to get the animal back into full stride. Meanwhile, Bobby Ussery found space on the rail with Prisoner's Base and was moving fastest of all at the finish, but not fast enough to catch Cabay. The stewards disqualified Cabay and made Prisoner's Base the winner.

THIRD RACE
Aqu - 32428
September 30, 1967

6 FURLONGS. (Near Man, July 17, 1963, 1.08⅗, 3, 112.)
Claiming. Purse $6,000. 3-year-olds and upward. Weights, 3-year-olds, 120 lbs., older 124 lbs. Non-winners of three races since July 29 allowed 3 lbs., of two races since then, 5 lbs., of a race since then, 7 lbs. Claiming price $8,500. 2 lbs. allowed for each $500 to $7,500. (Races when entered to be claimed for $6,500 or less not considered.)

Value to winner $3,900, second $1,200, third $600, fourth $300. Mutuel pool $564,243.

Index	Horse	Eqt A Wt	PP	St	¼	½	Str	Fin	Jockey	C'lg Pr	Owner	Odds $1
32334Aqu5—	[D]Cabay	b 3 106	3	4	4^{h}	$4^{1\frac{1}{2}}$	2½	$1^{1\frac{3}{4}}$	R Tanner	8500	S Nadler	[D]-10.20
32266Aqu—	Prisoner's Base	b 4 117	6	9	8½	6½	5^{1}	2½	R Ussery	8500	Big Lion Stable	5.40
32374Aqu3—	Wiggins Fork	b 4 117	7	7	6^{2}	$5^{1\frac{1}{2}}$	3½	3^{nk}	B Baeza	8500	S Marciano	1.80
32344Aqu6—	Wondrascope	b 5 117	1	8	10	8^{2}	7^{1}	4¾	A DeSpirito	8500	Windham Farm	50.50
32299LD7 —	Caught Short	b 5 117	10	10	7½	7^{1}	6^{1}	5^{3}	W Sh'maker	8000	D Shaer	9.30
32374Aqu8—	Resolute King	b 4 110	8	3	3^{2}	3½	8^{3}	6^{1}	F Toro	8500	A J Crevolin	60.20
32375Aqu7—	World Report	b 4 117	2	1	1^{h}	1^{h}	1^{h}	7½	J L Rotz	8500	M A Rothstein	2.40
32319Aqu3—	Last Chain	b 4 117	5	2	2^{3}	2^{2}	4^{h}	8^{2}	R Turcotte	8500	Little M Farm	6.50
32393Aqu13—	Olympia Jo	3 104	4	5	5½	9^{3}	9^{2}	$9^{2\frac{1}{2}}$	A Garramone	8000	Mrs P M Winchester	37.80
32319Aqu8—	Capitalino	5 115	9	6	9^{3}	10	10	10	O Rosado	8000	S A Calder	127.60

[D]-Disqualified and placed last.

Time .22⅕, .46⅕, 1.12 (with wind in backstretch). Track good.

$2 Mutuel Prices:

7-PRISONER'S BASE	12.80	5.80	4.60
8-WIGGINS FORK		3.80	3.20
1-WONDRASCOPE			11.00

Prisoner's Base—Dk. b. or br. g, by Turn-to—Old Game, by Menow. Trainer H. Jacobson. Bred by Greentree Stud (Ky.).

IN GATE AT 2.36. OFF AT 2.36 EASTERN DAYLIGHT TIME. Start good. First driving.

CABAY raced evenly for a half mile, drifted out after entering the stretch, bumped RESOLUTE KING and forced the latter on WIGGINS FORK, then disposed of WORLD REPORT and retained a clear advantage but was disqualified for fouling and placed last after a stewards' inquiry. PRISONER'S BASE, outrun early, saved ground during the stretch run and finished fast. WIGGINS FORK, steadied when caught in the roughing caused by CABAY near the three-sixteenths pole, could not better his position when clear. WONDRASCOPE lacked early foot but closed determinedly. CAUGHT SHORT broke slowly. RESOLUTE KING, prominent until reaching the stretch, checked when bumped by CABAY and failed to recover. WORLD REPORT made the pace until reaching midstretch but failed to stay. LAST CHAIN tired after entering the stretch. OLYMPIA JO was finished early. CAPITALINO showed nothing.

Scratched—32319Aqu7 Cretaceous.

Wiggins Fork was claimed by Three C. Stable, trainer M. Padovani.

THE FOURTH RACE

THIS IS a seven-furlong undertaking for two-year-olds that have never won an allowance race. Inasmuch as none of the entrants has ever raced seven furlongs, I see no reason to waste time on the thing. Seven furlongs is the second toughest distance on this or any other major track—the toughest being a mile race around one turn. Run like shorter sprints, with speed horses setting suicidal paces and come-from-behinders being forced to run faster than ever, these seven-furlong and mile races demand an unusual blend of speed and endurance. Until an animal has run the distance or longer, the player has no idea whether it can.

If you insist on looking for a bet in such a race, you brand yourself as a losing player. The intelligent choices you make in other kinds of races may net a profit, but your stubborn urge to bet on every race is sure to dissipate the profits in a tide of red ink.

---

7 FURLONGS. (Chute). (Rose Net, Sept. 17, 1962, 1.21⅕, 6, 114.)

4th Race Aqueduct — 7 FURLONGS (AQUEDUCT; Start ▾ / ▴ Finish)

Allowances. Purse $7,500. 2-year-olds which have never won a race other than maiden or claiming. Weight, 122 lbs. Non-winners of a race other than claiming since July 29 allowed 3 lbs., of such a race since July 1, 5 lbs., of such a race since May 31, 7 lbs.

Railbird — Ro. c (1965–Ky), Crafty Admiral—Pipeline, by Oil Capitol — H. Nadler — W. R. Corbellini — (C. Sawyer, Jr.) — **108**7 — 1967 6 1 3 0 $6,080

23Sep67–5Aqu fst 6½f.22⅘ .46⅘1.18⅗ Allowance 10 2 62¼ 53 41½ 2¾ RTanner7 107 9.90 86–13 Wellpoised 122¾ Railbird 107h Dynamic Turn 122¾ Closed well 10
19Sep67–5Aqu fst 6f .23 .45⅘1.11⅘ Clm 12500 1 1 21½ 32½ 33 21 RTanner7 109 11.60 83–14 Equivocate 1161 Railbird 1091½ Jack's Aloha 1123 Gamely 11
12Sep67–4Aqu fst 6f .23 .47 1.12⅗ Cl c–10000 13 10 117 910 69½ 55¾ BFeliciano 116 7.00f 74–20 Lord Tudor 106¾ Danny's Runaway 1163 Real Story 1191 Late bid 14
9Jun67–3Mth fst 5f .22⅕ .46⅘1.00⅗ Clm 7500 2 7 77½ 58½ 45 21¼ KKnapp 117 2.60e 86–22 Yankee Dot 1171¼ Railbird 117h Squad Boy 117nk Gamely 8
6Jun67–3Mth fst 5f .22⅕ .46⅘1.00 Clm 11000 2 9 98¾ 816 811 89½ BThornburg 117 2.70e 80–16 Cunning Fox 113¾ Buncombe 1123 Baruby 114no No speed 9
4May67–3Aqu fst 5f .23 .48 1.01⅗ Md 7500 4 9 88¾ 35 21½ 13½ BFeliciano 122 14.10 77–20 Railbird 1223½ Rainfall 120h Mr. Restless 1224 Drew clear 10
LATEST WORKOUTS Sep 29 Bel tr.t. 3f sly .36 h — Sep 25 Bel 4f fst .49 bg — Sep 21 Bel tr.t. 6f fst 1.15⅗ h — Sep 18 Bel 5f fst 1.01⅖ bg

Call A Cop — B. c (1965–Ky), by Traffic Judge—Flight Bird, by Count Fleet — Adele L. Rand — W. W. Stephens — (W. Stone) — **115** — 1967 3 1 0 0 $3,900

1May67–4Aqu fst 5f .22⅗ .46⅗ .59⅕ Md Sp Wt 4 2 13 14 15 15 JLRotz b 122 3.10 89–20 Call A Cop 1225 Tough Sledding 122¾ Agility 1228 Easy score 8
24Apr67–5Aqu sly 5f .23⅕ .47⅖ .59⅘ Md Sp Wt 4 9 78½ 65½ 57 46 BFeliciano b 122 4.70 80–24 Verbatim 1223½ Sounion 1222 Agility 122½ No late rally 9
17Apr67–3Aqu fst 5f .22⅘ .46⅕ .59⅖ Md Sp Wt 9 7 77¼ 77½ 58 45½ BFeliciano b 122 34.30 82–14 Flying Error 1222½ Happy Gold 1223 Chatham Center 122no Mild bid 10

Blighty * — Dk. b. or br. g (1965–Ky), by Black Beard—Bird Shot, by Chance Shot — F. E. Dixon, Jr. — J. S. Nash — (F. Aulick, Jr.) — **115** — 1967 4 1 1 1 $4,400

2Sep67–2Aqu fst 6f .22⅖ .46⅘1.12⅘ Clm 20000 5 4 46 44½ 32 33½ JLRotz 119 *2.80 75–16 Rare Sun 1172½ Mr. Hasty 1171 Blighty 1191 Wide for drive 11
8Aug67–7Sar fst 5½f.22⅖ .45⅗1.04⅖ Allowance 2 3 42½ 45½ 47 413 FToro 122 18.80 82–10 Pappa Steve 1229 Family Fun 1223 Hand To Hand 1221 No mishap 8
3Aug67–4Sar fst 5½f.22⅗ .46⅗1.05⅖ Md 20000 7 4 32½ 32 3nk 11 FToro 122 ♦5.70 90– 7 ♦Adrenalin 1221 ♦Blighty 1221 Mighty Hitter 1203½ Driving 10
3Aug67—♦Dead heat.
19Jun67–3Aqu sly 5f .23⅗ .47⅖1.00 Md 15000 7 9 42½ 33 33½ 26 ECardone 122 15.20 79–26 Earth's Greenbanner 1226 Blighty 1222 Kings Fame 1182½ Fair try 10
LATEST WORKOUTS Sep 25 Bel 5f fst 1.03⅖ b — Sep 20 Bel 6f fst 1.16⅕ h — Sep 15 Bel 5f fst 1.02⅗ h — Sep 12 Bel 5f fst 1.02⅗ h

Dixie Porter — Ch. c (1965–Fla), by Porterhouse—Dixie Lady, by Bull Lea — M. Guerrieri — G. Riola — (Llangollen Farm of Ocala) — **110**5 — 1967 8 2 0 1 $7,510

15Sep67–6Aqu fst 6f .23 .46⅗1.12 Allowance 5 3 3nk 44½ 79½1314 RTurcotte 115 5.70 69–19 Royal Exchange 1152 Licorice 1151½ Mr. Hasty 115h Bore out 13
30Aug67–6Aqu fst 6f .22⅕ .45⅗1.10⅘ Allowance 10 2 21½ 22 43½ 38½ RTurcotte 115 5.80 80–18 Captain's Gig 1222½ Dignitas 1176 Dixie Porter 1151 Weakened 10
21Jly 67–4Aqu fst 5½f.22⅘ .46⅖1.04⅖ Clm 16000 7 1 11½ 11½ 12 16 GMora5 114 *2.00 91–14 Dixie Porter 1146 Equivocate 1151 Real Story 1203 Won easily 8
17Jly 67–6Aqu fst 5½f.22⅗ .46⅗1.05⅘ Allowance 9 5 41 52 86½ 88¼ WBoland b 115 63.30 76–15 Out Of The Way 119¾ Beyond Price 1222½ Ben Ben 119h Tired 11
4Jly 67–5Aqu fst 5f .22⅖ .46 .59 Allowance 5 5 52½ 45 45 55½ MSorrentino 115 14.90 84–17 Hail To Garr 1191 Out Of The Way 1191 Join Forces 1192 No rally 9
20Jun67–3Aqu sly 5½f.22⅘ .46⅖1.04⅘ Allowance 3 2 2½ 21½ 36 514 RTurcotte 115 18.50 75–23 What A Pleasure 1173½ Sea Fable 1196 Wise Exchange 1174 Tired 6
6Jun67–4Aqu fst 5f .22 .46⅕ .59⅗ Md 18000 3 1 24 21½ 13 15 MVenezia 118 8.20 87–14 Dixie Porter 1185 Nickadinka 1183 Tiger Bright 1181½ Easily 9
22May67–4Aqu fst 5f .22⅘ .46⅕ .58⅕ Md Sp Wt 7 6 66¾ 78½ 711 613 MVenezia 122 104.40 81–14 WhatAPleasure1222 FavorablePath1224½ HailToGarr122nk No mis'p 10
LATEST WORKOUTS Sep 29 Aqu 3f sly .39 b — Sep 26 Bel tr.t. 3f fst .37 h — Sep 22 Bel tr.t. 4f fst .52⅖ b — Sep 14 Bel tr.t. 3f fst .37⅖ b

Mitey Prince — Dk. b. or br. c (1965–Ky), by Blue Prince—Ittie Bittie, by Mr. Music — B. C. Brittingham — W. H. Dixon — (M. Carter) — **122** — 1967 6 1 1 0 $4,710

23Sep67–6Atl fst 6f .22⅗ .46⅕1.12⅕ Allowance 6 5 2h 2h 2h 21¾ FToro b 120 10.50 79–22 Baker George 1181¾ Mitey Prince 120h Coral Atoll 118nk In close 11
15Sep67–6Aqu fst 6f .23 .46⅗1.12 Allowance 10 6 72 76½ 914 812 ORosado 122 24.30f 71–19 Royal Exchange 1152 Licorice 1151½ Mr. Hasty 115h Wide 13
7Sep67–6Aqu fst 6f .22⅕ .45⅗1.11⅖ Allowance 5 7 52¾ 78½ 69¼ 78¼ ORosado 122 9.70 78–17 Dignitas 1173 Count Flip 117nk Agility 1221 Fell far back 9
26Aug67–1Sar fst 6f .22⅘ .46 1.11⅕ Md Sp Wt 3 1 1h 11½ 14 16 ORosado 122 68.10 92– 7 MiteyPrince1226 MightyHitter1222 FourAndFrenchy1223 Easily 14
15Aug67–5Sar fst 6f .22 .45⅗1.12 Md Sp Wt 12 9 78½ 68 57½ 49½ ORosado 122 13.70f 78–10 Allardice 1222 Forever 1226 Sea O Galilee 1221½ Late gain 14
8Aug67–3Sar fst 5½f.22⅗ .46⅖1.05⅗ Md Sp Wt 10 11 1012 1011 107½ 612 FToro 122 117.20 77–10 Bold Native 1227 Endeavoring 1221 Wordy 122¾ No speed 12
LATEST WORKOUTS Sep 28 Bel 4f fst .48⅘ b — Sep 20 Bel 4f fst .47⅗ hg — Sep 13 Bel 3f fst .35⅖ h — Sep 1 Bel 6f fst 1.17 b

Principe — B. c (1965-Ky), by Princequillo—Black Panic, by Better Self — King Ranch — Max Hirsch — (King Ranch) — **122** — 1967 6 1 0 0 $3,575

15Sep67-6Aqu fst 6f .23 .46⅗1.12 Allowance 9 5 61½ 66 1011 1012 JLRotz b 122 7.20 71-19 Royal Exchange 1152 Licorice 1151½ Mr. Hasty 115h No speed 13
7Sep67-6Aqu fst 6f .22⅕ .45⅗1.11⅖ Allowance 8 1 73½ 68 54¾ 55¼ JLRotz b 122 2.20 81-17 Dignitas 1173 Count Flip 117nk Agility 1221 No late rally 9
22Aug67-4Sar fst 5½f.22⅖ .46 1.05 Md Sp Wt 2 2 1½ 1½ 14 17 JLRotz b 122 5.80 92-13 Principe 1227 Sea O Galilee 1221 Endeavoring 122h Easily 12
15Aug67-4Sar fst 6f .22⅖ .46⅕1.11⅗ Md Sp Wt 11 5 52½ 66 64 512 JLRotz 122 39.90 78-10 Captain'sGig1222 WindRiverLad1223 MightyHitter1226 No threat 14
27Jun67-3Aqu fst 5½f.22⅖ .46⅖1.05⅗ Md Sp Wt 10 9 97½111410 12 813 JLRotz 122 18.40 72-18 Skookum 122½ Noted Scholar 122½ Vitriolic 1222½ Never close 12
30May67-3Aqu fst 5f .23 .47 .59⅘ Md Sp Wt 5 5 96¾ 98 911 76¾ JLRotz 122 14.90 81-13 Hail To Garr 1222 Rob Win 122¾ Jayceetee 1221½ Greenly 10
LATEST WORKOUTS Sep 29 Bel tr.t. 3f sly .35⅗ h — Sep 27 Bel 4f fst .52 b — Sep 23 Bel 7f fst 1.32 b — Sep 19 Bel 4f fst .48⅖ b

Mr. Hasty — B. c (1965-Ky.), by Mr. Turf—Maggie James, by Count Turf — J. J. Amiel — C. McCreary — (J. J. Amiel) — **115** — 1967 8 1 1 1 $5,400

15Sep67-6Aqu fst 6f .23 .46⅗1.12 Allowance 2 13 105 87 55 33¼ HGustines b 115 45.20 79-19 Royal Exchange 1152 Licorice 1151½ Mr. Hasty 115h Slow start 13
2Sep67-2Aqu fst 6f .22⅖ .46⅘1.12⅘ Clm 20000 8 11 67 55 21½ 22½ HGustines b 117 6.80 76-16 Rare Sun 1172½ Mr. Hasty 1171 Blighty 1191 Made game try 11
30Aug67-6Aqu fst 6f .22⅕ .45⅗1.10⅘ Allowance 5 10 97½ 89 57½ 610 HGustines b 115 65.60 79-18 Captain's Gig 1222½ Dignitas 1176 Dixie Porter 1151 Sluggish start 10
15Aug67-6Sar fst 6f .22⅖ .45⅖1.11 Allowance 5 10 87½ 78½ 66½ 815 BFeliciano b 115 34.30 78-10 Bold Native 1225 Chompion 1225 Rooney's Sword 1192 No speed 10
27Jly 67-4Aqu fst 5½f.22⅘ .46⅗1.05⅘ Md 18000 9 5 42 32 13 13½ HGustines b 122 10.80 84-15 Mr. Hasty 1223½ Joelyn's Pet 117¾ Ten Cuidado 1182½ Easily 12
22Jly 67-3Aqu fst 5½f.22⅖ .46 1.05 Md Sp Wt 2 7 34½ 33½ 912 1012 JRuane b 122 43.50 76-11 Vitriolic 1225 ChathamCenter 1221¼ MaterialWitness 112no Stopped 11
24May67-3GS fst 5f .22⅖ .47⅕ .59⅘ Md 18000 2 6 44½ 55½ 78 811 HBlock 116 7.40 79-14 Winter Street 1162 Lomorn 113no Colonel Moore 1132¾ Tired 10
15May67-4Aqu fst 5f .22⅖ .45⅗ .58 Md Sp Wt 6 9 911 913 614 716 HGustines 122 29.00 79-13 Sea Fable 1224 Rooney's Sword 1223 Hail To Racing 1225 No threat 10
LATEST WORKOUTS Sep 29 Bel tr.t. 3f sly .35⅗ h — Sep 25 Bel tr.t. 6f fst 1.17 h — Sep 21 Bel tr.t. 4f fst .48⅗ h — Sep 11 Bel tr.t. 4f fst .49⅖ h

Rare Sun — Ch. g (1965-Va), by Midnight Sun—Rare Jade, by Hill Prince — Starlight Farm — L. H. Hunt — (Meadow Stud, Inc.) — **115** — 1967 6 2 0 0 $7,695

15Sep67-6Aqu fst 6f .23 .46⅗1.12 Allowance 7 10 128 109½1212 711 SHernandez 115 33.30 72-19 Royal Exchange 1152 Licorice 1151½ Mr. Hasty 115h No speed 13
2Sep67-2Aqu fst 6f .22⅖ .46⅘1.12⅘ Clm 20000 2 10 78 69 56 12½ ACorderoJr 117 4.40 79-16 Rare Sun 1172½ Mr. Hasty 1171 Blighty 1191 Won going away 11
22Aug67-6Sar fst 5½f.22⅕ .45⅖1.04⅗ Allowance 6 8 814 88½ 78 57½ ADeSpirito 122 29.60 86-13 Family Fun 1222½ Royal Exchange 1164 Mara Lark 1131 Slug. early 8
15Aug67-6Sar fst 6f .22⅖ .45⅖1.11 Allowance 4 9 101310 16 79½ 412 ADeSpirito 115 55.60 81-10 Bold Native 1225 Chompion 1225 Rooney's Sword 1192 Rallied 10
17Jly 67-6Aqu fst 5½f.22⅘ .46⅗1.05⅘ Allowance 4 8 87 63½ 53 75½ LGilligan 115 58.00 79-15 Out Of The Way 119¾ Beyond Price 1222½ Ben Ben 119h No mishap 11
10Jly 67-4Aqu fst 5½f.22⅗ .46⅗1.06⅖ M c-10500 5 10 75¾ 88¼ 54 11 ADeSpirito 118 14.60 81-16 Rare Sun 1181 What A Shape 1223½ Our Nail 122nk Up in time 12
LATEST WORKOUTS Sep 28 Bel 3f fst .34⅖ hg — Sep 23 Bel 7f fst 1.27⅘ h — Sep 14 Bel tr.t. 3f fst .37 h — Sep 11 Bel 5f fst 1.04⅗ b

Bugged — Ch. c (1965-Ky), by Nashua—Fly Trap, by Mahmoud — C. V. Whitney — I. G. Balding — (C. V. Whitney) — **122** — 1967 5 1 0 0 $4,000

7Sep67-6Aqu fst 6f .22⅕ .45⅗1.11⅖ Allowance 2 5 2½ 22 33 44¼ MVenezia 122 34.10 82-17 Dignitas 1173 Count Flip 117nk Agility 1221 Well up, tired 9
22Aug67-6Sar fst 5½f.22⅕ .45⅖1.04⅗ Allowance 1 5 43½ 43½ 88½ 812 HGustines b 122 4.00e 82-13 Family Fun 1222½ Royal Exchange 1164 Mara Lark 1131 Stopped 8
15Aug67-6Sar fst 6f .22⅖ .45⅖1.11 Allowance 2 8 32½ 34½ 34½ 614 HGustines b 122 7.60e 79-10 Bold Native 1225 Chompion 1225 Rooney's Sword 1192 Tired 10
8Aug67-1Sar fst 5½f.22⅖ .46⅕1.06 Md Sp Wt 11 4 1h 11½ 15 15 HGustines b 122 8.70 87-10 Bugged 1225 d-Very Funny 1224 Sea O Galilee 1222 Easily 12
1Aug67-4Sar sly 5½f.22⅖ .46⅗1.06⅖ Md Sp Wt 3 6 716 716 711 511 HGustines 122 15.40 74-15 •Federal Power 1223½ •Opulent 1223½ Improvisation 122½ No threat 8
LATEST WORKOUTS Sep 25 Bel 6f fst 1.14⅗ h — Sep 15 Bel 7f fst 1.28 h — Sep 4 Bel 5f fst 1.02⅘ b — Aug 30 Bel 5f fst 1.02⅕ b

Count Flip * — Dk. b. or br. c (1965-Ky), by One Count—Windup, by Better Self — Shelly Bee Stable — T. H. Heard, Jr. — (W. L. Jones, Jr.) — **117** — 1967 10 1 2 1 $7,812

15Sep67-6Aqu fst 6f .23 .46⅗1.12 Allowance 13 8 94½131213121213 LPincayJr b 117 4.10 70-19 Royal Exchange 1152 Licorice 1151½ Mr. Hasty 115h Wide 13
7Sep67-6Aqu fst 6f .22⅕ .45⅗1.11⅖ Allowance 3 8 87¾ 912 76½ 23 LPincayJr b 117 11.40e 83-17 Dignitas 1173 Count Flip 117nk Agility 1221 Finished fast 9
17Jly 67-6Aqu fst 5½f.22⅘ .46⅗1.05⅘ Allowance 3 9 1011 98 98½ 99¼ ADeSpirito b 122 30.20 75-15 Out Of The Way 119¾ Beyond Price 1222½ Ben Ben 119h No speed 11
4Jly 67-8Del fst 5½f.22⅘ .46⅗1.05⅕ Dover 3 9 109½1012 89½ 69½ GPatterson b 116 23.50 85-22 Clever Foot 116nk Subpet 1221½ Salerno 1191 Never a threat 10
21Jun67-8Mth fst 5½f.22⅘ .46 1.05⅘ TyroStakes 2 8 106¾ 87 65¾ 67½ JCulmone 115 46.00 80-21 Iron Ruler 1151¾ Royal Trace 1132 Four Fingers 115h No threat 12
5Jun67-5Aqu fst 5f .23 .46⅘ .59⅘ Md Sp Wt 5 4 2h 32 21 11 ADeSpirito 122 *3.00 86-15 Count Flip 1221 Carnaby Cat 122½ Agility 122¾ Going away 10
13May67-3Aqu fst 5f .22⅘ .46⅘ .59⅖ Md Sp Wt 5 7 66½ 65¾ 44½ 32¾ ADeSpirito 122 8.70 85-16 Ben Ben 122nk Favorable Path 1222½ Count Flip 1223 Rallied 10
3May67-7Aqu fst 5f .22⅕ .46 .58⅗ Youthful 5 8 65½ 711 59 49 ADeSpirito 117 13.60e 83-21 Kaskaskia 1226 Potomac 1221½ Wise Exchange 1221½ Never threat 8
24Apr67-3Aqu sly 5f .23⅖ .47⅖1.00 Md Sp Wt 2 8 813 713 514 28 ADeSpirito 122 16.60 77-24 Potomac 1228 Count Flip 1222 Out Of The Way 1222½ Rallied 9
3Apr67-4Aqu fst 5f .23⅕ .47⅗1.00⅖ Md Sp Wt 5 8 814 715 610 66½ LPincayJr 122 22.80 76-25 d-Captain Jud 1221½ Perfect Pass 122no Aqua Nail 1223 No threat 9
LATEST WORKOUTS Sep 27 Aqu 4f fst .50 b — Sep 22 Aqu 3f fst .37 b — Sep 14 Aqu 4f fst .49 b — Sep 5 Aqu 3f fst .37 bg

Critics Award — Ch. c (1965-Ky), by Hitting Away—Rave Notice, by Princequillo — Oxford Stable — J. P. Smith — (R. C. Wilson, Jr.) — **122** — 1967 4 1 0 0 $3,575

23Sep67-5Aqu fst 6½f.22⅘ .46⅘1.18⅗ Allowance 7 6 72½ 85 87½ 88¼ WShoemaker b 122 10.10 79-13 Wellpoised 122¾ Railbird 107h Dynamic Turn 122¾ No threat 10
30Aug67-5Aqu fst 6f .22⅖ .46⅕1.12⅗ Md Sp Wt 1 4 53½ 32 2½ 1¾ ACorderoJr b 122 18.70 80-18 Critics Award 122¾ Happy Gold 1221½ Very Funny 122nk Driving 14
22Aug67-4Sar fst 5½f.22⅖ .46 1.05 Md Sp Wt 11 8 96 916 89 69½ ACorderoJr 122 12.50 82-13 Principe 1227 Sea O Galilee 1221 Endeavoring 122h No threat 12
15Aug67-4Sar fst 6f .22⅖ .46⅕1.11⅗ Md Sp Wt 12 7 63½ 76½ 53½ 613 ACorderoJr 122 16.10 77-10 Captain'sGig1222 WindRiverLad1223 MightyHitter1226 No threat 14
LATEST WORKOUTS Sep 28 Bel tr.t. 5f fst 1.02⅗ b — Sep 20 Bel 7f fst 1.30 b — Sep 18 Bel tr.t. 3f fst .36 h — Sep 15 Bel 5f fst 1.01⅗ h

Captain Courageous — B. c (1965-Ky), by Sailor—Bold Princess, by Bold Ruler — Wheatley Stable — E. A. Neloy — (Wheatley Stable) — **122** — 1967 2 1 0 0 $3,575

30Aug67-6Aqu fst 6f .22⅕ .45⅗1.10⅘ Allowance 7 5 75½ 67 68½ 59½ BBaeza 122 4.20 79-18 Captain's Gig 1222½ Dignitas 1176 Dixie Porter 1151 Wide 10
19Aug67-1Sar sly 6f .22⅖ .45⅗1.12⅕ Md Sp Wt 8 4 21 2h 1h 11 WBoland 122 4.70 87-10 CaptainCourageous1221 Improvisation1221 RichStrike122nk Driving 12
LATEST WORKOUTS Sep 26 Aqu 3f fst .36⅗ b — Sep 21 Bel 4f fst .46⅖ h — Sep 17 Bel 3f sly .35⅖ h — Aug 28 Bel 4f sly .49 b

Shy Native — Ro. c (1965-Ky), by Native Dancer—Shy Dancer, by Bolero — J. D. Wimpfheimer — W. Sedlacek — (J. D. Wimpfheimer) — **117** — 1967 8 1 0 0 $3,835

23Sep67-5Aqu fst 6½f.22⅘ .46⅘1.18⅗ Allowance 6 9 108 95½ 64 63¾ EGuerin b 116 35.90 83-13 Wellpoised 122¾ Railbird 107h Dynamic Turn 122¾ Sluggish start 10
15Aug67-6Sar fst 6f .22⅖ .45⅖1.11 Allowance 7 5 913 914 912 715 ECardone b 119 31.20e 78-10 Bold Native 1225 Chompion 1225 Rooney's Sword 1192 Wide 01
7Aug67-7Sar fst 5½f.22⅕ .45 1.03⅗ Sanford 4 4 67 68½ 69 517 ECardone b 115 38.30 82-15 Exclusive Native 1154 Vitriolic 116¾ Forward Pass 12010 No speed 6
1Aug67-8Sar sly 5½f.23 .46⅘1.05⅖ Allowance 4 6 612 612 710 618 ECardone b 119 7.40 72-15 Palace Ruler 1226 Mara Lark 1153½ Chompion 1223 No speed 7
27Jun67-5Aqu fst 5½f.22⅘ .46⅘1.06⅕ Md Sp Wt 3 8 86¾ 85½ 3½ 1¾ ECardone b 122 8.40 82-18 Shy Native 122¾ Hail To Racing 1223 Chivalrous 1223½ Driving 11
20Jun67-1Aqu sly 5f .23⅖ .47⅕ .59⅕ Md Sp Wt 4 5 89½ 89½ 612 49½ ECardone b 122 12.80 79-23 Exclusive Native 1223½ Hand To Hand 1223 Nez Perce 1223 Rallied 10
12Jun67-5Aqu fst 5f .22⅗ .47 .59⅗ Md Sp Wt 7 2 1h 1h 78½ 913 ACorderoJr b 122 15.90 74-18 Beau Baron 1222½ Mighty Hitter 122no Jayceetee 122h Used up 10
5Jun67-5Aqu fst 5f .23 .46⅘ .59⅘ Md Sp Wt 9 7 1h 11 32 67¾ ACorderoJr b 122 6.50 78-15 Count Flip 1221 Carnaby Cat 122½ Agility 122¾ Tired 10
LATEST WORKOUTS Sep 19 Aqu 5f fst 1.01⅖ h — Sep 14 Aqu 5f fst 1.02 h — Sep 9 Aqu 5f fst 1.02 h — Sep 3 Aqu 4f fst .51⅗ b

Having said that to the compulsive bettors, I shall now cooperate with them to the extent of observing that the likeliest animal to play in this sort of race is a horse that (a) is in form and (b) has shown a tendency to gain ground in the stretch of six-furlong races. On that basis, the only possible play in this race would be Mr. Hasty. Count Flip, which gained considerable ground in the stretch on September 7, is clearly out of sorts. I ordinarily toss out a race in which a horse runs wide, as Count Flip did on September 15—but not when the animal finishes twelfth in a field of thirteen after showing absolutely no stretch run.

The Running of the Race

As THE CHART SHOWS, Mr. Hasty won this race at a good price. Those who use this victory as the basis of a system for playing two-year-olds in seven-furlong races will end as losers, although they will catch a few horses like Mr. Hasty.

FOURTH RACE **7 FURLONGS. (Chute). (Rose Net, Sept. 17, 1962, 1.21⅕, 6, 114.)**

Aqu - 32429

September 30, 1967

Allowances. Purse $7,500. 2-year-olds which have never won a race other than maiden or claiming. Weight, 122 lbs. Non-winners of a race other than claiming since July 29 allowed 3 lbs., of such a race since July 1, 5 lbs., of such a race since May 31, 7 lbs.

Value to winner $4,875, second $1,500, third $750, fourth $375. Mutuel pool $573,299.

Index	Horse	Eqt A Wt	PP	St	¼	½	Str	Fin	Jockey	Owner	Odds $1
32314Aqu^{3}	Mr. Hasty	b 2 115	5	7	9^{4}	$7\frac{1}{2}$	3^{1}	1^{nk}	R Turcotte	J J Amiel	7.90
31004Aqu^{1}	Call A Cop	b 2 115	2	4	4^{4}	3^{3}	2^{h}	$2^{2\frac{3}{4}}$	M Sor'tino	Adele L Rand	9.40
32314Aqu^{13}	Dixie Porter	2 110	3	1	1^{1}	$1^{1\frac{1}{2}}$	$1\frac{1}{2}$	$3^{1\frac{1}{2}}$	G Mora^{5}	M Guerrieri	11.00
32376Aqu^{6}	Shy Native	b 2 117	10	8	10	10	$6^{1\frac{1}{2}}$	4^{h}	E Guerin	J D Wimpfheimer	25.70
32376Aqu^{2}	Railbird	2 108	1	9	$5\frac{1}{2}$	$8^{1\frac{1}{2}}$	8^{2}	5^{nk}	R Tanner^{7}	H Nadler	4.20
31924Aqu^{5}	Captain C'geous	2 122	9	2	3^{h}	2^{h}	$4\frac{1}{2}$	6^{2}	B Baeza	Wheatley Stable	1.40
32251Aqu^{4}	Bugged	2 122	6	6	6^{h}	6^{h}	7^{1}	7^{1}	M Venezia	C V Whitney	28.30
32376Aqu^{8}	Critics Award	b 2 122	2	10	$8\frac{1}{2}$	$9\frac{1}{2}$	10	$8^{1\frac{1}{2}}$	W Sh'maker	Oxford Stable	41.20
32368Atl^{2}	Mitey Prince	b 2 122	4	3	$2\frac{1}{2}$	$4\frac{1}{2}$	$9\frac{1}{2}$	9^{nk}	F Toro	B C Brittingham	14.00
32314Aqu^{12}	Count Flip	b 2 117	7	5	$7^{1\frac{1}{2}}$	$5\frac{1}{2}$	5^{h}	10	L Adams	Shelly Bee Stable	7.00

Time .22⅕, .45⅗, 1.12, 1.25⅖ (with wind in backstretch). Track good.

$2 Mutuel Prices:

5-MR. HASTY	17.80	8.20	5.20
2-CALL A COP		10.00	7.00
3-DIXIE PORTER			6.60

B. c, by Mr. Turf—Maggie James, by Count Turf. Trainer C. McCreary. Bred by J. J. Amiel (Ky.).

IN GATE AT 3.12. OFF AT 3.12 EASTERN DAYLIGHT TIME. Start good. Won driving.

MR. HASTY, outrun until reaching the stretch, moved between horses during the drive, and, responding to brisk handling, won in the last sixteenth. CALL A COP saved ground from the start and reached the front between calls inside the final furlong but was unable to withstand the winner while easily second best. DIXIE PORTER set the pace until inside the last eighth but faltered when challenged by CALL A COP. SHY NATIVE lacked early foot and forced to race wide the last three-eighths, could not threaten the leaders. RAILBIRD, hustled after the start, tired after showing brief speed. CAPTAIN COURAGEOUS gave way during the stretch run. BUGGED, racing well out from the inner rail, was never dangerous. CRITICS AWARD broke slowly and raced wide approaching and entering the stretch. MITEY PRINCE was finished early. COUNT FLIP raced wide.

Scratched—32211Aqu^{3} Blighty, 32314Aqu^{10} Principe. 32314Aqu^{7} Rare Sun.

THE FIFTH RACE

IT LOOKS as if this race ought to attract some high-grade allowance sprinters. A glance at the list confirms it. Some of the best-known animals in the country are entered.

5th Race Aqueduct

6 FURLONGS AQUEDUCT (▼Start / ▲Finish)

6 FURLONGS. (Near Man, July 17, 1963, 1.08⅗, 3, 112.)
Allowances. Purse $12,000. 3-year-olds and upward listed in the Classified Division which have not won two races since July 29. Weights, 3-year-olds, 120 lbs., older 124 lbs. Non-winners of three races of $3,900 since Mar. 11 allowed 3 lbs., of two races of $4,875 since then, 5 lbs., of such a race in 1967, 7 lbs. (Maiden, claiming, optional and starter races not considered.)

(5th Aqu)—Coupled—Brunch and Wyoming Wildcat. Bold Hour and Full Of Fun.

Brunch
B. c (1964–Fla), by Intentionally—Munch, by Mustang — **117**
Tartan Stable J. A. Nerud (Tartan Farms)
1967 5 4 0 0 $18,525
1966 0 M 0 0

12Jly 67–6Aqu fst 7f .22⅖ .45 1.22⅘ Allowance 4 4 2h 2h 12 14 BBaeza 114 *0.80 92–13 Brunch 1144 Mister Pitt's Kid 1141 Brother Campbell 1141½ Easily 7
22Apr67–7Aqu fst 1⅛ .46⅗1.10⅘1.49⅗ WoodMem. 3 1 2h 2½ 916 925 MYcaza b 126 4.30 63–16 Damascus 1266 Gala Performance 1263 Dawn Glory 1261½ Stopped 9
13Apr67–8Aqu fst 1 .47 1.11⅘1.36⅘ Allowance 2 1 11½ 11½ 1½ 11½ WShoemaker 110 *0.60 87–16 Brunch 1101½ Dunderhead 1231½ Major Art 1115 Held safe margin 9
3Apr67–6Aqu fst 6f .23⅖ .47⅘1.12⅖ Allowance 3 1 1½ 11 11½ 14 WShoemaker 113 *0.30 81–25 Brunch 1134 Undermine 1131½ Blasting Charge 1082 Easily 7
.Mar67–3Hia fst 6f .22⅕ .45⅖1.10⅕ Md Sp Wt 2 2 12 12 14 16 RUssery 118 *0.90 93–13 Brunch 1186 Roman Stitch 1182 Nailon 1183¾ Drew out easily 12
LATEST WORKOUTS Sep 21 Bel tr.t. 4f fst .48⅗ h Sep 17 Bel tr.t. 5f fst 1.01⅗ b Sep 12 Bel tr.t. 4f fst .48⅕ h Sep 7 Bel tr.t. 4f fst .49 h

Bold Hour *
Dk. b. or br. c (1964–Ky), by Bold Ruler—Seven Thirty, by Mr. Music — **117**
G. D. Widener W. F. Mulholland (Erdenheim Farms Co.)
1967 6 2 1 0 $52,805
1966 9 4 3 0 $266,800

11Aug67–7Sar fst 1 .45⅖1.09⅘1.36⅕ JimDandy 4 4 33½ 33 31 45½ JLRotz 121 *2.70 87–12 GalaPerformance 114½ GreatPower 1192 Tumiga 1193 No excuse 12
15Jly 67–7Aqu sly 1¼ .47⅗1.12 2.03 DwyerH 4 5 44½ 32½ 611 614 JLRotz 125 5.40 69–18 Damascus 128¾ FavorableTurn 1122½ BlastingCharge 116h Bid, tired 9
1Jly 67–7Aqu gd 1 .45⅖1.09⅘1.36 SaranacH 6 5 61¾ 3¾ 1nk 11½ JLRotz 123 3.00 88–19 Bold Hour 1231½ Tumiga 123no Reason To Hail 119h Brisk drive 7
20Jun67–6Aqu sly 7f .23 .46⅘1.25⅕ Allowance 4 2 1h 1h 11½ 12 WBoland 112 *0.70 80–23 Bold Hour 1122 Sun Gala 1126 Major Art 110¾ Under mild drive 6
1Feb67–8Hia fst 7f .22⅘ .45⅖1.23 Bahamas 13 5 63 41¾ 12 2nk JLRotz 122 *1.60 94–13 Reflected Glory 115nk Bold Hour 1222 Cool Reception 1191 Gamely 16
21Jan67–8Hia my 7f .22⅗ .45⅕1.23⅘ Hibiscus 11 3 41½ 46 915 814 JLRotz b 122 *0.70 76–20 In Reality 1222 Reason To Hail 1152½ Native Guile 1122 Tired 14
12Nov66–8GS sly 1 1/16 .47⅖1.12⅕1.44⅕ Garden St. 12 1 14 13 11½ 23 JLRotz b 122 4.10e 81–29 Successor 1223 Bold Hour 1226 Proviso 122¾ Drifted out 12
15Oct66–7Aqu fst 1 .44⅘1.09⅖1.35 Champagne 8 2 1h 2h 57 49 JLRotz b 122 4.80 84–14 Successor 1221 Dr. Fager 1224 Proviso 1224 Speed, gave way 10
24Sep66–7Aqu fst 6½f .22⅘ .46 1.17⅗ Futurity 6 1 3nk 11½ 14 1½ JLRotz b 122 *1.40 92–18 Bold Hour 122½ Successor 1223½ Pinnacle 1222 Strong urging 7
27Aug66–6Sar fst 6½f .22⅖ .45⅗1.17⅕ Hopeful 1 2 1h 11 12 11¾ JLRotz b 122 2.70 92– 8 Bold Hour 1221¾ Great Power 122h Top Bid 1226½ Was never headed 5
LATEST WORKOUTS Sep 28 Bel tr.t. 4f fst .49 b Sep 24 Bel 7f fst 1.26 h Sep 19 Bel tr.t. 3f fst .37 h Sep 16 Bel 6f fs 1.14 b

It's Blitz *
B. c (1963–Fla), by Beau Gar—Blitz Kuchen, by Spy Song — **119**
B. Lobel A. A. Fiore (Hobeau Farm, Inc.)
1967 12 2 4 1 $20,125
1966 23 3 8 4 $19,893

16Sep67–6Aqu fst 6f .22⅖ .46 1.10⅖ Allowance 5 4 41¾ 43½ 69¾ 714 GMora5 b 114 26.50 77–16 Successor 1133 Golden Buttons 1191 Impressive 115h Tired 8
11Sep67–6Aqu fst 6f .22⅖ .45 1.10⅖ Allowance 7 2 23 44¼ 611 716 GMora5 b 110 18.80 75–21 Mr.Washington 1204 FirstAndFinest 1174 DemonDyno 115½ Tired 8
3Jun67–9Suf fst 6f .22⅖ .45⅗1.10⅕ Handicap 5 2 2h 3nk 2h 31 EGuerin b 115 2.70 89–16 Faultless Light 1121 Sandoval 123no It's Blitz 1153 Good try 6
17May67–7Aqu fst 7f .22⅕ .44⅕1.22⅕ RosebenH 3 4 1½ 2h 41½ 66¾ ECardone b 110 12.00 88–16 Indulto 113¾ Our Michael 1192½ Impressive 121no Used early 7
6May67–6Aqu sly 6f .22⅗ .46 1.11⅖ Allowance 4 1 1h 2½ 2h 2¾ ECardone b 121 *2.10 85–27 Gary G. 117¾ It's Blitz 1214½ Smooth Seas 1123 Bore out, hung 5
22Apr67–6Aqu fst 6f .22⅕ .45⅗1.10⅗ Allowance 1 3 11 1½ 11 1no ECardone b 119 11.60 90–16 It's Blitz 119no Ring Twice 1211½ Wyoming Wildcat 1195 Driving 6
13Apr67–6Aqu fst 6f .22⅕ .45⅖1.10⅘ Clm 25000 7 4 4¾ 4nk 41¼ 66¼ ECardone b 120 3.10 83–16 Auric 117nk Farmer's Son 113½ Smooth Seas 1171½ Speed, tired 8
4Apr67–6Aqu fst 7f .23 .46 1.23⅘ Clm 30000 4 3 11½ 1h 1½ 11½ ECardone b 115 8.50 87–21 It's Blitz 1151½ Auric 113¾ Sheet Anchor 115¾ Hard drive 7
28Mar67–6Aqu gd 6f .23 .46⅗1.11⅘ Clm 25000 6 4 1h 1h 2h 2h ECardone b 115 6.90 84–26 Notice Me 113h It's Blitz 1153 Auric 113n Led between calls 7
15Mar67–5Aqu sly 6f .23⅕ .47⅕1.12⅗ Clm 19000 2 6 1h 1h 1½ 2¾ ECardone b 117 2.10 79–24 Farmer's Son 121¾ It's Blitz 117½ Counsellor 1083 Gamely 6
LATEST WORKOUTS Sep 6 Bel 4f fst .48⅘ h Aug 29 Bel 6f fst 1.17 b Aug 21 Sar 6f sly 1.16 hg Aug 16 Sar tr.t. 4f fst .51 h

Golden Joey
Ch. h (1962), by Royal Serenade—Single Stroke, by One Hitter — **117**
Marion R. Frankel V. J. Nickerson (Mrs. M. Frankel)
1967 5 0 1 0 $1,100
1966 4 0 1 0 $2,125

26Sep67–5Atl fst 6f .22⅖ .44⅗1.09⅗ Allowance 1 3 11 11½ 11½ 2¾ GPatterson b 112 7.20 93–15 Lillington 117¾ Golden Joey 112nk Lane 1193½ Game effort 8
16Sep67–6Aqu fst 6f .22⅖ .46 1.10⅖ Allowance 2 6 Lost rider RUssery b 117 31.80 —— Successor 1133 Golden Buttons 1191 Impressive 115h Stumbled 8
4Sep67–6Aqu fst 6f .22 .45 1.09⅗ Allowance 5 4 33 34 511 622 LAdams b 115 32.40 73–14 Jim J. 115¾ Mr. Washington 1205 Successor 11310 Dropped back 6
12Aug67–7Sar fst 6f .22⅗ .46⅖1.11 Allowance 3 4 3nk 3½ 87½ 821 LAdams b 115 30.50 72–11 Spring Double 1211 Smooth Seas 1214 Sun Gala 1123½ Tired 8
5Aug67–7Sar fst 6f .22⅕ .45 1.09⅘ Allowance 9 4 52· 87½ 911 915 RUssery b 116 19.60 84– 6 Full Of Fun 1141 Demon Dyno 1152½ John Jacob 116h Fell back 9
2May66–4Aqu fst 6f .22⅗ .45⅗1.10⅘ Allowance 1 3 1h 2h 53¾ 613 GMineau5 b 114 9.10 76–19 Dark King 117h Ornamento 119no Flag Raiser 1241 Speed, stopped 6
23Apr66–6Aqu fst 6f .22⅕ .45⅖1.10⅕ Allowance 5 2 23 22 2h 42 RUssery b 117 4.00 90–14 Understudy 117h Hi-Hasty 1171 Black Mountain 1121 Weakened 8
16Apr66–6Aqu fst 6f .22⅕ .45⅕1.10⅕ Allowance 4 3 1½ 11½ 1½ 57¼ RUssery b 121 *0.80 85–14 Understudy 115nk A. Deck 1192 Linear B. 1171 Set pace, tired 7
9Apr66–6Aqu fst 6f .22⅖ .45⅘1.11⅕ Allowance 4 4 41½ 32 21 2nk RUssery b 117 *1.40 87–18 Chinatowner 114nk Golden Joey 117¾ Canal 119nk Game effort 10
16Jun65–8Mth fst 6f .21⅗ .45 1.10⅘ SelectH 2 5 31 2h 7101319 JSellers b 124 5.90 69–18 Country Friend 115nk Big Rock Candy 1145 Space Song 113½ Stop'd 13
9Jun65–7Mth fst 6f .21⅗ .44⅘1.11⅗ Allowance 4 3 21½ 41¼ 2½ 2nk JSellers b 124 2.50 84–19 Deutron 113nk Golden Joey 1242½ Cosimo 115nk Hung under impost 7
LATEST WORKOUTS Sep 24 Aqu 4f fst .48⅖ b Sep 20 Aqu 5f fst 1.02⅗ b Sep 14 Aqu 4f fst .47 h Sep 9 Aqu 4f fst .48⅗ b

Turn for Home
Ch. c (1963–Ky), by Turn-to—Her Honor, by Count Fleet — **107 10**
R. Lehman J. P. Conway (R. Lehman)
1967 1 0 0 0 ——
1966 11 3 2 2 $20,610

1Jly 67–6Aqu gd 6f .22⅗ .45⅘1.11⅕ Allowance 3 3 3¾ 55 58½ 66¾ HWoodhouse 115 18.40 80–19 Full Of Fun 1191 Kilmoray 108nk Flag Raiser 1243½ Fell back 6
26Sep66–8Aqu fst 1 .45⅕1.10⅕1.36 Allowance 1 3 716 819 Eased up LLoughry 115 11.40 —— Ring Twice 1183½ Understanding 111h Chinatowner 1202½ Far back 8
12Aug66–7Sar gd 1 .46 1.11 1.37 JimDandy 7 2 31½ 44½ 69 68¼ WBlum 114 11.80 81–16 Indulto 1192½ Imam 114½ Federalist Boy 1143½ Forced wide turn 7
23Jly 66–8Mth fst 1 1/16 .46⅘1.10⅘1.44⅖ Choice 9 4 32 33½ 35½ 3nk LLoughry 111 13.10 83–17 Tequillo 111no Impressive 122nk Turn for Home 111h Game try 10
16Jly 66–5Mth fst 1 70 .46⅗1.11⅗1.43 Allowance 5 1 2h 2h 32 33¾ JVelasquez 122 *1.20 82–18 Trish M. 1133½ War Horn 119nk Turn for Home 1221½ Bore out 7
9Jly 66–6Aqu fst 7f .22⅖ .45 1.24 Allowance 1 3 22 2½ 1h 1¾ WBlum 112 *1.30 86–19 Turn for Home 112¾ Valiant Bull 1175 New Outlook 1121½ Driving 7
23Mar66–9GP fst 1 1/16 .46⅗1.11⅕1.43⅕ F'tnYouth 5 3 44 57½11201125 LAdams b 114 25.90 71–18 Kauai King 1131¾ Amberoid 112nk Abe's Hope 116nk Close quarters 12
3Mar66–ExHia fst 1⅛ .46⅖1.10⅘1.50 Flamingo 5 1 11 2h 41½ 68½ LLoughry 122 —— 76–18 Buckpasser 122no Abe's Hope 1222¼ Blue Skyer 1222½ Used up 9
3Mar66—The Flamingo Stakes run between 7th and 8th races—No wagering.
18Feb66–9Hia fst 1⅛ .46⅕1.10⅖1.50⅗ Allowance 4 1 14 15 15 15 LLoughry5 110 *2.00 82–19 Turn for Home 1105 Clembo 115¾ Good Land 1122½ Easy score 9
LATEST WORKOUTS Sep 28 Bel 3f fst .36 b Sep 24 Bel 1m fst 1.45 b Sep 20 Bel 7f fst 1.29⅘ h Sep 15 Bel 3f fst .35 h

Brooklyn Bridge B. h (1962), by Swaps—Conniver, by Discovery
Templeton Stable J. C. Sweeney (W. Guest) **117** 1967 3 0 1 0 $3,150 / 1966 19 5 1 4 $39,104
5Aug67-7Sar fst 6f .22⅕ .45 1.09⅘ Allowance 2 3 41½ 45½ 76½ 89¼ ECardone 115 6.00 89-6 Full Of Fun 1141 Demon Dyno 1152½ John Jacob 116h Fell back 9
18Jly 67-7Aqu fst 6f .22⅖ .45⅗1.09⅘ Handicap 3 4 42½ 42 44½ 47½ RTurcotte 114 3.70 86-16 Flag Raiser 1215 Flying Tackle 1081½ Rego 1111 No late rally 6
20May67-6Aqu fst 6f .22⅕ .45⅔1.09⅗ Allowance 1 3 1½ 11 21½ 21½ RTurcotte 115 8.40 93-14 Aforethought 1151½ Brooklyn Bridge 1153 Voyager 105no Drifted out 8
3Dec66-7Aqu fst 1 .45⅗1.10⅗1.36 StuyvsntH 9 5 55½ 96½1014 1013 RTurcotte 115 14.40 75-20 Understanding 110no Mr. Right 116h Advocator 1143 Tired 12
31Oct66-7Aqu fst 6f .22⅕ .44⅘1.09⅘ SportPgeH 3 5 42½ 76½ 78 67 EFires 118 9.70 87-17 Impressive 126½ Vitencamps 1102 Hoist Bar 1131½ Weakened 8
15Oct66-6Aqu fst 6f .22⅗ .45⅖1.09⅘ Allowance 4 2 21½ 2½ 1h 1¾ BBaeza 124 3.60 94-14 Brooklyn Bridge 124¾ Odd Dancer 111½ Alexville 1181½ Driving 6
8Oct66-8Atl fst 7f .21⅗ .44⅕1.22 LongportH 1 8 41½ 65½ 85½ 812 BPhelps 117 7.20 81-23 Davis II 1174 Time Tested 1243½ Hoist Bar 1172½ Had poor start 8
29Aug66-7Aqu fst 6f .22⅖ .44⅘1.10⅖ FallHiWtH 8 6 64½ 56½ 46½ 23 RTurcotte 128 9.40 88-13 Impressive 1323 Brooklyn Bridge 128no Hoist Bar 1232½ Drifted out 10
20Aug66-7Sar fst 6f .22⅘ .45⅗1.10 Allowance 5 2 1h 1h 1h 1nk RTurcotte 117 4.60 98-10 Brooklyn Bridge 117nk Ornamento 112¾ Seaman 1248 Stiff drive 8
13Aug66-7Sar fst 6f .22⅗ .45⅗1.09⅘ Allowance 8 2 21½ 32 31½ 33½ RTurcotte 119 7.90 96-9 Ornamento 1102½ Seaman 121¾ Brooklyn Bridge 1192 Checked 10
LATEST WORKOUTS Sep 27 Bel 3f fst .36 h Sep 23 Bel 5f fst 1.01 h Sep 20 Bel 5f fst 1.01⅗ h Sep 14 Bel 4f fst .48⅘ h

Wyoming Wildcat * Ch. c (1963–Ky), by Gallant Man—Portage, by War Admiral
J. M. Roebling J. A. Nerud (Harbourton Stud, Inc.) **119** 1967 9 2 1 2 $18,615 / 1966 16 4 4 2 $39,624
28Aug67-7Aqu gd 6f .22⅗ .46⅘1.12⅗ FallHiwtH 3 5 89½ 76 87 86¾ HGustines 130 12.80 73-25 Indulto 132nk Full Of Fun 1341 Flag Raiser 1372½ Taken up sharply 8
23Aug67-6Sar fst 7f .22⅗ .45⅖1.22⅗ Allowance 6 3 23 32 31½ 34 BBaeza 115 *2.10 93-11 Sun Gala 110h Spring Double 1244 Wyoming Wildcat 1152 Bore out 8
10Jun67-6Aqu fst 7f .22⅗ .44⅘1.21⅕ Allowance 4 3 31½ 34 23 25 BBaeza 115 *1.30 90-12 d-Fl'gRais'r1245 Wyom'gWildc't115nk King'sJ't1151¾ Checked 6
10Jun67—Placed first through disqualification.
13May67-6Aqu fst 6f .22 .44⅘1.10⅖ Allowance 3 4 43½ 43½ 34 2½ BBaeza 117 3.30 90-16 Beaupy 121½ Wyoming Wildcat 117no Michigan Avenue 117¾ Rallied 7
22Apr67-6Aqu fst 6f .22⅕ .45⅗1.10⅗ Allowance 5 6 67½ 64 52 31½ WShoemaker 119 3.20 88-16 It's Blitz 119no Ring Twice 1211½ Wyoming Wildcat 1195 Rallied 6
25Mar67-6Aqu my 6f .22⅘ .47⅕1.12⅗ Paumon'kH 3 4 54½ 66½ 55 45½ WShoemaker 111 5.30 75-35 Our Michael 1163½ Beaupy 113nk Advocator 1171½ No rally 6
18Feb67-9Hia fst 6f .21⅗ .44⅕1.09⅗ Allowance 4 8 69½ 611 612 56 MYcaza 116 7.50 90-9 Impressive 1241½ Fleet Admiral 112¾ Country Friend 113½ No exc. 8
25Jan67-8Hia fst 7f .22⅕ .44⅗1.23⅕ RoyalPlmH 7 7 79¾ 89 811 88¼ DHidalgo 113 14.90e 85-15 Bold and Brave 116nk Bold Tactics 1141 Quinta 116no No factor 10
17Jan67-7Hia gd 6f .22⅖ .45⅘1.10⅖ Allowance 1 8 74 42½ 12 15 DHidalgo3 110 5.50 92-13 Wyoming Wildcat 1105 Jesterson 113no Wesley Ashcraft 113¾ Easily 11
LATEST WORKOUTS Sep 29 Bel tr.t. 3f sly .37⅖ b Sep 26 Bel 5f fst 1.01⅘ h Sep 16 Bel tr.t. 5f fst 1.01⅗ h Sep 11 Bel 4f fst .48⅖ b

Full of Fun × Ch. g (1962), by Jester—Mohduma, by Mahmoud
G. D. Widener S. E. Veitch (Erdenheim Farms Co.) **121** 1967 6 2 1 0 $26,282 / 1966 9 4 3 0 $19,525
9Sep67-8Aqu hd 1 1/16 Ⓣ 1.41⅗ Allowance 1 4 42½ 42 54 65¾ LGilligan 116 7.10 92-3 Spoon Bait 120no Gary G. 123nk Kentucky Kin 1163½ Speed, tired 8
28Aug67-7Aqu gd 6f .22⅗ .46⅘1.12⅗ FallHiwtH 2 2 23 21 11 2nk LGilligan 134 6.90 80-25 Indulto 132nk Full Of Fun 1341 Flag Raiser 1372½ Held on gamely 8
5Aug67-7Sar fst 6f .22⅕ .45 1.09⅘ Allowance 5 7 63 55½ 31 11 ALoguercio7 114 6.10 99-6 Full Of Fun 1141 Demon Dyno 1152½ John Jacob 116h Drew out 9
28Jly 67-6Aqu sf 1 1/16 Ⓣ 1.44 Allowance 4 1 1½ 1½ 42 610 JLRotz 118 2.90 76-18 Flag 1163½ Understanding 116no Forcejo 1161 Gave way badly 6
12Jly 67-8Mth fst 6f .21⅘ .44⅗1.10⅕ RumsonH 5 12 63 64½ 56 44 LGilligan 118 12.40 87-17 In Reality 1173½ Country Friend 118½ Quinta 118no Fair try 13
1Jly 67-6Aqu gd 6f .22⅗ .45⅘1.11⅕ Allowance 5 1 2nk 1h 11½ 11 JLRotz 119 6.00 78-19 Full Of Fun 1191 Kilmoray 108nk Flag Raiser 1243½ Hard drive 6
26Nov66-6Aqu gd 6f .22⅗ .45⅘1.10⅗ Allowance 2 1 25 26 24 1½ LGilligan 117 10.60 90-20 Full of Fun 117½ Taipan 1172 Aforethought 1153 Driving 6
19Oct66-5Kee my 7f .23 .45⅖1.23⅖ Allowance 6 3 32 32 1h 1nk KKnapp 116 2.60 91-19 Full of Fun 116nk Grand Central 1133½ Great Flame 1061½ Driving 6
22Sep66-7Aqu gd 6f .22⅖ .45⅗1.10⅖ Allowance 4 5 42½ 32½ 26 27 WBlum 117 3.80 84-23 Irish Ruler 1177 Full of Fun 1172½ Overflight 117½ Second best 7
LATEST WORKOUTS Sep 29 Bel 3f sly .39 b Sep 25 Bel 5f fst 1.00⅖ h Sep 21 Bel 3f fst .36⅗ b Sep 18 Bel 5f fst 1.01 h

Mr. Washington Dk. b. or br. c (1964–Ky), by Swoon's Son—Bent Twig, by Nasrullah
Pin Oak Stable E. Holton (Pin Oak Stud, Inc.) **120** 1967 6 5 1 0 $35,305 / 1966 0 M 0 0 —
11Sep67-6Aqu fst 6f .22⅖ .45 1.10⅖ Allowance 5 1 13 14 16 14 JLRotz 120 *0.60 91-21 Mr.Washington 1204 FirstAndFinest 1174 DemonDyno 115½ Easily 8
4Sep67-6Aqu fst 6f .22 .45 1.09⅗ Allowance 6 1 13 12 11½ 2½ HWoodhouse 120 *1.60 94-14 Jim J. 115½ Mr. Washington 1205 Successor 11310 Best of rest 6
4Jly 67-6Aqu fst 6f .21⅘ .44⅗1.10⅕ Allowance 1 2 13 14 14 1½ HWoodhouse 117 *0.30 92-17 Mr. Washington 117½ Jim J. 1123 d-Wallofroses 1144 Hard urged 7
22Jun67-5Aqu fst 6f .22 .44⅗1.10⅘ Allowance 4 2 12 13 14 13½ HWoodhouse 115 *0.30 89-17 Mr.Washington1153½ FirstAndFinest115no DeySovereign1241 Easily 6
14Jun67-6Aqu fst 6f .21⅗ .44⅗1.09⅘ Allowance 6 1 11 11½ 12 12½ RTurcotte 115 *1.10 94-14 Mr. Washington 1152½ Hail To Peace 1105 Yarak 1131 Easily 11
26Apr67-1Aqu fst 6f .22⅕ .45⅗1.10⅘ Md Sp Wt 11 1 11 12 16 17 HWoodhouse 122 5.20 89-17 Mr. Washington 1227 Minnesota Mac 122nk Iced Coffee 1222½ Easily 14
LATEST WORKOUTS Sep 27 Bel 4f fs .46⅖ h Sep 21 Bel 5f fst 1.00 b Aug 31 Bel 5f fst .57⅗ hg Aug 25 Bel 4f sl .48⅕ h

Impressive Dk. b. or br. c (1963–Ky), by Court Martial—High Voltage, by Ambiorix
Little M Farm W. A. Kelley (O. Phipps–Wheatley Stable) **119** 1967 10 1 1 3 $24,810 / 1966 18 8 4 0 $176,300
16Sep67-6Aqu fst 6f .22⅘ .46 1.10⅖ Allowance 3 3 31½ 33 41¾ 34 RTurcotte b 115 *1.30 87-16 Successor 1133 Golden Buttons 1191 Impressive 115h No excuse 8
12Jly 67-8Mth fst 6f .21⅘ .44⅗1.10⅕ RumsonH 3 2 21 31½ 32½105¼ KKnapp b 123 2.60 86-17 In Reality 1173½ Country Friend 118½ Quinta 118no Weakened 13
3Jun67-7Aqu fst 6f .22⅗ .45⅗1.09⅘ Allowance 5 1 2h 2½ 2½ 2no RTurcotte b 124 *1.10 94-15 Buz On 115no Impressive 124½ Aforethought 1192 Brushed in drive 9
30May67-7Aqu fst 1 .45⅘1.10 1.34⅗ Metrop'nH 4 1 1½ 11½ 11 35¾ RTurcotte b 113 15.40 89-13 Buckpasser 1301½ Yonder 1084½ Impressive 1131 Used in pace 6
17May67-7Aqu fst 7f .22⅕ .44⅕1.22⅕ RosebenH 6 1 2½ 1h 2½ 33¼ RTurcotte b 121 3.20 92-16 Indulto 113¾ Our Michael 1192½ Impressive 121no Drifted out 7
22Apr67-8GS fst 6f .21⅘ .45 1.10⅖ ChryHillH 8 6 43 3nk 3½ 53 RTurcotte b 124 3.10 89-20 Our Michael 118no Can He Run 1121¾ Irongate 1111 Lacked rally 8
12Apr67-7Aqu fst 6f .22⅗ .45⅘1.10⅕ TobogganH 1 1 1½ 1h 1h 44 RTurcotte b 126 *2.60 88-21 Advocator 1182½ Bold And Brave 117no Beaupy 1121½ Faltered str. 9
11Mar67-8Pim gd 6f .22⅘ .46⅕1.11⅕ Old Line H 1 3 1h 3½ 33½ 67¾ RTurcotte b 126 *0.70 86-14 Sub Call 1174½ Hansom Harve 120no FaultlessLight1132½ Stopped 7
18Feb67-9Hia fst 6f .21⅗ .44⅕1.09⅗ Allowance 8 1 1h 1h 12 11½ KKnapp b 124 2.30 96-9 Impressive 1241½ Fleet Admiral 112¾ Country Friend 113½ Driving 8
25Jan67-8Hia fst 7f .22⅕ .44⅗1.23⅕ RoyalPlmH 2 3 1h 32½1021 1027 RTurcotte b 126 4.30 56-15 Bold and Brave 116nk Bold Tactics 1141 Quinta 116no Tired 10
LATEST WORKOUTS Sep 25 Aqu 6f fst 1.13⅘ h Sep 21 Aqu 4f fst .51 b Sep 15 Aqu 3f fst .34⅘ h Sep 11 Aqu 7f fst 1.28⅗ h

Let us see if we can eliminate any on grounds of form, class, or the distance factor.

The first to go is Brunch, a sensational sprinter last spring, but idle since July. Workouts might prepare a Brunch to beat a softer field, but he needs racing sharpness for the animals in this race.

The same goes for Bold Hour, a stakes winner with good early speed. The colt's layoff of more than a month is a bad rap.

It's Blitz also goes out, having run too slowly in its last two races. Speed is essential for today's race.

Golden Joey is scratched. Turn for Home, whose only race in the last year occurred almost two months ago, is obviously not ready. Brooklyn Bridge is eliminated on grounds of idleness since early August. Wyoming Wildcat also lacks recent action. Impressive is scratched.

The contenders are Full of Fun (which runs as an entry with Bold Hour) and Mr. Washington. Full of Fun is a pretty nice sprinter, but that ninety-nine speed rating at Saratoga on August 5 was not representative. The Saratoga track was extraordinarily fast during 1967, and records were falling like ten-pins. A more typical sample of Full of Fun's talent was its race on a slightly off track last November 26.

Which means that Mr. Washington is as close to a sure thing you will find all year. This colt is one of the fastest animals in the world. While he tends to tire in the stretch and can be beaten by a fast finisher like the good Jim J., he figures to have everything his own way here. None of his rivals will be within hailing distance after half a mile.

The Running of the Race

MR. WASHINGTON was an overlay at 4–5 and won as Johnny Rotz pleased, leading from wire to wire.

FIFTH RACE
Aqu - 32430
September 30, 1967

6 FURLONGS. (Near Man, July 17, 1963, 1.08⅗, 3, 112.)
Allowances. Purse $15,000. 3-year-olds and upward listed in the Classified Division which have not won two races since July 29. Weights, 3-year-olds, 120 lbs., older 124 lbs. Non-winners of three races of $3,900 since Mar. 11 allowed, 3 lbs., of two races of $4,875 since then, 5 lbs., of such a race in 1967, 7 lbs. (Maiden, claiming, optional and starter races not considered.)
Value to winner $9,750, second $3,000, third $1,500, fourth $750. Mutuel pool $590,055.

Index	Horse	Eqt A Wt	PP St	¼	½	Str	Fin	Jockey	Owner	Odds $1
32278Aqu¹	Mr. Washington	3 120	8 1	1²	1²	1³	1³½	J L Rotz	Pin Oak Stable	.80
31988Sar⁴	Bold Hour	3 117	2 5	5³	5³	4½	2ʰ	W Shoemak'r	G D Widener	b--1.80
32271Aqu⁶	Full Of Fun	5 121	7 4	3ʰ	2ʰ	2ʰ	3¹	L Gilligan	G D Widener	b--1.80
31907Aqu⁸	Wyom'g Wildcat	4 119	6 7	7½	6¹	5⁴	4¾	D Hidalgo	J M Roebling	a--3.70
31687Aqu¹	Brunch	3 117	1 2	4²	3ʰ	3²	5⁷	B Baeza	Tartan Stable	a--3.70
31943Sar⁸	Brooklyn Bridge	5 117	5 6	6¹½	7⁴	7⁵	6¹	E Cardone	Templeton Stable	17.50
32323Aqu⁷	It's Blitz	b 4 119	3 3	2¹	4²	6³	7⁶	J Cruguet	B Lobel	48.50
31606Aqu⁶	Turn For Home	4 117	4 8	8	8	8	8	J Serrano†	R Lehman	66.60

a-Coupled—Wyoming Wildcat and Brunch, b-Bold Hour and Full of Fun.
†Ten pounds apprentice allowance waived.

Time .22, .45, 1.10⅕ (with wind in backstretch). Track fast.

$2 Mutuel Prices:

7-MR. WASHINGTON	3.60	2.40	2.40
2-BOLD HOUR (b-entry)		2.40	2.80
2-FULL OF FUN (b-entry)		2.40	2.80

Dk. b. or br. c, by Swoon's Son—Bent Twig, by Nasrullah. Trainer E. Holton. Bred by Pin Oak Stud, Inc. (Ky.).

IN GATE AT 3.44. OFF AT 3.44½ EASTERN DAYLIGHT TIME. Start good. Won easily.

MR. WASHINGTON, away alertly, saved ground and, establishing a good lead near midstretch, won with speed in reserve. BOLD HOUR raced evenly for a half mile and finished determinedly. FULL OF FUN had no mishap in a good effort. WYOMING WILDCAT lacked early foot. BRUNCH tired during the final furlong. BROOKLYN BRIDGE tired and raced wide entering the stretch. IT'S BLITZ had early speed but failed to stay. TURN FOR HOME, checked when caught between horses after the start, failed to recover.

Scratched—32323Aqu³ Impressive, 32385Atl² Golden Joey.

THE SIXTH RACE

HERE'S A RACE for fillies and mares on the grass. The $15,000 purse should attract some truly decent competition. By and large, our job is to find the classiest entrant. If it is in good condition, has already demonstrated its ability to run on sod, and is comfortably weighted, a bet will be in order.

6th Race Aqueduct

TURF COURSE
1 1-16 MILES
AQUEDUCT
Start Finish

1 1-16 MILES (Turf) (Shore, September 2, 1967, 1.40⅗, 3, 115.)
Allowances. Purse $15,000. Fillies and mares. 3-year-olds and upward listed in the Classified Division which have not won two races at a mile or over since May 31. Weights, 3-year-olds, 118 lbs., older 123 lbs. Non-winners of two races of $3,575 at a mile or over since April 20 allowed 3 lbs., of such a race of $4,875 since then, 5 lbs., of such a race of $3,900 since Mar. 11, 7 lbs. (Maiden, claiming, optional and starter races not considered.)

Fatal Step *
Ch. f (1963-Ky), by Flaneur II—Nature Walk, by Discovery
Mrs. G. S. Smith R. L. Dotter (Mrs. G. Smith) **116**
1967 15 2 3 4 $31,400
1966 22 3 5 5 $22.775

21Sep67-7Aqu hd 1 1/16 (T) 1.42⅘ f- Allow 4 7 65¼ 85½ 64½ 43 LAdams b 118 3.40 89- 8 Swim To Me 1161½ I'm All Ready 116no Spire 1111½ Mild late bid 9
8Sep67-7Aqu fst 7f .22⅗ .45 1.23⅗ f- Allow 1 9 917 912 45½ 3¾ LAdams b 120 8.10 87-17 Romanticism 120nk Silver True 113½ Fatal Step 1204 Rallied 9
2Sep67-6Aqu hd 1 1/16 (T) 1.40⅗ f- Allow 2 8 911 89½ 79 78¼ LAdams b 116 4.50 95— Shore 116½ Just Kidding 111¾ Mount Regina 120½ Never close 9
24Aug67-7Sar fm 1 1/16 (T) 1.41⅗ f- Allow 3 5 48½ 36½ 1h 2h LAdams b 116 5.20 92- 8 Hail The Queen 116h Fatal Step 1162 Swim To Me 116h Sharp 8
7Aug67-6Sar fst 1 .46 1.10⅗1.36⅖ f- Allow 1 8 813 89 86¾ 57¼ LAdams b 120 15.30 85-15 Reluctant Pearl 1163 Lady Pitt 1143 Belle De Nuit 120nk No threat 9
20Jly 67-7Aqu fst 7f .22⅗ .45⅖1.23⅗ f- Allow 4 8 812 89 73 11 LAdams b 118 6.30 88-15 Fatal Step 1181 Lady Dulcinea 114nk Boiseana 114½ Drew clear 8
10Jly 67-7Aqu fm 1 1/16 (T) 1.43⅘ f- Allow 1 7 714 711 55½ 31¼ LAdams b 118 4.80 86-13 Encanta 116½ Bubbles O'Tudor 118¾ Fatal Step 118½ Closed fast 7
22Jun67-7Aqu fst 7f .22⅗ .45 1.23⅘ f- Allow 1 7 715 716 77½ 56 LAdams b 116 3.80 81-17 Julie Potatoes 1162 Kerensa 1161½ Swift Lady 1161 No threat 7
13Jun67-7Aqu fst 7f .22⅘ .45⅖1.22⅘ f-H'dicap 1 6 611 610 53 31 LAdams b 113 8.10 91-14 Nature 117½ Cestrum 115½ Fatal Step 1133 Finished willingly 6
LATEST WORKOUTS Sep 18 Bel t.c. 5f fm 1.03⅖ b Sep 15 Bel 4f fst .52⅖ b Sep 7 Bel 3f fst .39 b Aug 31 Bel 4f fst .51 b

*Flor del Viento *
Dk. b. or br. m (1962), by Gulf Stream—Flight Plan, by Airborne
S. J. Lefrak J. R. Hastie (Haras Argentino) (Arg.) **116**
1967 13 1 1 1 $5,220
1966 7 2 0 0 $4,491

12Sep67-5Aqu fst 7f .23⅕ .47⅕1.25 f- 15000 2 6 42¼ 31½ 76½ 96¼ EBelmonte b 118 22.70 75-20 Needles Sword 114nk Unfair 114½ Air Whirl 1162½ Fell back 9
17Aug67-7Sar hd 1 1/16 (T) 1.41⅖ f- Allow 2 3 33½ 75 87¼ 814 ADespirito b 116 53.00 79- 7 Politely 120h Mount Regina 1202½ Aunt Tilt 1161 Used early 8
8Aug67-8Sar fm 1⅛ (T) 1.48⅘ Cl c-20000 10 4 41½ 42 41½1010 FToro b 113 10.40 79-11 Hardihood 1071½ Mostar 114no You're Tops 1161 Stopped 12
1Aug67-9Sar sly 1 .46⅘1.12⅗1.39⅗ Clm 23000 7 6 716 719 716 630 FToro b 112 6.00 46-15 Needles' Count 1143½ Sky Count 1071 Popsie Doodle 1065 No speed 7
17Jly 67-7Aqu sf 1⅛ (T) 1.51⅘ f- Allow 4 3 3½ 3½ 31 64¾ MYcaza b 115 10.70 71-24 Prides Profile 120½ Forty Merry's 1091 Shore 109½ Bid, tired 6
10Jly 67-7Del sf 1 (T) 1.41⅖ Clm 20000 2 4 31½ 24 1h 11¼ FToro b 112 *2.50 68-31 Flor Del Viento 1121¼ Random Shot 1189 Ky. Burgoo 1123½ Driving 7
23Jun67-6Del sf 1 (T) 1.40⅘ f- Allow 5 4 32 4¾ 52¾ 55 FToro b 113 2.60 66-31 Aunt Tilt 118¾ Longwood Lady 118¾ Bloody Mary 110h Weakened 6
13Jun67-8Del fm 1 (T) 1.36⅗ f- Allow 6 6 53 31½ 32 31¼ FToro b 11 6.40 91- 9 Alps 1121 Evora 112nk Flor Del Viento 1123½ No apparent mishap 6
24Apr67-8GP fm 1 (T) .47 1.36⅘ f Allow 1 4 412 47 36 46½ RHernandez 112 8.90 83-14 Funny Valentine 1125 Pituca 112no Camerola 1131½ Evenly late 6
LATEST WORKOUTS Sep 28 Bel tr.t. 5f fst 1.04 b Sep 25 Bel tr.t. 3f fst .37 h Sep 21 Bel 5f fst 1.02 h Sep 18 Bel tr.t. 4f fst .50 h

Green Glade
Ch. f (1964-Va), by Correspondent—Polyanthus, by Polynesian
Rokeby Stable E. Burch (P. Mellon) **111**
1967 6 2 0 3 $17,415
1966 11 2 2 2 $11.680

14Sep67-8Aqu fst 1 .47 1.11⅘1.36⅕ f- Allow 6 4 53½ 52¾ 47½ 39½ RTurcotte 120 7.30 77-17 Sumtex 1208 Nicki Baby 1161½ Green Glade 1203 No threat 7
2Sep67-7Aqu fst 1⅛ .49 1.12⅘1.50⅖ f-GazelleH 8 8 96 74¾ 61¾ 66 RTurcotte 112 26.60 78-16 Sweet Folly 1122½ Treacherous 116¾ Swiss Cheese 115h No mishap 13
22Aug67-7Sar fst 7f .22⅘ .45⅘1.23⅕ f-H'dicap 1 5 68 64 33½ 32¼ RTurcotte 111 13.20 92-13 Triple Brook 1231½ Sumtex 111¾ Green Glade 111no Rallied 7
12Aug67-5Sar fst 7f .23⅕ .46⅕1.23⅗ f- Allow 3 3 2h 2h 2h 1h EBelmonte 115 *0.70 92-11 Green Glade 115h Gateway Clipper 1154½ Gay Gobha 11310 Driving 8
3Aug67-8Sar fst 7f .22⅖ .45⅗1.23 f-Test 3 3 35½ 33 2h 32¼ BBaeza 113 3.50 93- 7 Treacherous 1151½ Silver True 118¾ Green Glade 1131 Faltered 8
3Aug67—The Test Stakes run in two divisions, 7th and 8th races.
18Jly 67-6Aqu fst 6f .22 .45 1.10 f- Allow 11 7 42½ 33 3½ 1¾ ECardone 109 3.50 90-16 Green Glade 109¾ Kathleen Gee 1095 Sweet Laura 114nk Driving 12
22Oct66-4GS fst 6f .22⅖ .45⅗1.11⅗ f- Allow 1 8 85½ 88 68½ 45½ BBaeza b 119 *1.20 80-20 La Chunga 1161 So Refined 1123½ Best Secret 1191 No excuse 9
8Oct66-7Aqu fst 1 .45⅖1.10⅖1.37⅖ f-Frizette 1 4 53 67½ 78 611 WBlum b 119 9.60e 70-17 Regal Gleam 119h Irish County 1194½ Pepperwood 1192 Brief speed 8
28Sep66-7Aqu fst 7f .22⅕ .45⅕1.24⅖ f-Astarita 7 5 55 54½ 31½ 31¼ WBlum b 116 5.60e 83-19 Irish County 1161 Pepperwood 116nk Green Glade 1164 Game try 10
LATEST WORKOUTS Sep 27 Bel t.c. 5f fm 1.00⅕ b Sep 24 Bel 6f fst 1.16 b Sep 20 Bel t.c. 3f fm .37 b Sep 11 Bel 3f fst .36 b

*Primarosa II
Ch. m (1960), by The Rabbi—Pontevedra, by Snob
R. A. Lopez J. A. Quintero (Haras Las Ortigas)(Arg.) **120**
1967 8 2 0 0 $16,025
1966 20 2 2 5 $16,190

14Sep67-7Aqu hd 1 1/16 (T) 1.42 f- Allow 7 2 21 2½ 1½ 12 FToro 116 5.20 96- 4 Primarosa II 1162 Shore 1182 Swim To Me 118h Under brisk drive 7
8Sep67-7Aqu fst 7f .22⅖ .45 1.23⅗ f- Allow 7 5 711 711 68 44¾ FToro 116 88.10 83-17 Romanticism 120nk Silver True 113½ Fatal Step 1204 Rallied 9
8Jly 67-7Aqu fm 1 3/16 (T) 1.54⅘ f-Sh'pByH 8 4 44½ 3h 62¼ 67½ MVenezia 107 53.40 88- 4 Indian Sunlite 1183½ Mount Regina 117nk Amerivan 1191 Bid, tired 10
16Jun67-8Mth fm*1 1/16 (T) 1.47⅗ f- Allow 6 1 11½ 1h 2½ 51¾ DBrumfield 115 4.70 89-13 Camerola 112no Lucaya II 120no Margarethen 1201¼ Speed, tired 7
9Jun67-7Aqu hd 1 1/16 (T) 1.42 f- Allow 7 2 21½ 23 63½ 77¼ ACorderoJr 118 14.80 89- 4 Mount Regina 118h Kerensa 1184 d-Prides Profile 116½ Impeded 10
1Jun67-8Aqu fm 1 1/16 (T) 1.43⅕ Clm 20000 5 1 11 11 1h 11 JLRotz 115 *2.50 90-10 Primarosa II 1151 Cleareye 116nk Good Ore 111nk Under brisk drive 10
19May67-7Aqu fst 7f .22⅖ .45 1.23⅗ f- Allow 3 4 49½ 613 712 712 JLRotz 116 32.80 76-18 Fizzy 1164 Julie Potatoes 120no Southside Miss 1161½ Dull try 7
11May67-7Aqu sly 6f .22⅘ .46⅖1.12⅕ f- Allow 7 6 814 812 919 916 JCamoretti 116 65.90 66-24 Cestrum 118¾ Bubbles O'Tudor 1161½ Southside Miss 1184 No speed 9
18Aug66-7Sar fm 1 1/16 (T) 1.42 f-H'dicap 3 4 44½ 55½ 69 612 RUssery 117 12.60 83- 5 Mount Regina 1222 Grand Splendor 110nk Snow Queen 1121½ Tired 6
9Aug66-8Sar fm 1⅛ (T) 1.48 f- Allow 2 3 42½ 41½ 86¼ 89¼ MYcaza 122 7.10 84- 7 Ho Ho 115nk Indian Sunlite 112½ Mount Regina 1191½ Speed, tired 9
LATEST WORKOUTS Sep 23 Bel tr.t. 7f fst 1.31⅗ h Sep 1 Bel tr.t. 5f fst 1.05 b

Swim to Me
B. m (1962), by King of the Tudors—Hukilau, by Native Dancer
Gedney Farm R. Sechrest (C. V. Whitney) **12C**
1967 20 5 0 4 $50.625
1966 13 1 1 2 $7,500

21Sep67-7Aqu hd 1 1/16 (T) 1.42⅘ f- Allow 2 9 75¼ 53 41 11½ RUssery b 116 3.60 92- 8 Swim To Me 1161½ I'm All Ready 116no Spire 1111½ Going away 9
14Sep67-7Aqu hd 1 1/16 (T) 1.42 f- Allow 2 7 66½ 55 43½ 34 RUssery b 118 2.50 82- 4 Primarosa II 1162 Shore 1182 Swim To Me 118h Mild late bid 7
6Sep67-7Aqu fst 1 .45⅗1.10 1.35⅗ f-MaskteH 2 8 812 812 915 918 HGustines b 109 19.00 72-18 Politely 115¾ Triple Brook 1173 Lady Pitt 115nk No speed 9
24Aug67-7Sar fm 1 1/16 (T) 1.41⅗ f- Allow 7 6 610 48 41¼ 32 EBelmonte b 116 3.70 90- 8 Hail The Queen 116h Fatal Step 1162 Swim To Me 116h In close 8
18Aug67-7Sar fst 6f .22⅖ .45⅖1.11⅕ f- Allow 4 9 911 812 26 11½ EBelmonte b 123 2.90 92-12 Swim To Me 1231½ Fennel 1184½ Tagend 1161 Won going away 9
13Jun67-7Aqu fst 7f .22⅘ .45⅖1.22⅘ f-H'dicap 6 1 2½ 2h 31 54½ HWoodhouse b 115 6.20 87-14 Nature 117½ Cestrum 115½ Fatal Step 1133 Well placed, tired 6
5Jun67-7Aqu fst 6f .22⅕ .44⅘1.09⅗ f-L.BelleH 4 5 77 76 78½ 76 HWoodhouse b 111 16.60 89-15 Triple Brook 115h Lady Swaps 1151 Mac's Sparkler 1222½ Trailed 7
29May67-6Aqu fst 6f .22⅘ .46⅖1.10⅘ f-H'dicap 1 6 69 63½ 36 34 JRuane b 122 7.30 85-18 Nature 1141 Just Kidding 1173 Swim To Me 1222 Stride late 6
20May67-7Aqu fst 1⅛ .48 1.11⅘1.49⅗ f-TopFl'tH 5 6 53 42½ 31½ 45½ JRuane b 110 34.60 82-14 Straight Deal 126¾ Mac's Sparkler 1224 Malhoa 112¾ Weakened 7
12May67-7Aqu sl 1 .47⅕1.12⅕1.37⅕ f-H'dicap 2 3 1½ 11 41½ 47¾ BBaeza b 113 5.20 75-26 StraightDeal126¾ Mac'sSparkler1234 ShimmeringGold1133 Weak'd 8
LATEST WORKCUTS Sep 2 Bel tr.t. 5f fst 1.04 b Aug 14 Sar tr.t. 5f fst 1.03 b Aug 8 Sar tr.t. 6f fst 1.15 h

Aunt Tilt * B. f (1963-Ky), by Tulyar—Kerala, by My Babu
Edith W. Bancroft F. Y. Whiteley, Jr. (Mrs. T. Bancroft) **123** 1967 9 2 0 2 $10,125 / 1966 17 2 3 6 $21,962
15Sep67-7Aqu fst 6f .23⅖ .47⅕1.11⅘ f- Allow 8 9 107¾ 87¼ 55½ 53¼ RTurcotte 114 6.60e 81-19 Regal Gleam 1111½ Cestrum 120no Ameri Belle 114nk Closed well 10
21Aug67-7Sar gd 1⅛.47⅘1.12⅗1.49⅗ f-DianaH ← 6 63½ 98¼ 913 820 RTurcotte 109 47.90 76-11 Prides Profile 114nk Straight Deal 1273 Malhoa 1112½ Slow start 9
17Aug67-7Sar hd 1 1/16 Ⓣ 1.41⅖ f- Allow 6 8 66½ 53½ 42¼ 32½ RTurcotte 116 22.50 90- 7 Politely 120h Mount Regina 1202½ Aunt Tilt 1161 Went well 8
12Jly 67-6Del gd 170.47⅖1.12⅗1.43 f- Allow 1 6 65 34½ 34½ 36¼ FLovato 115 7.80 79-18 Swinging Mood 1181¼ Cassino Vail 1085 Aunt Tilt 115½ Wide turn 7
1Jly 67-8Mth fst 1 1/16.47⅕1.11⅘1.44⅘ f-M.PtchrH 6 4 45¼ 52¼ 32 610 ENelson 112 53.40 71-17 Politely 1152¾ Straight Deal 1261 Indian Sunlite 1173½ Tired 7
23Jun67-6Del sf 1 Ⓣ 1.40⅘ f- Allow 4 6 63½ 51¾ 41¼ 1¾ FLovato 118 *2.50 71-31 Aunt Tilt 118¾ Longwood Lady 118¾ Bloody Mary 110h Poor start 6
9Jun67-8Mth fm*1 1/16 Ⓣ 1.47⅗ f- Allow 8 10 107 911 61¼ 51½ ENelson 118 4.20 89- 8 Star Garter 116h Panfilia 113¾ Devil's Candy 112h Late foot 10
29May67-8Del sf 1 Ⓣ 1.41 f- Allow 1 6 58 33 22½ 11¼ ENelson 112 2.50 70-30 Aunt Tilt 1121¼ Longwood Lady 1182½ Waterloo Bridge 118¾ Driving 6
12May67-8Pim fst 6f .23⅖ .47⅗1.13 f- Allow 1 7 66½ 52¾ 41¾ 41 NShuk 117 5.60 84-15 Waterloo Bridge 119h Misty's Baby 122h Penny Power 119¾ In close 7
LATEST WORKOUTS Sep 28 Bel 4f fst .50 b Sep 21 Bel 5f fst 1.03 b Sep 12 Bel 4f fst .49 b Sep 8 Bel tr.t. 4f fst .50 b

Recall * B. f (1964-Ky), by Renegad—Brookwood, by Brookfield
E. J. Wallis E. F. Schoenborn (S. B. Wilson) **111** 1967 14 5 0 0 $37,190 / 1966 11 4 1 1 $12,350
13Sep67-9Atl fm*1 1/16 Ⓣ 1.47 f- Allow 7 6 69 56 43½ 42½ RStovall 112 10.50 86-10 Margarethen 120h Alps 116½ Teetotaler 1182 Late foot 7
26Aug67-8Atl sf 1 1/16 Ⓣ 1.49⅘ f-Pag'ntH 5 5 45½ 52½ 69 717 RStovall 118 3.50 41-42 Farest Nan 1142¼ Miss Dilly Dally 1127 Sports Event 1101½ Tired 8
26Aug67—The Pageant Handicap run in two divisions—6th and 8th races.
18Aug67-8Atl fm*1 Ⓣ 1.39⅗ f- Allow 2 8 73¾ 42 4¾ 1¾ RStovall 114 10.30 90- 9 Recall 114¾ Lagoon Girl 116½ Devotedly 1121½ Under hard drive 10
1Aug67-8Mth fst 6f .22⅖ .45⅖1.09⅗ f- Allow 5 6 67 68 612 613 RStovall 121 4.70 81-16 Lagoon Girl 1144 T. V.'s Princess 1214 Mopolina 117½ Trailed 6
10Jun67-7Aqu fst 1⅛.47 1.10⅘1.49⅗ f-M.Goose 3 6 611 712 510 611 RStovall 121 93.30 77-12 Furl Sail 1213 Quillo Queen 121no Muse 1214½ Never a contender 11
27May67-7Aqu fst 1 .44⅖1.09⅕1.35⅗ f-Acorn 2 16 1616 1110 89 67 RStovall 121 14.00f 83-15 Furl Sail 1213 Quillo Queen 121½ Pepperwood 1213 Sluggish 17
19May67-8Pim fst 1 1/16.48 1.12⅗1.44 f-BlkEyeS. 6 9 96¼ 83¼ 77¾ 75½ RStovall 116 3.30 84-14 Farest Nan 1111 Back In Paris 111no Devotedly 1112 No mishap 10
10May67-7Aqu fst 7f .22⅖ .45⅘1.25 f- Comely 1 11 66 58½ 913 1011 RStovall 118 14.80 70-21 Gala Honors 113¾ Just Kidding 118nk Lake Chelan 1161 In close 11
26Apr67-7Aqu fst 6f .22⅕ .45⅕1.10⅗ f- Prioress 6 7 77½ 66½ 45½ 44¾ RStovall 121 6.90 85-17 Just Kidding 1214 Great Era 121½ Lake Chelan 121nk Rallied 7
LATEST WORKOUTS Sep 12 Atl 3f fst .35 h Sep 5 Atl 4f fst .48⅗ b Aug 17 Atl 3f fst .37 b Aug 13 Atl 6f fst 1.14⅗ h

Blue Thor X B. m (1960), by Blue Prince—Ambwithor, by Ambiorix
J. S. Pettibone T. H. Heard, Jr. (J. B. Randolph) **116** 1967 7 2 0 0 $11,575 / 1966 5 0 1 0 $2,000
14Sep67-7Aqu hd 1 1/16 Ⓣ 1.42 f- Allow 3 3 33 32½ 32½ 44 LGilligan b 116 10.30 92- 4 Primarosa II 1162 Shore 1182 Swim To Me 118h Well up, tired 7
2Sep67-6Aqu hd 1 1/16 Ⓣ 1.40⅗ f- Allow 7 4 44½ 55½ 67 67¾ LGilligan b 116 32.40 95— Shore 115½ Just Kidding 111¾ Mount Regina 120½ Fell back 9
29Mar67-9GP sf 1 1/16 Ⓣ 1.14 1.47 f-Suw'neeH 4 8 78¼ 811 813 514 JVasquez b 113 27.70 55-31 Cologne 1121½ Kerensa 1151 Indian Sunlite 1225 Showed nothing 8
15Mar67-8GP fm 1 Ⓣ .45⅖1.34⅗ f-OrchidH 8 5 612 413 412 49¼ WBlum b 115 13.40 92- 3 IndianSunlite117¾TurnToTalent1132½ShimmeringGold1133½ No th't 8
15Mar67—The Orchid Handicap run in two divisions, 8th and 9th races.
2Mar67-8Hia fm 1 1/16 Ⓣ 1.43 f- Allow 2 5 411 48½ 67 52 JVasquez b 121 3.70 88-11 Shimmering Gold 116no Star Garter 112nk Pollen 1121 Sore 9
16Feb67-9Hia fm*1 1/16 Ⓣ 1.45⅕ f- Allow 5 5 56 21 1h 13 JVasquez b 115 9.40 84-21 Blue Thor 1153 Blabla II 113h Lady C. C. O. 112½ Drifted out, clear 12
30Jan67-8Hia sf 1 1/16 Ⓣ 1.45⅖ f- Allow 6 6 41¼ 21½ 22 1no JVasquez b 112 7.10 78-22 Blue Thor 112no Flor Del Viento 1125 Treasure Chest 1153½ Driving 10
3Dec66-7Lrl fm 1 1/16 Ⓣ 1.45⅘ f-M.Dix'nH 8 5 84¼ 84 86 61¾ CRogers b 112 14.00 75-26 Swift Lady 111nk Teetotaler 112¾ Lady C. C. O. 109h No mishap 9
3Dec66—The Mason-Dixon Handicap, run in two divisions, 7th and 8th races.
LATEST WORKOUTS Sep 27 Aqu 6f fst 1.14 h Sep 22 Aqu 4f fst .48⅘ h Sep 21 Aqu 7f fst 1.30 b Sep 18 Aqu 5f fst 1.03⅕ b

---

Grass races are so deceptive that we had better examine each horse separately, and with great care:

Fatal Step: Has earned more than $2,000 per start this year, displaying the determination of a good horse, if not the desired blend of speed and stamina. Note that the only time Larry Adams kept her close to the early pace, the filly faded in the stretch. In the other races, he tried to save the horse for one run and invariably got to the wire too late. The July 20 victory at seven furlongs on the dirt track and the good repeat effort on September 8 should not be taken to mean that the filly prefers the shorter distance. Seven furlongs on the main course and today's mile-and-one-sixteenth on the grass are roughly equivalent tests of speed and endurance. Horses that can run on grass at all seem able to go a furlong or two further on such footing than on the dirt. Off her record, Fatal Step must be granted a chance to be in the running today, although victory would be surprising in a $15,000 race. CONTENDER.

Flor Del Viento: Poor performances in claiming company eliminate this one. NO BET.

Green Glade: Almost $3,000 per start this year, by virtue of stout performances in stakes races behind the likes of Triple Brook, Sumtex, Treacherous, and Silver True stamp Elliott Burch's filly as a classy animal. Unfortunately, this is her first effort on the turf. Would you bet on her to win, after noting her fine grass workout of three days ago? I would not, unless she had an enormous class advantage over the rest of the field. Neither would I bet against her, unless something else in the race turned out to be an established grass runner with a better record in stakes races. CONTENDER.

Primarosa II: This one likes turf, is in good form, and gives promise of climbing the class ladder. Must be considered a threat despite the weight, if only because of that last victory. CONTENDER.

Swim To Me: This mare's stakes performances have not been quite so impressive as Green Glade's, but she seems to improve by several lengths when she runs on grass. After losing to Primarosa II on September 14, she ran a real smasher on September 21. CONTENDER.

Aunt Tilt: The high weight may prevent this filly from duplicating her good August 17 performance, which found her running fairly close behind Politely and Mount Regina, either of which would be a strong favorite in today's field. NO BET.

Recall: The last two races in Atlantic City foretell trouble for this three-year-old against the older, higher-grade stock in today's field. NO BET.

Blue Thor: Tommy Heard's grass runner should be ready to run well today, if ever, after that long layoff and those two September tighteners. Off her Florida and Maryland performances, however, she just isn't good enough for this race. NO BET.

The contenders are Fatal Step, Green Glade, Primarosa II, and Swim To Me. The class edge goes to Green Glade, who has the extra advantage of Braulio Baeza and has shown that she can carry today's weight effectively against older horses of stakes calibre. Until she has actually run a race on turf, however, I would not bet on her. Being equally unwilling to bet against her, I hereby pass.

The Running of the Race

THE CROWD went to the form horse, Primarosa II, and made her a tepid 3–1 favorite. Hot tips on Blue Thor made her the second choice, with Swim To Me next.

Green Glade enjoyed the lawn. She was clearly the best animal in the race. Larry Adams made the customary late run on Fatal Step but didn't have a chance.

So I pass up another winner, after establishing that it had an excellent chance. I do this sort of thing all the time, much to the disgust of certain acquaintances who think I am part chicken.

"You," said a friend recently, "are no gambler."

I plead guilty. I do not get my jollies from gambling, but from winning. I therefore do what I can to reduce the possibility of loss to an absolute minimum. How? By betting on a horse only when it seems to me to be a genuine standout in its race.

Other experienced handicappers are less rigid. They keep an eye on the odds board. If a horse seems "probably best" in its field, even if no standout, and if its odds are high, they gamble. They believe, with reason, that the high odds more than compensate them for the relatively low percentage of winners.

I don't knock such procedures. I simply do not function that way. To me it is more fun to bet substantially on a really solid horse at modest odds than to spread the money thin in the quest for "action."

SIXTH RACE	1 1-16 MILES (Turf) (Shore, September 2, 1967, 1.40⅗, 3, 115.)

Aqu - 32431

September 30, 1967

Allowances. Purse $15,000. Fillies and mares. 3-year-olds and upward listed in the Classified Division which have not won two races at a mile or over since May 31. Weights, 3-year-olds, 118 lbs., older 123 lbs. Non-winners of two races of $3,575 at a mile or over since April 20 allowed 3 lbs., of such a race of $4,875 since then, 5 lbs., of such a race of $3,900 since Mar. 11, 7 lbs. (Maiden, claiming, optional and starter races not considered.)

Value to winner $9,750, second $3,000, third $1,500, fourth $750. Mutuel pool $605,866.

Index	Horse	Eqt A Wt	PP	St	¼	½	¾	Str	Fin	Jockey	Owner	Odds $1
32307Aqu³	Green Glade	3 112	3	2	1½	3³	1h	11	11½	B Baeza	Rokeby Stable	4.20
32360Aqu⁴	Fatal Step	b 4 116	1	1	5¹	5½	6³	5h	2¹½	L Adams	Mrs G S Smith	5.90
32318Aqu⁵	Aunt Tilt	4 123	6	8	8	8	7¹	4h	3nk	R Turcotte	Edith W Bancroft	8.70
32306Aqu¹	Primarosa II	7 120	4	3	2¹½	1h	2¹½	2h	4h	F Toro	R A Lopez	3.00
32299Atl⁴	Recall	3 111	7	6	7½	7½	5h	3¹	5¹	R Stovall	E J Wallis	16.60
32360Aqu¹	Swim To Me	b 5 120	5	7	6⁴	6³	3¹	6⁶	6⁸	R Ussery	Gedney Farm	4.00
32306Aqu⁴	Blue Thor	b 7 116	8	5	4¹	4h	8	7⁴	7⁸	J L Rotz	J S Pettibone	3.50
32286Aqu⁹	Flor D'l Viento	b 5 116	2	4	3¹	2h	4½	8	8	L Gilligan	S J Lefrak	66.40

Time 1.46⅕ (with wind in backstretch). Track soft.

$2 Mutuel Prices:

3-GREEN GLADE	10.40	6.40	4.40
1-FATAL STEP		6.80	5.00
6-AUNT TILT			7.00

Ch. f, by Correspondent—Polyanthus, by Polynesian. Trainer E. Burch. Bred by P. Mellon (Va.).

IN GATE AT 4.16. OFF AT 4.16 EASTERN DAYLIGHT TIME. Start good. Won driving.

GREEN GLADE, well placed from the start, was steadied after settling in the backstretch, regained command from PRIMAROSA II before reaching the final turn and retained a safe advantage while under brisk urging. FATAL STEP dropped back after beginning alertly, saved ground while outrun to the stretch and finished strongly. AUNT TILT lacked early foot but closed fast when kept to the inside during the drive. PRIMAROSA II prominent until near midstretch, faltered while racing in close quarters. RECALL raced wide approaching and entering the stretch. SWIM TO ME tired after making a bold challenge at the stretch turn. BLUE THOR gave way after a half mile. FLOR DEL VIENTO had early speed but failed to stay.

Overweight—Green Glade 1 pound.

THE SEVENTH RACE

THIS IS the big race of the day, the month, the year, the century. The fourteenth running of the Woodward Stakes has aroused more interest than any event since the match race between Nashua and Swaps in 1955.

The conditions are classic: weight-for-age, at a mile-and-a-quarter.

This means that a champion three-year-old—if it is a true champion—has a slight advantage in the weights. Horsemen agree that the traditional scale of weights, which imposes 126 pounds on horses aged four or more, but lets three-year-olds go with 120, is a pound or two wrong at this time of year. Good three-year-olds are now adults, or close to it, and can cover a distance of ground on equal terms with older animals of comparable quality with only a three- or four-pound weight concession.

This sounds like the splitting of hairs, and it is. But hair-splitting is the only known way to forecast the outcome of a race like the Woodward. In the absence of evidence to the contrary, one expects the leading entrants to be champions, in top condition, with champion riders. Even the slightest advantage in weights, pace or present form becomes significant. And a class advantage, if it can be recognized, becomes decisive.

As every reader of sports pages knows, the question at hand is whether the two fine three-year-olds of 1967, Damascus and Dr. Fager, can run with the mighty Buckpasser. Dr. Fager has already beaten Damascus. Damascus has beaten everything else in the age group, however. Furthermore, some folks think that Dr. Fager is not quite the wonder horse of the era and has been running against soft touches. It is possible to clarify these matters by means of handicapping. Let's run through the field and see what we can see.

7th Race Aqueduct

1¼ MILES
AQUEDUCT
Start Finish

1 1-4 MILES. (Gun Bow, July 25, 1964, 1.59⅗, 4, 122.)
Fourteenth running. THE WOODWARD. $100,000 added. Weight-for-age. 3-year-olds 120 lbs., older 126 lbs. By subscription of $100 each which shall accompany the nomination. $1,000 additional to start. The added money and all fees to be divided 65% to the winner, 20% to second, 10% to third and 5% to fourth. Starters to be named through the entry box at the usual time of closing. Trophies will be presented to the owner of the winner and the winning trainer and jockey. Closed Friday, September 1 with 18 nominations.

(7th Aqu)—Coupled—Hedevar and Damascus. Great Power and Buckpasser.

Hedevar × — **B. h (1962), by Count of Honor—Creme Brulee, by Double Jay**
Edith W. Bancroft F. Y. Whiteley, Jr (Mrs. T. Bancroft) — **126**

1967	9	3	1	3	$18,950
1966	6	3	2	0	$73,870

20Sep67–6Atl	fst 6f	.22	.44⅗	1.10	Allowance	7	3	$7^{3\frac{1}{4}}$	$6^{6\frac{1}{2}}$	3^{1}	$1^{\frac{1}{2}}$	WShoemaker	118	2.00	92–16	Hedevar $118^{\frac{1}{2}}$ Fearless Lee 118^{2} Al's Runner 112no	Bore in, lasted	8
23Jun67–8Del	gd 6f	.22	.45	1.10⅕	Allowance	6	1	1^{1}	1^{2}	1^{3}	1^{2}	TLee	122	1.80	94–17	Hedevar 122^{2} Sub Call $122^{5\frac{1}{2}}$ Lillington 116^{nk}	Easy score	6
10Jun67–8Aqu	fst 1	.45⅖	1.08⅘	1.34⅕	Allowance	6	1	1^{1}	$1^{1\frac{1}{2}}$	1^{2}	$3^{\frac{1}{2}}$	RTurcotte	116	3.60	96–12	Poker $116^{\frac{1}{2}}$ Ring Twice 118no Hedevar $116^{\frac{3}{4}}$	Faltered in drive	7
20May67–6Pim	fst 6f	.22⅗	.46	1.10⅘	Allowance	1	5	$5^{7\frac{1}{2}}$	$5^{5\frac{1}{2}}$	4^{6}	3^{4}	WShoemaker	b 117	1.70	92–11	Spring Double 119^{4} New Windsor 119no Hedevar $117^{2\frac{1}{2}}$	Rallied	6
13May67–7Pim	fst 6f	.22⅗	.45⅘	1.11⅕	Allowance	5	5	4^{4}	5^{6}	$4^{5\frac{1}{2}}$	$3^{2\frac{1}{2}}$	NShuk	119	*1.20	91–14	New Windsor 112no Mr. Judex $112^{2\frac{1}{2}}$ Hedevar $119^{\frac{1}{2}}$	Checked slightly	7
29Apr67–8GS	fst $1\frac{1}{16}$	.47	1.11⅘	1.44⅗	VlyForgeH	9	1	$1^{\frac{1}{2}}$	1^{h}	2^{1}	$6^{5\frac{1}{2}}$	NShuk	120	3.50	76–26	Stupendous 115^{h} Spring Double 113^{h} Point Du Jour 115^{nk}	Tired	10
22Apr67–8Aqu	fst 7f	.22⅖	.44⅘	1.22⅘	Allowance	6	1	$1^{1\frac{1}{2}}$	1^{3}	1^{3}	$1^{2\frac{1}{2}}$	WShoemaker	117	2.10	92–16	Hedevar $117^{2\frac{1}{2}}$ Handsome Boy 124^{h} Mr. Right $119^{\frac{3}{4}}$	Easy score	6
12Apr67–7Aqu	fst 6f	.22⅗	.45⅘	1.10⅕	TobogganH	7	4	$5^{3\frac{3}{4}}$	7^{7}	$6^{5\frac{3}{4}}$	8^{11}	WShoemaker	121	3.40	81–21	Advocator $118^{2\frac{1}{2}}$ Bold And Brave 117no Beaupy $112^{1\frac{1}{2}}$	Finished early	9
8Apr67–7Pim	fst 6f	.23⅕	.46⅖	1.11	Allowance	6	1	$5^{1\frac{3}{4}}$	$5^{1\frac{3}{4}}$	$2^{3\frac{1}{2}}$	2^{2}	NShuk	117	*1.00	93–14	Can He Run 117^{2} Hedevar 117^{2} Faultless Light $117^{1\frac{1}{2}}$	No excuse	8
30Jly 66–8AP	fst 1	.45⅖	1.09⅘	1.35⅘	ArlingtonH	7	5	2^{1}	$2^{\frac{1}{2}}$	$2^{\frac{1}{2}}$	2^{1}	WBlum	120	*1.20	86–15	Tronado 114^{1} Hedevar 120^{1} Time Tested $123^{\frac{3}{4}}$	Bore in near end	7

LATEST WORKOUTS Sep 29 Bel 3f sly .35⅗ h Sep 26 Bel 3f fst .40 b Sep 13 Bel 4f fst .48⅕ b Sep 3 Bel tr.t. 5f fst 1.05 b

Dr. Fager ⊗
B. c (1964–Fla), by Rough'n Tumble—Aspidistra, by Better Self — 120 — 1967 6 5 0 0 $363,744
Tartan Stable J. A. Nerud (Tartan Farms) — 1966 5 4 1 0 $112.338
2Sep67–8Rkm fst 1¼.46⅗1.11 1.59⅘ NHSwpClsc 1 1 11½ 2h 2h 11¼ BBaeza b 120 *0.20 115–17 Dr. Fager 1201¼ In Reality 1269 Barbs Delight 1152¾ Mild drive 5
15Jly 67–9Rkm fst 1⅛.46⅖1.10⅕1.48⅕ RkmSpec'l 5 1 16½ 13½ 13½ 14¼ BBaeza 124 *0.10 105–15 Dr. Fager 1244¼ ReasonToHail 1214¾ JackOfAllTrades 1128¼ Easily 7
24Jun67–8AP sly 1 .45 1.10⅖1.36 A.P.Classic 1 3 3nk 13 16 110 BBaeza 120 *0.40 83–25 Dr. Fager 12010 Lightning Orphan 1161¾ Diplomat Way 1187 Easily 6
30May67–7GS fst 1⅛.47 1.10⅗1.48 JrsyDerby 4 1 1½ 12 13 16½ MYcaza 126d-*0.30 97–14 d-Dr. Fager 1266½ In Reality 1268 Air Rights 12612 Crowded field 4
30May67—d-Disqualified and placed fourth.
13May67–7Aqu fst 1 .44⅕1.08 1.33⅘ Withers 8 4 21 2h 11½ 16 BBaeza 126 *0.80 99–16 Dr. Fager 1266 Tumiga 1265 Reason To Hail 1265 Easy score 8
15Apr67–7Aqu fst 1 .46⅕1.10⅖1.35⅕ Gotham 5 4 33 3nk 2h 1½ MYcaza 122 *1.30e 92–14 Dr. Fager 122½ Damascus 1225 Reason To Hail 1147 Driving 9
15Oct66–7Aqu fst 1 .44⅘1.09⅖1.35 Champagne 7 4 3½ 1h 13 21 WShoemaker 122 *1.00 92–14 Successor 1221 Dr. Fager 1224 Proviso 1224 Rank early, failed 10
5Oct66–7Aqu gd 7f .22⅘ .46 1.24⅘ Cowdin 1 10 31 32 21½ 1¾ WShoemaker 117 *0.80 82–22 Dr. Fager 117¾ In Reality 1171½ Successor 1172½ Slow start, driving 10
10Sep66–8Atl fst 7f .22⅗ .45⅖1.23⅕ Playground 3 6 1h 1½ 14 112 MYcaza 115 *0.90 87–24 Dr. Fager 11512 Glengary 1153½ Pointsman 115h Much the best 11
13Aug66–4Sar fst 6f .22⅗ .46⅖1.10⅖ Allowance 5 5 21½ 22 12 18 DHidalgo5 117 *0.90 96– 9 Dr. Fager 1178 Bandera Road 1172 Quaker City 1152 Easily 8
15Jly 66–3Aqu fst 5½f.22⅘ .46⅘1.05 Md Sp Wt 8 8 83 21 11½ 17 DHidalgo5 117 10.80 88–20 Dr. Fager 1177 Lift Off 1224 Rising Market 122½ Easily best 11
LATEST WORKOUTS Sep 28 Bel tr.t. 4f fst .47 b — Sep 22 Bel tr.t. 6f fst 1.12⅗ b — Sep 16 Bel tr.t. 5f fst .59⅘ b — Sep 11 Bel 4f fst .48⅖ b

Great Power ×
Dk. b. or br. c (1964–Ky), by Bold Ruler—High Voltage, by Ambiorix — 120 — 1967 12 4 1 0 $45,082
Wheatley Stable E. A. Neloy (Wheatley Stable–O. Phipps) — 1966 8 5 2 1 $118,765
23Sep67–6Aqu fm 1 1/16 Ⓣ 1.42⅕ Allowance 6 3 43 53¼ 811 811 BBaeza b 111 6.60 84– 5 Kentucky Kin 1161½ Flag 1161½ Pass The Brandy 112no Fell back 9
13Sep67–7Aqu fst 1 .44⅗1.08⅘1.34⅘ JeromeH 2 1 1½ 3½ 64¼ 913 WBoland b 119 17.30 81–14 High Tribute 113½ In Reality 1263½ Jim J. 1164 Early speed, tired 9
4Sep67–7Aqu fst 1⅛.48⅖1.12⅕1.48⅕ Aqueduct 2 1 12 1½ 43½ 48½ EBelmonte b 110 6.70 86–14 Damascus 1252 Ring Twice 119½ Straight Deal 1166 Used up 5
11Aug67–7Sar fst 1 .45⅖1.09⅘1.36⅕ JimDandy 11 2 2½ 2h 2h 2½ WBoland b 119 18.20 92–12 Gala Performance 114½ Great Power 1192 Tumiga 1193 Swerved str. 12
3Aug67–6Sar fst 7f .22⅗ .45 1.23 Allowance 3 4 21 2h 11½ 1¾ RUssery b 120 3.40 95– 7 Great Power 120¾ High Hat 118¾ Gala Performance 123¾ Driving 7
23Jun67–7Aqu sly 7f .22⅗ .45⅘1.24 Handicap 3 3 32 32½ 511 526 BBaeza b 124 *0.80 60–25 Air Rights 1154½ Reason To Hail 1195 Biller 1206 Lost action 5
20May67–8Pim fst 1 3/16.46⅖1.10⅘1.55⅕ Preakness 6 2 22 53½1014 1023 BBaeza b 126 16.50 74–11 Damascus 1262¼ In Reality 1264 Proud Clarion 126¾ Early speed 10
6May67–8GS sly 6f .22⅖ .45⅘1.10⅗ Del.VlyH 1 4 31 21½ 11½ 12¼ EBelmonte b 123 *1.60 91–23 Great Power 1232¼ Viking Dancer 116½ Right Card 1125 Driving 8
29Apr67–6GS fst 6f .22⅖ .46⅗1.11⅗ Allowance 3 4 31 21 2h 1nk BBaeza b 122 *0.40 86–26 Great Power 122nk Flying Tackle 122h Mr. Ed P. 1166 Hard drive 6
1Apr67–9GP fst 1⅛.48⅕1.12 1.50⅕ FlaDerby 4 2 41 53 76½ 811 BBaeza b 122 6.20 72–15 In Reality 1222½ Biller 122nk Reason To Hail 1223¼ Speed, tired 11
22Mar67–9GP fst 1 1/16.48 1.12 1.44⅖ FtnYouth 1 1 11 2h 3½ 51¾ BBaeza b 122 *0.50e 84–19 In Reality 122½ Biller 122½ Reason To Hail 119½ Speed to stretch 12
11Mar67–8GP fst 7f .22⅖ .44⅗1.22⅗ Allowance 1 5 11½ 11 14 14 HGrant b 117 *0.50 96–12 GreatPower1174 Light'gOrphan1152½ SouthernCharmer114no Easily 8
LATEST WORKOUTS Sep 20 Bel t.c. 5f fm 1.00⅗ h — Sep 11 Bel 4f fst .50⅖ b — Sep 2 Bel 4f fst .50 b — Aug 29 Aqu 6f fst 1.11⅘ h

Handsome Boy ×
Dk. b. or br. c (1963–Fla), by Beau Gar—Marullah, by Nasrullah — 126 — 1967 16 4 3 2 $260,215
Hobeau Farm H. A. Jerkens (Hobeau Farm, Inc.) — 1966 15 4 1 2 $110.517
16Sep67–9Det fst 1⅛.46⅕1.10⅖1.48⅖ Mich.1⅛H 11 2 2h 1h 1½ 2¾ EBelmonte b 123 d-0.80 98–18 Estreno II 112¾ d-Handsome Boy 1232 Tenzing II 110no Bore out 14
16Sep67–d-Disqualified and placed fourth.
19Aug67–8AP sly 1 .45⅖1.11 1.37⅗ Wash.PkH 5 3 2h 3½ 21½ 11 EBelmonte b 122 *1.70 75–21 Handsome Boy 1221 Pretense 1281½ Bold Tactics 116½ Driving 10
22Jly 67–7Aqu fst 1¼.46⅖1.09⅘2.00⅕ BrooklynH 1 1 13 13 15 18 EBelmonte b 116 5.30 97–11 Handsome Boy 1168 Buckpasser 1364½ Mr. Right 1133½ Easily 5
15Jly 67–8Mth sly 1¼.47⅘1.11⅘2.02 HaskellH 6 1 12 11½ 1½ 12½ JVasquez b 115 3.40 92–17 Handsome Boy 1152½ Amberoid 1187 Good Knight 1133½ Going away 9
4Jly 67–7Aqu fst 1¼.47⅘1.11⅘2.02⅕ SuburbanH 7 1 13 2h 22 44½ RTurcotte b 114 10.60 82–17 Buckpasser 133½ Ring Twice 1112½ Yonder 1091½ Set pace, tired 7
21Jun67–8Suf gd 1¼.46⅕1.10⅘2.02⅖ Mass.H 2 1 11½ 1h 1h 53 LMoyers b 116 *2.80e 90–19 Good Knight 1131 Understanding 114no Heronslea 1121¾ Faltered 12
12Jun67–7Aqu fst 1⅛.46⅖1.10 1.48 NassauC'ty 2 1 11½ 1½ 11½ 13½ EBelmonte b 114 4.30 96–18 Handsome Boy 1143½ Stupendous 114no Yonder 1144 Ridden out 7
7Jun67–7Aqu hd 1 3/16 Ⓣ 1.55 EdgemereH 7 1 16 14 13 32¼ ECardone b 111 7.00e 93– 5 Ginger Fizz 117nk Chinatowner 1142 Handsome Boy 111no Faltered 14
30May67–8Aqu fm 1 1/16 Ⓣ 1.41⅕ Handicap 3 2 2h 2h 21 55½ ECardone 117 5.60 94— Pass The Brandy 1121 Flag 1222½ Irish Rebellion 108½ Tired 7
20May67–6Aqu fst 6f .22⅕ .45⅖1.09⅗ Allowance 4 5 31 31 33 44½ ECardone 119 5.10 90–14 Aforethought 1151½ Brooklyn Bridge 1153 Voyager 105no Weakened 8
9May67–7Aqu gd 1⅛.47⅗1.12 1.50⅗ Allowance 3 1 1h 1h 23½ 26 EBelmonte 118 *0.60 77–25 Sette Bello 1186 Handsome Boy 1186 Bol 'N Jac 1183½ Tired 5
29Apr67–7Aqu fst 1⅛.46⅘1.11⅗1.49⅗ GreyLagH 4 2 43½ 63½ 62½ 41¼ EBelmonte 114 4.00 87–18 d-Advocator 1261¼ Moontrip 112no Amberoid 122h Lacked room 8
29Apr67—Placed third through disqualification.
22Apr67–8Aqu fst 7f .22⅗ .44⅘1.22⅘ Allowance 5 2 21½ 23 33 22½ EBelmonte 124 2.90 89–16 Hedevar 1172½ Handsome Boy 124h Mr. Right 119¾ Went well 6
15Apr67–8Aqu fst 1 .46⅖1.11⅕1.35⅘ Allowance 5 1 1½ 11½ 1h 21½ ECardone 118 *2.20 87–14 MisterWestgate1161½ HandsomeBoy1182½ SetteBello1164½ Game try 10
1Apr67–7Aqu fst 1 .46⅕1.10⅗1.35⅕ W'chester 1 3 31 52 53 66 RTurcotte b 119 5.30e 86–15 Advocator 1143 Our Michael 116no Model Fool 112½ Weakened 7
4Mar67–8Bow fst 1 1/16.47⅘1.12⅖1.43⅗ JCampb'lH 4 6 75¾ 87¾ 86¼ 67¼ LMoyers 115 5.90 88–16 Quinta 113no Model Fool 1155 Exceedingly 112nk Not a contender 9
LATEST WORKOUTS Sep 28 Bel 3f fst .36 b — Sep 25 Bel t.c. 5f fm .58⅕ h — Sep 21 Bel 1m fst 1.41 h — Sep 13 Bel t.c. 4f fm .46 h

Damascus ⊗
B. c (1964–Ky), by Sword Dancer—Kerala, by My Babu — 120 — 1967 13 10 2 1 $653,581
Edith W. Bancroft F. Y. Whiteley, Jr. (Mrs. T. Bancroft) — 1966 4 3 1 0 $25,865
4Sep67–7Aqu fst 1⅛.48⅖1.12⅕1.48⅕ Aqueduct 3 3 34 32 1h 12 WShoemaker 125 *0.30 95–14 Damascus 1252 Ring Twice 119½ Straight Deal 1166 Handily 5
19Aug67–6Sar sly 1¼.45⅘1.11 2.01⅗ Travers 4 3 3¹³ 16 110 122 WShoemaker 126 *0.20 100–10 Damascus 12622 Reason To Hail 1207 Tumiga 1175 Won eased up 4
5Aug67–8AP fst 1⅛.46 1.10⅕1.46⅘ AmercnDby 2 6 612 66¼ 14 17 WShoemaker 126 *0.80 101–16 Damascus 1267 In Reality 1203 Favorable Turn 1121½ Ridden out 7
15Jly 67–7Aqu sly 1¼.47⅗1.12 2.03 DwyerH 6 9 912 21 1h 1¾ WShoemaker 128 *0.50 83–18 Damascus 128¾ Favorable Turn 1122½ Blasting Charge 116h Driving 9
8Jly 67–8Del fst 1 1/16.47⅕1.10⅘1.42⅕ WduPontH 4 5 58 43 21 2no WShoemaker 121 *0.20 98–12 Exceedingly 113no Damascus 1214 Flag Raiser 1145 Hung 5
17Jun67–8Del fst 1⅛.47 1.11⅗1.49⅕ L.Richards 4 4 32½ 1½ 1h 13¼ RTurcotte 126 *0.10 91–13 Damascus 1263¼ Misty Cloud 1191½ Favorable Turn 1192½ Easily 6
3Jun67–8Aqu fst 1½.47 1.12⅖2.28⅘ Belmont 1 6 59½ 31 2h 12½ WShoemaker 126 *0.80 87–15 Damascus1262½ CoolReception126½ GentlemanJames1261 In hand 9
20May67–8Pim fst 1 3/16.46⅖1.10⅘1.55⅕ Preakness 2 9 811 86 13½ 12¼ WShoemaker 126 *1.80e 97–11 Damascus 1262¼ In Reality 1264 Proud Clarion 126¾ Ridden out 10
6May67–7CD fst 1¼.46⅗1.10⅘2.00⅗ Ky Derby 2 6 44 41½ 32 34 WShoemaker 126 *1.70 93– 7 Proud Clarion 1261 Barbs Delight 1263 Damascus 1261¼ Bid, hung 14
22Apr67–7Aqu fst 1⅛.46⅖1.10⅘1.49⅗ WoodMem. 4 3 45 42 11 16 WShoemaker 126 *0.70 88–16 Damascus 1266 Gala Performance 1263 Dawn Glory 1261½ Easily 9
15Apr67–7Aqu fst 1 .46⅕1.10⅖1.35⅕ Gotham 9 2 23 2h 1h 2½ WShoemaker 122 *1.30 91–14 Dr. Fager 122½ Damascus 1225 Reason To Hail 1147 Game try 9
25Mar67–7Aqu my 7f .22⅘ .46⅘1.25⅘ Bay Shore 1 4 46 45½ 22 12½ WShoemaker 115 2.40 77–35 Damascus 1152½ Disciplinarian 1171½ Nehoc's Bullet 1103 Driving 7
11Mar67–7Pim fst 6f .23⅗ .47⅖1.12⅕ Allowance 8 3 31½ 42 53¼ 1h NShuk 122 *0.60 89–16 Damascus 122h Solar Bomb 1221½ Last Cry 119½ Bumped late, up 8
LATEST WORKOUTS Sep 29 Bel 3f sly .34⅘ h — Sep 25 Bel 7f fst 1.27 b — Sep 24 Bel 3f fst .36⅕ b — Sep 20 Bel 7f fst 1.27⅖ b

Buckpasser ×
B. c (1963–Ky), by Tom Fool—Busanda, by War Admiral — 126 — 1967 5 3 1 1 $203,280
O. Phipps E. A. Neloy (O. Phipps) — 1966 14 13 1 0 $669,078
22Jly 67–7Aqu fst 1¼.46⅖1.09⅘2.00⅕ BrooklynH 3 3 33 23 25 28 BBaeza b 136 *0.70 89–11 Handsome Boy 1168 Buckpasser 1364½ Mr. Right 1133½ No excuse 5
4Jly 67–7Aqu fst 1¼.47⅘1.11⅘2.02⅕ SuburbanH 1 5 65 44 44 1½ BBaeza b 133 *0.50 87–17 Buckpasser 133½ Ring Twice 1112½ Yonder 1091½ Up final strides 7
17Jun67–7Aqu hd 1⅝ Ⓣ 2.41⅖ BwlGreenH 3 4 47½ 46½ 35 34½ BBaeza b 135 *0.40e 82–13 Poker 1121½ Assagai 1273 Buckpasser 135½ Failed to respond 5
30May67–7Aqu fst 1 .45⅘1.10 1.34⅗ Metrop'nH 5 3 32 34½ 21 11¼ BBaeza b 130 *0.30 95–13 Buckpasser 1301¼ Yonder 1084½ Impressive 1131 Scored easily 6
14Jan67–8SA fst 1⅛.46⅖1.10⅗1.48⅕ SFernando 3 3 37½ 44½ 32½ 11½ BBaeza b 124 *0.30 91–12 Buckpasser 1241½ Fleet Host 121¾ Pretense 118h With authority 6
31Dec66–6SA fst 7f .22⅗ .45⅕1.22 Malibu 2 9 76½ 54½ 21 1¾ BBaeza b 126 *0.40 93–15 Buckpasser 126¾ Drin 1201 Kings Favor 1171½ Slow start, driving 9
29Oct66–7Aqu fst 2 .49⅘1.15⅗3.26⅕ JCGoldCup 1 4 44½ 1h 11 11¾ BBaeza b 119 *0.30e 65–21 Buckpasser 1191¾ Niarkos 124½ O'Hara 1248 Drew out handily 7
19Oct66–7Aqu sly 1⅝.49⅖1.16 2.44⅕ Law. Real. 4 5 44½ 33½ 32½ 12½ BBaeza b 126 *0.20e 84–19 Buckpasser 1262½ Ring Twice 116½ Poker 11612 Was going away 5
1Oct66–7Aqu sly 1¼.47 1.11⅘2.02⅘ Woodward 4 6 64½ 31½ 1h 1¾ BBaeza b 121 *0.90e 84–24 Buckpasser 121¾ Royal Gunner 126¾ Buffle 1215 Ridden out 9
20Aug66–6Sar fst 1¼.47⅖1.11⅖2.01⅗ ...ers 6 5 512 43½ 21 1¾ BBaeza b 126 *0.30e 100–10 Buckpasser 126¾ Amberoid 1233½ Buffle 120no Under strong handl'g 6
6Aug66–8AP fst 1⅛.46⅘1.10⅗1.47 AmDerbyH 9 5 59½ 68 42 1nk BBaeza b 128 *0.60e 101– 9 Buckpasser 128nk Jolly Jet 1161 Advocator 1163 Driving 9
LATEST WORKOUTS Sep 26 Aqu 6f fst 1.11 h — Sep 21 Bel 1⅛m fst 1.49⅕ h — Sep 17 Bel 5f sly .59 h — Sep 13 Bel 1m fst 1.38⅖ b

Hedevar: This stablemate of Damascus is here to prevent Dr. Fager from stealing the race. As we all know, a front-runner like Dr. Fager enjoys an enormous advantage if nothing else in the field can run with him in the early stages. Under strong handling, the front-runner is throttled back, holding the lead with minimum exertion, while retaining fuel for the stretch battle. Hedevar used to be one of the best sprinters in the country. His present record does not show it, but he even held the world's mile record for a week—until Buckpasser set a new record. He still has enough early lick to make Dr. Fager run. The faster the early pace, the more trouble a speed horse like Dr. Fager will have at the end. Is this fair? Absolutely. If Dr. Fager can't beat a troop that includes other front-runners, he is no champion. To argue that Hedevar gives the stretch-running Damascus an unfair advantage over Dr. Fager is to overlook the presence of the stretch-running Buckpasser. Any help that Hedevar gives Damascus will also help Buckpasser. Be that as it may, Hedevar has no chance to win, but practically guarantees a test of Dr. Fager's true class.

Dr. Fager: The talented John Nerud has managed this colt splendidly. And it has not been an easy job. The horse is a prima donna, exceptionally difficult to rate, and given to swerving, biting other horses, and otherwise making life miserable for the rider who tries to conserve his energy. Much to everyone's surprise, including (I think) Nerud's, the colt has demonstrated that he can go today's distance. But he has not yet had to overcome really stern competition from wire to wire over such a long route. He will get it from Hedevar in today's early stages and from Buckpasser and Damascus later. Nerud has been saying that Dr. Fager can outrun Hedevar and Great Power (another speed horse) and still have more than enough left at the finish. Before deciding this for ourselves, let's look at the other entrants.

Great Power: Buckpasser's speedy stablemate, entered for the same reasons as Hedevar, but not as likely to figure in the running.

Handsome Boy: Allen Jerkens has done wonders with this colt. The high point was a front-running victory over Buckpasser in the Brooklyn Handicap, when favored with a weight advantage of twenty pounds. His failure to romp away from a cheap field at Detroit on September 16, plus today's high weight, make the horse's chances quite slim.

Damascus: An improving horse that was good to begin with. Lost the Gotham because Bill Shoemaker moved too fast too soon. Lost the Kentucky Derby because the crowd frightened him. Was much the best horse in both races and has proved this to my satisfaction in his four most recent starts. I find great significance in the record-shattering victory of August 5 when Damascus gave six pounds to the brave, speedy In Reality and won handily. On September 2, Dr. Fager was *given* six pounds by In Reality and won with some difficulty. On this basis, Damascus is a good 12 pounds better than Dr. Fager. Comparisons of this kind can not be made among cheaper horses, whose form fluctuates greatly. But champions usually run at their best or close to it: the

In Reality that gave six pounds to Dr. Fager was essentially the same animal that could not run with Damascus, even with a six-pound advantage. Therefore, I say that Damascus beats Dr. Fager today and has only one horse to fear. Guess who?

Buckpasser: A truly great horse, but hoof trouble has forced him to bypass opportunities to win many additional hundreds of thousands of dollars. I do not like the absence since July 22. Nor do I like the performances of July 4 and 22. I think the horse is past his peak, mainly because of infirmity. Even if he is in top condition or close to it, the recent lack of racing will hurt him in the kind of stretch battle to be expected from Damascus.

To me, it's Damascus by a clear margin. Frank Whiteley's colt has all the class he needs, plus sharp form, plus an edge in the weights. Buckpasser has not come close (this year) to matching the three-year-old's superior pace figures.

The Running of the Race

THE BUCKPASSER entry went off at 8–5. Damascus and Hedevar were 9–5. So was Dr. Fager. The race was like the forecast, only more so. Dr. Fager wilted after running the legs off Hedevar. Meanwhile, Shoemaker let Damascus dawdle twelve to fifteen lengths behind the pace. And when he asked the colt for some run, he got the most sensational burst of speed I have ever seen. Poor Buckpasser tried to come on in the stretch but was not the Buckpasser of old and had all he could do to beat the fading Dr. Fager for second money. The old Buckpasser would have made it close, but under today's weights would have been by no means a cinch to win. The Damascus of the late summer of 1967 was a horse for the ages. Incidentally, the track was rated as "fast" but was still a bit damp from recent rains. Yet Damascus came within a second of the track record.

SEVENTH RACE **1 1-4 MILES. (Gun Bow, July 25, 1964, 1.59⅗, 4, 122.)**

Aqu - 32432

September 30, 1967

Fourteenth running. THE WOODWARD. $100,000 added. Weight-for-age. 3-year-olds 120 lbs., older 126 lbs. By subscription of $100 each which shall accompany the nomination. $1,000 additional to start. The added money and all fees to be divided 65% to the winner, 20% to second, 10% to third and 5% to fourth. Starters to be named through the entry box at the usual time of closing. Trophies will be presented to the owner of the winner and the winning trainer and jockey. Closed Friday, September 1 with 18 nominations.

Value of race $107,800. Value to winner $70,070, second $21,560, third $10,780, fourth $5,390. Mutuel pool $648,902.

Index	Horse	Eqt A Wt	PP	¼	½	¾	1	Str	Fin	Jockey	Owner	Odds $1
32225Aqu^{1}	—Damascus	3 120	5	5^{1}	$5^{1\frac{1}{2}}$	4^{1}	$1^{\frac{1}{2}}$	1^{5}	1^{10}	W Sh'maker	Edith W Bancroft	a-1.80
31769Aqu^{2}	—Buckpasser	b 4 126	6	6	6	5^{3}	3^{4}	3^{6}	$2^{\frac{1}{2}}$	B Baeza	O Phipps	b-1.60
32217Rkm^{1}	—Dr. Fager	3 120	2	$1^{\frac{1}{2}}$	1^{h}	$1^{1\frac{1}{2}}$	2^{3}	2^{3}	3^{13}	W Boland	Tartan Stable	1.80
32329Det^{4}	—Handsome Boy	b 4 126	4	4^{5}	4^{5}	3^{1}	4^{3}	4^{12}	4^{20}	E Belmonte	Hobeau Farm	10.50
32341Atl^{1}	—Hedevar	5 126	1	2^{1}	2^{5}	2^{6}	5^{8}	5^{3}	5^{6}	R Turcotte	Edith W Bancroft	a-1.80
32377Aqu^{8}	—Great Power	b 3 120	3	3^{3}	3^{2}	6	6	6	6	R Ussery	Wheatley Stable	b-1.60

a-Coupled—Damascus and Hedevar, b-Great Power and Buckpasser.

Time .22⅖, .45⅕, 1.09⅕, 1.35⅗, 2.00⅗ (with wind in backstretch). Track fast.

$2 Mutuel Prices:				
	1-DAMASCUS (a-entry)	5.60	2.60	Out
	2-BUCKPASSER (b-entry)		2.80	Out

No Show Mutuels Sold.

B. c, by Sword Dancer—Kerala, by My Babu. Trainer F. Y. Whiteley, Jr. Bred by Mrs. T. Bancroft (Ky.).

IN GATE AT 4.50. OFF AT 4.50 EASTERN DAYLIGHT TIME. Start good. Won easily.

DAMASCUS, steadied after beginning alertly, saved ground while in hand for three-quarters, moved up determinedly thereafter and, taking command from DR. FAGER near the stretch turn, drew clear without the need of urging. BUCKPASSER, outrun until near the stretch turn but saving ground, responded readily during the drive but was no match for DAMASCUS and was under brisk handling to best DR. FAGER for the place. DR. FAGER went to the front before a quarter, was much used racing HEDEVAR into defeat and faltered when challenged by DAMASCUS. HANDSOME BOY tired before entering the stretch. HEDEVAR, away alertly, engaged DR. FAGER for three-quarters and had nothing left. GREAT POWER was finished early.

THE EIGHTH RACE

NOW WE COME down to earth with a thud. Seven furlongs for $10,500–$12,500 claimers. Let's knock off the horses that have been scratched plus those that haven't run good races at the distance in tough company, plus those that have been idle too long or are plainly out of trim.

8th Race Aqueduct

7 FURLONGS AQUEDUCT (Start ▼ … ▲ Finish)

7 FURLONGS. (Chute). (Rose Net, Sept. 17, 1962, 1.21⅕, 6, 114.) Claiming. Purse $7,000. 3-year-olds and upward. Weights, 3-year-olds, 120 lbs., older 124 lbs. Non-winners of two races since July 29 allowed 3 lbs., of a race since then or two races since July 1, 5 lbs., of a race since July 1, 7 lbs. Claiming price $12,500. 2 lbs. allowed for each $1,000 to $10,500. (Races when entered to be claimed for $8,500 or less not considered.)

Dion $12,500

Br. g (1962), by Obalr—Ros Clag, by Rosemont
Mrs. C. MacLeod, Jr. C. MacLeod, Jr. (Campanas Stable) **121**
1967 12 2 2 2 $13,025
1966 11 0 2 1 $2,750

16Sep67-3Aqu fst 6f .23 .46⅖1.11⅖ Clm 11500 8 8 85¼ 66½ 44¼ 31¼ RTurcotte b 119 4.80 85-16 Loop The Loop 121¾ Lynch 112½ Dion 119½ Made steady gain 10
9Sep67-4Aqu fst 6f .22 .45⅕1.11 Clm 10000 9 9 87¾ 77½ 33½ 11 RTurcotte b 117 7.00 88-16 Dion 1171 Metairie Padre 117¾ World Report 117¾ Hand drive 12
2Sep67-3Aqu fst 6f .23 .46⅗1.11⅗ Clm 8500 7 4 56½ 56 54¾ 22½ HWoodhouse b 117 3.60 82-16 Spruce Up 1172½ Dion 1173½ Bullyampa 119½ Made a fair effort 8
26Aug67-4Sar fst 7f .22⅖ .45⅖1.23 Clm 9000 3 5 4¾ 42½ 1h 32½ RTurcotte b 113 25.40 92- 7 Your Day 117h Upset Victory 1192½ Dion 1132 Led, tired 9
19Aug67-3Sar sly 6f .22⅖ .46⅕1.11⅖ Clm 8500 3 6 77¾ 77½ 45½ 57½ RTurcotte b 117 8.80 83-10 Bullyampa 113h Your Day 115nk Metairie Padre 1176½ No mishap 11
1Jly 67-5Aqu gd 7f .22⅘ .46 1.24⅘ Clm 10000 3 8 55½ 58½ 914 911 RTurcotte b 121 8.80 71-19 At First Blush 1192½ Dog Watch 1122 Chartist 121no Far back 9
3Jun67-5Aqu fst 6f .22⅗ .45⅗1.11 Clm 10000 4 3 65 810 89½ 88¼ LAdams b 121 7.30 80-15 Storm Crost 1212½ Mr.C.H.117½ Colbert II 1132½ Never close 9
27May67-8Aqu fst 6f .22⅖ .45⅗1.11⅕ Clm 11500 5 4 65 65 64¼ 55¼ ADeSpirito b 115 5.60 82-15 Prospect Street 117¾ Santo Domingo 1171 Big Rapids 113½ Wide 10
20May67-4Aqu fst 6f .22 .45⅗1.11⅕ Clm 10000 10 5 66 57 44½ 2no RTurcotte b 119 11.30 87-14 Beaustone 117no Dion 1191½ Last Chain 115h Sharp try 14
5May67-2Aqu fst 6f .22⅗ .45⅘1.11⅗ Clm 8500 5 3 32½ 44 2h 11½ RTurcotte b 117 8.20 85-19 Dion 1171½ Prospect Street 117½ McGun 1191½ Under strong drive 6
LATEST WORKOUTS Sep 29 Bel 3f sly .40 b Sep 25 Bel 5f fst 1.04 b Sep 15 Bel 3f fst .38⅘ b Sep 1 Bel 3f fst .37⅕ b

Demigod * $10,500

B. g (1961), by Gallant Man—Plotter, by Double Jay
C. Petigrow H. Jacobson (L. Combs 2d-Mrs. J. M. Olin) **106 7**
1967 14 3 1 1 $19,600
1966 24 4 2 3 $22,975

8Aug67-8Sar fm 1⅛ Ⓣ 1.48⅘ Clm 18000 9 11 1120 1217 1217 1226 LAdams 31.80 114 78-11 Hardihood 1071½ Mostar 114no You're Tops 1161 No speed 12
26Jly 67-8Aqu fst 1⅛.47⅕1.11⅘1.49⅗ Cl c-14000 9 8 89¼ 93¾ 62¾ 47½ WBoland 116 2.90 80-15 Snow Cap II 114h Koh-I-Noor 1082½ You're Tops 1155 Wide 10
5Jly 67-9Aqu gd 1⅛.49 1.14 1.51⅕ Clm 14000 1 8 64½ 66½ 55 26 ACorderoJr 119 *1.60 74-21 Kummel 1146 Demigod 119h Bombax 1142 Finished well 8
29Jun67-6Aqu fst 1 .46⅖1.11 1.36⅖ Clm 18000 9 7 67 66 57 46¼ WBoland 114 5.20 80-19 Needles' Count 118¾ Fiyalong 1162½ Macherio 1183 No threat 9
9Jun67-4Aqu fst 1⅛.48⅖1.12⅕1.51⅗ Clm 14000 4 5 54½ 44 1h 11¾ WBoland 116 *2.00 78-17 Demigod 1161¾ Emerald Lake 118nk Ganelon II 1164 Brisk drive 7
1Jun67-8Aqu fm 1 1/16 Ⓣ 1.43⅕ Clm 18000 9 10 1020 1017 1015 1021 WBoland 116 5.00 69-10 Primarosa II 1151 Cleareye 116nk Good Ore 111nk Not a contender 10
12May67-4Aqu sl 1⅛.47⅖1.13⅕1.52 Clm 14000 3 5 59 2½ 1½ 1¾ WBoland 115 3.00 76-26 Demigod 115¾ Needles' Count 1145 Sir Sanford 11410 Driving 5
3May67-8Aqu fst 1 .46⅘1.12 1.38 Clm 14500 7 3 34 33 32½ 1¾ WBoland 114 9.00 78-21 Demigod 114¾ Needles' Count 1171½ Koh-I-Noor 122½ Brisk drive 7
25Apr67-6Aqu sl 1 .47⅖1.12⅘1.38 Clm 15000 3 8 77 66½ 47 36¼ WBoland 113 8.50 72-28 Koh-I-Noor 116nk Emerald Lake 1166 Demigod 113nk Mild bid 8
LATEST WORKOUTS Sep 24 Aqu 3f fst .38 b Sep 20 Aqu 4f fst .50 b Sep 18 Aqu 4f fst .52⅗ b Sep 8 Aqu 3f fst .38⅗ b

Chartist * $10,500

Ch. c (1963-Ky), by To Market—Roodles, by Princequillo
L. Silver T. J. Gullo (W. M. Jeffords) **117**
1967 12 3 1 3 $14,225
1966 18 6 0 0 $12,035

16Sep67-3Aqu fst 6f .23 .46⅖1.11⅖ Clm 12500 9 6 75¼ 76¾ 54¾ 41¾ ACorderoJr b 121 *1.70 84-16 Loop The Loop 121¾ Lynch 112½ Dion 119½ Insufficient rally 10
19Aug67-8Sar sly 7f .23 .46⅕1.24 Clm 10500 12 5 61 43 43 13½ ACorderoJr b 115 *1.90e 90-10 Chartist 1153½ Get Gettin 1123½ Big Devil 1172 With something left 13
12Aug67-2Sar fst 6f .22⅖ .45⅘1.11⅕ Clm 9000 7 6 67 47 43½ 2h ACorderoJr b 113 *1.70 92-11 Get Gettin 119h Chartist 1135 Float Trip 1131½ Sharp 7
2Aug67-5Sar fst 6f .22⅘ .45⅗1.10⅗ Clm 6500 7 4 1h 1½ 12 14 ACorderoJr b 117 2.70 95- 8 Chartist 1174 Credential 1031 Cartabon 116¾ Speed to spare 9
8Jly 67-8Aqu fst 6f .22⅖ .45⅘1.11⅕ Clm 12500 2 7 68 67½ 811 815 JGiovanni b 119 24.90 72-14 Upset Victory 119nk Cuetip 117no Hobe Sound 1173½ Far off pace 8
1Jly 67-5Aqu gd 7f .22⅘ .46 1.24⅘ Cl c-10000 6 2 21 33½ 33½ 34½ ECardone b 121 12.40 77-19 At First Blush 1192½ Dog Watch 1122 Chartist 121no Hung 9
13Jun67-5Mth fst 6f .21⅘ .45⅗1.10⅗ Clm 13000 3 6 48 54½ 45 56¼ NReagan b 115 14.90 83-20 Do Sparkle 1152 Jeannie'sRuler 1182½ UpsetVictory 1151¼ No mish'p 9
30May67-4GS fst 6f .22⅘ .46⅕1.11⅕ Clm 12000 6 2 21 21½ 21 31½ MLukas b 114 7.40 86-14 Cuetip 116¾ Phantom Island 114¾ Chartist 1144¾ Fairly evenly 7
18May67-5GS fst 6f .22 .45⅕1.11 Clm 10000 1 7 52¾ 57 54¼ 33½ MLukas b 118 9.30 85-20 Arctic Aria 1121½ Buz On 1162 Chartist 118nk Finished well 8
LATEST WORKOUTS Sep 27 Bel tr.t. 3f fst .37 h Sep 22 Bel tr.t. 4f fst .51 h Sep 9 Bel tr.t. 6f fst 1.19 b Aug 9 Sar 3f fst .35⅗ h

Loop the Loop * $12,500

Ch. g (1962), by Windy City II—Hula, by Polynesian
A. G. Vanderbilt W. C. Freeman (A. G. Vanderbilt) **124**
1967 12 2 3 0 $10,550
1966 5 0 1 1 $1,400

16Sep67-3Aqu fst 6f .23 .46⅖1.11⅖ Clm 12500 10 4 41 2h 1h 1¾ EGuerin b 121 8.60 86-16 Loop The Loop 121¾ Lynch 112½ Dion 119½ Under strong handling 10
4Sep67-4Aqu fst 6f .22⅖ .45⅖1.10⅗ Clm 16500 4 6 43¼ 813 714 712 HGustines b 120 10.80 78-14 Get Gettin 1082½ A. Deck 115h Santo Domingo 108½ Tired 8
17Aug67-8Rkm fst 6f .22⅖ .45⅘1.11⅕ Allowance 4 7 43¼ 42¼ 32½ 1no MHole b 112 4.40 88-15 Loop The Loop 112no Silver Joey 113½ Ye Ye Prince 113nk Driving 8
8Aug67-8Rkm fst 6f .22⅕ .45⅕1.11⅕ Allowance 5 8 74¼ 55 53¼ 77¾ MHole b 112 5.60 80-19 Rorque 112nk Someticco 1192¼ Lady Backbone 1071½ No mishap 9
1Aug67-8Rkm fst 6f .22⅗ .45⅘1.11⅕ Allowance 2 4 1½ 41 43 56¼ MHole b 114 4.80 82-19 Low Son 1141¼ Someticco 1191 Shiny Whistle 1111¼ Weak'd 9
18Jly 67-4Aqu fst 6f .22⅖ .45⅕1.10 Clm 25000 1 5 2½ 55½ 69½ 612 EBelmonte b 117 9.40 81-16 Active Alibi 103h Crossing The T. 1173½ Mountainside 1172 Fell back 6
15Apr67-5Aqu fst 6f .22⅗ .45⅗1.10⅕ Allowance 1 5 43½ 34½ 32 32¼ JLRotz b 121 8.50 90-14 Bologna Gellis 111¾ d-Right Card 1111½ LoopTheLoop121h Crowded 8
15Apr67—Placed second through disqualification.
30Mar67-6Aqu sl 6f .23 .46⅘1.12⅗ Clm 15000 2 2 31½ 2½ 2h 2no JLRotz b 114 4.40 80-33 Storm Crost 113no Loop The Loop 1148 Counsellor 110½ Bore in 7
13Mar67-4Aqu fst 6f .23 .46⅗1.12 Clm 12500 3 4 2½ 2h 21 31¾ JLRotz b 117 5.40 81-18 d-CharlieTooley 117nk CorredorII 1171½ LoopTheLoop117¾ Impeded 9
13Mar67—Placed second through disqualification.
LATEST WORKOUTS Sep 23 Aqu 4f fst .50 b Sep 15 Aqu 3f fst .37⅗ b Sep 10 Aqu 4f fst .50 b Sep 2 Aqu 4f fst .49 b

*Paulonio $12,500
B. h (1962), by Licencioso—Paula, by Borneo II
A. S. Bowman, Jr. C. V. B. Cushman, Jr. (Haras El Huerton) (Chile)
117
1967 12 0 0 0 ——
1966 11 3 2 1 $5,510

9Sep67-2Fai fm*1 1/16 Ⓣ 2.00⅘ Allowance 3 Fell CChavis b 141 6.30 —— Mighty Stroke 143nk Mako 141h Kyrenia 1381 Stumbled first turn 17
26Aug67-4Sar fst 7f .22⅖ .45⅖1.23 Clm 10000 7 9 97¾ 74¾ 52¾ 56½ JCruguet b 117 12.20 88- 7 Your Day 117h Upset Victory 1192½ Dion 1132 Slow start 9
19Aug67-8Sar sly 7f .23 .46⅕1.24 Clm 12500 11 13 11⁷⁄₁¹19¾ 84¼ 711 JCruguet b 119 27.80 79-10 Chartist 1153½ Get Gettin 1123½ Big Devil 1172 Began very slowly 13
8Jly 67-5Del fm 1 1/16 Ⓣ 1.44⅕ Allowance 6 2 51¾ 68½ 622 626 MNGonzalez b 114 38.30 57-24 FanJet 1151½ AmberPrince 1121½ GreenFelt 1124½ Studdish at post 6
26Jun67-7Del fm 1 1/16 Ⓣ 1.44⅕ Clm 13500 6 7 68 68 58 57 JCruguet 116 29.50 76-19 Cavans Rose 1111 Change Maker 1222 Double Strings 114h No threat 7
13Jun67-8Mth fst 1 1/16 .48 1.12⅗1.45⅕ Allowance 11 9 86¾ 98½1015 99¾ SHernandez 113 146.40 69-20 Swoonaway 1154½ Wrong Card 112½ Put-In-Bay 115½ No threat 12
6Jun67-8Del fm 1 1/16 Ⓣ 1.42⅗ Allowance 5 4 48½ 512 617 617 SBrooks b 113 30.00 74-14 Federalist Boy 1133 Classic Work 1194 Zapata 119nk No speed 7
1Jun67-8Del fst 6f .22⅕ .45⅖1.10⅕ Allowance 5 5 63½ 57¾ 813 816 NShuk b 113 104.30 78-19 Sub Call 1225 Slade 107¾ Al's Runner 1164½ Dropped far back 8
6May67-7Pim fm 1 1/16 Ⓣ 1.12 1.44⅗ Allowance 6 4 613 821 831 827 PIGrimm b 113 49.20 65- 9 Lucky Turn 122no Al Sirat 1224 Ginger Fizz 1173 Far back 8
26Apr67-5Pim gd 1 1/16 .47 1.11⅘1.43⅕ Allowance 5 3 44 45 58½ 59 ENelson b 115 14.10 85-12 Bay Hawk 119¾ Tide Mill 115h Pretko 119h Raced trifle wide 5
LATEST WORKOUTS Sep 19 Bel tr.t. 6f fst 1.16 h Sep 13 Bel 5f fst 1.01⅕ h Sep 7 Bel tr.t. 3f fst .37 h Sep 2 Bel 5f fst 1.03 b

*Koh-I-Noor ✻ $12,500
Ch. g (1961), by Major Portion—Glitter, by Golden Cloud
Mrs. F. H. Merrill F. H. Merrill (Lord Carnarvon) (Ire.)
117
1967 25 10 4 2 $44,410
1966 12 4 2 1 $14,110

30Aug67-9Aqu fst 1⅛.47⅘1.11⅘1.51⅕ Cl c-10000 6 2 23 24 24 25 ACorderoJr 118 3.40 75-18 Joe Di Rosa 1185 Koh-I-Noor 1183½ Sectario 118½ Fair try 9
19Aug67-8Sar sly 7f .23 .46⅕1.24 Clm 12500 6 10 43½ 86¾ 95¾ 49 RTanner10 109 9.00 81-10 Chartist 1153½ Get Gettin 1123½ Big Devil 1172 Shuffled back on turn 13
16Aug67-9Sar fm 1⅛ Ⓣ 1.48 Clm 16000 7 5 52½ 54¼ 99½ 811 EBelmonte 118 3.30 82- 8 Venturado 1141½ Volandero 118no Cleareye 116nk Weakened 9
8Aug67-4Sar fst 6f .22⅘ .46⅕1.10⅘ Clm 16000 2 7 88¾ 89¾ 66½ 57½ RTanner10 114 8.30 86-10 Cuetip 1173 Bugler 1213 A. Deck 121½ No apparent mishap 9
26Jly 67-8Aqu fst 1⅛.47⅕1.11⅘1.49⅗ Clm 15000 4 2 24 23 1h 2h RTanner10 108 3.50 88-15 Snow Cap II 114h Koh-I-Noor 1082½ You're Tops 1155 Sharp 10
15Jly 67-9Aqu sly 1 1/16.48 1.12⅕1.51 Hcp 7500s 3 3 2h 31 23 47¾ MYcaza 128 *1.60 73-18 Bombax 115¾ Austral II 1084 Wondrascope 1143 Speed, tired 7
6Jly 67-8Aqu fm 1 1/16 Ⓣ 1.44⅕ Clm 20000 4 3 45 54¾ 62¼ 63¼ BBaeza 120 *3.30 84-15 Macherio 118nk Mostar 118h Coronel White 114no Rough trip 10
21Jun67-6Aqu sf 1 1/16 Ⓣ 1.44⅖ Clm 20000 10 2 2h 1½ 1h 32½ BBaeza 114 5.10 81-16 Sheet Anchor 1212 Flag 118¾ Koh-I-Noor 1141½ Tired in drive 10
13Jun67-6Aqu hd 1⅛ Ⓣ 1.48⅗ Allowance 1 2 21 54 56 611 ACorderoJr 118 6.60 81- 8 Blasting Charge 113¾ Beau Legs 120h Fast Count 1184 Stopped 8
1Jun67-6Aqu fm 1 1/16 Ⓣ 1.43⅕ Clm 18000 5 4 1½ 11 13 15 BBaeza 116 *1.50 90-10 Koh-I-Noor 1165 Solemn Nation 116½ Shady Living 1202 Easily 9
LATEST WORKOUTS Sep 29 Bel tr.t. 3f sly .39 b Sep 23 Bel tr.t. 3f fst .38⅗ b Sep 20 Bel tr.t. 3f fst .38 b Aug 15 Sar trt. 6f fst 1.18 b

Bullyampa ✻ $10,500
Ch. g (1963-Ky), by Hasseyampa—Lovely Princess, by Royal Serenade
E. Mittman W. L. Dorsey (W. H.-R. E. Courtney)
113
1967 11 6 2 2 $23,425
1966 3 1 0 0 $3,150

23Sep67-3Aqu fst 6f .22⅖ .46⅖1.11 Clm 9000 7 3 31 3nk 1h 2½ LPincayJr b 113 3.30 86-13 Santo Domingo 117½ Bullyampa 1132 Wiggins Fork 1152 Sharp 8
16Sep67-2Aqu fst 6f .22⅖ .45⅘1.11⅗ Clm 8500 3 4 44½ 44½ 2½ 11½ ACorderoJr b 119 *2.10 85-16 Bullyampa 1191½ Wiggins Fork 117¾ Last Chain 1101¼ Drew out 9
7Sep67-8Aqu fst 7f .23 .46 1.24⅕ Clm 6500 1 8 1½ 11 13 12 EBelmonte b 121 *3.10 85-17 Bullyampa 1212 Chai Cha-Na 1152½ Highly Pleased 117nk Mild drive 14
2Sep67-3Aqu fst 6f .23 .46⅗1.11⅗ Clm 8000 6 5 45 33 24 36 ACorderoJr b 119 *1.70 79-16 Spruce Up 1172½ Dion 1173½ Bullyampa 119½ Well placed, hung 8
19Aug67-3Sar sly 6f .22⅖ .46⅕1.11⅖ Clm 7500 10 5 42½ 42½ 1½ 1h HGustines b 113 *2.40 91-10 Bullyampa 113h Your Day 115nk Metairie Padre 1176½ Driving 11
12Aug67-4Atl fst 6f .23 .46⅗1.11 Clm 5500 7 6 31½ 1h 13 16 CBaltazar b 115 *1.70 87-14 Bullyampa 1156 Good 'N' Green 107no Silver Monarch 117h Easily 11
27Jun67-4Aqu fst 7f .23 .45⅖1.24⅕ Cl c-6500 1 7 1h 13 13 3½ ACorderoJr b 119 *1.60 84-18 McGun 121no Wrapped Up 119½ Bullyampa 1192 Clear lead, tired 11
17Jun67-1Aqu fst 7f .22⅖ .45 1.23⅗ Cl c-5000 6 5 52 32½ 11 13½ ACorderoJr b 119 *0.80 88-15 Bullyampa 1193½ Prestigio II 119½ Flipaway 119h Easy score 10
10Jun67-5Aqu fst 6f .22⅕ .45⅕1.11 Clm 5000 5 5 52¾ 42 11½ 14 ACorderoJr b 117 *2.80 88-12 Bullyampa 1174 Predicador 1171 Sum Farce 117no Something left 13
LATEST WORKOUTS Sep 28 Bel 4f fst .49 b Sep 12 Bel 4f fst .48⅕ h Aug 29 Bel 5f fst 1.01⅕ h Aug 16 Bel 4f fst .48 h

Prospect Street ✻ $12,500
Ch. g (1963-Ky), by Nashua—Tapis Vert, by Mahmoud
O. Cohen V. Blengs (Mereworth Farm)
117
1967 13 1 4 0 $10,650
1966 7 1 0 0 $2,940

23Sep67-2Aqu fst 6f .23 .46⅘1.11⅘ Clm 10000 2 7 58 21 22 22 JLRotz b 117 4.20 82-13 Crying Towel 1172 Prospect Street 1172 Counsellor 117½ Good try 9
11Sep67-5Atl fst 1 1/16.47⅕1.12⅗1.44⅖ Allowance 6 3 42½ 67½ 611 616 HGrant b 120 11.00 69-18 SwampRabbit113¾ HappyHilarious1161½ BanquetHall1181 Tired 7
7Aug67-7Atl fst 1⅛.48⅘1.13⅕1.51⅗ Allowance 1 2 1h 32 77 911 WGavidia b 119 4.00 69-15 VictoryStep 113½ d-TraderRic 111nk HappyHilarious 1142½ G've way 8
28Jly 67-7Mth sly 1 1/16.48 1.12⅘1.44⅗ Allowance 5 7 76¼ 611 613 619 JCombest b 123 8.10 63-22 Enchanted Easter 1127 Dance Toledo 1146 Hatchery 1121½ No speed 10
19Jly 67-6Mth fst 170.47⅘1.12⅕1.42⅘ Allowance 7 2 1h 2h 42 63 WGavidia b 114 10.50 84-16 Readership 114½ Atoll's Sun 111h English Muffin 1111½ Tired 8
14Jly 67-7Mth fst 170.47⅕1.12⅗1.43⅘ Allowance 7 2 8 1013 912 89¾ 68 HGrant b 123 10.10 75-19 Lutza'sKil'r114½ Ench'ntedEaster1123½ SandAndCor'l1161½ No sp'd 10
5Jly 67-8Aqu fm 1⅛ Ⓣ 1.48⅕ Allowance 9 6 88 914 924 936 LGilligan b 118 22.10 58- 6 Isokeha 1233 Salmon River 110nk Undermine 1151½ Far back 9
5Jly 67—The Morning Telegraph Time 1.50⅘.
23Jun67-6Aqu sly 1⅛.47⅖1.12⅗1.53⅖ Allowance 3 2 2h 2½ 2h 2no ACorderoJr b 118 *1.90e 69-25 Happy Lark 111no Prospect Street 118½ Yirrkala 1045 In front, mis'd 6
30May67-5Aqu fst 1⅛.46⅘1.11⅗1.51⅕ Allowance 1 2 23 22 11 25 LGilligan b 120 6.90 75-13 Isokeha 1205 Prospect Street 1203 Turn To Dad 1132½ Tired 9
LATEST WORKOUTS Sep 19 Atl 4f gd .50 b Sep 7 Atl 4f fst .48 h Aug 28 Atl 4f my .51⅗ b Aug 23 Atl 5f sly 1.06 b

Mr. Elwood W. × $10,500
B. g (1961), by Blazing Count—Reckless Miss, by High Lea
Clara L. Ostriker E. Jacobs (Mrs. G. R. Bryson)
106[7]
1967 1 0 1 0 $1,000
1966 30 6 6 7 $31,230

19Sep67-4Aqu fst 6f .22⅗ .46⅕1.11 Cl c-5000 2 2 21½ 23 32 24¾ WShoemaker 117 5.00 83-14 Cartabon 1124½ Mr. Elwood W. 1171 Fair Valley 116nk Fair try 11
7Dec66-9Aqu fst 1⅛.47⅘1.13 1.51⅗ Clm 10500 3 1 14 12 11½ 1¾ LPincayJr 116 *2.50 78-24 Mr. Elwood W. 116¾ Cool Oasis 1153½ Walk Out 1176 Fully extended 7
5Nov66-9Aqu fst 1⅛.48⅕1.12⅘1.51⅗ Hcp 5000s 6 3 41½ 21½ 2h 33½ JLRotz 122 10.30 74-13 Aerie 1131½ Direct Action 1132 Mr. Elwood W. 1222½ Good effort 9
22Oct66-9Aqu fst 1⅛.47⅘1.13 1.52⅘ Hcp 5000s 5 1 13 14 12 12½ JLRotz 117 6.30 72-16 Mr. Elwood W. 1172½ Nike Site 1121 Aerie 1141½ Brisk drive 11
8Oct66-9Aqu fst 1⅛.47⅘1.13⅕1.52 Hcp 5000s 5 2 3h 2½ 66 612 WShoemaker 120 3.80 64-17 Ruperto 121h Aerie 1142½ Hy-Nat 1132½ Well placed, tired 10
3Oct66-9Aqu fst 1⅛.48 1.12⅗1.52⅗ Clm 9500 4 2 21½ 21 1h 13 WShoemaker 118 4.80 73-19 Mr.ElwoodW. 1183 Listen to Reason 118no MainCount1141½ Driving 10
10Sep66-9Aqu fst 1⅛.47⅕1.12⅗1.53⅕ Hcp 5000s 7 1 12 11½ 2½ 44¾ WBlum 120 *3.20 65-23 Nike Site 1121½ Flannel 1093 Atlantic 119nk Clear lead, tired 10
29Aug66-9Aqu fst 1⅛.47⅘1.12⅗1.53⅕ Cl c-9000 4 1 13 1½ 21 2h DHidalgo 116 3.80 70-13 Sir Sanford 118h Mr. Elwood W. 1161 EnfantTerrible 1141½ Bore out 7
23Aug66-4Sar sly 1 .46⅘1.12⅕1.38⅘ Clm 9000 2 1 13 13 1½ 11½ DHidalgo5 109 6.60 80-15 Mr. Elwood W. 1091½ Sir Sanford 1185 No Kidding 1208 Driving 7
12Aug66-9Sar gd 1⅛.47⅗1.12⅘1.52⅕ Clm 6500 6 1 13 11½ 13 16 DHidalgo5 115 *2.30 84-16 Mr. Elwood W. 1156 Express Stop 1142 Rao Raja 1183½ Easily 7
LATEST WORKOUTS Sep 26 Aqu 7f fst 1.30 b Sep 18 Bel 3f fst .36⅖ h Sep 14 Bel 3f fst .37 b Sep 3 Bel 6f fst 1.16 b

Big Luxury $12,500
Ch. g (1961), by Big Money—Luxury Liner, by Swing and Sway
G. Maccheroni R. Jacobs (J. A. Bell, Jr.)
117
1967 12 4 1 3 $11,115
1966 12 0 2 3 $2,277

23Sep67-9Aqu fst 1⅛.46⅘1.11⅘1.50⅗ Hcp 5000s 3 1 1½ 11½ 21½ 33¾ RTurcotte b 110 21.40 79-13 Swing Rex 116¾ Austral II 1163 Big Luxury 1101½ Speed, tired 9
16Sep67-9Aqu fst 1 3/16.47⅗1.13 1.59⅗ Hcp 3500s 5 1 13 11½ 33½ 63¾ ALoGuercio b 112 6.10 68-16 Swing Rex 1133 Fuzzie King 1253 Jet Formation 114nk Used up 9
12Sep67-9Aqu fst 1 .45⅘1.09⅘1.36⅗ Cl c-3500 8 1 14 14 16 16 ALoGuercio7 b 113 *1.70 85-20 Big Luxury 1136 Manga Reva 1162 Willow Creek 1164 Easily 14
6Sep67-1Aqu fst 6f .23 .46⅘1.11⅗ Clm 3500 12 4 21½ 21½ 2h 1½ RTurcotte b 121 3.20 85-18 Big Luxury 121½ Don't Walk 114¾ Festival King 114h Driving 14
30Aug67-2Aqu fst 6f .22⅘ .46⅕1.12 Clm 3500 10 5 41½ 43½ 56 54½ ACordero7 b 112 6.30 78-18 Fair Valley 1171 Ash Blue 121½ Speedy Admiral 117h Wide 14
29Jly 67-8Aqu fst 6f .22⅕ .45⅗1.11⅖ Clm 4500 5 3 1½ 11½ 11½ 1½ ACordero7 b 110 9.30 86-14 Big Luxury 110½ Prevalent 108nk Rogo 112½ Long, hard drive 8
19Jly 67-1Aqu fst 6f .22⅖ .45⅘1.11⅗ Cl c-3500 9 2 1½ 1½ 2½ 2½ ACordero7 b 108 3.40 82-13 Lord Birchfield 1242½ Big Luxury 108nk Fair Valley 1182 Swerved 9
4Jly 67-2Aqu fst 7f .23 .46⅕1.25⅗ Clm 3500 4 5 4¾ 2h 33½ 33½ ACorderoJr b 117 5.20 74-17 Lord Birchfield 121h Sum Farce 1173½ Big Luxury 1172½ Hung 9
21Jun67-2Aqu gd 6f .22⅖ .46 1.11⅗ Clm 3500 10 3 34 34½ 26 59½ WBoland b 119 5.70 74-21 Match Wits 1193½ Party Giver 119h Pippin 1144 Speed, tired 13
22Apr67-7Mid hd*1¾ Ⓣ 2.13⅗ Allowance 1 3 12 21 2¾ 34½ CO'Brien3 b 159 —— —— Marcoton 1463½ Macumba 1271 Big Luxury 1592 Weakened 11
LATEST WORKOUTS Aug 19 Sar tr.t. 4f fst .50⅗ h Aug 15 Sar tr.t. 4f fst .49⅖ h Aug 10 Sar tr.t. 3f fst .37 h

Beaustone * $10,500 Dk. b. or br. c (1963–NJ), by Beauridge—Lodestone, by Johns Joy **113** 1967 18 1 1 4 $9,665
Brandy Hills Farm F. E. McMillan (W. Lynch) 1966 23 3 5 5 $21,100
9Sep67-3Aqu fst 7f .22⅘ .45⅘1.23⅘ Clm 12500 4 7 76½ 76 55½ 57½ ADeSpirito b 119 16.40 81–16 UpsetVictory 1173 OneNightStand 119¾ AtFirstBlush 115¾ No threat 7
30Aug67-9Aqu fst 1⅛.47⅗1.11⅘1.51⅕ Cl c-10000 4 4 34½ 34½ 37 613 WBoland b 118 9.00 67–18 Joe Di Rosa 1185 Koh-I-Noor 1183½ Sectario 118½ Fell back 9
19Aug67-8Sar sly 7f .23 .46⅕1.24 Clm 12500 8 7 106½10⁹½ 74 913 WBoland b 119 16.20 77–10 Chartist 1153½ Get Gettin 1123½ Big Devil 1172 Never a threat 13
5Aug67-8Sar fst 6f .22⅘ .45⅗1.10⅘ Clm 12500 7 5 87¼ 65½ 43½ 45¼ WBoland b 117 18.40 89– 6 Santo Domingo 1172½ Itsago 110nk Savin Rock 1122½ Finished well 8
25Jly 67-9Aqu fst 1⅛.46⅘1.11 1.50⅘ Cl c-10000 11 7 66½ 54½ 44 54½ RTurcotte b 118 7.80 77–11 Joe Di Rosa 1181½ Sectario 1162½ Daily Reminder 118h No mishap 12
12Jly 67-9Aqu fst 1⅛.46⅖1.10⅕1.48⅗ Clm 11500 7 4 45 37½ 210 216 BBaeza b 116 4.00 77–13 Lochoir 11816 Beaustone 116½ Neparoo 1181½ No real threat 8
28Jun67-9Aqu fst 1⅛.49 1.13⅗1.51⅘ Clm 11500 1 2 2½ 21 31¼ 35 JGiovanni b 116 *2.50 72–17 Pomidoro 118h Artist's Award 1205 Beaustone 1162½ Bid, tired 6
14Jun67-9Aqu fst 1⅛.47⅗1.12 1.50⅗ Clm 11500 4 4 31 2h 2h 41 JGiovanni b 116 3.70 82–14 Bombax 118no Spartanburg 118¾ Cormier 116nk Well up, hung 8
27May67-8Aqu fst 6f .22⅘ .45⅗1.11⅕ Clm 11500 9 5 77 77 54 42¼ JRuane b 119 *1.40e 85–15 Prospect Street 117¾ Santo Domingo 1171 Big Rapids 113½ Rallied 10
20May67-4Aqu fst 6f .22 .45⅗1.11⅕ Clm 10000 7 7 89¼ 79½ 67 1no JRuane b 117 9.80 87–14 Beaustone 117no Dion 1191½ Last Chain 115h Hard drive 14
LATEST WORKOUTS Sep 27 Bel 6f fst 1.15 h Sep 22 Bel 6f fst 1.14⅖ h Aug 29 Bel 3f fst .35⅘ h Aug 16 Sar 3f fst .36⅘ h

One Night Stand $12,500 Ch. g (1963–Ky), by Sailor—Olympia Gal, by Olympia **117** 1967 22 1 1 1 $7,460
Syl George Stable E. W. King (T. Gentry) 1966 17 2 2 2 $9,375
16Sep67-3Aqu fst 6f .23 .46⅖1.11⅖ Clm 12500 3 5 53 44 75¾ 73 LGilligan b 118 10.70 83–16 Loop The Loop 121¾ Lynch 112½ Dion 119½ Had no mishaps 10
9Sep67-3Aqu fst 7f .22⅘ .45⅘1.23⅘ Clm 12500 7 3 65 55 45 23 JRuane b 119 30.80 86–16 UpsetVictory 1173 OneNightStand 119¾ AtFirstBlush 115¾ Rallied 7
2Sep67-6Atl fst 7f .23 .46⅕1.23 Clm 14000 6 2 62¾ 78¼ 610 613 RBroussard b 117 17.30 75–13 Bag Of Ice 1132½ Soleil II 1132½ Siempre Listo 1192½ Fell back 7
25Aug67-5Sar fm 1 1/16 Ⓣ 1.41⅘ Clm 18000 3 7 711 79½ 712 717 JRuane b 112 36.10 74– 7 Lancastrian 116¾ Cleareye 1125½ Volandero 1161½ Trailed 7
16Aug67-9Sar fm 1⅛ Ⓣ 1.48 Clm 16000 6 2 21 32 89 913 JRuane b 118 52.10 80– 8 Venturado 1141½ Volandero 118no Cleareye 116nk Used up 9
8Aug67-8Sar fm 1⅛ Ⓣ 1.48⅘ Clm 18000 8 2 2h 21 96½1111 JRuane b 114 81.30 78–11 Hardihood 1071½ Mostar 114no You're Tops 1161 No speed 12
3Aug67-9Sar sf 1 1/16 Ⓣ 1.42 Allowance 2 7 79 813 812 724 JRuane b 116 72.10 66–10 Isokeha 1233½ Royal Comedian 1172 You're Tops 1162 No speed 7
18Jly 67-4Aqu fst 6f .22⅘ .45⅕1.10 Clm 22500 6 1 63 66½ 58 58 RTurcotte b 115 31.40 85–16 Active Alibi 103h Crossing The T. 1173½ Mountainside 1172 No factor 6
12Jly 67-6Aqu fst 7f .22⅘ .45 1.22⅘ Allowance 6 1 53 56½ 79 613 LAdams 121 71.20 79–13 Brunch 1144 Mister Pitt's Kid 1141 Brother Campbell 1141½ Wide 7
LATEST WORKOUTS Sep 28 Bel tr.t. 4f fst .49 h Sep 21 Bel tr.t. 4f fst .48 h Sep 7 Bel tr.t. 4f fst .48⅘ h

North Rim * $11,500 B. g (1963–Va), by Tillman—North River, by By Jimminy **110⁵** 1967 6 0 0 1 $1,875
A. Stempel A. J. Danko (Meadow Stud, Inc.) 1966 13 1 0 1 $5,375
23Sep67-2Aqu fst 6f .23 .46⅘1.11⅘ Clm 10000 6 2 86¾ 87 56 44¾ RTanner7 b 110 7.20 79–13 Crying Towel 1172 Prospect Street 1172 Counsellor 117¾ Rallied 9
16Sep67-3Aqu fst 6f .23 .46⅖1.11⅖ Clm 12500 1 1 2½ 86¾ 97½106 GMora5 113 29.40 80–16 Loop The Loop 121¾ Lynch 112½ Dion 119½ Brief foot, tired 10
29Aug67-8Aqu fst 1 .46⅕1.11⅗1.38⅗ Clm 15000 6 2 55½ 55 69½ 613 RTurcotte 117 16.90 62–25 Walk Out 117¾ Willup 111½ A. Deck 1163 Dropped back early 7
5Aug67-7Mth fst 6f .22⅘ .45⅘1.10 Allowance 3 4 31½ 53¼ 79 715 MAristone 113 45.60 77–18 Isgala 1171¼ Swoonland 113¾ Garden King 1174½ Brief factor 8
22Jly 67-6Aqu fst 6f .22⅘ .45⅕1.09⅗ Allowance 3 1 67½ 610 618 617 LAdams 118 18.50 78–11 Dey Sovereign 121nk Who Called 1126 First And Finest 1171 Trailed 6
15Jly 67-6Aqu sly 6f .22⅘ .45⅗1.11 Allowance 6 1 54 45 47½ 311 MAristone 115 53.00 77–18 Kilmoray 1152½ Rebellious 1108 North Rim 115¾ Fair try 6
25Jly 66-6Aqu fst 7f .22⅘ .45⅖1.24⅕ Clm 18000 6 1 43½ 44½ 54 58½ LAdams b 116 8.40 77–16 Beaustone 1092½ Sole Support 1222 Holly Man 111¾ Raced wide 7
11Jly 66-4Aqu fst 6f .23 .47 1.12⅕ Cl c-14000 3 2 33½ 33 23 68½ WBlum 116 *1.40e 73–21 Royal Harbinger 116½ Textonian 1161½ Deal 111no Stopped 7
28Jun66-8Aqu fst 6f .22⅘ .45⅗1.11⅖ Clm 20000 5 2 3½ 3nk 3nk 32 WBlum b 116 3.60 84–19 Bandera Beau 1151¼ Indian Fighter 115½ North Rim 116nk Tired 9
18Jun66-8Suf fst 6f .22⅘ .45⅗1.10⅖ Handicap 3 2 2h 3½ 1h 42 JSpinale 115 5.80 92–12 Flame Tree 124nk It's Blitz 1091 Mister Westgate 113¾ Weakened 7
LATEST WORKOUTS Sep 28 Bel 3f fst .36⅖ h Sep 14 Bel 4f fst .49⅗ b Sep 7 Bel 3f fst .35⅗ h Sep 2 Bel 3f fst .36 h

Counsellor * $12,500 Dk. b. or br. c (1963–Md), by Cavan—Guirvita, by Roman **117** 1967 12 1 0 4 $7,430
Anita C. Heard T. H. Heard, Jr. (Max Hirsch) 1966 12 2 2 1 $8,975
23Sep67-2Aqu fst 6f .23 .46⅘1.11⅘ Cl c-10000 1 9 43½ 43 33½ 34 BBaeza 117 6.40 80–13 Crying Towel 1172 Prospect Street 1172 Counsellor 117¾ No mishap 9
19Aug67-8Sar sly 7f .23 .46⅕1.24 Clm 12500 5 6 71¼ 98½1213 1221 LAdams 119 24.40 69–10 Chartist 1153½ Get Gettin 1123½ Big Devil 1172 Disliked the slop 13
8Aug67-4Sar fst 6f .22⅘ .46⅕1.10⅘ Clm 15000 4 8 66½ 78¾ 88 714 EBelmonte 119 31.50 80–10 Cuetip 1173 Bugler 1213 A. Deck 121½ Never a contender 9
22May67-6Aqu fst 6f .22⅕ .45⅕1.10⅘ Allowance 3 3 43½ 88½ 911 97½ ACorderoJr b 119 19.10 81–14 VelvetFlash 114no •RightCard 109nk •PriceOfGlory 117nk Tired 9
11May67-6Aqu sly 1⅛.46⅘1.13⅖1.53⅘ Allowance 6 3 410 59 610 625 ACorderoJr 120 8.80 44–24 Blas'gCharge11310SolemnNation123noRuffledFeathers1144 No fac'r 7
29Apr67-5Aqu fst 7f .22⅘ .46⅗1.24⅖ Allowance 8 1 57 57 53½ 38 ATCordero 121 16.80 76–18 Gaylord'sFeather110h FavorableTurn1178 Counsellor1212½ No m'h'p 8
18Apr67-6Aqu my 7f .23⅘ .46⅘1.25 Cl c-14000 3 3 2½ 21 1½ 12 BBaeza 119 *1.60 81–25 Counsellor 1192 Well To Do 1215 •Beaustone 1154 Drew clear 5
10Apr67-6Pim fst 6f .23⅕ .46⅖1.11⅗ Clm 16500 7 6 64¾ 68 66¾ 53¼ ARussello7 108 9.50 89–16 Mr. Judex 1081 Transvaal 116¾ Rebellious 114½ Forced outside 7
30Mar67-6Aqu sl 6f .23 .46⅘1.12⅗ Clm 15500 6 4 57½ 513 511 38 ARussello7 110 *2.10 72–33 Storm Crost 113no Loop The Loop 1148 Counsellor 110½ Rallied 7
15Mar67-5Aqu sly 6f .23⅕ .47⅕1.12⅘ Clm 19000 6 4 2h 31 33 31¼ ARussello7 108 5.50 78–24 Farmer's Son 121¾ It's Blitz 117½ Counsellor 1083 Wide 6
LATEST WORKOUTS Sep 29 Aqu 4f sl .50⅖ b Sep 21 Bel 5f fst 1.01 hg Sep 17 Bel tr.t. 5f fst 1.02⅘ b Sep 13 Bel tr.t. 4f fst .51⅖ b

Horses Shown Below Are on the "Also Eligible" List and Are Not Listed in Order of Post Positions.

Upset Victory * $12,500 Ch. h (1962), by Dedicate—Best of Show, by Billings **121** 1967 19 3 4 6 $21,560
Flo-Henny Stable L. S. Barrera (E. G. Burke) 1966 23 6 8 3 $33,310
20Sep67-9Aqu fst 1⅛.48 1.12 1.51 Clm 12500 3 4 41½ 11½ 12 2nk LPincayJr b 118 *2.40 81–14 Ganelon II 111nk Upset Victory 1181½ Sky Count 1071½ Couldn't last 6
14Sep67-4Aqu fst 6f .22⅘ .45⅘1.10⅘ Clm 15000 11 2 63½ 43¾ 45¾ 411 FAlvarez b 114 5.80 81–17 Crossing The T. 1145½ Space Song 1183½ Storm Crost 1081¼ No rally 11
9Sep67-3Aqu fst 7f .22⅘ .45⅘1.23⅘ Clm 11500 5 4 33 33 11½ 13 BBaeza b 117 *0.90 89–16 UpsetVictory 1173 OneNightStand 119¾ AtFirstBlush 115¾ Easily 7
26Aug67-4Sar fst 7f .22⅘ .45⅖1.23 Clm 10000 2 8 76¾ 85¼ 4¾ 2h MYcaza b 119 *2.70 95– 7 Your Day 117h Upset Victory 1192½ Dion 1132 Sharp try 9
19Aug67-8Sar sly 7f .23 .46⅕1.24 Clm 12500 1 11 54½ 54½ 53½ 611 HGustines b 119 6.00 79–10 Chartist 1153½ Get Gettin 1123½ Big Devil 1172 Lacked a rally 13
8Aug67-4Sar fst 6f .22⅘ .46⅕1.10⅘ Clm 16000 3 9 98¾ 68¼ 55½ 67¼ MYcaza b 119 7.70 86–10 Cuetip 1173 Bugler 1213 A. Deck 121½ Drifted out stretch 9
8Jly 67-8Aqu fst 6f .22⅘ .45⅘1.11⅕ Cl c-12500 7 4 57½ 56 4¾ 1nk WBoland b 119 3.20 87–14 Upset Victory 119nk Cuetip 117no Hobe Sound 1173½ Up in time 8
24Jun67-8Aqu gd 6f .22⅘ .45⅕1.10⅘ Clm 12500 4 7 69½ 66½ 47 25 JVasquez b 119 2.50 84–18 Space Song 1195 Upset Victory 1193½ Chillicoot 124½ Rallied 7
20Jun67-7Mth sl 6f .22⅘ .46 1.11⅕ Clm 13000 3 6 610 57 52½ 21 JVasquez b 112 3.70 85–21 JoeTheBarber1141 UpsetVictory112¾ RowdyDowdy1111½ Closed fast 7
LATEST WORKOUTS Sep 7 Bel tr.t. 4f fst .50 h Sep 2 Bel tr.t. 4f fst .52 b Aug 15 Sar tr.t. 4f fst .53⅗ b

Vail Pass $12,500 B. h (1962), by Hill Prince—Vermiglia, by Owen Tudor **117** 1967 9 0 2 1 $5,100
A. J. Giordano S. J. Smith (Meadow Stud, Inc.) 1966 26 2 3 6 $14,000
23Sep67-4Aqu fst 7f .22⅘ .45⅕1.22⅘ Clm 14000 3 7 73¾ 74¾ 23 23 RTurcotte b 113 10.20 90–13 A. Deck 1173 Vail Pass 1131 Bugler 1242 Made good effort 12
6Sep67-6Aqu fst 7f .23⅘ .46⅕1.23⅘ Allowance 5 4 73¾ 75½ 811 56½ LPincayJr b 117 13.10 81–18 Hornbeam 113¾ Undermine 113h London Jet 1152 Bothered 8
19Aug67-8Sar sly 7f .23 .46⅕1.24 Clm 12500 3 8 93¼ 76½107¾1115 RTurcotte b 119 4.00 75–10 Chartist 1153½ Get Gettin 1123½ Big Devil 1172 Mild bid, tired 13
3Aug67-5Sar fst 7f .23⅘ .46⅕1.22⅘ Clm 15000 2 7 55 44 43½ 49½ HGustines b 117 2.00 86– 7 Peter Piper 117no Simpleton 1174½ Bigamo 1165 Off sluggishly 7
14Jly 67-6Aqu fst 7f .22⅘ .45 1.23 Allowance 4 3 52½ 52 31½ 23 HGustines b 117 17.50 90–20 Command Performer 117¾ Vail Pass 117nk Terresto 1123 Gamely 6
7Jly 67-8Aqu fst 6f .22 .45 1.10⅘ Clm 18000 2 7 77¼ 76¾ 56¾ 36¼ EBelmonte b 115 14.30 86–15 Active Alibi 103nkSpace Song 1156 Vail Pass 1151 Late gain 9
28Jun67-5Aqu fst 6f .22⅘ .45⅗1.10⅘ Clm 15000 2 7 77¾ 75 55½ 43¾ RTurcotte b 115 31.10 85–17 Space Song 1152½ Garden King 119nk Rebellious 1161 No mishap 8
28Feb67-7Hia fm 5½f Ⓣ 1.04⅖ Clm 20000 8 10 119½1011 68½ 54 RTurcotte b 116 81.80 92–10 CrossingTheT. 1121½ RomeExpress 116½ AdmiralClove 116½ Rallied 12
24Feb67-7Hia fst 7f .23⅕ .46⅕1.23⅖ Allowance 9 10 1112111411191116 KKnapp b 113 44.90 76–15 Irongate 1211½ Tom Poker 1138 Wondrascope 1131½ No speed 12
LATEST WORKOUTS Sep 29 Bel tr.t. 3f sly .38 b Sep 18 Bel 6f fst 1.17⅖ b Sep 11 Bel t.c. 3f fm .38 b Sep 1 Bel tr.t. 3f fst .38 b

On those grounds, out go Dion (distance), Demigod (scratched), Loop the Loop (scratched), Paulonio (form), Koh-I-Noor (idleness), Bullyampa (class), Mr. Elwood W. (class), Big Luxury (class), Beaustone (form), One Night Stand (scratched), North Rim (distance). Let us now examine the survivors.

Chartist: Although Tom Gullo dropped this consistent colt down to $6,500 to burgle a purse at Saratoga—and got away without losing the animal—there is nothing really cheap about Chartist. He belongs in this company, likes the distance, and has Shoemaker in the irons. CONTENDER.

Prospect Street: After failing repeatedly in mediocre allowance company at Jersey tracks, this Nashua gelding showed a touch of zip in a claiming sprint here just one week ago. Its true class, condition, and distance preference are so obscure that I have to make more guesses than I like. The sum of the guesses is that the horse would be a real threat at seven furlongs if it were in its May and June form, but that it is not. If it had gained even a foot in the stretch of its race last week, I'd fear it today. NO BET.

Counsellor: Another animal that came to life in the second race last Saturday after running poorly for months. Apparently that $10,000 claimer was overpriced. I now feel better about eliminating Prospect Street and do not hesitate to do the same with Counsellor. NO BET.

Upset Victory: Beat this kind of field at this distance under Baeza three weeks ago. Whether it can do the same today with Fernando Toro and 121 pounds remains to be seen. CONTENDER.

Vail Pass: Ran a tremendous race behind A. Deck last week. Gets Baeza today. CONTENDER.

The contenders are Chartist, Upset Victory, and Vail Pass. The competition is so keen that I think we can toss out Upset Victory on grounds of overweighting. Inasmuch as Vail Pass has run faster against better horses than Chartist has faced, the edge goes to Vail Pass and Baeza.

The Running of the Race

VAIL PASS was slightly less than 5–2, Chartist slightly more. Upset Victory was third favorite at 11–2. Shoemaker got more early speed out of Chartist than could possibly have been expected and lasted well enough to beat Vail Pass by two lengths. But Beaustone, a longshot and then some, chose this day to wake up and won with plenty to spare. Such things happen. You can't win them all.

EIGHTH RACE
Aqu - 32433
September 30, 1967

7 FURLONGS. (Chute). (Rose Net, Sept. 17, 1962, 1.21⅕, 6, 114.)
Claiming. Purse $7,000. 3-year-olds and upward. Weights, 3-year-olds, 120 lbs., older 124 lbs. Non-winners of two races since July 29 allowed 3 lbs., of a race since then or two races since July 1, 5 lbs., of a race since July 1, 7 lbs. Claiming price $12,500. 2 lbs. allowed for each $1,000 to $10,500. (Races when entered to be claimed for $8,500 or less not considered.)

Value to winner $4,550, second $1,400, third $700, fourth $350. Mutuel pool $551,132.

Index	Horse	Eqt	A	Wt	PP	St	¼	½	Str	Fin	Jockey	C'lg Pr	Owner	Odds $1
32266Aqu⁵	Beaustone	b 4	4	113	9	11	10¹	7½	3²	1³	W Boland	10500	Brandy Hills Farm	46.70
32320Aqu⁴	Chartist	b 4	4	117	2	7	1h	1¹	1½	2²	W Sh'maker	10500	L Silver	2.90
32375Aqu²	Vail Pass		5	117	12	10	12⁴	11¹	5²	3no	B Baeza	12500	A J Giordano	2.40
32320Aqu³	Dion	b 5	5	121	1	12	6¹	6½	4½	4nk	R Turcotte	12500	Mrs C MacLeod Jr.	15.80
31927Aqu²	Koh-I-Noor		6	117	4	9	11½	12¹½	6½	5h	R Ussery	12500	Mrs F H Merrill	14.00
32374Aqu²	Bullyampa	b 4	4	113	5	8	5½	2½	2h	6nk	E Belmonte	10500	E Mittman	7.30
32353Aqu²	Upset Victory	b 5	5	121	13	1	8²	8¹	7¹	7¹	F Toro	12500	Flo-Henny Stable	5.50
32373Aqu³	Counsellor		4	117	11	2	9½	10½	8h	8³	L Adams	12500	Anita C Heard	f-22.20
32202Fai	Paulonio	b 5	5	117	3	13	13	13	9¹	9nk	J Cruguet	12500	A S Bowman Jr.	147.70
32339Aqu²	Mr. Elwood W.		6	106	7	4	3h	4h	10h	10²½	R Tanner⁷	10500	Clara L Ostriker	14.10
32373Aqu⁴	North Rim	b 4	4	110	10	3	7h	9½	11³	11⁵	G Mora⁵	11500	Sunwood Stable	f-22.20
32380Aqu³	Big Luxury	b 6	6	117	8	5	4h	5½	12¹	12⁶	E Cardone	12500	G Maccheroni	25.10
32373Aqu²	Prospect Str't	b 4	4	117	6	6	2h	3h	13	13	J L Rotz	12500	O Cohen	16.80

f-Mutuel field.

Time .23, .46⅕, 1.12, 1.24⅘ (with wind in backstretch). Track fast.

$2 Mutuel Prices:

9-BEAUSTONE	95.40	24.20	12.40
2-CHARTIST		5.00	3.20
10-VAIL PASS			3.60

Dk. b. or br. c, by Beauridge—Lodestone, by Johns Joy. Trainer F. E. McMillan. Bred by W. Lynch (N. J.).

IN GATE AT 5.24. OFF AT 5.24 EASTERN DAYLIGHT TIME. Start good. Won handily.

BEAUSTONE steadily worked his way forward under good handling, responded to mild urging during the stretch run and, disposing of the leaders inside the last eighth, won going away. CHARTIST set the pace until inside the stretch but was unable to stay with BEAUSTONE. VAIL PASS lacked early foot but closed gamely. DION could not better his position when set down through the stretch. KOH-I-NOOR outrun for a half mile. NORTH RIM was never dangerous. BIG LUXURY stopped during the stretch run. PROSPECT the final furlong. UPSET VICTORY away fast raced early and was unable to stay in serious contention. COUNSELLOR dropped back after beginning alertly. PAULONIO broke slowly. MR. ELWOOD W. tired after a half mile. NORTH R IM was never dangerous. BIG LUXURY stopped during the stretch run. PROSPECT STREET gave way before entering the stretch.

Scratched—31962Sar¹² Demigod, 32320Ayu¹ Loop The Loop, 32320Aqu⁷ One Night Stand.

Chartist was claimed by Mrs. W. A. Kelley. Trainer W. A. Kelley.

THE NINTH RACE

THE LAST RACE on the program is one of those starter handicaps we were talking about in the last chapter.

If you look over the past performances, you will find plenty of good reasons for doubting that Swing Rex can win its fifth race in succession. Among the most compelling arguments is the exceedingly tough time the gelding had last week. At its age it should not be expected to win again today, at a longer distance, and under 120 pounds. But as I tried to tell you in the chapter on the subject, the only way I know to play this kind of race is to play the horse that won a starter handicap most recently. That makes Swing Rex the bet.

9th Race Aqueduct

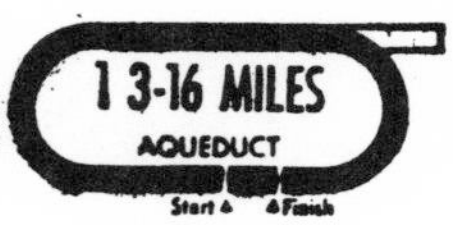

1 3-16 MILES. (Divine Comedy, November 5, 1960, 1.55⅘, 3, 116.)
Starters handicap. Purse $7,500. 3-year-olds and upward which have started for a claiming price of $3,500 or less since Sept. 16, 1966.

*Tulyaric *

B. h (1962), by Branding—Lady Tulyar, by Tulyar **113** 1967 25 1 6 3 $12,640
J. C. Toomey J. E. Rich (Haras El Pelado) (Arg.) 1966 24 3 4 1 $4,499

15Sep67-9Aqu	fst	1⅛	.48⅖	1.14	1.52⅘	Clm	6500	2	2	2^{1}	1^{1}	1^{2}	1^{1}	ACaceres	b 118	9.00	72-19	Tulyaric 118^{1} Big Shot 118^{1} PrestigioII 118^{4}	Driving	8
8Sep67-9Aqu	fst	1⅛	.47⅗	1.12⅗	1.52⅘	Clm	6500	9	7	6^{13}	$7^{7\frac{1}{2}}$	$4^{\frac{1}{2}}$	$4^{2\frac{1}{4}}$	RCun'gham[7]	b 111	15.40	70-17	Ruperto 114no World Guide 114^{2} Flannel 118^{nk}	Wide stretch	10
26Aug67-9Sar	fm	1⅛ Ⓣ			1.48⅗	Hcp	5000s	12	7	$6^{2\frac{1}{4}}$	$6^{5\frac{1}{2}}$	$7^{3\frac{3}{4}}$	6^{15}	HWoodhouse	b 111	9.30f	75- 7	Domitrix 117^{2} Spartanburg 122^{4} Austral II 114^{3}	No threat	13
19Aug67-9Sar	sly	1⅛	.48⅕	1.13⅕	1.52⅗	Hcp	3500s	8	4	$4^{1\frac{3}{4}}$	$3^{3\frac{1}{2}}$	3^{3}	3^{8}	HWoodhouse	b 111	14.70	73-10	Sudden Storm 115^{2} Awesome 109^{6} Tulyaric 111^{1}	Bid, tired	8
12Aug67-9Sar	fst	1⅛	.47⅕	1.12⅕	1.51⅘	Hcp	5000s	8	10	10^{12}	10^{11}	$10^{6\frac{1}{4}}$	6^{12}	HWoodhouse	b 109	36.80	73-11	Age Of Reason 112^{1} Austral II 112^{2} Sectario $117^{\frac{1}{2}}$	No threat	12
5Aug67-9Sar	fst	1⅛	.47	1.12	1.51⅘	Hcp	3500s	3	5	5^{11}	$6^{6\frac{1}{2}}$	3^{3}	$3^{2\frac{3}{4}}$	HWoodhouse	b 109	25.90	82- 6	Agraria 120^{nk} Came To Play $112^{2\frac{1}{2}}$ Tulyaric $109^{\frac{1}{2}}$	Closed well	10
8Jly 67-9Aqu	fst	1 3/16	.47⅘	1.12⅗	1.58⅗	Hcp	3500s	8	8	9^{11}	$9^{9\frac{1}{2}}$	7^{9}	7^{14}	RTurcotte	b 112	25.40	72-14	Fuzzie King 124^{1} Encantado 114^{2} Awesome $114^{2\frac{1}{2}}$	Never in content'n	10
24Jun67-9Aqu	gd	1 3/16	.48	1.12⅗	1.59⅕	Hcp	3500s	5	5	$5^{3\frac{3}{4}}$	$4^{\frac{3}{4}}$	$2^{1\frac{1}{2}}$	$9^{8\frac{1}{2}}$	LGilligan	b 113	9.40	75-18	Fuzzie King 120^{3} Lord Saybrook 115^{nk} Discretion 100no	Tired	11
16Jun67-9Aqu	fst	1⅛	.48⅕	1.12⅘	1.52	Clm	6500	8	5	$4^{3\frac{1}{2}}$	3^{1}	$2^{1\frac{1}{2}}$	2^{4}	RTurcotte	b 118	10.20	72-14	Ronnie's Rebel 118^{4} Tulyaric 118^{h} Highly Pleased 118^{5}	Gamely	10
2Jun67-9Aqu	fst	1⅛	.47⅖	1.12	1.52⅕	Clm	6500	1	3	4^{8}	$4^{5\frac{1}{2}}$	2^{4}	$4^{2\frac{1}{4}}$	LAdams	b 118	5.90	73-18	Joe Di Rosa $118^{\frac{1}{2}}$ Ronnie's Rebel $120^{1\frac{1}{2}}$ Abolengo II 118^{nk}	Hung	9

LATEST WORKOUTS Sep 29 Bel tr.t. 3f sly .39 b Sep 26 Bel tr.t. 3f fst .37 h Sep 14 Bel tr.t. 3f fst .40 b Sept 7 Bel tr.t. 3f fst .37 h

Sudden Storm *

Gr. g (1961), by Huzzah—Dontellella, by Burning Dream **116** 1967 26 6 2 5 $27,780
Martionette Stable W. P. King (Mr.-Mrs. L. G. Burns) 1966 35 2 7 6 $10,634

26Sep67-9Aqu	fst	1⅛	.48	1.12	1.51⅕	Cl	c-10000	1	4	$3^{3\frac{1}{2}}$	3^{3}	$6^{3\frac{1}{2}}$	$7^{2\frac{3}{4}}$	RTanner[7]	b 113	5.60	77-11	Bitter $118^{\frac{3}{4}}$ Pomidoro 118no Neparoo $114^{\frac{3}{4}}$	Speed, tired	8
20Sep67-9Aqu	fst	1⅛	.48	1.12	1.51	Clm	10500	1	5	5^{3}	6^{11}	6^{12}	$5^{7\frac{1}{4}}$	RTurcotte	b 116	2.60	74-14	Ganelon II 111^{nk} Upset Victory $118^{1\frac{1}{2}}$ Sky Count $107^{1\frac{1}{2}}$	Dull effort	6
9Sep67-9Aqu	fst	1⅛	.47⅗	1.12	1.52⅕	Hcp	5000s	8	8	7^{10}	6^{9}	$6^{6\frac{1}{2}}$	$3^{3\frac{1}{2}}$	RTurcotte	b 116	11.40	71-16	Austral II 113^{3} Joe Di Rosa $119^{\frac{1}{2}}$ Sudden Storm 116^{2}	Late rush	8
2Sep67-9Aqu	fst	1 3/16	.48⅗	1.13⅗	1.58⅗	Hcp	3500s	2	3	3^{1}	$1^{\frac{1}{2}}$	$2^{\frac{1}{2}}$	2^{1}	RTurcotte	b 118	6.40	85-16	Gallazo 121^{1} Sudden Storm $118^{1\frac{1}{2}}$ Fuzzie King 126^{5}	Gamely	8
19Aug67-9Sar	sly	1⅛	.48⅕	1.13⅕	1.52⅗	Hcp	3500s	4	5	$5^{3\frac{3}{4}}$	2^{3}	$2^{1\frac{1}{2}}$	1^{2}	RTurcotte	b 115	*1.00	81-10	Sudden Storm 115^{2} Awesome 109^{6} Tulyaric 111^{1}	Going away	8
4Aug67-9Sar	sly	1⅛	.48⅕	1.13⅕	1.52⅘	Clm	6000	1	4	4^{3}	$3^{1\frac{1}{2}}$	$1^{1\frac{1}{2}}$	1^{8}	RTurcotte	b 114	*1.90	80-20	Sudden Storm 114^{8} Abolengo II 116^{4} Sir Sanford $118^{2\frac{1}{2}}$	Easily	9
13Jly 67-3Aqu	fst	1	.46⅘	1.11⅘	1.37⅕	Clm	8500	2	4	4^{3}	$5^{4\frac{1}{2}}$	$5^{8\frac{1}{2}}$	$5^{9\frac{3}{4}}$	BBaeza	b 117	4.70	72-17	Bigamo $117^{\frac{3}{4}}$ Razonable 120^{h} Highly Pleased 117^{8}	No threat	6
30Jun67-9Aqu	sly	1 3/16	.49⅗	1.14⅘	2.00⅗	Cl	c-6500	4	3	$1^{1\frac{1}{2}}$	$1^{1\frac{1}{2}}$	1^{1}	$1^{\frac{1}{2}}$	LGilligan	b 120	*2.20	76-22	Sudden Storm $120^{\frac{1}{2}}$ Bent Spur $118^{2\frac{1}{2}}$ Flannel 113^{8}	Driving	5
23Jun67-9Aqu	sly	1⅛	.48⅖	1.13⅘	1.54⅕	Clm	6500	2	5	5^{6}	$2^{1\frac{1}{2}}$	$2^{\frac{1}{2}}$	1^{h}	LGilligan	b 118	9.80	65-25	Sudden Storm 118^{h} Bigamo 118^{6} Direct Action 113^{1}	Just up	7
3Jun67-9Mth	fm	1 1/16 Ⓣ			1.44⅗	Cim	8500	4	7	$4^{2\frac{1}{2}}$	4^{5}	5^{8}	$6^{5\frac{3}{4}}$	ACaceres	b 112	36.20	86- 4	Bursun $115^{1\frac{3}{4}}$ Clatterbox $114^{1\frac{1}{4}}$ Officer Sweeney 117^{nk}	No mishap	11
27May67-9Aqu	fst	1 3/16	.48⅖	1.13⅕	1.59	Hcp	3500s	8	5	$4^{2\frac{1}{2}}$	4^{4}	$7^{6\frac{1}{2}}$	7^{13}	LGilligan	b 114	34.20	71-15	Parkway North 119^{4} Gallazo 118^{h} Gypsy Baron 117^{nk}	Factor, tired	9
19May67-9Aqu	fst	1⅛	.48⅕	1.12⅘	1.53⅗	Cl	c-6500	7	10	10^{11}	11^{11}	$9^{8\frac{1}{2}}$	9^{13}	BBaeza	b 116	9.40	55-18	d-Tulyaric 116^{1} Razonable 116^{2} Abolengo II 114^{h}	Never close	11

LATEST WORKOUTS Aug 31 Bel tr.t. 5f fst 1.05 b Aug 12 Sar tr.t. 6f fst 1.17⅗ b Aug 1 Sar tr.t. 4f fst .51⅖ h

By the Sword

Ch. g (1964-Ky), by Amerigo—Granule, by Slide Rule **105** 1967 13 M 1 1 $1,725
F. Sorantino E. W. King (Mrs. F. W. Armstrong) 1966 3 M 0 0 ——

20Sep67-6Aqu	hd	1⅛ Ⓣ			1.50	Allowance		4	8	$7^{5\frac{3}{4}}$	7^{9}	8^{11}	8^{15}	JRuane	b 112	54.40	70-14	Bracer 118^{1} Fath II 117^{4} Mighty Nimrod 112^{2}	Never a factor	8
8Sep67-8Aqu	hd	1⅛ Ⓣ			1.47⅘	Allowance		1	9	$9^{7\frac{1}{4}}$	8^{9}	$7^{7\frac{1}{2}}$	6^{12}	JRuane	b 111	61.90	84- 4	Vladivostok 116^{8} Turn To Dad 112^{nk} Demetrios II $120^{1\frac{1}{2}}$	No threat	10
1Sep67-1Aqu	fst	7f	.23	.46⅘	1.26⅕	Md	6500	4	14	14^{12}	11^{11}	$7^{6\frac{1}{2}}$	$4^{4\frac{1}{4}}$	JRuane	b 120	20.00f	71-21	Tankard $120^{2\frac{1}{2}}$ Mister G. R. $118^{\frac{3}{4}}$ Paul's Option 120^{1}	Rallied	14
15Aug67-8Sar	fm	1⅛ Ⓣ			1.48⅗	Allowance		7	7	$9^{8\frac{1}{4}}$	$11^{9\frac{3}{4}}$	12^{14}	12^{20}	BFeliciano	b 110	36.30e	70-10	Ski Lift $109^{3\frac{1}{2}}$ Hatchery $113^{1\frac{1}{2}}$ Shah 110^{1}	Never a threat	12
5Aug67-9Sar	fst	1⅛	.47	1.12	1.51⅘	Hcp	3500s	9	7	8^{14}	$8^{9\frac{1}{2}}$	$8^{7\frac{1}{4}}$	$8^{9\frac{1}{4}}$	JRuane	b 107	45,00	76- 6	Agraria 120^{nk} Came To Play $112^{2\frac{1}{2}}$ Tulyaric $109^{\frac{1}{2}}$	No speed	10
24Jly 67-2Aqu	fst	1⅛	.47	1.12⅗	1.53⅖	Clm	4500	9	8	8^{11}	5^{7}	1^{1}	2^{2}	JRuane	b 117	13.40	67-17	Col. Pyncheon 117^{2} By The Sword $117^{\frac{3}{4}}$ Jed 117^{5}	Drifted out on turn	11
17Jly 67-9Aqu	fst	1 3/16	.48⅘	1.13⅘	1.59⅗	Cl	c-3500	2	4	4^{6}	$5^{9\frac{1}{2}}$	5^{21}	5^{29}	HGustines	b 109	3.70	52-15	Bold Stand 116^{1} Eight Up 116^{14} Willow Creek 116^{6}	Fell back	7
10Jly 67-1Mth	fst	6f	.22⅕	.45⅗	1.12⅖	Clm	3500	10	9	$10^{8\frac{1}{4}}$	10^{17}	$8^{8\frac{1}{4}}$	5^{4}	JVelasquez	b 113	4.10	76-16	Fear Nothing $113^{\frac{1}{2}}$ Orcinus 103^{2} Thailand $115^{1\frac{1}{2}}$	Rallied	12
5Jly 67-1Aqu	gd	1⅛	.47⅕	1.12⅖	1.53⅕	Md	6000	6	7	7^{15}	9^{19}	6^{16}	5^{19}	EBelmonte	b 112	*3.00	51-21	Oglethorpe 114^{2} Never Never Miss 114^{8} Mister G. R. 110^{6}	Wide	11
22Jun67-3Aqu	fst	7f	.22⅘	.46⅕	1.26⅕	Md	7500	6	7	$6^{4\frac{1}{2}}$	6^{6}	$5^{4\frac{1}{2}}$	5^{6}	BBaeza	b 115	12.80	69-17	Wyatt $115^{\frac{1}{2}}$ Paul's Option $115^{1\frac{1}{2}}$ Eagle Cloud 111^{h}	Rough trip	14
12Jun67-1Aqu	fst	1⅛	.47⅘	1.13	1.54⅕	Md	4500	10	10	10^{21}	9^{13}	$6^{5\frac{1}{2}}$	3^{4}	BBaeza	b 114	5.50	61-18	Jed $114^{3\frac{1}{2}}$ Socialsnif $112^{\frac{1}{2}}$ By The Sword 114^{6}	Poor start	10
7Jun67-9Mth	fm*	1 1/16 Ⓣ			1.49⅖	Clm	7500	5	5	8^{11}	9^{20}	9^{23}	9^{25}	DHidalgo	b 114	23.40	57-16	Long Valley $114^{\frac{1}{2}}$ Wheels Down 112^{5} Ativon $109^{\frac{3}{4}}$	Far back	10

LATEST WORKOUTS Sep 18 Bel tr.t. 5f fst 1.04 b Sep 14 Bel tr.t. 5f fst 1.03⅕ b Sep 11 Bel tr.t. 4f fst .51 h Aug 24 Sar 7f fst 1.29 h

Jet Formation *

B. g (1963–Fla), by Bolivar II—Missinformation, by Jet Master
H. A. Cohen S. S. Sahagian (H. S. Nichols) 110
1967 13 4 1 2 $9,800
1966 6 1 1 0 $4,125

16Sep67-9Aqu fst 1 1/16 .47⅗1.13 1.59⅗ Hcp 3500s 4 8 712 69 46½ 36 PBrandt b 114 3.80 71–16 Swing Rex 113³ Fuzzie King 125³ Jet Formation 114nk In close 9
30Aug67-7Rkm fst 1¼ .47⅗1.12 2.03 Hcp 4000s 6 6 612 14½ 16 19 PBrandt b 122 3.60 99–15 JetFormation 122⁹ ShahOfMorocco 108¾ IceJam 120²½ Mild drive 7
23Aug67-8Rkm fst 1 3/16 .47⅖1.12⅘1.58⅕ Hcp 4000s 9 5 57½ 42 12½ 2½ PBrandt b 123 2.50 87–19 Ice Jam 116½ Jet Formation 123¾ Shah Of Morocco 110⅜ Failed 9
14Aug67-9Rkm fst 1⅛ .47⅕1.12 1.51⅘ Hcp 2500s 6 6 613 56½ 12 12½ PBrandt b 126 3.20 87–18 Jet Formation 126²½ Prince Tuck 114¾ Flakey 107¹½ Kept driving 6
7Aug67-6Rkm gd 1⅛ .47⅘1.12⅕1.53 Hcp 2500s 1 1 11½ 12 12½ 1½ PBrandt b 123 3.00 81–22 Jet Formation 123½ Persian Knight 114⁶ Big Poona 128¹½ Driving 6
1Aug67-10Rkm fst 1 1/16 .48⅕1.12⅗1.44⅗ Clm 2500 10 1 13 14½ 112 118 PBrandt b 118 6.20 88–19 Jet Formation 118¹⁸ Sooner's Son 115¹½ CountNelson115nk Mild dr. 11
18Jly 67-5Rkm fst 1 1/16 .47⅘1.12⅘1.46⅘ Clm 4000 2 2 22 23½ 46 68¾ TSisum b 115 3.00 68–18 Cherry Tree 117no War Alert 115⁶½ Red Salmon 115½ Early speed 7
10Jly 67-3Rkm fst 1 1/16 .47⅕1.11⅗1.44⅘ Clm 3500 6 1 1h 1h 22 35 TSisum b 115 4.40 82–15 SmoothFlying 115³½ OzarkJet 115¹½ JetFormation 115¹ Weakened 7
28Jun67-7Suf fst 6f .22⅘ .46⅕1.11⅗ Clm 6250 7 9 87 98¼ 910 87½ TDunlavy b 114 22.10 76–19 LightGraph117¹½ HalfStoned 114½ Maid'sAdventure109h No speed 9
24Jun67-4Suf fst 6f .22⅕ .45⅗1.10⅘ Clm 7500 3 6 64½ 79½ 711 712 TDunlavy b 114 7.40 75–19 Circumspect 112³¾ Slapstick 114²½ Bronzeuary 114² No speed 8

Willow Creek

B. c (1963–NY), by Auditing—Lynmouth, by Better Self
R. B. Rakow J. Rigione (Miss Barbara Van Tuyl) 110
1967 15 1 0 6 $11,765
1966 13 2 1 0 $7,330

18Sep67-9Aqu fst 1 3/16 .48⅕1.12⅘1.59 Clm 3500 7 7 76 54 1½ 13½ ACorderoJr b 113 3.90 84–15 Willow Creek 113³½ Victaray 113³ Eiffel II 117² Ridden out 11
12Sep67-9Aqu fst 1 .45⅘1.09⅗1.36⅗ Clm 3500 10 11 910 711 413 33 ECardone b 116 15.30 77–20 Big Luxury 113⁶ Manga Reva 116² Willow Creek 116⁴ Rallied 14
7Aug67-9Sar fst 1⅛ .47⅘1.13⅕1.54 Cl c-3500 4 5 43½ 32 45 413 CErrico b 115 11.20 61–15 Kalonji 115³ Real Beat 117⁵ Royal Rick 107⁵ Well up, wide 9
29Jly 67-9Aqu gd 1 .45⅕1.09⅘1.36⅗ Clm 3500 6 10 1014 713 610 49 JLRotz b 118 9.90 76–14 Don't Walk 111⁸ From The Top 118no Porky 118¹ Stride too late 14
24Jly 67-9Aqu fst 1⅛ .47⅘1.12⅘1.52⅕ Clm 3500 4 7 55½ 41½ 52¾ 33¼ ECardone 115 9.80 72–17 Jimmy Miller 117nk Kalonji 115³ Willow Creek 115² Wide 8
17Jly 67-9Aqu fst 1 3/16 .48⅘1.13⅘1.59⅗ Clm 3500 7 6 56½ 35 38½ 315 ADeSpirito 116 8.20 66–15 Bold Stand 116¹ Eight Up 116¹⁴ Willow Creek 116⁶ No threat 7
10Jly 67-9Aqu fst 1⅛ .47 1.12⅖1.51⅘ Clm 3500 8 7 716 78¾ 611 515 ADespirito 118 6.20 62–16 Came To Play 120²½ Eight Up 118⁸ Victaray 118² Slow start 8
15Jun67-9Aqu fst 1⅛ .46⅗1.11⅕1.51⅘ Clm 4500 8 6 613 711 69½ 68¼ ECardone 116 3.80e 68–13 d-Victaray 114¾ Real Beat 116¾ Campari II 118½ Roughed 10
18May67-9Aqu fst 1⅛ .47⅖1.12 1.52⅘ Clm 4500 1 2 24 24 23 33½ ECardone 114 5.40 68–20 Joe Di Rosa 116¹ Hy-Nat 122²½ Willow Creek 114⁶ Even try 12
4May67-9Aqu fst 1⅛ .48 1.12⅕1.53⅗ Clm 4500 5 2 2½ 1h 1h 3½ ECardone 114 28.00 67–20 Yucal 118½Scarlet Stone 114no Willow Creek 114nk Held on well 11

LATEST WORKOUTS Sep 28 Bel tr.t. 4f fst .50 h Sep 24 Bel tr.t. 5f fst 1.03 b Sep 16 Bel tr.t. 4f fst .52 b Sep 11 Bel tr.t. 3f fst .38 b

Awesome ×

B. g (1963–Va), by Bryan G.—Weird, by Tulyar
Mrs. F. E. McMillan F.E. McMillan (R. R. Dodderidge) 108
1967 24 5 2 2 $19,080
1966 21 1 2 4 $5,248

8Sep67-9Aqu fst 1⅛ .47⅗1.12⅗1.52⅘ Cl c-6500 5 3 32½ 31 106¾ 911 ORosado b 118 9.70 61–17 Ruperto 114no World Guide 114² Flannel 118nk Early speed 10
2Sep67-9Aqu fst 1 3/16 .48⅗1.13⅗1.58⅗ Hcp 3500s 6 2 2h 2½ 68 815 ORosado b 110 6.80 71–16 Gallazo 121¹ Sudden Storm 118¹½ Fuzzie King 126⁵ Bore out 8
19Aug67-9Sar sly 1⅛ .48⅕1.13⅕1.52⅗ Hcp 3500s 3 1 1½ 13 11½ 22 ORosado b 109 17.60 79–10 Sudden Storm 115² Awesome 109⁶ Tulyaric 111¹ Good effort 8
12Aug67-9Sar fst 1⅛ .47⅕1.12⅕1.51⅘ Hcp 5000s 9 5 56½ 55½ 75½1016 ORosado b 109 66.10 69–11 Age Of Reason 112¹ Austral II 112² Sectario 117½ Tired 12
5Aug67-9Sar fst 1⅛ .47 1.12 1.51⅘ Hcp 3500s 1 1 13 13 43½ 67 LAdams b 113 19.90 78– 6 Agraria 120nk Came To Play 112²½ Tulyaric 109½ Used early 10
29Jly 67-9Aqu sf 1 3/16 Ⓣ 1.59⅗ Hcp 5000s 3 1 1½ 2h 67½1117 RTurcotte b 110 24.10 55–27 Austral II 110nk Came To Play 112² Sectario 119¾ Early sp'd, tired 13
22Jly 67-9Aqu fst 1 3/16 .46⅗1.11⅕1.58⅖ Hcp 3500s 1 2 23 24 43½ 54½ LAdams b 112 3.90 82–11 Encantado 114¹½ Eagle's Scream 110¹ Fuzzie King 128¹½ Weak'd 8
15Jly 67-9Aqu sly 1⅛ .48 1.12⅕1.51 Hcp 7500s 2 1 1h 21 56½ 615 RTurcotte b 111 4.50 66–18 Bombax 115¾ Austral II 108⁴ Wondrascope 114³ Used early 7
8Jly 67-9Aqu fst 1 3/16 .47⅘1.12⅗1.58⅗ Hcp 3500s 1 1 13 13 1h 33 WBoland b 114 *2.20 83–14 Fuzzie King 124¹ Encantado 114² Awesome 114²½ Clear lead, weak'd 10
29Jun67-9Aqu fst 1⅛ .47⅕1.12⅕1.52⅘ Cl c-5000 3 1 12 14 15 14 LAdams b 120 4.90 72–19 Awesome 120⁴ Victaray 118nk Sir Rodolph 118¹½ Mild drive 8
22Jun67-9Aqu fst 1 3/16 .49⅘1.14⅕1.59⅘ Clm 5000 4 1 11 1½ 1½ 11½ LAdams b 118 11.60 80–17 Awesome 118¹½ Victaray 118² Ruperto 118⁵ Kept to drive 6

LATEST WORKOUTS Sep 27 Bel 1m fst 1.48 b Sep 22 Bel 4f fst .53 b Sep 1 Bel 4f fst .50 b

Fuzzie King ×

Br. h (1961), by Martins Rullah—Blue Fuzz, by Kings Blue
Pomponio Stable J. P. McCormick (Mrs. M. Zipkin) 123
1967 14 8 1 2 $27,955
1966 7 2 0 2 $6,825

16Sep67-9Aqu fst 1 3/16 .47⅗1.13 1.59⅗ Hcp 3500s 2 5 411 46 23 23 RWitmer b 125 *3.00 74–16 Swing Rex 113³ Fuzzie King 125³ Jet Formation 114nk Gamely 9
2Sep67-9Aqu fst 1 3/16 .48⅗1.13⅗1.58⅗ Hcp 3500s 8 8 87¼ 74 33½ 32½ RWitmer b 126 *2.30 83–16 Gallazo 121¹ Sudden Storm 118¹½ Fuzzie King 126⁵ Rallied 8
22Jly 67-9Aqu fst 1 3/16 .46⅗1.11⅕1.58⅖ Hcp 3500s 6 6 613 34 13 32¼ RWitmer b 128 *2.00 84–11 Encantado 114¹½ Eagle's Scream 110¹ Fuzzie King 128¹½ Faltered 8
8Jly 67-9Aqu fst 1 3/16 .47⅘1.12⅗1.58⅗ Hcp 3500s 6 5 63¾ 45½ 3½ 11 RWitmer b 124 2.90 86–14 Fuzzie King 124¹ Encantado 114² Awesome 114²½ Won going away 10
24Jun67-9Aqu gd 1 3/16 .48 1.12⅗1.59⅕ Hcp 3500s 1 6 64¼ 52¾ 11½ 13 RWitmer b 120 4.70 83–18 Fuzzie King 120³ Lord Saybrook 115nk Discretion 100no Ridden out 11
29Apr67-3Pim fst 1⅛ .48 1.12⅘1.50⅘ Hcp 3500s 5 5 56 31 11½ 1¾ RWitmer b 122 *1.40 97–11 Fuzzie King 122¾ Showdown Man 105⁷ Gallazo 121³ Hard urged 6
22Apr67-4Pim fst 1 1/16 .47⅖1.12 1.45⅕ Hcp 3500s 6 5 56 2h 14 16 RWitmer b 114 *2.40 84–16 Fuzzie King 114⁶ Crown Keys 113¹ Regal Lover 128¹ Easily 7
8Apr67-4Pim fst 1⅛ .47 1.11⅗1.51⅘ Hcp 4000s 4 7 611 410 36 1½ RWitmer b 112 3.10 92–14 Fuzzie King 112½ Crown Keys 114¹½ Discretion 104⁵ Handy score 8
25Mar67-7Pim fst 1 1/16 .47⅘1.12⅘1.59⅗ Hcp 5000s 4 6 42 42 35 46 RWitmer b 113 6.90 69–24 Regal Lover 117¹ Bombax 119⁴ Gray Prince 114¹ No mishap 10
13Mar67-5Pim fst 1⅛ .48⅕1.13⅕1.51⅗ Cl c-5000 5 5 fog 1h 11 JBrockleb'nk b 122 5.30 93–14 Fuzzie King 122¹ Dodgertown 113⁸ Two Wings 114³½ Driving 7

LATEST WORKOUTS Sep 23 Atl 6f fst 1.15 b Aug 29 Atl 7f fst 1.27 b Aug 26 Atl 6f my 1.17⅖ b

* Gallazo *

B. h, (1962), by Naucide—Crackling, by Krakatao
J. S. Kroese F. J. McManus (Haras Tarapaca) (Chile) 121
1967 15 4 2 1 $19,085
1966 4 0 0 0 ——

16Sep67-9Aqu fst 1 3/16 .47⅗1.13 1.59⅗ Hcp 3500s 9 7 612 59 816 914 WBoland 125 5.90 63–16 Swing Rex 113³ Fuzzie King 125³ Jet Formation 114nk Slow start 9
2Sep67-9Aqu fst 1 3/16 .48⅗1.13⅗1.58⅗ Hcp 3500s 3 6 42 41½ 1½ 11 JCruguet 121 3.30 86–16 Gallazo 121¹ Sudden Storm 118¹½ Fuzzie King 126⁵ Driving 8
25Aug67-7Sar fm 1⅝ Ⓣ 2.39⅗ SenecaH 7 10 98½ 911 1020 1026 JCruguet 110 24.50 70– 7 Paoluccio 109nk Assagai 126¾ Isokeha 111¹½ Showed nothing 11
12Aug67-8Sar fm 1 1/16 Ⓣ 1.41⅖ Allowance 7 6 56 65¼ 41 42¼ JCruguet 116 20.00 91– 7 Mystic Lad 118½ Understanding 116¾ High Hat 109¹ Lacked room 9
25Jly 67-7Del sf 1½ Ⓣ 2.36 Hcp 5000s 4 5 38 1h 12 11½ JCruguet 124 2.80 68–33 Gallazo 124¹½ Mamborro 116¹ Royal Trumpeter 109⁷ Mild drive 7
18Jly 67-7Del sf 1⅜ Ⓣ 2.21 Hcp 5000s 7 5 46½ 2h 1h 1no TLee 122 5.30 57–43 Gallazo 122no Mamborro 115⁴ Sand And Stars 119nk Hard drive 12
7Jly 67-9Del fst 1½ .51⅕1.16⅖2.32⅘ Hcp 4000s 1 1 2h 12 13 13 JCruguet 117 2.70 91–16 Gallazo 117³ Sand And Stars 122³ Bar Gossip 112¹⁰ Easily 6
24Jun67-9Aqu gd 1 3/16 .48 1.12⅗1.59⅕ Hcp 3500s 3 4 43½ 96¾ 94¾ 65¼ WBoland 117 *4.20 78–18 Fuzzie King 120³ Lord Saybrook 115nk Discretion 100no Roughed 11

LATEST WORKOUTS Sep 29 Bel 5f sly 1.06 b Sep 26 Bel 4f fst .53⅘ b Sep 23 Bel 5f fst 1.05 b Sep 21 Bel tr.t. 3f fst .40 b

Swing Rex *

Br. g (1961), by Bold Ruler—Harmonica, by Snark
F. G. Rivera F. Martin (Hartland Farm) 120
1967 23 6 1 3 $26,985
1966 3 0 0 0 $160

23Sep67-9Aqu fst 1⅛ .46⅘1.11⅘1.50⅗ Hcp 5000s 4 3 44 21½ 11½ 1¾ ACorderoJr 116 3.80 83–13 Swing Rex 116¾ Austral II 116³ Big Luxury 110¹½ Hard drive 9
16Sep67-9Aqu fst 1 3/16 .47⅗1.13 1.59⅗ Hcp 3500s 7 3 34½ 32 13 13 ACorderoJr 113 4.40 77–16 Swing Rex 113³ Fuzzie King 125³ Jet Formation 114nk Mild drive 9
7Sep67-9Aqu fst 1⅛ .48⅕1.12⅗1.51⅕ Cl c-5000 4 1 11 12 13 18 ACorderoJr 118 *1.70 80–17 Swing Rex 118⁸ Chantajista 118¾ Big Shot 118¹½ Easy score 8
28Aug67-9Aqu gd 1⅛ .48⅘1.14 1.54⅖ Clm 3500 6 3 2½ 11 13 16 ACorderoJr 120 2.30 64–25 Swing Rex 120⁶ Victaray 109¹⁰ Suerte Fue 116½ Easily best 9
4Aug67-2Sar fst 1⅛ .47⅗1.12⅘1.51⅕ Clm 5000 3 1 12 13 51¾ 411 ORosado b 118 *1.80 77–10 Plow 118⁵½ Eight Up 118nk Ruperto 118⁵ Set pace, tired 7
31Jly 67-9Sar fst 1⅛ .47⅘1.12⅗1.52⅕ Clm 3500 3 1 15 15 15 17 ACorderoJr b 118 1.80 83–12 Swing Rex 118⁷ Kalonji 118¹⁶ Rao Raja 118½ Speed to spare 7
29Jun67-9Aqu fst 1⅛ .47⅕1.12⅕1.52⅘ Cl c-5000 1 2 32½ 46 35½ 45¾ HWoodhouse b 118 6.10 66–19 Awesome 120⁴ Victaray 118nk Sir Rodolph 118¹½ Fell back 8
16Jun67-9Aqu fst 1⅛ .48⅕1.12⅘1.52 Clm 6500 10 1 2½ 2h 43 715 CErrico 118 23.40 61–14 Ronnie's Rebel 118⁴ Tulyaric 118h Highly Pleased 118⁵ Weakened 10
6Jun67-2Aqu fst 7f .22⅗ .45⅕1.23⅘ Clm 6250 10 6 53 43½ 35 67¾ HGustines 117 16.30 79–14 Hamorton 114³ Raider Radka 121nk Gay Orchid 117½ Weakened 12
25May67-9Aqu sl 1⅛ .47⅘1.13⅗1.52⅗ Cl c-5000 3 1 1½ 11½ 1h 34 ECardone 116 *1.90 69–24 Yucal 120³ No Snakes 119¹ Swing Rex 116³ Set pace, tired 8
19May67-9Aqu fst 1⅛ .48⅕1.12⅘1.53⅗ Clm 6500 11 4 4nk 31 82½ 77½ JTartaglia10 106 37.40 60–18 d-Tulyaric 116¹ Razonable 116² Abolengo II 114h Speed, tired 11

LATEST WORKOUTS Sep 29 Bel tr.t. 3f sly .39 b Sep 22 Bel tr.t. 3f fst .36⅘ h Sep 14 Bel tr.t. 4f fst .48⅖ h Sep 3 Bel tr.t. 3f fst .37 h

NINTH RACE
Aqu - 32434
September 30, 1967

1 3-16 MILES. (Divine Comedy, November 5, 1960, 1.55⅘, 3, 116.)

Starters handicap. Purse $7,500. 3-year-olds and upward which have started for a claiming price of $3,500 or less since Sept. 16, 1966.

Value to winner $5,200, second $1,600, third $800, fourth $400. Mutuel pool $557,236.

Index	Horse	Eqt	A	Wt	PP	St	¼	½	¾	Str	Fin	Jockey	Owner	Odds $1
32380Aqu¹	Swing Rex		6	120	8	2	2½	3½	3²	2h	1½	E Belmonte	F G Rivera	2.80
32263Aqu⁹	Awesome	b	4	108	5	1	1³	1¹½	1²	1¹½	2⁵½	E Cardone	Mrs F E McMillan	17.00
32326Aqu³	Jet Formation	b	4	113	4	4	4⁴	2¹	2²	3⁶	3⁴	L Adams	H A Cohen	3.70
32398Aqu⁷	Sudden Storm	b	6	116	2	3	3h	4³	4¹	4h	4²½	R Turcotte	Martoinette Stable	5.90
32326Aqu²	Fuzzie King	b	6	123	6	7	6³	5½	5¹½	5⁴	5⁷	R Witmer	Pomponio Stable	2.50
32317Aqu¹	Tulyaric	b	5	113	1	6	5h	6⁵	6⁵	6⁶	6⁴	A Caceres	J C Toomey	19.40
32350Aqu⁸	By The Sword	b	3	108	3	8	8	7¹⁰	7	7	7	J Ruane	F Sorrentino	44.90
32326Aqu⁹	Gallazo		5	121	7	5	7½	8	Bled			J Cruguet	J S Kroese	5.60

Time .24, .48, 1.12, 1.38⅕, 1.58⅖ (with wind in backstretch). Track fast.

$2 Mutuel Prices:

8—SWING REX	7.60	5.40	3.60
5—AWESOME		12.60	6.80
4—JET FORMATION			3.80

Br. g, by Bold Ruler—Harmonica, by Snark. Trainer F. Martin. Bred by Hartland Farm.

IN GATE AT 5.56. OFF AT 5.56 EASTERN STANDARD TIME. Start good. Won driving.

SWING REX, reserved and well placed until reaching the stretch, responded readily during the drive and won from AWESOME in the last sixteenth. AWESOME, away fast, set the pace under steady rating and held on determinedly during the drive but could not withstand SWING REX while easily second best. JET FORMATION tired during the final furlong. SUDDEN STORM raced fairly well without mishap. FUZZIE KING was never dangerous. TULYARIC had no excuse. BY THE SWORD was far back the entire trip. GALLAZO bled.

Scratched—32335Aqu¹ Willow Creek. Overweights—By The Sword 3 pounds, Jet Formation 3.

A SUMMING UP

How did we do on the day? I had Worklamp ($12.40), Mr. Washington ($3.60), Damascus ($5.60), Vail Pass (loser), and Swing Rex ($7.60). A profit of $19.20 on $2.00 bets, or $192 on $20.00 bets. Or $1,920 on $200 bets. An exceptionally good day. No cause whatever to regret passing up Fire Escape ($20.00), Mr. Hasty ($17.80), Green Glade ($10.40), or the daily double ($151).

PART SIX

Handicapping Another Full Card

THURSDAY, SEPTEMBER 19, 1968, was neither the most nor the least challenging day of the long Atlantic City racing season. Call it a typical Thursday. Of the seven sprints on the main track and the two middle-distance affairs on the grass, three were run under allowance conditions and the rest were claimers. No really good horse appeared, but the overall quality was only a cut below what you see on a Thursday at New York or Los Angeles.

Let's take this cloudy afternoon as it comes, handicapping each race as best we can, and see whether we can leave with more green than we had when we arrived.

THE FIRST RACE

THIS RACE is at seven furlongs, for $5,000 maiden fillies, aged three and four. The handicapping problem is severe.

1st Atlantic City

Start ▼ 7 FURLONGS ATLANTIC CITY ▲Finish

7 FURLONGS (Chute). (Chit Chat, Aug. 12, 1958, 1.20⅗, 6, 114.) Maidens. Claiming. Purse $3,500. Fillies. 3- and 4-year-olds. Weights 3-year-old 116 lbs., 4-year-olds 119 lbs. Claiming price $5,000.

Barbee Vee $5,000 — Ch. f (1964-Md), by Prepared—Potville, by Greek Ship — Vale-Rio Stable B. Lepman (Vale-Rio Stable) **114**5 — 1968 5 M 0 1 $4 / 1967 5 M 0 0 —

9Sep68-1Atl fst 7f .23 .46⅗1.25⅖ f-M 5000 8 11 74¾ 79½ 1018 1023 GCusimano5 b 114 8.10 53-18 She Rates 116nk Maestro's Miss 1164½ Miss Parker 1163½ Reared
23Aug68-1Atl fst 6f .22⅗ .46⅕1.12⅕ Md 5000 9 2 32 35 54¾ 68¾ DKassen b 115 4.40 72-19 Amore Luigi 111nk Maori Hero 1202 Sufico 1162 Used in pace
5Aug68-1Atl fst 6f .22⅘ .47 1.13 f-M 5000 3 4 11 1½ 21½ 32½ DKassen b 120 16.50 74-17 Debby's Tune 1162 Roulette Queen 117½ BarbeeVee120no Weakened
26Jly 68-1Mth fst 6f .22⅖ .46⅖1.12⅘ Md 5000 7 4 2h 11 33½ 59¼ DKassen b 115 7.50 69-23 Our Beulah 1111½ Battle Emperor 1156 Implicit 1101½ Used early
11Jly 68-1Mth fst 6f .22 .45⅘1.13⅖ f-M 5000 2 6 2h 1½ 2½ 74½ DKassen b 121 28.30 70-19 Royal Bessie 1161½ Festa Burga 111h Miss Parker 116no Used up
9Nov67-1GS fst 6f .22⅗ .47 1.13⅘ Md 4500 9 4 64½ 711 812 816 EMonacelli b 112 46.50 59-24 Choicy Pet 1121½ Darlin's Bob 117no Eagle Nest 1171 No threat
1Sep67-1Atl gd 6f .23 .47 1.12⅖ Md 4500 7 12 1011 1012 1018 1120 AAgnello b 110 70.60 60-22 BeyMahmoud 1143½ Galleon 1204½ Bobby'sBrother 1171¼ No speed
30May67-7Del fst 6f .22⅘ .47 1.12⅗ Allowance 3 5 2h 32½ 814 815 DDSmith b 111 29.20 67-19 TwistOfTime122hCheerf'lApproach122no•BirthdayCard1226 Stopped
27Apr67-1GS sly 6f .23⅗ .48⅖1.14⅗ Md 10000 8 3 41¼ 68½ 713 822 JJohnson 113 21.40 49-30 Olympia Jo 1133½ Galleon 120h Inagreement 1204½ Fell back
22Apr67-3GS fst 6f .22⅗ .46⅗1.12⅗ Clm 7500 5 4 73¾ 78¾ 79½ 618 RBroussard 116 26.20 63-20 Sky Dive 1162 Ethical 1111½ Quick Jump 1161 No mishap
LATEST WORKOUTS Sep 18 Atl 4f fst .52 b — Sep 1 Atl 3f fst .37⅖ b

Everglades Pry $5,000 — Ch. f (1965-Fla), by Fouquier—Juldee, by Selalbeda — R. DeSantis R. DeSantis (H. A. Dabson) **109**7 — 1968 7 M 0 0 — / 1967 0 M 0 0 —

14Sep68-1Atl fst 6f .23 .46⅘1.11⅗ f- 4000 9 11 1110 1113 1115 1118 JCastillo7 b 107 7.90 66-14 Little Tag 1144 Pauline Puppet 1102 Dadley's Image 1173½ Far back
24Aug68-1Atl fst 6f .22⅖ .46⅕1.12 f- 4000 11 10 810 1011 1115 1114 RLaTorre7 b 107 103.10 68-13 Computed 107¾ Sy-Bee 1102 Pied-A-Terre 1141½ Showed nothing
16Aug68-4Atl fst 6f .22⅖ .45⅕1.10⅘ f- 4500 8 8 87¼ 813 817 820 RLaTorre7 b 107 185.20 68-18 El Esmeralda 1186 Swiss Maid 106¾ Woman's Rights 118no Trailed
8Aug68-4Atl fst 1⅛.48⅗1.13⅘1.54 Md 5000 7 6 56 717 820 841 GCusimano5 b 106 27.80 27-19 Bob's Guide 114nk Bailey's Comet 11420 Impy Sailor 114nk Far back
30Jly 68-3Del fst 170.47⅖1.13⅗1.45⅕ Md 7500 1 7 718 717 721 624 FLovato 110 60.60 50-23 Kalakaua 115nk Invincible Ed 1151½ Winter Man 1152½ Never close
10Jly 68-1Del fst 6f .22⅘ .47⅗1.14⅕ f-M 7500 12 12 1215 1214 1116 1115 RKotenko 113 110.90 59-19 PollyComeHome113h DubiousDebut'te1131½ RoyalS'ffle113h No sp'd
27Jun68-1Del my 6f .23⅕ .47⅘1.14 Md 7500 5 12 1213 1018 1118 1118 LGino 110 70.70 57-24 Prophet'sSide1091¾ DerbyDancer108h PollyComeHome1103 No speed
LATEST WORKOUTS Sep 11 Atl 4f fst my .50 b — Sep 5 TL 4f fst .47⅘ h

Paul's Bandit $5,000 — Dk. b. or br. f (1965-Ky), by Bandit—First Honey, by Beau Pere — Mr.-Mrs. B. M. Harrison-J. Gauthier J. Gauthier (O. R. Harrod) **116** — 1968 1 M 0 0 — / 1967 1 M 0 0 —

6Sep68-1Atl fst 6f .22⅖ .45⅗1.11⅘ Md 5000 1 9 55½ 813 1115 1115 EGuerin b 115 23.10 68-18 Dadley'sImage1142 RunningTom1173 LaVictroienne1142 Fell back
17Jly 67-1Del fst 5½f.22⅖ .47⅘1.07⅗ Clm 5000 9 5 55 68¼ 813 921 RRincon b 111 56.30 61-21 South C Prince 1143½ Lomorn 1137 Rapallo Sky 1115 No factor

Nanny Sel $5,000 — Ch. f (1965-Ky), by Bolero—Fancy One, by One Hitter — Valley Farm H. Young (L. Katz) **116** — 1968 10 M 0 0 — / 1967 3 M 0 0 —

3Sep68-1Atl fst 7f .22⅕ .45 1.23⅗ Md 6500 4 11 109½ 914 913 815 DHidalgo b 110 99.30 70-17 Misty Jac 1133 Rechazado 1164½ Maestro's Miss 1042½ No speed
20Aug68-4Atl fst 7f .22⅗ .44⅗1.23⅖ Md 7500 9 3 610 617 616 613 DHidalgo b 111 90.10 73-16 French Cafe 1181½ Sentinel 1145½ Misty Jac 111nk Never close
22Jly 68-7Mth fst 170.47 1.11⅖1.42 Clm 10000 5 7 711 614 616 621 DHidalgo 110 40.20 70-14 Naughty Joke 1159 Baker George 1173 Jodie R. 1153½ Never close
3Jun68-2Mth fst 6f .22⅕ .45⅘1.11⅘ f-MdSpWt 2 9 913 814 88 511 MMiceli 114 54.00 72-14 Mertensia 1152½ Desiring 1147 Five Six Quebec 1141½ Slow start
9May68-4GS fst 170.46⅘1.12⅕1.43⅕ f-MdSpWt 8 7 712 79 57½ 714 WGavidia 115 89.20 64-18 Jim N' Pam 1161½ Helen Jennings 1153 Drover's Dream 1152 No sp'd
24Apr68-3GS fst 6f .22⅖ .46 1.12 f-MdSpWt 2 8 813 78¼ 69 610 RBroussard b 116 15.30 74-14 Sequela 115no Drover's Dream 1158 Millie's Pride 1151½ No speed
28Mar68-1GP fst 7f .22⅗ .45⅘1.24⅗ f-MdSpWt 10 4 1011 1215 918 714 HGrant b 119 110.00 72-10 Pub Crawler 1193¾ Raylut 114½ Misty Jac 1191¼ Never close
12Mar68-5GP fst 7f .22 .45 1.26⅖ f-MdSpWt 7 12 1212 1117 1013 810 DBrumfield b 119 12.80e 67-17 Joy Mixa 120¾ Turf Cutter 119¾ Between The Axe 119½ No speed
13Feb68-4Hia fst 6f .22⅗ .46⅗1.12⅕ f-MdSpWt 3 9 98 87¼ 108¼ 107½ DBrumfield b 118 10.60 75-13 Connie H. 118¾ Grain Goddess 118nk Young N' Sassy 118h No speed
19Jan68-4Hia sly 6f .22⅖ .46⅖1.12⅗ f-MdSpWt 5 9 1112 813 87 54¼ LAdams b 118 65.80 77-11 Seen Afar 118no Topmost 118½ Le Doina 1183 Mild late rally
LATEST WORKOUTS Jly 28 Mth 3f fst .35⅗ h

Tony's Heather $5,000 — B. f (1965-NJ), by Tony's Chance—Heathereast, by Heather Broom — A. J. Repici G. F. Jabalee (E. J. O'Connell) **116** — 1968 2 M 0 0 — / 1967 0 M 0 0 —

12Sep68-1Atl fst 6f .22⅘ .46⅘1.12⅖ Md 4500 8 5 51¾ 1014 1120 1131 EMonacelli 112 14.50 49-21 Cool Caper 1155 Tax Load 1164 You Will Score 1142½ Tired
5Sep68-3Atl fst 6f .23 .46⅗1.12 Cl c-3500 3 5 61¾ 64¾ 68½ 713 EMaple 110 5.40 69-19 El Casey 108nk Cool Caper 1127 Phylsjohn 1131¼ Showed little
LATEST WORKOUTS Sep 11 Atl 3f my .36⅕ h — Sep 2 Atl 5f fst 1.01⅗ h — Aug 15 Atl 5f fst 1.05 bg

Millie's Pride $5,000 — Ro. f (1965-Va), by Sherluck—Chemuka, by Palestine — Mrs. T. J. Brogan E. Yowell (M. Church 3d) **116** — 1968 9 M 1 2 $1.77 / 1967 3 M 0 0 $21

26Aug68-5Atl fst 6f .22⅗ .46⅕1.11⅖ f-MdSpWt 2 6 56 56 57½ 59¼ WBlum b 116 5.10 76-16 Shirly Swift 1163 Right Busy 116no High Sails 116nk No threat
12Aug68-3Atl fst 6f .22 .45⅗1.12 f-MdSpWt 1 7 56½ 610 66½ 54½ WBlum b 116 8.50 77-14 Lightning Blue 116¾ Bubble Case 1183 Right Busy 117½ No mishap
29Jly 68-3Mth fst 6f .22⅗ .46⅕1.11⅗ f-MdSpWt 3 3 1½ 1½ 44½ 35 JVasquez b 115 9.70 79-17 Still 115½ Right Busy 1174½ Millie's Pride 115no Hard used
15Jly 68-2Mth fst 6f .22 .45⅖1.11⅕ f-MdSpWt 9 11 109½ 913 79 78¾ CBaltazar b 115 8.30 77-13 Director 115h Model Sister 1102½ Gosh A' Mighty 115h No factor
12Jun68-1Mth sly 6f .22 .45⅘1.12⅕ Md 7500 4 2 68 69½ 58 57 JVelasquez 112 4.20 74-16 Tote The Mail 1172 Convivia 113½ Sea Chant 1183½ No mishap
23May68-1GS fst 6f .22⅕ .45⅗1.11⅘ Md 7500 4 6 43½ 39 46 23 JVasquez 110 *2.30 82-15 Geormel 1133 Millie's Pride 1102 Happy Medium 110½ Rallied
16May68-2GS fst 6f .22⅘ .46⅕1.11⅘ Md 10000 1 5 2h 44¼ 46½ 57¾ GPatterson 111 5.40 77-17 Athena's Lark 1111¼ Hopeful Bid 1162½ Country Day 1223½ Gave way
24Apr68-3GS fst 6f .22⅖ .46 1.12 f-MdSpWt 8 2 32 42¼ 45½ 38 CBaltazar 115 10.00 76-14 Sequela 115no Drover's Dream 1158 Millie's Pride 1151½ Tired
26Feb68-3Hia fst 6f .22⅖ .46⅕1.11⅗ f-MdSpWt 9 7 1013 1018 913 815 DBrumfield 118 12.00 71-15 CourtCircular1182 NativeEmpress1182 FourthWonder1183½ Stopped
18Aug67-4Atl fst 5½f.22⅕ .45⅘1.05⅕ f-MdSpWt 1 7 83½ 812 710 69½ JCombest 117 4.70 83-15 Purple Thrush 1174½ Double Ripple 117nk Lanoka 1171¼ No threat
LATEST WORKOUTS Sep 15 Atl 5f fst 1.01⅗ h — Sep 11 Atl 4f my .50⅘ b — Sep 7 Atl 3f sly .48 b — Aug 24 Atl 3f fst .36 b

La Victroienne $5,000 — Dk. b. or br. f (1965-Va), by Victory Morn—Berlette, by Decathlon — J. A. Bell 3d W C. Freeman (Cherry Blossom Farm) **116** — 1968 3 M 0 1 $45 / 1967 0 M 0 0 —

6Sep68-1Atl fst 6f .22⅖ .45⅗1.11⅘ Md 5000 11 1 31½ 32½ 34½ 35 GPatterson 114 12.10 78-18 Dadley'simage1142 RunningTom1173 LaVictroienne1142 Evenly
14Aug68-1Atl fst 6f .22⅗ .46⅕1.12⅕ Md 5000 7 2 42 69½ 917 1021 GPatterson 111 *2.70 60-13 Law And Chancery 1159 Nappy's Girl 1132½ Conjurer 116¾ Brief sp'd
7Aug68-1Atl fst 6f .22⅖ .46⅖1.12⅕ Md 5000 5 5 2h 21 35 611 GPatterson 111 12.50 70-15 Little Miss Muffet 1125 Buzzaway 1115 Cool Caper 116½ Weakened
LATEST WORKOUTS Sep 14 Atl 4f fst .49 b — Aug 31 Atl 4f fst .51⅕ b — Aug 27 Atl 5f fst 1.01 h — Jly 31 Del 4f fst .49 hg

laid Doll * **$5,000** B. f (1964–NJ), by Scotch Bull—Togadru, by Escadru
Helene Kane A. Caccese (G. F. Veirman) **112**7

1968	3	M	0	0	——
1967	15	M	5	2	$4,415

Sep68–1Atl	fst 6f	.22⅘ .46⅘1.12⅖	Md	5000	3	7	4¾	34½	59	619	FMartinez7	110	6.90	61–21	Cool Caper 1155 Tax Load 1164 You Will Score 1142½	Tired 11
Aug68–1Mth	my 6f	.22⅕ .46⅖1.12⅗	Md	5000	7	7	43½	77½	914	1224	RTanner5	110	9.80	55–21	Implicit 1183 Woman's Rights 1176 Carry Away 1202	Stopped 12
May68–1GS	fst 6f	.22⅕ .45⅘1.12⅕	Md	5000	1	8	913	1124	Pull'd up		JVasquez	117	8.10	——	Rising Rage 111½ Silver Beakey 1161½ Black Copper 117nk	Unr'ly post 11
Nov67–1GS	fst 6f	.23 .47 1.13⅘	Md	5000	11	1	11	1h	21	25	JVelasquez	116	*1.10	70–26	Tony's India 1135 Plaid Doll 1161 Colts Neck Dandy 1153	Gamely 12
Oct67–1GS	fst 6f	.22⅘ .47⅖1.13⅕	Md	5000	11	1	12	14	11½	23½	WGavidia	115	4.50	74–22	Mendota Hills 1143½ Plaid Doll 115h Tubelo 1143	Gamely 12
Oct67–1GS	fst 6f	.22⅘ .47 1.12⅘	Md	5000	6	3	11½	13	32½	813	WGavidia	115	7.20	67–23	Carr Bairn 1183½ Mendota Hills 1141½ Masked Jim 1181¼	Used up 12
Sep67–1Atl	fst 6f	.22⅖ .45⅖1.11⅖	f–M	5000	2	3	13	16	14	21	DCaraballo7	110	5.40	84–15	Dads Dearie 1131 Plaid Doll 1104 Cornishrose 1082	Gamely 12
Sep67–1Atl	gd 6f	.23 .47 1.12⅖	Md	5000	9	1	2h	3nk	35	49¼	WGavidia	114	6.90	71–22	BeyMahmoud 1143½ Galleon 1204½ Bobby'sBrother 1171¼	Tired 12
Aug67–1Atl	sly 6f	.22⅕ .45⅖1.11	Md	5000	3	2	1h	13	21	26	WGavidia	113	5.40	81–14	Navy Strut 1176 Plaid Doll 1133 Press Release 1172	Gamely 12

LATEST WORKOUTS Sep 6 Atl 5f fst 1.00⅖ b Aug 30 Atl 6f fst 1.15⅖ b Aug 17 Atl 4f fst .49⅗ b Aug 14 Atl 3f fst .37 b

rctic Gem **$5,000** Dk. b. or br. f (1965–Md), by Star Ice—Janet B., by Chrysler II
F R. Hertig M. Benson (Mr.–Mrs. F. R. Hertig) **116**

1968	1	M	0	0	——
1967	3	M	0	0	——

Sep68–1Atl	fst 6f	.22⅖ .45⅗1.11⅘	Md	5000	8	11	109¼	611	58	57¼	JGiovanni	114	40.80	76–18	Dadley'sImage1142 RunningTom1173 LaVictroienne1142	No threat 12
Nov67–4GS	fst 6f	.22⅘ .47⅗1.14⅗	f–MdSpWt		8	12	1218	1014	1015	1012	WMcKeever5	111	254.80	59–27	Flaming Fields 1161½ Properly 1162½ Weeki Wacki 116¾	Never close 12
Oct67–3GS	fst 6f	.22⅘ .46⅘1.12⅗	f–M	10500	6	9	96½	913	913	813	JLeonard	117	121.00	68–19	Forever Cheery 1082 Coila 1131 Royal Souffle 1133½	No speed 12
Oct67–1GS	fst 6f	.22 .46 1.12⅗	Md	12500	8	10	1015	1021	1120	1116	CBaltazar	114	63.60	65–20	Mineola Lad 1171¼ Amore Luigi 1131½ Jimmy Bennett 112½	No sp'd 12

LATEST WORKOUTS Sep 18 Atl 3f fst .37 b Sep 14 Atl 4f fst .49 b Sep 5 Atl 3f fst .37 b Aug 31 Atl 5f fst 1.04⅗ b

air Boadicea **$5,000** Gr. f (1964–NJ), by My Warrior—Bijou Fol, by Royal Gem
Mrs. G. S. Howell G. S. Howell (Mr.–Mrs. G. S. Howell) **112**7

1968	8	M	0	2	$970
1967	6	M	0	0	$175

May68–1Mth	gd 6f	.22⅖ .46⅕1.14	Md	5000	12	9	813	820	712	57¼	RSage5	b 112	*2.90	65–14	El Robarb 115¾ Le Prop 1154 Very Wise 1221¼	Not a threat 12
May68–1Pim	fst 6f	.23⅖ .47 1.13⅖	Md	8500	12	11	1111	813	711	47¾	EWalsh	b 115	8.80	75–18	Curling Stone 1126 Swearing In 1221¾ Buzzaway 107no	Rallied 12
May68–4Pim	fst 6f	.23⅗ .47⅖1.13⅕	f–	5000	4	12	129½	1212	1212	99½	EWalsh	b 115	27.00	74–18	Ivajay 1151½ Pianissima 1121¼ Broken Needle 1152½	Never close 12
Apr68–5Bow	fst 6f	.22⅖ .45⅗1.10⅘	f–	5000	8	11	1113	911	77¾	54½	EWalsh	b 113	31.60	88–10	Miss Race 1141¾ Ivajay 1141¾ Doesn't She 116¾	Late rally 11
Apr68–3Bow	fst 1 1/16	.48⅕1.12⅗1.45	Md Sp Wt		7	4	53½	57	48	109	RSage7	b 110	11.70	79–11	First Hunt 1111 Kurrewa 1125 Parthia's Star 1221	Fell back 12
Apr68–4Bow	fst 6f	.22⅖ .46 1.12	Md	5000	11	1	108¼	611	54	35	HDittfach	b 115	4.60	82–18	Rule Breaker 1205 Pulltight Knob 120h Fair Boadicea 115¾	No exc. 12
Mar68–4Bow	fst 7f	.23⅗ .47⅕1.27	Md Sp Wt		7	6	63¼	55	31	3½	HDittfach	b 115	47.50	69–22	Sun Porch 115½ Barbers Son 120h Fair Boadicea 1151½	Wide 10
Mar68–3Bow	fst 6f	.22⅗ .46 1.11⅕	Md Sp Wt		5	11	99¼	910	811	711	HDittfach	b 115	34.30	80–11	Blinkin Excuse 1134 Rose Bluff 115no Festive Dancer 1201½	No sp'd 12
Dec67–4Lrl	gd 6f	.23⅕ .48⅗1.14⅖	f–MdAllow		7	8	75¼	43½	46	45½	HDittfach	b 113	53.90	74–18	Boob Tube 117½ Astrobelle 1174½ Nade's Girl 113½	No mishaps 11

Only three of the starters have tried this difficult distance and only one of these—Fair Boadicea—has shown any aptitude for it. But Fair Boadicea has not raced since May and can be granted little chance against fit rivals, even cheap ones.

Are any of her rivals really fit? And are the fit ones likely to respond well to the problems of a seven-furlong race?

Running down the track program we note a couple of jockey changes which might have some bearing on the situation. Tony's Heather is to be steered by the eminent Joe Culmone, who is choosy about his mounts. And Plaid Doll's people have forsaken the seven-pound apprentice allowance to use the talented Eddie Maple. We should keep these changes in mind when considering the horses' prospects.

A look at the past performances permits me to eliminate all but three of the starters.

Barbee Vee has early speed but no endurance. Everglades Pry and Paul's Bandit have never showed a lick of speed at any distance. Nanny Sel has been competing with higher-priced males but not vigorously enough to suggest that today's sharp drop in class will make a winner of her.

Tony's Heather has been a professional racer for only two weeks and today she faces a field of her own sex for the very first time. The presence of Culmone means that someone thinks the filly will benefit from her last two outings and from the more congenial company. Could this filly take it all? Could be, but I wouldn't bet a penny on it. If stabbing at longshots were the same as handicapping, the stabbers would be riding in taxis and the handicappers would be walking. Out goes Tony's Heather.

And so does Plaid Doll. She has been racing the boys but looks like anything but a seven-furlong horse. Moreover, her physical condition is suspect. Note how sparsely and poorly she has raced this year.

So we are left with the following:

Millie's Pride: Eddie Yowell's Sherluck filly closed bravely against $7,500 male maidens on May 23, behaving very much as if she would appreciate a longer race. On August 12 she offered a similar clue in a race against some of the most expensive female maidens on the grounds. Dropping today into the least formidable field of her career, she must be accepted as a contender, but I refuse to bet on her. She never has put together two decent races in succession. Furthermore, she has had twelve good chances to break her maiden and has come close to it only once. Worse still, her people have been unable to find the key to her. When her rider pushes her close to the early pace, she fades in the stretch. She closes well only when allowed to fall hopelessly behind in the early going. That is, she doesn't close well enough to make up for her laggard early stride. So she is a dubious item, class drop or not. If nothing more promising can be found, I'd pass this race altogether. No Bet.

La Victroienne: In her last outing Mike Freeman's novice came to life a little. If she were entered against the same kind of males today, she would rate as a contender simply on the basis of that last effort. Because today's field is a softer one, she deserves respect. But can she get the distance? Her record contains no evidence to that effect. I much prefer her to Millie's Pride, however. A lightly raced, apparently improving horse is generally a better bet than one that has failed repeatedly to fulfil its promise. If it were compulsory to bet on this race and the only two contenders were La Victroienne and Millie's Pride, I'd take La Victroienne. Fortunately, betting is never compulsory. No Bet.

Arctic Gem: This one ran her best race on September 6, behind La Victroienne. Her best, therefore, was none too hot. Since that was her first outing of the year, she might improve today. I might be tempted to buy a ticket if any of her workouts had been especially good. But they were only fair, and that dismal 1967 record inspires no confidence at all. No Bet.

In my fervid opinion, we should sit this race out. If you are the sort who simply must play, our analysis might lead you to bet on La Victroienne, but you would do so without encouragement from me.

The Running of the Race

MILLIE'S PRIDE was favored at 3–2. Arctic Gem and La Victroienne each went at slightly better than 4–1. The favorite wore herself out trying to catch Plaid Doll in the early going and finished a poor fourth. Arctic Gem was never in contention. La Victroienne won with the ease of a 3–5 shot. Joe Culmone took second with Tony's Heather, demonstrating that the horse had indeed been wound up for this particular race.

FIRST RACE 7 FURLONGS (Chute). (Chit Chat, Aug. 12, 1958, 1.20⅗, 6, 114.)

Atl - 35936
September 19, 1968

Maidens. Claiming. Purse $3,500. Fillies. 3- and 4-year-olds. Weights 3-year-olds 116 lbs., 4-year-olds 119 lbs. Claiming price $5,000.

Value to winner $2,100, second $700, third $455, fourth $245. Mutuel pool $53,656.

Index	Horse	Eqt A Wt	PP St	¼	½	Str	Fin	Jockey	Cl'g Pr	Owner	Odds $1
35837Atl³	—La Victroienne	3 116	7 5	4¹	45	11½	16	G Patterson	5000	J A Bell 3d	4.20
35882Atl¹¹	—Tony's Heather	3 116	5 3	5½	5²	4½	2½	J Cuimone	5000	A J Repici	32.70
35810Atl⁸	—Nanny Sel	b 3 116	4 9	10	8²	5³	33½	M Miceli	5000	Valley Farm	18.60
35667Atl⁵	—Millie's Pride	b 3 116	6 4	34	2½	3²	45	W Blum	5000	Mrs T J Brogan	1.50
35882Atl⁶	—Plaid Dcll	b 4 119	8 1	1¹	1²	2²	5²	E Maple†	5000	Helene Kane	10.40
34601Mth⁵	—Fair Boadicea	b 4 119	10 2	61½	6¹	7½	6ⁿᵏ	M Hole†	5000	Mrs G S Howell	9.80
35900Atl¹¹	—Everglades Pry	3 109	2 10	8ʰ	9½	9³	7ⁿᵒ	J Castillo⁷	5000	R Desantis	89.10
35837Atl⁵	—Arctic Gem	3 116	9 6	95	7ʰ	8ʰ	8ⁿᵏ	J Giovanni	5000	F Hertig	4.20
35855Atl¹⁰	—Barbee Vee	b 4 114	1 7	2½	3²	6½	94	G Cusimano⁵	5000	Vale-Rio Stable	9.70
35837Atl¹¹	—Paul's Bandit	b 3 116	3 8	7ʰ	10	10	10	E Guerin	5000	Mrs-G M Harrison	40.60

†Seven pounds apprentice allowance waived.

Time .22⅗, .46, 1.12⅖, 1.25⅖. Track fast.

$2 Mutuel Prices:

9—LA VICTROIENNE	10.40	6.40	5.40
7—TONY'S HEATHER		21.20	15.20
5—NANNY SEL			10.20

Dk. b. or br. f, by Victory Morn—Berlette, by Decathlon. Trainer W. C. Freeman. Bred by Cherry Blossom Farm (Va.).

IN GATE AT 1.32. OFF AT 1.32 EASTERN DAYLIGHT TIME. Start good. Won easily.

LA VICTROIENNE rallied into contention from the outside entering the stretch, quickly gained command while coming in slightly and drew out to win as her rider pleased. TONY'S HEATHER rallied in upper stretch and lacked a further response. NANNY SEL, slow to find best stride, finished willingly in the middle of the track. MILLIE'S PRIDE raced forwardly from the start, lodged her bid from the outside leaving the quarter pole and weakened. PLAID DOLL sprinted clear early and tired. FAIR BOADICEA was never a factor. ARCTIC GEM was always outrun. BARBEE VEE was through after a half.

Scratched—Hasty Marcha, 35855Atl³ Miss Parker, Miss Scribe, 35891Atl⁹ Adaptable Spin, 35867Aqu⁷ Long On Looks, 35691Atl¹² Elegant Bey

THE SECOND RACE

THIS RACE is at six furlongs, for $3,500 three-year-olds. The program shows that the riders have played musical chairs for this one. Each of the apparent contenders will be ridden by someone other than the guy who was aboard last time.

2nd Atlantic City

6 FURLONGS ATLANTIC CITY (Start / Finish)

6 FURLONGS. (Bright Holly, September 2, 1961, 1.08⅖, 3, 112.)
Claiming. Purse $3,500. 3-year-olds. Weight 120 lbs. Non-winners of two races since August 10 allowed 3 lbs., a race 5 lbs., a race since July 10, 8 lbs. Claiming price $3,500.

Shrapnel $3,500 — Ch. f (1965–Ky), by Federal Hill—Ammo, by War Admiral — Pennyacres Farm G. G. Delp (Fayette Farm) — **104^5** — 1968 1 M 0 0 — / 1967 0 M 0 0 —
9Sep68-3Atl fst 6f .22⅖ .46⅕1.11⅗ f-MdSpWt 10 7 10^11 10^14 10^13 10^14 GCusimano^5 112 6.40 70–18 Bubble Case 117^nk Gosh A' Mighty 117¾ Right Busy 117^2 No factor
LATEST WORKOUTS Sep 17 Atl 5f fst 1.01⅗ hg Sep 8 Atl 3f fst .38 b Sep 5 Atl 6f fst 1.14⅘ h Aug 31 Atl 5f fst 1.01 b

Fleet Tony * $3,500 — Ch. g (1965–Ariz), by Fleeting—Sistony, by Two Ton Tony — R. W. Woodward R. W. Woodward (L. Madison) — **112** — 1968 14 1 5 3 $2,7.. / 1967 0 M 0 0 —
14Sep68-7ShD fst 3½f.22⅖ .35 .41 Clm 2500 3 9 86¾ 76 66 CCSmith b 116 31.90 84–13 Strength De Fer 116½ Whosit 116¾ Eternal Knot 114^1 No factor
6Aug68-7Wat fst 5½f.23⅘ .48⅕1.09 Clm 2500 10 1 52¼ 42 21½ 25 FGorgone^5 b 115 *2.20 67–34 Muffinsville 116^5 Fleet Tony 1152½ Dora De 115^1 Wide
25Jly 68-7Wat my 6f .24⅕ .49⅖1.17⅘ Allowance 7 2 2^h 31 56 89¼ DCornelison b 114 18.60 52–43 Roman Affaire 112¾ Jet Count 121^2 Steel City 114½ Tired
18Jly 68-6Wat fst 6f .23⅖ .47⅗1.15⅗ Allowance 5 5 42½ 43½ 33 34 JChoina b 116 6.70 68–38 Star Bonus 1141½ Roman Affaire 1112½ Fleet Tony 116^2 Evenly
4Jly 68-7Wat fst 6f .23⅘ .48⅕1.16 Clm 5000 5 2 21½ 22 2½ 45 EKelly b 115 5.40 65–31 Bold Tor 121^1 San Martin 114^1 Press Conference 102^3 Tired
27Jun68-6Wat sl 6f .23⅗ .48⅕1.16⅗ Allowance 4 8 84¾ 66 54 43¾ EKelly 120 4.00 63–44 Madison Heights 113¾ Circle Eye 114^3 Tom Tywdd 116no Rallied
20Jun68-7Wat fst 6f .24 .48⅖1.16⅖ Allowance 5 2 52 54 55 24 EKelly 120 10.30 64–42 San Martin 115^4 Fleet Tony 120^nk Five Moons 115^1 Rallied
13Jun68-8Wat fst 6f .23⅘ .48⅕1.16⅗ Allowance 2 7 64 54¾ 43 35 GGillespie 120 5.20 62–34 Bladen 120^4 Circle Eye 114^1 Fleet Tony 120½ Mild rally
6Jun68-8Wat fst 6f .24 .48⅗1.16⅗ Allowance 8 6 53 42 2½ 2½ EKelly 120 37.70 66–35 Tongues Of Fire 117½ Fleet Tony 120^1 Bladen 120^1 Game effort

Big To Do * $3,500 — Dk. b. or br. g (1965–Md), by Trojan Monarch—Annamax, by Maxim — R. De Santis R. De Santis (Mrs. J. P. Jones) — **112** — 1968 1 0 0 0 — / 1967 3 1 0 0 $1,9..
5Sep68-2Atl fst 6f .22⅗ .46⅕1.12 Clm 3500 9 4 41½ 42¼ 54½ 66½ DHidalgo 112 25.90 75–19 Balaroja 1121¼ Barry's Beau 110¾ Timidity 115^2 Factor, tired
3Jly 67-2Del gd 5½f.22⅖ .47⅖1.07⅖ Cl c-5500 6 1 21½ 24 48½ 922 AAgnello^5 115 2.60 61–20 Lomorn 115^7 Dandy D. 116^nk Boone's Special 1161½ Speed, tired
20Jun67-1Del sl 5½f.22⅘ .48⅖1.08⅗ Md 5000 3 4 11½ 11 13 13½ EDonnally 120 *1.70 77–26 Big To Do 1203½ Nostar 117^1 Michaelrulla 120^2 Easily
5Jun67-2Del fst 5f .22⅖ .47 1.00⅖ Clm 7000 5 10 10^16 77 74¾ 63¼ EDonnally 114 2.90 84–14 King Dandy 114^nk Rocky Serenade 114^2 Reddito 111^h Green
LATEST WORKOUTS Sep 14 Atl 4f fst .48 h Sep 11 Atl 3f my .38 b Aug 29 Atl 3f fst .36 b Aug 19 Atl 5f fst 1.02⅗ b

Gerenade $3,500 — Ch. f (1965–Md), by Nade-Claro, by Chaos — Mrs. R. B. Archer R. B. Archer, Jr. (Mrs. A. Riggs 4th) — **109** — 1968 0 M 0 0 — / 1967 0 M 0 0 —
LATEST WORKOUTS Aug 2 Del 4f my .49⅘ bg Jly 27 Del 3f fst .37⅕ b Jly 23 Del 3f fst .37 b

Timidity $3,500 — B. c (1965–Ill), by Key Issue—Aptatally, by Appliable — E. D. Serotini N. J. Moran (Dr. M. R. Mitchell) — **112** — 1968 17 0 2 2 $2,8.. / 1967 16 4 2 3 $6,9..
12Sep68-2Atl fst 6f .22⅘ .46⅗1.13 Clm 3500 8 6 51¼ 31½ 44 63¾ CBaltazar b 112 4.30 73–21 Atoll's Star 112^nk Hereditament 109no O'Caladate 1152½ Tired
5Sep68-2Atl fst 6f .22⅗ .46⅕1.12 Clm 3500 2 6 52½ 52¼ 41½ 32 EGuerin b 115 8.20 80–19 Balaroja 1121¼ Barry's Beau 110¾ Timidity 115^2 Finished well
22Aug68-4Atl fst 6f .22⅕ .45⅖1.11⅖ Clm 5000 7 8 76¾ 56½ 55 44¾ EGuerin b 115 55.90 80–15 Geormel 118^2 Soybean Sam 115¾ Clever Kid 119^2 Rallied
15Aug68-2Atl fst 6f .22⅘ .46⅗1.12⅗ Clm 5000 1 10 84 117¾ 95¾ 97 CBaltazar b 115 27.40 72–19 Barren Isle 110¾ Hallucinaction 115¾ Mr. W. Harrison 117¾ No fact.
7Aug68-9Atl fst 7f .22⅗ .46 1.24⅕ Clm 6500 2 9 86 75 69¾ 516 MMiceli b 116 73.00 66–15 String Tie 116^10 Bowl Fresh 117no Barren Isle 112^6 No threat
27Jly 68-3Mth fst 6f .22⅕ .45⅖1.11 Clm 6500 2 8 68 511 59 511 DHidalgo b 110 41.20 76–15 River Sty 108no Birdsofafeather 1171½ That Guy 114^7 No threat
15Jly 68-5Mth fst 6f .21⅘ .44⅗1.10⅗ Clm 6500 8 6 67½ 512 614 717 DHidalgo b 115 11.20 72–13 Clever Kid 122no Twisty Clem 117^10 String Tie 122^3 Far back
11Jly 68-5Mth fst 6f .22⅖ .45⅕1.11 Cl c-5000 3 6 52¾ 34 26 29 JVasquez b 114 *1.80 78–19 Janette O. 109^9 Timidity 114^5 Royal Sovereign 115no Second best
4Jly 68-4Mth fst 6f .22⅘ .47⅖1.13⅖ Clm 5000 8 7 51¾ 3^nk 31 21¼ RTanner^5 b 109 8.30 74–22 Geormel 1181¼ Timidity 109^2 Andeverything 114^2 Forced wide
28Jun68-9Mth sly 170.47⅗1.13⅘1.46⅖ Clm 5000 4 4 33½ 36 78 76½ RTanner^5 b 110 3.80 62–25 Morning Coat 114½ Masked Gal 107^nk Easy Spending 120^2 Fell back
20Jun68-3Mth gd 6f .23 .47⅖1.13 Clm 5000 6 9 74¾ 53¾ 45½ 35½ RTanner^5 b 109 6.60 71–26 String Tie 1171½ Andeverything 114^4 Timidity 1091½ Rallied
LATEST WORKOUTS Aug 31 Atl 5f fst 1.03⅘ b Aug 27 Atl 4f fst .50⅘ b Aug 20 Atl 5f fst 1.05 b Aug 2 Mth 6f sly 1.20 b

Mr. W. Harrison * $3,500 — Dk. b or br. c (1965–Ky), by Mr. Turf—Patricia Bailey, by Big Dipper II — W. P. Rosso R. J. Durso (J. J. Amiel) — **115** — 1968 10 1 1 1 $4,2.. / 1967 5 M 0 0 —
30Aug68-3Atl fst 6f .22⅘ .46 1.11⅕ Clm 3500 6 10 95¾ 94¼ 77 56½ RBroussard b 117 3.40 79–17 Implicit 112^2 Balaroja 112^3 Rejjy 118¾ Had no mishap
15Aug68-2Atl fst 6f .22⅘ .46⅗1.12⅗ Clm 5000 4 9 104¼ 65½ 52½ 31½ RBroussard b 117 26.40 77–19 Barren Isle 110¾ Hallucinaction 115¾ Mr. W. Harrison 117¾ Good try
7Aug68-9Atl fst 7f .22⅗ .46 1.24⅕ Clm 6500 1 7 3^nk 43 59½ 922 EMonacelli b 119 10.50 60–15 String Tie 116^10 Bowl Fresh 117no Barren Isle 112^6 Early foot
24Jly 68-9Mth sly 1 1/16.47⅗1.13⅗1.48⅘ Clm 7000 2 6 76½ 613 716 623 PKallai b 120 5.50 38–22 Ben Dorada 117^9 Only Always 1112½ Bowl Fresh 112no No threat
13Jly 68-2Mth fst 6f .22⅕ .46 1.12⅕ Md 6500 8 5 44½ 4^nk 2^h 13 PKallai b 113 6.20 81–16 Mr W. Harrison 113^3 Rechazado 115½ Prim Point 110½ Driving
3Jly 68-1Mth sl 170.47⅕1.13⅘1.45⅗ Clm 3500 6 1 2^h 1^h 11½ 21 PKallai b 112 5.80 72–17 Jerry'sBrandy117^1 Mr.W.Harrison1122½ d-FieldsOfClover108^h Gam'y
29Jun68-1Mth gd 6f .22⅕ .46⅕1.13⅘ Md 5000 7 5 31 21 21½ 42 EMonacelli b 115 *1.80 71–21 Take Advantage 1101½ Dukesun 115^nk Assembly Point 115^nk Weak'd
15Jun68-3Mth fst 6f .22⅕ .45⅖1.12 Clm 6500 5 6 62¾ 69½ 59 413 EMonacelli b 114 39.30 69–14 Clever Kid 117^4 Hallucinaction 117^4 Bowl Fresh 114^5 In close
4Jun68-2Mth fst 6f .22⅕ .45⅘1.11⅘ Md Sp Wt 5 8 54¼ 76¾ 75½ 68½ EMonacelli b 115 47.80 74–16 Silent Arrow 115^nk MakeItEasy 118^2 PunctualCowboy 1151¾ No exc.
27May68-2GS fst 6f .22⅘ .46⅘1.12 Md c-5000 1 5 33 35 715 711 JVasquez b 116 3.60 73–13 Noble Fleet 1121½ Computed 106^5 Tea Caddy 1161½ Brief speed
13Dec67-4Aqu sly 6f .22⅘ .47⅖1.13⅗ Md Sp Wt 1 9 65 98½ 10^12 919 NTurcotte b 122 38.10f 56–28 Maggie's Pet 117^6 Dagger Counter 1221½ Ambifort 122^1 Swerved
LATEST WORKOUTS Aug 24 Atl 5f fst 1.01⅘ h Aug 4 Atl 4f fst .49 b Aug 13 Atl 3f fst .36 b Jly 20 Mth 4f gd .50 b

Rejjy

$3,500 B. g (1965–Md), by Rejected—Hurrican Minny, by Tuscany
Mrs. S. M. Pistorio L. W. Jennings (Mrs. S. M. Pistorio) **112**
1968 8 1 0 1 $3,395
1967 0 M 0 0 ——

Sep68-2Atl fst 6f .22⅘ .46⅗1.13 Clm 3500 12 10 95 77 78 42¾ WBlum b 117 3.10 74–21 Atoll's Star 112nk Hereditament 109no O'Caladate 1152½ Rallied 12
Aug68-3Atl fst 6f .22⅘ .46 1.11⅘ Clm 3500 3 6 54½ 51½ 44½ 35 HGrant b 118 11.90e 81–17 Implicit 1122 Balaroja 1123 Rejjy 118¾ Had no mishap 12
Aug68-9Atl fm*1⅛ Ⓣ 1.12⅗1.52⅗ Clm 5500 6 8 810 814 914 816 RBroussard b 117 9.90 78– 6 Lady Wolfram 1081½ Count Curious 1122 Past Post 1145 Far back 11
Jly 68-9Mth fm 1₁₆ Ⓣ 1.12⅗1.45⅗ Clm 7500 9 6 67½ 715 814 823 RBroussard b 117 14.20 —— Only Always 1103 Slicky Jim 115¾ Trueno 115no Never close 9
Jly 68-9Mth sly 1₁₆.47⅗1.13⅗1.48⅘ Clm 7000 8 8 913 916 614 519 RBroussard b 120 4.20 42–22 Ben Dorada 1179 Only Always 1112½ Bowl Fresh 112no No factor 9
Jly 68-1Mth fst 6f .21⅘ .46 1.12⅘ Md 5000 11 7 67¾ 43 1h 15 RBroussard b 117 *2.40 78–22 Rejjy 1175 Implicit 1101½ Jocasta 1102 Easily best 12
Jun68-1Mth fst 6f .22⅕ .46⅕1.12⅕ Md 5000 5 5 54 65 58½ 46½ CBaltazar 115 6.50 74–23 Heliofleet 1151½ Ben Dorada 1153½ Royal Sovereign 1151½ No mishap 12
Apr68-1GS gd 6f .23 .47⅖1.14⅖ Md 5000 11 8 107½ 84¾ 65½ 44 RBroussard 116 5.40 68–20 Soybean Sam 1151½ Base Royal 115½ Song Of Hope 1152 In close 12
LATEST WORKOUTS Sep 18 Atl 3f fst .35⅗ b Sep 9 Atl 5f fst 1.01 b Sep 6 Atl 3f fst .36⅖ b Aug 26 Atl 4f fst .49⅗ bg

Top Nail

$3,500 B. c (1965–Ky), by Royal Levee—Shoenail, by Nail
Ida Geller J. J. Quarter (Pebblebrook Farm) **112**
1968 2 0 0 0 ——
1967 5 1 0 0 $3,060

Sep68-2Atl fst 6f .22⅘ .46⅕1.12 Clm 3500 1 10 85 88½ 88¾ 77½ MMiceli 112 4.80 74–19 Balaroja 1121½ Barry's Beau 110¾ Timidity 1152 Never threat 11
Aug68-3Atl fst 6f .22⅘ .46 1.11⅘ Clm 3500 5 9 64½ 62¾ 56½ 66¾ ESantana 113 4.80 79–17 Implicit 1122 Balaroja 1123 Rejjy 118¾ Had no mishap 12
Aug67-2Sar fst 6f .23 .46⅘1.13⅕ Clm 9000 6 10 74¾ 32 31½ 44½ JLRotz 115 7.70 77–16 Flag Of Freedom 1162 Lord Tudor 1161 Mr. Restless 1151½ Used up 10
Aug67-4Sar fst 5½f.22⅘ .47⅖1.07 Md 6500 12 5 43 1½ 2h 1no JLRotz 118 *1.60e 82–15 Top Nail 118no Evade The Law 12210 Steel Girder 1224 All out 12
Jly 67-1Aqu gd 5½f.22⅗ .47 1.06⅗ Md 7000 6 9 97½ 88 55½ 44½ GMora5 115 5.60 76–14 Mr. Restless 118no Jamie Dee 1223 Jack's Aloha 1221½ No threat 12
Jun67-3Aqu sly 5f .23⅘ .47⅘1.01⅕ Md c-8500 10 9 74½ 810 812 58¾ HGustines 122 3.10 70–25 Jelou 1192½ Evade The Law 118nk Aqua Nail 1224 Sluggish start 10
Jun67-3Aqu fst 5f .22⅘ .47⅕ .59⅘ Md 9000 10 10 87¾ 85¾ 66½ 66½ HGustines 118 46.10 79–14 Rockem Back 1222½ Boxing Prince 1221½ Farmer Snob 122¾ Slow st. 10
LATEST WORKOUTS Sep 17 Atl 3f fst .35⅖ hg Sep 14 Atl 4f fst .49 b Aug 24 Atl 5f fst 1.02 b Aug 21 Atl 6f fst 1.15⅘ bg

Royal Sovereign *

$3,500 B. c (1965–Va), by Warhead—Mad Again, by Sun Again
B. Lepman B. Lepman (F. Neusch) **112**
1968 13 1 0 2 $3,450
1967 0 M 0 0 ——

Aug68-3Atl fst 6f .22⅘ .46 1.11⅘ Clm 3500 8 1 106¾ 84½ 88 88 EMaple 112 7.60 78–17 Implicit 1122 Balaroja 1123 Rejjy 118¾ Never a factor 12
Aug68-2Atl fst 6f .22⅗ .45⅗1.11⅗ Clm 3500 7 2 32 45 45 43½ CBurr 115 26.80 82–15 Cypark 115nk Barry's Beau 1102½ Dot's Libertine 113½ Evenly 10
Aug68-1Atl fst 7f .22⅘ .45⅕1.23⅗ Clm 3500 4 7 55½ 57 48 715 CBurr 112 18.60 70–15 Seen Afar 10710 Dot's Libertine 112¾ Janssen 1122 Tired 12
Aug68-1Atl fst 6f .22⅘ .45⅘1.11⅘ Clm 3500 4 9 11121111511118 916 CBaltazar 112 5.90 67–20 Soybean Sam 1126 Barry's Beau 115h Craig's Date 112nk No speed 11
Jly 68-9Mth fm 1₁₆ Ⓣ 1.13 1.46⅗ Clm 4500 6 4 53¾ 44½ 54½ 94 PKallai 115 27.50 —— Lady Wolfram 112no Jerry's Brandy 1171½ Judge Colie 1172 Tired 12
Jly 68-5Mth fst 6f .22⅘ .45⅕1.11 Clm 4500 5 3 21 24 39 314 PKallai 115 13.30 73–19 Janette O. 1099 Timidity 1145 Royal Sovereign 115no Tired 7
Jly 68-4Mth fst 6f .22⅘ .47⅖1.13⅗ Clm 5000 4 4 21½ 5¾ 64½ 510 JVasquez 117 4.20 65–22 Geormel 1181½ Timidity 1092 Andeverything 1142 Gave way 8
Jun68-2Mth sly 6f .22⅘ .47⅗1.14⅗ Md 5000 5 3 42 32½ 11½ 12½ JVasquez 115 4.10 70–25 RoyalSovereign1152½ TurnAndGo1102½ Bailey'sComet1152½ Driving 12
Jun68-1Mth fst 6f .22⅕ .46⅕1.12⅕ Md 5000 7 1 22 21 36 35 JVasquez 115 11.00 76–23 Heliofleet 1151½ Ben Dorada 1153½ Royal Sovereign 1151½ Weakened 12
Jun68-1Mth fst 6f .22⅘ .46 1.11⅗ Md 5000 11 1 2h 4nk 55 514 RBroussard b 117 9.70 70–14 Barnesville 1157 Llanfab 1155 Implicit 115½ Tired 12
May68-2GS sly 170.46⅘1.13⅕1.44⅘ Md 6000 8 2 41011281229 1027 RBroussard b 117 *2.70 43–22 Base Royal 1156 Pat's Pat 1151 Endow 1201 Dropped back 12
LATEST WORKOUTS Aug 5 Atl 3f fst .36 b Jly 31 Mth 3f fst .38⅖ b

Maverick County *

$3,500 B. g (1965–Md), by Espumoso—Sandra's Choice, by New Moon
R. Christopher W. A. Gaines (C. H. Smith) **112**
1968 17 1 2 0 $3,090
1967 11 1 1 0 0 $1,500

Sep68-2Atl fst 6f .22⅘ .46⅗1.13 Clm 3500 1 8 73¾111110121012 RNolan b 112 153.80 65–21 Atoll's Star 112nk Hereditament 109no O'Caladate 1152½ No factor 12
Aug68-1Atl fst 7f .22⅘ .45⅕1.23⅗ Clm 3500 12 3 65½112112271238 PRomero7 b 108 188.00 47–15 Seen Afar 10710 Dot's Libertine 112¾ Janssen 1122 No factor 12
Jly 68-1Mth fst 6f .22 .45⅘1.13⅕ Clm 3500 7 9 712 614 612 718 MBeneito b 116 69.10 58–23 PetesGesture1136 JohnnyTango113nk Dot'sLibertine1137 No speed 11
Jly 68-1Mth fst 6f .22⅕ .45⅘1.13⅕ Clm 3500 7 4 76½ 9101015 917 PRomero7 b 108 47.80 59–21 Barry'sBeau1112 RockySerenade1146 Dot'sLibertine1132½ Far back 11
Jun68-3Mth fst 170.48⅕1.13⅘1.45⅘ Clm 3500 2 1 21 46½ 615 629 PRomero7 108 15.50 43–18 Easy Spending 1157 Open Throttle 115½ Gatlin 11212 Gave way 8
Jun68-2Mth fst 6f .22⅗ .46⅗1.13⅗ Clm 3500 8 1 31½ 31½ 42½ 45½ PRomero7 108 30.80 69–18 Spent Fury 1133½ Final Hour 113¾ Dot's Libertine 1131 Tired 10
Jun68-2Mth fst 6f .22⅕ .45⅘1.13⅕ Clm 3500 6 8 42½ 44½ 49 512 PRomero7 b 108 75.90 73–12 Landquest 1103 Andeverything 1139 PetesGesture 116no Fractious st. 11
Jun68-3Mth fst 6f .22⅕ .45⅘1.10⅘ Clm 3500 8 3 34 711 916 728 MMiceli b 113 21.30 60–14 Clever Kid 1169 Andeverything 1136 Winged Prince 1169 Brief sp'd 9
May68-9GS fst 1₁₆.46⅘1.12⅕1.45⅕ Clm 4000 3 2 47½ 819 Eased JKDaly 112 88.90 — GoldenMustang 1121 Lanoka 1118 Forever Cheery 1136 Far back 8
May68-2GS gd 6f .22⅘ .47 1.12⅘ Clm 3500 1 9 42½ 46½ 818 920 WBlum 114 5.30 61–22 String Tie 1147 Miss Parker 109½ Brandy Glen 1092 Brief foot 10
Apr68-1Aqu fst 7f .22⅗ .46 1.25⅗ Clm 3500 6 7 46 56½ 818 726 RNolan b 117 3.40 53–16 ♦Myolivia 11710 ♦Johnny Tango 11910 Crow Hill 1171 Wide 9
Mar68-5Nar fst 6f .23⅕ .47⅕1.14⅗ Clm 5000 3 4 33 33½ 44½ 45½ PErnst b 118 5.30 68–27 Extra Line 1121½ Mr. N. J. G. 1151 Scef 1122¾ No mishap 8
LATEST WORKOUTS Sep 18 Atl 3f fst .38⅖ b Sep 9 Atl 4f fst .51 b

With It

$3,500 B. g (1965–Va), by Roman Tread—Corinthia, by Bright Sword
Asbell-Blom T. Bromley (V. M. Onet) **112**
1968 22 1 2 4 $5,285
1967 13 2 2 3 $2,627

Sep68-2Atl fst 6f .22⅘ .46⅗1.13 Clm 3500 3 7 21 54 65 85½ TLee • b 112 41.00 72–21 Atoll's Star 112nk Hereditament 109no O'Caladate 1152½ Tired 12
Aug68-9Atl fm*1⅛ Ⓣ 1.13⅗1.53⅗ Clm 4000 5 1 21 88¾ 818 832 GPatterson b 110 33.50 58–10 Judge Colie 1123 Past Post 114no Count Curious 113¾ Stopped 8
Aug68-2Atl fst 6f .22⅗ .45⅗1.11⅗ Clm 3500 3 8 88 812 78¾ 67¾ GPatterson b 112 12.00 78–15 Cypark 115nk Barry's Beau 1102½ Dot's Libertine 113½ No mishap 10
Aug68-1Del fst 6f .22⅘ .46⅗1.13⅗ Clm 3000 3 6 57½ 43½ 43 31¾ RBaker10 b 109 8.90 77–20 Scarlet Dancer 1101½ Cypark 119h With It 110h Finished willingly 11
Aug68-2Del gd 170.47 1.13⅗1.45⅗ Clm 3000 9 2 2½ 69 819 921 RLatorre7 b 109 3.60 51–20 Hath Charms 1111 Scalping Knife 1112½ Eric's Find 1205 Tired 12
Jly 68-3Del fst 6f .22⅘ .46⅘1.12⅘ Clm 3750 7 3 45½ 47 55¾ 44½ GPatterson b 113 8.90 76–22 O'Caladate 1204 Isolated 113½ Truwil 112h Raced on outside 8
Jly 68-3Del fst 6f .22⅗ .46⅘1.13⅗ Clm 4500 2 8 63¾ 78 35 63¼ GPatterson b 113 27.60 74–20 Home Chat 113nk Copyreader 1132 M. D. Wim 113nk Had no mishap 12
Jly 68-2Del fst 6f .22⅘ .47⅕1.13⅘ Clm 3500 1 3 53½ 64¾ 79 85¾ GPatterson b 113 14.60 70–19 Family Trouble 116no Noble Zone 1111 Joy's Secret 1152½ In close 10
Jly 68-5Mth fst 6f .22⅘ .45⅕1.11 Clm 4000 7 4 62¾ 710 721 728 WGavidia b 114 34.90 59–19 Janette O. 1099 Timidity 1145 Royal Sovereign 115no Far back 7
Jly 68-1Mth fst 6f .22⅕ .46⅖1.13⅕ Clm 3500 10 1 34½ 54½ 67½ 511 CGonzalez b 113 9.60 65–21 Barry'sBeau1112 RockySerenade1146 Dot'sLibertine1132½ Tired 11
Jun68-5Mth sly 6f .22 .46 1.12 Clm 5000 7 3 613 714 918 925 CGonzalez b 114 35.60 57–20 Judge Colie 1122 Rocky Serenade 1144 Soybean Sam 1152 No speed 10

Do Behave

$3,500 Dk. b. or br. c (1965–Fla), Ambehaving—Be Nice, by Attention
Prestileo-Rodriguez C. Rodriguez (Dr. J. Lee) **112**
1968 5 0 1 1 $1,350
1967 15 2 1 3 $7,055

Sep68-6Atl fst 6f .22⅗ .46 1.11⅗ Clm 5000 2 5 3nk 42 57 98½ CBaltazar b 115 5.70 76–19 Soybean Sam 1171½ Implicit 1171½ Gay Port 118nk Speed, tired 11
Aug68-7Atl fst 7f .22⅘ .45⅕1.24⅘ Clm 7250 4 4 1h 43 58½ 912 CBaltazar b 113 4.50 72–19 Light Stepper 115½ Mopeta 1102 Title Bout 1173½ Speed, tired 11
Aug68-7Atl fst 7f .22⅕ .45⅕1.24⅗ Clm 7000 10 1 14 12 11 22 CBaltazar b 112 26.60 79–18 String Tie 1172 Do Behave 112nk Bells And Whistles 109no Gamely 12
Aug68-5Mth fst 6f .22⅕ .46⅕1.12⅕ Cl c-5000 7 1 31½ 2h 21½ 53¼ WGavidia b 115 5.10 78–17 Moon Crest 115h Base Royal 115no Barren Isle 115nk Weakened 9
Jly 68-4Mth sl 6f .22⅘ .46⅗1.11⅘ Clm 5000 4 1 21½ 23 37 313 PWhitemen b 115 10.30 70–23 Laba Daba 11512 Base Royal 1151¼ Do Behave 115nk Held the plac'g 8
Oct67-5Atl fst 6f .22⅘ .45⅘1.13⅘ Cl c-5000 2 5 33 31½ 1h 2¾ JVasquez 119 *0.60 73–22 Janssen 114¾ Do Behave 119¾ Judge Colie 114no Failed to last 9
Sep67-4Atl fst 6f .22⅘ .46⅖1.12⅘ Clm 8500 7 7 73 66 68 64¾ GCusimano10 105 23.30 73–20 Hallucinaction 115h Swimmin'Hole 1182 Gen.Foretudor 115¾ No thr't 9
Sep67-4Atl fst 6f .22⅕ .45⅕1.11⅘ Cl c-6500 8 7 76 68 65½ 53½ WGavidia 119 4.20 80–12 Lanoma Cindy 109½ Stameejip 1161 Commanding Khal 116nk Late ft. 8
Aug67-3Atl gd 6f .22⅗ .46 1.11⅗ Cl c-5000 1 6 21 1h 14 18 WGavidia 115 2.70 85–16 Do Behave 1158 Sister Ramona 1131½ Lucky Bill 115¾ Won easily 12
Aug67-5Atl sly 6f .22⅕ .45⅕1.10⅘ Clm 6500 6 2 76¾ 712 55½ 35½ WGavidia 113 21.40 82–14 Swimmin' Hole 1204½ Atoll's Star 1151 Do Behave 113¾ Rallied 9
Aug67-5Atl fst 5½f.22⅘ .46 1.05⅘ Clm 7000 8 3 52¾ 53¾ 76½ 54½ WGavidia 115 35.80 86–15 Regality 108nk Swimmin' Hole 1201½ Air Gage 1151½ No mishaps 10
LATEST WORKOUTS Sep 13 Atl 4f fst .51⅗ b Jly 21 Mth 4f fst .51 b

Horses Shown Below Are on the "Also Eligible" List and Are Not Listed in Order of Post Positions

Royal Sargent $3,500 Dk. b. or br. c (1965–Fla), by Tres Sargentos—Royal Brat, by Royal Serenade (G. E. Allen, Jr.) G. E. Allen, Jr. W. Rideout **105**^{7}

1968	7	M	0	1	$7
1967	7	M	2	1	$49

12Sep68–6Atl	fst 6f	.22⅖	.46⅕	1.12⅖	Clm 4000	7	2	$6^{4\frac{3}{4}}$	8^{15}	8^{22}	8^{27}	JCastillo^{7}	b 104	153.90	53–21	Barren Isle 112^{1} Clever Kid 115^{2} Step Blue 115½	Tired
8Aug68–6Atl	fst 6f	.22⅕	.45⅘	1.12	Clm 5000	8	6	$8^{8\frac{1}{2}}$	10^{16}	10^{19}	10^{28}	JCastillo	b 115	92.40	54–19	Petes Gesture 119^{2} Creswood Dip 117½ O'Caladate 122^{2}	Far back
12Jun68–1Mth	sly 6f	.22	.45⅘	1.12⅕	Md 7500	2	6	$4^{5\frac{1}{2}}$	$7^{9\frac{3}{4}}$	6^{12}	9^{18}	DKassen	b 115	18.10	63–16	Tote The Mail 117^{2} Convivia 113½ Sea Chant 118$^{3\frac{1}{2}}$	Fell back
16May68–2GS	fst 6f	.22⅘	.46⅕	1.11⅘	Md 10000	3	6	4^{nk}	3^{4}	$3^{6\frac{1}{2}}$	$4^{7\frac{1}{4}}$	DKassen	b 116	29.50	78–17	Athena's Lark 111$^{1\frac{1}{4}}$ Hopeful Bid 116$^{2\frac{1}{2}}$ Country Day 122$^{3\frac{1}{2}}$	Weaken'd
23Apr68–6GP	fst 6f	.22⅕	.45⅗	1.12⅗	Md 7500	2	5	4^{4}	5^{9}	3^{9}	$3^{7\frac{1}{2}}$	SMiller	b 120	24.70	73–18	Glory Ed 120^{6} Lindsey–Jan 120$^{1\frac{1}{2}}$ Royal Sargent 120^{1}	Fair try
18Apr68–6GP	fst 6f	.22⅘	.46⅖	1.12⅗	Md 10000	12	1	3^{nk}	3^{2}	4^{5}	$5^{9\frac{1}{4}}$	SMiller	b 120	127.50	72–16	Barren Isle 120^{4} Jack King 120¾ Second Sin 120$^{2\frac{1}{2}}$	Speed, tired
10Apr68–6GP	fst 7f	.22⅕	.45⅗	1.24⅖	Clm 7500	2	10	$10^{5\frac{3}{4}}$	12^{20}	12^{37}	12^{39}	KKorte	b 116	110.00	48–13	Tim Tom 116$^{4\frac{1}{2}}$ Mrs. Mehle 107no Half Space 106¾	Showed nothing
1Jun67–1Sem	fst 3½f	.24	.36	.42	Md Sp Wt	8	3		$8^{4\frac{3}{4}}$	$7^{6\frac{3}{4}}$	$6^{4\frac{1}{2}}$	PTuccio	b 120	10.60	84–11	MountainSpirits117$^{1\frac{1}{2}}$MarkOfPisces120^{nk}FilleDeMayor117^{h}	No sp'd
25May67–1Sem	fst 3½f	.24	.36	.42⅖	Md Sp Wt	1	2		$5^{3\frac{1}{2}}$	5^{6}	$7^{3\frac{3}{4}}$	PTuccio	b 120	*2.30	83–10	Admiral's Flower 117no Violet B. 117no May's Honor 117^{1}	Dull try
9May67–2Sem	fst 3½f	.24	.36⅖	.42⅖	Md Sp Wt	3	2		3^{nk}	2^{1}	2^{1}	PTuccio	b 120	*1.50	——	Sheragate 117^{1} Royal Sargent 120^{1} Izzy's Choice 120½	Gamely
1May67–1Sem	fst 3½f	.23⅖	.35⅖	.42	Md Sp Wt	2	3		2^{3}	$2^{2\frac{1}{2}}$	2^{1}	PTuccio	b 120	6.20	——	Royal Leona 117^{1} Royal Sargent 120^{1} Shuking 120½	Gamely

The following starters can be eliminated for good and sufficient reason: Shrapnel (a maiden filly on which Buddy Delp seems to have given up after one woeful race), Fleet Tony (an unimposing refugee from West Virginia), Gerenade (an unraced filly from Delaware), Mr. W. Harrison (totally inactive this month after a vigorous but unproductive August campaign), Top Nail (no signs of life this year), Maverick County (form), With It (form), and Royal Sargent (form). The contenders are:

Big To Do: After laying off for more than a year, this gelding managed to beat five horses of today's class on September 5 and has had two tidy workouts in the meantime. Improvement is predictable and should make it a factor in the early running. But the rest of the field would have to be rather poor to assure it of victory. Before deciding what to do about this horse, we'd better look at the rest. Contender.

Timidity: This colt has had seventeen chances this year without winning once. Nick Moran's decision to try cheaper competition has not paid off. The horse has run no better against $3,500 claimers than he did before. The switch from Chuck Baltazar to the less modish Jiminez is not a good omen. If all the other contenders are like Big To Do, with early speed and not much else, Timidity might have a slim chance. When at his uninspired best, the colt likes to come from slightly off the pace. He never seems to close fast enough, though. Let's say that he's a possible, provided the others are mainly tiring speedballs and no good closer is in the pack. Contender.

Rejjy: Last week this gelding gave every sign of readiness, gaining authoritatively in the closing stages of a race against horses like those it faces today. On July 5 it showed that it does its best work when the rider is able to hustle it into contention before the final furlong. The switch from the topnotch Walter Blum to the younger but quite competent Eddie Maple should work no great hardship. Eddie is perfectly capable of helping Rejjy demonstrate a stretch kick far more formidable than Timidity's. Moreover, unless Big To Do improves phenomenally, Rejjy looks ready to eat it alive in the stretch. So far, Rejjy looks like a decent bet. Contender.

Do Behave: One might be tempted to think of this colt as the class of the race, if his last couple of efforts had not been so disappointing. The increased stamina that should have been in evidence on August 23 was nowhere to be found. The drop into $5,000 company on September 5 helped not at all. Today's additional drop should move the animal ahead a few lengths—if anything can—but I see no justification for a bet. Note that the hot Blum—second only to apprentice George Cusimano among riders at this meeting—has replaced Chuck Baltazar as this colt's jock. They'll be all-out for the win, but not with any money of mine. No Bet.

To make the outlook as clear as possible, let's consider the pace factor. If Do Behave were truly the class of the race, he would beat off any challengers in the early stages and win as easily as he did here on August 28, 1967. But he has deteriorated greatly since then. His recent figures show that a wire-to-wire victory today would require a sharp reversal of form. Much more probably, he and Big To Do will beat each other, with the fit Rejjy coming along at the end. Rejjy should be able to run as fast today as on August 30—faster, if necessary. That much speed seems beyond the powers of the other contenders.

The Running of the Race

Do Behave, a 2–1 favorite, tired himself while putting away Big To Do. Rejjy, the strong horse in the stretch, won without great difficulty, paying an attractive $11.00. Timidity also came along at the end, but not rapidly enough to get closer than third spot.

SECOND RACE   6 FURLONGS. (Bright Holly, September 2, 1961, 1.08⅖, 3, 112.)

Atl - 35937

September 19, 1968

Claiming. Purse $3,500. 3-year-olds. Weight 120 lbs. Non-winners of two races since August 10 allowed 3 lbs., a race 5 lbs., a race since July 10, 8 lbs. Claiming price $3,500.

Value to winner $2,100, second $700, third $455, fourth $245. Mutuel pool $98,235.

Index	Horse	Eqt A Wt PP St	¼	½	Str	Fin	Jockey	Cl'g Pr	Owner	Odds $1
35883Atl4	Rejjy	b 3 112 7 5	6²	3¹	2²	1¹¾	E Maple	3500	Mrs S M Pistorio	4.50
35833Atl9	Do Behave	b 3 113 11 1	3½	2³	1h	2⁷	W Blum	3500	Prestileo–Rodriguez	2.10
35883Atl6	Timidity	b 3 112 5 11	11¹	10¹	4¹	3½	C Jiminez	3500	E D Serotini	13.80
35829Atl6	Big To Do	3 112 3 6	1h	1½	3⁵	4¹½	F Lovato	3500	R DeSantis	5.40
35883Atl8	With It	b 3 112 10 2	4h	5²	5h	5h	C Baltazar	3500	Asbell–Blom	40.50
35829Atl7	Top Nail	3 113 8 12	12	6¹½	6²	6²	H Block	3500	Ida Geller	4.70
35701Atl5	Mr.W.Harrison	b 3 115 6 9	7h	8½	7¹	7¹	P Kallai	3500	W P Rosso	6.00
35887Atl8	RoyalSargent	b 3 105 12 3	10h	9¹	8²	8³	J Castillo⁷	3500	G E Allen Jr	209.70
	—Gerenade	3 110 4 10	8½	11²	9h	9³	D Hidalgo	3500	Mrs R B Archer	92.70
35883Atl10	M'verickCounty	b 3 112 9 4	9¹	12	11½	10¹½	R Nolan	3500	R Christopher	201.50
35919ShD6	Fleet Tony	b 3 115 2 8	2¹	4²	10²	11²	E Guerin	3500	R W Woodward	47.10
35857Atl10	Shrapnel	b 3 105 1 7	5¹	7h	12	12	G Cusimano⁵	3500	Pennyacres Farm	13.60

Time .22⅖, .46⅕, 1.11⅗. Track fast.

$2 Mutuel Prices:

7-REJJY	11.00	4.80	3.20
11-DO BEHAVE		4.40	3.00
5-TIMIDITY			5.00

B. g, by Rejected—Hurrican Minny, by Tuscany. Trainer L. W. Jennings. Bred by Mrs. S. M. Pistorio (Md.). IN GATE AT 2.00. OFF AT 2.00 EASTERN DAYLIGHT TIME. Sart good for all but TOP NAIL. Won driving.

REJJY, away in good order, followed the pace to the stretch, came outside for the drive and wore down DO BEHAVE. The latter, close up from the start, gained command in upper stretch then could not contain the winner. TIMIDITY ralied belatedly. BIG TO DO set the pace for a half and tired. WITH IT was through early. TOP NAIL was off poorly. MR. W. HARRISON was never a factor. FLEET TONY vied for the early lead and retired.

Scratched—35887Atl8 Royal Sargent, 35883Atl9 Second Act, 35846Atl8 Smorgsie, 35701Atl2 Interrogate.

Overweights—Shrapnel 1 pound, Fleet Tony 3, Gerenade 1, Top Nail 1, Do Behave 1.

THE THIRD RACE

THIS RACE is at six furlongs, for $5,000 maiden males, aged two. Glance at the records and you notice that the field includes a few starters that have run fairly well in better company. Knowing that these animals have held their own in races against previous winners, there is no need to waste time on entrants that have been running poorly against maidens.

3rd Atlantic City

6 FURLONGS — ATLANTIC CITY (Start / Finish)

6 FURLONGS. (Bright Holly, September 2, 1961, 1.08⅖, 3, 112.)
Maidens. Claiming. Purse $3,500. Colts and geldings. 2-year-olds. Weight 118 lbs. Claiming price $5,000.

Baron Bedros $5,000 — B. c (1966–Md), by Bronze Babu—Tom Gal, by Nirgal — 118 — 1968 3 M 0 0 —
G. H. Burt G. H. Burt (Glade Valley Farms, Inc.)
5Sep68–1Atl fst 6f .22⅗ .46⅗1.12⅗ Md 5000 4 11 96¾11141212 1016 EWalsh b 118 34.50 63–19 Demi'sPrince 1185 RoyallyInclined 1182½ Bill Flood 1184½ No speed 12
4Jly 68–3Mth fst 5½f.23⅗ .48 1.08 Clm 7500 8 9 97¼ 913 81¼ 711 MMiceli b 114 12.30 66–22 I Miss 111½ Slim's Pride 1091½ Ariel Hiatus 1166 Never close 9
18Apr68–3Bow fst 5f .23 .46⅕ .59⅗ Md Sp Wt 1 8 611 615 617 611 AAgnello 119 8.70 81–10 Lord Brandon 1191 d-Rock Break 119¾ Tearing Around 1192 No sp'd 8
LATEST WORKOUTS Sep 18 Atl 3f fst .37⅕ b Sep 14 Atl 5f fst 1.03⅕ b Sep 4 Atl 3f fst .36⅘ b Aug 30 Atl 4f fst .51 b

Ted's Angel $5,000 — Dk. b. or br. g (1966–NJ), by Sailor Beware—Night Angel, by Rounders — 118 — 1968 6 M 0 0 $245
T.-S. Smith E. H. Barney (Dr. A. R. Gemberling)
5Sep68–1Atl fst 6f .22⅗ .46⅗1.12⅗ Md 5000 9 5 43¼ 24 47½ 412 RPerna b 118 86.90 67–19 Demi'sPrince 1185 RoyallyInclined 1182½ Bill Flood 1184½ Weakened 12
31Aug68–1Atl fst 6f .22⅖ .45⅘1.11⅘ Clm 5000 4 6 75¾ 713 815 816 RPerna b 114 49.70 67–15 Crafty Boy 1141½ Xalapa's Last 1141½ Mytar 1172 Showed nothing 11
20Aug68–3Atl fst 6f .22⅖ .46 1.12⅖ Md 7000 11 5 1211121811141117 RPerna 114 147.10 63–16 Samslena 1114 Robe Of Honour 113no Delica Tessie 1083½ No speed 12
10Aug68–2Atl fst 5½f.22⅗ .47⅖1.07⅖ Clm 5000 4 5 25 54½ 68 911 RPerna 113 40.60 71–17 Roguery 1134½ Restforall 107nk Delong Pike 113½ Brief speed 10
25Jly 68–3Mth sl 5½f.23⅗ .49 1.08⅘ Md 7000 1 3 2h 98½ 912 918 RPerna 114 29.90 55–23 Uncle Herbie 1182 Mitty Star 115½ Spurs Image 1153½ Brief speed 9
9Jly 68–4Mth fst 5½f.23⅕ .46⅘1.06⅘ Md Sp Wt 4 8 96¾ 924 826 829 RPerna 118 18.00 54–21 Hit Or Miss 1189 Robe Of Honour 1181¼ Make It Big 118¾ Far back 10
LATEST WORKOUTS Sep 14 Atl 4f fst .51 b Aug 31 Atl 5f fst 1.03 b Aug 27 Atl 3f fst .37 b Aug 7 Atl 3f fst .39 b

Restforall $5,000 — Gr. g (1966–Tenn), by Pete's Pet—Valerius, by Galerius — 118 — 1968 4 M 1 1 $1,155
J. S. Abrams W. H. Foales (J. E. Roper)
6Sep68–2Atl fst 6f .22⅕ .45⅖1.11⅖ Clm 5000 8 2 11 1½ 24 311 GPatterson b 114 18.60 74–18 Xalapa's Last 1149 Hillsbo Errard 1142 Restforall 1143 Used up 9
28Aug68–2Atl fst 6f .22⅗ .47⅕1.13 Clm 5000 12 1 1h 31 12161222 FMartinez7 b 109 9.10 55–16 Golden Asset 114¾ Nou Secret 1173½ Demi's Prince 1172½ Bore out 12
10Aug68–2Atl fst 5½f.22⅗ .47⅖1.07⅖ Clm 5000 1 4 15 12 21 24½ FMartinez7 b 107 16.00 77–17 Roguery 1134½ Restforall 107nk Delong Pike 113½ Best others 10
26Jly 68–3Mth fst 5½f.24⅖ .46⅗1.06⅗ Clm 6500 3 6 32½ 48½ 718 824 WTichenor b 114 49.40 60–23 King Bolero 1182 Que Intersante 114¾ Ariel Hiatus 11710 Stopped 9
LATEST WORKOUTS Sep 17 Atl 3f fst .36⅘ b Sep 11 Atl 6f my 1.15⅗ b Aug 27 Atl 5f fst 1.03 b Aug 23 Atl 6f fst 1.17 b

Shabash $5,000 — Dk. b. or br. c (1966–Fla), by Outing Class—Indian Night, by Ambiorix — 118 — 1968 2 M 0 0 —
J. Haynie L. W. Donovan (Tartan Farms)
30Aug68–2Atl fst 6f .22⅗ .45⅗1.10⅗ Clm 7500 12 7 108¼1016 920 921 JBelmonte 114 38.70 68–17 Sure N' Swift 1175 Top Fighter 1174 Florida Fling 11/6 No speed 12
23Aug68–5Atl fst 6f .22⅘ .46⅕1.12⅕ Clm 7500 8 9 814 815 818 714 JBelmonte 113 17.70 67–19 Private Barge 1183 Top Fighter 117nk Roguery 1192 No speed 9
LATEST WORKOUTS Aug 29 Atl 4f fst .49⅕ b Aug 19 Atl 5f fst 1.00⅖ h Aug 12 Atl 5f fst 1.04 b Jly 27 Mth 4f fst .50 b

Arturito $5,000 — Dk. b. or br c (1966–Ky), by Arturo A.—New Lede, by Tudor Minstrel — 118 — 1968 9 M 1 3 $1,460
A. H. Pollack A. G. Goodman (L. Combs 2d–Fourth Estate Stable)
6Sep68–2Atl fst 6f .22⅕ .45⅖1.11⅖ Clm 5000 9 4 54½ 58½ 711 716 WTichenor b 114 5.60 69–18 Xalapa's Last 1149 Hillsbo Errard 1142 Restforall 1143 Tired 9
8Aug68–2Atl fst 5½f.22⅖ .46⅖1.06⅕ Md 7500 1 9 109¼1017 1015 1026 CBaltazar b 116 7.10 62–19 Florida Fling 118¾ Screech 1143 Wandering Reef 113¾ No speed 12
30Jly 68–3Mth fst 5½f.23 .47⅖1.07 Md c-5000 8 2 41 31½ 21 2½ CBaltazar b 118 6.10 81–16 Baby James 118½ Arturito 1182½ Slievenamon 1182½ Strong finish 12
25Jly 68–1Aqu gd 5½f.23⅕ .47⅗1.07 Md 6000 1 1 1h 2h 22½ 34 HVelez b 118 21.40 74–18 Private Park 1224 Best Deal 119h Arturito 118¾ Weakened 12
12Jun68–4MP fst 4½f.23 .47 .53⅗ Md 6500 2 4 21 42¼ 35 MShirota b 116 6.80 79–12 Away Up High 1173 Four K's 1162 Arturito 116nk Well placed, tired 10
6Jun68–5MP fst 4½f.23⅕ .46⅖ .52⅖ Md Sp Wt 5 4 44 57 67½ MShirota b 116 16.30 82–10 Fussy Bob 116¾ Bo Tree 1164 The Pauper King 116nk Fell back 10
28May68–3MP sl 4½f.23 .50 .56⅘ Md 7500 2 2 2½ 23 38½ MShirota b 116 18.30 59–32 Sir Realist 1198 Peter Platterpus 116½ Arturito 1161 Bid, tired 8
14May68–5CD gd 5f .23⅕ .47⅕1.00⅗ Md Sp Wt 3 4 33 65½ 815 813 MShirota b 120 30.10 74–16 Mr.Putnam1201¼BabyJaneGray1171½Gregg'sPlaymate1202 Tired 8
8May68–3CD fst 5f .23 .46⅗1.00 Md Sp Wt 2 6 64¼ 613 617 619 MShirota b 120 17.30 71–17 Uhlan 1202 Polar Traffic 120no Sir Realist 120nk Never close 6
LATEST WORKOUTS Sep 18 Atl 3f fst .36⅖ b Sep 14 Atl 4f fst .50 b Sep 11 Atl 4f my .50 b Sep 1 Atl 4f fst .48⅖ h

Sunny Year $5,000 — Ch. g (1966–Va), by Next Year—Sunny Hook, by Sun Again — 118 — 1968 8 M 1 1 $1,245
M. R. Farm J. S. Salvaggio (Mrs. J. P. Jones)
5Sep68–1Atl fst 6f .22⅗ .46⅗1.12⅗ Md 5000 3 6 75¾ 812 811 915 RFerraro 118 5.50 64–19 Demi'sPrince 1185 RoyallyInclined 1182½ Bill Flood 1184½ Dull try 12
16Aug68–2Atl fst 5½f.22⅖ .45⅘1.05⅘ Md 7000 2 9 98¾ 912 77 65¾ RFerraro 114 29.80 84–18 Try N' See 118nk Que Intersante 1143 Lido Away 1162 No factor 12
7Aug68–1Del fst 6f .22⅘ .47⅖1.15 Cl c-4000 8 9 86¾ 66 44 42½ EMaple 116 *1.40 67–25 CutItShort113¾ HideawayDancer1161 PicturesqueOcala116¾ Wd. tn. 12
2Aug68–1Del gd 5½f.22⅕ .47⅕1.07⅕ Clm 5000 11 10 79½ 610 48½ 34¾ EMaple 113 *2.60 78–20 Frank's Claudia 113¾ Mystic Moonlight 1094 Sunny Year 113nk Ral'd 12
16Jly 68–1Del fst 5½f.22⅖ .47⅖1.07⅖ Clm 4500 1 8 98¾ 66¾ 46 23½ EMaple 115 27.50 78–20 Now Doris 1123½ Sunny Year 115no Boone's Twist 120no Rallied 12
3Jly 68–1Del gd 5½f.22⅗ .47⅗1.07⅕ Clm 6000 11 11 1210 1011 810 612 FLovato 116 18.40e 71–22 RoadToKo-Ro-Ba1163 RoyalMerit1163 Boone'sTwist120¾ Wide 12
21Jun68–4Del fst 5½f.22⅕ .46⅘1.06⅘ Clm 6500 6 8 88 811 814 67¾ RFitzgerald 113 18.20e 77–17 ThomasJ.1174 ♠–RoadToKo-Ro-Ba113¾ ♠–R'ketDestro'r113¾ No th't 12
13Jun68–3Del fst 5f .22⅕ .47 1.00 Clm 7500 5 8 715 717 613 614 RFitzgerald 113 14.30e 75–20 Ruckus 1086 Trojan Max 1143¾ Glory Train 1141 Showed nothing 10
LATEST WORKOUTS Aug 30 Atl 4f fst .50 b Jly 27 Del 4f fst .51⅖ b

Mistic Jay $5,000 Dk. b. or br. c (1966–Ky), by Poppy Jay—Mystic Mist, by King's Pawn **118** 1968 6 M 0 0 —

S. R. Madonna C. P. Coco (Dr. W. S. Karutz)

15Aug68-3Tim fst 5¾f.23⅘ .49⅕1.11⅕ MdSpWt 7 8 814 815 717 717 FManco b 118 54.30 67–21 Heap Big Brave 1186 Default 1185 Bulge 118h Never close 8

26Jly 68-1Del fst 5½f.22⅘ .47⅘1.07⅗ Clm 4500 6 5 810 91510221018 FManco b 114 52.50 63–21 Clytemnestra 1052 Tucquan 1134 Stockade 1133 No speed 12

11Jly 68-1Del fst 5½f.22⅘ .48⅖1.08⅖ Md 5000 7 2 94¾ 98¼11151118 JChoquette b 120 36.10 59–24 Frank's Claudia 1121 NouSecret1201 AuldLangSyne1202 No factor 12

8Jly 68-2Del fst 5½f.22⅘ .47 1.07 Clm 6500 3 4 55 89½ 912 917 JChoquette b 113 22.30 67–19 Please John 116no No Flitter 1134 Miramar Chief 116no Far back 9

3Jun68-6Del fst 5f .22⅘ .47⅗1.00⅖ Md Sp Wt 10 8 121312161221 E'd RFitzgerald 120 128.20 —— Swift Don 1208 Ana Pole 120nk Carolina Model 1171 Trailed 12

8May68-3ShD fst 3½f.22⅖ .34⅘ .41 Md Sp Wt 10 7 711 712 716 DJohnstonJr 118 16.10 74–10 Doge Do Little 118½ Get Sis 115¾ Goose Gun 1155½ Never close 10

LATEST WORKOUTS Sep 13 Atl t.c. 6f fm 1.17 b

High And Away $5,000 B. c (1966–Ky), by Hitting Away—Cassarate, by Abernant **118** 1968 3 M 0 0 $225

Locust Hill Farm F. A. Bonsal (Mrs. S. S. Janney)

5Jun68-4Del fst 5f .22⅕ .47 1.00 Md Sp Wt 9 5 44 47½ 511 513 WJPassmore b 120 9.30 76–17 Bushido 120½ Sail Lark 1204 Never Wink 1206 Showed little 11

13May68-3Pim fst 5f .22⅗ .46⅘ .59⅖ Md Sp Wt 5 2 2½ 54½ 57½ 710 TLeee 119 13.80 84–17 Run Like Mad 119¾ Stool Pigeon 1195 Swift Don 1191 Speed, tired 12

26Apr68-3Pim fst 5f .22⅗ .47⅖1.01 Md Sp Wt 7 3 22 35½ 35 43½ TLee 119 9.80 82–21 Imprimis 119nk Run Like Mad 1191 Stool Pigeon 1192¼ Tired 12

LATEST WORKOUTS Sep 16 Atl 5f fst 1.04⅘ b Sep 12 Atl 6f fst 1.19⅖ b Sep 8 Atl 4f fst .50 b Sep 3 Atl 3f fst .37⅗ b

Brillant Boy $5,000 B. c (1966–Fla), by Shining Sceptre—Frivolette, by Gold Teddy **111**7 1968 3 M 0 0 —

Boronia Farm Margaret MacLennan (Dr. M. Humphries)

5Sep68-1Atl fst 6f .22⅗ .46⅗1.12⅗ Md 5000 2 7 64¼ 610 511 613 RLaTorre7 111 112.30 66–19 Demi'sPrince 1185 RoyallyInclined 1182½ Bill Flood 1184½ No factor 12

3Jly 68-1Del gd 5½f.22⅗ .47⅗1.07⅕ Clm 6000 2 5 42½ 56½11191232 FValdizan 116 57.00 51–22 RoadToKo-Ro-Ba1163 RoyalMerit1163 Boone'sTwist120¾ Tired 12

10Jun68-4Del fst 5f .22⅖ .47⅕ .59⅘ Md Sp Wt 1 4 64¼ 917 925 938 GBrogan5 115 51.40 52–17 Paula's Lark 120h d-Caicos 120h Inkosana 1206 Fell far back 9

Singing Serenada $5,000 B. c (1966–Fla), by Prince Cohen—Tupesta, by Tudor Pasha **118** 1968 2 M 0 0 —

J. B. Rowe J. B. Rowe (Mr.-Mrs. P. Falkenstein)

1Aug68-4Mth fst 5½f.23 .47 1.06⅘ Md 7500 2 10 10111016 917 914 KKorte 118 68.40 70–17 Lustihood 1162 Que Intersante 1184 Double Dividend 118nk No sp'd 12

24Jly 68-3Mth fst 5½f.23⅗ .48⅕1.07⅗ Md 7500 12 12 1117111911151016 PRomero7 111 98.40 63–17 SureN'Swift118nkTulegAppointment1143½BraveGreek118no No sp'd 12

LATEST WORKOUTS Sep 17 Atl 5f fst 1.04 bg Sep 14 Atl 5f fst 1.02⅖ b Sep 7 Atl 5f sly 1.05 b Sep 3 Atl 3f fst .38 b

Devil Encanto $5,000 B. g (1966–Fla), by Encanto—Ett's Devil, by Devil Diver **118** 1968 8 M 0 0 —

D. E. Taylor W. J. Sacco (D. E. Taylor-H. L. Cherry)

28Aug68-2Atl fst 6f .22⅗ .47⅕1.13 Clm 5000 5 11 117½ 86¾ 79½ 79¾ EMaple b 114 21.20 67–16 Golden Asset 114¾ Nou Secret 1173½ Demi's Prince 1172½ No factor 12

10Aug68-2Atl fst 5½f.22⅗ .47⅖1.07⅖ Clm 5000 10 9 99¾ 911 79 57¼ MMiceli b 113 27.40 75–17 Roguery 1134½ Restforall 107nk Delong Pike 113½ Mild gain 10

8Aug68-1Atl fst 5½f.22⅘ .47⅕1.06⅘ Md 5000 6 10 129 111310131012 MMiceli b 118 52.20 73–19 Royal Ram 118nk Crafty Boy 1192 Demi's Prince 1184 Far back 12

2Jly 68-3Mth fst 5½f.23⅗ .48⅘1.08⅗ Md 6000 8 8 812 813 814 717 RSage5 b 113 25.10 57–21 River Carry 114¾ Wandering Reef 1134 The Peddler 1184½ No speed 8

27Jun68-1Mth sly 5½f.23 .48⅕1.08 Md 6500 9 10 10131015 912 813 RTanner5 b 113 18.50 64–19 Par Game 1183 Ship K. 1141¼ Wandering Reef 118¾ No speed 11

20Jun68-2Mth gd 5½f.24 .49 1.09⅕ Md 6500 6 7 89¾ 714 69½ 58¾ RTanner5 b 113 12.50 62–26 Fraternizing 1182 Linky 1162 Bol 'N Ball 118¾ Not a threat 10

13Jun68-4Mth sly 5f .22⅘ .47⅗1.00 Md 6500 3 1 412 612 69½ 613 AECordero5 113 8.20 77–20 Azhi Dahaka 1183 Duk's Fancy 1186 Xalapa's Last 1181½ No factor 10

10Jun68-3Mth fst 5f .22⅗ .46⅗ .59⅖ Clm 10000 3 8 65¼ 58 611 716 AECordero 114 43.50 77–12 He's A Smasher 1174½ King Bolero 1181 Dr. Allan S. 1172 Tired 8

LATEST WORKOUTS Sep 16 Atl 6f fst 1.16 b Sep 12 Atl 3f fst .36⅖ h Sep 8 Atl 3f fst .37⅕ b Sep 4 Atl 4f fst .48⅘ h

Horses Shown Below Are on the "Also Eligible" List and Are Not Listed in Order of Post Positions.

Sails Unfurled $5,000 Gr. g (1966–Ky), by Tudor Grey—Rosy Outlook, by Succession **118** 1968 4 M 0 1 $530

E. D. Sauselen J. P. Considine (E. D. Sauselen)

3Sep68-3Tim fst 5¾f.23⅘ .49⅕1.12⅖ Clm 7500 5 5 42½ 32 34½ 43½ RRincon 113 5.30 74–21 C.K'.sMooney 114no Boone'sTwist 1171½ DaringFlight 1122 No rally 6

6Aug68-4Del fst 6f .23 .47⅖1.13⅖ Md 10000 4 5 2h 2h 76½1112 WJPassmore 120 17.00 66–20 VictoriaIsland 1201 DandyDevelin 1204 RocketDestroyer 120h Used 12

30Jly 68-4Del fst 5½f.22⅗ .48⅕1.08 Md 8000 9 4 22½ 24 22½ 33¾ HPilar 120 80.00 75–23 Lucky Enuff 113¾ Tricky's Note 1203 Sails Unfurled 120½ Good try 12

20Jun68-1Del fst 5½f.22⅗ .47 1.07⅖ Md 8500 7 5 42½ 712 8101116 RRincon 120 15.90 66–23 Private Barge 1206 Rebel John 120no Brandy Sling 1201 Stopped 12

LATEST WORKOUTS Jly 25 Del 5f fst 1.03 bg Jly 20 Del 5f my 1.06⅗ b

Therefore, out go Baron Bedros, Ted's Angel, Arturito, Sunny Year, Mistic Jay, Brilliant Boy, Singing Serenada, and Devil Encanto. Shabash, no match for the $7,500 winners that humiliated him in his two races, might do better in today's weak field but has neither raced nor worked this month. Out he goes. High And Away, which showed mild promise in three losses to expensive Maryland and Delaware maidens, has not raced since June. He has had four workouts in September but was not impressive enough to turn my head. He may prove in time to have a touch of class but need not be feared today, when he likely will come up short. The real contenders seem to be:

Restforall: Dropping into its first maiden race, this gelding seems to prefer the lead but has not been able to stay there against the animals it has been meeting. On the other hand, it showed real improvement in its last race, producing more speed than ever and holding it over a longer distance. Its September 11 workout in the mud was outstandingly good for a horse of its age and station in life.

Sails Unfurled: A horse that can't win at Timonium is sure to have an even worse time in New Jersey. But this gelding's record is full of angles. The Timonium race was for $7,500 winners, meaning that at least a few members of the field were probably superior to the $5,000 maidens in today's race. Note also that Sails Unfurled displayed a little early foot in its July and August races at Delaware. I would regard the newcomer as a sleeper—and pass this race entirely —if there were not certain holes in it. For one thing, it beat only two horses in the Timonium race. Secondly, although it was gaining on the leader at the end, something else was moving even more rapidly and took third position from it. Thirdly, its record contains not a single local workout. Sails Unfurled may be a sleeper, but Restforall looks like a better bet today.

The Running of the Race

HIGH AND AWAY, favored at 2.70–1, wore himself out chasing Sails Unfurled and finished fifth. Sails Unfurled, 7–2, ran a fine race, holding second place from start to finish and gaining throughout the stretch run. But the winner was Restforall, who paid $7.60. It broke well, was three lengths in front after a quarter mile, and, as the chart says, it lasted.

THIRD RACE   **6 FURLONGS. (Bright Holly, September 2, 1961, 1.08⅖, 3, 112.)**
Atl - 35938   Maidens. Claiming. Purse $3,500. Colts and geldings. 2-year-olds. Weight 118 lbs.
September 19, 1968   Claiming price $5,000.
Value to winner $2,100, second $700, third $455, fourth $245. Mutuel pool $86,231.

Index	Horse	Eqt A Wt	PP	St	¼	½	Str	Fin	Jockey	Cl'g Pr	Owner	Odds $1
035838Atl[3]—Restforall		b 2 118	3	3	1³	11½	1¹	1¾	G Patterson	5000	J S Abrams	2.80
35812Tim[4] –Sails Unfurled		2 118	12	2	2ʰ	25	2³	2³	M Miceli	5000	E D S.....elen	3.50
35838Atl[7]—Arturito		b 2 118	5	6	8³	7²	51½	3½	D Hidalgo	5000	T–S Smith	33.60
35828Atl[4]—Ted's Angel		b 2 118	2	7	41½	41½	41½	41½	R Perna	5000	A H Pollack	6.60
35700Atl[9]—[DH]Shabash		2 118	4	8	7ʰ	9⁴	71½	5	E Maple	5000	J Haynie	[DH]-14.10
34922Del[5]—[DH]HighAndA'		b 2 118	8	4	31½	33	3ʰ	5½	W Blum	5000	Locust Hill Farm	[DH]-2.70
35828Atl[10]—Baron Bedros		b 2 118	1	10	6²	6ʰ	6½	71½	E Walsh	5000	G H Burt	126.60
35828Atl[9]—Sunny Year		b 2 118	6	11	9²	8ʰ	8³	8⁴	R Ferraro	5000	M R Fain	6.60
35682Atl[7]—Devil Encanto		b 2 118	11	12	11¹	11³	11⁵	9ⁿᵏ	E Santana	5000	D E Taylor	45.60
35530Tim[7] –Mistic Jay		b 2 118	7	9	10²	10²	10ʰ	10²	R Hernandez	5000	S Madonna	151.80
35828Atl[6]—Brilliant Boy		2 118	9	5	5½	5½	9½	11³	H Blockt	5000	Boronia Farm	92.80
35504Mth[9]–Singing Serenada		2 118	10	1	12	12	12	12	F Lovato	5000	J B Rowe	63.50

†Seven pounds apprentice allowance waived. [DH]—Dead heat.

Time .22⅖, .46⅕, 1.13. Track fast.

$2 Mutuel Prices:

3–RESTFORALL	7.60	4.00	3.00
12–SA .S UNFURLED		4.60	3.00
5–ARTURITO			4.60

Gr. g, by Pete's Pet—Valerius, by Galerius. Trainer W. H. Foales. Bred by J. E. Roper (Tenn.).

IN GATE AT 2.26. OFF AT 2.26 EASTERN DAYLIGHT TIME. Start good. Won driving.

RESTFORALL gained the lead from the inside soon after the start, drew well clear on the final turn and lasted over SAILS UNFURLED. The latter raced closest to the pace from the start and was gaining steadily at the end. ARTURITO rallied belatedly. TED'S ANGEL finished with good energy along the inside. SHABASH rallied to finish on even terms with HIGH AND AWAY. The latter displayed some early speed, tired and dead-heated with SHABASH. SUNNY YEAR failed to menace.

Scratched—35812Atl[7] Make It Big, 35828Atl[12] Clever Star, 35828Atl[7] Shining Link, 35864Atl[8] Been There.

THE FOURTH RACE

HERE IS A race for three-year-old fillies in the $5,000–$6,000 range. The distance is six furlongs. Among the possibly significant jockey switches are Walter Blum replacing a green apprentice on Melanion's Gal and the sizzling George Cusimano taking over Half Space from Joe Culmone (and getting that filly a five-pound apprentice allowance in the bargain).

4th Atlantic City

6 FURLONGS. (Bright Holly, September 2, 1961, 1.08⅖, 3, 112.) Claiming. Purse $3,800. Fillies. 3-year-olds. Weight 119 lbs. Non-winners of two races since August 3 allowed 3 lbs., a race 6 lbs. Claiming price $6,000. 1 lb. allowed for each $250 to $5,000.

(4th Atl)—Coupled—Wild Nail and Pied-A-Terre.

Melanion's Gal * $6,000

Ch. f (1965–Fla), by Melanion—Kensington Gal, by Head Play
S. J. V. Stable J. A. Wulforst (Sunshine Stud Farm) **116**

1968	18	1	3	4	$6,560
1967	18	2	2	1	$6,445

13Sep68-6Atl	fst 6f	.22⅖ .45⅗1.11⅗	f-	7000	6	2	1^{h}	2^{½}	2^{1½}	6^{4½}	FMartinez[7]	b 107	7.40	79-18	Landquest 118½ Trojan's Broom 118^{2} Seen Afar 115^{h}	Tired 9
21Aug68-3Atl	fst 6f	.23 .46⅗1.11⅘	f-	5000	1	2	1^{2}	1^{2}	1^{3}	1^{1¾}	HGrant	b 118	8.50	83-18	Melanion's Gal 118^{1¾} Seen Afar 116½ Rapallo Sky 113^{3}	Driving 6
15Aug68-2Atl	fst 6f	.22⅘ .46⅗1.12⅗	Clm	5000	3	5	1^{1}	1^{1}	3^{½}	6^{4¼}	RGabriella	b 110	25.30	75-19	Barren Isle 110¾ Hallucinaction 115¾ Mr. W. Harrison 117¾	Used up 11
3Aug68-1Mth	my 6f	.22⅕ .46⅖1.13	f-	c-4000	4	6	1^{3}	1^{1}	1^{h}	3^{2¼}	RBroussard	b 117	*2.10	75-19	Negro Oro 112^{1¾} My Fair Beebe 114½ Melanion's Gal 117¾	Weak'd 12
27Jly 68-2Mth	fst 6f	.21⅘ .45⅗1.12⅕	f-	4000	2	5	2^{h}	1^{h}	2^{½}	4^{2}	RBroussard	b 117	*2.00	79-15	Cute Style 115^{nk} Devil's Dolly 108^{nk} Little Chickadee 115^{1½}	Used up 12
20Jly 68-2Mth	fst 6f	.22⅗ .46⅖1.13	f-	4000	7	3	2^{h}	1^{3}	1^{3}	2^{nk}	RBroussard	b 117	*3.00	77-17	My Fair Beebe 112^{nk} Melanion's Gal 117^{1} Little Tag 115^{2}	Missed 12
13Jly 68-1Mth	fst 6f	.22 .45⅖1.13	f-	4000	7	3	3^{4}	2^{3}	2^{3}	3^{3¼}	RBroussard	b 117	3.60	74-16	FamilyRoom 115^{1¼} BlossomHeath 111^{2} Melanion'sGal 117^{1}	Hung 10
6Jly 68-2Mth	fst 6f	.22⅖ .47 1.13⅘	f-	4000	7	4	1^{1}	1^{2}	2^{½}	4^{7½}	RBroussard	b 17	3.10	65-23	Colina Real 118^{2½} Chime Song 115^{2½} Next Left 111^{2½}	Hard used 10
28Jun68-3Mth	sly 6f	.22⅗ .47⅕1.13⅕	f-	4000	2	2	1^{2}	1^{1½}	1^{h}	2^{5}	RBroussard	b 117	10.60	71-25	Janette O. 110^{5} Melanion's Gal 117^{4½} Centuple 114½	Best of rest 11
8Jun68-3Mth	fst 6f	.22⅕ .46 1.12⅕	f-	4500	4	6	3^{1}	4^{4}	5^{10}	5^{8½}	RSage[5]	b 107	14.30	72-17	Royal Stella 117^{3½} Miss Patty Sue 117^{4} Little Tag 114no	Tired 10

LATEST WORKOUTS Sep 10 Atl 4f fst .47⅕ h Sep 5 Atl 3f fst .36 b Aug 14 Atl 4f fst .49 b

Great Tabi Kat * $6,000

Ch. f (1965–Ky), by Great One—Tobu Tabi, by Sub Fleet
H. W. McGrath J. J. Greely, Jr. (H. W. McGrath) **116**

1968	9	1	1	2	$4,265
1967	15	2	1	0	$5,630

9Sep68-6Atl	fst 7f	.22⅖ .45⅗1.24⅗	f-	5500	2	3	1^{2}	1^{1}	1^{3}	3^{3¾}	EMaple	b 116	*4.20	76-18	Lanoka 110^{3} Half Space 113¾ Great Tabi Kat 116^{2½}	Faltered str. 12
17Aug68-1Atl	fst 6f	.22 .46⅗1.12	f-	4000	2	3	1^{2}	1^{3}	1^{4}	1^{3}	DKassen	b 114	6.90	82-15	Great Tabi Kat 114^{3} Lolla B. 112^{2} Lenape Road 114½	Steady drive 12
10Aug68-1Atl	fst 6f	.22⅕ .47 1.12⅘	f-	4000	8	3	2^{h}	1^{½}	2^{h}	2^{1}	DKassen	b 114	7.40	77-17	Little Chickadee 114^{1} Great Tabi Kat 114^{2} Flow Gently 114^{1¼}	Gam'y 12
27Jly 68-2Del	fst 6f	.22⅘ .46⅘1.12⅘	Clm	5000	7	1	1^{3}	1^{h}	3^{3}	5^{7¼}	GCusimano[5]	b 104	5.30	74-20	Coray 104^{3} Code Of The Hills 115^{1½} Noble's Mill 111¾	Used up 8
15Jly 68-5Del	fst 6f	.22⅗ .46⅗1.12⅖	f-	6250	9	5	5^{4}	10^{12}	9^{13}	9^{16}	BThornburg	b 112	17.30	67-19	Lolla B. 116^{5} Sheilas Sweetie 114½ Lady Lewis 112^{3}	Tired 10
26Jun68-6Del	fst 6f	.22⅘ .46⅘1.14⅗	f-	6500	7	5	2^{2}	3^{3½}	6^{5½}	5^{5¼}	BThornburg	b 112	5.40	67-20	Bryagin 112¾ Sheilas Sweetie 119½ Clip Clip 107^{3}	Bore out 8
19Jun68-4Del	fst 6f	.22⅖ .46⅖1.12⅘	f-	7000	1	2	1^{2}	2^{½}	2^{½}	3^{4}	BThornburg	b 113	5.70	77-16	Pony Keg 108^{3} Bryagin 113^{1} Great Tabi Kat 113^{nk}	Speed, tired 8
30May68-4Del	sly 6f	.22⅗ .47 1.13⅖	Clm	7500	2	2	1^{2½}	3^{1}	4^{4½}	4^{4¾}	CBaltazar	b 111	6.10	73-20	Mighty Me 116^{1¼} Sam Bolero 116^{3} Struck 112½	Speed, tired 11
9May68-7CD	sly 6f	.21⅘ .46 1.11⅘	f-	8250	5	2	2^{h}	1^{h}	3^{1}	4^{7}	EFires	b 113	7.00	80-22	April Sister 116^{5} Dear Ethel 113^{2} Jubilee Lady 113^{h}	Tired 6

LATEST WORKOUTS Sep 5 Atl 5f fst 1.03 b Jly 24 Del 3f fst .37 b

Half Space * $6,000

Dk. b. or br. f (1965–Fla), by Ambehaving—Ballylo, by Ballydam
R. Chabok M. A. Buxton (Meadowbrook Farm, Inc.) **108^{5}**

1968	17	1	2	1	$4,975
1967	12	6	2	0	$14.342

9Sep68-6Atl	fst 7f	.22⅖ .45⅗1.24⅗	f-	5500	5	9	10^{6½}	8^{8¼}	5^{4}	2^{3}	JCulmone	113	13.40	77-18	Lanoka 110^{3} Half Space 113¾ Great Tabi Kat 116^{2½}	Closed well 12
14Aug68-6Atl	fst 7f	.22⅗ .45⅖1.24⅕	f-	6500	6	3	6^{5¾}	6^{9½}	7^{13}	8^{18}	JCulmone	114	12.80	64-13	LittleMissMuffet114^{2½} BundleOfTwigs116^{3½} JanetteO.113^{2}	Tired 10
31Jly 68-9Mth	fm 1$\frac{1}{16}$ Ⓣ	1.12⅗1.45⅗	Clm	7500	2	4	4^{2½}	4^{7}	5^{8}	6^{14}	EMonacelli	110	16.40	——	Only Always 110^{3} Slicky Jim 115¾ Trueno 115no	Brief foot 9
18Jly 68-7Mth	fst 6f	.22⅖ .45⅗1.11⅘	Clm	8000	1	5	4^{3}	4^{3½}	4^{7½}	5^{8¾}	EMonacelli	110	29.60	74-21	Old Watts 115¾ Landquest 112^{2} Cotton To Market 115^{1½}	Tired 8
9Jly 68-5Mth	fst 6f	.22⅕ .45⅘1.12⅘	f-	c-6000	7	6	7^{7}	7^{13}	7^{14}	7^{9¼}	MMiceli	111	4.80	69-21	Double The Bet 116^{nk} Landquest 114^{1} Pied-A-Terre 113^{2½}	No factor 12
10Apr68-6GP	fst 7f	.22⅕ .45⅗1.24⅖	Cl	c-7500	12	2	9^{3¾}	5^{1¾}	3^{4}	3^{4½}	CPerret[5]	106	*1.60	82-13	Tim Tom 116^{4½} Mrs. Mehle 107no Half Space 106¾	Held on evenly 12
28Mar68-4GP	fst 6f	.22⅖ .45⅘1.10⅘	f-	10000	4	6	7^{6}	6^{4}	6^{7}	6^{13}	MMiceli	116	4.30	77-10	Istrue 116^{7} Incassable 116^{1} Alretta's 116^{2}	No factor 10
21Mar68-4GP	fst 6f	.22 .45⅗1.12⅖	f-	12500	4	9	8^{9¼}	3^{7}	2^{1½}	1^{h}	PMaxwell	116	4.30	82-14	Half Space 116^{h} Formal Deb 116^{4} Miss Hambra 107½	Stiff drive. 10
18Mar68-4GP	fst 7f	.22⅗ .45⅖1.23⅗	f-	13000	6	2	9^{7}	9^{8¼}	9^{11}	8^{8¾}	RNono	112	9.20	82-15	Some Wind 113^{3} Only Always 113¾ Ladypuggy 116^{h}	No speed 9
12Mar68-7GP	fst 6f	.22⅗ .45⅘1.11⅘	f-	Allow	6	2	5^{1¼}	3^{1}	6^{5½}	5^{8}	MMiceli	115	6.60	77-17	Mrs.Peterkin 113^{h} MarshHarbour 113^{6} PatteeCanyon 108^{1}	Tired 7

LATEST WORKOUTS Sep 18 Atl 3f fst .38 b Sep 7 Atl 3f sly .39 b Aug 31 Atl 4f fst .51⅕ b Aug 20 Atl 3f fst .38 b

Wild Nail * $6,000

Dk. b. or br. f (1965–Md.), by Nail—Fedela, by Requested
Indian Mills Stock Farm B. W. Perkins (H. Dixon) **113**

1968	26	7	6	2	$19,257
1967	6	M	1	3	$1,560

7Sep68-1Atl	sl 6f	.23⅕ .47⅕1.13⅗	f-	c-4000	6	4	1^{h}	2^{½}	3^{3}	2no	GPatterson	b 119	*2.90	74-22	Craig's Date 113no Wild Nail 119^{1¼} Pied-A-Terre 114^{3}	Came again 11
29Aug68-7Tim	fst 5¾f	.23⅗ .48⅗1.11⅕	Clm	5000	3	2	2^{1}	3^{1½}	4^{2}	2^{h}	RKimball	b 117	6.80	84-23	Soft Weather 111^{h} Wild Nail 117^{h} Duly Noted 113¾	Wide 8
16Aug68-8Tim	fst 5¾f	.24 .48⅘1.11⅕	Clm	5000	7	6	4^{2}	4^{2¾}	5^{5½}	6^{4¾}	JKratz	b 119	3.60	79-23	Copyreader 116^{h} Federal Grant 119^{2½} C.B.'s Boy 111^{1}	No mishap 8
3Aug68-2Del	fst 6f	.22⅗ .47 1.13⅗	f-	c-4000	4	5	2^{2}	2^{h}	1^{4½}	1^{¾}	RLatorre[7]	b 112	3.10	77-19	Wild Nail 112¾ M. D. Wim 116^{3} Crooked Course 113^{nk}	Driving 10
26Jly 68-4Del	fst 6f	.22⅖ .46⅘1.13⅖	f-	3500	7	3	5^{5½}	6^{3¾}	3^{1}	1^{nk}	RLatorre	b 109d-	*3.00	78-21	d-Wild Nail 109^{nk} Miss Loppy 113^{4} Carlyn Profit 113^{3}	Bore in 12
26Jly68—d-Disqualified and placed second.																
19Jly 68-3Del	fst 6f	.22⅖ .46⅖1.13	Clm	3000	7	2	1^{4}	1^{3}	1^{2}	1^{h}	RLatorre[10]	b 104	*1.10	80-17	Wild Nail 104^{h} Pipe Of Port 115^{h} Brenda's Dare 114^{7}	Driving 11
13Jly 68-3Del	fst 6f	.22⅖ .46⅗1.13	Clm	3750	2	8	5^{5½}	5^{8}	5^{8½}	7^{7}	JGiovanni	b 115	5.20	73-15	Cypark 117^{1} Gremmie 117^{1} Pet For Me 112^{1½}	Had no mishaps 12
4Jly 68-1Del	gd 6f	.22⅗ .47⅕1.14⅖	f-	4500	4	6	6^{2¾}	6^{6}	4^{5}	2^{h}	DRWright[5]	b 114	*4.50	73-23	Trojan's Broom 116^{h} Wild Nail 114^{nk} Coray 113^{1½}	Strong finish 12
20Jun68-2Del	fst 6f	.22⅗ .47⅖1.14⅘	f-	3000	2	2	2^{h}	2^{h}	2^{h}	1^{1}	RFitzgerald	b 118	*1.10	71-23	Wild Nail 118^{1} Pet Vest 112¾ Stick On 107½	Hard drive 12
15Jun68-1Del	fst 6f	.22⅖ .46⅘1.13⅖	Clm	3500	7	2	2^{½}	1^{1}	1^{3}	1^{4}	RFitzgerald	b 115	5.90	78-13	Wild Nail 115^{4} Coin A Phrase 109^{3} Miss Loppy 110^{nk}	In hand 11

Athena's Lark $5,000

Dk. b. or br. f (1965–Ala), by T. V. Lark—Royal Athena, by Olympia (F. W. Hooper) **109** 1968 9 1 0 0 $2,675 / 1967 2 M 0 0

A. J. Repici   G. F. Jabalee

9Sep68–6Atl	fst 7f .22⅖ .45⅗1.24⅗ f—	4500 10	4	3² 3¹ 2³ 6⁷¼	EMonacelli	111	,36.10	72–16 Lanoka 110³ Half Space 113¾ Great Tabi Kat 116²½	Speed, tired 12
31Aug68–2Atl	fst 6f .23 .46½1.11¾ f—	c-3500 6	2	5⁴ 7¹⁰ 7¹⁰ 6⁵¾	JVelasquez	b 114	*2.50	77–15 My Fair Beebe 117ⁿᵏ Now Listen 114ⁿᵒ Craig's Date 114½	Dull 7
14Aug68–6Atl	fst 7f .22⅖ .45⅖1.24⅗ f—	6500 7	10	Bolted	CBaltiazar	b 113	9.60	—— LittleMissMuffet114²½ BundleOfTwigs116³½ JanetteO.113²	Eased 10
25Jly68–6Mth	gd 6f .22⅖ .45⅗1.12¾ f—	8000 9	7	7⁴½ 7¹⁴ 7¹⁴ 7¹⁴	EMonacelli	113	14.90	66–16 Landquest 112¹½ Star Angle 111½ Dey's Captain 117²	No speed 9
10Jly68–5Mth	fst 1 .47½1.12⅖1.39⅖ f—	10000 6	2	3⁵ 3¹½ 4⁶ 6¹⁵	EMonacelli	109	4.20	61–15 Casey's Clarice 111¹½ Lancerrae 112³ La Picada 115⁷	Tired 6
24Jun68–2Mth	fst 6f .22 .45½1.11 f—	10000 3	1	2½ 2½ 3²½ 3⁷½	EMonacelli	109	d10.30	79–18 Reel Irish 116³ Libamah 112⁴½ d–Athena's Lark 109½	Bore out 8
24Jun68–d–Disqualified and placed fourth.
24May68–7GS	sly 6f .22⅖ .46⅗1.12 f—	11500 5	1	3² 6⁹ 6⁹½ 5⁸	JVelasquez	118	4.30	76–22 Formal Deb 116¹½ Good Bet 1183½ Lady Lewis 112ⁿᵏ	Brief speed 7
16May68–2GS	fst 6f .22⅖ .46⅗1.11⅘ Md	10000 2	4	3ⁿᵏ 2ʰ 1¹½ 1¹½	JVelasquez	111	5.50	85–17 Athena's Lark 111¹½ Hopeful Bid 116²½ Country Day 122³½	Driving 11
8May68–2GS	fst 6f .22 .45⅗1.12½ f–MdSpWt	4	5	108¹11¹³10¹⁰ 7⁷½	JVelasquez	115	13.30	75–16 Stormy Pink 115² Young N' Sassy 115ⁿᵒ Mertensia 115½	No threat 12
25Aug67–4Atl	sly 6f .22⅖ .45⅕1.10⅗ f–MdSpWt	7	1	76½ 8¹⁴ 68½ 6¹⁰	JVelasquez	117	20.90	78–14 Double Ripple 117² Hear The Fear 117¾ Formal Deb 117ⁿᵏ	No threat 9

LATEST WORKOUTS   Sep 16 Atl 3f fst .38 b   Aug 24 Atl 4f fst .48½ b   Aug 17 Atl 4f fst .49⅗ bg   Aug 12 Atl 4f fst .50⅖ b

Ricles $6,000

Ch. f. (1965–Fla), by Alcibiades II—Orevent, by Fervent (Harbor View Farm) **113** 1968 7 0 0 1 $927 / 1967 1 1 0 0 $2,405

Rose Hill Stable   J. Griffin

11Sep68–5Atl	fst 6f .22 .44⅗1.11⅜ Clm	6500 1	7	9⁸ 7¹¹ 59½ 55½	VTejada	113	34.20	78–17 Soybean Sam 116¾ DerbyDancer109¹½ LauraWinston115³	Late foot 10
4Sep68–6Atl	fst 6f .23⅖ .45⅗1.11⅕ f—	7000 8	1	7²½ 55 7⁷ 7³¼	MMiceli	113	12.10	82–20 Landquest 115¹ Seen Afar 115¹½ Bundle Of Twigs 110ⁿᵒ	No threat 9
31Aug68–6Atl	fst 6f .22⅖ .45⅛1.11 Clm	6500 4	4	6⁶ 7¹⁰ 6⁷ 54½	MMiceli	107	45.00	82–15 Cohesian 119² Gay Youth 111½ That Guy 116½	Some late foot 9
25Jly68–6Mth	gd 6f .22⅖ .46⅕1.12⅖ f—	c-7500 3	4	4¹½ 6¹³ 8¹⁷ 8²⁰	CBaltazar	112	6.60	60–16 Landquest 111²½ Star Angle 111½ Dey's Captain 117²	Brief speed 9
16Jly68–5Mth	fst 6f .21⅖ .45 1.11⅞ f—	8500 9	5	4⁵ 58½ 76 45½	CGonzalez	110	46.10	79–17 Rubia 111ⁿᵒ Aqua Val 113² Merci Bien 117³½	Mild late gain 9
16Jly68–d–Dead heat.
2Jly68–4Mth	fst 6f .22⅖ .47 1.13⅗ f—	7500 6	4	6²½ 64½ 7¹¼ 43½	CBaltazar	114	*3.00	72–21 Dey's Captain 116½ Rapallo Sky 116½ Star Angle 111²	No mishap 12
30Apr68–5GS	fst 6f .22⅖ .45⅛1.12⅗f—	7500 10	3	10⁷¼ 9⁷¾ 5²½ 3¹½	RBroussard	116	24.80	79–18 Ifu Say So 116¹½ Ebbie's Imp 116½ Ricles 116ⁿᵏ	Blocked repeatedly 11
17Jly67–1Mth	sl 5½f .23 .47⅕1.07⅛ f–M	5500 8	4	4²½ 3² 1² 1²	RBroussard	117	11.70	81–20 Ricles 117² Starcrossed 117³ Bobbie's Runner 113⁴½	Driving 12

LATEST WORKOUTS   Sep 3 Atl 3f fst .36 b   Jly 23 Mth 6f fst 1.17⅗ b

Ash Leaf * $6,000

Ch. f (1965–NJ), by Celtic Ash—Maralal, by Royal Charger (J. Fieramosca) **113** 1968 10 0 2 1 $2,740 / 1967 6 2 0 1 $4,510

A. Nini   J. Kulina

9Sep68–6Atl	fst 7f .22⅖ .45⅗1.24⅗ f—	5500 9	5	2² 2¹ 3³½ 46½	GPatterson	b 113	6.20	74–16 Lanoka 110³ Half Space 113¾ Great Tabi Kat 116²½	Speed, tired 12
24Aug68–3Atl	fst 7f .22⅖ .45 1.23⅗ f—	6500 2	7	4² 54½ 56 5¹⁰	GPatterson	110	24.10	75–13 Celtic Song 113⁵ Seen Afar 113¹½ Xmas In July 114²½	Tired 8
7Aug68–9Atl	fst 7f .22⅖ .46 1.24⅛ Clm	6500 11	11	96½ 85½ 7¹³ 54½	WGavidia	113	15.40	62–15 String Tie 116¹⁰ Bowl Fresh 117ⁿᵒ Barren Isle 1126	Not a threat 11
29Jly68–4Mth	fst 6f .22⅖ .46½1.12 f—	6000 9	1	6⁴½ 6⁵½ 55½ 45½	PKallai	112	7.50	77–17 Bundle Of Twigs 113² Rapallo Sky 113¹½ Moon Chase 113¹½	Evenly 9
9Jly68–5Mth	fst 6f .22⅖ .45⅗1.12⅖ f—	6500 1	8	6⁵ 59½ 5¹² 55¾	RTanner⁵	b 109	7.30	72–21 Double The Bet 116ⁿᵏ Landquest 114¹ Pied–A–Terre 113²½	Late f't 12
6Jun68–6Mth	fst 6f .22⅖ .46 1.12½ f—	6500 4	1	2¹½ 3⁴½ 34½ 3¹½	JVelasquez	b 111	*2.20	79–17 Casey's Clarice 115ʰ Star Angle 111½ Ash Leaf 111⁵½	No rally 10
28May68–5GS	sly 6f .22⅖ .47⅛1.13⅗ f—	6750 2	3	2³½ 24 2¹ 2ⁿᵏ	JVelasquez	b 114	3.30	76–24 Tudor Isle 112ⁿᵏ Ash Leaf 114²½ Rapallo Sky 122¹	Coming again 7
10May68–5GS	fst 6f .22⅖ .46⅖1.11⅘ f—	8250 2	3	5²½ 66 6⁵½ 57½	WGavidia	114	9.20	78–15 Good Bet 116¹½ Little Chickadee 113½ Ebbie's Imp 112½	Tired 6
3May68–4GS	fst 6f .22⅖ .46 1.12 f—	8500 5	4	4²½ 54½ 24 54½	JVelasquez	b 114	*2.20	81–12 Sister John 116¹ Lenape Road 118² Behoove 116ⁿᵒ	Went evenly 8
23Apr68–2GS	fst 6f .22⅖ .46⅗1.12½ f—	8000 10	2	3½ 3³ 1ʰ 2¹½	JVelasquez	b 116	4.70	81–12 Lenape Road 112¹½ Ash Leaf 116²½ Little Chickadee 112ʰ	Gamely 12

LATEST WORKOUTS   Sep 1 Atl 3f fst .35⅗ b   Jly 27 Mth 5f fst 1.02⅘ b   Jly 22 Mth 4f fst .49 b

Rapallo Sky * $6,000

Dk. b. or br. f (1965–Md), by Correspondent—Valerie J., by Great Circle (C. W. Hancock) **113** 1968 18 2 5 3 $11,985 / 1967 22 4 2 4 $8,820

S. Branca   J. J. Dougherty

21Aug68–3Atl	fst 6f .23 .46⅗1.11⅘ f—	5000 2	5	55¼ 55¼ 33¼ 32½	FLovato	b 113	4.40	81–18 Melanion's Gal 118¹½ Seen Afar 116¼ Rapallo Sky 113³	Fair try 6
14Aug68–6Atl	fst 7f .22⅖ .45½1.24⅗ f—	6000 1	9	8⁷½ 79½ 5⁷½ 4⁸	JVasquez	b 112	6.10	74–13 LittleMissMuffet114²½ BundleOfTwigs116³½ JanetteO.113²	No threat 11
7Aug68–9Atl	fst 7f .22⅖ .46 1.24⅘ Clm	6500 3	8	109³106½ 59½ 4¹⁶	JVasquez	b 112	3.40	66–15 String Tie 116¹⁰ Bowl Fresh 117ⁿᵒ Barren Isle 1126	Not a factor 11
29Jly68–4Mth	fst 6f .22⅖ .46½1.12 f—	6500 8	8	88½ 77½ 6⁵½ 2²	JVasquez	b 113	*2.70	80–17 Bundle Of Twigs 113² Rapallo Sky 113¹½ Moon Chase 113¹½	Hung 9
16Jly68–5Mth	fst 6f .21⅖ .45 1.11⅘ f—	8500 5	4	88½ 7¹¹ 65 66	RTanner⁵	b 109	5.40	79–17 Rubia 111ⁿᵒ Aqua Val 113² Merci Bien 117³½	Mild bid, tired 9
2Jly68–4Mth	fst 6f .22⅖ .47 1.13⅖ f—	7500 4	12	10⁶ 75 5½ 2½	JVasquez	b 116	7.80	74–21 Dey's Captain 116½ Rapallo Sky 116½ Star Angle 111²	Gamely 12
22Jun68–5Mth	fst 6f .22⅖ .44⅗1.10½ Clm	9000 9	11	118¹ 87 6⁵½ 66	WTichenor	b 109	30.20	80–17 Bunty Escar 1096 ♣Rubia 111² ♣Crolicy 1107	Lacked early foot 12
11Jun68–7Mth	fm*1 ① .48½1.40 f—	10000 10	7	715¹⁰16¹⁰16¹⁴ 9¹⁸	RSage	b 105	9.20	80– 3 Bungalow 109¹ Who Cabled 113⁴ Cecebe 118⁶	Showed nothing 10
28May68–5GS	sly 6f .22⅖ .47⅛1.13⅗ f—	c–7000 1	7	71² 49 42½ 32¾	HGrant	b 122	3.70	73–24 Tudor Isle 112ⁿᵏ Ash Leaf 114²½ Rapallo Sky 122¹	Held evenly 7
14May68–6GS	fst 6f .22⅖ .46⅖1.12⅖ f—	6000 7	8	99¼ 53¾ 2½ 1²½	JVelasquez	b 116	5.90	81–18 Rapallo Sky 116²½ Neat Dish 116³ Dey's Captain 114¹	Driving 9

Horses Shown Below Are on the "Also Eligible" List and Are Not Listed in Order of Post Positions.

Royal Stella $5,750

Ch. f (1965–Fla), by Royal Dinner—Stella J., by Gay Bacon (J.–J. Byrd) **112** 1968 9 3 M 1 1 $8,995 / 1967 2 0 0 1 $375

Caccese–Sitar   A. Caccese

5Sep68–6Atl	fst 6f .22⅖ .46 1.11¾ Clm	5000 9	4	6²½ 53½ 35 43	EMaple	112	6.30	81–19 Soybean Sam 117¹½ Implicit 117¹½ Gay Port 118ⁿᵏ	No rally 11
22Jun68–2Mth	fst 6f .21⅖ .45½1.12½ Clm	6250 4	5	48 32½ 3ⁿᵏ 42½	RSage⁵	b 109	*2.80	79–17 Dey's Captain 111² Drums 114ⁿᵒ Swoon Free 114ⁿᵏ	No mishap 12
8Jun68–3Mth	fst 6f .22⅖ .46 1.12½ f—	5000 6	3	2ʰ 1³ 1³ 1³½	VSpuzzo	b 117	*0.90	84–17 Royal Stella 117³½ Miss Patty Sue 117⁴ Little Tag 114ⁿᵒ	Mild drive 10
23May68–2GS	fst 6f .22⅖ .46 1.12½ f—	5500 10	2	2¹ 11½ 1³ 1²½	JVelasquez	b 116	*3.20	83–15 Royal Stella 116²½ Carlyn Profit 112²½ War Fever 114ʰ	Driving 10
11May68–5GS	fst 6f .22⅖ .45⅗1.11⅖ Clm	5500 7	2	2¹½ 21½ 24 5²½	RSage⁷	b 105	16.70	80–13 Sly Bandit 116²½ Jolly Fella 112³½ Rocky Serenade 112½	Weakened 10
30Apr68–5GS	fst 6f .22⅖ .45⅗1.12⅗f—	7250 5	9	3ⁿᵏ 3⁴ 4² 11¹³	RPerna	b 116	12.60	68–18 Ifu Say So 116¹½ Ebbie's Imp 116½ Ricles 116ⁿᵏ	Gave way badly 11
26Apr68–6GS	gd 6f .22⅖ .45⅗1.13¼ Clm	6500 7	7	2¹½ 2² 3⁴	WBlum	b 113	4.60	74–18 Marvina's Will 111ʰ Sly Bandit 116⁴ Royal Stella 113ⁿᵒ	Poor start 7
26Mar68–3GP	gd 6f .22⅖ .46½1.12¾ Md	7500 7	4	11½ 13 14 1ʰ	RWholeyJr⁵	b 110	4.90	81–12 Royal Stella 110ʰ Fast Skipper 120² Fojo 120½	All out 12
2Jan68–4TrP	fst 6f .21⅖ .45 1.11⅕ f—	6500 1	4	14 13 1½ 2ⁿᵏ	RTanner⁷	b 109	19.20	77–24 Our Soca 118² d–Mrs. Mehle 113³ Royal Stella 109²½	Impeded 9
2Jan68–Placed second through disqualification.
5Dec67–1TrP	fst 6f .22 .45⅜1.11 Md	c–5000 12	1	2² 2¹ 3⁵ 4¹⁴	JHarrison	116	*2.40	69–20 Trim Ruler 114³¾ Lightning Rullah 119⁴ Ed Farrell 119⁶	Tired 12

LATEST WORKOUTS   Aug 30 Atl 6f fst 1.13⅗ hg   Aug 24 Atl 5f fst 1.00⅖ hg   Aug 17 Atl 3f fst .36⅖ b

Dadley's Image $5,000

Ch. f (1965–SC), by V–Two—Dadley, by Final Touch (W. P. Buyck) **112** 1968 5 1 0 1 $2,555 / 1967 0 M 0 0 ——

Red Brick Stable   D. C. LeVine

14Sep68–1Atl	fst 6f .23 .46⅗1.11⅘ f—	c–4000 4	5	11½ 11 2½ 36	PlGrimm	117	2.20	78–14 Little Tag 114¹ Pauline Puppet 117² Dadley's Image 117³½	Used up 12
6Sep68–1Atl	fst 6f .22⅖ .45⅗1.11⅘ Md	5000 3	6	2¹½ 2½ 2½ 1²	PlGrimm	114	6.70	83–18 Dadley'sImage114² RunningTom117³ LaVictroienne114²	Driving 12
21Aug68–3Atl	fst 6f .23 .46⅗1.11⅘ f—	5000 5	1	3³ 3⁵ 59½ 6¹³	GPatterson	113	17.80	70–18 Melanion's Gal 118¹½ Seen Afar 116½ Rapallo Sky 113³	Tired 6
16Aug68–1Atl	fst 6f .22⅖ .45⅗1.11⅘ Md	5000 1	8	2ʰ 2ʰ 3⁴ 68½	PlGrimm	113	7.50	77–18 Tea Caddy 116⁶ Pimpernel Gem 113² Native Lark 111ⁿᵏ	Tired 12
9Aug68–1Atl	fst 6f .22⅖ .45⅗1.12 Md	5000 1	9	10¹³10¹⁵ 89½ 69½	PlGrimm	113	23.80	72–16 Woman's Rights 117⁵ Phantom Spv 111ʰ Wace 109³½	No factor 12

LATEST WORKOUTS   Aug 30 Atl 5f fst 1.03⅖ b   Jly 24 Rkm 4f fst .49⅖ h

---

I think we can eliminate Wild Nail, although she was a consistent winner against cheaper stock in Delaware, and her local debut was quite impressive. It seems probable that today's class is too rich for her blood. Also, I think she should have had a workout since her last race.

Athena's Lark seems to have gone to pot. Her last race was an improvement over that August 31 disgrace, but she doesn't figure to bother $6,000 fillies.

Ricles looks like the kind that needs another furlong to do her best and cannot be taken too seriously today, despite the drop into softer competition. Ash Leaf might benefit from today's shorter journey but has not been sharp since May, and it looks as if $3,500 company might be the only solution. Dadley's Image seems outclassed. The likelier prospects are:

Melanion's Gal: This speedster has not beaten $6,000 animals but neither, for that matter, has any other entrant in this race. As her good races for Howard Grant and Ray Broussard indicate, she needs strong handling or else she goes to pieces in the stretch. She'll get such handling from Walter Blum. The big question is whether some other rapid starter will be able to hook her early and wear her out. Pending the answer to that question, we have to like Melanion's Gal, excusing her last defeat under an apprentice rider, and noting with respect that she is returning to action only six days later. Contender.

Great Tabi Kat: A beaten favorite ten days ago, when she conked out in the stretch of a longer race, this front-runner appears capable of spoiling Melanion Gal's afternoon. And vice versa. If they were the only two starters in the race, however, I'd vote for Melanion's Gal. Her victory of August 21 was a tick swifter than Great Tabi Kat's of August 17 and was against better opposition. So we can rule out Great Tabi Kat as a winner here, but we shall also be wary of the effects on Melanion's Gal of the inevitable early duel with Great Tabi Kat. No Bet.

Half Space: This filly won at the distance in March but does not really shape up as a threat. Her recent form has been that of an animal best suited to longer races. No doubt she'll be running at the leaders in the final yards of today's skirmish, but I can't see her as the winner. No Bet.

Rapallo Sky: In shape, this one could probably catch a tiring Melanion's Gal. But there is no evidence that she is in shape. She has neither raced nor worked out in the past month. I make her a contender only because of her late-charging style and her potential suitability to today's class and distance. But I would not bet on a claiming racer who has been idle so long and whose record shows no victories after lengthy vacations. No Bet.

Royal Stella: In May and June this filly easily defeated a couple of fields like the one she meets today. Her latest two races, against strong males, proved that she is too much for $5,000 fillies to handle. I'd choose her unhesitatingly if her physical soundness were not suspect. Why did she lay off between June and September? Then, after those three excellent August workouts and that splendid effort of September 5, why has she been idle? No Bet.

Every one of these contenders is seriously flawed. Melanion's Gal is being asked to beat off Great Tabi Kat and stick it out against the onrushing Royal Stella, Rapallo Sky, and Half Space. Considering Half Space's preference for a longer distance and the dubious fitness of Royal Stella and Rapallo Sky, it is easy enough to make Melanion's Gal a selection. But there is a difference between making a selection and making a bet. For me, this is not a playable race. Those who insist on buying tickets will probably do best to back both Melanion's Gal and the likeliest of the come-on horses, Royal Stella.

The Running of the Race

HALF SPACE was the best filly in the race and would have won if given an extra furlong. She was eating up the victorious Melanion's Gal at the finish. Great Tabi Kat took the early lead but could not hold it when Melanion's Gal got rolling. Neither Rapallo Sky nor Royal Stella showed much. Note that the crowd seemed to see the race much as we did, making Melanion's Gal a lukewarm favorite, with Royal Stella next.

FOURTH RACE **6 FURLONGS. (Bright Holly, September 2, 1961, 1.08⅖, 3, 112.)**

Atl - 35939 Claiming. Purse $3,800. Fillies. 3-year-olds. Weight 119 lbs. Non-winners of two races since August 3 allowed 3 lbs., a race 6 lbs. Claiming price $6,000. 1 lb. allowed for each $250 to $5,000.

September 19, 1968

Value to winner $2,280, second $760, third $495, fourth $265. Mutuel pool $115,881.

Index	Horse	Eqt	A	Wt	PP	St	¼	½	Str	Fin	Jockey	Cl'g Pr	Owner	Odds $1
35896Atl[6]	—Melanion's Gal	b	3	116	1	6	$2^{1\frac{1}{2}}$	$1^{\frac{1}{2}}$	1^{3}	$1^{1\frac{1}{2}}$	W Blum	6000	F J V Stable	2.70
35860Atl[2]	—Half Space		3	108	3	7	$6^{\frac{1}{2}}$	$6^{\frac{1}{2}}$	5^{h}	$2^{1\frac{1}{2}}$	G Cusimano[5]	6000	R Chabok	5.60
35860Atl[4]	—Ash Leaf	b	3	113	7	8	$5^{\frac{1}{2}}$	5^{3}	6^{2}	$3^{\frac{3}{4}}$	J Giovanni	6000	A Nini	15.60
35629Atl[3]	—Rapallo Sky	b	3	113	8	10	$9^{\frac{1}{2}}$	8^{1}	8^{3}	$4^{\frac{1}{2}}$	P Kallai	6000	S Branca	7.00
35[illegible]33Atl[4]	—Royal Stella		3	112	10	3	3^{3}	3^{6}	$2^{\frac{1}{2}}$	5^{h}	M Hole	5750	Sitar-Caccese	3.60
35900Atl[3]	—Dadley's Image		3	112	9	1	8^{h}	7^{3}	$7^{\frac{1}{2}}$	6^{h}	J C Cruz	5000	Red Brick Stable	41.10
35860Atl[3]	—Great Tabi Kat	b	3	116	2	2	$1^{1\frac{1}{2}}$	2^{2}	3^{2}	7^{nk}	E Maple	6000	H W McGrath	7.50
35846Atl[2]	—Wild Nail	b	3	113	4	4	4^{3}	4^{1}	4^{h}	8^{2}	M Aristone	6000	Indian Mills Stock F'rm	17.40
35860Atl[6]	—Athena's Lark		3	111	5	5	7^{1}	9^{5}	9	9	E Monacelli	5000	A J Repici	44.00
35877Atl[5]	—Ricles		3	113	6	9	10	10	Bled		V Tejada	6000	Rose Hill Stable	6.10

Time .22⅕, .45⅗, 1.12. Track fast.

$2 Mutuel Prices:			
1-MELANION'S GAL	7.40	4.80	3.80
3-HALF SPACE		5.40	4.00
7-ASH LEAF			6.40

Ch. f, by Melanion—Kensington Gal, by Head Play. Trainer J. A. Wulforst. Bred by Sunshine Stud Farm (Fla.)

IN GATE AT 2.53. OFF AT 2.53 EASTERN DAYLIGHT TIME. Start good. Won driving.

MELANION'S GAL, close up from the start while along the inside, came out and around GREAT TABI KAT to take command entering the stretch and held HALF SPACE safe. The latter, slow to gain best stride, finished with good energy. ASH LEAF was going well at the end. RAPALLO SKY was void of early speed. ROYAL STELLA went evenly. GREAT TABI KAT sprinted clear soon after the start and tired. RICLES bled.

Scratched—35627Sar[9] Ruling Light, 35824Atl[3] Bundle Of Twigs, 35896Atl[7] Polly Come Home, 35824Atl[5] Star Angle, 35846Atl[3] Pied-A-Terre, 32893Aqu[3] Seewinkel. Overweight—Athena's Lark 2.

THE FIFTH RACE

THIS RACE is a six-furlong claimer for $4,000–$5,000 three-year-olds. Several of the starters can be discarded on grounds of recent inactivity. They are Creswood Dip, Jimmy Bennett, and Coral Atoll. Easy Spending, a middle-distance runner, does not belong in this field and also is eliminated.

5th Atlantic City

6 FURLONGS ATLANTIC CITY (Start / Finish)

6 FURLONGS. (Bright Holly, September 2, 1961, 1.08⅖, 3, 112.)
Claiming. Puse $3,700. 3-year-olds. Weight 122 lbs. Non-winners of three races since July 24 allowed 3 lbs., two races 5 lbs., a race 7 lbs. Claiming price $5,000. 1 lb. allowed for $250 to $4,000.

Sufico $5,000 — B. g (1965-Ky), by Royal Serenade—Susie Dear, by Porterhouse — **117** — 1968 2 1 0 1 $2,735
M. R. Fain J. S. Salvaggio (Dr. W. S. Karutz) — 1967 0 M 0 0
13Sep68-1Atl fst 1⅛.47⅗1.12⅗1.52⅘ Md c-4000 12 2 1½ 13 1½ 1¼ WBlum 113 6.10 74-18 Sufico 1131¼ Endow 1115 Brother R. 1093 Under urging 12
23Aug68-1Atl fst 6f .22⅗ .46⅕1.12⅕ Md 5000 7 4 46 56½ 43¼ 32¼ WBlum 116 5.50 79-19 Amore Luigi 111nk Maori Hero 1202 Sufico 1162 Mild rally 10
LATEST WORKOUTS Aug 17 Atl 4f fst .49⅘ b Aug 14 Atl 4f fst .48⅖ h Aug 10 Atl 5f fst 1.02⅖ b Aug 7 Atl 3f fst .36⅘ b

Hereditament $4,250 — B. g (1965-Ky), by Terra Firma—Switch Off, by Condiment — **112** — 1968 13 1 1 3 $3,300
H. J. Ross M. McGee (H. P. Morancy) — 1967 7 1 0 0 $1,225
12Sep68-2Atl fst 6f .22⅘ .46⅗1.13 Clm 3500 7 11 116 66 33½ 2nk FMartinez7 b 109 9.20 77-21 Atoll's Star 112nk Hereditament 109no O'Caladate 1152¼ Sharp 12
5Sep68-2Atl fst 6f .22⅗ .46⅕1.12 Clm 3500 8 8 95¼ 74¼ 74¾ 54½ BPhelps b 114 30.20 77-19 Balaroja 1121¼ Barry's Beau 110¾ Timidity 1152 Mild gain 11
29Aug68-4Atl fst 6f .22⅘ .46 1.11⅗ Clm 4000 4 7 108 1012111311012 BPhelps b 114 76.50 72-16 Moon Crest 1173½ Soybean Sam 117½ Black Nade 115nk Never close 12
25May68-3MP sl 7f .23⅗ .48 1.31⅗ Clm 3750 6 1 25 310 33 413 NCartwright b 118 *1.90 47-43 Chlo Jay 1126½ Baggage Smasher 116½ DougCrowe 1125½ Dull effort 7
15May68-9CD fst 1 .46⅗1.11 1.38 Clm 3500 5 1 3nk 11 13 11 BPhelps b 113 *2.10 83-14 Hereditament 1131 Defoliate 1124 No Sugar 112nk Under drive 7
6May68-7CD fst 7f .24 .47⅗1.26⅗ Clm 4000 4 1 44½ 43½ 22 32¾ HArroyo5 b 110 *2.40 71-21 One Last Bid 118¾ Tracer Bullet 1222 Hereditament 110nk Hung 7
3May68-6CD fst 6f .22⅕ .46⅕1.12⅕ Clm 5000 1 4 3½ 64½ 52½ 77¾ DRichard b 115 5.60 77-17 Count Book 118nk Pav-Iron 1132 Bend 1152 Speed in spots 12
25Apr68-3Kee fst 7f .23 .46⅗1.25 Clm 5000 2 5 25 42½ 1½ 32 DRichard b 112 11.50 81-15 Up The Limit 114no Blinker 1082 Hereditament 1123¼ Gamely 9
6Apr68-1GP fst 6f .22 .44⅘1.11⅗ Clm 6000 11 1 9⁵¾ 917 916 714 HPilar b 112 34.60 72-12 Regal Randi 106¾ Barren Isle 1115½ Glory Ed 116¾ No speed 12
27Mar68-4GP fst 7f .22 .44⅗1.23 Clm 7000 1 9 912 1019 717 817 DRichard b 112 99.10 77-15 Fleet Again 11110 Top Tick 1161 Neat Dish 113no No speed 12
16Feb68-4Hia fst 7f .23⅕ .46 1.24⅘ Clm 10000 4 4 97¼ 1011 1214 1213 DRichard b 112 48.00 72-14 Unique Rascal 116nk Patricia G. G. 1071 Tudor Pitch 1161 No speed 12
LATEST WORKOUTS Aug 3 Del 5f fst 1.03⅖ b

Creswood Dip $4,500 — Dk. b. or br. g (1965-Md), by Ambehaving—Spartan Queen, by Pavot — **113** — 1968 7 1 1 0 $3,035
P. Cresci J. B. Rowe (P. Cresci-S. D'Ippolito) — 1967 7 1 0 1 $3,040
15Aug68-2Atl fst 6f .22⅘ .46⅗1.12⅗ Clm 5000 8 7 73 86¼ 119¾ 1110 WBlum b 117 4.20 69-19 Barren Isle 110¾ Hallucinaction 115¾ Mr. W. Harrison 117¾ Dull try 11
8Aug68-6Atl fst 6f .22⅕ .45⅘1.12 Clm 5000 6 3 31½ 3nk 2½ 22 WBlum b 117 5.60 80-19 Petes Gesture 1192 Creswood Dip 117½ O'Caladate 1222 Gamely 10
15Jly 68-1Mth fst 6f .22⅗ .45⅘1.11⅘ Clm 3500 3 3 1½ 14 15 14¼ KKorte b 113 11.50 83-13 Creswood Dip 1134¼ Implicit 1104½ El Robarb 115nk Ridden out 12
6Jun68-3Mth fst 6f .22⅘ .46⅖1.12⅕ Clm 5000 6 5 42¾ 53½ 76¾ 713 PRomero7 b 108 19.50 68-21 Hallucinaction 1144¼ Rocky Serenade 1142 Morning Coat 109½ Tired 8
1Jun68-4Mth fst 6f .21⅘ .45⅕1.11⅗ Clm 5500 7 8 810 810 66 612 PRomero5 b 108 68.80 73-15 Wild Fella 1176 Soybean Sam 1151 Drums 114nk Showed nothing 8
23Mar68-6GP fst 6f .22⅗ .46⅕1.12 Allowance 1 12 1014 1015 1123 1221 JDonahue b 115 153.00 63-16 Happy Tivo 1151 Versemaker 117¾ Paint Rock 1141½ Far back 12
4Jan68-3TrP fst 6f .22⅘ .45⅘1.11⅕ Alw 6500s 8 1 4nk 75¼ 1010 1011 HViera 115 132.00 71-18 Dieter 1152 Carlstoe 1203 Monkey Dollar 115nk Brief speed 11
1Nov67-1GS fst 6f .22⅗ .46⅗1.13⅕ Clm 5000 8 2 42½ 56½ 33½ 34 FLovato b 114 *2.40 74-23 Dot'sLibertine 1143 GreatTabiKat 1131 CreswoodDip 1142 Rallied 12
27Oct67-2GS fst 6f .22⅗ .46⅖1.13⅕ Md 5000 3 4 23 2½ 12 11 FLovato b 117 3.90 78-19 Creswood Dip 1171 Did Sport 1103½ Happy Holligan 117½ Driving 12
LATEST WORKOUTS Aug 31 Atl 5f fst 1.01 b

Tea Caddy $5,000 — B. g (1965-Va), by Craigwood—Midnight Tea, by Mister Black — **117** — 1968 8 1 1 1 $3,755
Audley Farm Stable J. B. Dodson (Audley Farm) — 1967 0 M 0 0
11Sep68-5Atl fst 6f .22 .44⅘1.11⅗ Clm 6500 6 9 54½ 59½ 611 78 RLaTorre7 111 38.80 76-17 Soybean Sam 116¾ DerbyDancer1091¼ LauraWinston1153 No threat 10
30Aug68-6Atl fst 6f .22⅗ .46⅕1.10⅘ Clm 7000 2 8 1h 41¼ 32 49 RLaTorre7 107 16.40 79-17 Mopeta 1128 Derby Dancer 109nk Forkful 114¾ Failed to stay 8
23Aug68-7Atl fst 7f .22⅖ .45⅖1.23⅘ Clm 7500 9 6 41½ 66 9121014 CGonzalez 114 8.70 70-19 Light Stepper 115½ Mopeta 1102 Title Bout 1173½ Speed, tired 11
16Aug68-1Atl fst 6f .22 .46⅕1.11⅗ Md 5000 10 3 33 3½ 11 16 CGonzalez 116 *1.60 85-18 Tea Caddy 1166 Pimpernel Gem 1132 Native Lark 111nk Easily 12
9Aug68-1Atl fst 6f .22⅕ .45⅗1.12 Md 5000 6 4 52½ 43½ 32 45¾ CGonzalez 116 7.90 76-16 Woman's Rights 1175 Phantom Spy 111h Wace 109¾ Tired 12
27May68-2GS fst 6f .22⅘ .46⅘1.12 Md 5000 2 6 54¾ 45 37 36½ CBaltazar 116 8.40 78-13 Noble Fleet 1121½ Computed 1065 Tea Caddy 1161½ Held on 12
19Apr68-4Bow fst 7f .23⅕ .46⅕1.24⅗ Md 7000 9 2 62¾ 610 717 718 CBaltazar 118 *3.70 64-14 Judy's Prince 118nk Wish Mart 1205 Jolley Clare 114nk No excuse 11
18Mar68-1Bow my 6f .23 .47⅗1.15⅕ Md 5000 5 8 76¾ 75 63¾ 41½ GCusimano5 115 4.30 69-24 d-Sailor's Rest 120h d-Johnny Cee 1201¼ Miss Mito 115nk Bothered 11
18Mar68—Placed second through disqualifications.
LATEST WORKOUTS Jly 30 Mth 5f fst 1.03 b Jly 23 Mth 6f fst 1.17⅖ bg

Cool Caper $5,000 — B. g (1965-NJ), by Star Ice—Parchesi, by Bless Me — **117** — 1968 12 1 1 4 $4,410
Mildred Mayer J. O'Brey, Sr. (E. F. Placilla) — 1967 0 M 0 0 ——
12Sep68-1Atl fst 6f .22⅘ .46⅘1.12⅗ Md 4500 11 1 2h 2½ 1½ 15 ESantana 115 *2.40 80-21 Cool Caper 1155 Tax Load 1164 You Will Score 1142½ Easily 11
5Sep68-3Atl fst 6f .23 .46⅗1.12 Clm 3500 6 4 2½ 2h 2h 2nk ESantana 112 11.10 82-19 El Casey 108nk Cool Caper 1127 Phylsjohn 1131½ Made sharp try 9
29Aug68-1Atl fst 6f .23 .47 1.12⅘ Clm 3750 1 Lost rider ESantana 113 6.30 —— Sy-Bee 1093 You Will Score 1133 Smorgsie 1123 Stumbled start 10
23Aug68-3Atl fst 6f .22⅘ .46⅗1.11⅗ Clm 3500 6 5 65½ 67 69 311 ESantana 112 28.20 75-19 Fort Worth 12210 El Casey 108½ Cool Caper 1121½ Passed tired ones 7
14Aug68-1Atl fst 6f .22⅗ .46⅕1.12⅕ Md 5000 4 6 84 912 815 817 TLee 116 4.80 64-13 Law And Chancery 1159 Nappy's Girl 1132½ Conjurer 116¾ Far back 11
7Aug68-1Atl fst 6f .22⅗ .46⅖1.12⅕ Md 5000 10 3 46 46 58 310 ESantana 116 13.80 71-15 Little Miss Muffet 1125 Buzzaway 1115 Cool Caper 116½ Fair try 12
1Aug68-1Mth fst 1⁷⁰.47⅕1.13 1.45 Md 5000 4 7 911 913 917 915 CBurr b 116 14.60 61-17 ReelPrince 114½ WarDiamond 1172 HighChieftain 116nk No speed 12
18Jly 68-1Mth fst 6f .22⅘ .47 1.13⅗ Md 5000 8 9 2½ 43½ 21 34 ESantana 115 4.20 71-21 Jamies Dream 1151 Blarie 1113 Cool Caper 115½ Good effort 12
2Jly 68-1Mth fst 6f .22⅗ .46⅘1.13⅗ Md 5000 6 6 63 68½ 59½ 38¾ RTanner5 110 8.50 66-21 Gertie Glink 1136 Blarie 1202½ Cool Caper 1103 Mild late gain 12
12Jun68-1Mth sly 6f .22 .45⅘1.12⅕ Md 7500 1 10 910 912 814 615 MBeneito 117 9.70 66-16 Tote The Mail 1172 Convivia 113½ Sea Chant 1183½ No threat 11
LATEST WORKOUTS Jly 30 Mth 4f fst .54 b Jly 24 Mth 3f fst .38 bg

Step Blue $5,000 Gr. g (1965–Va), by Roman Tread—Tens' Rocket, by Blue Rocket (C. H. McIntosh) **115** 1968 10 1 2 3 $5,120
W. P. Bell W. P. Bell 1967 4 M 1 0 $600

12Sep68–6Atl fst 6f .22⅖ .46⅕1.12⅖ Clm 5000 8 1 32½ 35 35 33 TLee b 115 37.70 77–21 Barren Isle 1121 Clever Kid 1152 Step Blue 115½ Evenly 9
3Sep68–5Tim fst 7f .24⅕ .48⅕1.30 Clm 5000 2 4 79¼ 712 814 726 CCSmith b 117 12.90 55–21 Isolated 114nk Panafly 1178 M. D. Wim 113½ Bore out turns 7
22Jun68–6Del fst 6f .22⅘ .46⅕1.12⅕ Clm 6000 5 7 78½ 79 68½ 611 GPatterson b 118 4.40 73–18 Walkin Dud 1104 Copyreader 115½ Heather Nade 118nk No factor 7
8May68–1Pim fst 6f .23⅘ .47⅗1.13⅘ Md 5000 6 1 51¾ 42¾ 3½ 11¼ TLee b 112 *2.30 81–20 Step Blue 1121¼ Fleetfoot Moran 112nk Jolley Clare 1122¼ Driving 11
19Apr68–1Bow fst 7f .22⅖ .45⅕1.24 Md 7000 8 4 36 35 23½ 21 GPatterson b 118 6.90 84–14 Masked Gal 1151 Step Blue 1181½ Winning Wave 110¾ Wide 12
3Apr68–1Bow fst 1 1/16 .49⅕1.14⅗1.47⅖ Md 5000 10 5 1h 11½ 1½ 33¼ CCSmith b 120 9.20 73–15 Michelle'sTuscany 120nk Abbeylands II 1133 StepBlue 120½ Weak'd 12
25Mar68–1Bow fst 1 1/16 .48⅘1.14⅗1.49⅕ Md 5000 6 3 75¼ 78½ 77¼ 54¼ CCSmith 120 9.80 63–16 Lady Jadoran 1151¼ Windsor Calm 1201 Frank 'N Dee 115½ No thr't 12
28Feb68–3Bow fst 1 1/16 .49⅕1.14 1.47⅘ Md 5000 3 5 64 56 54½ 45 CCSmith 120 4.80 69–16 Rush Hour 1201 Windsor Calm 120no Six N's 1204 No mishap 12
23Feb68–1Bow fst 6f .23 .47⅕1.14⅕ Md 5000 1 7 41¾ 44¼ 53¼ 3¾ CCSmith 120 3.80 75–20 That's That 110¾ Jack's Mt. 120h Step Blue 120no Late rally 12
8Feb68–1Pim fst 6f .24⅕ .48⅘1.16⅕ Md 5000 10 8 53¼ 49 46 22½ CCSmith 120 4.90 66–30 Rulla Springs 1082½ Step Blue 1201½ Ruddle 1152¼ Wide, closed well 12
11Dec67–3Lrl sly 6f .23⅘ .49⅕1.14⅗ Md 8000 8 6 74½ 88¼ 712 612 HDittfach 116 17.70 67–24 Joe's Cavan 1206 Dime To Dare 1201½ Drums 1161½ No threat 12
LATEST WORKOUTS Sep 10 Atl 4f fst .48⅘ h

Jimmy Bennett $4,500 B. c (1965–NJ), by John Smith—Running Lady, by Lotowhite (Mrs. L. Diantonio) **106[7]** 1968 11 1 0 0 $3,475
S. Butti B. L. Williams 1967 11 M 1 2 $2,045

1Aug68–5Mth fst 6f .22⅕ .46⅕1.12⅕ Clm 5000 8 7 910 910 912 79¾ DDSmith 115 43.90 71–17 Moon Crest 115h Base Royal 115no Barren Isle 115nk No factor
25Jly 68–4Mth sl 6f .22⅖ .46⅗1.14⅘ Clm 5000 3 8 77 78½ 610 514 DDSmith 115 16.20 69–23 Laba Daba 11512 Base Royal 1151¼ Do' Behave 115nk Not a contend'r
13Jly 68–2Aqu fst 7f .22 .44 1.22⅘ Clm 6500 12 7 1012121813201322 HGustines b 112 47.80f 72– 9 Graystet 1146 Coatai 1173 Phantom Island 110½ No speed 1
9Jly 68–7Mth fst 6f .22⅕ .45⅗1.11⅘ Clm 7500 9 10 1112111411201117 RTanner5 b 109 43.90 66–21 Carr Bairn 1192 Pop N Go 116½ Shy Fox 1161½ Showed nothing 12
22Jun68–5Mth fst 6f .21⅘ .44⅘1.10⅘ Clm 8000 11 3 12111111 99¾ 711 HPilar b 110 29.70 77–17 Bunty Escar 1096 •Rubia 1112 •Crolicy 1172 Was never close 12
17Jun68–9Mth fm*1 1/16 Ⓣ 1.16⅖1.50⅘ Clm 11000 5 6 97¼107¾11121015 SGuerra b 111 43.10 —— GoldenMustang1142½Marcia'sMistake1122¼N'ghtyJoke1172 No sp'd 11
28May68–6GS sly 1 1/16 .48⅖1.14 1.47 Clm 10500 1 7 88¾1021 1020 923 VTejada b 112 41.50 47–24 Mortek 114¾ Bells And Whistles 1186 Not Too Modest 1182 Far back 10
22May68–4GS fst 6f .22⅗ .46 1.11⅘ Clm 10000 8 5 87¾ 814 811 67 DHidalgo b 116 10.80 78–13 Bells And Whistles 1141 Trueno 1181 Regal Randi 1112½ No speed 8
30Apr68–8Aqu fst 1 .46 1.10⅘1.37 Clm 10000 6 5 63½ 43½ 44½ 45¼ MYcaza b 116 8.80 78–19 Marcia's Mistake 112¾ Buford's Duke 1142 On With It 1112½ No rally 9
12Apr68–1Aqu fst 7f .22⅗ .45⅗1.26 Md 7500 9 6 54 54 3nk 13 MYcaza b 115 *2.60 76–21 Jimmy Bennett 1153 Elbee 1131½ Judson S. 1131 Going away 14
4Apr68–1Aqu fst 6f .22 .45⅘1.12⅖ Md 7500 6 7 77¼ 86½ 44 46¾ MYcaza b 122 11.20 79–18 Taillevent 1224 Chivalrous 122¾ Gay Port 1222 Mild bid 14
LATEST WORKOUTS Jly 31 Mth 3f fst .36⅖ b Jly 23 Mth 3f fst .36⅘ b

Coral Atoll $5,000 Ch. c (1965–Ky), by Atoll—Island Lass, by Blenheim II (S. D. Petter, Jr.) **119** 1968 11 3 0 0 $9.85
F. P. Dyer L. Charron 1967 6 2 1 1 $7,07

17Aug68–3Atl fst 6f .22 .45⅖1.10⅘ Clm 9500 7 1 63¼ 67½ 711 711 WBlum b 116 5.50 77–15 Crolicy 1172 Flying Blind 1152½ I. J.'s Mito 1142 Fell back
6Aug68–6Atl fst 6f .23 .46⅗1.12⅗ Cl c-7500 7 1 85¼ 54 65¼ 1h RBroussard b 117 *1.10 79–20 Coral Atoll 117h Aweigh My Lads 116nk Doug Oswald 116nk In time
27Jly 68–5Mth fst 6f .21⅗ .44⅖1.10⅘ Clm 10000 1 5 69½ 513 46½ 1h RBroussard b 117 3.00 88–15 Coral Atoll 117h Four Straight 114¾ Twisty Clem 1133 Driving
25Jun68–6Mth fst 6f .22 .45⅗1.11⅗ Clm 7500 1 5 67 46 31 11¾ RBroussard b 117 5.10 84–17 Coral Atoll 1171¾ Calwood 116¾ By The Numbers 1195 Driving clear
3Jun68–7Mth gd 1 Ⓣ .48⅘1.41⅖ Clm 11000 3 7 79¾1116 1121 1130 RBroussard b 117 3.70 45–25 Not Too Modest 117nk Bungalow 1107 Creative 1144½ Dull try 1
21May68–6GS fst 6f .22⅕ .45⅖1.10⅗ Clm 14000 7 3 75 56½ 67 56 RBroussard b 116 5.70 85–14 Fleet Again 1162 Get Em John 1142½ I. J's Mito 111½ Even race
3May68–7GS fst 6f .23 .46⅖1.11⅘ Clm 15000 2 5 42 45 58½ 54¾ RBroussard 116 3.10 80–17 Some Wind 111½ Star Nell 1111 I. J's Mito 1112¼ Brief factor
23Apr68–5GS fst 6f .22⅖ .45⅘1.11⅖ Clm 16000 2 5 21 32½ 44½ 94½ WBlum 116 *2.00 82–12 Blue Field 1143¼ Star Nell 111no Undespairing 120no In close
LATEST WORKOUTS Aug 31 Atl 4f fst .50 b Aug 25 Atl 4f fst .49⅖ b Aug. 5 Atl 3f fst .36⅗ b Jly 26 Mth 3f sl .38 b

Cypark $4,500 Dk. b or br. g (1965–Md), by Beechpark—Cycount, by Cyclotron (F. M. Clagett) **110[5]** 1968 8 3 1 0 $7,120
Mrs. T. M. Cochran A. J. Cochran 1967 0 M 0 0 ——

5Sep68–2Atl fst 6f .22⅗ .46⅕1.12 Cl c-3500 4 2 1½ 1h 3½ 910 CBaltazar 117 *3.30 72–19 Balaroja 1121¼ Barry's Beau 110¾ Timidity 1152 Tired abruptly 1
22Aug68–2Atl fst 6f .22⅗ .45⅗1.11⅖ Clm 3500 9 1 11 1½ 11½ 1nk CBaltazar 115 3.70 85–15 Cypark 115nk Barry's Beau 1102½ Dot's Libertine 113½ Lasted 1
10Aug68–1Del fst 6f .22⅖ .46⅗1.13⅖ Clm 3000 1 3 13 1½ 12½ 21¼ WJPassmore 119 2.80 77–20 Scarlet Dancer 1101¼ Cypark 119h With It 110h Failed to last 1
31Jly 68–3Del fst 6f .22⅘ .46⅘1.12⅘ Clm 3750 8 2 2h 2h 35 713 BPhelps 120 3.20 68–22 O'Caladate 1204 Isolated 113½ Truwil 112h Forced pace, tired 8
13Jly 68–3Del fst 6f .22⅖ .46⅗1.13 Clm 3750 1 1 12 11½ 13 11 WJPassmore 117 6.70 80–15 Cypark 1171 Gremmie 1171 Pet For Me 1121½ Held safe margin 1
5Jly 68–2Del fst 6f .22⅗ .46⅘1.13 Clm 4250 3 1 11½ 11½ 12 1nk WJPassmore 113 45.90 80–17 Cypark 113nk Pet For Me 1113½ Mopeta 1191 Long hard drive 1
27Jun68–2Del my 6f .23⅖ .48 1.15⅕ Cl c-3000 9 5 73¾ 56 66 75¾ WJPassmore 119 6.60 63–24 O'Caladate 119¾ Sheet Music 119no Little Sunshine 1142 No factor 1
17Jun68–2Del fst 6f .23⅕ .47⅕1.14 Clm 3750 5 6 11 2h 22 83¾ GBrogan5 108 19.80 71–16 Tourlanx'sIdol 113noShoalAhead1221¼Mother'sBeau122nk Tired 12
LATEST WORKOUTS Jly 27 Del 3f fst .37⅗ b

Easy Spending $5,000 B. g (1965–Va), by Craigwood—Mighty Tag, by Mighty Story (Audley Farm) **105[10]** 1968 16 4 0 3 $11,660
A. Rosoff G. Auerbach 1967 9 2 1 0 $3,875

10Sep68–9Atl fst 1⅛ .48 1.12⅘1.52 Clm 5000 6 1 11 31 89 814 WBlum 113 *3.00 64–15 d-Count Curious 113no Judge Colie 1162 Decamar 115nk Used up 8
27Aug68–9Atl fm*1⅛ Ⓣ 1.13⅗1.53⅖ Clm 5000 8 2 11 1½ 1h 57¾ JVelasquez 113 3.60 82–10 Judge Colie 1123 Past Post 114no Count Curious 113¾ Tired 8
19Aug68–3Atl fst 1⅛ — — 1.53⅗ Cl c-3500 3 2 2½ 33 57½ 69½ MMiceli 115 *2.50 60–15 Instomatic 104½ Bob's Guide 1172 Janssen 1123 Speed, tired 8
9Jly 68–6Mth fst 6f .21⅗ .45 1.12⅗ Clm 6000 5 8 814 816 916 913 BPearl 113 21.10 66–21 Clever Kid 1191½ Hallucinaction 1173 Swoon Free 114no No speed 9
28Jun68–9Mth sly 170 .47⅗1.13⅘1.46⅖ Cl c-4500 3 2 22 23 21½ 3¾ CBaltazar 120 *2.80 68–25 Morning Coat 114½ Masked Gal 107nk Easy Spending 1202 No excuse 8
19Jun68–3Mth fst 170 .48⅕1.13⅘1.45⅘ Clm 3500 4 2 11 1½ 12 17 CBaltazar 115 *1.40 72–18 Easy Spending 1157 Open Throttle 115½ Gatlin 11212 Easily 8
5Jun68–3Mth fm 1⅛ Ⓣ 1.13⅖1.52⅗ Clm 6500 3 1 1½ 37 78¼ 719 CBaltazar 111 3.60 —— Golden Mustang 1174½ Some Bully 1132½ MistyWave1075 Used up 9
31May68–9Mth fst 170 .47⅖1.12⅖1.43⅗ Clm 5000 5 2 21 32½ 55½ 37 CBaltazar 120 8.80 76–14 Some Bully 1152½ Sailor's Rest 1184½ Easy Spending 1201 Weakened 10
15May68–9Pim fm 1 1/16 Ⓣ 1.13⅕1.47⅕ Clm 5000 12 1 12½ 11 11 12¾ JGiovanni 115 9.20 79–15 Easy Spending 1152¾ Judge Glenn 1158 Paper Spin 115nk Driving 12
6May68–9Pim fst 1 1/16 .48⅕1.14⅘1.49 Clm 5000 3 2 1½ 2½ 811 811 JGiovanni 115 5.10 54–19 Don't Spank Me 110h Phantom Jet 1071¼ Gemro 1122 Tired abruptly 12
25Apr68–9Pim gd 1 1/16 .48⅕1.14⅕1.50⅗ Clm 5000 1 1 11½ 22 24 32 JGiovanni 117 3.10 55–27 Run 'N' Catch 1121 Lady Rhonda 1081 Easy Spending 1172 Gamely 9
LATEST WORKOUTS Sep 18 Atl 3f fst .38⅗ b Sep 14 Atl 4f fst .49⅘ b Sep 12 ShD 4f fst .50⅗ bg Sep 9 Atl 3f fst .37 b

Horses Shown Below Are on the "Also Eligible" List and Are Not Listed in Order of Post Positions.

O'Caladate * $5,000 Dk. b. or br. g (1965–Fla), by O'Calaway—Pretty Date, by Prince Simon **117** 1968 8 3 0 2 $7,240
D. B. Schmeck W. A. Manzi (Ocala Stud Farm, Inc.) 1967 11 2 2 2 $8,420

12Sep68–2Atl fst 6f .22⅘ .46⅗1.13 Cl c-3500 11 1 41¼ 2½ 2½ 3nk EWalsh b 115 5.10 77–21 Atoll's Star 112nk Hereditament 109no O'Caladate 1152½ No rally 12
30Aug68–3Atl fst 6f .22⅘ .46 1.11⅘ Clm 3500 9 3 3nk 3½ 33½ 45¾ EWalsh b 117 *2.80 80–17 Implicit 1122 Balaroja 1123 Rejjy 118¾ Wide throughout 12
22Aug68–4Atl fst 6f .22⅕ .45⅖1.11⅖ Clm 5000 8 1 2h 32 44½ 58¾ EWalsh b 119 4.00 76–15 Geormel 1182 Soybean Sam 115¾ Clever Kid 1192 Tired 8
8Aug68–6Atl fst 6f .22⅕ .45⅘1.12 Clm 5000 5 4 21 2h 3½ 32½ GPatterson b 122 *2.70 79–19 Petes Gesture 1192 Creswood Dip 117½ O'Caladate 1222 Tired 10
31Jly 68–3Del fst 6f .22⅘ .46⅘1.12⅘ Clm 3750 1 5 1h 1h 15 14 EWalsh b 120 5.20 81–22 O'Caladate 1204 Isolated 113½ Truwil 112h Drew out easily 8
19Jly 68–2Del fst 6f .22⅗ .46⅕1.13⅕ Clm 3000 8 2 1h 1h 14 1nk EWalsh b 119 4.10 79–17 O'Caladate 119nk Count Walnut 1143 Jack's Mt. 115no Tiring, lasted 11
5Jly 68–2Del fst 6f .22⅗ .46⅘1.13 Clm 4250 11 7 66 56½ 811 99½ EWalsh b 116 *3.20 70–17 Cypark 113nk Pet For Me 1113½ Mopeta 1191 Wide early, tired 11
27Jun68–2Del my 6f .23⅖ .48 1.15⅕ Clm 3000 10 4 21 1h 12 1¾ EWalsh b 119 *1.30 69–24 O'Caladate 119¾ Sheet Music 119no Little Sunshine 1142 Driving 12
23Aug67–6Atl sly 6f .22 .46 1.11⅘ Allowance 3 3 22 21½ 44 67 PKallai b 120 11.00 76–20 Ocean Bar 116nk Natula Pass 1164 Colonel Moore 1142½ Weakened 9
12Aug67–5Atl fst 5½f .22⅗ .46⅕1.05 Clm 16000 8 1 2h 11 2h 22 PKallai b 119 *1.00 92–14 Gambling Bob 1152 O'Caladate 1192 Clowntown 1151 No excuse 9
LATEST WORKOUTS Sep 7 Atl 5f sly 1.02 b Aug 17 Atl 4f fst .47 h

---

Sufico: Although this gelding's only victory was against cheap maidens at a mile and a furlong, it set a respectable early pace and should be granted a chance for part of today's purse. A peculiarity of this field is that none of the legitimate contenders has the credentials of a $5,000 sprinter. Many, like Sufico, have beaten only maidens. No Bet.

Hereditament: That stout stretch run last week qualifies this one for consideration, but the horse really looks as if it belongs in $3,500 company at seven furlongs. No Bet.

Tea Caddy: Since breaking its maiden in August, the Audley Farm entrant has proved itself unequal to $6,500 competition. It apparently is capable of running away from cheapies if the early pace is leisurely—as it did on August 16. As we proceed we'll see whether this field is cheap enough and slow enough to make Tea Caddy a winner. Contender.

Cool Caper: Two weeks ago this one ran a stout race against $3,500 winners. Seven days later it trounced cheap maidens in a slow race: At this stage of their careers, Tea Caddy looks like more horse. But let's reserve decision on Cool Caper until we see what else is running. Contender.

Step Blue: That was not a bad race on September 12, especially by contrast with this one's awful performance at Timonium a few days earlier. If the Bell gelding has any real speed, it has been well concealed during recent months. No Bet.

Cypark: Here we have the speed of the field. It's cheap speed, as the two most recent races show, but speed it is, nevertheless. Notice that the gelding covered the distance in 1.11⅗ after getting the half in .45⅗ on August 22, but collapsed after a much slower half on September 5. The supposition is that some other horse collared Cypark in the latter race, discouraging the front-runner entirely. Cypark can be discarded if some other entrant in today's race is capable of hooking it. But if it is the only horse that can go the half mile in .45⅗, it must be given a good chance to last. Contender.

O'Caladate: Not quite fast enough to catch Cypark but likely to be a threat if Cypark's speed does not hold up. Contender.

Cypark looks to have the early pace all its own way. Today's rider, the live George Cusimano, can be counted on to hold the animal together. Cypark may not win, but it is difficult to name any member of this field with a bettable chance of beating it. Unless some other horse comes up with more early speed than any of them have recently shown, the Cochran entrant looks like a nice bet, especially at the odds.

The Running of the Race

THE CROWD liked the recently idle Coral Atoll well enough to send him as a 1.70–1 favorite. The reason, of course, was the colt's former class. Second choice, and for better reason, was Tea Caddy. Cypark went at a generous 12.20–1, beat off the challenge of Tea Caddy, and won going away. This race is an excellent example of the kind of situation in which cheap speed carries the day. Had any horse in the race a recent record of high early speed, Cypark would not have been worth a nickel.

FIFTH RACE **6 FURLONGS. (Bright Holly, September 2, 1961, 1.08$\frac{4}{5}$, 3, 112.)**

Atl - 35940 Claiming. Puse $3,700. 3-year-olds. Weight 122 lbs. Non-winners of three races since July 24 allowed 3 lbs., two races 5 lbs., a race 7 lbs. Claiming price $5,000. 1 lb. allowed for $250 to $4,000.

September 19, 1968

Value to winner $2,220, second $740, third $480, fourth $260. Mutuel pool $87,487.

Index	Horse	Eqt	A	Wt	PP	St	¼	½	Str	Fin	Jockey	Cl'g Pr	Owner	Odds $1
35829Atl^{9}	—Cypark		3	110	9	1	$2^{1\frac{1}{2}}$	1^{h}	1^{h}	$1^{\frac{3}{4}}$	G Cusimano^{5}	4500	Mrs T M Cochran	12.20
35891Atl^{1}	—Sufico		3	117	1	6	$5^{\frac{1}{2}}$	$5^{1\frac{1}{2}}$	3^{2}	2^{h}	R Hernandez	5000	M R Fain	13.60
35877Atl^{7}	—Tea Caddy		3	117	4	3	1^{h}	2^{4}	2^{5}	3^{3}	C Baltazar	5000	Audley Farm Stable	4.40
35883Atl^{2}	—Hereditament	b	3	112	2	9	$8^{\frac{1}{2}}$	$8^{\frac{1}{2}}$	6^{3}	4no	D Hidalgo	4250	H J Ross	11.30
35887Atl^{3}	—S[illegible] Blue	b	3	115	6	8	$6^{\frac{1}{2}}$	4^{2}	5^{h}	$5^{1\frac{1}{2}}$	G Patterson	5000	W P Bell	8.00
35602Atl^{7}	—Coral Atoll	b	3	119	8	11	$10^{1\frac{1}{2}}$	$7^{\frac{1}{2}}$	8^{2}	6^{2}	E Maple	5000	F P Dyer	1.70
35882Atl^{1}	—Cool Caper		3	117	5	4	4^{h}	6^{h}	$7^{\frac{1}{2}}$	7^{2}	E Santana	5000	Mildred Mayer	10.10
35883Atl^{3}	—O'Caladate	b	3	117	11	2	$3^{\frac{1}{2}}$	$3^{1\frac{1}{2}}$	4^{h}	$8^{\frac{1}{2}}$	W Blum	5000	D B Schmeck	6.90
35583Atl^{11}	-Creswood Dip	b	3	113	3	7	7^{2}	9^{1}	$9^{\frac{1}{2}}$	9^{nk}	F Lovato	4500	P Cresci	17.80
35505Mth^{7}	-Jimmy Bennett		3	106	7	10	11	11	11	$10^{\frac{1}{2}}$	J Castillo^{7}	4500	S Butti	130.20
35872Atl^{8}	—Easy Spending		3	105	10	5	9^{1}	10^{3}	10^{1}	11	J Colasacco^{10}	5000	A Rosoff	59.40

Time .22$\frac{3}{5}$, .45$\frac{4}{5}$, 1.11$\frac{3}{5}$. Track fast.

$2 Mutuel Prices:			
10–CYPARK	26.40	13.80	7.40
1–SUFICO		12.80	7.20
4–TEA CADDY			4.60

Dk. b. or br. g, by Beechpark—Cycount, by Cyclotron. Trainer A. J. Cochran. Bred by F. M. Clagett (Md.).

IN GATE AT 3.24. OFF AT 3.24 EASTERN DAYLIGHT TIME. Start good. Won driving.

CYPARK vied with TEA CADDY from the start while outside that one and was going away at the end. SUFICO rallied to pressure in the drive and was up on the outside for the place. TEA CADDY alternated in setting and pressing the pace to deep stretch while along the inside and weakened slightly. HEREDITAMENT rallied belatedly along the inner rail. STEP BLUE failed to menace. CORAL ATOLL was never a factor. COOL CAPER was through early.

Scratched—35342Mth^{8} Noted Scholar, 35833Atl^{2} Implicit, 35897Atl^{10} Loveagate, 35741Rkm^{1} Rallier, 35887Atl^{4} Heliofleet.

Tea Caddy was claimed by J. C. Irvin, trainer J. P. Dumesnil Jr.

THE SIXTH RACE

THIS IS an allowance affair at six furlongs, for three- and four-year-olds that have not won more than one allowance race in which first prize was as high as $2,400. Forgive me if I seem to upstage you, but I see in one glance at the past-performance records that this race is going to fool practically everybody—and is going to play special havoc with persons who follow the superficial rules of conventional handicapping.

6th Atlantic City

6 FURLONGS — ATLANTIC CITY (Start / Finish)

6 FURLONGS. (Bright Holly, September 2, 1961, 1.08⅗, 3, 112.) Allowances. Purse $4,800. 3- and 4-year-olds which have not won $2,400 twice other than maiden or claiming. Weights 3-year-olds 118 lbs., 4-year-olds 122 lbs. Non-winners of $6,600 allowed 2 lbs., $3,600 since July 26, 4 lbs., a race since August 3, 6 lbs., $2,400 at any time 9 lbs. (Maiden and claiming races not considered.)

Tower Of Strength

B. g (1965–Md), by Native Dancer—Ivory Tower, by Hill Prince — A. G. Vanderbilt — W. C. Freeman — (A. G. Vanderbilt) — **114**

1968	4	1	2	1	$5,305
1967	7	1	1	2	$5,285

12Sep68-7Atl	fst 7f .22⅘ .45⅘1.24	Allowance	1	3	21 2h 11½ 2½	GPatterson	b 115	*1.10	82–21	Zymurgy 113½ Tower Of Strength 1156 A Latin Spin 1092	Gamely	6
27Aug68-7Atl	fst 6f .22⅖ .45⅗1.10⅘	Allowance	3	5	43½ 34 32 12	GPattetrson	b 114	2.50	88–10	TowerOfStrength 1142 AmberEagle 1141¼ PebbleDrive 1182½	Driv'g	11
20Aug68-7Atl	fst 6f .22⅖ .45 1.10	Allowance	8	6	61¾ 32 32 21½	GPatterson	b 114	*2.60	90–16	SayTheWord 1181½ TowerOf Strength 1141 FourStraight 1145	Game	11
13Aug68-5Atl	fst 6f .22⅕ .45 1.10⅘	Allowance	2	8	33½ 45 34 35	GPatterson	b 114	3.20	83–15	MartialMelody117no RoyalPath II 1165 TowerOfStrength1147	Poor st.	8
20Dec67-7Lrl	fst 7f .23 .47⅖1.26⅕	Allowance	7	6	43½ 21½ 22 21½	CBaltazar	b 117	3.50	86–16	JoyousJohn1171½TowerOfStr'gth1171½Danny'sRunaway114nk	G'mely	10
6Dec67-6Lrl	fst 7f .23 .47 1.26⅗	Allowance	8	9	53¾ 47 34 34	JGiovanni	b 117	*2.10	82–15	Shay Jay 1222½ Final Encore 1151½ Tower Of Strength 1173	Hung	9
23Nov67-8Lrl	fst 7f .22⅘ .46⅖1.24⅘	MdFut'rity	3	5	72¾ 68¾ 58½ 56	JGiovanni	b 112	26.40	89–19	Dancer's Image 124no Martins Jig 1175 Sky Sailor 1241	No mishap	13
18Nov67-6Lrl	fst 6f .22⅗ .46⅗1.12⅕	Allowance	4	5	56¼ 35 57½ 38	GPatterson	b 117	23.20	83–15	Promise 1228 SecondAdventure 122h TowerOfStrength 117¾	No mis.	9
30Oct67-7Lrl	fst 6f .23 .47⅕1.12⅖	Allowance	10	6	42 45 44½ 59	CBaltazar	119	8.90	81–20	Captain Courageous 1192½ Bailar 1196 Wood-Pro 102½	Tired	11
19Oct67-4Aqu	gd 6f .22⅖ .46⅖1.13⅕	Md Sp Wt	8	4	31½ 1½ 12½ 1no	JRuane	122	30.30	77–22	Tower Of Strength 122no Gaynamene 122h Outspan 1223½	All out	9
11Oct67-5Aqu	my 6f .22⅘ .46⅗1.11⅘	Md Sp Wt	5	13	106¼1217 919 918	JRuane	122	34.90	66–19	Pamir 1222½ Trumpet Tudor 1222 Outspan 1223	Showed nothing	13

LATEST WORKOUTS Sep 8 Atl 5f fst 1.02⅗ b — Sep 4 Atl 4f fst .54 b — Aug 19 Atl 3f fst .40 b — Aug 8 Atl 6f fst 1.14⅕ h

*Martial Melody

B. c (1965), by Red God—Aria II, by Tudor Minstrel — Golden Vale Farm — A. Scruton — (P. Burns) (Ire.) — **114**

1968	7	2	0	2	$6,825
1967	4	M	0	0	$430

22Aug68-7Atl	fst 6f .22⅗ .45⅕1.09⅘	Allowance	4	2	2h 31½ 34½ 33¼	RBroussard	b 117	4.40	90–15	Carr Bairn 1201¼ Biddeford 1122 Martial Melody 1171¼	Weakened	8
13Aug68-5Atl	fst 6f .22⅕ .45 1.10⅘	Allowance	4	2	21½ 21 1h 1no	RBroussard	b 117	*1.60	88–15	MartialMelody117noRoyalPathII1165TowerOfStrength1147	Driving	8
30Jly 68-6Mth	fst 6f .22 .44⅗1.10⅕	Allowance	2	3	21½ 25 34 69¼	PKallai	b 115	5.90	81–16	Happy Ridan 1173½ I Did 115no I Am Slipping 114½	Speed, tired	9
23Jly 68-7Mth	fst 6f .22⅕ .45⅕1.10⅕	Allowance	1	5	1½ 2½ 2h 32	PKallai	b 115	14.30	89–16	Coati II. 1162 Say The Word 120h Martial Melody 1153	Good try	10
3Jly 68-5Mth	gd 6f .22⅖ .46⅕1.12	Md Sp Wt	6	1	1½ 1½ 1½ 11½	RBroussard	b 117	3.90	82–17	MartialMelody 1171½ CountryDay 1221 Eagle'sSwoop 1171	Driving	8
18Jun68-7Mth	fst 6f .21⅘ .44⅘1.11⅗	Allowance	6	3	32 24 33 57¼	WGavidia	b 113	6.30	77–23	A Latin Spin 1163 Bold Star 114no Coati II 1161¾	Well up, tired	7
11Jun68-5Mth	fm*5f Ⓣ .47 .59⅗	Clm 14000	12	4	41 32 33½ 53	WGavidia	b 115	45.30	94– 3	Master Steve 112h Creativity 111nk Flying Blind 118¾	Wide	12
17Jly 67-6Mth	gd 5½f.22⅕ .46⅖1.06⅕	Md Sp Wt	11	3	26 25 23 53¼	BThornburg	b 118	29.70	83–18	Three Carrswold 118½ Swoon Free 118h d-Bright Ray 1182	Bumped	11

17Jly67—Placed fourth through disqualification.

3Jly 67-4Mth	sl 5½f.23 .47⅖1.07⅖	Md Sp Wt	5	4	42 75¾ 911109¾	CBaltazar	b 118	35.90	70–23	Winged T. 1181¼ I Did 118nk Olympia Blood 1181¼	Couldn't keep up	12

LATEST WORKOUTS Sep 17 Atl 3f fst .37 b — Sep 14 Atl 4f fst .49⅖ b — Sep 9 Atl 5f fst 1.06 b — Sep 4 Atl 3f fst .38⅕ b

Say The Word *

Dk. b. or br. g (1964–Ky), by Federal Hill—Saygosh, by Sayasolpax — Indian Mills Stock Farm — B. W. Perkins — (Elcee-H Breeding Farms, Inc.) — **118**

1968	13	3	4	0	$14,220
1967	1	M	0	0	$225

14Sep68-7LD	fst 5f .22⅖ .46 .58	Handicap	7	1	51¾ 54 67 710	MAristone	119	2.70	88– 8	Naughty Jester 1181 GoldenArrow1133 WinningShotJr.1192	Tired	7
20Aug68-7Atl	fst 6f .22⅖ .45 1.10	Allowance	2	2	1½ 11½ 12 11½	MAristone	118	*2.60	92–16	SayTheWord 1181½ TowerOfStrength 1141 FourStraight 1145	Driv.	11
15Aug68-8Atl	fm*5½f Ⓣ .46⅕1.04⅖	Allowance	3	3	4nk 41½ 54½ 76	WBlum	112	4.60	85– 9	Night Cloud 1222 Manipulation 113no Parkesburg 1221	In close	8
9Aug68-8Atl	fst 6f .22 .44⅖1.10	KgNept'nH	6	1	22 26 34 44¾	MAristone	112	17.50	87–16	Chicot 1153½ Kaskaskia 1141 Bowler King 115nk	Lost whip	7

9Aug68—The King Neptune Handicap run in two divisions, 6th and 8th races.

2Aug68-8Mth	sl 1 .47⅕1.12⅖1.39⅗	Allowance	6	1	16 18 14 21½	MAristone	118	3.10	73–21	Carr Bairn 1201½ Say The Word 1183 Gamarette 1135	Gamely	8
23Jly 68-7Mth	fst 6f .22⅕ .45⅕1.10⅕	Allowance	8	1	2½ 1½ 1h 22	MAristone	120	8.70	89–16	Coati II. 1162 Say The Word 120h Martial Melody 1153	Gamely	10
12Jly 68-7Mth	fst 170.46⅕1.11⅖1.42⅘	Allowance	1	1	14 12 33½ 716	MAristone	118	4.00	71–21	Mortek 113¾ I Did 1127 Manipulation 1222½	Used up	8
2Jly 68-5Mth	fst 6f .22⅖ .46⅕1.12⅕	Allowance	1	1	11 11½ 1h 21	MAristone	120	3.40	80–21	Squall Line 1161 Say The Word 120h Winds At War 1124	Gamely	8
28Jun68-8Mth	sly 170.46⅗1.12⅖1.43⅕	Allowance	10	1	13 13 1½ 25	MAristone	118	11.40	80–25	Sumter 1095 Say The Word 1182 Meadows Hope 1122½	Gamely	10
18Jun68-7Mth	fst 6f .21⅘ .44⅘1.11⅗	Allowance	5	1	1½ 14 12 44¾	MAristone	120	3.80	79–23	A Latin Spin 1163 Bold Star 114no Coati II 1161¾	Hard used	7

LATEST WORKOUTS Sep 10 Atl 4f fst .48 b — Sep 2 Atl 5f fst 1.01 b — Jly 29 Mth t.c. 3f fm .37⅖ b — Jly 20 Mth 3f gd .38 b

Amber Eagle

B. g (1965–Ky), by Bald Eagle—Amber Honey, by Ambiorix — Miss M. Zarnes — J. R. Wyatt — (H. F. Gggenheim) — **114**

1968	9	2	2	0	$7,360
1967	2	M	0	0	——

12Sep68-7Atl	fst 7f .22⅘ .45⅘1.24	Allowance	6	1	11 1h 21½ 58½	EMaple	115	2.40	74–21	Zymurgy 113½ Tower Of Strength 1156 A Latin Spin 1092	Used up	6
3Sep68-6Atl	fst 6f .22⅕ .45⅖1.10⅘	Allowance	6	2	21½ 22 2h 11½	EMaple	114	6.40	88–17	Amber Eagle 1141½ Rangatira 1142 Laba Daba 1091	Driving clear	8
27Aug68-7Atl	fst 6f .22⅖ .45⅗1.10⅘	Allowance	8	1	1½ 1h 11 22	EMaple	114	36.30	86–10	TowerOfStrength 1142 AmberEagle 1141½ PebbleDrive 1182½	Sharp	11
20Aug68-7Atl	fst 6f .22⅖ .45 1.10	Allowance	7	1	3½ 43½ 67 59½	EMaple	114	22.90	82–16	SayTheWord 1181½ TowerOf Strength 1141 FourStraight 1145	Tired	11
6Aug68-7Del	fst 6f .21⅘ .45⅘1.11⅗	Allowance	4	1	13½ 14 13½ 22½	CRogers	115	3.50	84–20	Pio Pico 1152½ Amber Eagle 115½ Ace Lover 1152½	Faltered in drive	7
25Jly 68-8Del	fst 6f .22⅖ .46 1.11⅖	Allowance	4	8	3½ 31 99¼ 816	CRogers	111	69.50	72–22	Sikkim 1221¼ Light The Fuse 1172 Sub Call 1223	Gave way abruptly	9
28Jun68-7Del	sf 1 Ⓣ 1.38⅘	Allowance	3	1	11 21 712 715	CRogers	113	21.40	66–17	Great White Way 122nk Keep Shipping 119no Peach II 122½	Stop'd	7
14Jun68-4Del	fst 6f .22⅕ .46 1.13	Md Sp Wt	12	1	1½ 14 13 11	CRogers	113	62.00	80–23	Amber Eagle 1131 Winter Man 1103½ Kalakaua 1131¼	Driving	12
29Apr68-4Pim	fst 6f .23 .46⅘1.14	Md Sp Wt	4	3	35½ 59 89¼ 87½	CCooke	112	29.50	72–17	Withering Fire 111no Sam Bolero 114¾ King's Shilling 112h	Tired	12
11Oct67-1Aqu	my 6f .22⅗ .46⅖1.12	Md Sp Wt	7	5	53½ 55½13281318	RTurcotte	122	11.00	65–19	Second Adventure 122¾ Man Of Action 1225 RoyalJest 122½	Tired	14
6Sep67-5Aqu	fst 6f .22⅘ .47 1.12⅗	Md Sp Wt	14	4	1½ 1h 42½1310	ACorderoJr	122	17.90	70–18	Grimaldi 122½ Stage Door Johnny 122¾ Forever 122h	Stopped	14

LATEST WORKOUTS Aug 4 Del 4f fst .49 b

Terry's Song ✻

Dk. b. or br. c (1965–Ky), by Terrang—Myrtle's Song, by Spy Song
M. Gache J. O'Brey, Sr. (R.-P. Tackett)
107 5

1968	24	2	4	2	$13,875
1967	11	1	2	1	$5,075

4Sep68-9Atl	hd	*1 1/16 (T)	1.13⅗ 1.46⅕	Clm	15000	2	3	3 4	7 7	7 13	7 19	ESantana	115	12.20	74– 5	Voluntario III 117 2 Cleareye 116 6 Doctor Will 112 4	Tired	8
24Aug68-4Atl	fst	1 1/16	.47⅖ 1.12 1.44⅗	Clm	12500	6	2	2 4	2 1½	1 2	1 8	JVelasquez	115	2.80	84–13	Terry's Song 115 8 Top Trojan 112 1½ Ben Dorada 107 nk	Mild drive	7
19Aug68-7Atl	fm	1 1/16 (T)	1.11⅕ 1.44	Clm	11000	7	4	4 3½	5 5½	5 7½	4 4	TLee	110	6.10	82–14	Francis Son 114 nk Boffo 112 3 Crown Chief 118¾	No mishap	9
12Aug68-7Atl	fm	*1⅛ (T)	1.13⅕ 1.51⅗	Clm	12500	7	3	1 h	2 3	2 5	3 10	ESantana	116	10.30	89– 2	Not Too Modest 118 8 Ponciana 111 2 Terry's Song 116 1	Gave way	8
2Aug68-6Mth	sl	1 1/16	.48 1.12⅗ 1.44⅘	Clm	14000	3	4	4 6½	4 7½	5 12	4 17	RBroussard	117	5.00	64–21	Naughty Joke 114 3 Not Too Modest 119 3½ Top Trojan 112 10	No mish'p	8
20Jly 68-7Mth	fst	1 1/16	.47⅖ 1.12⅘ 1.46⅗	Allowance		4	7	6 8	4 3½	3 2	6 3¾	ESantana	113	20.30	68–17	Fenian Lad 115 no Ful O'Dance 115 nk Mineola Lad 115½	Bid, hung	7
6Jly 68-5Mth	fm	1 1/16 (T)	1.12⅘ 1.44⅘	Clm	13500	4	4	2 5	2 1½	1 1	2 4	DKassen	114	15.90	——	Creative 115 4 Terry's Song 114 1½ The Magic Dragon 113 1½	Gamely	8
24Jun68-7Mth	fm	1 1/16 (T)	1.12⅕ 1.44⅖	Clm	11000	4	6	4 3	3 1	4 6	2 6	RTanner5	110	10.30	——	Not Too Modest 119 6 Terry's Song 110 2 Till And Toil 110 3	Wide	8
17Jun68-9Mth	fm	*1 1/16 (T)	1.16⅖ 1.50⅘	Clm	13000	4	4	3 2	11 8¾	10 12	9 14	DHidalgo	115	9.10	——	GoldenMustang 114 2½ Marcia'sMistake 112 2¼ N'ghtyJoke 117 2	Stop'd	11
4Jun68-5Mth	fm	5f (T)	.47⅕ .59⅖	Clm	15000	6	8	8 8	8 6¾	7 5¾	7 6½	JCulmone	115	16.50	83–16	Bobanroll 115 2½ Formal Deb 115 nk Big Frolic 115 1	No threat	8
8May68-7GS	fst	1 1/16	.47⅗ 1.12⅕ 1.44⅗	Allowance		6	3	4 4½	6 10	6 12	6 15	RPerna	113	19.30	67–16	Mineola Lad 113 no Mr. Will Power 111 2 Lady Carene 108¾	Far back	7
3May68-7GS	fst	6f	.23 .46⅖ 1.11⅘	Clm	15000	7	1	7 4¼	7 12	7 16	6 11	JVelasquez	118	5.90	74–17	Some Wind 111½ Star Nell 111 1 I. J's Mito 111 2¼	Showed little	7

LATEST WORKOUTS Sep 13 Atl 5f fst 1.03⅗ b Aug 30 Atl 5f fst 1.02⅕ b Aug 18 Atl 3f fst .36⅗ b Aug 10 Atl 4f fst .49 b

With Confidence ✻

Ch. g (1965–Ky), by Watch Your Step—Palestra, by Palestine
G. French L. W. Jennings (S. G. Miller, Jr.)
114

1968	16	3	3	2	$13,815
1967	5	1	0	1	$1,895

10Sep68-6Atl	fst	7f	.22⅖ .44⅘ 1.22⅖	Allowance		8	1	2 h	1 1	1 4	1 4	WBlum	b 115	2.30	91–15	With Confidence 115 4 Amerigold 115 1 Bukhhalter 117½	Easily	8
3Sep68-6Atl	fst	6f	.22⅕ .45⅖ 1.10⅘	Allowance		3	6	7 8¼	7 7	7 8	5 4½	RBroussard	b 117	*2.60	83–17	Amber Eagle 114 1½ Rangatira 114 2 Laba Daba 109 1	Never threat	8
20Aug68-7Atl	fst	6f	.22⅖ .45 1.10	Allowance		1	5	5 1¾	6 6½	5 5½	4 7½	MMiceli	b 114	3.20	84–16	SayTheWord 118 1½ TowerOfStrength 114 1 FourStraight 114 5	In cl.	11
8Aug68-7Atl	fst	7f	.22⅖ .45 1.23⅗	Allowance		4	3	1 ½	2 ½	3 1½	4 2¼	MMiceli	b 109	3.80	83–19	Know 112 h Biddeford 112 2 Naughty Joke 111 nk	Early speed, tired	7
23Jly 68-7Mth	fst	6f	.22⅕ .45⅕ 1.10⅕	Allowance		5	9	10 7	10 12	8 6¼	7 5¾	RBroussard	b 117	*1.80	86–16	Coati II. 116 2 Say The Word 120 h Martial Melody 115 3	Slow early	10
17Jly 68-4Aqu	fst	7f	.23⅕ .46 1.22⅕	Clm	25000	6	4	5 2½	4 2	4 1¼	2 ½	RBroussard	b 117	9.10	94–11	HappyGold 116½ WithConfidence 117½ ArmedWarrior 109 1	Game try	7
11Jly 68-7Mth	fst	6f	.22⅕ .45⅖ 1.11	Allowance		1	6	6 4½	6 9¼	6 6	5 4½	RBroussard	b 117	11.00	82–19	Jaikyl 122 3 Revitup 118 no I Am Slipping 113 h	Never a threat	7
4May68-6GS	fst	170	.46⅖ 1.11⅘ 1.43⅕	Allowance		9	3	1 h	2 ½	2 1	5 7½	JVelasquez	b 114	*1.50	70–19	Eddie's Delight 114 1 Space Bird 114 4½ Revitip 114 2	Tired abruptly	9
27Apr68-5GS	fst	6f	.22⅖ .45⅘ 1.11⅕	Allowance		7	10	10 8¾	10 8¼	6 7	3 5½	RBroussard	b 116	4.50	82–18	Balustrade 113 3½ Zymurgy 114 2 With Confidence 116½	Rallied	10
2Apr68-9GP	fst	6f	.22⅕ .45 1.10⅘	Clm	25000	4	3	6 6	4 6½	4 5	3 2½	CPerret5	b 111	8.60	87–14	Welland Rd. 118 2½ Mezzo Forte 116 h With Confidence 111 1	Rallied	7

LATEST WORKOUTS Sep 16 Atl 4f fst .47⅗ b Sep 1 Atl 3f fst .36 b Aug 27 Atl 4f fst .49 b Aug 19 Atl 3f fst .37 b

Third Monarch ✻

B. c (1964–Fla), by Fair Ruler—Triple Bells, by Triplicate
Lin-Drake Farm J. P. Conway (Ocala Stud Farms, Inc.)
116

1968	9	2	0	0	$3,555
1967	8	1	0	0	$1,690

5Sep68-6Aqu	fst	7f	.23⅕ .46⅕ 1.24⅕	Clm	20000	7	1	5 2¼	8 6½	8 6	8 5¾	BThornburg	114	15.60	79–21	Happy Monday 117 h Puppet State 114¾ Bugler 116 nk	Fell back	8
21Aug68-5Sar	sl	6f	.22⅖ .46⅖ 1.11⅘	Clm	15000	9	1	4 2¼	2 2	2 ½	1 3½	MYcaza	b 119	13.10	89–17	Third Monarch 119 3½ Tolk 119½ Loop The Loop 117 2	Easily	9
13Aug68-9Sar	fm	1 1/16 (T)	1.41⅕	Clm	18000	4	1	1 3	1 2	4 4½	7 18	DBThomas5	109	10.40	76– 7	Lancastrian 120 5 Misty Lad 114 h Magic Beat 120 8	Stopped badly	10
27Jly 68-8Aqu	fm	1 1/16 (T)	1.43⅕	Allowance		7	3	3 1	5 5¼	8 6¾	8 9	HWoodhouse	118	40.00	78– 8	Ruth's Rullah 112 2½ Jade Amicol 113 1½ Royal Jest 113 1½	Tired	9
4Jly 68-5Aqu	fst	6f	.22⅗ .45 1.09⅗	Allowance		5	2	3 2	4 4	3 4½	5 6	CLedezma	121	25.90	89–11	Noblest Roman 114 h Lucky Richard 117 5 Tennis Champ 112¾	Tired	6
14May68-8GS	fst	170	.47⅖ 1.12⅕ 1.42⅖	Allowance		7	3	4 1½	4 3	4 5	5 3¼	JVelasquez	117	4.40	79–18	Birthday Card 117 no Jumping Jack 117 nk Mr.Scipio 117 3	No rally	7
4May68-7GS	fst	6f	.22⅘ .46 1.10⅘	Allowance		8	5	6 3½	7 4¼	4 1¼	4 3¼	EGuerin	115	23.20	87–19	Make It 113 h Spring Double 113 h Baitman 113 3	Bid, tired	9
19Apr68-9GP	fst	6f	.22⅗ .45⅗ 1.10⅘	Allowance		4	3	2 h	2 ½	1 h	1 nk	HMoreno	115	*1.60	90–13	ThirdMonarch 115 nk RomanTrooper 116 4 PatteeCanyon 107 2	Driving	8
3Apr68-8GP	fst	6f	.22⅕ .44⅘ 1.09⅘	Allowance		8	3	1 1	2 ½	2 3	4 7¼	EGuerin	115	47.20	88–16	Jodybo 108 3½ Valam 119 2 Navy Strut 113 1¾	Speed to stretch	9
22Jun67-6AP	fst	6f	.22⅗ .45⅘ 1.10⅖	Clm	15000	1	1	4 2¼	6 6¾	6 12	6 19	HArroyo5	b 111	45.00	72–15	O Be Joyful 116½ Carlo Fordo 118 3 Kingdom Jr. 118 2	Early speed	8

LATEST WORKOUTS Sep 16 Atl 5f fst 1.00 b Sep 11 Atl 4f my .48⅖ b Sep 2 Bel 3f fst .36⅗ b Aug 29 Bel 4f fst .52 b

A Latin Spin

B. c (1964–Md), by Spin—Alluring, by Tiger
J. A. Manfuso J. de Murguiondo (J. A. Manfuso)
116

1968	10	1	1	1	$6,200
1967	9	1	3	1	$5,340

12Sep68-7Atl	fst	7f	.22⅘ .45⅘ 1.24	Allowance		2	5	6 4½	3 3	4 3	3 6½	FMartinez7	109	9.90	76–21	Zymurgy 113½ Tower Of Strength 115 6 A Latin Spin 109 2	Rallied	6
29Aug68-7Atl	fst	7f	.22⅖ .45⅕ 1.22⅗	Allowance		7	3	8 6¼	9 9¾	7 9	6 8½	DKassen	116	35.40	81–16	Perfect Tan 107 1½ Cup Race 116 3 Waking Dawn 112 2	Never threat	10
15Aug68-7Atl	fst	6f	.22⅖ .45⅕ 1.09⅗	Allowance		6	4	5 7½	7 11	8 12	7 12	DKassen	118	16.90	82–19	Happy Ridan 117 6 Carr Bairn 120½ Perfect Tan 107 1	Never close	8
1Aug68-6Mth	fst	6f	.22 .45⅕ 1.10⅘	Allowance		3	4	4 2¼	5 3¼	4 3½	4 1¼	DKassen	118	5.70	87–17	Full Capacity 112½ Man Of Action 112 no Coati II 118¾	Gaining	6
17Jly 68-5Mth	fst	1 1/16	.48 1.12⅖ 1.44⅖	Allowance		6	7	7 11	7 12	7 10	6 15	DKassen	120	13.80	68–15	Sly Bird 113 4 In-Clava-Tator 113 3 Perfect Tan 111 5	Stumbled st.	7
10Jly 68-7Mth	fm	1 1/16 (T)	1.12⅖ 1.44⅕	Allowance		5	3	4 3	3 2	4 3	4 5¼	DKassen	120	24.40	——	Harleigh Green 118 nk Sir Omni 111 h Homa The Fair 111 5	Tired	8
27Jun68-7Mth	sly	170	.47⅕ 1.12⅖ 1.43⅕	Allowance		3	5	7 9½	4 7	4 3	5 5	DKassen	121	7.60	80–19	Doctor Art 112 3 ♦Atoll's Sun 119 nk ♦Perfect Tan 117 nk	Mild bid	9
18Jun68-7Mth	fst	6f	.21⅘ .44⅘ 1.11⅗	Allowance		7	2	4 4	5 7½	2 2	1 3	DKassen	116	*3.00	84–23	A Latin Spin 116 3 Bold Star 114 no Coati II 116 1¾	Well in time	7
12Jun68-7Mth	sly	6f	.22⅕ .45 1.11⅗	Allowance		4	1	4 ¾	4 4	4 4	4 3¼	DKassen	118	2.70	82–16	Celtuity 113½ Tuinadek 113¾ Coati II 118 2	No late response	7
5Jun68-5Mth	fst	6f	.22 .44⅗ 1.10⅕	Allowance		8	2	4 1¼	4 3½	4 3½	2 4½	DKassen	b 118	24.90	86– 9	Straight Ahead 115 4½ A Latin Spin 118¾ Wise Road 115¾	Rallied	8

LATEST WORKOUTS Sep 7 Atl 5f sly 1.06 b Aug 13 Atl 3f fst .37 b Jly 27 Mth 4f fst .52 b

Rather than labor through the records of each contestant, let me say at once that the standout in this field is a horse that the average player would eliminate on sight. The horse is Third Monarch, and the supposed rap against him is that he is moving into allowance company after failing to set the world on fire in claiming races. But the facts are that he outclasses this field. And his record proves it!

When he beat a field of $15,000 animals at Saratoga on August 21, Jim Conway's colt was competing for a $7,200 purse. Compare that with today's $4,800 purse. Third Monarch is dropping 33⅓ percent in class off that Saratoga victory. As to his failure against $20,000 animals on September 5—forget it. The purse on that occasion was $10,000.

Nothing Third Monarch faces today has ever come close to winning a $7,000 purse. If Third Monarch is in shape, he should romp. His workout line proves that he is in elegant shape. Enough said. He is the best bet of the day, and very likely the best of the month.

If you now are asking indignantly how anyone is supposed to know that high-priced claiming races in New York are classier than moderate allowance races in New Jersey, I have a two-part answer. Firstly, one gets to know these things with experience. Secondly, one need not wait to accumulate the experience. A file of result charts contains the necessary information about the purse values and true class of a horse's recent races.

The Running of the Race

ALLOWED TO GET AWAY at almost 12–1, Third Monarch won by six lengths.

SIXTH RACE   **6 FURLONGS.** (Bright Holly, September 2, 1961, 1.08⅖, 3, 112.)

Atl - 35941

September 19, 1968

Allowances. Purse $4,800. 3- and 4-year-olds which have not won $2,400 twice other than maiden or claiming. Weights 3-year-olds 118 lbs., 4-year-olds 122 lbs. Non-winners of $6,600 allowed 2 lbs., $3,600 since July 26, 4 lbs., a race since August 3, 6 lbs., $2,400 at any time 9 lbs. (Maiden and claiming races not considered.)

Value to winner $2,880, second $960, third $625, fourth $335. Mutuel pool $125,847.

Index	Horse	Eqt A Wt PP St	¼	½	Str	Fin	Jockey	Owner	Odds $1
35833Aqu8	Third Monarch	4 116 7 3	5$1\frac{1}{2}$	1h	1^3	1^6	F Lovato	Lin–Drake Farm	11.70
35888Atl5	Amber Eagle	3 114 4 1	2$\frac{1}{2}$	2$\frac{1}{2}$	2h	2^3	E Maple	Miss M Zarnes	13.20
35888Atl2	Tower Of St'ngth b	3 114 1 8	7^6	6^2	6^5	3$\frac{1}{2}$	G Patterson	A G Vanderbilt	3.90
35862LD7	Say The Word	4 118 3 2	1^2	3^3	3^3	4no	M Aristone	Indian Mills Stock Farm	2.70
35869Atl1	With Confidence b	3 114 6 6	6^1	5$1\frac{1}{2}$	5$\frac{1}{2}$	5$1\frac{1}{2}$	W Blum	G French	2.40
35888Atl3	A Latin Spin	4 116 8 4	4h	4h	4h	6^6	M Hole	J A Manfuso	26.90
35827Atl7	Terry's Song	3 107 5 7	8	8	7^1	7^3	G Cusimano5	M Gache	27.40
35642Atl3	Martial Melody b	3 117 2 5	3$\frac{1}{2}$	7^1	8	8	R Broussard	Golden Vale Farm	4.40

Time .22⅖, .45⅕, 1.09⅖. Track fast.

$2 Mutuel Prices:

7–THIRD MONARCH	25.40	10.00	4.80
4–AMBER EAGLE		11.20	6.20
1–TOWER OF STRENGTH			3.40

B. c, by Fair Ruler—Triple Bells, by Triplicate. Trainer J. P. Conway. Bred by Ocala Stud Farms, Inc. (Fla).

IN GATE AT 3.51. OFF AT 3.51 EASTERN DAYLIGHT TIME. Start good. Won ridden out.

THIRD MONARCH, never far back, raced SAY THE WORD into defeat from the outside approaching the quarter pole, repulsed several bids by AMBER EAGLE and drew off in the final furlong. AMBER EAGLE pressed the early pace while between horses and was not up to the winner. TOWER OF STRENGTH rallied belatedly. SAY THE WORD made the early pace and weakened. WITH CONFIDENCE could not menace. A LATIN SPIN had no mishap. MARTIAL MELODY was through early.

Overweight—Martial Melody 3 pounds.

THE SEVENTH RACE

HERE IS ANOTHER allowance race, this time at seven furlongs. It is open to any horse aged three or more that has not won two races of this grade during 1968.

7th Atlantic City

7 FURLONGS ATLANTIC CITY (Start ▼ / Finish)

7 FURLONGS (Chute). (Chit Chat, Aug. 12, 1958, 1.20⅗, 6, 114.)
Allowances. Purse $5,500. 3-year-olds and upward which have not won $2,500 twice other than maiden, claiming, optional or starter in 1968. Weights 3-year-olds 119 lbs., older 122 lbs. Non-winners of $6,600 in 1968 allowed 3 lbs., $4,900 since July 4, 6 lbs., $2,700 since April 10, 9 lbs., $2,925 twice in 1967–68, 11 lbs. (Maiden, claiming, optional and starter races not considered.)

Springwood *

B. h (1963-Va), by Third Brother—Slash Cottage, by To Market — Rockbridge Stable — J. P. Simpson — (R. W. Wood) — **113**

1968 5 0 0 0 $375
1967 14 2 2 2 $12,350

3Sep68-8Tim	fst 1	.48⅖ 1.15⅕ 1.40⅘	Allowance	6	5	510	67½	611	613	RKimball	b 113	7.00	74–21	Bachelor Of Arts 1164 Sly Bandit 1172¾ FuzzieKing 1221¼	No factor	6
22Aug68-8Tim	fst 7f	.23⅘ .47⅘ 1.27⅕	Allowance	8	7	58½	58½	720	819	RKimball	b 115	2.10	76–21	Guss Gray 115h Mr. Judex 11510 Bronze Bout 1153	No speed	8
12Aug68-8Atl	fst 6f	.22⅖ .45⅖ 1.10⅕	Allowance	3	7	66½	68½	67	56¾	GPatterson	b 115	5.80e	84– 9	Trish M. 117no Misty Cloud 115nk Golden Buttons 1122½	No mishap	8
5Aug68-7Atl	fst 7f	.22⅘ .46 1.24⅕	Allowance	3	5	33½	811	912	912	FLovato	b 117	*2.20e	70–17	Woodford 1131½ Trish M. 1172 Hespero 112¾	Gave way badly	9
25Jly 68-8Del	fst 6f	.22⅖ .46 1.11⅖	Allowance	3	9	98¾	98	58	46¼	RKimball	b 112	5.90e	82–22	Sikkim 1221¼ Light The Fuse 1172 Sub Call 1223	Forced circle field	9
19Aug67-9Det	my 170	.47⅕ 1.11⅗ 1.42⅘	Frontier H	1	8	76	713	615	512	CNicholson	b 115	7.20	73–27	Carpenter's Rule 111no Royal Course 1132 Errante II 1145	No factor	8
12Aug67-8Det	fst 6f	.23 .45⅘ 1.10⅘	Allowance	2	7	67	53	41	2¾	CNicholson	b 119	3.70	85–17	Bonny Johnny 117¾ Springwood 1191 Jet Avenger 1121	Held gamely	7
19Jly 67-7Mth	fm 1 1/16 Ⓣ	1.45⅘	Allowance	5	4	44½	54	66¾	67½	DBrumfield	b 120	27.30	78–14	Gary G. 1222 Quite An Accent 1202½ Decacean 1112½	Fell far back	7
8Jly 67-6Aqu	fst 1	.44⅗ 1.09⅖ 1.35⅗	Allowance	7	5	79	87¼	77½	78¾	ECardone	b 118	95.50	81–14	Mr. Right 116nk Wrong Card 118½ Jack Of All Trades 1143	No threat	9
29Jun67-8Mth	fm 5f Ⓣ	.58	Allowance	3	5	53½	52½	62¾	73¾	JJohnson	b 116	24.50	93– 8	Arctic Aria 118¾ Roving Satellite 1181 New Windsor 1141	Fell back	7
13Jun67-8Mth	fst 1 1/16	.48 1.12⅗ 1.45⅕	Allowance	6	4	53	88½	914	88¼	BThornburg	b 122	20.90	71–20	Swoonaway 1154½ Wrong Card 112½ Put-In-Bay 115½	No threat	12

LATEST WORKOUTS Sep 18 Atl 3f fst .36⅗ b — Sep 15 Atl 5f fst 1.00⅖ h — Sep 13 Atl 3f fst .36 b — Sep 11 Atl 3f my .37⅖ b

Castle Rullah

Dk. b. or br. c (1964-Ky), by Amarullah—Rededicate, by Dedicate — Kinsella-Zehnder, Jr. — J. J. Sarner, Jr. — (W. H.-D. L. White) — **108⁵**

1968 1 0 0 0 ——
1967 25 5 1 5 $28,705

30Aug68-7AP	fst 6f	.22⅗ .45⅘ 1.10⅕	Allowance	6	8	86	810	88½	68¼	DBrumfield	b 113	30.30	84–16	Gin-Rob 107h Bold Tactics 112nk Suteki 1222½	Never a factor	8
15Nov67-7Spt	fst 1 1/16	.48⅖ 1.13⅗ 1.46⅘	Handicap	6	1	1½	1h	1½	1h	ECoffman	b 120	*0.70	84–21	Castle Rullah 120h Thackeray 118no Jeffer 1141¾	Hard drive	6
8Nov67-8Spt	fst 1	.48⅖ 1.13 1.39⅖	Handicap	8	1	11½	1½	11½	14	ECoffman	b 115	3.60	86–23	Castle Rullah 1154 Bebarjay 1161½ Laffin Mango 115h	Easily	10
28Oct67-8Spt	gd 6½f	.22⅕ .45⅘ 1.17⅗	Snaro H	4	7	65½	75¾	88½	78¼	RMundorf	b 112	14.00	82–21	Royal Course 1222 Gamin 1161 Great McGow 113¾	No threat	11
18Oct67-6Kee	fst 6f	.21⅘ .45⅖ 1.11	Allowance	5	4	46¼	43½	33	33½	DRichard	b 117	3.50	84–23	CountryFriend120no RoyalHarmony1073½ CastleRullah117nk	Fair try	7
11Oct67-6Kee	fst 6f	.21⅘ .45⅘ 1.11⅕	Allowance	7	5	69	67¼	43½	1¾	DRichard	b 115	7.90	87–18	Castle Rullah 115¾ Model Prince 113¾ Country Friend 1221½	Driving	8
16Sep67-7CD	fst 1	.46⅕ 1.10⅘ 1.36	Allowance	4	5	56½	44	34	34	DBrumfield	b 121	7.80	89–13	Gay Flight 118¾ Mr. Ed. P. 1183¼ Castle Rullah 1213½	No rally	8
4Sep67-8CD	fst 7f	.23 .46 1.24	Allowance	9	3	2½	13	1h	31¾	DBrumfield	b 116	4.60	85–18	Air Boat 107nk Mr. Ed. P. 1191½ Castle Rullah 1165½	Weakened	9
16Aug67-7AP	fst 6f	.22⅕ .45⅕ 1.09⅗	Allowance	6	2	67	66¾	56	33½	CPerret5	b 112	8.60	91–10	Mr. Ed P. 1192 Jeronia 1171½ Castle Rullah 112nk	Closed well	7

Trish M. *

Ch. g (1963-Ky), by Royal Serenade—Our Margobee, by Crafty Admiral — Charfran Stable — D. Dodson — (Charfran Stable) — **116**

1968 18 1 4 4 $12,510
1967 16 4 3 3 $27,350

26Aug68-7Atl	fst 7f	.22⅗ .45⅕ 1.22⅘	Allowance	5	4	54	45	43	41¾	DKassen	b 117	7.10	87–16	Baitman 117¾ Relics Of Wars 114¾ Bar Tab 105nk	No late response	7
19Aug68-8Atl	fst 7f	.22⅘ .45 1.22⅗	Allowance	5	3	32	42½	33	33½	RBroussard	b 117	3.70	87–15	Woodford 1172½ Isgala 1191 Trish M. 117nk	Held on evenly	7
12Aug68-8Atl	fst 6f	.22⅖ .45⅖ 1.10⅕	Allowance	8	4	55	54½	41½	1no	RBroussard	b 117	3.20	91– 9	Trish M. 117no Misty Cloud 115nk Golden Buttons 1122½	Driving	8
5Aug68-7Atl	fst 7f	.22⅘ .46 1.24⅕	Allowance	5	7	54½	33	32	21½	RBroussard	b 117	2.90	80–17	Woodford 1131½ Trish M. 1172 Hespero 112¾	Made game try	9
23Jly 68-8Mth	fst 1 1/16	.48 1.12 1.44⅗	Allowance	3	3	1h	1h	2h	44¼	CBaltazar	b 117	*1.60	78–16	WingsOfMorn'g1221¼ WithoutWarning1171 GoodKnight1152	Tired	8
11Jly 68-7Aqu	fm 1 1/16 Ⓣ	1.42⅗	Allowance	2	4	48	55	43½	54½	RTurcotte	b 116	6.40	85–10	Crafty Look 118¾ Mimado II 1162 Ginger Fizz 123¾	No rally	7
1Jly 68-8Mth	fst 6f	.22⅕ .45⅘ 1.11⅖	Allowance	4	9	87¼	76¼	42	31	RBroussard	b 117	3.00	84–21	Isgala 117½ Charles Elliott 117½ Trish M. 1171¼	Finished well	9
17Jun68-8Mth	fst 6f	.22⅕ .45⅗ 1.10⅘	Allowance	2	7	74¼	63½	44	3½	RBroussard	b 117	10.00	87–18	Flower's Boy 117no Night Cloud 112½ Trish M. 1175	Rallied	8
10Jun68-8Mth	fst 6f	.22⅕ .45 1.09⅖	Allowance	2	6	53	53¼	63	69¾	CBaltazar	b 117	14.10	85–12	Bowler King 1176 Flower's Boy 117nk Golden Buttons 113¾	Tired	7
30Apr68-8GS	fst 6f	.22⅗ .46⅕ 1.11	Allowance	5	7	78½	55½	68	56	RBroussard	116	11.40	83–18	On Your Mark II 1133½ Swoonland 113½ Bowler King 113h	No threat	7
17Apr68-9GP	fm*1 1/16 Ⓣ	1.43⅗	Allowance	2	3	32	1½	11	22	..roussard	123	2.80	——	I'm Smiley 1092 Trish M. 1231½ Hardihood 1235	Failed to last	7

LATEST WORKOUTS Sep 16 Atl 6f fst 1.14 b — Sep 11 Atl 3f my .38 b — Sep 8 Atl 6f fst 1.17⅖ b — Aug 25 Atl 3f fst .37⅗ b

Pretty Tweetsie ×

B. g (1964-Ky), by Barbizon—Tweetsie Dee, by Helioscope — H. W. Dietrich — B. P. Bond — (Brown Hotel Farms, Inc.) — **116**

1968 9 6 1 1 $20,085
1967 9 2 2 3 $7,800

6Sep68-8Atl	sly 6f	.22 .44⅘ 1.10⅘	Allowance	1	4	13	16	15	12½	JCulmone	b 114	*0.80	88–22	PrettyTweetsie1142½BrotherCampbell1161½MistyCloud1164½	Driving	7
24Aug68-5Atl	fst 6f	.22 .44⅖ 1.09⅕	Cl c-12500	6	1	13	15	16	112	GPatterson	b 118	*0.80	96–13	Pretty Tweetsie 11812 War Horn 120¾ Bet Lite 111h	Won easily	8
17Aug68-6Atl	fst 6f	.22⅕ .45⅖ 1.10	Clm 12500	10	4	12	13	15	13	GPatterson	b 114	8.20	92–15	Pretty Tweetsie 1143 Last Cry 1177 Chear-up II 113½	Driving	12
13Aug68-7Atl	fst 6f	.22 .44⅘ 1.11	Cl c-8000	7	3	13	16	14	14½	GCusimano5	b 111	*1.50	87–15	PrettyTweetsie1114½ SpadeAndShovel1161¼ Winamac1143	Driving	9
7Aug68-8Del	fm 5f Ⓣ	.58⅗	Allowance	4	2	1h	53½	53½	55¾	WJPassmore	b 112	*1.50	——	Parkesburg 1122¾ Chip Off It 1091 Bronze Bout 110½	Bolted	6
29Jly 68-7Del	fst 6f	.22⅗ .46 1.12	Clm 17500	6	5	1½	1½	2½	33¾	GCusimano5	b 107	*1.90	81–18	Big Devil 116¾ Mr. Judex 1103 Pretty Tweetsie 1071	Bumped start	8
17Jly 68-7Del	fst 6f	.22 .45⅖ 1.11⅗	Clm 20000	2	2	13	13½	13	2½	GCusimano5	b 107	*1.60	86–18	BrotherCampbell112½ PrettyTw'tsie107nk MakeltPlat'm1165	Failed	6
26Jun68-5Del	fst 6f	.22⅕ .45⅕ 1.12	Clm T1500	1	2	13½	14½	13½	13½	GCusimano5	b 110	*0.90	85–20	Pretty Tweetsie 1103½ Star Spin 1121 Gusoldboy 1151¾	Handily	6
31May68-6Del	gd 6f	.22⅕ .46⅕ 1.13⅕	Cl c-7500	2	3	13	14	11½	11	WPeake	b 115	2.20	79–24	PrettyTweetsie1151 ArabianLegend1131¼ TrustingJewel 1181	Driv'g	7

LATEST WORKOUTS Sep 13 Atl 3f fst .36⅗ b — Sep 4 Atl 3f fst .34⅗ b — Aug 3 Atl 4f fst .46⅖ h — Jly 27 Del 3f fst .37⅖ b

Bar Tab *

B. g (1964-Md), by Trojan Monarch—Tabarina, by The Yuvaraj — Bear Creek Farm — J. L. Skinner — (J. L. Skinner) — **111**

1968 15 5 4 2 $24,335
1967 18 5 1 4 $15,130

31Aug68-8Tim	fst 1	.47⅖ 1.13⅘ 1.40⅕	Handicap	7	8	915	813	512	45½	NShuk	b 111	6.40	84–18	Terrible Tiger 1172¼ Corn Caster 1191¼ Barnesville 1142	Rallied	10
26Aug68-7Atl	fst 7f	.22⅗ .45⅕ 1.22⅘	Allowance	1	7	77	67	53½	31½	Alliescu7	b 105	16.10	87–16	Baitman 117¾ Relics Of Wars 114¾ Bar Tab 105nk	Finished will'gly	7
14Aug68-8Tim	fst 1	.48⅖ 1.14⅖ 1.40⅕	Allowance	7	5	47	47	410	312	Alliescu7	b 106	5.30	78–22	Wallofroses 1089 Barnesville 1193 Bar Tab 106no	Wide, tired	8
3May68-8Pim	fm 1 1/16 Ⓣ	1.13⅕ 1.45⅘	Allowance	1	2	65	611	512	514	ENelson	b 112	7.40	72–15	Rock Talk 1192 Exceedingly 122¾ Fuzzie King 1151½	No speed	6
20Apr68-8Bow	fst 1 1/16	.46⅘ 1.11 1.42	JBCamp'lH	2	5	54	56	66¼	77	AAgnello	b 103	48.10	96– 8	In Reality 1221 Barbs Delight 117½ Peter Piper 1172	No threat	7
10Apr68-8Bow	fst 7f	.22⅗ .45⅗ 1.23	Allowance	9	4	57	44½	46½	42¼	ENelson	b 115	3.40	88–11	Great White Way 117h Noah's Ark 1121¼ Great Depths 1151	Hung	10
25Mar68-7Bow	fst 1 1/16	.47⅘ 1.13⅖ 1.45⅘	Allowance	5	5	52¼	2h	2h	22	PIGrimm	b 112	*1.20	82–16	Tom Stone 1122 Bar Tab 112½ Star Spin 1093	Held gamely for place	6
16Mar68-6Bow	fst 1 1/16	.47 1.12⅗ 1.45⅗	Allowance	1	5	55	32½	22	21	PIGrimm	b 119	3.40	84–19	Navy Admiral 1191 Bar Tab 119no Happy Hilarious 114no	Rallied	6
6Mar68-8Bow	fst 7f	.23⅕ .45⅘ 1.23	Allowance	8	1	52½	23	23	2½	PIGrimm	b 119	*1.50	89–15	James Bay 114½ Bar Tab 1195 Black Verse 107h	Made game effort	8
22Feb68-7Bow	fst 6f	.22⅗ .45 1.10⅗	Clm 25000	3	4	35	35	33	1¾	ENelson	b 118	3.50	94–19	Bar Tab 118¾ Whistling Kettle 1083 Steel Trap 1152	Driving	6

LATEST WORKOUTS Sep 7 Tim 3f my .37⅘ b — Jly 27 Del 3f fst .37 b

Proud Sailor ✻ Dk. b. or br. c (1964–Ky), by Sailor—In Shape, by Sayajirad 116 1968 9 2 0 0 $5,850
Mrs. R. L. Reineman C. P. Sanborn (R. L. Reineman) 1967 5 1 1 1 $3,635
17Aug68–7Atl fst 7f .22⅗ .45⅗1.23⅗ Allowance 5 9 914 913 710 612 GCusimano5 108 40.10 73–15 Court Her 1157 Hedevar 1182 Flower's Boy 115nk Never close 9
20Jly 68–9Mth fst 1 .48⅗1.12⅘1.37⅘ Allowance 2 8 810 816 816 826 DRichard 114 66.60 58–17 Spring Double 119¾ Exclusive Native 1143 Besieger 1196 Trailed 8
5Jly 68–4Aqu fst 6f .21⅘ .44⅖1.09⅖ Allowance 1 5 613 617 614 613 WBoland 121 34.50 83–13 Tanrackin 121no Allardice 1171½ Beau Marker 1141½ Trailed 6
8Jun68–7Mth fm 1 Ⓣ .47⅕1.36⅗ OceanprtH 6 6 715 69½ 612 512 CBaltazar 111 17.90 87– 1 Country Friend 1164 Burning Bridges 1111¾ Vis-A-Vis 1094 No thr't 7
8Jun68—The Oceanport Handicap, run in two divisions, 7th and 8th races.
25Apr68–9GP fm*1 Ⓣ 1.36⅘ Allowance 4 7 79½ 614 67¾ 412 HMoreno 114 8.50 —— Mara Lark 1064 Maverick III 1182½ Sir Winzalot 1205 No factor 7
11Apr68–9GP fst 7f .22⅖ .45⅘1.24⅖ Allowance 6 8 77¼ 75¼ 31½ 11½ HGrant 118 *1.50 87–13 Proud Sailor 1181½ Circuit Court 113no Naturally Rare 1105 Driving 8
28Mar68–8GP fst 7f .22⅖ .45⅖1.23⅘ Allowance 1 9 65½ 46½ 23 12¾ HGrant 119 2.00 90–10 Proud Sailor 1192¾ Kona 1144 Neecap 114½ Under mild drive 9
14Mar68–7GP fst 6f .22⅗ .46 1.11⅕ Allowance 10 10 912109½ 610 44¾ HGrant 119 6.50 83–13 Fly The Green 1074 Pebble Drive 117¾ Sean Home 115h Bumped st. 12
29Feb68–6Hia fst 6f .22 .45⅕1.10⅖ Allowance 7 8 811 814 813 812 TBarrow 115 57.00 80–15 Tom Pippin 119¾ Chartist 1171½ Hill Turn 1142 Trailed the field 8
LATEST WORKOUTS Sep 10 Atl 3f fst .35⅗ h Sep 2 Atl 5f fst 1.03⅖ b Aug 29 Atl 4f fst .49⅘ b Aug 16 Atl 3f fst .36 b

Hornbeam ✻ Gr. g (1964–Ky), by Roman Line—Tiare Lei, by Native Dancer. 111 1968 2 0 0 0 ——
Watermill Farm V. J. Nickerson (L. L. Haggin 2d) 1967 16 1 4 3 $20,100
7Sep68–6Aqu fst 6f .23 .46⅕1.10⅘ Allowance 1 7 52 41¼ 35 58¼ ECardone b 117 38.60 81–18 Terresto 1122 Trade In 1176 Golden Buttons 117h Bid, tired 9
20Aug68–6Sar fst 6f .22⅕ .45⅘1.10⅗ Allowance 8 6 64¾ 75¼ 74 85 ECardone b 117 37.70 90– 9 Shy Native 109nk Balouf 117h Bossy 1192 Not a threat 9
12Dec67–7Aqu sly 1 .46 1.12⅗1.40 Allowance 5 4 42½ 41½ 42 49¼ DThomas5 b 108 3.20 59–36 Needles' Count 1165 Just About 1094 Terrific Traffic 110nk Weak'd 7
1Dec67–6Aqu gd 7f .23⅖ .47⅕1.25 Allowance 1 6 55¼ 23 21½ 21¾ AGarramone7 b 108 *0.90 79–24 Rougeway 1191¾ Hornbeam 1089 Undermine 1192 No excuse 6
8Nov67–6Aqu fst 7f .22⅗ .46⅕1.24⅖ Allowance 5 6 55¾ 42½ 23 2nk JLRotz b 117 4.10 84–22 Peace Pipe 122nk Hornbeam 1176 Salmon River 1171½ Drifted out 7
28Oct67–6Kee fst 1 1/16 .46⅖1.10⅕1.42⅗ FayetteH 13 12 1017 812 66½ 65¾ PAnderson b 113 47.00 87–15 Swoonaway 1192 Hy Frost 1161½ Miracle Hill 1151½ Slow early 13
18Oct67–6Aqu sly 7f .22⅗ .45⅖1.24⅕ Allowance 1 6 44 22 2½ 2½ JLRotz b 118 *1.50 84–23 Kissing Bair 114½ Hornbeam 118nk Nehoc's Bullet 1145 Gamely 6
11Oct67–6Aqu my 1 .46⅗1.11⅖1.36⅖ Allowance 5 3 31½ 1½ 12 2¾ JCruguet b 112 2.00 85–19 Ski Lift 123¾ Hornbeam 1124 Shadow Brook 1124½ Couldn't last 7
6Oct67–7Aqu fst 7f .23⅕ .46⅕1.23 Allowance 5 3 63¼ 35½ 36 313 JLRotz b 118 3.60 78–19 Peter Piper 1176½ Velvet Flash 1146 Hornbeam 1183 Wide 6
27Sep67–8Aqu fm 1 1/16 Ⓣ 1.43⅕ Allowance 4 6 65¼ 64 4¾ 31¾ JLRotz b 113 6.50 88–10 Royal Comedian 113¾ Royal Concert 1181 Hornbeam 1132 Closed well 8
18Sep67–7Aqu fst 7f .22⅘ .45⅗1.23 Allowance 6 9 87 55½ 57 44½ MSorrentino b 117 7.30 86–15 Prinkipo 113¾ First And Finest 1201¾ Major Art 1132 Rallied 9
LATEST WORKOUTS Sep 14 Aqu 4f fst .49 b Sep 4 Aqu 4f gd .49 b Aug 31 Aqu 6f fst 1.15 b Aug 27 Aqu 4f fst .50 b

Relics Of Wars ✻ Blk. c (1964–NJ), by Cosmic Bomb—My Liebschen, by War Age 113 1968 9 1 1 1 $6,950
Mrs. J. Genova T. L. Klapproth (Mrs. J. Genova–G. Buonocore) 1967 21 3 1 4 $17,087
13Sep68–5Aqu fst 1 .45⅘1.10⅘1.36⅘ Clm 25000 4 1 11 1½ 11 1nk BThornburg b 117d–18.50 83–19 d-RelicsOfWars117nk RoyalMedal117no SkyCount1191½ Drifted out 11
13Sep68—d-Disqualified and placed third.
5Sep68–6Aqu fst 7f .23⅕ .46⅕1.24⅕ Clm 25000 1 8 21 3½ 41 74¼ DBThomas5 b 113 9.70 81–21 Happy Monday 117h Puppet State 114¾ Bugler 116nk Slow st., used 8
26Aug68–7Atl fst 7f .22⅗ .45⅕1.22⅘ Allowance 3 3 1½ 11 1h 2¾ GCusimano b 114 13.60 88–16 Baitman 117¾ Relics Of Wars 114¾ Bar Tab 105nk Sharp try, mis'd 7
17Aug68–7Atl fst 7f .22⅗ .45⅗1.23⅗ Allowance 3 3 33 56½ 813 817 CBurr b 113 19.70 68–15 Court Her 1157 Hedevar 1182 Flower's Boy 115nk Brief speed 9
27Jly 68–7Mth fst 1 1/16 .47⅘1.12 1.44⅖ Allowance 6 1 11½ 2½ 32½ 77¼ CBurr b 115 35.20 76–15 Sir Beau 1123½ Primo Richard 117h Balustrade 113no Tired 9
17Jly 68–7Mth fst 6f .22– .45⅕1.10⅘ Handicap 7 3 52¼ 66 76¾ 67½ DHidalgo b 120 9.80 80–15 Gee Sparkler 112½ Do Sparkle 117no Sarolsa 1152 Showed little 8
11Jly 68–8Mth fst 6f .22 .44⅘1.10⅘ Allowance 1 7 42¼ 66½ 79 712 RTanner5 b 112 6.80 76–19 Night Cloud 1173 Admiral Tudor 112½ Wallofroses 117¾ Tired 8
8Feb68–8Hia fst 7f .23 .45⅘1.23⅗ Allowance 4 2 12 12½ 1½ 1¾ CHMarquez b 113 60.60 91–18 RelicsOfWars113¾ Gaylord'sFeather1131¾ MajorArt1134½ Driving 12
3Feb68–9Hia fm 1⅛ Ⓣ 1.48⅘ Allowance 2 3 65½ 912 917 922 BThornburg b 114 45.60 77– 4 More Scents 113no War Censor 1193 Tequillo 113nk Far back 9
23Dec67–9TrP fst 6f .22⅖ .45⅘1.10⅘ CyCGableH 4 8 42 87¼ 711 711 HPilar b 111 37.60 73–26 Jeronia 1173¼ Country Friend 119¾ Sikkim 1203 Brief factor 11
9Dec67–9TrP fst 6f .21⅘ .44⅕1.09⅕ GoldCo'stH 3 5 55 77½1010119½ HPilar 113 32.40 82–17 Jeronia 114nk Glassell B. 1121 Sikkim 122¾ Never a factor 12
25Nov67–9TrP fst 170 .47 1.11⅕1.41 CtyMiamiH 7 2 1h 1h 65½ 79¾ JVasquez 114 *2.80 82–16 Icy Nino 1122¾ Hydrology II 1142½ Shade II 115½ Used early 9
LATEST WORKOUTS Sep 18 Atl 3f fst .35⅖ b Sep 10 Atl 4f fst .47 h Aug 25 Atl 3f fst .36⅘ b Aug 21 Atl 5f fst 1.00 h

---

We can eliminate Springwood, who has been finishing last at Timonium, Castle Rullah, the recent arrival, Bar Tab who needs more distance, and Proud Sailor, idle for a month. The live ones are:

Trish M.: This gelding is speedy, especially in the late stages, but has won only one of its 18 races this year. It will probably have a good chance today, if the front-runners beat each other early and no other pace-forcing type has enough class. The rider is Ray Broussard, who knows Trish M. Contender.

Pretty Tweetsie: On September 6, this recent acquisition of Bernie Bond's proved that his speed is not the cheap variety. By winning an allowance race as decisively as he did, he established his class. Unless another starter in today's race can match his extreme early speed, he must be recognized as the likely winner. True, he has never gone seven furlongs, but he seems to have a world of energy, and—unlike others of his type—often has plenty of run left at the end of his six-furlong races. Contender.

Hornbeam: Having given this animal two races in tough company, Lefty Nickerson shipped it to New Jersey in quest, no doubt, of a killing. In its best 1967 form, the gelding would have a chance to catch Pretty Tweetsie. But this is another year and Hornbeam's form is not yet established. Moreover, Pretty Tweetsie seems to have the early pace locked up, which would make things difficult even for a sharp Hornbeam. No Bet.

Relics Of Wars: On August 26, this colt ran on the front end of a race like today's, losing narrowly in the last yards. Here, then, is Pretty Tweetsie's competitor for the early lead. And here is final confirmation that it should be Pretty Tweetsie all the way. When Relics of Wars runs the first half-mile in .45⅕, he tires later. But Pretty Tweetsie can run the half much more rapidly than that and have plenty of pep at the finish. No Bet.

Note that this race is a handicapping problem similar to the fifth, won by Cypark. A fit speed horse, faster than any other front-runner in its race, is always a stern threat on a fast track.

The Running of the Race

PRETTY TWEETSIE, a deserving favorite at 1.10–1, ran the first half in .44⅖, six lengths ahead of Relics of Wars, and lasted to win by a nose from the onrushing Hornbeam.

SEVENTH RACE   **7 FURLONGS** (Chute). (Chit Chat, Aug. 12, 1958, 1.20⅗, 6, 114.)

Atl - 35942

September 19, 1968

Allowances. Purse $5,500. 3-year-olds and upward which have not won $2,500 twice other than maiden, claiming, optional or starter in 1968. Weights 3-year-olds 119 lbs., older 122 lbs. Non-winners of $6,600 in 1968 allowed 3 lbs., $4,900 since July 4, 6 lbs., $2,700 since April 10, 9 lbs., $2,925 twice in 1967-68, 11 lbs. (Maiden, claiming, optional and starter races not considered.)

Value to winner $3,300, second $1,100, third $715, fourth $385. Mutuel pool $139,745.

Index	Horse	Eqt A Wt	PP	St	¼	½	Str	Fin	Jockey	Owner	Odds $1
35844Atl[1]	Pretty Tw'tsie	b 4 116	4	3	1[2]	1[6]	1[3]	1[no]	J Culmone	H W Dietrich	1.10
35851Aqu[5]	Hornbeam	b 4 111	7	2	3[3]	3[5]	2[3]	2[3½]	C Baltazar	Watermill Farm	11.90
35732AP[6]	Castle Rullah	b 4 108	2	5	5[h]	4[h]	4[4]	3[3½]	G Cusimano[5]	Kinsell–Zehnder Jr	11.50
35895Aqu[3]	Rel's Of Wars	b 4 113	8	1	2[6]	2[1½]	3[1½]	4[2]	W Blum	Mrs J Genova	3.30
35669Atl[4]	Trish M.	b 5 117	3	7	6[h]	5[2]	5[2]	5[2]	R Broussard	Charfran Stable	4.90
35817Tim[6]	Springwood	b 5 113	1	6	4[1]	6[4]	6[5]	6[4]	M Miceli	Rockbridge Stable	88.10
35606Atl[6]	Proud Sailor	4 116	6	8	8	8	7[1]	7[1]	F Lovato	Mrs R L Reineman	69.20
35661Tim[4]	Bar Tab	b 4 113	5	4	7[5]	7[4]	8	8	P I Grimm	J L Skinner	6.70

Time .23, .44⅖, 1.09, 1.22⅕. Track fast.

$2 Mutuel Prices:

4-PRETTY TWEETSIE	....	4.20	3.60	3.20
7-HORNBEAM	....		8.00	5.20
2-CASTLE RULLAH	....			5.40

B. g, by Barbizon—Tweetsie Dee, by Helioscope. Trainer B. P. Bond. Bred by Brown Hotel Farms, Inc. (Ky.).

IN GATE AT 4.18. OFF AT 4.18 EASTERN DAYLIGHT TIME. Start good. Won driving.

PRETTY TWEETSIE sprinted to a long lead early, set a brisk pace, raced wide on the turn and into the stretch and just lasted over HORNBEAM. The latter gained steadily under strong pressure, saved ground in the drive and just missed. CASTLE RULLAH could not menace though finishing with good energy. RELICS OF WARS pressed the pace to the stretch and faltered. TRISH M. was never a factor. BAR TAB was never a factor.

Scratched—35676Atl[7] Olympian Idle. Overweights—Trish M. 1 pound, Bar Tab 2.

THE EIGHTH RACE

THIS RACE IS for fillies and mares under allowance conditions over a mile and one-sixteenth of grass. Some of the starters have not raced on the turf course and have no record of good grass workouts to redeem them. So we can eliminate Pendulous, Queen of Action, and Gay Sailorette. Flo Alligator also does not figure, being an unacclimated newcomer to Jersey racing. And Alps, an established grass runner, has been inactive for almost a month.

8th Atlantic City

TURF COURSE
1 1-16 MILES
ATLANTIC CITY
Start ▲ ▲ Finish

ABOUT 1 1-16 m. (Turf). (Fan Jet, September 7, 1966, 1.44⅘, 6, 113.)
Allowances. Purse $5,500. Fillies and mares. 3-year-olds and upward which have not won $2,925 twice at a mile or over since November 5 other than maiden, claiming, optional or starter. Weights 3-year-olds 118 lbs., older 122 lbs. Non-winners of $6,600 over a mile since June 30 allowed 3 lbs., $4,875 at a mile or over July 1, 5 lbs., any over a mile since June 30 allowed 3 lbs., $4,875 at a mile or over since July 1, 5 lbs., any race of $4,300 in 1968 or $6,500 in 1967, 7 lbs., $3,900 twice in 1968, 9 lbs., $2,600

Chriscinca

Dk. b. or br. f (1964–Fla), by Ambehaving—Be Nice, by Attention — A. A. Muller — B. Lepman — (Dr. J. M. Lee) — **117** — 1968 14 2 2 4 $28,730 — 1967 20 3 2 5 $16,735

12Sep68–9Atl fm 1 Ⓣ .46⅗1.36⅕ f– Allow 3 6 64¼ 65½ 42½ 42¾ CBaltazar b 117 7.10 87–12 T.V.'s Princess 119nk Baby Jane II 113½ Who Cabled 1172 Rallied 7
16Aug68–8Atl fm*1 1/16 Ⓣ 1.12⅗1.45 f– Allow 1 7 78¼ 76¼ 56 46 CBaltazar b 120 *1.50 93– 1 T.V.'s Princess 1135 Alps 118no d-Malluca 1201 Passed tired ones 8
16Aug68—Placed third through disqualification.
10Aug68–8Atl fst 1 1/16 .46⅖1.10⅘1.44 f-MargteH 1 6 715 511 37 28 CBaltazar b 113 15.60 79–17 Lady Diplomat 1128 Chriscinca 1132 Telepathy 1131½ Second best 11
3Aug68–7Mth fst 1 1/16 .47 1.12⅖1.45⅘ Allowance 5 6 54½ 52 36 47¾ HGrant 118 11.30 68–15 Harleigh Green 1194 Becacean 119nk Mystic's Desire 1143½ Weak'd 8
12Jly 68–7Aqu fm 1 1/16 Ⓣ 1.42⅕ f– Allow 4 5 58 54½ 56 69½ JLRotz 118 3.20 82– 8 May's Guide 1204 Shore 1203 Shirley Heights 118nk No excuses 8
17Jun68–7Mth fm*5f Ⓣ .48⅖1.01⅗ f– Allow 3 9 99¾ 811 68 31½ RBruno b 120 *2.20e 85–13 Miss Buffum 113h Voluntarily 1131½ Chriscinca 120nk Rallied 9
7May68–7GS fst 1 1/16 .46⅘1.11⅗1.43⅗ f– Allow 7 4 39 310 310 316 WGavidia b 118 6.80 71–18 T.V.'s Princess 11210 Sarolsa 1156 Chriscinca 1185 Held on 7
15Apr68–9GP fm 1 1/16 Ⓣ 1.12⅕1.43⅕ f– Allow 7 4 32 42 51¼ 11¼ RWholeyJr5 b 118 *♦2.20 88–13 ♦Ring Francis 1231¼ ♦Chriscinca 1181¼ Star Garter 1171½ Bumped 8
15Apr68—♦-Dead heat.
27Mar68–9GP fm 1 1/16 Ⓣ 1.10⅖1.41⅘ f-Suwan'eH 4 9 912 711 58½ 64 EFires b 113 7.50 91– 5 Ludham 1101¾ Farest Nan 113no Ring Francis 1111¾ Slow early 11
13Mar68–9GP fm 1 Ⓣ 1.35⅘ f-OrchidH 4 7 611 22 12 1nk EFires b 109 17.60 94– 9 Chriscinca 109nk Ring Francis 1093 Farest Nan 1133 Driving 14
LATEST WORKOUTS Sep 9 Atl 5f fst .59⅗ h — Sep 3 Atl 3f fst .35⅗ b — Aug 28 Atl 4f fst .50 b — Aug 9 Atl 3f fst .35 h

Pendulous *

Ch. f (1965–Ky), by Fulcrum—Saddle Saga, by Bernborough — P. D. DePaul — C. L. Robbins — (E. K. Thomas) — **109** — 1968 18 2 5 4 $17,932 — 1967 13 2 1 4 $8,155

28Aug68–8Atl fst 6f .22⅕ .45⅕1.10⅖ f– Allow 2 4 54 57 57 41¾ EMaple b 114 *2.30e 88–16 Clover Blossom 1091½ Dragnetta 117h Pillgrim'sPride114nk Late f't 8
15Aug68–6Atl fst 6f .22⅖ .45⅖1.10⅕ f– Allow 6 2 54 55 56½ 57 GCusimano5 b 109 5.00 84–19 Light Face 114nk Dragnetta 117nk It's A Pilot 1165 Never threat 6
10Aug68–8Atl fst 1 1/16 .46⅖1.10⅘1.44 f-MargteH 11 11 1120 712 512 615 RPerna b 109 16.40 72–17 Lady Diplomat 1128 Chriscinca 1132 Telepathy 1131½ No speed 11
22Jly 68–8Mth fst 6f .21⅖ .44⅕1.10⅖ f– Allow 1 5 65¾ 47 45½ 31¾ ESantana b 114 3.90 88–14 Light Face 114h Clover Blossom 116¾ Pendulous 1142 Rallied 7
13Jly 68–8Rkm fst 6f .21⅗ .44⅗1.10⅘ f-Rockette 1 6 58¼ 59 37½ 33½ ADeSpirito b 116 24.40 86–15 Twice Cited 1202 Indian Love Call 1141½ Pendulous 1163 Evenly 11
19Jun68–6Mth fst 6f .21⅘ .45 1.11⅗ f– Allow 4 6 64¼ 45½ 32½ 2nk RTanner5 b 109 11.50 84–18 Ronchu 113nk Pendulous 1091¾ Dragnetta 1125 Sharp try 7
1Jun68–8Mth fst 6f .21⅕ .44⅕1.10⅗ f-MWoodfd 4 9 78 910 1012 811 PKallai b 114 60.50 78–15 First Noel 1162 Twice Cited 116½ Singing Tune 1142½ Never close 10
27Apr68–8GS fst 6f .22⅕ .45⅘1.11⅕ f-BRossH 10 8 107¾ 119 99¼ 98½ PGrove b 111 56.90 79–18 Guest Room 1181½ Miss Swapsco 1211½ Brouillard 1171 No factor 11
17Apr68–6Bow fst 7f .23⅕ .46⅕1.23⅘ f– Allow 4 1 4¾ 2h 1½ 1½ PGrove b 118 2.00 86–11 Pendulous 118½ Inge 114nk Double Ripple 1144 Drifted out lasting 6
10Apr68–4Bow fst 6f .22⅗ .45⅖1.09⅗ f– Allow 1 4 32 33½ 32½ 21½ ENelson b 110 *2.20 97–11 Patrician Lady 1101½ Pendulous 1103½ Tabbit 113½ Game try 7
10Apr68—The Morning Telegraph Time 1.10⅕.
27Mar68–8Bow fst 6f .22 .45⅖1.10⅗ f– Allow 3 7 76¼ 84¼ 42 32½ PGrove5 b 109 15.20 91–14 Singing Rain 1182½ Solometeor 118h Pendulous 1091 Rallied 10
22Mar68–8Bow fst 7f .23⅖ .47 1.25⅕ Allowance 3 3 4nk 79¼ 78 712 PGrove5 b 109 6.30 67–20 Barbachino 1192 Boronia Gold 107h Mitey Prince 1152½ Tired 8
LATEST WORKOUTS Sep 14 Atl 4f fst .49⅕ b — Aug 6 Atl 3f fst .36⅗ b — Aug 2 Mth 4f sly .53 b

Who Cabled

Ch. m (1963–NJ), by Whodunit—First Cable, by Royal Palm — Cosens-Murphy — B. W. Perkins — (J. Murphy) — **117** — 1968 14 2 5 4 $20,136 — 1967 16 0 2 5 $4,980

12Sep68–9Atl fm 1 Ⓣ .46⅗1.36⅕ f– Allow 2 1 1h 11 2h 3¾ RBroussard b 117 4.30 89–12 T.V.'s Princess 119nk Baby Jane II 113½ Who Cabled 1172 W'kened 7
31Aug68–8Rkm fst 1 1/16 .47⅕1.11⅘1.45 f-P.Dor'nH 3 3 2½ 12 31 45 MArstone 111 4.90 81–17 Femtastic 107½ Queen Viking 1084½ Gay Sailorette 119no Weakened 11
23Aug68–8Atl fm 1 1/16 Ⓣ 1.12⅖1.43⅗ f– Allow 4 2 21½ 11 21 2h MAristone 116 5.70 88–12 Midnight Model 118h Who Cabled 1161¾ Gallarush 1081½ Gamely 6
6Aug68–8Atl fst 6f .22⅕ .45⅘1.11⅖ f– Allow 3 3 23 2½ 11½ 21½ JVasquez 115 3.10 83–20 La Meme Chose 1171½ Who Cabled 1153 Reel Irish 113½ Gamely 7
26Jly 68–8Mth fm 1 Ⓣ .49 1.40⅘ f– Allow 1 1 1½ 11 2h 24 JVasquez 121 3.40 74–22 Malluca 1144 Who Cabled 1211½ Midnight Model 1191½ Best others 9
10Jly 68–9Mth fm 1 Ⓣ .48⅘1.39⅖ f– Allow 4 1 2h 1h 11½ 2no JVasquez 121 *d1.20 85–15 Vitrinome 117no d-Who Cabled 1211½ Amherst 116¾ Bore out 8
10Jly68—d-Disqualified and placed third.
2Jly 68–8Mth fm 1 Ⓣ .48 1.38 f– Allow 1 1 11 11½ 1½ 2no JVasquez 121 5.10 91– 9 Miss Buffum 115no Who Cabled 1211 Cecebe 115½ Failed to last 8
20Jun68–6Mth gd 1 .47⅗1.13⅘1.40⅘ f– Allow 3 2 21½ 11½ 14 17 JVasquez 115 *2.80 69–26 Who Cabled 1157 Bungalow 1091 Minnie Baby 115¾ Mild drive 8
11Jun68–7Mth fm*1 Ⓣ .48⅕1.40 f– 12000 9 1 14 14 1½ 21 RTanner5 113 7.80 97– 3 Bungalow 1091 Who Cabled 1134 Cecebe 1186 Long lead, tired 10
31May68–7Mth fst 6f .22⅕ .45⅗1.11⅗ f– Allow 3 6 64 67 812 813 PKallai 112 3.10 71–14 Prim Lady 121nk Talented 1122½ Doubledoor 1141½ No factor 8
27May68–6GS fst 6f .22⅖ .45⅖1.10⅖ Clm 11500 7 1 1½ 13 16 14½ JVasquez 112 3.80 92–13 Who Cabled 1124½ Upset Victory 113½ War Horn 112h Mild drive 8
18May68–5GS fst 6f .22⅗ .46⅕1.11 Clm 12500 11 2 1h 21½ 23 34½ MAristone 112 13.30 84–15 Demon Doug 1162½ Royal Harbinger 1142 Who Cabled 112¾ Good try 11
LATEST WORKOUTS Sep 11 Atl 3f my .36 b — Sep 7 Atl 4f sly .53⅖ b — Aug 19 Atl 3f fst .35⅗ b — Aug 14 Atl 4f fst .49⅖ b

Flo Alligator B. m (1963–Fla), by Fair Ruler—Mama Honey, by Johns Joy — G. Victor — A. E. Mettz — (G. Victor) — **113** — 1968 10 2 0 0 $8,075 — 1967 19 0 3 2 $6,100

27Aug68–8AP	m 1 1/16 Ⓣ	1.13⅗1.44⅘	f– Allow	3	6	614	617	614	614	JRLopez	b 112	13.40	73–13	Dark Stream 1052 Babys Future 107¾ Marble Step 1227	No speed	7
17Aug68–8AP	sf 1⅛ Ⓣ	1.14⅖1.52⅗	f–MatronH	2	8	89½	89½	617	616	JRLopez	b 110	43.50	62–33	Ludham 1226 Pattee Canyon 1105 Harem Lady 1103	Showed nothing	8
8Aug68–8AP	fm 1 1/16 Ⓣ	1.12⅖1.44⅗	Allowance	3	6	510	613	616	518	DGargan	b 112	15.20	71–15	SwingingMood 1173 Courageously 1143½ DarkStream 105nk	No sp'd	6
25Jly 68–8AP	fm 1 1/16 Ⓣ	1.14⅕1.47⅖	f– Allow	6	6	715	7½	68	57	DGargan	b 117	11.30	66–27	Marble Step 1122¾ Swinging Mood 1191¼ Irish Ebony 113h	Far back	7
2Jly 68–8AP	fm 5½f Ⓣ	.48⅘1.04⅗	f– Allow	1	8	815	817	818	820	DGargan	b 114	42.40	72–11	TimelyMiss 1174½ MissDebutante 1221½ MissSwapsco 1103	Far back	8
2Mar68–9Hia	fm 1 1/16 Ⓣ	1.44⅗	f– Allow	5	8	85¼	98	73	52	RGrubb	b 113	13.60	80–11	Our Dear Ruth 113no Chriscinca 1131½ Doc Nan 108no	Late gain	11
24Feb68–4Hia	gd 7f .24⅖	.47⅘1.25	f– Allow	5	7	83½	74¼	53	1½	RGrubb	b 112	15.60	84–12	Flo Alligator112½ American Dream1131½ Sports Event114h	Driving	8
16Feb68–8Hia	fm 1 1/16 Ⓣ	1.42⅖	f– Allow	8	7	77	76	86¼	74½	RGrubb	b 113	23.30	88– 7	Shade II 117no Mount Regina 113¾ Baby Jane II 1131½	No threat	11
7Feb68–7Hia	fm 1 1/16 Ⓣ	1.46⅕	f– Allow	7	10	116	84¼	96	92½	DRichard	b 112	47.10	71–24	Mount Regina 113nk Our Dear Ruth 112nk Spire 112h	Wide thruout	12

Gallarush Br. m (1962), by Gallant Man—Why the Rush, by Sir Gallahad III — Mrs. H. H. Hecht — G. G. Delp — (Forest Retreat Farms, Inc.) — **106**5 — 1968 8 1 2 2 $10,500 — 1966 17 0 3 3 $14,875

12Sep68–9Atl	fm 1 Ⓣ	.46⅗1.36⅕	f– Allow	4	7	54	54½	56½	53½	GCusimano5	108	3.20	86–12	T.V.'s Princess 119nk Baby Jane II 113½ Who Cabled 1172	No threat	7
23Aug68–8Atl	fm 1 1/16 Ⓣ	1.12⅖1.43⅗	f– Allow	1	3	44	44	45	31¾	GCusimano5	108	2.90	86–12	Midnight Model 118h Who Cabled 1161¾ Gallarush 1081½	Rallied	6
10Aug68–8Atl	fst 1 1/16 .46⅖	1.10⅘1.44	f–MargteH	7	9	916	915	714	515	GCusimano	108	6.10	72–17	Lady Diplomat 1128 Chriscinca 1132 Telepathy 1131½	No speed	11
26Jly 68–8Del	fm 1 Ⓣ	1.39	f– Allow	5	3	31	22	24	2¾	GCusimano5	116	*0.70	79–23	Perfect Looker 121¾ Gallarush 116no I Be Dandy 111nk	Gamely	6
10Jly 68–7Del	fst 170 .46⅖	1.11⅖1.42⅕	f– Allow	2	3	39½	37	39½	33¾	GCusimano5	108	3.00	85–19	Sale Day 1081¾ Miss Spin 1132 Gallarush 1086	Going well end	6
3Jly 68–8Del	gd 1 1/16 .47	1.12⅖1.45⅗	Clm 22500	5	3	36½	1½	14	11¼	GCusimano5	106	*1.10	81–22	Gallarush1061¼ MakeItPlatinum1105 BrotherCampbell116¾	Mild dr.	5
18Jun68–8Del	fm 1 Ⓣ	1.36⅗	f– Allow	8	6	612	311	38	22¼	GCusimano5	107	1.70	90–12	Lady Diplomat 1192¼ Gallarush 107h Teetotaler 1193	Rallied	8
6Jun68–8Del	fm 1 Ⓣ	1.36⅘	f– Allow	6	4	55¼	34	55¾	48½	GCusimano5	b 107	9.20	82– 9	Teetotaler 118no Patrician Lady 1104¼ Your It 1124¼	Wide	7
9Aug66–8Sar	fm 1⅛ Ⓣ	1.48	f– Allow	8	7	85½	74	73¼	64¾	BBaeza	b 115	9.40	88– 7	Ho Ho 115nk Indian Sunlite 112½ Mount Regina 1191½	No mishap	9
28Jly 66–7Aqu	fm 1 1/16 Ⓣ	1.45⅘	f– Allow	4	8	75	75	55	44	ORosado	115	11.40	73–23	Grand Splendor 1102½ Barletta 115¾ In the Dell 109¾	Late foot	9

LATEST WORKOUTS — Sep 8 Atl 5f fst 1.01 b — Sep 3 Atl 5f fst .58⅘ h — Aug 29 Atl 3f fst .35⅖ b — Aug 21 Atl 4f fst .48⅘ b

Gay Sailorette Dk. b. or br. f (1964–Ky), by Sailor—Gay Rig, by Turn-to — Mrs. R. L. Reineman — C. P. Sanborn — (R. L. Reineman) — **117** — 1968 6 2 0 1 $11,242 — 1967 12 1 2 3 $30,785

31Aug68–8Rkm	fst 1 1/16 .47⅕	1.11⅘1.45	f–P.Dor'nH	4	11	1112	107¼	67	35	HGrant	b 119	*1.50	81–17	Femtastic 107½ Queen Viking 1084½ Gay Sailorette 119no	Rallied	11
22Aug68–8Atl	fst 7f .22⅕	.44⅗1.22⅖	f– Allow	2	6	31	1h	1h	1nk	HGrant	b 118	*1.60	91–15	Gay Sailorette 118nk Regal Hostess 117¾ Telepathy 1171½	Driving	7
13Aug68–8Atl	fst 6f .22	.45⅕1.10⅘	f– Allow	2	3	55	32½	11½	16	HGrant	b 118	2.50	88–15	Gay Sailorette 1186 Amherst 1124 Narova 1125	Mild drive	7
6Aug68–7Atl	fst 6f .22⅕	.45⅘1.11⅗	f– Allow	1	9	98¾	77½	45½	41	HGrant	b 118	4.30	83–20	Rubia 115¾ Sequela 113nk Lady Jester 113no	Best stride late	10
30Jly 68–8Mth	fst 6f .22	.45 1.10⅘	f– Allow	8	10	109¾	810	67	66	DKassen	b 117	9.40	82–16	It's A Pilot 1122½ Threadneedle 1121¼ Lady Jester 112½	Slow start	10
19Apr68–9GP	fst 6f .22⅗	.45⅗1.10⅘	Allowance	2	6	42	44	43½	57	CPerret5	b 104	2.90	83–13	ThirdMonarch115nk RomanTrooper1164 PatteeCanyon1072	Tired	8
12Aug67–6Sar	fst 1¼ .47	1.11⅗2.03⅕	f–Alabama	12	13	1313	119¼	96¾	814	GOverton	b 121	56.50	78–11	Gamely 1182 Treacherous 1144 Muse 1141½	Wide late stages	13
2Aug67–8AP	fst 1 .44⅖	1.09⅘1.35⅖	f–PckrUpH	9	8	610	54½	41¾	1nk	GOverton	b 112	25.50	86–19	Gay Sailorette 112nk Court Circuit 1122¾ Grand Coulee 113h	Driving	12
24Jly 67–8AP	fst 1 .45⅖	1.09⅗1.34⅘	f– Allow	1	7	716	56½	24	23½	GOverton	b 113	8.20	85–14	Grand Coulee 1153½ Gay Sailorette 1133½ Fine Thanks 115h	Gamely	7
4Jly 67–8Mth	fst 1⅛ .47⅗	1.12⅕1.52⅕	f–MthOaks	11	10	912	1013	1021	1114	HBlock	b 112	27.80e	69–24	Quillo Queen 1213½ Secret Promise 112¾ SwissCheese 121no	No speed	12
17Jun67–8Mth	fst 170 .46⅗	1.11⅗1.43⅖	f–Post-Deb	8	7	98¼	1014	1017	912	WGavidia	b 112	13.50	72–18	T. V.'s Princess 1121¾ Amherst 1122¼ Forty Merry's 1121½	No threat	10

LATEST WORKOUTS — Sep 18 Atl 3f fst .36 b — Sep 16 Atl 3f fst .38 b — Sep 12 Atl 6f fst 1.19 b — Aug 29 Atl 4f fst .49⅘ b

Alps * B. m (1962), by Pavot—Alyxia, by Alycidon — W. M. Jeffords, Jr. — O. White — (Mrs. W. M. Jeffords) — **117** — 1968 6 0 1 0 $2,050 — 1967 12 3 2 1 $31,725

23Aug68–8Atl	fm 1 1/16 Ⓣ	1.12⅖1.43⅗	f– Allow	5	6	54	56	34	43¼	GPatterson	b 113	*1.20	85–12	Midnight Model 118h Who Cabled 1161¾ Gallarush 1081½	Evenly	6
16Aug68–8Atl	fm*1 1/16 Ⓣ	1.12⅗1.45	f– Allow	5	6	46½	32½	24	25	GPatterson	b 118	12.90	94– 1	T.V.'s Princess 1135 Alps 118no d-Malluca 1201	Finished well	8
2Jly 68–8Del	fm 1 1/16 Ⓣ	1.43	Allowance	1	5	614	811	812	811	GPatterson	b 117	11.40	78–16	Decacean 118nk Sol Naciente II. 112½ Exceedingly 1221	No factor	8
18Jun68–8Del	fm 1 Ⓣ	1.36⅗	f– Allow	1	4	712	515	615	615	GPatterson	b 119	4.60	77–12	Lady Diplomat 1192¼ Gallarush 107h Teetotaler 1193	Dull try	8
6Jun68–8Del	fm 1 Ⓣ	1.36⅘	f– Allow	3	5	66¼	78½	66¼	711	GPatterson	b 118	*2.00	80– 9	Teetotaler 118no Patrician Lady 1104¼ Your It 1124¼	Bore in	7
7May68–7GS	fst 1 1/16 .46⅘	1.11⅗1.43⅗	f– Allow	2	3	411	414	415	522	GPatterson	b 118	10.20	65–18	T.V.'s Princess 11210 Sarolsa 1156 Chriscinca 1185	Far back	7
9Dec67–8Lrl	gd*1 1/16 Ⓣ	1.47	f–ChrysmH	8	8	86¾	63¼	41½	1½	ORosado	b 111	13.10	88–16	Alps 111½ Swinging Mood 126nk Penny Power 1133	Under brisk drive	10
15Nov67–8Lrl	fm 1 1/16 Ⓣ	1.43⅖	f– Allow	7	5	54¾	52¾	33½	24	GPatterson	b 118	3.20	85–11	Margarethen 1164 Alps 118½ Ranch Maid 109no	Best others	7
30Oct67–8Lrl	fm*1 1/16 Ⓣ	1.46⅗	f– Allow	1	3	55	52½	42	33¼	GPatterson	b 118	1.90	87–10	Star Garter 1201¼ Extra Place 1132 Alps 1181½	Made fair effort	6
6Oct67–8Atl	hd 1 1/16 Ⓣ	1.44⅖	f– Allow	4	5	68	67	44	1no	BThornburg	b 118	3.50	85–19	Alps 118no Star Garter 120h Teetotaler 1181½	Up final yards	7

LATEST WORKOUTS — Sep 13 Atl 3f fst .39 b — Sep 1 Atl 5f fst 1.01 h — Aug 27 Atl 4f fst .50⅖ b — Aug 20 Atl 5f fst 1.01 h

Again, we find a single front-running type, sure to have the early pace all its own way. Look at the record of Who Cabled. Nothing else in the race has her early foot. She is, of course, an habitual decelerator in the home stretch. Nevertheless, she must be regarded as the winner here—unless one of the off-pace runners has a real edge in class. Chriscinca might once have qualified on those grounds but has failed too often in allowance company to be regarded as a terrible threat today. If you have trouble reposing entire confidence in the weak Who Cabled, you might consider betting on her *and* Chriscinca.

The Running of the Race

GAY SAILORETTE was favored, which would have been a plausible state of affairs had the race been on the main track. She finished next to last. Who Cabled, the second favorite, won easily, drawing away. Chriscinca arrived third, behind the longshot Flo Alligator.

EIGHTH RACE
Atl - 35943
September 19, 1968

ABOUT 1 1-16 m. (Turf). (Fan Jet, September 7, 1966, 1.44⅘, 6, 113.) Allowances. Purse $6,500. Fillies and mares. 3–year–olds and upward which have not won $2,925 twice at a mile or over since November 5 other than maiden, claiming, optional or starter. Weights 3–year–olds 118 lbs., older 122 lbs. Non–winners of $6,600 over a mile since June 30 allowed 3 lbs., $4,875 at a mile or over July 1, 5 lbs., any over a mile since June 30 allowed 3 lbs., $4,875 at a mile or over since July 1, 5 lbs., any race of $4,300 in 1968 or $6,500 in 1967, 7 lbs., $3,900 twice in 1968, 9 lbs., $2,600

Value to winner $3,900, second $1,300, third $845, fourth $455. Mutuel pool $115,074.

Index	Horse	Eqt A Wt	PP	St	¼	½	¾	Str	Fin	Jockey	Owner	Odds $1
35890Atl[3]	Who Cabled	b 5 117	3	2	2⁵	11½	1⁵	1⁵	1⁶	R Broussard	Cosens–Murphy	2.90
35706AP[6]	Flo Alligator	b 5 113	4	7	7	7	6	2½	W Blum	G Victor	26.80
35890Atl[4]	Chriscinca	b 4 117	1	4	4h	5³	4h	2h	3²½	C Baltazar	A Muller	3.60
35890Atl[5]	Gallarush	6 106	5	3	3½	4h	5h	5h	4no	G Cusimano⁵	Mrs H H Hecht	5.40
35652Atl[4]	Alps	b 6 117	7	5	6²	6²	6⁴	4½	5¾	M Miceli	W M Jeffords Jr	6.20
35868Rkm[3]	Gay Sailorette	b 4 117	6	6	5²	3½	2½	3¹	6	F Lovato	Mrs R L Reineman	2.30
35688Atl[4]	Pendulous	b 3 110	2	1	1h	2³	3¹	Bled		E Maple	P DePaul	12.30

Time .24, .48⅕, 1.12⅖, 1.38⅖, 1.45. Track hard.

$2 Mutuel Prices:

3–WHO CABLED	7.80	4.60	3.60
4–FLO ALLIGATOR		14.60	6.20
1–CHRISCINCA			4.00

Ch. m, by Whodunit—First Cable, by Royal Palm. Trainer B. W. Perkins. Bred by J. Murphy (N.J.).

IN GATE AT 4.44. OFF AT 4.44 EASTERN DAYLIGHT TIME. Start good. Won easily.

WHO CABLED raced PENDULOUS into early defeat from the outside, drew well clear and won with speed to spare. FLO ALLIGATOR, slow to gain best stride, finished fast. CHRISCINCA went evenly. GALLARUSH failed to menace. ALPS was never a factor. GAY SAILORETTE had no excuses. PENDULOUS vied for the early lead from the inside and bled.

Scratched—35870Atl[6] Queen Of Action. Overweight—Pendulous 1 pound.

THE NINTH RACE

THE FINAL RACE of the afternoon is another turf event, same distance, for $6,500–$7,500 claimers.

Out go Moon Hit (a maiden), Pampadonna (a cheap filly), Zurk (unimpressive on grass), Nantagos (physically suspect), Dosila (long idle), Enchanted Easter (no races or works since September 2), and Sabair (poor recent form). The others are:

TURF COURSE
1 1-16 MILES
ATLANTIC CITY
Start Finish

9th Atlantic City

ABOUT 1 1-16 m. (Turf). (Fan Jet, September 7, 1966, 1.44⅘, 6, 113.) Claiming. Purse $4500. 3-year-olds and upward. Weights 3-year-olds 118 lbs., older 122 lbs. Non-winners of two races since August 10 allowed 3 lbs., a race 6 lbs. (Races where entered for $5,000 or less not considered.) Claiming price $7,500. 1 lb. allowed for each $250 to $6,500.

Moon Hit $6,500 — Dk. b. or br. g (1964–Va), by Moonsun—She's Got It, by Johnstown — H. J. Rose H. J. Rose (W. R. Helwick) — 107 5 — 1968 2 M 1 0 $760 — 1967 11 M 3 1 $3,150

13Sep68–1Atl fst 1⅛ .47⅗1.12⅗1.52⅘ Md c-5000 6 11 119½ 99¾ 610 612 MMiceli b 120 *1.50 62–18 Sufico 1131¼ Endow 1115 Brother R. 1093 Had no excuse 12
29Aug68–2Atl fst 1⅛ .48⅘1.13⅘1.53⅘ Md 5000 2 7 63 42 21 2h MMiceli b 122 4.00 72–16 Sacra Via 111h Moon Hit 1221½ Jolty 1142 Sharp effort 12
3Nov67–4GS sly 1 1/16 .48⅗1.13⅘1.47⅖ Md Sp Wt 3 7 65½ 66¾ 65¾ 710 WBlum b 118 3.40 58–32 Victory String 1151½ Jolly Heir 1211½ Panajoy 1181 No speed 8
17Oct67–7GS fst 170 .47⅗1.13⅕1.44⅕ Allowance 6 7 76½ 78¼ 55½ 56¾ WGavidia b 114 11.80 66–20 Lexingtonian 114nk Listen Mr. 1163 C'est L'Amour 1142 No factor 9
10Oct67–6Atl fm 1 Ⓣ 1.40 Clm 12500 9 10 911 87¾ 68 33¼ WGavidia b 113 11.10e 68–30 Dale Hill 110¾ Bey Mahmoud 1152½ Moon Hit 1132 Stride late 10
14Sep67–6Atl fst 1⅛ .48 1.12⅘1.52⅕ Clm 7000 1 5 55 44 31 2h CBaltazar b 114 10.30 77–19 Fair Page 11?h Moon Hit 1142 Consistently 120nk Sharp, missed 8
2Sep67–5Atl fst 1⅛ .48 1.11⅗1.49⅘ Clm 10000 3 6 78¾ 515 514 59 GPatterson b 115 20.90 80–13 IleD'Levant 108nk SwampRabbit 115no Atoll'sSun 1151¾ No threat 7
21Aug67–1Atl fst 1⅛ .48 1.13 1.52⅘ Md 5000 11 8 88¼ 35 2½ 2nk GPatterson b 117 3.90 74–13 Nawab II 122nk Moon Hit 1173 Celestial Shot 1173½ Sharp try 12
28Jly 67–7Mth sly 1 1/16 .48 1.12⅘1.44⅗ Allowance 3 9 1012 1018 921 827 PKallai 113 19.70e 55–22 Enchanted Easter 1127 Dance Toledo 1146 Hatchery 1121½ No speed 10
14Jly 67–7Mth fst 170 .47⅕1.12⅗1.43⅗ Allowance 4 10 912 1014 910 79½ KKnapp b 112 50.90 73–19 Lutza'sKil'r114½ Ench'ntedEaster112¾ SandAndCor'l1161½ No sp'd 10
LATEST WORKOUTS Sep 11 Atl 4f my .51⅗ b Sep 5 Atl 5f fst 1.03 b Aug 28 Atl 3f fst .37⅗ b Aug 24 Atl 6f fst 1.17 b

Jolly Heir * $7,500 — B. g (1963–Ky), by Mister Gus—Demree, by Revoked — J. Marzano P. Dunne (R. L. Reineman) — 114 5 — 1968 9 2 1 2 $7,620 — 1967 16 1 1 3 $5,86?

3Sep68–9Atl fm*1⅛ Ⓣ 1.12⅗1.52⅖ Clm 6000 4 3 31½ 2½ 11½ 15 HGrant b 118 *1.20 95– 8 Jolly Heir 1185 Yoga 1192 Model Soldier 1165 Kept to drive 10
22Aug68–9Atl fm 1 1/16 Ⓣ 1.12 1.44⅕ Clm 6500 5 6 58 32 15 15 GCusimano b 116 d40.00 85–15 d–Jolly Heir 1165 Rucapequen 1162 KingOfMomus110h Caused jam 12
22Aug68—d–Disqualified and placed last.
15Aug68–9Atl fst 1⅛ .48⅗1.12⅘1.51⅕ Clm 6250 6 7 79 914 921 926 RPerna b 115 34.40 56–19 Imparcial II 1183½ Saguaro 1166 Ridgid 109½ No factor 10
3Aug68–2Mth sf 1 Ⓣ .51⅕1.47⅖ Cl c-5000 2 4 48½ 24 25 27 HGrant b 119 *2.00 38–55 Diplomate II 1167 Jolly Heir 1198 Ridgid 1122 Best of rest 9
17Jly 68–9Mth fm 1 Ⓣ 1.14 1.40⅕ Clm 4500 1 3 32½ 3½ 1h 21½ HGrant b 118 *2.80 79–11 d–Meredrum 1111½ Jolly Heir 1181 Jovial Jeff 116h Impeded 11
17Jly 68—Placed first through disqualification.
24Jun68–9Mth fm 1 1/16 Ⓣ 1.12 1.46 Clm 5000 2 2 32 32 21 42¾ HGrant b 118 2.70 —— Air Spinner 113no Bey Mahmoud 118¾ d–Saguaro 1132 Bid, tired 12
24Jun68—Placed third through disqualification.
23Apr68–8GP fm*1 Ⓣ 1.39⅖ Allowance 3 4 31½ 3nk 33 33¼ HGrant b 118 7.30 —— Physical Fitness 112¾ Cant Elope 1072½ Jolly Heir 118no Held on 6
11Apr68–5GP fst 7f .22⅘ .46⅖1.24⅖ Allowance 2 6 77¼ 67½ 56½ 59 HGrant b 118 8.50 78–13 Physical Fitness 1093 Mornay II 1141½ Neecap 1124 Never close 7

Pampadonna * $6,500 — B. f (1964–Va), by Duc de Fer—Lady Pampa, by Hassyampa — Krispi Ranch L. Nichols (Mac Sweetie Stable) — 109 — 1968 19 5 5 3 $13,505 — 1967 18 1 0 3 $3,795

2Sep68–4Rkm fst 1 1/16 .47⅖1.12⅘1.46 Cl c-5000 6 1 1h 53 711 717 ERobart 119 5.70 64–28 Big Poona 1141 Time Lapse 106h Victory Imp 1148½ Hard used 8
24Aug68–5Rkm fst 1 1/16 .47⅕1.12⅗1.45⅘ Cl c-3750 7 1 12 13 15 112 HHinojosa 114 *1.60 82–18 Pampadonna 11412 Mr. Hot Shot 1172¼ Caius Julius 114no Mild dr. 9
16Aug68–9Rkm fst 1 1/16 .47⅗1.12⅗1.46⅗ f– 3500 7 3 32 21½ 22 23½ DMadden 120 3.20 74–19 Scairt 1123½ Pampadonna 1201¼ Quicketia 1154 Game effort 7
10Aug68–5Rkm fst 1 1/16 .47 1.12⅕1.45⅗ Clm 3250 3 2 22½ 21½ 2h 11¼ DMadden 112 7.80 83–15 Pampadonna1121¼ HastyVic1096½ ReadyOrNot1141½ Driving clear 8
31Jly 68–10Rkm fst 1 1/16 .47⅗1.12⅘1.47⅘ Clm 3500 8 3 3nk 2h 21 31½ DMadden 114 12.90 70–18 Robie J. C. 1171¼ Red Salmon 114nk Pampadonna 1142 Went well 11
24Jly 68–10Rkm fst 1⅛ .48 1.12⅘1.53⅕ Clm 4000 9 4 61¾ 42½ 79¼ 820 DMadden 112 10.30 55–17 Real And Ideal 1173 Yasa Boy 1141¼ Ole Buck Green 1141¾ Tired 9
16Jly 68–10Rkm fst 1 1/16 .47⅘1.13 1.47⅕ Cl c-2500 8 1 1½ 12 12 14 LMoyers 112 *2.10 75–19 Pampadonna 1124 Sarapat 114¾ Bicarb Jr. 1172½ Easily best 9
3Jly 68–6Suf fst 1 1/16 .47⅗1.13 1.47⅖ Clm 2500 8 1 12 12½ 12 13 LMoyers 109 *1.70 72–22 Pampadonna 1093 Ozark Jet 1142¼ Disatate 1122 Easily best 9
7Jun68–2Suf fst 6f .22⅗ .46⅗1.12⅗ Clm 2500 3 4 54½ 55 33 23¾ LMoyers 112 *1.00 74–22 Sporty Cast 1173¾ Pampadonna 1123 Ole Buck Green 1142 Gamely 10
24May68–5Suf gd 6f .22⅗ .46⅖1.12⅘ f– 3500 8 5 43½ 56½ 45 35¼ LMoyers 115 *2.10 72–21 I Think So 1122 Safe Corner 1072¼ Pampadonna 1152½ No mishap 10
LATEST WORKOUTS Sep 15 LD 5f fst 1.04 b Jly 29 Rkm 5f fst 1.05 b

***Zurk** * $7,000 — Dk. b. or br. g (1964), by Palor—Zarmoria, by Uranio — J. Skop R. J. Cremen (Haras Uruguay) (Uru.) — 114 — 1968 12 1 1 0 $3,693 — 1967 20 5 2 1 $20,960

7Sep68–6Tim fst 1 .48 1.14⅗1.41 Clm 7500 2 2 23½ 21½ 12 2nk WJPassmore b 114 5.80 86–19 Jayette 114nk Zurk 1143½ Say You Can 1171½ Failed to last 8
31Aug68–3Tim fst 1 .48⅕1.15⅕1.41⅖ Clm 7500 5 4 37 42½ 45½ 46¼ WJPassmore b 119 3.50 78–18 Nightstick 1094 South Branch 1111 Acceptance 1041¼ Tired 6
8Aug68–6Del fst 170 .47 1.13⅕1.44 Clm 6250 4 3 37 23 3½ 1h EWalsh b 115 19.90 80–22 Zurk 115h Two Wings 113¾ Nuthin To Eat 1114 Up final strides 9
29Jly 68–5Del fst 6f .22⅗ .46⅖1.12⅕ Clm 6000 7 8 811 88 511 58¼ EMaple b 115 51.40 76–18 Guss Gray 1142½ Cohesian 122¾ Broken Needle 1142 Slow start 8
10Jly 68–9Del fm 1 Ⓣ 1.37⅖ Hcp 5000s 8 5 714 718 714 719 RKotenko b 109 94.20 69–15 Carolina Game 110½ King Barney 1133 Paxton Road 1133 No speed 9
14Jun68–7Del fst 6f .22 .46 1.12⅖ Cl c-5000 8 12 1224 1118 1215 1213 SHernandez b 115 37.80 70–23 Cohesian 1154 Gigante 1181½ Chief Embrey 115½ No speed 12
8May68–7Pim fm 5f Ⓣ .46 .58⅕ Clm 7000 1 9 918 921 923 918 RHernandez b 114 14.50 80–10 Mr. Albermarle 1143 Rule Of Facts 1071 Accredit 107¾ Trailed 9
1Apr68–6GP fst 6f .22⅖ .45⅖1.11⅖ Clm 7500 6 12 1214 1216 1115 1014 RHernandez b 116 10.20 73–19 Gilgar 1112½ Scotch Sailor 1161 Pretty Bug 111½ Never close 12
17Feb68–10Hia fst 1⅛ .46⅖1.10⅘1.50⅖ Clm 9000 9 6 615 919 913 914 ECardone b 112 8.40 69–17 Harsh Hajokah 1143 Ruperto 1133½ •Sound Box 116h No factor 12
6Feb68–10Hia gd 1⅛ .46⅗1.11⅗1.51⅕ Clm 9000 6 4 34½ 33½ 54 77½ RTurcotte b 112 8.60 71–17 Mr. Elwood W. 116h Sound Box 112no Bigamo 1123 Well up, tired 12
LATEST WORKOUTS Sep 18 Atl 3f fst .37⅗ b Aug 20 Tim 7f fst 1.35⅖ b Aug 7 Del 5f fst 1.03 b Aug 6 Del 3f fst .39⅗ b

*Nantagos $6,500   B. c (1964), by Crepello—Just Wyn, by Stardust   J. M. Olin   J. W. Thompson   (The Burton Agnes Stud) (Ire.)   112   1968 5 0 0 0 — / 1967 5 0 0 1 $1,875

*Dosiia $6,500   Dk. b. or br. m (1962), by Carapalida—Doremi, by Bahram   O. T. Dubassoff   H. S. Clark   (Haras Malal Hue) (Arg.)   109   1968 8 0 0 1 $710 / 1967 8 0 0 1 $455

Enchanted Easter * $7,500   Ch. c (1964-Ind), by Beau Busher—Easter Babe, by Trymenow   Salma Katz   R. Nixon   (R. Fortune, Jr.)   116   1968 14 0 0 0 — / 1967 5 1 1 1 $22,200

*Pomidoro $7,500   Gr. g (1962), by Postin—Entrevaux, by British Empire   A. L. Bigelow   L. D'Casseries   (Haras Chillon) (Peru)   116   1968 9 0 0 2 $1,150 / 1967 18 4 4 0 $24,600

Sabair * $7,500   Ch. c (1965-Fla), by Jabneh—Criteria, by Questionnaire   S. Gaynor   J. Clark   (Mrs. S. C. Tingle)   107⁵   1968 14 3 0 2 $12,115 / 1967 14 3 0 1 $62

*Saguaro $6,500   Ch. h (1961), by Terek—Gironde, by Dichato   A. E. Fortugno   J. L. Denest   (M. Etchepare) (Chile)   112   1968 21 5 3 1 $15,570 / 1966 14 1 3 3 $2,900

Jolly Heir: I do not like this horse's failure to work out since his last race, which was on September 3. Otherwise, I'd assume that here is definitely the one to beat. The rise in class should be no problem for an animal able to win as decisively as Jolly Heir did last time. But because we have a right to be suspicious about his physical condition, we had better not concede the victory yet. Contender.

Pomidoro: Moving down to a much lower class of competition after showing a lot of early speed, this six-year-old deserves careful consideration. His last race came after a month of freshening and indicated that the rest had helped him. His return to the starter's gate today—only three days later—is an especially good sign of fitness. Finally, he figures to carry his speed further against today's easier field. Contender.

Saguaro: This consistent seven-year-old seems to need a little more yardage than today's race provides. His strong performance on September 9 does not necessarily mean that he can handle legitimate $7,500 stock on the grass course. That he has a chance is undeniable, but I am a bit afraid of today's distance and class. No Bet.

It seems apparent enough that, if Pomidoro runs the first three quarters of a mile in 1.11, as he did on September 6, no other horse in the race will be within reach of him. For the third time on this program, we find a front-runner in the enviable position of being able to dictate the manner in which the race will be run. Pomidoro's tendency to falter is less likely to be exploited today than in his recent races against better horses.

The Running of the Race

JOLLY HEIR, the 7–5 favorite and the only animal in the field with a prayer of catching Pomidoro, showed absolutely nothing and finished fifth. As suspected, his failure to race or work since September 3 meant that something was wrong. Pomidoro had everything his own way. He ran the first three quarters in 1.13⅗, throttled all the way back, and won by five lengths.

NINTH RACE
Atl - 35944
September 19, 1968

ABOUT 1 1-16 m. (Turf). (Fan Jet, September 7, 1966, 1.44⅘, 6, 113.) Claiming. Purse $4500. 3-year-olds and upward. Weights 3-year-olds 118 lbs., older 122 lbs. Non-winners of two races since August 10 allowed 3 lbs., a race 6 lbs. (Races where entered for $5,000 or less not considered.) Claiming price $7,500. 1 lb. allowed for each $250 to $6,500.

Value to winner $2,700, second $900, third $585, fourth $315. Mutuel pool $92,518.

Index	Horse	Eqt	A	Wt	PP	St	¼	½	¾	Str	Fin	Jockey	Cl'g Pr	Owner	Odds $1
35914Atl^{7}	Pomidoro	b	6	116	8	2	$1^{1\frac{1}{2}}$	1^{3}	1^{3}	1^{4}	1^{5}	C Jiminez	7500	A L Bigelow	4.10
35863Atl^{1}	Saguaro		7	113	10	6	6^{6}	4^{h}	4^{1}	2^{h}	$2^{1\frac{1}{2}}$	W Blum	6500	A E Fortugno	4.00
35891Atl^{6}	Moont Hit	b	4	107	1	7	7^{h}	7^{2}	6^{3}	$4^{\frac{1}{2}}$	3^{1}	R Sage^{5}	6500	H J Rose	28.70
35809Rkm^{7}	Pampadonna		4	112	3	1	2^{3}	$2^{\frac{1}{2}}$	$3^{1\frac{1}{2}}$	$3^{1\frac{1}{2}}$	4^{2}	M Hole	6500	Krispi Ranch	35.70
35818Atl^{1}	Jolly Heir	b	5	114	2	3	$5^{1\frac{1}{2}}$	5^{1}	$5^{1\frac{1}{2}}$	6^{4}	$5^{1\frac{1}{2}}$	G Cusimano^{5}	7500	J Marzano	1.40
35656Sar^{9}	Nantagos	b	4	112	5	5	4^{2}	3^{3}	$2^{1\frac{1}{2}}$	5^{h}	6^{3}	E Maple	6500	J M Olin	40.70
35886Atl^{5}	Sabair	b	3	112	9	8	9^{3}	9^{5}	8^{5}	7^{3}	7^{3}	G Patterson†	7500	S Gaynor	33.10
35376Del^{4}	Dosila	b	6	109	6	4	$3^{\frac{1}{2}}$	6^{5}	7^{3}	8^{h}	$8^{1\frac{1}{2}}$	F Lovato	6500	O T Dubasoff	15.40
35851Tim^{2}	Zurk	b	4	114	4	10	10	10	10	9^{5}	9^{5}	E Walsh	7000	J Skop	15.00
35809Atl^{6}	Ench'tedE'st'r	b	4	116	7	9	8^{2}	8^{1}	9^{h}	10	10	H Block	7500	Selma Katz	6.60

†Five pounds apprentice allowance waived.

Time .23⅘, .48⅗, 1.13⅗, 1.39⅘, 1.46⅕. Track hard.

$2 Mutuel Prices:			
8-POMIDORO	10.20	5.80	4.80
10-SAGUARO		4.80	4.60
1-MOON HIT			13.00

Gr. g, by Postin—Entrevaux, by British Empire. Trainer L. D'Casseries. Bred by Haras Chillon (Peru.).

IN GATE AT 5.14. OFF AT 5.14 EASTERN DAYLIGHT TIME. Start **good for all but ZURK. Won driving.**

POMIDORO went to the front from the outside in the run to the clubhouse turn, was nicely rated on the pace and was not menaced to the end. SAGUARO advanced steadily around horses leaving the backstretch and finished evenly. MOON HIT was forced extremely wide attempting to rally into the stretch and could not threaten. PAMPADONNA pressed the pace to the end of the backstretch and tired. JOLLY HEIR was never a factor. ZURK stoumbled at the start. ENCHANTED EASTER showed nothing.

Scratched—35903Atl^{3} Law School, 35886Atl^{3} Banker Barn, 35897Atl^{1} Helioroad, 35698Rkm^{9} Bold Ship.
Overweights—Pampadonna 3 pounds, Sacuaro 1.
Zurk was claimed by Pennyacres Farm. Trainer G. G. Delp

A SUMMING UP

It has been an enlightening day. The advance dope stood up more firmly than it usually does, enabling us to look like geniuses in the seven playable races. The victories by three unopposed front-runners were especially instructive and should stand the reader in good stead whenever he encounters a similar situation in the future. The victory by Third Monarch, who paid $25.40 but should have been 2–1, was another valuable experience.